The
MODERN FAMILY
COOK BOOK

By META GIVEN

FOR DAILY USE IN THE AMERICAN HOME

INCLUDES

Menus for one week in every month of the year, and a simple recipe for every cooked food listed in the menus. All menus are planned to measure up to the U. S. Government's basic seven food groups.

526 Clam Chowder

J. G. FERGUSON AND ASSOCIATES
CHICAGO

THIS BOOK IS DEDICATED TO

DR. EVELYN G. HALLIDAY
and
DR. LYDIA J. ROBERTS
of the University of Chicago

whose contributions to the field of Home
Economics have won nation-wide
recognition, and to whom the author ac-
knowledges a great personal debt.

TABLE OF CONTENTS

LIST OF ILLUSTRATIONS

TABLES

ACKNOWLEDGMENTS

Building a cook book is something like building a house. . . . First, the plans go through a stage of dreaming, then the builder collects practical ideas from houses already built—from architects, building specialists and home builders. When the decision finally is made to go ahead, the blueprint is drawn, embodying the results of dreams, observations and consultations.

Once the blueprint is ready, material is assembled, workmen are called in . . . and the house begins to grow. As work progresses, friends and neighbors drop in, giving the builder the benefit of their experiences, knowledge and skill—pointing out weak spots and ways of strengthening them—adding their bit to the plans of the builder. So when the house is finished . . . it bears the marks of many hands.

And so it has been with the construction of this cook book in which many participated. For many good features in the book, I have them to thank; for all that is faulty, I take the blame.

Therefore, I am grateful to Marguerite Lyon, Author and Columnist for chapter heading ideas, to Mata Roman Friend, Author and Home Economist in Business, for suggestions on organization and content. To the following Food Specialists for reading certain chapters and making recommendations for improvement: Katherine Bele Niles of the Poultry and Egg National Board, Inez S. Willson, formerly of the National Live Stock & Meat Board, Venona Schwartz, formerly of the American Meat Institute, Rachel Reed, formerly of Borden Company, Toni Delay and Frederica Beinert of the Cereal Institute, Dr. Lydia J. Roberts and Dr. Evelyn G. Halliday of the University of Chicago and Dr. Helen Mitchell, formerly of the Federal Security Agency, and Dr. Margaret Doyle of the University of Chicago, for revising the Diet Pattern Chapter for this last edition.

Special thanks are also due to my co-workers for their able assistance: To Elaine Bechtel for rewriting original materal and some editorial work, Amy C. Jackson, Ruth Dahlberg Smith, Ingrid B. Nielsen, Mary L. Wright and Vivian Hewitt for the development of recipes; Elma R. Crain for planning menus to conform to a diet pattern; Helen A. Swadey for capable help in the complete revision of this last edition.

I also wish to gratefully acknowledge all organizations who supplied some of the illustrations, credit is given on pages where the pictures appear.

INTRODUCTION

MRS. HOMEMAKER, THIS BOOK IS WRITTEN FOR YOU. . . .
in full appreciation of your problems of running a home. These problems
would challenge a psychologist, an expert on child training, an interior
decorator, a skilled seamstress, a trained nurse. In addition your problems demand nutritional knowledge and cooking skill for their solution.
Unless you belong to the 10 per cent whose budget is not strictly limited,
you are daily faced with the necessity of budgeting the income of one
average husband—a problem to stagger any financier!

It's impossible to pick out just one of your numerous functions and
say that it is more important than all the rest. But if we had to do it, we'd
venture to say that the function of dietitian and cook comes near the
top of the list. "Show me what you eat and I'll tell you what you are," is
an old true saying that is better understood today than ever before. Our
health and happiness, social effectiveness, even business and pro-
fessional success is profoundly influenced by the state of our nutrition.

Family meals are not just a means of satisfying hunger. As a modern
homemaker you must plan meals with a long view, knowing you are not
just filling empty stomachs, but building health for your whole family.
Properly planned meals will increase resistance and prevent many ill-
nesses; they will keep your youngsters keen and vigorous; they will help
them grow and work and play; and you will find that an improved
diet makes your own work seem lighter, and your husband's too.

This book was planned to help you deal with your food problems. A
careful analysis shows them to be of four kinds—PLANNING, BUYING,
COOKING, SERVING. For this reason, we have four parts to this book,
each filled with helpful suggestions written in simple language, each
headed by a "CREED" expressing the importance and the dignity of
the homemaker's tasks.

In planning meals, good nutrition is the first consideration. Therefore,
we have included the lastest information on nutrition in the chapter
called, THE DIET PATTERN. Here, you will learn the whys and hows
of planning the kinds of meals your family needs to develop and maintain health at a high level. The food needs are expressed in a "PAT-
TERN" which anyone can follow in selecting the day's food. It is
important to give meals other characteristics, such as appetizing combinations of flavors, colors and textures, as well as variety. To help the
busy homemaker plan for these qualities as well as nutritional needs, a

menu has been included for one week in every month of the year. Recipe Numbers are given with each food suggested.

Since most families have less money than they could conveniently use, it is worthwhile to learn how to "STRETCH THE FOOD DOLLAR". A garden where possible, careful buying and good storage, as well as thoughtful use of leftovers may release many a dollar for additional foods or for other purchases.

The third section is on the actual cooking. The object of this section is to help homemakers to be more than "rule-of-thumb" cooks. Information on why foods are cooked in certain ways is included. The ingredients in the recipes are listed in the order in which they are used in the mixing.

Each woman should feel herself to be a hostess to her family. This is the grand climax of a procession of achievements. A woman who is a good planner, a wise purchaser, an excellent cook and a gracious hostess to her family is truly a MASTER HOME BUILDER.

Our menus are tailored to YOUR BUDGET. Our Introductory Chapters were written to answer YOUR questions. Our recipes were tested and retested in our kitchens so you should have success with them every time.

MRS. HOMEMAKER, THIS BOOK IS YOUR BOOK.

The Meal Planner's Creed

The health of my family is in my care; therefore—

I will spare no effort in planning the right kinds of food in the right amounts.

Spending the food dollar for maximum value is my job; therefore—

I will choose from the variously priced foods to save money without sacrificing health.

My family's enjoyment of food is my responsibility; therefore—

I will increase their pleasure by planning for variety, for flavorful dishes, for attractive color, for appetizing combinations.

My family's health, security, and pleasure depend on my skill in planning meals; therefore—

I will treat my job with the respect that is due it.

THE DIET PATTERN

THIS vital chapter might have been called "What Every Meal-Planner Ought to Know." In it you will find the facts about food and its nutritive value, presented in a down-to-earth manner that takes them out of the laboratory and brings them right into your kitchen. These are the basic things You *as planner and cook should know about food, if you want to see* YOUR *family enjoy the radiant health which comes from a well-chosen diet!*

ELEMENTS OF THE DIET

A well-balanced diet is made of a great variety of foods. These foods supply us with the energy we need for our daily work and play, and also with the elements we require for growth and maintenance, and for the regulation of body processes. If one or more of these elements is persistently lacking, or is present in insufficient quantity, the health of the body will suffer—not suddenly or dramatically, but gradually, over a long period. This is the "hidden hunger" which is revealed not by hunger pangs, but by such signs as fatigue and lowered vitality. "Hidden hunger" may be present even when the appetite is satisfied.

Because of the many important interrelationships between them, the nutrients in foods cannot be rigidly classified as to the type of function they perform. In general, however, the essential foodstuffs which must be supplied by an adequate diet fall into five classes:

1. *Carbohydrates and fats*—furnish heat and energy—an excess over needs will be stored in the form of body fat.

2. *Protein*—builds and repairs body tissues, serves in the formation of certain important regulatory substances.

3. *Minerals*—serve as constituents of the bones and teeth, giving these tissues their strength and hardness; they are also necessary constituents of the soft tissues and the blood, and serve important regulatory functions in the body.

3

4. *Vitamins*—serve as body regulators necessary for normal growth and the maintenance of health.

5. *Bulk*—aids in elimination of body waste.

Added to these is *water*, which although not a food in the ordinary sense, plays an important role in regulating body processes, and we have the foundation stones on which we build healthy bodies.

PLANNING THE DIET

The menus used in this book have been built to include all the basic foods which supply the individual's needs for protein, minerals, vitamins, and energy. Here is the DIET PATTERN* used in building them:

1. 1 quart milk for each child and 1 pint for each adult (2 cups evaporated milk are the approximate equivalent of 1 quart fresh milk).
2. 1 serving of citrus fruit, or tomatoes, or tomato juice.
3. 1 other fruit, either fresh, canned or dried.
4. 1 green (preferably leafy) or yellow vegetable, raw or cooked.
5. 1 other vegetable, either fresh, canned, or dried (aside from potato).
6. 1 serving of potato.
7. Whole grain or enriched cereal—bread, breakfast food, cake, etc.
8. 1 serving of meat, fish or cheese. Liver or other meat sundry weekly.
9. 1 egg daily if possible; otherwise at least 3 or 4 times weekly.
10. 3 to 5 tablespoons of butter, or oleomargarine fortified with vitamin A.

When these basic ingredients have been incorporated into the daily menus, the body's requirements for health are met, as far as is known today. After these minimum requirements are met you can go ahead and add anything your family likes to provide extra energy value or for variety and palate appeal. This may be something extra, like a savory gravy, pie, cake or some other dessert; or it may be more of the same—an extra serving of vegetable, or of meat, or potato, or more bread or cereal. Each of these extras will add some additional food value, as well as pleasing flavor and the bulk that makes you feel satisfied when you have finished eating.

Of course, the basic foods should not be selected for food value alone— texture, color and flavor must all be considered, as well as seasonability and economy. For example, a meal in which all the foods are white or light colored has little eye appeal. In such a menu, yellow turnips (rutabagas) will be more appetizing in appearance than white ones. In making substitutions, which may be necessary from time to time for a variety of reasons (such as family food preferences or unavailability of certain foods on local markets) try

---

*This DIET PATTERN is in agreement with the standard set up by the Committee on Food and Nutrition of the National Research Council, which was organized to advise U.S. Governmental Agencies on nutrition problems connected with the National Defense Program.

to substitute only foods from the same class in the DIET PATTERN. In the case above, for instance, both yellow and white turnips come under number 5 in the diet pattern, and so would beets or carrots which might be substituted. Or, as another example—if you can't get water cress when it appears on the menu, use another salad green instead. Other changes should be made in the same manner.

CALORIC REQUIREMENTS

A diet which supplies the essential proteins, minerals and vitamins, and which also provides for normal growth in children or maintains the adult body at its normal weight, is supplying the correct number of calories.

The energy requirements of children are high in proportion to their size —they need calories to grow, as well as to meet their high activity requirements. In addition to the elements necessary for body building their diet must supply sufficient calories to provide for a steady increase in weight. During the period of rapid growth in adolescence, when both growth and activity levels are high, there is a need for a high calorie diet—many extra foods may be necessary to supplement the basic diet pattern.

The energy requirements of adults also vary with their activity. It is generally recommended that an individual should try to bring his weight to that which corresponds to the life insurance average for his height at age 30, and that he maintain it at that figure thereafter. Variations from normal weight should not exceed 10 per cent in either direction.

In cases where weight must be reduced or increased due to pronounced variation from the normal, it is always wise to consult a physician, since other factors besides diet may play a part in producing the abnormality. It is safe to say, however, that in both reducing and gaining diets, but especially in the former, care should be taken to see that the full daily requirement of vitamins and minerals is met.

PROTEIN REQUIREMENT

Protein is necessary for the building and the upkeep of muscles and other body tissues, and to provide materials for the building of certain important regulatory substances such as hormones and enzymes. Protein may also be used, in part, as a source of heat and energy, along with carbohydrate and fat.

Normal growth, upkeep, and repair of body tissues requires that the body be supplied constantly with more protein. There are many sources of protein —most foods contain some of this foodstuff, but in many cases the amount is small and the quality is poor. This is true of most fruits, for instance. Foods of animal origin—meat, fish, poultry, milk, cheese, eggs—are excellent sources of high quality protein. Legumes, grains and nuts are also good protein sources.

An adequate diet containing a variety of foods, such as will be secured if the "pattern" (p. 4) is followed, will provide plenty of protein for the normal healthy adult. Growing children and expectant and nursing mothers, all of whom are creating extra protein, need generous amounts of high quality protein such as is found in meat, milk, and eggs. In addition to supplying protein, these foods also supply important nutrients for bone-building and for blood.

FUNCTIONS OF VITAMINS

The body is quick to feel any lack or insufficiency of calories in the diet, but it may go for long periods of time with an inadequate supply of vitamins before noticeable effects are observed. A continued deficiency of vitamins may cause serious consequences, however, for these substances are of the utmost importance in regulating some of the fundamental bodily functions.

Vitamins are no longer quite the mysterious substances they once seemed to be, for scientists have been able to isolate and study them, and to produce many of them in the laboratory. New experimental techniques have made it possible to learn much about the specific "jobs" of certain vitamins. Nevertheless, there is still much to be learned, especially about the way the different vitamins act together and with other substances in the complicated mechanism of the body.

All of the vitamins play important roles in promoting normal growth and development, and in maintaining health and vigor—and the attractive appearance and good disposition that go with radiant good health. In planning an adequate diet we need consider only certain vitamins, however. If the food we eat contains sufficient quantities of vitamins A, D, and C and of thiamine, riboflavin and niacin, and, in addition, provides for adequate protein and mineral intake, it will also supply sufficient quantities of the lesser known vitamins.

Some of the functions of these important vitamins are listed below:

Vitamin A—this vitamin helps keep the mucous membranes of the body in good condition. It has special functions in connection with the eye—in additon to its effect on the mucous membranes, it is a constituent of a pigment which is a part of the mechanism by which we see in dim light. Vitamin A is also important in the production of tooth enamel, and in normal bone formation.

Vitamin D—this vitamin promotes absorption of calcium from the intestinal tract, and is necessary for the efficient utilization of calcium and phosphorus in building strong bones and teeth. This vitamin is sometimes called the "sunshine vitamin," because certain substances in the skin are converted into vitamin D when exposed to sunlight or ultra-violet light.

Lack of vitamin D in childhood produces rickets. It is not definitely known what importance vitamin D has in the diet of the adult, but it seems that a certain amount is necessary to enable the body to use the calcium and phosphorus present in food.

Vitamin C (ascorbic acid)—this vitamin is essential for the normal formation of the intercellular "cementing" substances of the body—in this way it exerts a function on the structure of bones, cartilage and teeth, and in the maintenance of the normal strength of the capillary walls.

A continued low intake of vitamin C results in such symptoms as lack of energy, fleeting pains in the joints, bleeding gums. A severe lack of vitamin C results in scurvy.

Thiamine (vitamin B_1)—one of the primary functions of this vitamin is the role which it plays in the utilization of carbohydrate by the body. Thiamine also promotes normal appetite and normal motility of the digestive tract.

A lack of thiamine results in such symptoms as fatigue, lassitude, and loss of appetite. A severe deficiency of the vitamin causes beriberi.

Riboflavin (vitamin B_2, vitamin G)—this vitamin is part of an enzyme system which functions in the fundamental processes of the utilization of food by the body.

Lack of riboflavin results in a form of dermatitis, in fissures at the corners of the mouth, and in certain abnormalities of the tongue and of the eyes.

Niacin (nicotinic acid)—this vitamin is also a part of an enzyme system involved in the utilization of food by the body.

Lack of niacin results in pellagra, a disease characterized by dermatitis, by digestive disorders, and, in severe cases, by mental derangement. This deficiency disease, once common in the southern part of this country, is much less frequent in occurrence since the discovery of niacin.

The last three vitamins listed are all members of a group of vitamins known as the "vitamin B-complex". Once this group was thought to be a single vitamin, but it is now known to be made up of a number of different factors. Among the members of the vitamin B-complex are *pyridoxine, pantothenic acid, para-aminobenzoic acid, choline, biotin, inositol, folic acid,* and *vitamin B_{12}*. Like all vitamins, these substances are necessary for normal growth and development, and specific functions are known for some of them —vitamin B_{12} is used in the treatment of pernicious anemia, for example. It is not necessary to pay particular attention to these vitamins in planning meals, however, because the normal healthy adult will receive sufficient quantities of all of them in an adequate diet such as will be obtained if the "pattern" is followed.

FOOD SOURCES OF THE VITAMINS

Since large supplies of pure vitamins and vitamin concentrates have become available, it has become popular to "take" all the vitamins in the form of tablets, pills, or capsules. This practice is neither necessary nor desirable, unless done under a physician's supervision. All of the vitamins, with the possible exception of vitamin D, can be obtained from an ordinary adequate diet by a healthy individual.

Vitamin D is available in few foods except fish liver oils and vitamin D-enriched foods, such as milk and certain breakfast cereals. Just what constitutes an adequate daily supply of vitamin D for adults has not been established, but 400 I. U. is the amount suggested for children and for expectant and nursing mothers. To be on the safe side, this should be supplied in some fish liver oil or vitamin D concentrate throughout the year. Theoretically, it can safely be discontinued during the summer months if the person is much in the sun; but in practice, the sunshine is not always of good quality due to smoke and haze, and the body may fail to manufacture sufficient vitamin D even when frequently exposed to the sun.

The following list gives some of the best sources of certain of the vitamins:

Vitamin A—fish liver oils, liver, butter, eggs, cream, milk. Most yellow vegetables and fruits and green leafy vegetables contain *carotene*, a substance which can be converted into vitamin A in the body.
Vitamin C—citrus fruits, tomatoes, fresh strawberries, cantaloupe, raw cabbage, and other fresh fruits and vegetables.
Thiamine—whole grains, meat—especially pork—liver, enriched cereals, breads and flours, nuts, eggs, legumes, many vegetables.
Riboflavin—milk, liver, whole grains, eggs, cheese, enriched breads and flours, legumes, green leafy vegetables.

It should be noted that some foods may be valuable sources of certain vitamins, even though they do not contain particularly large amounts of that vitamin. For instance, a medium size potato contains only about one-fourth as much vitamin C as a medium size orange. If eaten regularly and abundantly, however, potatoes may supply important amounts of this vitamin. In northern countries such as Finland, where it is difficult to obtain an adequate supply of citrus fruits and tomatoes, potatoes are the principal source of vitamin C.

FUNCTIONS OF MINERALS

Minerals are building materials and are essential to body growth, maintenance and repair; they are also important in regulating the functions of the body. A wide variety of mineral substances are found in the body—it is not definitely known, however, whether all of them are truly "essential", or whether they are merely present "accidentally". Many of these minerals, if they are essential, are needed in such small amounts that it is unlikely there would ever be any shortage of them in the diet.

Among the minerals needed in relatively large quantites in the body are *calcium* and *phosphorus*. These minerals work together in bone building, with the collaboration of vitamins A, C, and D. Both of them serve other important functions in addition—calcium is necessary for normal blood coagulation, for example, and phosphorus is a constituent of many important regulatory substances. Adequate supplies of these minerals are vital for the child, the adolescent, and for the pregnant or nursing mother. In the child and adolescent they are needed to make hard, straight bones and sound teeth; in pregnancy and lactation they are required to give the baby a good start and also to preserve the mother's health, since she must share her own body calcium with her child. A generous supply of calcium and phosphorus during pregnancy will help to put an end to the old superstition that the mother must lose "a tooth for every child." Adults require these same minerals in somewhat smaller quantities to help *keep* their teeth and bones sound and healthy.

Iron and *copper* are partners in blood building. Iron is a constituent of hemoglobin, the substance in the red blood cells which carries oxygen to all parts of the body. The presence of copper is necessary for the utilization of iron in forming hemoglobin. New red blood cells must continually be manufactured by the body, and this is impossible without a sufficient supply of iron. Nutritional anemia, evidenced by such signs as low vitality and a tendency toward easy fatigue, may result if insufficient amounts of iron are present in the diet.

Iodine is needed by the thyroid gland to keep it functioning normally, and it is the activity of the thyroid that regulates the utilization of the foods we consume. Excessive thyroid activity causes the metabolic rate (the rate at which food is converted into energy by the body) to go up, with resulting nervousness and loss of weight; subnormal thyroid activity causes it to go down followed by a gain in weight and often by lethargy or over relaxation.

FOOD SOURCES OF MINERALS

Most foods contain a certain quantity of minerals, and an adequate diet will provide sufficient quantities of most of the essential ones. In planning our meals it is necessary to give special consideration to three important minerals, however. These are *calcium, iron,* and *iodine.*

Although many foods contain some calcium, it is difficult to obtain the necessary quantities of this mineral unless milk and other dairy products, such as cheese, are included in the diet. These foods, in addition to being a rich source of calcium, also provide other important body building nutrients, too.

The body is very efficient in its use of iron—normally the iron in the body is conserved and may be used over and over again. It is especially important that plenty of iron be supplied in the food during childhood, and during pregnancy when new tissues are being formed. An adequate supply of iron is important for girls and women throughout the reproductive period.

Sufficient iodine to maintain normal thyroid activity and normal metabolism is found in sea foods and in garden produce and drinking water in many parts of the country. In the Great Plains area in the center of the country and around the Great Lakes, however, it is desirable to supplement the possible deficiency by using preparations such as iodized salt.

Although *phosphorus* is needed in relatively large quantities, it is widely distributed among our foods, and if the diet provides sufficient protein and calcium, the phosphorus requirement will be met.

A list of foods which are important sources of minerals is given below.

Calcium—cheese, buttermilk, sweet milk, cauliflower, chard, cabbage, carrots, egg yolk, onions, green beans, asparagus.
Phosphorus—beans, cheese, egg yolk, lentils, liver, milk, peas, whole grains.
Iron—asparagus, beans, cauliflower, celery, chard, dandelion greens, egg yolk, heart, liver, lettuce, kidneys, oatmeal, oysters, red meat, whole wheat.
Copper—cocoa, liver, oysters, peas, apricots.
Iodine—sea foods.

In planning meals with adequate mineral intake it should be remembered that, as in the case with vitamins, a food which is eaten regularly in relatively large quantities may be an important source of a mineral, and may provide as much as another "rich" source of that mineral which is eaten only occasionally. An example is milk, which, though low in iron per serving, will provide almost as much iron in a week of three servings a day as will a single serving of liver which is very high in iron.

CONSERVING MINERALS AND VITAMINS

The mineral content of foods is more stable than the vitamin content, which is greatest when the food is perfectly fresh, and gradually is lost on exposure to air. The longer fresh fruits and vegetables are allowed to stand after picking, the greater the vitamin loss. Of course, this is true to a much smaller extent of vegetables and fruits which have skins, like oranges, apples, tomatoes and potatoes. Nor does it apply to canned foods, which are sealed in air-tight containers almost immediately after picking. Vitamin loss is especially rapid after the fruit or vegetables have been peeled, and they should be eaten or cooked promptly after paring. Dry foods such as flour, cereals, etc., are relatively stable sources of the vitamins which they contain.

Both minerals and vitamins may be lost from fruits and vegetables if, after paring, they are allowed to stand in water which is later discarded. And they lose still more when cooked in water, through dissolving out into the water. For this reason it is recommended that all vegetables be cooked in the smallest amount of water which will make them palatable and appealing, and that the "pot liquor" or cooking water which must be drained off before serving be used for soup or a vegetable cocktail, since it contains minerals and vitamins in solution.

Asparagus, beans, carrots, cabbage and peas are only a few of the vegetables whose pot liquors, either hot or chilled, make a delicious beverage. The pot liquor from pared potatoes has less flavor but contains just as large a quantity of vitamins and minerals as the more flavorful pot liquors; it should be saved and used when water is required for soup, gravy, or even for cooking other vegetables. Two of the few exceptions to the rule that all pot liquor should be utilized are spinach and beet cooking water. Due to the high oxalic acid content of spinach and the "earthy" taste of the beet skin these are unpalatable and may be discarded.

WHY USE MENUS?

● ● ● ● ● ● ● ● ●

TODAY many homemakers have a puzzled attitude toward balanced diets. It can be summed up something like this: "Our grandparents got along without worrying about balanced menus—they didn't even know about vitamins and minerals, and they seemed none the worse for it—so why should I fuss about what my family eats so long as I put enough on the table to fill them up?" You will find a satisfying answer to this question by reading this chapter.

● ● ● ● ● ● ● ● ●

The chief reason why grandmother's unscientific method of filling up her family and letting it go at that was nutritionally successful in so many cases, is that in those days folks had bigger appetites. Everyone worked harder—physically harder—than most of us do now. Eighty years ago, 80 per cent of the population lived on farms; and in those days there were few of the labor-saving devices which all of us take for granted in this age of electricity and Diesel engines. Men and women, boys and girls, all worked with their hands and it made them hungry. They lived in colder, draughtier houses too, and needed food to keep them warm as well as to make energy. Vitamins and minerals are found rather sparingly in most foods, and the smaller the meals we eat the more difficult it is to get them in sufficient quantities for health. Our grandparents ate more food and automatically obtained more of these precious food elements.

The food they ate was different from our food, too. They had far less variety than we enjoy, but since 80 per cent of them lived on farms, the limited variety of foods they ate was fresh from field and garden and orchard, with all its vitamin value intact. In winter root vegetables, cabbage and apples from cellar and pit, and canned and dried foods tided them over till spring. Even the city folk, living in small cities, were much nearer to their source of supply than we are today. Now city dwellers, unless they have a garden of their own at the edge of the city, seldom see a fresh food in a market that is less than 24 hours old, while many are much older, because they pass through many hands. This means that a large proportion of the vitamin content has vanished.

Put these 2 facts together and you will see why our forebears got along as well as they did with no special effort or knowledge on their part. Not only were their foods richer in essential vitamins and minerals than the foods we eat, but they ate more of them. They ate more not only because they worked hard and were made hungry by the exercise, but also because their foods gave them more of the appetite-stimulating vitamins.

Another condition that influences present-day diets both for worse and for better is that a vastly greater variety of foods is available to us. Grandmother had only a few basic foods to work with, and if her family wanted enough to fill up, they had to eat what was set before them. If Johnny disliked greens, Johnny had no other choice and got no encouragement in developing food dislikes. Nowadays it is so easy to replace a disliked food with another food which may be far less valuable nutritionally. To this extent the wide variety of foods we enjoy may affect our diet for the worse.

On the other hand, the possibilities of good nutrition are increased today because we have access to so many fresh foods the year around which were formerly not available at all or were available only for brief seasons. For example, when grandfather was a boy, oranges were such a rarity in the North and East that many children saw them only in their Christmas stockings; whereas today we can drink fresh orange juice every day of the year if we wish. The same is true to a smaller extent of many other fresh fruits and vegetables, and even of dairy products; and of canned foods of all kinds. If we use this variety wisely we can improve our nutrition and make our meals more attractive too. But our tastes and preferences, due to pressures and habits of modern life, cannot be depended upon as a guide to the wisest choice amongst this abundance; and this is where scientifically planned menus are helpful.

Finally, food costs more today than it did a generation ago; and this, unfortunately, is particularly true of the protective foods—milk, eggs, meat, green vegetables, and fresh fruit. Even the farm family encounters this problem with foods they do not raise; and city families are confronted with it at every turn. Because she can save the most money by cutting down on just these protective foods, the homemaker who is not guided by a definite menu plan for a well-balanced diet may easily fall into this false economy at the expense of the health of her family.

Thus the changing conditions of life which have made us an urban instead of a rural nation have added the extra task of *meal-planning for health* to the homemaker's essential activities. It is with the object of lightening her burden that the following menus have been planned.

Here are the ways in which our carefully worked-out menus help both the homemaker and her whole family:

1. They outline a day-by-day diet which provides the essential food elements in quantities sufficient to develop and maintain buoyant health. Because of the smaller quantities of food which almost all of us consume nowadays, and because of the smaller vitamin and mineral content of much of that food, it is difficult to do this by haphazard selection of the foods the family happens to fancy.

2. They provide for a reasonable variety, not only in the foods themselves but in their methods of preparation. Thus the family may be kept interested in the basic protective foods which must be eaten daily for health.

3. They utilize seasonable foods. The summertime season for fresh fruits and vegetables is so short that it is good practice to serve them very often while they last. Few families would object to strawberry shortcake or strawberries and cream every day during their brief season. This is also an economy measure, for fresh foods in season are usually low in price.

4. They suggest ways of using inexpensive foods, especially inexpensive cuts of meat, with which many women are unfamiliar but which are just as delicious and satisfying as the more expensive ones, when well cooked. The frequent use of these inexpensive cuts will make it possible to enjoy the choicer ones on special occasions—on holidays, and when "company" comes.

5. They call the homemaker's attention to new recipes, new food combinations, perhaps even to foods which she has never tried before; and thus they build up her recipe repertoire, make her a more versatile cook, and satisfy her with a sense of new achievement.

6. They answer that daily recurring question: "What shall I serve today?" —and they answer it so reliably that the homemaker no longer needs to be uncertain about her choice of food.

In short, these menus are designed to help women deal confidently and successfully with the changing world in which they live, so far as food and nutrition are concerned.

HOW TO USE THESE MENUS

THE menus you will find in the 21 pages of this book are not meant for "slavish" following. You may want to vary them, to exercise your own imagination and ingenuity, and to adapt them to your family's preferences and to the food supply available to you. For example, if you raise your own corn or strawberries, you will probably serve corn or strawberries during their season much oftener than they are called for here. If you have your own chickens, you may be able to serve eggs or egg dishes every day instead of 3 or 4 times a week, and to indulge in a chicken dinner much oftener than we have allowed it. But regardless of your supply, if Susie happens to be allergic to strawberries, you will have to skip strawberries for Susie even in their season, and give her instead some of the other fresh fruits in season at the same time.

These menus will free you from the pressure of having to plan 3 meals a day every day of the week. Even though you prefer to make your own adjustments, they furnish a basic plan to guide you.

The menus are designed to give satisfactory nutrition at medium to low levels of cost, to suggest variety, methods of preparation and service which will enable the family to enjoy their meals day after day.

Should you desire to make a few changes in these menus, use all of the above factors to guide you.

1. HOW TO BEGIN MEAL PLANNING

Due to shortage of space in this book, representative MENUS have been planned for but ONE WEEK IN EACH MONTH OF THE YEAR. These are merely to give you a RIGHT START in meal planning. So when a homemaker follows the menus for a week, what shall she do for menus for the remaining 21 to 24 days of the month? Here are 2 suggestions:

1. Use these menus as a guide in connection with the DIET PATTERN, p. 4. Make up your own menus for the rest of the month, substituting different vegetables, salads, meats and desserts.

2. Or use these menus again the 2nd, 3rd and 4th week as well as the remaining days in the month. When food is well cooked and attractively

served, the average healthy family does not tire of meals repeated 4 times, when each repetition is a week apart. One advantage in such repetition is:

(a) That the seasonal foods will continue in season and enable you to take advantage of them.

(b) That it saves the homemaker time in making up menus from scratch. However, it isn't much of a trick to make substitutions now and then to give the meal a "NEW LOOK".

Suppose the family does not approve of beets, which appear on tonight's dinner menu, but prefer carrots or kohlrabi. Either of these 2 vegetables are nutritionally acceptable as they come within the same class, see DIET PATTERN, p. 4. Or if veal on tomorrow's menu is impossible to get at your butcher's, then use lamb or chicken, and you can be sure your family will not be deprived of any nutrients in these substitutions, as they come in the same class.

We have not included menus for holiday meals except the Thanksgiving Day Dinner. One reason is that only 2 holidays fall on the same day every year, namely, Thanksgiving and Easter Sunday. However, we have not left the homemaker without help. If roast goose is the piece de resistance on your Christmas Dinner table, we supply a good recipe for roast goose. If roast ham is what you want to serve New Years or Easter, you can find recipes for that, too.

2. HOW TO MAKE SUBSTITUTIONS OF FOODS

You may occasionally wish to substitute other foods for those in a given menu, whether because strawberries give Susie the hives, or because pork chops are not the best meat buy on the day they are suggested, or because you have less, or even more to spend than usual. This can easily be done, but to keep the menu well balanced nutritionally, be sure to substitute something from the same class of food. That is, if you take out a fresh fruit, put another fresh fruit in, not a pudding; if you take out a leafy green vegetable, substitute another vegetable of the same type, such as cabbage for lettuce or spinach for broccoli.

3. HOW TO ADJUST QUANTITIES

The menus have been designed for a family of five—husband, wife and three children. If there are fewer in your family, you can adjust the amounts of food you allow in proportion. A family consisting of father, mother and only one child will consume roughly about three-fifths—slightly over one-half—as much food as a family of five.

The recipes in many cases can be adjusted in the same way. But where this is difficult or impossible, or if you simply prefer not to bother with changing recipes, you can make the full amount and count on serving the left-overs at another meal, replacing some food of the same type called for in

16

the menu for that meal. If what is left over is vegetable, let it replace a vegetable, not meat or eggs or a citrus fruit. Utilizing left-overs intelligently is a real art, involving careful storing, careful re-heating, and careful serving to make them as attractive as they were the first time. But if your family doesn't like to eat left-overs, it will pay you to practice reducing recipes to fit the number of mouths you have to feed, so that all will be consumed in the first meal.

If one member of the family is a baby, there will be a difference in the kinds of food he eats. Milk forms the major part of his diet during his first year; after that he will continue to need a quart of milk a day, but will gradually begin to eat the same foods the rest of the family eats, in gradually increasing amounts. After the first year, the baby may be figured as using up his full share of the food allowed for the family, though actually, for a year or two, his servings will continue to be a trifle smaller than those of his older brothers and sisters. The supposition is that father and his adolescent son will want larger servings, mother and little sister smaller ones, than the average figured on, depending of course upon their physical activity.

A number of times the menus suggest a recipe which will be sufficient for two meals, based on average appetites. Perhaps for your particular family the quantities may be too skimpy, or too large, according to the food needs and the activities of the various members. You will probably be able to judge from the recipes whether quantities are about right, or whether they need to be adjusted.

Of course it is often convenient to have a little too much, in case unexpected guests drop in about dinner time; and perhaps Junior may have been playing football, thus acquiring a double-barrelled appetite. On the other hand, sometimes a rather small meal provides welcome opportunity for using up leftovers.

Since all the recipes are based on what we assume to be average folks with average activities and average appetites, there is very likely to be some deviation from the needs of your family. So it is up to you, as you use the book, to exercise your native ingenuity in adapting both menus and recipes to the special needs of your special household.

4. HOW TO SWITCH MENUS

If the noon meal is the big meal of the day in your home, in most cases you can simply switch the dinner and luncheon menus, and serve dinner at noon and luncheon as the evening supper.

If your husband's boss or some other special guest is coming to dinner on a week-day evening and you want to do something extra for him which doesn't appear on the menu for the day, perhaps you can switch it with Sunday's dinner. This usually provides for something a little "special" and may just fill the bill. In making such exchanges from day to day, you need to plan carefully about left-overs—both those already on hand and those which you will have as a result of the switch. This may mean adjustments for two or three days—but you have the menus to use as a basis and a little juggling will usually do the trick successfully.

5. HOW TO PLAN AHEAD WITH THE MENUS

Don't be content to study the menus just one day at a time. Look ahead to the next day—that will enable you to get ready in advance if there is any preliminary preparation to be done, and will save you work. For example, there may be a dried bean dish tomorrow, and in that case the beans should be put to soak overnight. You may save a trip to the store tomorrow, too, by ordering tomorrow's supplies along with today's.

If you have storage facilities for more than enough food for a day or two, study the whole week's menus at a time. Then make a list of the foods required for each menu, referring to the individual recipes for exact amounts when it is necessary, then make your market list for the whole week, or for half the week, according to your convenience. Some homemakers form a habit of making 2 lists. On one they put staple items and canned or packaged foods which can safely be bought and stored, and on the other, foods like meat, fruit and fresh vegetables, which should be bought more or less from day to day.

Sometimes you will be able to make considerable savings by buying enough potatoes or apples for a whole week, or a month, or even longer. But this is never practical unless you have suitable and sufficient storage space to take care of them.

Another advantage in planning ahead is that it helps you to arrange for family assistance. You will know which meals require help and be able to assign tasks in advance, so other members of the family can plan their activities accordingly.

6. HOW TO ADJUST THE MENUS TO YOUR CANNING PROGRAM

If you are in a position to can fruits and vegetables yourself, you will save money and will have greater variety, and in some cases better flavor. This is particularly true with jams, jellies, preserves and pickles. They add zest to meals at which they are served, and add calories and some slight food value besides. If they have been economically put up at home, they may be served even more often than they appear on the menus, to pep up the flavor of the whole meal. If they must all be bought, they become a luxury item, and it may be necessary to serve them less often than we have indicated.

Where home canning and preserving have been done, keep a list of the products you have on hand, and check off each jar or can as it is used. Try to use them according to a schedule, so your strawberry jam will not be all gone while you still have a big supply of grape jelly on hand. Unless you have reason to suppose that the strawberry jam won't keep well this year, due to some seasonal difference in the fruit, this is an unnecessary sacrifice of variety.

Of course the same thing goes for canned vegetables and fruits. If the family is unusually fond of your canned peaches, put up an extra amount to satisfy them, but don't serve canned peaches to the exclusion of other kinds of fruit and thus exhaust your supply long before spring comes.

7. HOW TO GET COOPERATION FROM THE FAMILY

You can use the Diet Pattern and the menus together as the basis for a sort of educational game which will teach every member of the family more about nutrition, and how to choose foods. Help them to see how the food they eat and enjoy fits into the "pattern" of what they must eat to be healthy and strong. For if they do not cooperate with you by eating the food you provide, they will not be well fed, no matter how carefully you plan their diet; and one way of increasing their willingness to eat the right food is to interest them in its choice and the reasons behind it.

JANUARY

A WEEK'S GUIDE USING SEASONAL FOODS IN THRIFTY BALANCED MENUS

(See Index for recipes to make foods suggested in menus)

MONDAY

Breakfast—Orange Juice
Rolled Oats 168 with Thin Cream
Toast with Butter, Jelly 704, 709
Coffee for Adults   Milk for Children

Luncheon—*Cream of Navy Bean Soup 954
Hot Corn bread 34 and Butter
Raw Apples
Tea for Adults   Milk for Children

Dinner—Poached Eggs 391 on Beef Hash 511
Baked Acorn Squash 1101
Head Lettuce, French Dressing 841
Bread and Butter
Whipped Strawberry Gelatine 320
Vanilla Crisps 208
Coffee for Adults   Cocoa for Children.

TUESDAY

Breakfast—½ Grapefruit
Hot Whole Wheat Cereal 168 with Thin Cream
Cinnamon Toast 55
Coffee for Adults   Milk for Children

Luncheon—Spinach Chowder 974
Toasted Cheese Sandwiches 885
Fresh or Canned Pears
Tea for Adults   Milk for Children

Dinner—Curried Lamb 528
Baked Potatoes 1067 Butter
Buttered Parsley Carrots 1012
Stuffed Prune Salad 770
Bread and Butter
Pumpkin Custard 232
Coffee for Adults   Milk for Children

WEDNESDAY

Breakfast—Freshly Sliced Oranges
Poached Eggs on Toast 391
Jelly 709
Coffee for Adults   Cocoa for Children

Luncheon—Tomato Rarebit 192
Shredded Cabbage and Celery Salad 779
Sliced Bananas with Thin Cream
Tea for Adults   Milk for Children

THURSDAY

Breakfast—Grapefruit Juice
Hot Rice 174 with Brown Sugar and Thin Cream
Whole Wheat Toast with Butter
Coffee for Adults   Milk for Children

Luncheon—Baked Beans 1001
Boston Brown Bread 33
Pickles 720 and Celery
Stewed Apricots 274
Cocoa for All 4

*Navy bean soup is best for children when strained.

Dinner—Pan-fried Liver **601**
Mashed Potatoes **1077**
Green Onions
Creamed Peas **1060**
Whole Wheat Bread and Butter
Butterscotch Pudding **352**
Coffee for Adults   Milk for Children

Dinner—Escalloped Potatoes and
  Ham **539**
Buttered Onions **1047**
Grated Carrot and Raisin Salad
  743
Bread and Butter
Apple Dumplings **259**
Coffee for Adults   Milk for Children

FRIDAY

Breakfast—Grapefruit Juice
Scrambled Eggs **396**
Whole Wheat Toast and Butter
Coffee for Adults   Cocoa for Chil-
  dren

Luncheon—Spicy Bread Crumb
  Griddle Cakes **37**, Syrup **924**
Pork Sausage Patties **565**
Grape Tapioca **369**
Tea for Adults   Milk for Children

Dinner—Veal à la King **582**
American Fried Potatoes **1073**
Buttered Spinach **1094**
Olives and Radishes
Bread and Butter
Cupcakes **118**
Coffee for Adults   Milk for Children

SATURDAY

Breakfast—Tangerines
Whole Wheat Muffins **48** with
  Butter
Fried Sliced Luncheon Meat
Jelly **704** or **709**
Coffee for Adults   Cocoa for Chil-
  dren

Luncheon—Macaroni with Cheese
  Sauce **179**
Stewed Tomatoes **1111**
Celery Cabbage, Raw
Bread and Butter
Cupcakes **118**
Tea for Adults   Milk for Children

Dinner—Quick-baked Pike **415**
Parsley Buttered Potatoes **1069**
Green Beans with Onions **987**
Bread and Butter
Peach Salad **757**
Cocoa Puff **349**
Coffee for Adults   Milk for Children

SUNDAY

Breakfast—Grapefruit Halves
Prepared Cereal with Thin Cream
Toast with Butter
Jam **702** or **703**
Coffee for Adults   Milk for Children

Dinner—Baked Ham Slice
Baked Sweet Potatoes **1085**
Buttered Brussels Sprouts **1008a**

Bread and Butter
Crabapple Pickles **721**
Dried Fruit Whip **286**
Coffee for Adults   Milk for Children

Supper—Molded Vegetable Salad
  817
Bacon Muffins **44** with Butter
Cocoa for All **4**

FEBRUARY

A WEEK'S GUIDE USING SEASONAL FOODS
IN THRIFTY BALANCED MENUS

(See Index for recipes to make foods suggested in menus)

MONDAY

Breakfast—Stewed Dried Peaches 283
Soft-cooked Eggs 394
Toast with Butter, Jelly 704 or 709
Coffee for Adults Milk for Children

Luncheon—Tomato and Cabbage Soup 975
Crackers
Whole Wheat Bread and Butter
Cottage Cheese with Marmalade 712
Tea for Adults Milk for Children

Dinner—Meat Soufflé 405
Buttered Carrots 1012
Green Pepper Sticks Radishes
Creamed Potatoes 1070
Bread and Butter
Grapefruit Fluff 322
Coffee for Adults Milk for Children

TUESDAY

Breakfast—Tangerines
Prepared Cereal with Top Milk
Toast with Butter, Jelly 704 or 709
Coffee for Adults Cocoa for Children

Luncheon—Kidney Bean Loaf 995
with Chili Sauce 725a
Lettuce Sandwiches 875
Fruit Cocktail, or Fruit Cup 287
Hermits 202
Tea for Adults Milk for Children

Dinner—Braised Spareribs with Gravy 556
Mashed Potatoes 1077
Buttered Beets 1005 Celery
Bread and Butter
Dutch Apple Pie 637
Coffee for Adults Milk for Children

WEDNESDAY

Breakfast—Halved Grapefruit
*Scrambled Eggs 396
Biscuits and Butter, Jam 711
Coffee for Adults Cocoa for Children

Luncheon—Spinach Chowder 974
Melba Toast 58
Cranberry Sauce 282
Oatmeal Drop Cookies 204
Tea for Adults Milk for Children

THURSDAY

Breakfast—Applesauce 261
Bran Muffins 45 and Butter
Broiled Bacon 544
Jelly 704 or 709
Coffee for Adults Milk for Children

Luncheon—Hot Tomato Bouillon 977
Grilled Cheese Sandwiches 884
Sliced Bananas in Orange Juice
Tea for Adults Milk for Children

*Stir lightly, don't beat, for white-and-gold-streaked scrambled eggs.

Dinner—Meat Balls, Sauerkraut 488
Potato Dumplings 1078
Bread and Butter
Shredded Lettuce with Mayonnaise 843
Molded Raspberry Cream 334
Coffee for Adults   Milk for Children

Dinner—Pot Roast of Veal with Gravy 576
Carrot Sticks
Baked Potatoes 1067
Buttered Spinach 1094
Bread and Butter
Brown Sugar Custard 227
Coffee for Adults   Milk for Children

FRIDAY

Breakfast—Prune Juice
Rolled Oats with Thin Cream 168
Toast with Butter, Jam 702 or 712
Coffee for Adults   Milk for Children

Luncheon—Baked Eggs in Bacon Rings 381
Toast and Butter
Orange Waldorf Salad 756
Peanut Butter Cookies 222
(Save Half for Saturday's Luncheon)
Chocolate Ice Cream
Tea for Adults   Milk for Children

Dinner—Lamb Patties 525
Quick Escalloped Potatoes 1075
Buttered Peas 1060
Bread and Butter
Baked Apples 266 or 267
Coffee for Adults   Milk for Children

SATURDAY

Breakfast—Tomato Juice 719a
Griddle Cakes 38, syrup 924
Coffee for Adults   Cocoa for Children

Luncheon—Beans au Gratin 986
Bread and Butter
Garden Salad 795
Peanut Butter Cookies 222
Stewed Dried Apricots 274
Tea for Adults   Milk for Children

Dinner—Heart Chop Suey 624
Boiled Rice 174
Lettuce, 1000 Island Dressing 848
Bread and Butter
Frozen Berries and Cookies
Coffee for Adults   Milk for Children

SUNDAY

Breakfast—½ Grapefruit
Broiled Bacon 544
Apple and Pineapple Rolls 32
Coffee for Adults   Milk for Children

Dinner—Braised Pork Chops, Gravy 549
Mashed Potatoes 1077
Buttered Broccoli 1007
Head Lettuce, Russian Dressing 846

Bread and Butter
Cottage Pudding 353 with Lemon Sauce 934
Coffee for Adults   Milk for Children

Supper—Cottage Cheese Salad 789
Jelly Sandwiches 896a
Cookies
Tea for Adults   Milk for Children

Cottage cheese loses its sweet flavor quickly. Be sure it's fresh.

MARCH

A WEEK'S GUIDE USING SEASONAL FOODS IN THRIFTY BALANCED MENUS

(See Index for recipes to make foods suggested in menus)

MONDAY

Breakfast—Freshly Sliced Pared Oranges
Poached Eggs **391**, Toast, Butter
Coffee for Adults   Milk for Children

Luncheon—Beef Bouillon   **977a**
Soda Crackers
Apple and Pineapple Rolls   **32**
Cottage Cheese Salad   **789**
Tea for Adults   Milk for Children

Dinner—Veal Paprika   **585**
Mashed Potatoes   **1077**
Buttered Corn with Green Pepper
. **1025**
Celery Hearts
Whole Wheat Bread and Butter
Golden Feather Cake   **118**
(Save Half for Tuesday Dinner)
Raspberries Frozen or Canned
Coffee for Adults   Milk for Children

TUESDAY

Breakfast—Sliced Bananas
Whole Wheat Cereal   **170**
Toast with Butter
Jelly   **709**
Coffee for Adults   Milk for Children

Luncheon—Grilled Cheese and Bacon Sandwiches   **852**
Bread and Butter Pickles   **726**
Lettuce with French Dressing   **841**
Applesauce   **261**   Gum Drop Cookies   **201**
Cocoa for All   **4**

Dinner—Lamb Scallop   **534**
Hashed Brown Potatoes   **1082**
Cucumber and Onion Salad   **793**
Bread and Butter
Cottage Pudding   **353**   with Lemon Sauce   **934**
Coffee for Adults   Milk for Children

What a piquant contribution homemade pickles give to a meal!

WEDNESDAY

Breakfast—Stewed Prunes   **301**
Scrambled Eggs   **396**
Toast with Butter
Coffee for Adults   Cocoa for Children

Luncheon—Toasted Rice   **176**
Stewed Tomatoes   **1111**
Whole Wheat Bread and Butter
Molded Peach Salad   **759**
Tea for Adults   Milk for Children

THURSDAY

Breakfast—½ Grapefruit   French Toast   **56**
Syrup   **924**
Coffee for Adults   Milk for Children

Luncheon—Split Pea Soup   **961a**
Soda Crackers
Grated Carrot Salad   **742**
Doughnuts   **128**
(Save Half for Friday Dinner)
Tea for Adults   Milk for Children

For occasional use it's practical to buy mint jelly.

Sometimes a salad goes formal in its arrangement, and that is just what has happened to this Whole Meal Fruit Salad (773). The salad shown is a single serving, arranged on a dinner-size plate—a grand dish for Sunday night supper on a warm spring or summer day.

Simple garnishes are the magic that make servings of plain rennet or custard deluxe. Scrolls and squiggles of whipped cream, cut-outs from sheets of firm gelatin, apricot purée, candied cherry, mint leaves, pre-toasted sliced marshmallows, corn flakes stuck in mounds of whipped cream and pear halves with slivers of candied ginger have garnished the simple desserts in this picture.

Use a homemade paper pattern to cut the pastry for this impressive Fish Shell with Salmon-Lobster Filling (436). The back of your paring knife makes the realistic markings in the unbaked filled shell.

Dozens of foods which were once available only in their brief seasons are now on hand the year around . . . in the Frozen Food Cabinets at the corner grocery; besides these, there are other delicious perishable foods from far away places. To be able to eat peaches and cream, strawberry shortcake, oyster or shrimp cocktails, fresh-frozen vegetables, fish, poultry or meat at any time the appetite craves them . . . is really something to be thankful for.

Dinner—Frankfurter and Lima Bean
   Casserole **594**
Buttered Cabbage **1008**
Cranberry Relish **745a**
Bread and Butter
Chocolate Blanc Mange **344**
Coffee for Adults   Milk for Children

Dinner—Spanish Sausage **566**
Mashed Potatoes **1077**
Buttered Green Beans **985**
Whole Wheat Bread and Butter
Canned Plums **718**
Coffee for Adults   Milk for Children

FRIDAY

Breakfast—Orange Juice
Rolled Oats **168** with Light
   Cream
Toast with Butter
Jam **711**
Coffee for Adults   Milk for Children

Luncheon—Eggs Benedictine **386**
Celery
Canned Pears **717a**
Tea for Adults   Milk for Children

Dinner—Codfish Balls **423**
Harvard Beets **1006**
Celery Cabbage Salad **784**
Bread and Butter
Doughnuts **128**
Baked Apples **267**
Coffee for Adults   Milk for Children

SATURDAY

Breakfast—Sliced Bananas
Farina with Light Cream
Toast with Butter, Jam **708**
Coffee for Adults   Milk for Children

Luncheon—Peanut Butter and Water
   Cress Sandwiches **898**
Orange and Cocoanut Salad **754**
Cocoa for All **4**

Dinner—Tomato Hamburgers **496**
Creamed Potatoes **1070**
Head Lettuce with 1000 Island Dress-
   ing **848**
Bread and Butter
Mincemeat Custard **229**
Coffee for Adults   Milk for Children

SUNDAY

Breakfast—Canned Grapefruit Juice
Quick Streusel Coffee Cake **54**
Pan-fried Canadian Bacon
Coffee for Adults   Milk for Children

Dinner—Sauerbraten **505**
Potato Dumplings **1078**
Buttered Cauliflower **1019**
Pickled Crabapples **721**
Whole Wheat Bread **90** and But-
   ter

Mince Pie **650**
Coffee for Adults   Milk for Children

Supper—Cream of Carrot Soup **948**
Soda Crackers
Waldorf Salad **772**
Ginger Ice Box Cookies **213**
(Save Half for Monday)
Tea for Adults   Milk for Children

Pot roast goes "high-hat" in sauerbraten.

APRIL

(See Index for recipes to make foods suggested in menus)

MONDAY

Breakfast—Sliced Bananas
Bran Muffins 45
Pan-broiled Link Sausage 563a
Apple Butter 701
Coffee for Adults Cocoa for Children

Luncheon—Hot Tomato Bouillon 977
Crackers
Pea and Cheese Salad 798
Canned Pineapple and Cookies
Tea for Adults Milk for Children

Dinner—Barbecued Spareribs 555
Parsley Buttered Potatoes 1069
Creamed Celery 1021
Tossed Vegetable Salad 825
Bread and Butter
Bread Pudding 339
Coffee for Adults Milk for Children

TUESDAY

Breakfast—Pineapple Juice
Rolled Oats 168 with Top Milk
Toast with Butter, Jelly 704a
Coffee for Adults Milk for Children

Luncheon—Cream Tomato Soup 960
Crackers
Peanut Butter Sandwiches 895
Prune Whip 302
Tea for Adults Milk for Children

Dinner—Pot Roast of Veal 576
  with Gravy 468
Boiled Potatoes 1068
Buttered Green Cabbage 1008
Olives and Radishes
Bread and Butter
Tapioca Cream 367
Coffee for Adults Milk for Children

WEDNESDAY

Breakfast—Tomato Juice 719a
Poached eggs 391 on Toast, Bacon
Coffee for Adults Cocoa for Children

Luncheon—Cream of Beet Soup 947
Crackers
Grapefruit-avocado Salad 752
Oatmeal Cookies 204
(Save Half for Thursday)
Tea for Adults Milk for Children

THURSDAY

Breakfast—Stewed Raisins 305
French Toast 56
Jelly 709
Coffee for Adults Milk for Children

Luncheon—Cream of Potato Soup 957
Crackers
Stewed Apricots 274
Oatmeal Cookies 204
Tea for Adults Milk for Children

26

Dinner—Lamb Patties 525
Creamed Potatoes 1070
Buttered Carrots 1012
Wilted Lettuce 827
Bread and Butter
Cherry Pie 645 or 646
Coffee for Adults   Milk for Children

Dinner—Pineapple Juice
Old-fashioned Baked Beans 1001
Boiled Potatoes 1068
Cole Slaw 786
Whole Wheat Bread 90   and Butter
Grapefruit Shortcake 288
Coffee for Adults   Milk for Children

FRIDAY

Breakfast—Sliced Bananas on Prepared Cereal with Top Milk
Toast with Butter
Jelly 704
Coffee for Adults   Cocoa for Children

Luncheon—Green Beans au Gratin 986
Melba Toast 58
Pineapple Date Salad 766
Tea for Adults   Milk for Children

Dinner—Tomato Juice Cocktail 24
Braised Pork Shoulder Steak 478a
Mashed Potatoes 1077
Pineapple Cole Slaw 787
Whole Wheat Bread and Butter
Rice Pudding 366
Coffee for Adults   Milk for Children

SATURDAY

Breakfast—Freshly Sliced Peeled Oranges
Cooked Whole Wheat Cereal 170 with Thin Cream
Scrambled Eggs 396
Toast with Butter
Coffee for Adults   Milk for Children

Luncheon—Grilled Cheese and Bacon Sandwiches 852
Vegetable Slaw 807
Applesauce 261
Tea for Adults   Milk for Children

Dinner—Tuna and Celery Fondue 438
Buttered Green Beans and Potatoes 985
Tossed Vegetable Salad 825
Cornsticks 46 and Butter
Lemon Chiffon Pudding 359
Coffee for Adults   Milk for Children

SUNDAY

Breakfast—Canned Grapefruit Sections
Wheat Biscuits with Top Milk
Toast with Butter
Quince Honey 713
Coffee for Adults   Cocoa for Children

Dinner—Beef and Vegetable Pie 501

Tossed Vegetable Salad 825 and 841
Whole Wheat Bread and Butter
Peach Meringue 292
Coffee for Adults   Milk for Children

Supper—Grilled Denver Sandwiches 886 Bread and Butter Pickles
Fruit Buttermilk 13

27

MAY

A WEEK'S GUIDE USING SEASONAL FOODS IN THRIFTY BALANCED MENUS

(See Index for recipes to make foods suggested in menus)

MONDAY

Breakfast—Stewed Rhubarb 307
Prepared Cereal with Top Milk
Whole Wheat Toast with Butter
Coffee for Adults   Cocoa for Children

Luncheon—Cold Fruit Plate with Cottage Cheese 749
Crackers
Chocolate Blanc Mange 344
Milk for All

Dinner—Meat Croquettes 513
Parsley Buttered Potatoes 1069
Creamed Green Beans 985
Green Onions   Radishes
Bread and Butter
Strawberry Shortcake 309
Coffee for Adults   Milk for Children

TUESDAY

Breakfast—Stewed Prunes 301
Scrambled Eggs 396
Whole Wheat Toast with Butter
Coffee for Adults   Milk for Children

Luncheon—Potato-carrot Soup 972
Croutons 61
Cabbage and Raisin Slaw 740
Canned Sliced Peaches 717
Tea for Adults   Milk for Children

Dinner—Baked Liver and Vegetables 609
Buttered Greens 1038
Bread and Butter
Radishes and Green Onions
Lemon Pie 670
Coffee for Adults   Milk for Children

The richest man can buy no more valuable vegetable than cabbage.

WEDNESDAY

Breakfast—Sliced Bananas on Prepared Cereal with Thin Cream
Toast with Butter
Coffee for Adults   Cocoa for Children

Luncheon—Pineapple and Date Salad No. 1 766
Bacon and Tomato Sandwiches 851
Tea for Adults   Milk for Children

THURSDAY

Breakfast—Tomato Juice 719a
Poached Eggs 393 on Toast, Bacon
Coffee for Adults   Milk for Children

Luncheon—Spinach Chowder 974
Peanut Butter-jelly Sandwiches 897
Sugared Fresh Pineapple 299
Vanilla Crisps 208
(Save ⅔ for Friday and Sunday)
Tea for Adults   Milk for Children

Be generous with peanut butter; it's generous with vitamin B₁.

28

Dinner—Veal Fricassee 584
Buttered New Peas 1060
Hot Rolls and Butter
Cornstarch Pudding 350
Coffee for Adults   Milk for Children

Dinner—Baked Macaroni and Cheese
  177 or 178
Tossed Vegetable Salad 825
Buttered Beets 1005
Whole Wheat Bread and Butter
Strawberry and Banana Fruit Cup
  287
Coffee for Adults   Milk for Children

FRIDAY

Breakfast—Sugared Strawberries
Rolled Oats 168 with Top Milk
Cinnamon Toast 55
Coffee for Adults   Milk for Children

Luncheon—Spinach Mold with
  Cheese Sauce 1100
Bread 88 and Butter
Applesauce 261
Vanilla Crisps 208
Tea for Adults   Milk for Children

Dinner—Fried Round Steak 471
  Gravy 468
Mashed Potatoes 1077
Escalloped Tomatoes 1109
Wilted Lettuce 827
Bread and Butter
Stewed Rhubarb 307 and Sponge
  Cake 93
Coffee for Adults   Milk for Children

SATURDAY

Breakfast—Grapefruit Juice
French Toast 56
Syrup 924
Coffee for Adults   Milk for Children

Luncheon—Olive and Egg Sand-
  wiches 891
Pan-fried Bananas 280a
Tea for Adults   Milk for Children

Dinner—Spanish Pork Chops 551
Buttered Fresh Asparagus 981
Pickled Peaches 727
Bread and Butter
Frozen Raspberries and Butter Cook-
  ies 221
Tea for Adults   Milk for Children

SUNDAY

Breakfast—Sugared Fresh Pineapple
  299
Soft-cooked Eggs 394
Whole Wheat Toast with Butter
Coffee for Adults   Milk for Children

Dinner—Stuffed Lamb Breast 532
Boiled Rice 174
Buttered New Peas and Carrots
  1060
Tomato and Lettuce Salad 806

Ice Box Rolls 66
(Save Part of Dough for Monday)
Strawberries and Cream
Vanilla Crisps 208
Coffee for Adults   Milk for Children

Supper—Salted Crackers, Cheese
  Slices
Fruit Cup 287
Buttermilk for All

Juicy fresh pineapple——choose one whose spines pull out easily.

29

JUNE

A WEEK'S GUIDE USING SEASONAL FOODS IN THRIFTY BALANCED MENUS

(See Index for recipes to make foods suggested in menus)

MONDAY

Breakfast—Canned Orange and Grapefruit Juice
Prepared Cereal with Top Milk
Toast with Butter
Coffee for Adults   Milk for Children

Luncheon—Red Raspberry and Cottage Cheese Salad **771**
Toast and Butter
Cinnamon Blanc Mange **345**
Tea for Adults   Milk for Children

Dinner—Cold Meat Loaf **489**
Escalloped New Cabbage **1010**
American Fried Potatoes **1073**
Sliced Tomatoes and Cucumbers
Whole Wheat Bread and Butter
Applesauce **261**
Oatmeal Cookies **204**
(Save Half for Tuesday Lunch)
Iced Tea for Adults   Milk for Children

TUESDAY

Breakfast—Stewed Prunes **301**
Soft-cooked Eggs **394**
Whole Wheat Toast with Butter
Coffee for Adults   Milk for Children

Luncheon—Cream of Pea Soup **956**
Soda Crackers
Strawberries with Cream
Oatmeal Cookies **204**
Tea for Adults   Milk for Children

Dinner—Pot Roast of Veal with Gravy **576**
Parsley Buttered Potatoes **1069**
Green Beans **985** in Brown Sauce **902**
Hot Baking Powder Biscuits **26** and Butter
Tomato and Lettuce Salad **806**
Sugared Fresh Pineapple **299**
Coffee for Adults   Milk for Children

WEDNESDAY

Breakfast—Applesauce **261**
French Toast **56** and Butter
Broiled Bacon **544**
Coffee for Adults   Milk for Children

Luncheon—Creamed Peas **1060**
Carrot Sticks
Chipped Beef Sandwiches **853**
Rice Cream **364**
Tea for Adults   Milk for Children

THURSDAY

Breakfast—Strawberries with Cream
Scrambled Eggs **396**
Toast with Butter
Jelly **709**
Coffee for Adults   Milk for Children

Luncheon—Bacon and Peanut Butter Sandwiches **851a**
Wilted Lettuce **827**
Pears with Chocolate Sauce **926**
Tea for Adults   Milk for Children

Try chocolate sauce with your pears; you've a treat in store.

30

Dinner—Braised Shortribs of Beef 478a
Boiled Potatoes   **1068**
Bread and Butter
Grated Carrot and Raisin Salad   **743**
Cherry Cobbler   **644**
Coffee for Adults   Milk for Children

Dinner—Pork Chop Suey   **562**
Rice   **174**
Whole Wheat Bread and Butter
Sliced Tomatoes and French Dressing   **841**
Brown Sugar Custard   **227**
Coffee for Adults   Milk for Children

FRIDAY

Breakfast—Tomato Juice   **719a**
Rolled Oats   **168**   with Thin Cream
Toast with Butter, Jelly   **710**
Coffee for Adults   Milk for Children

Luncheon—Cream of Asparagus Soup   **946**
Soda Crackers
Buttered Beets   **1005**
Sugared Fresh Pineapple   **299**
Tea for Adults   Milk for Children

Dinner—Quick-baked Catfish   **415**
Escalloped Potatoes   **1074**
Buttered Greens   **1038**
Cornbread and Butter   **34**
Radishes and Green Onions
Sliced Bananas with Top Milk
Coffee for Adults   Milk for Children

SATURDAY

Breakfast—Sugared Strawberries with Cream
Prepared Cereal with Top Milk
Cinnamon Toast   **55**
Coffee for Adults   Milk for Children

Luncheon—Green Beans   **985**   on Toast with Welsh Rarebit   **193**
Radishes
Bread and Butter
Stewed Rhubarb   **307**
Tea for Adults   Milk for Children

Dinner—Swiss Steak   **508**
Mashed Potatoes   **1077**
Creamed New Cabbage   **1008**
Lettuce with Russian Dressing   **846**
Whole Wheat Bread and Butter
Watermelon
Coffee for Adults   Milk for Children

SUNDAY

Breakfast—Sugared Red Raspberries
Poached Eggs   **391**
Toast with Butter
Coffee for Adults   Milk for Children

Dinner—Stuffed Lamb Breast   **531**
Buttered New Peas   **1060**
Whole Wheat Bread and Butter
Raw Cauliflower Salad   **783**

Fresh Strawberry Pie   **660**
Coffee for Adults   Milk for Children

Supper—Bacon Sandwiches   **849**
Tossed Vegetable Salad   **825**
Cantaloupe Wedges
Iced Tea or Coffee   Milk for Children

Watermelon joins the procession of wonderful summer fruits.

JULY

A WEEK'S GUIDE USING SEASONAL FOODS IN THRIFTY BALANCED MENUS

(See Index for recipes to make foods suggested in menus)

MONDAY

Breakfast—Cantaloupe Wedges
Pan-broiled Sausage Links
Toast with Butter
Preserves **714 or 715**
Coffee for Adults   Milk for Children

Luncheon—Jellied Bouillon **978**
Crackers
Kohlrabi **1039** with Cheese Sauce **920**
Whole Wheat Bread **90** and Butter
Red Plums
Chilled Cocoa for All **4**

Dinner—Meat Soufflé **405**
Quick Escalloped Potatoes **1075**
Broiled Tomatoes **1110**
Head Lettuce, French Dressing
Bread and Butter
Sugared Fresh Sour Cherries
Coffee for Adults   Milk for Children

TUESDAY

Breakfast—Sliced Bananas on Prepared Cereal with Top Milk
Poached Eggs **391** on Toast
Coffee for Adults   Milk for Children

Luncheon—Cucumber, Onion and Pickle Sandwiches **873**
Cottage Cheese
Prune and Orange Jelly **332**
Milk for All

Dinner—Curried Lamb **528**
Boiled Rice **174**
Buttered Peas **1060**
Tomato and Lettuce Salad **806**
Whole Wheat Bread and Butter
Red Raspberries and Cream
Coffee for Adults   Milk for Children

WEDNESDAY

Breakfast—Sugared Fresh Blackberries
Bacon
Whole Wheat Toast with Butter
Marmalade **712**
Coffee for Adults   Milk for Children

Luncheon—Tomato and Cabbage Soup **975**
Crisp Crackers
Fruit Salad **750**
Iced Tea for Adults   Milk for Children

THURSDAY

Breakfast—Chilled New Apple Sauce **261**
Scrambled Eggs **396**
Toast with Butter
Coffee for Adults   Milk for Children

Luncheon—Kidney Bean Salad **797**
Bacon Sandwiches **849**
Cantaloupe Wedges
Iced Tea for Adults   Milk for Children

If you can't buy kohlrabi, use turnips or cabbage instead.

32

Dinner—Boiled Fresh Tongue 625
Buttered Spinach 1094
Hashed Brown Potatoes 1082
Grated Carrot and Raisin Salad 743
Bread and Butter
Lime Fluff 289
Coffee for Adults   Milk for Children

Dinner—Baked Pork Chops with
Apples 548
Creamed Potatoes No. 1 1070
Creole Wax Beans 989
Whole Wheat Bread and Butter
Jelly Roll 97
Hot or Iced Coffee   Milk for Children

FRIDAY

Breakfast—Canned Grapefruit Sections
Prepared Cereal with Cream
Toast with Butter, Jelly 705
Coffee for Adults   Milk for Children

Luncheon—Fresh Corn and Tomato
Casserole 1032
Bread and Butter
Cantaloupe and Cherry Salad 741a
Cold Baked Custard 226
Hot or Iced Tea   Milk for Children

Dinner—Lamb Patties 525
Parsley Buttered Potatoes 1069
French Bowl Salad 818
Bread and Butter
Peach Shortcake 310
Hot or Iced Coffee   Milk for Children

SATURDAY

Breakfast—Plums, Fresh Red or Blue
Soft-cooked Eggs 394
Toast with Butter
Jelly 710
Coffee for Adults   Milk for Children

Luncheon—Baked Beans in Tomato
Cups 1003
Rye Melba Toast 58
Blackberries with Cream
Iced Tea for Adults   Milk for Children

Dinner—Veal à la King 582
Buttered 171 or Crisp Noodles
173a or Toast
Cole Slaw 786
Rye Bread and Butter
Chocolate Marshmallow Pudding
347
Coffee for Adults   Milk for Children

SUNDAY

Breakfast—Sliced Peaches on Prepared Cereal with Milk
Toast with Butter, Jam 703
Coffee for Adults   Milk for Children

Dinner—Steak Roll 507
Mashed Potatoes 1077
Fried Corn 1028
Whole Wheat Bread and Butter
Celery and Radishes

Devil's Food Cake 109 and Ice
Cream
Coffee for Adults   Milk for Children

Supper—Tossed Vegetable Salad
825
Melba Toast 58
Fresh Apricots
Iced Tea for Adults   Milk for Children

33

AUGUST

A WEEK'S GUIDE USING SEASONAL FOODS
IN THRIFTY BALANCED MENUS

(See Index for recipes to make foods suggested in menus)

MONDAY

Breakfast—Stewed Fresh Plums **298**
Fried Eggs **390**
Toast with Butter, Jam **702**
Coffee for Adults   Milk for Children

Luncheon—Creamed Carrots and Celery on Toast **1014**
Sliced Tomatoes
Pears
Hot or Iced Tea   Milk for Children

Dinner—Pan-fried Liver **602** and Bacon **545** with Riced Potatoes **1068a**
Buttered Green Beans **985**
Bread and Butter
Sliced Cucumber Salad **790**
Pineapple Bavarian **329**
Coffee for Adults   Milk for Children

TUESDAY

Breakfast—White Grapes
Prepared Cereal with Top Milk
Toast with Butter
Jelly **710**
Coffee for Adults   Milk for Children

Luncheon—Cabbage **1008** in Cheese Sauce **920**
Sliced Tomatoes with French Dressing **841**
Whole Wheat Bread and Butter
Watermelon
Hot or Iced Tea   Milk for Children

Dinner—Stuffed Veal Rolls **578** with Gravy
Boiled Potatoes **1068**
Pickled Beets and Onions **774**
Bread and Butter
Fresh Peach Cobbler **656**
Coffee for Adults   Milk for Children

WEDNESDAY

Breakfast—Sliced Peaches
Prepared Whole Cereal with Thin Cream
Toast with Butter
Broiled Bacon **544**
Coffee for Adults   Milk for Children

Luncheon—Parsley Butter Sandwiches **876**
Orange Waldorf Salad **756**
Caramel Blanc Mange **343**
Hot or Iced Tea   Milk for Children

THURSDAY

Breakfast—Grapefruit Juice
Soft-cooked Eggs **394**
Cinnamon Toast **55**
Coffee for Adults   Milk for Children

Luncheon—Beet Borsht **962**
Crisp Crackers
Sliced Bananas with Lemon Sauce **934**
Hot or Iced Tea   Milk for Children

Good old-fashioned lemonade has the pulp; don't strain it.

34

Dinner—Braised Beef Balls 478
Creamed Potatoes 1070
Buttered Spinach 1094
Bread and Butter
Baked Fresh Pears 295
Coffee for Adults   Milk for Children

Dinner—Roast Boston Style Pork
   Butt 542
Roast Potatoes 1083
Buttered Peas 1060
Whole Wheat Bread 90 and Butter
French Bowl Salad 818
Cantaloupe Wedges
Coffee for Adults   Milk for Children

FRIDAY

Breakfast—Cantaloupe
Prepared Cereal with Top Milk
Toast with Butter, Jam 703
Coffee for Adults   Milk for Children

Luncheon—Creamed Eggs 383 on
   toast
Sliced Tomatoes and Lettuce Wedges,
   French Dressing 841
Fresh Pears
Hot or Iced Tea   Milk for Children

Dinner—Cold Sliced Fresh Boston
   Style Pork Butt 542
Corn on the Cob 1024
Okra and Tomatoes 1056
Grated Carrot, Apple, and Orange
   Salad 745
Bread and Butter
Fresh Peach Tarts 654
Coffee for Adults   Milk for Children

SATURDAY

Breakfast—Grapefruit Juice
Prepared Cereal with Top Milk
Toast with Butter
Broiled Bacon 544
Coffee for Adults   Milk for Children

Luncheon—Tuna Salad 837
Buttered Summer Squash 1102
Whole Wheat Bread and Butter
Fresh Plums
Chilled Cocoa for All 4

Dinner—Irish Stew 529
Lettuce with French Dressing 841
Bread and Butter
Fresh or Canned Apricots
Brownies 194
Coffee for Adults   Milk for Children

SUNDAY

Breakfast—Sliced Bananas with Top
   Milk
French Toast 56
Syrup 924
Coffee for Adults   Milk for Children

Dinner—Chicken Fricassee 690
Mashed Potatoes 1077
Corn on the Cob 1024

Whole Wheat Bread and Butter
Tomato and Cucumber Salad 805
Peach Blossom Pie 678
Coffee for Adults   Milk for Children

Supper—Olive and Egg Sandwiches
   891
Prune Milk Shake 20   Cookies

Eat first what you need; finish with what you prefer.

SEPTEMBER

A WEEK'S GUIDE USING SEASONAL FOODS
IN THRIFTY BALANCED MENUS

(See Index for recipes to make foods suggested in menus)

MONDAY

Breakfast—Melon Wedges
Cooked Whole Wheat Cereal 168
  or 170 with Thin Cream
Toast with Butter
Broiled Bacon 544
Coffee for Adults   Milk for Children

Luncheon—Cream of Lima Bean and
  Carrot Soup 952
Whole Wheat Toast and Butter
Lettuce with French Dressing 841
Fruit Cup 287
Cocoanut Fingers 219
Tea for Adults   Milk for Children

Dinner—Hot Beef Sandwiches 861a
Gravy 468
Parsley Buttered Carrots 1012
Mashed Potatoes 1077
Celery
Caramel Mousse 243
Iced Tea for Adults   Milk for Children

TUESDAY

Breakfast—Sliced Peaches
Prepared Cereal with Top Milk
Toast with Butter
Orange Marmalade 712
Coffee for Adults   Milk for Children

Luncheon—Stuffed Tomato Salad
  No. 1 801
Carrot Butter Sandwiches 871
Fresh Pears
Tea for Adults   Milk for Children

Dinner—Braised Spareribs 556
Creamed Potatoes 1070
Buttered Peas 1060
Whole Wheat Bread and Butter
Tossed Vegetable Salad 825
Apple Crumble 258
Coffee for Adults   Milk for Children

WEDNESDAY

Breakfast—Concord Grapes
Griddle Cakes 36 and Bacon
Syrup 924
Coffee for Adults   Milk for Children

Luncheon—Baked Eggs in Tomato
  Cups with Bacon 382
Whole Wheat Bread and Butter
Baked Prune Pudding 379
Milk for All

THURSDAY

Breakfast—Melon Wedges
Rice Cooked in Milk 175
Toast with Butter
Jelly 710
Coffee for Adults   Milk for Children

Luncheon—Stuffed Green Peppers
  No. 4 1066
Bread and Butter
Baked Peaches 290
Milk for All

This month is the time to can grape juice for beverage and jelly.

36

Dinner—Steak and Kidney Pie 620
Buttered Summer Squash 1102
Cole Slaw 786
Bread and Butter
Apple Snow 264
Coffee for Adults   Milk for Children

Dinner—Veal and Spaghetti 583
Pan-broiled Tomatoes 1110
Whole Wheat Bread and Butter
Shredded Lettuce with French Dress-
    ing 841
Lemon Pineapple Fluff 323
Coffee for Adults   Milk for Children

Cook skins, seeds and flesh, if summer squash is tender.

FRIDAY

Breakfast—Grapefruit Juice
Rolled Oats 168 with Top Milk
Poached Eggs on Toast 391
Coffee for Adults   Milk for Children

Luncheon—Salmon Salad 832
Muffins 42 and Butter
White Grapes
Milk for All

Dinner—Beef Pot Roast 498
Roast Potatoes 1083
Buttered Green Beans 985
Tomato and Lettuce Salad 806
Bread and Butter
Frozen Peach Cream 246
Coffee for Adults   Milk for Children

SATURDAY

Breakfast—Sliced Bananas in Freshly
    Squeezed Orange Juice
Prepared Cereal with Milk
Toast with Butter
Jelly 710
Coffee for Adults   Milk for Children

Luncheon—Creamed Chipped Beef
    518 on Toast
Celery
Baked Apples No. 1 266
Tea for Adults   Milk for Children

Dinner—Braised Lamb Shanks 478a
Baked Potatoes 1067
Cucumber and Radish Salad 791
Buttered Spinach 1094 or Mus-
    tard Greens 1038
Bread and Butter
Baked Custard 226
Coffee for Adults   Milk for Children

SUNDAY

Breakfast—Canned   Orange   and
    Grapefruit Juice
Prepared Cereal with Thin Cream
French Toast 56 Syrup 924
Coffee for Adults   Milk for Children

Dinner—Veal Birds 580
Creamed Potatoes 1070
Fried Eggplant 1036

Tomato and Lettuce Salad 806
Whole Wheat Bread and Butter
Plum Dumplings 297
Coffee for Adults   Milk for Children

Supper—Parsley Omelet 401
Bread and Butter
Grapes and Angel Food Cake 91
Tea for Adults   Milk for Children

Use the least possible water to cook vegetables, except strong ones.

OCTOBER

A WEEK'S GUIDE USING SEASONAL FOODS IN THRIFTY BALANCED MENUS

(See Index for recipes to make foods suggested in menus)

MONDAY

Breakfast—Freshly Sliced Oranges
Cooked Cracked Wheat Cereal   170
Toast with Butter, Jelly   704a
Coffee for Adults   Milk for Children

Luncheon—Cream of Tomato Soup
960
Orange Bread   40a   Butter
Grated Carrot Salad   742
Grapes
Tea for Adults   Milk for Children

Dinner—Braised Pig Hocks   561
Boiled Potatoes   1068
Buttered Rutabaga   1114
Lettuce with French Dressing   841
Bread and Butter
Baked Apples   266 or 267
Coffee for Adults   Milk for Children

TUESDAY

Breakfast—Orange Juice
Rolled Oats   168   with Milk
Toast with Butter
Jam   701
Coffee for Adults   Milk for Children

Luncheon—Corn Fritters   1026
with Syrup   924
Celery
Baked Apples   267
Tea for Adults   Milk for Children

Dinner—Boiled Bologna   598
Baked Potatoes   1067
Escalloped Tomatoes   1109
Bread and Butter
Lettuce with French Dressing   841
Brown Sugar Custard   227
Coffee for Adults   Milk for Children

Select pumpkins for Hallowe'en—a small one for the table.

WEDNESDAY

Breakfast—Stewed Prunes   301
French Omelet   400
Toast with Butter, Jelly   709
Coffee for Adults   Milk for Children

Luncheon—Macaroni, Tomato and
Green Pepper Casserole   1113
Toast with Butter, Honey
Concord Grapes
Tea for Adults   Milk for Children

THURSDAY

Breakfast—Grapefruit Juice
Prepared Cereal with Milk
Toast with Butter, Jam   702
Coffee for Adults   Cocoa for Children

Luncheon—Vegetable Soup   945
Crisp Crackers   Butter
Oatmeal Cookies   204
Applecot Sauce   263
Tea for Adults   Milk for Children

If milk stands in the sun 1 hour, ½ of vitamin B_2 is gone.

Dinner—Spanish Liver **611**
Buttered Parsnips **1057**
Whole Wheat Bread and Butter
Cole Slaw **786**
Sliced Bananas with Butterscotch
  Sauce **925**
Coffee for Adults   Milk for Children

Dinner—Lamb Shoulder Chops with
  Dressing **522**
Creamed Potatoes **1070**
Buttered Spinach **1094**
Whole Wheat Bread and Butter
Frosted Cup Cakes **118** and **136**
(Save Half for Saturday)
Coffee for Adults   Milk for Children

FRIDAY

Breakfast—Freshly Sliced Oranges
Hot Whole Wheat Cereal with Thin
  Cream **168** or **170**
Toast with Butter, Jelly **709**
Coffee for Adults   Milk for Children

Luncheon—Cream of Lima Bean and
  Carrot Soup **952**
Crisp Crackers or Toast
Lettuce Wedges with 1000 Island
  Dressing **848**
Pears
Tea for Adults   Milk for Children

Dinner—Veal Chop Suey **581**
Boiled Rice **174**
Buttered Carrots **1012**
Bread and Butter
Sliced Cucumber Salad **790**
Cherry Tapioca **372**
Coffee for Adults   Milk for Children

SATURDAY

Breakfast—Tomato Juice **719a**
French Toast **56**
Syrup **924**
Broiled Sausages **563a**
Coffee for Adults   Milk for Children

Luncheon—Eggs **395** with Cheese
  Sauce **920** on Toast
Tomato Aspic Salad **814**
Sliced Pineapple
Tea for Adults   Milk for Children

Dinner—Salmon Loaf **431**
Potatoes O'Brien **1080**
Buttered Peas **1060**
Whole Wheat Bread and Butter
Celery and Radishes
Frosted Cup Cakes **118** and **136**
Coffee for Adults   Milk for Children

SUNDAY

Breakfast—Sliced Bananas
Poached Eggs **391** with Bacon
  Curls **545**
Toast with Butter, Jam **701**
Coffee for Adults   Cocoa for Children

Dinner—Tomato Juice Cocktail **24**
Roast Duck **692** with Gravy **468**
Mashed Potatoes **1077**
Buttered Rutabaga **1114**

Radishes
Whole Wheat Bread and Butter
Apple Delight **312** with Custard
  Sauce **930**
Coffee for Adults   Milk for Children

Supper—Date, Cream Cheese, and
  Shredded Lettuce Salad **747**
Bread and Butter
Pineapple Buttermilk **13**

Cut soup vegetables small—shorter cooking, more flavor and vitamins.

NOVEMBER

A WEEK'S GUIDE USING SEASONAL FOODS
IN THRIFTY BALANCED MENUS

(See Index for recipes to make foods suggested in menus)

MONDAY

Breakfast—Sliced Bananas on Prepared Cereal with Milk
Cinnamon Toast **55**
Coffee for Adults   Cocoa for Children

Luncheon—Tomato Clam Chowder **965**
Crisp Crackers or Toast
Jam Meringue Puff **358**
Tea for Adults   Milk for Children

Dinner—Meat Loaf **489**
Quick Escalloped Potatoes **1075**
Baked Hubbard Squash **1106**
Whole Wheat Bread and Butter
Shredded Lettuce with Dressing **841**
Applesauce Cake **103**
(Save Half for Tuesday Dinner)
Coffee for Adults   Milk for Children

TUESDAY

Breakfast—Tomato Juice   **719a**
Hot Rolled Oats with Milk   **168**
Toast with Butter
Marmalade   **712**
Coffee for Adults   Milk for Children

Luncheon—Tuna Fish Salad   **837**
Bread and Butter
Sliced Bananas with Lemon Sauce **934**
Tea for Adults   Milk for Children

Dinner—Roast Fresh Boston Style Pork Butt   **542**
Mashed Potatoes   **1077**
Savory Creamed Spinach   **1096**
Bread and Butter
Apple Sauce Cake   **103**
Coffee for Adults   Milk for Children

WEDNESDAY

Breakfast—Freshly Sliced Peeled Oranges
Soft-cooked Eggs **394**
Toast with Butter, Jelly   **704a**
Coffee for Adults   Milk for Children

THANKSGIVING DAY

Breakfast—Grapefruit Halves
Prepared Cereal with Thin Cream
Toast with Butter, Jam   **703**
Coffee for Adults   Cocoa for Children

Thanksgiving Day is but one of 365 when we should be thankful.

40

Luncheon—Oxtail Soup 943
Carrot Raisin Sandwiches 872
Baked Apricot Whip 277
Tea for Adults   Milk for Children

Dinner—Beef Stew with Vegetables 502
Cole Slaw 786
Whole Wheat Bread and Butter
Rice Cream 364
Coffee for Adults   Milk for Children

Thanksgiving Dinner—Roast Turkey 695 with Dressing 697, 698, 700 and Gravy 468
Mashed Potatoes 1077
Buttered Onions 1047
Cranberry Sauce 282
Head Lettuce with 1000 Island Dressing 848
Whole Wheat Bread and Butter
Pumpkin Pie 679
Coffee for Adults   Milk for Children

Supper—Oyster Bisque 970
Crisp Crackers or Toast
Canned Peaches
Milk for All

Breakfast—Stewed Prunes 301
Cooked Whole Wheat Cereal 168 or 170 with Milk
Toast with Butter
Orange Marmalade 712
Coffee for Adults   Milk for Children

Luncheon—Turkey à la King, Toast
Head Lettuce, French Dressing 841
Cranberry Sauce 282
Tea for Adults   Milk for Children

Dinner—Baked Perch 415 Tartar Sauce 915
Mashed Potatoes 1077
Stewed Tomatoes 1111
Grapefruit Salad 753
Bread and Butter
Apple Dumplings 259
Coffee for Adults   Milk for Children

Breakfast—Stewed Apricots 274
Hot Rolled Oats 168 with Milk
Toast with Butter, Jelly 704
Coffee for Adults   Milk for Children

Luncheon—Escalloped Cabbage 1010 with Broiled Bacon 544
Bread and Butter
Waldorf Salad 772
Gingersnaps 199
(Save Some for Sunday)
Tea for Adults   Milk for Children

Dinner—Chicken Rice Soup 940
Croutons 61
Pea and Potato Casserole 1061
Carrot and Cabbage Salad 780
Bread and Butter
Lemon Chiffon Pudding 359
Coffee for Adults   Milk for Children

Breakfast—Tomato Juice **719a**
Scrambled Eggs **396**
Toast with Butter, Broiled Bacon
544
Coffee for Adults   Milk for Children

Dinner—Chicken Pie **691**
Candied Sweet Potatoes **1087**
Buttered Green Beans **985**
Whole Wheat Bread and Butter

Lettuce Wedges with 1000 Island
Dressing **848**
Pineapple Upside Down Cake **121**
Coffee for Adults   Milk for Children

Supper—Peanut Butter and Jelly
Sandwiches **897**
Gingersnaps **199**
Canned Peaches **717**
Cocoa for All **4**

DECEMBER

A WEEK'S GUIDE USING SEASONAL FOODS
IN THRIFTY BALANCED MENUS

(See Index for recipes to make foods suggested in menus)

MONDAY

Breakfast—Grapefruit Halves
Griddle Cakes **36**
Syrup **924**
Coffee for Adults   Milk for Children

Luncheon—Bacon   Omelet **399,**
Tomato Sauce **916**
Bread and Butter
Canned Fruit Salad **750** and **842**
Chocolate Wheat Pudding **348**
Tea for Adults   Milk for Children

Dinner—Diced Meat Roast **480**
Mashed Potatoes **1077**
Buttered Rutabaga **1114**
Tossed Vegetable Salad **825**
Bread and Butter
Apricot Bavarian **314**
Coffee for Adults   Milk for Children

TUESDAY

Breakfast—Stewed Dried Apricots
274
Cooked Cracked Wheat Cereal **170**
Toast with Butter, Jelly **704a**
Coffee for Adults   Milk for Children

Luncheon—Beef and Noodle Soup
939
Crisp Crackers
Lettuce, 1000 Island Dressing **848**
Dutch Apple Cake **356** with
Lemon Sauce **934**
Tea for Adults   Milk for Children

Dinner—Beef   Stew   **502**   and
Dumplings **26b**
Orange Waldorf Salad **756**
Bread and Butter
Floating Island **234**
Coffee for Adults   Milk for Children

For flavor and color dried apricots are superior to canned.

WEDNESDAY

Breakfast—Freshly Sliced Oranges
Poached Eggs on Toast **391**
Coffee for Adults   Milk for Children

Luncheon—Broccoli   **1007**   with
   Cheese Sauce   **920**
Toast and Butter
Celery
Sugar Cookies for Children   **224**
(Save Half for Saturday's Lunch)
Fruit Cup   **287**
Holiday Fruit Cake   **124**   for Adults
Tea for Adults   Milk for Children

Dinner—Braised Pork Chops   **549**
Gravy   **468**
Mashed Potatoes   **1077**
Buttered Carrots   **1012**
Cole Slaw   **786**
Whole Wheat Bread and Butter
Escalloped Apples   **269**
Coffee for Adults   Milk for Children

THURSDAY

Breakfast—Dates in Cooked Wheat
   Cereal   **169**   with Milk
Toast with Butter, Jelly   **709**
Coffee for Adults   Milk for Children

Luncheon—Cream of Tomato Soup
   960
Melba Toast with Butter   **58**
Sweet Potato Salad   **800**
Canned Peaches
Tea for Adults   Milk for Children

Dinner—Creamed Shrimp   **462**
Boiled Rice   **174**
Buttered Spinach   **1094**
Whole Wheat Bread and Butter
Prune and Orange Jelly   **332**
Coffee for Adults   Milk for Children

FRIDAY

Breakfast—Freshly Sectioned Grape-
   fruit
Pan-fried Mush   **172,**   Bacon   **544**
Honey and Butter
Coffee for Adults   Milk for Children

Luncheon—Carrot Soufflé   **1018**
Watermelon Pickles   **731**
Whole Wheat Bread and Butter
Pears
Inexpensive Fruit Cake   **124**
Tea for Adults   Milk for Children

Dinner—Spanish Sausage   **566**
Riced Potatoes   **1068a**
Pan-fried Onions   **1050a**
Bread and Butter
Shredded Lettuce with Mayonnaise
   843
Apple Cobbler
Coffee for Adults   Milk for Children

SATURDAY

Breakfast—Dried Fruit Compote
   284
Prepared Cereal with Milk
Toast with Butter, Jam   **701**
Coffee for Adults   Cocoa for Chil-
   dren

Luncheon—Green Beans   **985**   with
   Cheese Sauce   **920**
Bread and Butter   **90**
Orange Cocoanut Salad   **754**
Sugar Cookies   **224**
Tea for Adults   Milk for Children

Dinner—Braised Spareribs   **556**
Sauerkraut with Apples   **1092**
Parsley Buttered Potatoes   **1069**
Bread and Butter
Lemon Pineapple Fluff   **323**
Coffee for Adults   Milk for Children

Breakfast—Baked Apple **267**
Broiled Sausage Patties **565**
Toast with Butter, Jelly **709**
Coffee for Adults   Milk for Children

Dinner—Roast Chicken **687**,
  Dressing **698**
Gravy **468**
Mashed Potatoes **1077**
Creamed Brussels Sprouts **1008a**

Whole Wheat Bread and Butter
Tomato Aspic Salad **814** Lettuce
Steamed Fruit Pudding **377** with
  Lemon Sauce **934**
Coffee for Adults   Milk for Children

Supper—Egg Salad Sandwiches **889**
Dill Pickles **724**
Pears **717a**
Cocoa for All **4**

FOOD FOR CHILDREN

— • — • — • — • —

WHAT! No pumpkin pie for the younger generation—not even on Thanksgiving? But the youngsters won't feel slighted if you'll bake some of the pumpkin custard filling for them in custard cups and dress it up with some dainty special garnish, so they can have their VERY OWN dessert on the great day. This is just one of many suggestions you'll find in this chapter for fitting the family's regular menus to Junior's measure, to his benefit and yours.

— • — • — • — • — • — • —

In most homes it is not convenient or practical for the children to eat meals entirely different from those prepared for the grown-ups. From the time the baby begins to receive solid food, the objective should be to teach him to like and to eat all the foods that are good for him. This does not mean he will eat everything his parents eat, and in just the same form; for actually a child's meals should be tailored to fit him just as much as his clothes are. What it does mean is—that food prejudices should be prevented from developing in the growing child if he is to grow up healthy, well-nourished and happy.

One of the most important influences on the child's attitude toward food is his parents' attitude. If the father dislikes vegetables and says so, the child who is devoted to his father is more than likely to copy his dislike and his refusal of vegetables. If the mother dislikes some particular food and never serves it at home, the child will never become acquainted with it, and may never learn to like it.

Parents who, with the welfare of their children foremost in mind, conquer their own food dislikes lest they influence the children, are benefiting not only the youngsters but themselves in the long run; since it is difficult to eat a well-balanced diet if one has a number of food prejudices, to say nothing of the social embarrassments they cause to both guest and hostess.

45

FEEDING THE PRE-SCHOOL CHILD

The youngster from babyhood on to five or six years of age is being introduced to a vast variety of unfamiliar foods. Foods which most children welcome from the very first are meats, which he will be served daily, and sweets, which he should be given very sparingly, and only after meals. Most other foods he will learn to like as he becomes familiar with them.

To introduce a child to a new food, give him a small quantity of it—not more than a tablespoonful at first—in addition to his regular meal. After two or three trials he should be ready to accept the new food as an old friend. Don't try to start him on more than one new food at a time.

The small child should never be given any highly seasoned foods. A small amount of salt is all that will be required to make food palatable. Vegetables for the family should be cooked with about half the usual amount of salt, and after the child's portion has been taken out the grown-ups can add more to suit their taste. Pepper and other spices are not required by a perfectly healthy, unsophisticated palate and most small children dislike them. They should never be offered to the little child.

Other taboos for the pre-school child are coffee or tea in any form; they should not be used even as flavorings in such foods as puddings or sauces for the child. Rich gravies should be avoided, and the child should get no pastry, as both contain a large proportion of fat, which slows down the time of digestion. When other members of the family have pie, some of the filling may be saved out for the child, unless it is too rich in itself. A custard cup of pumpkin filling will be more acceptable to any child than the filling scooped out of a piece of pie, because it seems like his own.

It is desirable for the pre-school child to have his heaviest meal in the middle of the day rather than with the rest of the family in the evening. His evening meal may be very light, with a milk soup, cereal and milk, or even bread and milk, as its basis. And it may be more convenient for him to finish his meal and be put to bed before the rest of the family have dinner.

FEEDING THE SCHOOL CHILD

After his school life begins, the child's diet will gradually begin to conform more closely to the grown-up pattern, though condiments, or stimulants such as tea and coffee, and rich foods like pastry should still be avoided.

From eight or nine years on, the growing child's caloric requirement will be nearly the same as an adult's, and during adolescence the boy's requirement often exceeds his father's, unless his father is very active.

If the child has been trained from babyhood to accept and enjoy a variety of foods, including the important vegetables, both raw as in salads and cooked, he will present no special feeding problems during the school years or afterward.

Breakfast is an important meal for the child and he should never be allowed to hurry off without it in the morning. It must be remembered that breakfast, even when the child declares that he is not hungry for it, must be depended on to supply from ¼ to ⅓ of the day's caloric and nutrient needs. If less is eaten, morning hunger and inefficiency develop. The other two meals of the day can hardly supply the nutrients and calories the deficient breakfast fails to provide.

Preferably the breakfast should be a hot one, or contain at least one hot dish. Especially in cold weather, an all-cold breakfast does not give the quick warmth and energy that should help to start the day right. Hot whole-grain restored or enriched cereal, with plenty of milk or cream and a little sugar, is a good everyday breakfast dish. If the hot cereal is omitted, a cup of hot cocoa or hot milk should be included in the breakfast menu for the child.

A child who is never hungry for breakfast will find his appetite stimulated by getting up half an hour earlier than usual and taking some brisk exercise. His morning household tasks, if done before breakfast, will prove a great appetizer.

Because many American children take their lunch and eat it away from home, the school lunch is an important dietary consideration. It should be planned just as carefully as a home luncheon to provide its fair share of the day's requirement. Sandwiches should be made with whole-grain bread, if possible, or with enriched white bread. Sandwich fillings should not be limited to the simple sliced meat or cheese, jelly or jam, which is the easiest thing to prepare. There are many delicious chopped raw vegetable spreads which add much food value; and combinations of these with meat and cheese are good. The lunch box should always contain some fruit, either a raw apple, orange or banana, or other fruit which may be conveniently eaten from the hand, or a little covered jar of stewed or canned fruit.

Unless a hot dish is provided at school, the lunch box should contain a thermos bottle. The hot drink provided may be a hot milk beverage, cocoa or a milk soup; or in hot weather cold milk or a milk beverage may be preferred.

The Food Shopper's Creed

The health of my family is in my care; therefore—

I will base my market list on meals planned according to the "DIET PATTERN," p. 4.

I will choose foods of quality and in quantities that will provide the nutritive elements planned for.

Stretching the food dollar is part of my responsibility; therefore—

I will take advantage of what the seasonal markets offer in variety, quality and price, to the end that I may exchange my dollar for maximum values.

My family's enjoyment of food is my responsibility; therefore—

I will use the possibilities of the market to provide variety, excellent quality and novelty within the limits of my food budget.

Purchasing food is an important link in the business of feeding my family; therefore—

I will make every effort to weigh possibilities offered by various markets, by various foods, and the forms in which they are offered from season to season, to the end that I may take pride in a job well done.

STRETCHING THE FOOD DOLLAR

MEMORIZING this brief chapter will be time well spent. It will help you to become a good manager. Adopt it as your homemaking creed, and put it into practice every day. It will help you stretch your food budget so both ends will meet every time.

There are various ways to make the budget allowance for food go farther. By putting them into action you may be able to shave a dollar or two a week from the estimated weekly budget allowed for these menus. This depends to some extent on the type of community in which you live.

MAKE IT YOURSELF!

In any kind of store, it is poor economy to buy cooked meats, cakes, cookies, jellies, preserves, pickles and the like. In so doing, you are paying not only for the food itself, but for the time and labor that went into cooking and packaging it. When your time is your own, it is economy to buy the raw materials and make the cake or other food yourself.

SHOP AROUND

If there are several grocery stores in your neighborhood, make it a practice to patronize all of them. By buying each food where it is least expensive and best for the price, you will save pennies every day—and if you take care of the pennies, the dollars will last much longer. Watch for specials.

CASH-AND-CARRY

To fall back on in emergencies, an account at a credit-and-delivery grocery may be useful; but for day-to-day buying, cash-and-carry is more economical. In credit-and-delivery you are paying for the delivery boy and his truck, and you are paying for the privilege of deferred payment even though you pay cash, since prices are the same for all.

BUY IN QUANTITY

Every woman knows that in buying hand lotion, for example, a bottle containing 12 ounces will cost much less than twice as much as a bottle containing 6 ounces. Exactly the same principle applies to food. A 10-pound bag of sugar costs less per pound than 10 pounds bought 1 pound at a time. This is because in buying the one pound you are paying not only for the food but for the same amount of labor in packing and labeling that went into the larger bag.

More or less the same principle applies to fresh foods too, such as apples and potatoes. If you buy a sack of potatoes all at once, rather than 2 or 3 pounds every day, it saves a lot of handling by the retailer, who makes you a premium price that may save you several cents per sack.

If you have facilities for storing potatoes by the sack, apples by the barrel, sugar in 10 or 50-pound lots, and canned foods by the case, you can save a little each month. When added up at the end of the year, this will mount to a tidy sum to spend on the occasional extras which make living a little more luxurious.

BUDGET YOUR INCOME

The difficulty with quantity buying is frequently that of getting together the larger amount of cash to pay for the food all at once, instead of in driblets. There is only one way to meet this problem, and that is by a system of budgeting firmly followed.

The simplest of these systems involves keeping a careful account of a month's expenditures, and then dividing the next month's income into portions to meet the various large items. A convenient way of doing this is to have a group of envelopes labeled with the family's big expenses: rent, gas, light and heat, groceries, milk, taxes, clothing for the various members of the family, and so on. Divide the actual cash of the income between these envelopes, then let the expenditures fit the allowance. Not all the expenses will need to be considered every month in all probability, but those which must be met at a certain future date should have a fraction of the whole sum put aside each month. By following this plan scrupulously, the money needed to pay for food will be on hand and can be paid out in large as well as in small sums, provided the total is not exceeded. The same system may be followed by the week.

This simple budget system has the advantage of being based on past experience of *your* family, rather than on the theory of some remote budget-planner who never had to deal with Junior's shoes or Sister's tooth-straightening.

HAVE YOUR OWN GARDEN

Not everyone is so fortunately situated as to have a big back yard or vacant lot close at hand; but many people, even city dwellers, can locate a spot where they can have a small kitchen garden. There, at the expense of a dollar's worth of seeds, some good outdoor exercise and a lot of family fun, they can raise a little or a lot of their fresh vegetable supply for the summer months.

The advantage to be derived is more than just the saving of a few dollars;

it is that the kitchen garden will supply perfectly fresh foods—something which most people who raise nothing for themselves seldom experience.

Any family which is suitably situated and has some experience and managing ability, can keep a few good laying chickens, or even a good milk cow, and be sure that their feed and keep will be much less than the value of the food they produce in exchange.

TIN CANS AND
THEIR CONTENTS*

* * * * * * * * *

NOW that commercial canning of foods is so scientific in method and produces foods of such uniformly high quality, it's definitely out of date to look down on a can opener. With that once despised gadget, any enterprising bride can serve a creditable meal, full of vitamins, minerals AND flavor. Of course she may not know just how to buy canned goods to get the right amounts and avoid leftovers; but she can learn how by studying this chapter.

* * * * * * * * *

Foods packed in tin cans are so widely used nowadays that a discussion of them seems important. A total of nearly 500 different kinds of food are packed in tin cans and glass jars, including numerous varieties of vegetables, fruits, fish and shellfish, meats and so on. Some of these are luxury items, but many are everyday foods used in every household in the country.

Commercially canned foods keep well because the food is sealed in airtight containers and then processed to destroy spoilage organisms present in the food. No preservatives are used. Unless the can itself becomes damaged from outside causes, foods thus canned will keep for months without spoilage.

The cans themselves are made of thin sheets of steel, thinly plated with tin. Certain kinds of food are packed in cans made from tin plate lined with "enamel" to prevent discoloration. There is no effect on the food itself from contact with the can, and even after the can is opened, it is the safest place to keep that leftover, because the inside of the can is more sterile than any container into which the food might be put. The only reason for transferring the contents to another container is to keep the appearance more attractive.

---

*Information contained in this chapter adapted from publications of National Canners Association, Washington, D. C.

Commercial canning preserves the vitamin content of foods to a high degree, because the cans or glass jars are sealed before the food is processed, thus excluding oxygen from the food while it is being heated. This is true also of home-canned food if the raw or blanched food is sealed before processing. Neither canned nor freshly cooked food has the same vitamin value as the raw food. The liquid in the can contains considerable nutritive value, especially minerals which may have dissolved out in the processing, and it should not be discarded. It may be evaporated by boiling and served with the food, or saved for use in soups or sauces. It contains pure water with juice from the food itself, plus seasonings, sugar or other ingredients used in the product.

It is not necessary to cook or even to heat vegetables after they are removed from the can if they are to be served cold, as in a salad. They may be served straight from the can if desired.

TIN CAN AND GLASS JAR SIZES

Tin can and glass jar sizes have been fairly well standardized by most packers until there are only about 34 sizes now in general use. Many of these are used for certain foods or types of food; some are used only in certain sections of the country. Therefore, not all of these sizes are commonly encountered by housewives over the country. It is a good plan to use the following TABLE to learn these sizes and their contents, in order to be able to purchase the right amount of food needed.

Various Canned Foods in Common Household and Jar Sizes

	Product	Container Sizes	Net Weight
Fruits	Apples; Apple sauce; Berries; Cherries; Grapes; Grapefruit; Orange sections; Fruit Cocktail; Fruits for Salad; Sliced Peaches; Pears; Pineapple Chunks; Crushed; Tidbits	8Z Tall No. 303 No. 2 No. 2½	8¼ to 8¾ 1 lb. 1 lb. 4 oz. 1 lb. 13 oz.
	Apricots, Whole, Med. size	No. 2 No. 2½	1 lb. 4 oz. 1 lb. 13 oz.
	Apricot Halves, Med. size	No. 2 No. 2½	1 lb. 4 oz. 1 lb. 13 oz.
	Peach Halves, Med. size Pear Halves, Med. size	No. 2 No. 2½	1 lb. 4 oz. 1 lb. 13 oz.
	Pineapple, Sliced	No. 1 Flat No. 2 No. 2½	9 oz. 1 lb. 4 oz. 1 lb. 14 oz.
	Plums; Prunes	No. 2 No. 2½	1 lb. 4 oz. 1 lb. 14 oz.
	Figs	No. 2 No. 2½	1 lb. 4 oz. 1 lb. 14 oz.
	Cranberry Sauce	No. 300	1 lb.
	Olives, Ripe*	8Z Tall Pint No. 1 Tall Quart	4½ oz. 9 oz. 1 lb. 2 oz.
Juices	Apple; Cherry; Cranberry; Grape; Grapefruit; Grapefruit-Orange; Pineapple; Prune; Tangerine; Carrot; Sauerkraut; Tomato; Vegetable; Vegetable Cocktail Lemon; Lime	No. 211 Cylinder No. 2 No. 303 Cylinder No. 2 Cylinder No. 3 Cylinder 5Z	12 oz. 1 pt. 2 oz. 1 pt. 3 oz. 1 pt. 7 oz. 1 qt. 14 oz. 5 oz.

*The number of olives per container varies as to the size of olives.

VARIOUS CANNED FOODS IN COMMON HOUSEHOLD AND JAR SIZES

	Product	Container Sizes	Net Weight
Vegetables	Asparagus Cuts; Beans, Green and Wax, Kidney, Lima; Beets; Carrots; Corn; Hominy; Okra; Onions; Peas; and Carrots; Black Eye Peas; Pimientos, Peppers, Red, Sweet; Pumpkin; Sauerkraut; Spinach and other Greens; Squash; Succotash; Sweet Potatoes; Tomatoes; Mixed Vegetables; Potatoes, White, Cut, Sliced	8Z Tall No. 1 Picnic No. 2 Vacuum No. 303 No. 2 No. 2½	8½ oz. 10¼ oz. 12 oz. 1 lb. 1 lb. 4 oz. 1 lb. 13 oz.
	Asparagus Spears	No. 1 Square No. 2 No. 2½	1 lb. 1 lb. 3 oz. 1 lb. 13 oz.
	Potatoes, White Whole	No. 2	1 lb. 4 oz.
	Beans, Baked; With Pork; in Sauce	No. 300 Jumbo	15½ oz. 1 lb. 10 oz.
	Mushrooms	2 Z 4 Z 8 Z	3½ oz. 6¾ oz. 12½ oz.
Vegetables and Fruits	Infant (Strained) Homogenized Junior (Chopped)		4½ oz. 4½ oz. 7½ oz.
Meats	Infant (Strained) Junior (Chopped)		3½ oz. 3¼ oz.
Soups	Infant & Junior		4½ oz.
Soups		No. 1 Picnic No. 303 No. 300 Cylinder No. 303 Cylinder No. 3 Cylinder	10½–12 oz. 1 lb. 1 lb. 2 oz. 1 lb. 5 oz. 3 lb. 2. oz.

Note: The net weight of various foods in the same size can or glass jar will vary with the density of the food. For most part minimum weights are shown in the table.

VARIOUS CANNED FOODS IN COMMON HOUSEHOLD AND JAR SIZES

	Product	Container Sizes	Net Weight
Meats	Chili Con Carne	No. 300	15½ to 16 oz.
	Corned Beef	No. 1	12 oz.
	Corned Beef Hash	1 lb.	1 lb.
	Deviled Ham	No. ¼	3 oz.
	Deviled Meat; Potted Meat; Meat Spreads	No. ¼ No. ½	2 to 3¼ oz. 5½ oz.
	Veal Loaf	7 oz.	7 oz.
	Tongue, Lunch	No. ½ No. 1	6 oz. 12 oz.
	Tongue, Ox		1 to 2 lb.
	Hams, Whole (Small) (Medium to Large)		9 to 11 lb. 11 to 13 lb.
	Poultry, Chicken; Turkey; (Boned)		4½ oz. 6 oz. 11 oz.
	Sausage, Pork; Frankfurters	8Z	8 oz. 12 oz.
	Vienna Sausage	No. ½	4 oz. 9 oz.
Fish and Shellfish	Clams	No. 1 Picnic No. 300	10½ oz. 15 oz.
	Crabmeat	Squat	6½ oz.
	Mackerel	1 lb. Tall	1 lb.
	Salmon	½ lb. Flat 1 lb. Flat 1 lb. Tall	7¾ oz. 15½ oz. 1 lb.
	Sardines Sardines (Pilchards)	No. ¼ No. 1 Oval	3¾ oz. 15 oz.
	Shrimp (Medium Size)	8Z Short No. 1 Picnic	5 oz. 7 oz.
	Tuna	No. ½ No. 1	7 oz. 13 oz.

CARE OF FOOD IN THE HOME

* * * * * * *

ALMOST as important as the actual cooking of foods is their storage. Fresh fruits and vegetables, meats, dairy products, and cake and other cooked foods are stored in the home for periods varying from a few hours to several weeks or months (as potatoes and apples). The manner in which they are cared for influences not only their appearance, flavor, and general quality, but their food value as well.

* * * * * * * *

Carelessness in caring for and storing foods after they are brought into the home may result in various forms of deterioration and spoilage such as withering, discoloration, molding and decay. This brings about marked loss of natural flavor, attractive appearance, and vitamin content, and sometimes the complete loss of the food itself.

In the majority of cases, only enough of the perishable foods should be brought into the home for one or two days' supply, and they should be stored carefully until used. The kind of storage space a family needs for foods depends on the source of supply. A refrigerator, either mechanical or ice is desirable to prevent spoilage and waste. But a farm family with a garden planted to provide a succession of fresh vegetables all summer, and which has a large, unheated storage cellar for winter vegetables, can get along with a medium size refrigerator for dairy products and the most perishable foods. The storage cellar is a good place to store root vegetables, potatoes, apples and all canned foods in the winter; and in the summer when rains, heat or drought make it necessary to harvest larger amounts of vegetables than can be consumed in one day, the cellar will keep the excess in good condition for a few days. In normal weather fresh vegetables require no refrigeration if gathered the day they are eaten, with the possible exception of the highly perishable ones such as lettuce, radishes and spinach.

The city homemaker has a different problem in obtaining and caring for foods. Her grocer buys fresh vegetables and fruits daily, and if he has adequate refrigeration facilities for storing them to preserve their freshness, it is to her advantage to purchase these foods shortly before she needs them, so as not to burden her refrigerator with them. If she lives in a house rather than an apartment, it may be possible and practical for her, too, to have an unheated storage space as well as an efficient refrigerator. But she is more likely to be entirely dependent on her refrigerator for food storage than is the farm homemaker. Many foods keep best in the refrigerator, as the low temperature slows down the action of organisms and enzymes which cause spoilage. Some foods do not require refrigeration but need a cool dry place; others require a cool moist place, such as a cellar; still others keep well at room temperature. Usually it is advisable to clean the foods before storing, and to remove soft or damaged specimens; but sometimes washing is not recommended, as for berries or grapes, until just before serving.

FRESH VEGETABLES

Salad greens. Salad vegetables include not only lettuce, endive, cress, escarole, romaine, cabbage, parsley and mint, but also any green or leafy vegetables such as spinach, celery and green onions which may be eaten raw as well as cooked. When any of these leafy vegetables are brought into the kitchen they should be trimmed immediately to remove bruised or soiled leaves. If they are in tight heads, like *cabbage, head lettuce, celery* or *French endive,* washing is not necessary, but store in an enamelware or glass container of a size and shape to hold them and a variety of other fresh foods without crushing. In the older type mechanical refrigerator this container needs a tight-fitting cover to prevent drying out; one usually comes with the refrigerator and is called a hydrator. A bag of plastic or other waterproof material is a good container for bulky fruits or vegetables to be placed in this type of refrigerator; the ends should be folded together tightly to exclude air. Lacking a hydrator or a plastic bag, the trimmed vegetables may be wrapped in cheesecloth wrung out of cold water and then in waxed paper. In an ice refrigerator, and in some of the late-model mechanical ones, either a well-ventilated cover or none at all is advised for salad greens. Just before serving, the whole heads may be washed in cold water, and any discoloration at the stem end may be cut off.

Greens which grow in loose heads, like *leaf lettuce* and *curly endive,* should be washed carefully to remove any sand or dirt, then drained well and the excess water removed by shaking them loosely in a towel. Then the head should be put away just like head lettuce. *Parsley,* although it does not grow in heads, should be treated in the same way. *Spinach* requires special care in washing; the roots should be trimmed off and each leaf washed separately to avoid any grittiness in the cooked or raw vegetable. *Cress—*It is best to use the day purchased. Here is the best way to keep it a few hours: Untie the string and swish cress gently through cold water, then shake off excess water. Now stand cress up in bowl or wide-mouth jar that has several folds of wet paper toweling in bottom. Then cover cress with a piece of wet paper toweling or the jar lid and place in refrigerator. Light and air wilt and yellow the leaves. *Mint* keeps several days if, after it is washed and the excess water shaken off, it is placed in a tall screw-top glass jar, tightly covered and stored in the refrigerator. *Green onions* may be kept in the same way as mint, but not longer than a few hours. *Chives,* which are usually purchased growing in little pots may be kept in a cool corner of the kitchen or in a window. They should never be watered from the top, as this causes the spears to turn yellow. To water them, set the pot in a shallow dish of cold water for a few minutes each morning.

Greens should never be allowed to freeze in the refrigerator, for freezing makes the leaves limp and watery. When trimming head lettuce, save 2 or 3 good outer leaves—do not wash; wrap these snugly around whole or cut head to retard "pink color."

Cucumbers and *radishes,* though not belonging to the family of greens, are favorite salad materials. Cucumbers should be washed, dried, and placed in the refrigerator, and should not be peeled, if peeling is desired, until time for use. Any portion of the cucumber which is not required for that meal should be cut off and not peeled; a piece of waxed paper may be fastened over the cut end with a rubber band. Radishes should be washed and most all leaves removed before placing in the refrigerator. The outer fresh leaves of radishes may be added to spinach to give a delicious new flavor; the heart leaves may be left attached to radishes when they are served, for they are attractive in appearance and have an appealing peppery flavor. Just before serving, cut off the tap root and elaborate, if desired, by cutting into petals. Left-over radish roses have no food value and the flavor rapidly deteriorates because of the many cuts on their surface.

Other green vegetables. All green vegetables should be cooked the same day they are bought, if possible, to avoid vitamin loss. *Green beans* should not be washed before storing in the refrigerator, but should be washed, trimmed and broken just before cooking time. *Peas* should be left in their pods if they must be stored for a few hours; if the pods are very soiled they may be washed and dried before putting them into the refrigerator. After shelling, peas quickly lose freshness and vitamin content, so they should be shelled just before cooking time. Each spear of *asparagus* should be swished gently through cold water and all the scales along the stalk removed if any sand seems to be caught under them. If the spears are not crisp, the ends may be placed in cold water for a few minutes after trimming with a sharp knife; then they may be drained and placed in the refrigerator. To be at its best, asparagus should not be kept more than a few hours after gathering or purchasing.

Root vegetables such as potatoes, carrots, turnips, parsnips and beets, require only to be kept in a cool place where the air is not too dry. In cold weather storing them is no problem, but in hot weather refrigeration is desirable for carrots and beets, so it is wise to buy them in small quantities, unless you have a cellar or a large refrigerator. When cool storage space is available outside the refrigerator, root vegetables should not be washed until just before paring; and they should never be pared until just before cooking time. When carrots and beets are stored in the refrigerator, carrot tops should be cut off close to the shoulder, and beet tops about 2½ inches from the beet. Young, tender beet tops may be washed, stored and cooked like spinach. Carrots may be washed but not scraped before storing; beets should be washed carefully, to avoid breaking the skin or tap root.

FRUITS

Apples are considered to be a semi-perishable fruit. Due to their waxy, air-tight covering, they keep well out of the refrigerator in a cool not too dry place, so long as skins are not bruised or broken. In winter, both cooking and eating apples will keep for weeks in a cool cellar or similar storage place, and even in warm weather cooking apples may be kept in such a place for a week or more. They should never be allowed to freeze. Eating apples keep in the best condition in the refrigerator if the weather is warm, and most people prefer them chilled. They may be washed and dried, and then placed in the hydrator.

Bananas should never be kept in the refrigerator as the cold darkens them. If several days' supply of bananas is bought at one time, a good plan is to buy full-ripe ones to be eaten immediately, yellow-ripe ones for the next day or two, and green-tipped ones to be kept longest. They ripen quite rapidly in a warm room; ripening may be slowed down by keeping them in a cooler place, but not in the refrigerator.

Berries of all kinds are quite perishable. One or two soft or moldy berries in a basket will spoil others, so it is always best to turn them out of the basket and pick them over as soon as they are brought home. Discard all soft ones and put the rest, without washing, into a clean bowl; cover and place in the refrigerator. They should not be washed until just before serving. *Raspberries* and *blackberries* need no other preparation for serving than looking over for hulls and damaged fruit, than washing and draining. *Strawberries* and *dewberries* may be sandy, so *before hulling*, they should be washed as follows: Place the berries in a large bowl and run cold water gently over them; swish them gently through the water and lift them out with outspread fingers to drain in a colander. Badly soiled berries may need several washings, but this should not be done until just before serving time. If the berries have blemishes, these should be cut out when the berries are hulled. Some people prefer strawberries left whole, sprinkled with sugar, and served almost immediately; some like them sugared and left to stand until the juice begins to be drawn out; others want their berries sliced or crushed with sugar, to make them very juicy. Berries have a more intense flavor at room temperature, but some persons prefer them chilled. Their flavor deteriorates if they are allowed to stand more than half an hour after preparing.

Grapes should be picked over to discard any damaged ones, and then stored in the refrigerator *without washing,* in a covered bowl or hydrator. When ready to serve, wash by holding the bunch under the cold water faucet, and shake dry in a clean dry towel. Most people like them chilled in warm weather or warmed to room temperature when the day is cold.

Melons, if fully ripe, should be kept in the refrigerator, but if they seem hard, they will ripen slowly outside the refrigerator. Since they absorb both flavors and odors from other food and give off their own odor, it is desirable to keep them in a plastic bag if possible. After cutting, a piece of waxed paper may be spread over the cut surface before returning the melon to the bag. For the best flavor and appearance, a melon should be cut just before serving, and most people like melon cold.

Peaches should never be washed or rubbed before storing, as the removal of the bloom or fuzz hastens spoiling. Perfectly sound peaches may be kept in the refrigerator for a day or two, but if they show any fresh bruises, they should be consumed the same day. Wash, pare and slice them just before serving; or if they are to be sugared, let them stand half an hour with the sugar on them after slicing, either in or out of the refrigerator, depending on the temperature preferred. Peaches are very perishable and need special care to avoid waste. *Apricots, nectarines* and *plums* require similar care, but are less perishable.

Oranges, grapefruit and *lemons* may be kept either in or out of the refrigerator. It is preferable not to cut or squeeze them until just before they are to be served, because the "edge" of their fine flavor as well as some vitamin content may be lost when the juice or cut fruit stands a few hours.

Dried fruits have such a low moisture content that they keep well at room temperature. If the room is fairly cool and dry, so much the better. If not packaged, they should be wrapped tightly in waxed paper or moisture-proof cellophane to preserve the moisture they have.

Canned fruits. Commercially canned fruits will keep for months in any cool, dry place. The same applies to home-canned fruit put up in tin, but home-canned foods in glass require slightly different storage conditions. They should be stored in a place that is not only cool, but dark and slightly damp. If the air is too dry, the rubber rings may dry out and crack, permitting organisms to enter. Light bleaches the color of the foods. Therefore, glass jars of canned food which must be stored in a light place either should be wrapped in tan-colored heavy wrapping paper or should be shielded from the light by hanging a tan or cream-colored window shade over the front of the storage shelves.

MEAT

Fresh meat. All fresh meat should be refrigerated, and since under average home refrigeration it loses its fine flavor if kept too long, it is never wise to buy more meat than is needed for two or three days, with the idea of keeping it in the uncooked state. Meat should go into the coldest spot in the refrigerator, under the freezing compartment or the ice compartment. It is not harmed by freezing. Meats bought in the frozen state, such as chops and steaks, should be kept frozen until ready for use. It is best not to refreeze after thawing.

The smaller the proportion of cut surfaces exposed on a piece of meat, the better it keeps. Thus meat in one large piece, like a standing rib roast, will keep in good condition in the refrigerator for a longer time than meat cut in small pieces as for stewing. Ground meat, which has a very high proportion of cut surface, loses flavor and juiciness rapidly, and should be used as soon as possible after purchasing.

As soon as fresh meat is brought into the home, it should be unwrapped and wiped off with a damp cloth—never washed in water. Then it may be placed on a clean dry plate or shallow refrigerator dish, and covered lightly or not at all; a piece of waxed paper laid over the meat is sufficient, or a loosely fitting refrigerator-dish cover may be used. Meat should never be closely covered or tightly wrapped in waxed paper, because a little drying of the surface retards bacterial growth and is therefore to be desired. If the meat is left wrapped in the butcher's original paper, cold penetration is slowed up and the paper will absorb some of the meat juices.

Cured meats. Old-fashioned country style *ham* and similar products (smoked picnics and smoked butts) may be kept out of the refrigerator in any dark, cold place, except in hot weather, when refrigeration is desirable. But most all hams nowadays have a mild cure and require about the same care as fresh meat before cooking, especially after they have been cut. *Sliced bacon* should be left in its original wrapping, or wrapped in clean waxed paper and kept in the refrigerator in the coldest place. Only the amount to be used for the meal should be removed from the refrigerator. If the whole package is taken out and allowed to warm up, moisture will condense on the bacon and lessen its keeping qualities. It is not advisable to keep bacon, even in the refrigerator, longer than a week or two, as the fat tends to become hard and easily broken, and both appearance and flavor deteriorate. *Corned beef* should be treated just like fresh meat. *Sliced cold cuts* such as salami and bologna, should be stacked compactly, wrapped in waxed paper, and kept in the coldest part of the refrigerator.

Ready-to-serve canned meats. If sliced canned meats are left over from one meal to another, the slices should be piled together and wrapped securely in waxed paper before placing in the refrigerator. They should be kept the shortest possible time, for there is a loss in flavor.

Cooked meat. After cooking, any kind of meat should be made into the most compact parcel possible, and wrapped tightly in waxed paper or placed in a dish with a tight-fitting cover. Because the surface has already been dried out by cooking, no further drying is desirable, and there may be not only loss of meat flavor but absorption of other flavors if the meat is left uncovered in the refrigerator.

POULTRY

Like fresh meat, poultry should go immediately into the coldest available place in the refrigerator. Before storing, it should be drawn, cleaned, washed and thoroughly drained, then covered lightly with waxed paper. If the bird is to be stuffed for roasting, do this the day it is to be cooked. In recent months experimental work has proven that it is unsafe to stuff the bird the day before it is cooked, even though the stuffed, trussed bird is kept in refrigerator. In cold weather, if the refrigerator is crowded, any safe cold place will keep the bird in good condition; but the thermometer reading should be 50° or lower. If the bird is cut up for frying, stewing, or broiling, cover lightly with waxed paper and store in refrigerator until cooking time.

DAIRY PRODUCTS AND EGGS

Fresh milk and *cream* should always be stored in the original containers, since the bottles or cartons are sterilized before being filled and the inside is therefore as clean as possible. If the outside of the container is soiled, it should be thoroughly washed with cold water, and dried, before placing in the refrigerator. Milk and cream belong in the coldest place in the refrigerator, and the manufacturer usually indicates where this place is by making it tall enough to accommodate bottles.

Evaporated and *sweetened condensed milk* should be kept in the can after opening, but the can should be well cleaned on the top and outside before it is opened, and any drip should be wiped off before the opened can is put away. Cover the opening with a hood of waxed paper and fasten on with a rubber band. Condensed milk keeps almost indefinitely even when open if it is well cared for. Evaporated milk, however, should be used within a few days, for once opened it spoils almost as quickly as fresh milk.

Butter should have a special glass or enamelware container with a close-fitting cover, because it absorbs food odors readily. If the quarter-pound sticks are wrapped separately in parchment, leave them wrapped until needed. Oleomargarine should be given care similar to butter, but it is not so perishable.

Cheese, whether natural or packaged, requires refrigeration as soon as it is cut. Processed packaged cheeses are pasteurized and change very little, either in aroma or in texture when kept unopened without refrigeration for several months; but as soon as they are exposed to the air, organisms can enter and the cheese should thereafter be refrigerated.

All cut natural cheeses, whether packaged or not, require refrigeration because they are not pasteurized. Natural cheeses such as Camembert, Brie, Roquefort and Liederkranz, which are cut and then packaged, are quite perishable and should be kept in the refrigerator even before opening; when kept cold, they hold their natural flavor well without giving off much aroma. The soft types, like Camembert and Brie, should be allowed to warm up to room temperature before serving, since this semi-liquid softness is characteristic of such cheese when well ripened, and its flavor is best in this soft state. One way to keep cheese like the cheddar type is in the refrigerator. That old-time way of wrapping it in a cloth dipped in vinegar helps retard the development of mold which often appears on cheese, but it changes the appetizing aroma and flavor. A better way of retarding mold formation is to keep the cheese in a plastic bag.

Eggs should always be refrigerated, not only by the housewife, but by the poultryman and the dealer. This not only prolongs their freshness, it also helps keep the yolk in the center of the egg, which is so desirable for stuffed eggs or for hard-cooked eggs which are sliced for garnishing. If eggs are to be separated, they should be separated as soon as removed from the refrigerator as they separate more easily while cold. The yolks may be used at once or covered and returned to the refrigerator; but the whites should be allowed to warm up to room temperature before beating in order to get the greatest possible volume.

COOKED FOODS

Some cooked foods are much more perishable than others. It is not advisable to keep bought foods containing custard more than a few hours, as the combination of eggs, milk and sugar is irresistible to bacteria; however, there is no danger from homemade custards, custard pies and cream puffs which are kept overnight in the refrigerator. Baked custards should be removed from the pan of hot water in which they are baked and stood on cake racks till cool; then covered and kept in the refrigerator until they are served. Soft custards may be rapidly cooled by setting the top of the double boiler in a pan of cold water; when cool, pour the custard into a clean sterile jar, cover tightly with a screw-top lid and place in the refrigerator until serving time. Custard is best both in flavor and in texture if served the same day it is made.

White sauce may often be made conveniently ahead of time and stored until just before use. The sauce should be cooled thoroughly by placing the pan in cold or iced water, stirring frequently as it cools to prevent skin from forming on top. Then it may be poured into a sterile glass jar and stored like soft custard. When ready to use, reheat it over boiling water, adding a little milk if needed to bring it to the desired consistency.

Gelatine desserts of the plain fruit variety keep better than those made with whipped cream or whipped evaporated milk, but it is best not to keep even these longer than a day or two. They should be kept constantly in the refrigerator, and if possible should be covered to prevent absorption of foreign odors and flavors, and drying out of the surface.

Leftover cooked foods should be placed in clean, covered containers (bowls, refrigerator dishes, or glass jars) and kept in the refrigerator. If small quantities of several vegetables or cooked or canned fruits are left, they may be combined in one container and used for soup or salad. Leftovers should always be used as soon as possible for the sake of flavor, appearance, and nutritive value.

BAKED GOODS

Homemade *cake* keeps best if it is transferred from the baking pans to cake coolers soon after removal from the oven, then frosted as soon as it is barely cooled. Frosting helps to keep cake fresh and moist. Of the various types of icings, a cooked fudge or panocha icing will keep in good condition longest; butter icing is next best; and a seven-minute frosting is most perishable—it is at its best for only a few hours. Whether iced or not, the cake itself will keep in best condition if covered so as to be virtually air-tight. Cake boards and covers do the job very satisfactorily. But it should be remembered that cake is at its very best when perfectly fresh, as soon as it has lost the oven heat. Bought *cake* should be kept the same way; if possible, it should be left or replaced in its original wrapper.

Cookies should be stored in a cookie jar or covered tin pail. This helps to keep crisp cookies crisp and soft ones soft. Only one kind of cookie should be put into a cookie jar at one time, or there will be an interchange of flavors between different kinds which makes all of them taste nondescript. The cookie jar should be thoroughly washed out, scalded and carefully dried between batches.

To have the best quality, *pie* should be made in a sufficient quantity for just one meal, for no pie can be stored with very satisfactory results. The crust becomes soaked on standing, and the filling, whether it is a fruit or custard type, becomes unattractive in appearance and loses the fine edge of its flavor. Mince, pumpkin and chiffon pies may if necessary be kept overnight; but they are at their best within a few hours after preparation. Of course they should be stored in the refrigerator and should be covered.

Bread keeps best if left in its original wrapping, or if wrapped snugly in waxed paper. Then it should be stored either in a clean dry bread box or, if none is available, in a closed container in the refrigerator. Bread that is kept in the refrigerator shows less tendency to become moldy. If the bread is always kept wrapped, the bread box is much easier to care for than if the unwrapped loaf is placed in it; in the latter case, the box will require frequent washing in hot, soapy water, rinsing in scalding water and thoroughly drying to keep it sweet and free from mold spores.

MISCELLANEOUS FOODS

Coffee should preferably be kept in the home not longer than a week, so a family of five should not purchase more than a week's supply at a time. If the coffee is purchased in a paper bag, transfer it immediately to a clean dry glass or tin container. Cover it tightly, and never leave the cover off for a minute longer than necessary when measuring coffee into the pot. The volatile substances which give coffee its pleasing flavor and aroma escape very quickly when exposed to air. Keep the tightly closed coffee container in the refrigerator, or other cool dark place. A good plan is to let it stand upside down, so the rising aroma cannot escape through the crack around the lid but will be trapped in the upturned bottom of the container.

Syrups, such as molasses, honey, maple syrup and corn syrup, and also *jellies, jams, preserves* and *pickles,* need no refrigeration so long as they are unopened, though they keep best in a cool, fairly dry place. After opening, the jars or bottles should be thoroughly cleaned on the outside to remove any sticky smears where bacterial growth might start, and the tops should be covered with a layer or two of strong waxed paper, secured with a rubber band or a piece of string. If convenient, they should be stored in the refrigerator; but if the remainder is to be consumed within a few days, this is not necessary, provided a cool place is available outside the refrigerator. Honey should never be kept cold unless you particularly like it very thick; if refrigerated over a long period, it is liable to crystallize. Crystallized honey can be restored to its liquid state by setting the jar in a pan of hot water for a few minutes to melt.

Both *mayonnaise and French dressing,* and the various types of cooked salad dressing (either bought or homemade), should be stored in the refrigerator, but not in the coldest spot. Keep them tightly covered and the outside of the container clean. Homemade French dressing should be taken out before using and allowed to warm up enough so that it can be mixed well by shaking before adding to the salad.

Shortenings and oils. Hydrogenated shortenings, especially those made from vegetable oils, are very stable and need no refrigeration to keep them in good condition. These shortenings should be kept tightly covered, for if exposed to the air they will collect dust and will eventually contract and crack on the surface, though they may not become rancid. If their storage place is so hot that they melt at any time, their texture will be changed. After these shortenings have once been melted and used for deep fat frying, they should be carefully strained into the original container, cared for in the same way as before using, and not used for any other purpose than frying.

Lard should be stored in the refrigerator, if possible. It is softer than the hydrogenated vegetable fats, and is relatively easy to handle even when chilled.

Cooking and salad oils (olive, cottonseed and corn oils) may be kept in the refrigerator to prevent rancidity, though if they are used within a few weeks, there is little danger of their becoming rancid in any cool place.

Spices and extracts should always be kept tightly covered, in a cool, dark, dry place. Both light and heat affect the volatile substances which give them flavor and aroma, and some manufacturers are now putting out their flavoring extracts in dark bottles to exclude a maximum of light. It is not advisable to buy spices in large quantities, because even under the best storage conditions they lose their potency in time. They should be replaced every six months if possible.

Nuts contain a rather high percentage of oil, and if stored in a warm place they soon become rancid and discolored. Shelled nutmeats should be placed in a clean dry glass jar, covered tightly, and stored in the refrigerator. Nuts in the shell may be kept in any cool, dry place. Neither should be expected to keep indefinitely.

Dry *bread crumbs* are a great convenience to have on hand. They can readily be made from any stale mold-free bread by drying it out thoroughly in a very slow oven and then rolling it to fine crumbs with a rolling pin or putting it through a food mill or rubbing it over a coarse grater to obtain crumbs. When rolling the bread, crumbs will be prevented from flying if the dry bread is placed in a paper sack and rolled in the sack. Put the crumbs immediately into a clean dry glass jar and cover with a screw-top in which several holes have been punched, or with 2 or 3 thicknesses of cheesecloth tied on with string or fastened securely with a rubber band. Keep in a cool dry place. Crumbs should not be stored in an air-tight container, or they will become stale and musty in flavor. Stored as directed they will keep several weeks without deteriorating.

The Cook's Creed

The health of my family is in my care; therefore—

> I will preserve as far as possible the nutritive elements in the foods which are delivered to me.

My family's enjoyment of food is in my care; therefore—

> I will preserve and enhance the attractive qualities of the foods with which I work.

Stretching the food dollar is part of my responsibility; therefore—

> I will take such care of foods that none will spoil. I will use left-overs with thought and skill.

A well-prepared dish and an appetizing meal are a creative achievement; therefore—

> I shall derive happiness from work itself.

Good food is of prime importance to my family; therefore—

> I shall take pride in doing an outstanding job of cooking.

MEASUREMENTS

WHEN recipes were written in such terms as "butter the size of a walnut," judgment developed through long experience was of primary importance to the cook. Today, when we have standardized measuring cups and spoons, and recipes standardized to conform with standard measurements, judgment is still an indispensable quality in a cook who hopes to free herself from slavish following of recipes, and to have the fun of creating new dishes.

Measuring cups and spoons and detailed instructions enable even the beginner to cook acceptable dishes while she develops her knowledge of how mixing and cooking affect raw materials. They enable her, as well as the experienced cook, to approximately duplicate a product. Cakes made by two persons, following the same recipe, will always differ somewhat because the two cooks will fill their measuring cups and spoons a little differently, will use different degrees of vigor in beating and mixing, and will spend different lengths of time on the process. One may use a fine-grained sugar, the other a coarse; one a large egg, the other a small; one an aluminum baking pan an inch wider or a quarter of an inch deeper than the tin or glass pan used by the other. One may have a better insulated oven than the other, with a more constant temperature and more level racks. The two cakes they produce will differ somewhat in texture, color, lightness and even in flavor, yet both may be excellent cakes. Such variations are part of the charm of home-cooked foods.

Below are some tables which will aid the homemaker in standardizing her own measurements, and in making adjustments in the recipes she uses.

TABLE 2
EQUIVALENT WEIGHTS AND MEASUREMENTS

1 bushel	4 pecks
1 peck	8 quarts
1 gallon	4 quarts
1 quart	2 pints
	4 cups
1 pint	2 cups
1 cup	16 tablespoons or 8 fluid ounces
¾ cup	12 tablespoons or 6 fluid ounces
⅔ cup	10 tablespoons plus 2 teaspoons
½ cup	8 tablespoons or 4 fluid ounces
⅓ cup	5 tablespoons plus 1 teaspoon
¼ cup	4 tablespoons or 2 fluid ounces
⅛ cup	2 tablespoons or 1 fluid ounce
1 tablespoon	3 teaspoons or ½ fluid ounce

TABLE 3
EQUIVALENT WEIGHTS AND MEASURES OF SOME FOODS*

1 lb. all-purpose flour, sifted..........	4	cups
unsifted	3½	cups
1 lb. cake flour, sifted...............	4½ to 2⅔ cups	
unsifted	4	cups
1 lb. whole wheat flour, unsifted.......	3½	cups
1 lb. corn meal	3	cups
1 lb. granulated sugar	2¼	cups
1 lb. brown sugar	2¼	cups firmly packed
1 lb. fat (any kind)	2	cups
¼ lb. butter	1	stick or ½ cup
1 lb. coffee.....................	about 80	tablespoons
	or 5½	cups, coarse grind
1 lb. cocoa	about 64	tablespoons
	or 4	cups
1 oz. baking chocolate (bitter)	1	square equals ¼ cup grated
1 lb. chopped walnuts, shelled	4	cups
1 lb. American cheese, grated	4	cups loosely packed
1 cup egg whites	8-10 egg whites	
1 cup egg yolks	12-14 egg yolks	
1 cup fresh whole eggs	5 to 6 eggs	
1 tablespoon dried egg white plus 2 tablespoons water equals 1 fresh egg white.		

*Variations in all these amounts may be caused by the quality of the foods themselves, and by the manner of measuring.

1½ tablespoons dried egg yolk plus 1 tablespoon water equals 1 fresh egg yolk.

2 tablespoons dried whole egg plus 2 tablespoons water equals 1 fresh egg.

1 oz. baking powder .... 2⅔ tablespoons

1 oz. baking soda .... 2 tablespoons

1 oz. cream of tartar .... 3 tablespoons

TABLE 4

SUBSTITUTIONS

1 cup all-purpose flour minus 2 tablespoons equals 1 cup cake flour—both sifted before measuring.

¼ cup cocoa plus 1½ teaspoons shortening equals 1 oz. bitter chocolate.

1 cup vegetable shortening plus ½ teaspoon salt is approximately equal to 1 cup butter in salty flavor.

1 cup sweet milk, or ½ cup evaporated milk and ½ cup water, plus 1 tablespoon lemon juice or vinegar, equals 1 cup sour milk.

1 tablespoon corn starch equals 2 tablespoons flour for thickening.

4 to 6 lemons equal 1 cup juice.

TABLE 5

HOW TO MEASURE VARIOUS INGREDIENTS

Flour .... Measure after sifting. Lift lightly into cup; do not shake or tap down but level off with edge of spatula.

Corn meal or farina ... Measure like sugar.

Granulated sugar .... Lift lightly into cup and level off.

Brown sugar .... Pack down firmly into cup before leveling off.

Baking powder ..... Dip measuring spoon into can and level off with spatula.

Soda .... Like baking powder.

Fat .... Pack into cup so as to eliminate all air pockets. Level off with knife or spatula. Butter which is divided into ¼ pound sticks may be measured by estimate: ¼ lb. equals ½ cup, etc.

Grated cheese .... Measure loosely packed in cup. Or if recipe calls for ¼ lb. cheese, grated, weigh the cheese before grating, or estimate the weight.

Liquids .... Measure in glass cup having the top marking below rim of cup; place cup on level surface or hold at eye level while pouring liquid in.

BEVERAGES

● ● ● ● ● ● ● ●

REMEMBER that hospitable old neighbor who kept the coffee pot sim-mering on the back of the stove all day, "just in case somebody drops in?" Now modern culinary knowledge does not approve of that practice, but this chapter recognizes the social value of serving beverages such as coffee and tea, when made by orthodox methods. Beverages especially for the small fry have a place in this chapter, too.

● ● ● ● ● ● ● ● ●

A hot drink on a cold day and a cold drink on a hot one can make really important contributions to comfort and morale. They are also socially valu-able, being practically indispensable for all the between-meal refreshments which are served to guests, as well as for planned entertainments.

COFFEE

Most adults consider coffee an important starter for the day, so every homemaker should be able to make it well and have it equally good every time. General rules for making good coffee by any method are about the same, and are as follows:

(1)   Start by buying coffee of the proper grind for the type of coffee maker used. Buy coffee in fairly small quantities—not more than enough for a week; the amount for your family depends on how much coffee it consumes. It is poor economy to buy coffee in large quantities as some of the "coffee good-ness" is lost every time the container is opened. The best way to keep coffee bought in a paper bag is to transfer it immediately to a perfectly clean, dry, odorless glass jar with an air-tight lid. Store in refrigerator, standing it up-side down so the rising aroma will not find its way out and escape so fast when the jar is turned up and opened.

(2)   Use fresh, clean, pure water. Perfect coffee cannot be made with

hard water which contains traces of many minerals, or with water that tastes strongly of chlorine. Water with a flavor of its own is not desirable for cooking. If it leaves a mark on pots and pans in the form of a lime deposit or a stain of iron rust, get a filter for your faucet, or better still, a "Domestic Water Softener" which is a good investment even just for coffee making.

(3)   Be sure the coffee maker—vacuum, drip, percolator or old-fashioned coffee pot—is kept odorlessly clean by washing with hot, soapy water and scalding thoroughly after each using. Never allow grounds to stand in it for several hours, and never use the grounds twice.

Instant coffee requires no equipment other than a coffee cup. It is a convenience to have on hand, but container must be kept tightly sealed. When boiling water is poured over instant coffee, it dissolves almost instantaneously, producing a beverage which many cannot tell from regular coffee.

There also are coffees available from which all or most of the caffeine has been removed. Caffeine is the stimulating element in coffee, so persons who drink coffee for its stimulating effect are not satisfied with this type. Beverages made from cereal grains are also used as coffee substitutes, but the flavor is quite different from that of coffee. Some of these preparations sold under trade names are made like regular coffee, others are made like instant coffee.

TEA

Like coffee, tea is aromatic and loses flavor and fragrance rapidly if exposed to air. Therefore, store it in a tightly covered container. Good tea is the small or medium-sized leaves, free of stems and dust. Inferior tea selling at a lower price is usually poor economy as a much larger quantity of it is often necessary to produce a good flavor.

Always use a glass, china or pottery tea pot for brewing tea. Metal imparts some of its own flavor. Two pots are usually needed, or the tea may be brewed in a tightly covered enamelware saucepan, then strained into a heated pot for serving. Measure the tea leaves into the pot or pan, then pour freshly boiling water over it. Cover and allow it to brew or steep for 3 to 5 minutes in a warm place. Then strain the liquid into a pot which has been heated by rinsing with boiling water, and serve at once. Or place tea ball or tea bag into the pot and pour boiling water over it. When the tea has steeped the required time, or until it is the desired strength, lift out ball or bag. Tea made in a cup using a tea ball or tea bag is seldom as good in flavor or aroma as tea brewed in the pot, but the "cup method" is a convenient one.

FRUIT DRINKS

Fruit punches and various cold drinks are especially refreshing on a hot day, and the fruit juice which they contain makes a real contribution to nutrition. The possible combinations are nearly unlimited, as almost any fruit juice will combine harmoniously with almost any other. Many persons like punches which have charged water or ginger ale added to the fruit juice mixture, but plain water with plenty of ice makes a less expensive and a more convenient beverage.

MILK DRINKS

Various milk drinks are especially valuable because they are a means of getting more milk into the diets both of children and of adults. In hot cocoa and chocolate, chilled cocoa or chocolate milk, milk shakes, malted milks, and eggnogs, milk plays the most important role. But many persons have never discovered how deliciously milk, and buttermilk too, can combine with fruit juices and thin fruit purées to make the most flavorful and refreshing of cold drinks. This is an excellent way of using juices of canned fruits which have been drained for use in salads or for other purposes.

In making cold drinks with milk, have the milk and the other ingredients thoroughly chilled before combining. If it is necessary to keep the mixed drink for a time before serving, let it stand in the refrigerator. Ice should never be added to a milk drink, as it dilutes it. And in serving fruit-milk drinks, bear in mind that curdling may take place if the mixture is allowed to stand.

When a very acid fruit juice, such as orange or lemon, is added to milk, the danger of curdling may be lessened and the richness of flavor increased by using a little cream with the milk. Or evaporated milk may be substituted for fresh milk, in the proper dilution.

1

SPICED OR MULLED APPLE CIDER

1 quart sweet apple cider ,
8 whole allspice
8 whole cloves
1 stick cinnamon, if desired

Few grains salt
¼ cup brown sugar, well packed

Put cider into a 3-qt. saucepan, add the spices, salt and sugar, and cover; heat very slowly to the boiling point. Heat should be so low that it takes the cider about half an hour to come to a boil. Remove from heat, strain, and serve steaming hot. 5 servings.

2

COCOA FOR ADULTS

2 tablespoons cocoa
2 tablespoons sugar
Pinch salt
½ cup boiling water

2 cups scalded milk or
1 cup. evaporated milk and
1 cup boiling water
¼ teaspoon vanilla

Mix cocoa, sugar and salt together in top of a double boiler, then blend to a smooth paste with the ½ cup boiling water. Place over direct heat, bring to a boil and cook rapidly for 1 minute, stirring constantly to form a syrup. Add rest of liquid and heat to scalding over boiling water. Remove from heat and add vanilla. Whip for a minute with an egg beater and serve steaming hot. 3 servings.

3   COCOA FOR CHILDREN

1½ tablespoons cocoa   3 cups scalded milk or
 2 tablespoons sugar   1½ cups evaporated milk
   Pinch salt   and 1½ cups boiling water
¾ cup boiling water   ¼ teaspoon vanilla

Make by same method as Cocoa for Adults. About 4 servings.

4   HOT OR CHILLED COCOA FOR ALL

3½ tablespoons cocoa   5 cups scalded milk or
¼ cup sugar   2½ cups evaporated milk
⅛ teaspoon salt   and 2½ cups boiling water
1¼ cups boiling water   ½ teaspoon vanilla

Blend cocoa, sugar and salt in top of a double boiler, then mix to a paste with the 1¼ cups boiling water. Place over direct heat, bring to a boil and cook rapidly for 1 minute, stirring constantly to form a syrup. Add 3 cups scalded fresh milk or 1¾ cups evaporated milk and 1¾ cups boiling water, and heat to scalding over boiling water. Remove from heat, add half the vanilla and whip. Serve the 2 adults from this mixture. Then add remaining liquid, reheat, add rest of vanilla and serve the 3 children. About 7 servings.

This method makes it possible to serve full-strength cocoa to adults and half-strength to children without making two lots of cocoa.

To make chilled cocoa, place pan of hot cocoa in cold water to cool quickly. Then pour into a sterile jar or bottle, cover tightly and place in coldest spot in refrigerator for at least 2 hours before serving.

5   CHOCOLATE SYRUP
(*For hot or cold chocolate*)

5 squares baking chocolate   1¾ cups sugar
  (5 oz.)   ¼ cup light corn syrup
2 cups boiling water   ½ teaspoon salt

Melt chocolate over hot water; add boiling water and cook over direct low heat, stirring constantly until smooth and thick, about 2 minutes. Add sugar, corn syrup and salt, and then cook briskly for 3 or 4 minutes, stirring occasionally. Cool. Pour into clean glass jar. There should be 2¾ cups; if less, add boiling water. Cover jar, cool and store in refrigerator.

To use this syrup as flavoring for hot chocolate or cold chocolate milk, allow about 1 tablespoon to a cup of milk, or to suit taste. If used as sauce on ice cream, stir in ¼ cup butter while sauce is hot.

6   HOT CHOCOLATE

2 squares baking chocolate	4 cups scalded milk *or*
1⅓ cups boiling water	2 cups evaporated milk and
⅓ cup sugar	2 cups boiling water
Pinch salt	½ teaspoon vanilla

Melt chocolate over hot water, add 1⅓ cups boiling water, then cook 5 minutes to a smooth paste, stirring occasionally. Add sugar and salt to hot milk, then combine with the chocolate syrup and continue cooking 5 minutes over boiling water. Add vanilla, whip for a minute with egg beater and serve steaming hot. Addition of marshmallows or whipped cream makes a richer, more interesting drink. 5 to 6 servings.

7   CHOCOLATE MALTED MILK

⅓ to ½ cup chocolate syrup (5)	4 tablespoons malted milk powder
	1 quart cold milk

Blend chocolate syrup and malted milk powder thoroughly. Add milk and beat with rotary egg beater or shake until thoroughly mixed. Serve immediately. 5 servings.

8   OLD-FASHIONED "BOILED" COFFEE
(*Using Egg*)

Measure 2 level tablespoons of regular or coarse grind coffee into the pot for each measuring cup (8 oz.) of water. To 5 or 6 tablespoons of coffee, stir in about ½ tablespoon of beaten egg or egg white, or add the inner linings from 2 egg shells. Pour on the required amount of boiling water, cover and bring to a boil. Remove from heat immediately and let stand on the back of the stove 4 or 5 minutes before pouring.

9   PERCOLATOR METHOD
(Measure 2 level tablespoons coffee for each cup of water used)

1. Measure fresh cold water into percolator. Place over heat until water boils. Remove from heat.
2. Measure regular-grind coffee into basket.
3. Insert basket into percolator, cover, return to heat and percolate slowly 6 to 8 minutes.
4. Remove coffee basket and serve coffee at once.

10   DRIP METHOD
(Measure 2 level tablespoons coffee for each cup of water used)

1. Preheat pot by scalding with hot water.
2. Measure drip-grind coffee into filter section.
3. Measure fresh boiling water into upper container. Cover.
4. When dripping is completed, remove upper section. Stir brew and serve.

10a   VACUUM METHOD
(Measure 2 level tablespoons coffee for each cup of water used)

1. Measure fresh cold water into lower bowl. Place over heat.
2. Place filter in upper bowl. Add vacuum-grind coffee.
3. When water boils, reduce heat or turn off electricity. Insert upper bowl with slight twist.
4. Let most of water rise into upper bowl. Stir water and coffee thoroughly. In 1 to 3 minutes, remove from heat.
5. When brew returns to lower bowl, remove upper bowl. Serve the coffee at once.

NOTE: COFFEE STRENGTHS AND ICED COFFEE

Two level tablespoons of coffee (approximately equal to 1 heaping tablespoon per cup) will make good strength coffee. For weaker or stronger coffee, reduce or increase the quantity of coffee used. For iced coffee, make coffee of double strength and pour the hot coffee over ice.

11   EGGNOG

4 eggs	1½ teaspoon vanilla
¼ cup sugar	¼ teaspoon salt
1 quart milk, chilled	Nutmeg

77

Beat 3 whole eggs and 1 yolk until very thick and light in color. Add 3½ tablespoons sugar, beating in thoroughly. Stir in milk, vanilla, and salt and pour the mixture into glasses. Beat remaining egg white until almost stiff, add remaining sugar and beat until stiff. Top each glass of eggnog with a spoonful of meringue, sprinkle with nutmeg if desired, and serve immediately. 5 servings.

12   CARAMEL EGGNOG

6 tablespoons granulated sugar	3 cups milk, chilled
1½ cups boiling water	¾ cup evaporated milk, chilled
3 eggs, separated	¼ teaspoon salt, or to taste
2 tablespoons granulated sugar	

Place the 6 tablespoons sugar in a skillet and heat, stirring frequently, until an amber liquid is formed. Slowly add the boiling water and stir until caramel dissolves; remove from heat and chill. Just before serving, beat egg yolks until very thick and lemon-yellow, and beat egg whites separately, gradually adding the 2 tablespoons sugar, until very stiff and smooth. Combine chilled caramel syrup with the milk and evaporated milk. Fold egg whites into yolks, and quickly stir in the milk mixture and salt. Serve at once. 5 servings.

13   FRUIT BUTTERMILK

3 cups thick buttermilk	juice from canned fruit
1½ cups canned fruit juice *or*	3 tablespoons sugar, or to taste

Combine all ingredients and stir until sugar dissolves. Serve well chilled. Will not curdle on standing. 5 servings.

Red cherry, apricot, pineapple, peach, and grape juice all combine well with buttermilk; or mixed juices may be used.

14   FRUIT JUICE MEDLEY

Juice of 3 medium oranges	2 cups ice water
Juice of 2 lemons	Sugar to suit taste
1 cup pineapple juice	

Combine all ingredients and serve well chilled. 5 to 6 servings, depending on size of glasses.

15   FRUIT PUNCH

Almost any combination of fruit juices, in any proportions, makes a delicious beverage when well iced. If the sweetened juice from canned fruit is used, the juice of a lemon diluted with water improves the flavor. Sugar may always be added to suit the taste when required. A sprig of mint or a half slice of lemon hung over the edge of the glass, or a red cherry dropped into each glass, makes a pleasing garnish. Various fruit punch combinations are suggested in the menus.

15a   GRAPE JUICE FLOAT

3 cups grape juice	¼ cup sugar, or to taste
½ cup lemon juice	1 cup ginger ale
1 cup apple cider	1 pint orange ice

Combine grape juice, lemon juice and cider and sweeten to suit taste. Just before serving add ginger ale. Fill glasses about ¾ full and drop a scoop of orange ice on top. Serve immediately. 5 to 6 servings.

16   LEMONADE

½ cup freshly squeezed lemon juice	⅓ cup sugar, or to taste About 4 cups ice water

Remove seeds from lemon juice but do not strain. Add sugar and water and stir quickly until sugar dissolves. Serve immediately, as the flavor deteriorates on standing. Amount of water and sugar both may be varied to suit personal tastes. 5 servings.

17   LEMON SYRUP

1½ cups sugar	1½ cups unstrained lemon juice
4 cups water	

Combine sugar and water in a saucepan and bring to boil; boil briskly for 5 minutes. Cool. Add unstrained lemon juice, stir thoroughly and pour into a clean glass jar. Cover jar and store in refrigerator. Makes about 5½ cups.

To prepare lemonade with this syrup, use about ½ cup of the syrup for each 8-oz. glass of lemonade, filling up with ice water and cracked ice. About 11 servings.

Note: Do not keep longer than a few hours, as it will lose both flavor and some vitamin content. Useful chiefly in preparing ahead of time for a large party.

18   LIMEADE

        5 small limes   5 cups ice water
        ⅔ cup sugar

Grate off a little of the green rind from limes: Then squeeze out the
juice, remove seeds but do not strain juice. Combine rind with lime juice
and sugar; add water and serve in glasses of cracked ice with a sprinkling
of grated rind on top. May be served hot, diluted with more water, if
desired. 5 servings.

18a   HOT MILK

        1 quart milk   ½ tablespoon vanilla
        2 tablespoons sugar   Cinnamon or nutmeg
        ¼ teaspoon salt

Heat milk just to scalding with the sugar and salt. Remove from heat
and stir in vanilla. Serve hot, with a sprinkling of cinnamon or nutmeg
over each serving. (If preferred, omit the sugar and vanilla, increase the
salt to suit the taste, and sprinkle with nutmeg.) 5 servings.

19   HOT SPICED MILK

        ¼ cup moist shredded   ½ teaspoon cinnamon
          cocoanut   ½ teaspoon nutmeg
        1 tablespoon butter   2 tablespoons honey
        4 cups milk

Brown cocoanut in melted butter in a 3-qt. saucepan, stirring to obtain
even color. Add milk, spices, and honey and heat to scalding. Strain
out cocoanut and serve immediately. Cocoanut may be left in if desired,
but should in that case be chopped before browning. 5 servings.

19a   MOLASSES NOG

        2 cups evaporated milk   2 or 3 tablespoons sorghum or
        2 cups ice water   light molasses
          Dash salt   Dash of nutmeg, ginger or
                                              cinnamon

Combine milk, water, salt and molasses, stirring well. Pour into
glasses and sprinkle a dash of the preferred spice on top. 5 servings.

20   PRUNE MILK SHAKE

1½ cups prune purée, about   ¹⁄₁₆ teaspoon salt
     ½ lb. dried prunes (285)   4½ cups milk, chilled
6 tablespoons lemon juice   Sugar to taste

Mix the prune purée thoroughly with the lemon juice and salt. Add
milk and beat with rotary beater; add sugar to suit the taste, amount depends on sweetness of prunes. Chill before serving. 5 or 6 servings.

21   PINEAPPLE EGG PUNCH

1 quart milk, chilled   ⅛ teaspoon salt
2 eggs, separated   9-oz. can crushed pineapple
½ cup sugar

Scald 1 cup of the milk in a double boiler. Beat egg yolks until thick
and light-colored with sugar and salt. Pour scalded milk over egg yolk
mixture, stirring until blended; then chill. Just before serving, add rest
of milk and the pineapple, pulp and juice. Then beat egg whites until
stiff. Fold them into rest of mixture. Serve at once. 5 servings.

22   HOT TEA

Choose a good grade of tea of variety your family prefers. Allow 1
teaspoon tea for each cup to be brewed. Place this in a clean, scalded
china, earthenware or glass tea pot. Pour over it the desired amount of
furiously boiling water—should be freshly boiled—, cover and let stand
on back of stove 2 to 5 minutes, or until it has reached desired strength.
Stir thoroughly and strain into another clean pot which has been rinsed
in hot water to warm it. Serve with lemon and sugar or cream and
sugar. A good plan, when a number of people with varying tastes are to
be served, is to provide a pot of hot water with which the guests may
dilute the tea to suit their own taste.

Note that the strength of the tea is determined less by the amount of
tea used than by the length of time it is permitted to steep. One teaspoon
tea is sufficient to make a cup of very strong tea.

23   ICED TEA

Prepare just as directed for Hot Tea, letting it steep to a good strength.
Pour the freshly made hot tea directly over ice cubes or cracked ice in
tall glasses or a pitcher. It is better to have the hot tea too strong than
too weak, since it may easily be diluted by adding ice water, while it is

impossible to make it stronger without brewing more hot tea. Serve with lemon wedges, sugar, and a sprig of mint if desired.

23a   SASSAFRAS TEA

The bark from the roots of the sassafras plant is used for making sassafras tea. It can be purchased in most grocery stores in the early spring. To make sassafras tea, estimate how much bark would be required to make ¾ cup if finely chopped, but leave the pieces of bark whole. Place in a clean enamelware saucepan and pour 5 cups boiling water over it. Cover and let stand in a warm place until steeped to the desired strength and color. Then strain the tea into a hot china or earthenware teapot, and serve with sugar, or sugar and cream. 5 servings.

24   TOMATO JUICE COCKTAIL

1 quart tomato juice	1 teaspoon vinegar
¾ teaspoon Worcestershire	½ teaspoon prepared horse-
½ teaspoon salt	radish
½ teaspoon sugar	¼ teaspoon celery salt
1 teaspoon lemon juice	

Thoroughly mix the tomato juice and seasonings. Chill before serving. Makes 1 quart.

25   VEGETABLE JUICE COCKTAIL

If any of the cooking water or "pot liquor" must be poured off after cooking vegetables, save it in a covered jar in the refrigerator until enough has accumulated to make appetizer cocktails for the family. A combination of several such pot liquors is especially desirable. Add some tomato juice or sauerkraut juice if desired, season to suit taste (probably no salt will be needed since cooking water is generally salted), and serve ice cold.

Use pot liquors as soon as possible, as their flavor and vitamin value deteriorate, though the mineral content is not affected by standing.

BREADS

GOOD home-made bread is easy to make, and it's fun! It's a real thrill, too, to see crusty golden-brown rolls and loaves as good as Grandma's come out of your very own oven. Perhaps that's why more and more women, in cities as well as rural districts, are serving more and more home-made bread, both the quick and yeast varieties. Bread of either sort, when made with either whole wheat flour or the new enriched white flour, is among the most nutritious of foods, because it is eaten so regularly and in such generous quantities. Read this chapter carefully to get new slants on the staff of life.

Breads are divided into two distinct classes, quick breads (baking powder or soda) and yeast breads. There is very little similarity between them, either in appearance, flavor or texture, but they have one thing in common: they are both universally popular, especially when home-made.

Quick breads are just that; they can be made on the spur of the moment, whereas yeast breads require time for rising and more time for shaping than quick breads and must be started a few hours before the meal. On the other hand, yeast breads keep much better than quick breads, so it is quite practical to bake enough for two or three days' supply at one time.

QUICK BREADS

Quick breads are especially popular for breakfast, because they can be mixed up in a jiffy and baked while the family drinks its orange juice. The same qualities that make them so good for breakfast, make them equally appealing for luncheon and dinner; so most of them—biscuits, muffins, and popovers especially—are right at home in any meal.

In addition to biscuits, muffins and popovers, the quick bread group includes griddle cakes, waffles, cornbread, and some kinds of fancy loaves—nut bread, fruit bread and the like are often made with baking powder or soda instead of yeast. Some kinds of doughnuts are also made with baking powder and may therefore be classed as quick breads.

The technique of making quick breads is simple but exacting. Once you have learned to make tender, flaky biscuits, light, even-textured muffins, and spongy, golden-brown pancakes, it is easier to make them right than to make them wrong. So it is important to get the right start and acquire the right habits at the very beginning.

Biscuits: The essence of good biscuit-making technique, for both baking powder and sour milk soda biscuits, is accurate measuring of ingredients and thorough, speedy mixing. This produces a dough that is soft and well mixed. A well blended dough results in a fine even texture; a soft dough makes the lightest, tenderest biscuit. Here are the steps in the process:

1. Sift the flour before measuring, and then sift again *three times* with the measured baking powder and salt. If baking powder is not thoroughly distributed through the flour, it may make brown speckles on the surface of the baked biscuit.

2. Add the solid shortening all at once and cut it in with a pastry blender or 2 knives, or rub it in with the finger tips until the mixture has a texture ranging from that of coarse cornmeal to that of grains of rice.

3. Add the milk all at once, and stir briskly until the dry ingredients are thoroughly dampened; the dough will stiffen up rather suddenly, and should not be stirred any more.

4. Turn the dough out onto a lightly floured board and knead it quickly about 12 to 15 times, using just enough flour to prevent sticking to the board and hands. The surface will still be sticky.

5. Roll or pat the dough out to the desired thickness—⅜ to ¾ inch, depending on whether you want a thin crusty biscuit or a thick one with a tender center between its crisp crusts.

6. Cut out biscuits with a lightly floured cutter, and with the same motion, lift them onto a lightly greased baking sheet and shake the biscuit out of the cutter.

7. Bake in a hot oven (450-475° F.) from 8 to 12 minutes.

8. Serve immediately when done. Biscuits should be eaten piping hot, so hot they melt the butter instantly. Biscuits can be re-heated by sprinkling lightly with water, closing securely in a paper bag, and placing in a hot oven for 10 to 12 minutes, but they are never quite so good as when first baked.

Shortcakes are made just like biscuits, but generally have a little sugar added. They may be somewhat richer too, sometimes made with thin cream instead of milk. Some people make shortcakes thick and break them open; some roll them thin and lay two together before baking; some prefer crusty shortcakes and therefore bake thin ones separately and lay two of these together when serving. Large shortcakes may be baked in round or square cake pans, and split before serving.

Various types of pinwheel biscuits are popular. These are made by rolling regular biscuit dough out thin and into a rectangular shape, sprinkling or spreading with a mixture of sugar and cinnamon, nuts, orange rind and

84

sugar, chopped fruit, meat, grated cheese, or any desired filling, and rolling up like a jelly roll. The roll is then sliced and the slices set on end in baking pans or in muffin pans, and baked as usual.

Muffins: Like biscuits, muffins require speed in mixing. The principal difficulty to guard against is over-manipulation, which is the cause of most of the common faults of poor muffins. The actual process, again, is a simple one:

1. Sift measured dry ingredients together three times, the last time into the mixing bowl.
2. In another bowl, beat the eggs; add the milk and melted shortening.
3. Pour these liquid ingredients all at once into the dry ones.
4. Stir quickly until the flour is *just* dampened; then give 4 or 5 more quick stirs. The batter should *not* be smooth, but a little lumpy.
5. Dip the batter quickly into buttered muffin pans, filling them about ⅔ full.
6. Bake in a hot oven (425° F.) about 20 minutes, until golden brown.
7. Serve immediately.

A perfect muffin has a rounded top, not a peaked one, and the crumb is even-textured, without any vertical tunnels. Peaks and tunnels are typical of an over-mixed muffin, which will also tend to be tough and heavy.

When raisins, chopped dates, nuts or other fruits are added to muffins, it should be done with those last few stirs; no extra stirring should be done.

Popovers: These are a less common type of hot bread which is very enjoyable as an occasional treat. Unlike muffins, there is no danger of over-beating the batter, and in fact it should be beaten thoroughly and vigorously to insure sufficient "popping." Another requirement is that muffin pans be heated sizzling hot before the batter is poured in.

Cornbread: Cornbread has different characteristics in different parts of the country, because of the variations in ingredients and the methods of baking. The South likes it made with 100 per cent cornmeal; but as we move farther North, the tendency is to mix the corn meal with a larger and larger proportion of white flour.

Whatever the composition of the cornbread, however, most people like it to have a crisp brown crust. This is obtained by using heavy iron or cast aluminum pans (a large skillet is perfectly satisfactory), and having them heated sizzling hot before greasing them and pouring in the batter. This starts cooking immediately and develops the desired crustiness. Corn bread should be served piping hot with plenty of butter.

Griddle cakes: A good recipe will produce good griddle cakes under most conditions. Poor ones are usually due to the griddle temperature, which, if too high, produces cakes mottled with dark and light patches, and if too low, produces pale cakes that are also likely to be heavy and tough. If the griddle is just right, baking will be quick and even, giving a smooth golden-brown surface and a tender "inside." This calls for a griddle heated only moderately hot; a griddle thermometer should register between 300° and 325° F.

Griddle thermometers are available in many department stores. They are set in a small frame which permits the bulb to rest directly on the griddle and register the exact temperaure of the baking surface, thus eliminating the guesswork which usually spoils at least the first baking of cakes.

Another precaution to take in baking cakes is to avoid too much grease on the griddle. Very little or none is required to prevent sticking, and an excess tends to make the cakes spotty and greasy, and also causes more smoking and makes the griddle harder to clean.

Griddle cakes may be kept hot in the top of a double boiler placed over hot water until the whole batch is baked and ready to be served.

Waffles: Waffle batter is quite similar to pancake batter, but a little stiffer and usually richer. The extra fat is sufficient to make it unnecessary to grease the modern electric waffle iron. Some greasing is necessary with the old-fashioned waffle iron which is heated on the kitchen range, because it is washed after using, whereas the electric model is never washed and the grease remains in the pores of the grids.

Since most electric waffle irons have their own heat indicator, it is easy to regulate them. The iron should be moderately hot to bake well. It needs to be well-filled in order to bake evenly, but care should be taken not to over-fill it unless there is a special rim which will catch the overflow effectively. It is usually possible to fill it just to capacity by using a ⅓ or ½ cup measure as a dipper. Experience will teach you just how much your own iron will accommodate.

Waffles should be served and eaten the instant they are removed from the iron. They quickly lose their crispness if allowed to stand. Stacking them is the surest way to destroy that desirable crisp freshness. If they are allowed to cool for use as sandwiches, they should be placed on a cake cooler so they can cool without sweating.

YEAST BREAD

Good home-made bread, the sort with which Grandmother used to perfume the house once or twice every week in the good old days, is not only easy to make, but fun, and so satisfying to eat that it is well worth the extra time and attention which yeast dough demands.

Essentials for good bread are either fresh live dried granular yeast or moist compressed yeast, and a good hard wheat, all-purpose or bread flour. Soft wheat flours make good breads, but a different technique and different recipes are needed. Butter used as the shortening, and milk or part milk as the liquid, will add to both flavor and food value, but are not essential. Nor is white bread the only kind that can be successfully made at home. Whole wheat or part whole wheat bread is no harder to make, and the home-made whole wheat loaf is so good that you will find it a big help in teaching your family to like whole grain breads.

86

The bread-making technique is simple and straightforward. Here are the basic steps in the process:

1.   Start the action of the yeast before combining it with the other ingredients. This is done by letting it soak in lukewarm water with a little sugar.°
Both compressed yeast and the new fast granular yeast should be treated in this way, and the soaking time is the same for both types, about 5 minutes. The only difference is that compressed yeast must be crumbled into the water.

2.   Scald the milk. The purpose of scalding is to destroy enzymes and "pasteurize" the milk, thus protecting both the yeast and the dough. Then cool the mixture to lukewarm, adding the salt and the rest of the sugar.

3.   Combine the lukewarm liquid with the softened yeast. If the yeast is overheated at any time it will be injured or even destroyed; if it is too cold, it will act very slowly. An even warmth of slightly less than body temperature (about 85° F.) is best throughout the process.

4.   Stir in about half the sifted flour until well mixed.

5.   Stir in the cooled melted shortening.

6.   Add the remaining flour to make a smooth soft dough. The softer the dough can be kept, the lighter and more tender the bread will be when baked.

7.   Turn the dough onto a lightly floured board, pastry cloth or table top and knead until it is smooth and elastic, adding as little extra flour as possible. Kneading will require about 10 minutes. Do it lightly and quickly, giving the dough a quarter turn each time you knead.

8.   Place the dough in a well-greased clean mixing bowl large enough to let it double in bulk without overflowing. To prevent formation of a thin crust on top, which will make streaks in the dough and the bread, brush the surface lightly with melted fat before setting to rise. Cover with a damp cloth and place in a cozy spot (85° and free from draughts) to rise. Let the dough rise well, until fully doubled in bulk (except whole wheat dough, which should increase its bulk by slightly more than one-half). When sufficiently risen, the pressure of a finger will leave a deep dent in the dough, which will not spring back.

9.   After one rising, the dough is usually kneaded down and allowed to rise again, slightly less than the first time, before shaping into loaves or rolls; but this is not essential.

10.   Knead the dough down, divide and shape, placing in greased pans.

°Yeast should not be softened in warm milk, or brought into contact with shortening in any way before some flour is added to the mixture. Fat seems to form a film around the yeast cells through which the tiny plants have difficulty in fermenting. Women who melt their shortening in the milk as it is being scalded, and add the yeast to this mixture when it has cooled to lukewarm, are likely to get a slow-rising dough. Best results are obtained by softening the yeast in warm water which contains a little sugar to start the activity of the yeast plants; and no shortening should be added to the dough until about half of the flour has been incorporated.

11. Let the loaves or rolls rise until doubled in bulk, in the same cozy place, covered with a supported clean towel (not touching the rolls). If they are brushed lightly with melted butter before baking, an attractive glossy brown surface will result.

12. Bake in a moderately hot oven (400-425° F.), according to the recipe used.

13. Turn the bread or rolls out onto a cake rack to cool at room temperature unless rolls are to be eaten immediately. Bread should never be cut while hot.

Refrigerator rolls require slightly different proportions of ingredients; usually a little less yeast is used. The kneaded dough may be allowed to rise once in a cozy place, and then kneaded down, covered with securely tied waxed paper, and stored in the refrigerator; or it is sometimes placed in the refrigerator immediately after kneading, without allowing it to rise first. Rising will take place, but at a very much retarded rate, in the refrigerator. About 2 hours before rolls are required, the refrigerator dough should be shaped, placed in pans, and allowed to rise in a warm place until fully doubled in bulk before baking, which is usually done in a moderately hot oven (400° F.). Dough will remain in good condition for several days, so freshly baked rolls may be had each day from the same batch of refrigerator dough.

Rolls: Many different kinds of rolls may be made from the same type of yeast dough. Plain buns, cloverleaf rolls, Parkerhouse rolls and similar plain bread rolls may be made from a plain bread dough. Sweet rolls—pecan rolls or schnecken, cinnamon rolls, butterfly rolls and the like—usually call for a sweeter, richer dough, but they also may be made from a plain dough if preferred.

Other types of yeast bread: Many coffee cakes are made from yeast dough. This may be sweeter, richer and also lighter than ordinary bread dough. Yeast doughnuts are also quite common, though many of them have been displaced by the baking powder type; but all filled doughnuts, such as Bismarcks, require yeast dough.

ENRICHED BREAD AND FLOUR

It is no longer necessary to force whole wheat bread and whole wheat flour on people who prefer white. During World War II most white flour was enriched by the addition of certain vitamins and iron, making it more nearly equal in food value to the whole wheat flour.

The added vitamins are factors of vitamin B complex: thiamine or vitamin B_1, which aids in utilization of carbohydrates by the body and stimulates appetite; nicotinic acid, which prevents pellagra; and in some cases riboflavin —which however is always present in any bread made with milk. Iron is also added. All these elements are present in the germ and other parts of the wheat kernel which are discarded in the refining process.

Here is the way to get the family to the table promptly when the meal is ready: Tempt them with fragrant, crunchy-crusted, tender, sizzling-hot, hot breads! At upper right—Plain Muffins (42) then from top to bottom: Cornsticks (46), Baking Powder Biscuits (26), Whole Wheat Muffins (48) baked in loaf-shaped muffin pans and Orange Pinwheel Biscuits (29).

The hot broiled sausage doesn't steal away a bit of the goodness from the hot crisp waffles and comb honey—in fact they add to the complete satisfaction of this ideal array of breakfast foods.

Old-fashioned Gingerbread doesn't require modernization to be welcome on any table, but if you want something a little different, bake it in a deep round cake pan or in individual Mary Ann Molds, and serve it warm with a lavish garnish of whipped cream, orange sections, and walnut halves **(123).**

Old-Fashioned Marble Cake **(111)** *always has its dark part darkened with molasses and spices, because that's the way Grandma used to make it.*

ABOVE—*For a truly regal-looking cake, bake Red Devil's Food Cake* (109) *increasing the ingredients by one-half to have 3 layers. Then put layers together with Dark Chocolate Frosting* (138) *and cover the whole with fluffy white Seven-Minute Icing* (145).

BELOW—*The same recipe which produces delicate white Angel Food Cake* (91) *makes cocoa angel food if you reduce the cake flour to ¾ cup and add to it ¼ cup cocoa.*

© Swan's Down Cake Flour.

It is therefore less essential today that people learn to like whole wheat bread, because they can get the vitamins and much of the mineral content from white breads made with enriched flour.

QUICK BREADS

26   BAKING POWDER BISCUITS

2 cups all-purpose flour	½ teaspoon salt
3 teaspoons baking powder, see p. 122	⅓ cup shortening
	¾ to ⅞ cup milk

Sift flour, measure, and resift 3 times with baking powder and salt, the last time into a 3-qt. mixing bowl. Add shortening and cut in with pastry blender or 2 knives until particles are size of rice grains. Add milk all at once and stir vigorously until dough just stiffens up. The larger amount of milk will probably be required in cold weather; dough should be rather soft. Turn out onto floured board or pastry cloth, knead from 12 to 15 times; then roll or pat out ⅜ to ¾-inch thick (according to whether you want thin crusty biscuits or fat soft ones). Cut out with biscuit cutter dipped in flour, lift onto a greased baking pan. Brush tops with melted butter. Bake in hot oven (450° F.) 10 to 15 minutes, depending on thickness, or until they are golden brown. Serve immediately. 12 to 15 medium-sized biscuits.

Note: To save trouble in cleaning up after biscuits, try turning dough out onto a piece of waxed paper sprinkled with flour. Knead and pat the dough out on this paper, and after the biscuits are cut out, the paper may be thrown away.

26a   BUTTERMILK BISCUITS

2½ cups all-purpose flour	1 teaspoon salt
1½ teaspoons baking powder, see p. 122	⅓ cup plus 1 tablespoon shortening
½ teaspoon baking soda	1 cup buttermilk

Sift flour, measure and resift 3 times with rest of dry ingredients, the 3rd time into mixing bowl. Cut in shortening with a pastry blender, or rub in with finger tips. Stir in buttermilk. When thoroughly mixed, turn onto lightly floured board, knead a dozen times, and roll from ½ to ¾-inch thick. Cut with floured biscuit cutter and place on a greased baking sheet; brush tops with melted butter. Bake in a hot oven (450° F.) 12 to 15 minutes. Serve piping hot. 14-16 biscuits, 2¼ inches in diameter.

26b　　　　　　　　　DROP DUMPLINGS

1½ cups all-purpose flour	½ teaspoon salt
2¼ teaspoons baking powder, see p. 122	¾ cup milk
	Chopped parsley, if desired

Sift flour, measure and resift 3 times with baking powder and salt, the 3rd time into the mixing bowl. Add milk all at once and stir rapidly until well blended. If desired, add about 1 teaspoon finely chopped parsley. Drop by teaspoonfuls on top of stewed chicken, or beef or lamb stew, dipping spoon into the hot broth each time before dipping into the batter, to prevent sticking. As soon as dumplings are all in, cover the stew and boil moderately for 12 minutes without uncovering. Then remove dumplings to a hot platter, arranging them around the outside and the stew in the center. Even if the meat is well done, it should not be removed from the kettle before the dumplings are added, and there should be at least 3 cups of boiling liquid so there will be enough gravy left after cooking the dumplings. 5 servings.

27　　　　　　　　　BUTTERSCOTCH PINWHEELS

2 cups all-purpose flour	¼ cup melted butter
½ teaspoon salt	⅓ cup brown sugar, packed
3 teaspoons baking powder, see p. 122	¼ cup white corn syrup
⅓ cup shortening	½ teaspoon cinnamon
¾ cup milk	¼ cup chopped nuts

Sift flour, measure, and resift 3 times with salt and baking powder. Cut in shortening, add milk all at once, and stir quickly until dough stiffens. Turn out onto floured board and knead 6 times. Roll dough out carefully in a 12 x 8-inch rectangle, about ⅜-inch thick. Brush with ⅓ the butter, sprinkle with ⅓ the sugar mixed with cinnamon, and roll up from long side like jelly roll. Cut in 16 slices. Put ¾ teaspoon each of butter, brown sugar syrup and nuts in each of 16 small buttered muffin pans; place 1 slice in each cut-side down. Bake in moderately hot oven (425° F.) 15 to 20 minutes or until browned. Serve hot with butter. 16 small pinwheels.

28 CHEESE BISCUITS

1½ cups all-purpose flour
2¼ teaspoons baking powder,
    see p. 122
½ teaspoon salt
¼ cup shortening

½ cup milk
¼ cup grated sharp cheese
    blended with
2 tablespoons butter

Sift flour, measure, and resift 2 times with baking powder and salt. Cut in shortening with pastry blender or 2 knives, until particles are size of navy beans. Add milk all at once and stir quickly until dough stiffens. Turn out on floured board and knead for about 20 seconds. Roll out ¼-inch thick and cut in 1½-inch rounds. Spread ⅔ of cheese mixture between pairs of biscuits, sandwich-fashion, and the rest on top, and transfer to a baking sheet. Bake in a hot oven (450° F.) 12 minutes or until biscuits are golden brown. Serve piping hot. If preferred, the cheese mixture may be cut into the sifted dry ingredients and distributed through the dough in mixing. 15 to 18 biscuits.

29 ORANGE PINWHEEL BISCUITS

2 tablespoons butter
½ cup orange juice
½ cup sugar
1 teaspoon grated orange rind

1 recipe of Baking Powder
    Biscuits (26)
2 tablespoons sugar
½ teaspoon cinnamon

Combine butter, orange juice, ½ cup sugar and grated rind, and heat just until butter melts and mixture is well blended. Pour into a baking pan measuring about 6 by 10 by 2 inches. Roll out biscuit dough ⅜-inch thick, in a 9 x 12 inch rectangle, and sprinkle with the 2 tablespoons sugar and cinnamon mixed together. Roll up as for jelly roll starting at wide side and cut into 12 equal slices. Lay slices close together in the orange syrup, cut side down. Bake in a hot oven (450° F.) 20 to 25 minutes until golden brown. 12 pinwheels.

30 WHOLE WHEAT BISCUITS

1 cup all-purpose flour
2¼ teaspoons baking powder,
    see p. 122
¾ teaspoon salt

1 cup whole wheat flour
⅓ cup butter or other
    shortening
¾ cup milk

Sift the white flour, measure, and resift 3 times with baking powder and salt, the last time into mixing bowl. Stir in the unsifted whole wheat flour. Cut in shortening with a pastry blender. Add milk all at once and stir vigorously until dough just stiffens up; then turn out onto a lightly floured board and knead 6 times. Roll or pat out to thickness of ⅜ to ½-inch, and cut out with biscuit cutter. Place on greased baking sheet. Bake in a hot oven (450° F.) about 12 minutes. Twelve 2-inch biscuits.

31   SHORTCAKES

Use recipe for Baking Powder Biscuits (26), but add 1 tablespoon more shortening and, if desired, 1 or 2 tablespoons sugar, to be sifted with the flour mixture. For an extra-tender shortcake, substitute cream for the milk.

32   APPLE AND PINEAPPLE ROLL

2 cups all-purpose flour	¼ cup granulated sugar
3 teaspoons baking powder, see p. 122	1½ teaspoons cinnamon
	1½ cups chopped peeled apple
½ teaspoon salt	1 No. 2 can crushed pineapple, drained
⅓ cup shortening	
⅔ cup milk	1 tablespoon melted butter
2 tablespoons butter, melted	3 tablespoons brown sugar

Sift flour, measure and resift with baking powder and salt 3 times. Cut in shortening with pastry blender or 2 knives. Add milk all at once and stir just until dough stiffens; then turn out onto floured board, knead half a dozen times, and roll out in rectangular sheet ¼-inch thick. Spread with the 2 tablespoons melted butter, sugar and cinnamon. Mix apple and pineapple and sprinkle over dough. Roll dough up tightly like jelly roll starting at the wide side. Pour the 1 tablespoon melted butter into bottom of 9-inch square baking pan, and sprinkle brown sugar evenly over it. Cut roll in 1-inch slices, and place close together in baking pan, cut-side up. Bake in a moderately hot oven (425° F.) 25 to 30 minutes or until done and well browned. 9 to 12 slices, depending on size.

This roll may be served as coffee cake or with whipped cream as a dessert for luncheon or dinner.

33   BOSTON BROWN BREAD

1 cup corn meal	1 teaspoon salt
1 cup whole rye flour	¾ cup molasses or sorghum
1 cup whole wheat flour	2 cups buttermilk
1 teaspoon soda	½ cup seedless raisins

Spoon corn meal and the flours into cup to measure and turn into sifter. Add soda and salt and sift into 3-qt. mixing bowl. Return bran remaining in sifter to mixture and stir well.

Combine molasses and buttermilk, add to the dry ingredients, and stir until dry ingredients are just dampened, then beat hard for a minute. With the last few stirs, add the washed and dried raisins. Pour batter into well-buttered molds, filling them ⅔ full. Put on lids. Steam for 50 to 60 minutes, or until springy when pressed and no longer sticky. To improvise a steamer, set a rack in the bottom of a deep kettle, cover the bottom with boiling water, and place molds on the rack; cover tightly. Replenish water as it boils away. Cool in the molds for a few minutes; then turn out and serve warm. Makes enough for three 2½-cup molds—10 to 12 servings.

Note: 1-pound baking powder cans are excellent molds; punch holes in their lids to allow steam to escape.

34   SOUTHERN CORN BREAD

1½ cups yellow corn meal	1⅓ cups buttermilk
¾ teaspoon soda	2 eggs, separated
1 teaspoon salt	¼ cup melted shortening

Sift corn meal, soda, and salt together. Add buttermilk to well-beaten egg yolks and add to corn meal mixture; beat well. Add hot melted shortening and again beat well. Fold in stiffly beaten egg whites. Turn immediately into a piping hot, greased, heavy 10-inch skillet. Bake in a hot oven (450° F.) 25 to 30 minutes. Serve at once with butter. 5 servings.

35   SPOON CORN BREAD

2¼ cups milk	⅔ cup corn meal
2 tablespoons butter	3 eggs, separated
1 teaspoon salt	

Heat milk to scalding; add butter and salt, and slowly stir in corn meal. Cook for 1 minute, stirring constantly. Remove from heat and cool a few minutes; then stir into well-beaten egg yolks. Fold in stiffly beaten egg whites and pour into a greased 4-cup casserole. Bake in a moderate oven (375° F.) for 35 to 40 minutes. Serve from baking dish, with plenty of butter. 5 servings.

36   GRIDDLE CAKES OR PANCAKES

2 cups all-purpose flour	3 tablespoons sugar
5 teaspoons baking powder, see p. 122	2 eggs
	2 cups milk
1 teaspoon salt	1/3 cup melted shortening

Sift flour, measure and resift with baking powder, salt and sugar. Beat eggs in mixing bowl, add milk and mix. Stir in melted shortening; then add flour mixture all at once and beat until perfectly smooth. Have griddle heated only moderately hot, or to a temperature of 300-325° F. if you have a griddle thermometer. Grease lightly with unsalted fat. Pour out 1/4 cup batter for each cake. Bake until top-side is full of air bubbles and under side is golden brown, then turn and bake until brown on other side. A spatula or pancake turner is desirable for turning cakes. Serve at once with butter and syrup (924), honey, or sugar and sausages or bacon, if desired. About 25 cakes.

Note: If thinner cakes are desired, add 1/4 cup more milk.

37   SPICY BREAD CRUMB GRIDDLE CAKES

1 cup sifted dry bread crumbs	1 cup all-purpose flour
3 tablespoons melted butter	2 1/4 teaspoons baking powder,
2 tablespoons brown sugar	see p. 122
1 teaspoon cinnamon	1/2 teaspoon salt
2 cups milk	3 eggs, separated

Mix together bread crumbs, butter, sugar and cinnamon and brown slightly in a saucepan over low heat, stirring constantly. Remove from heat. Stir 1 cup of the milk into the mixture and let soak until milk is absorbed. Sift flour, measure, and resift twice with baking powder and salt. Beat egg yolks, add rest of milk, and stir in dry ingredients. When smooth, stir in crumb mixture. Then lightly fold in the stiffly beaten egg whites. Bake on a lightly greased moderately hot griddle and serve immediately with butter and sugar or syrup (924). 12 to 15 cakes (1/4 cup batter to a cake).

38   EVAPORATED MILK GRIDDLE CAKES

1 cup all-purpose flour	1/4 cup shortening
1 1/2 teaspoons baking powder, see p. 122	1/4 cup boiling water
1/2 teaspoon salt	1 egg, beaten
2 teaspoons sugar	3/4 cup evaporated milk

Sift flour, measure, and resift twice with baking powder, salt and sugar. Melt shortening in the boiling water and stir into the beaten egg; add milk, stir and add all at once to the flour mixture, stirring briskly until well mixed. Bake on a moderately hot, slightly greased griddle. Makes about 20 cakes, 3 inches in diameter.

39 CORN MEAL GRIDDLE CAKES

1½ cups all-purpose flour
¾ cup yellow corn meal
4½ teaspoons baking powder,
  see p. 122
1 teaspoon salt

2 tablespoons sugar
1 egg
2 cups milk
¼ cup melted shortening

Sift flour, measure, and resift twice with all dry ingredients. Beat egg, add milk and pour all at once into dry ingredients. Beat with egg beater until smooth. Stir in melted shortening. Bake on a moderately hot griddle, very lightly greased, until golden brown on under side and dry-looking on top; then turn and bake until other side is brown. Makes about 2 dozen 4-inch cakes.

40 NUT BREAD

2½ cups cake flour
3 teaspoons baking powder,
  see p. 122
½ teaspoon salt

½ cup sugar
1 egg, beaten
1 cup milk
1 cup chopped nuts

Sift flour, measure, and resift twice with baking powder, salt and sugar. Combine well-beaten egg and milk and add all at once to dry ingredients, stirring quickly until flour is all dampened, but not until smooth. Quickly fold in nuts just enough to distribute. Turn into buttered loaf pan (8 by 4 by 2½ inches), pushing well into corners. Bake in a slow oven (300° F.) 20 minutes; then increase heat to moderate (375° F.) and bake 25 to 30 minutes longer or until nicely browned and well done. 1 loaf.

40a FLORIDA ORANGE BREAD

3 medium juice oranges
½ cup sugar
¼ cup water
1 tablespoon butter
1 cup orange juice
1 egg, well beaten

2½ cups all-purpose flour
2½ teaspoons baking powder,
  see p. 122
¼ teaspoon soda
½ teaspoon salt

Grease a 9 x 5 x 3-inch loaf pan. Start oven 10 minutes before baking; set to moderately slow (325° F.). Wash and dry oranges. Pare off thin rind with a sharp knife, cutting around the orange, then cut yellow rind in very thin slivers with scissors. There should be ½ cup. Combine sugar and water, add rind and stir constantly over heat until sugar dissolves. Boil gently for 5 minutes. Peel and syrup should measure ⅔ cup. Add butter and stir until melted. Sift flour, measure and resift 3 times with next 3 ingredients. Combine peel mixture, orange juice and beaten egg; add to dry ingredients all at once and mix just enough to moisten ingredients. Batter should be lumpy. Turn into prepared pan and place in heated oven. Bake 1¼ hours or until loaf tests done. 15 servings.

41   PEANUT BREAD

1¾ cups all-purpose flour	⅓ cup peanut butter
1 teaspoon soda	1 egg, well beaten
½ teaspoon salt	1 cup buttermilk
1 cup brown sugar, packed	

Sift flour, measure and resift 3 times with soda and salt. Blend sugar into peanut butter. Stir in well-beaten egg and beat until smooth. Add flour mixture and buttermilk alternately, beating until smooth after each addition. Turn into buttered loaf pan 4″ x 8″ x 2½″. Bake in a moderate oven (350° F.) 1 hour or until well browned. 1 loaf.

42   PLAIN MUFFINS

2 cups all-purpose flour	1 egg
½ teaspoon salt	1 cup milk or ⅓ cup evapo-
2¼ teaspoons baking powder, see p. 122	rated milk and ⅔ cup water
	3 tablespoons melted butter
2 tablespoons sugar	

Sift flour, measure, and resift 3 times with next 3 ingredients, the last time into a mixing bowl. Beat egg thoroughly, add milk and melted butter and pour into a "well" in the dry ingredients. Stir quickly until the dry ingredients are just dampened; then give 4 or 5 more stirs. Batter should not be smooth. Spoon batter quickly into buttered muffin pans, filling about ⅔ full. Bake in a moderately hot oven (425° F.) 20 minutes or until golden brown. Serve immediately. Makes 12 medium-size muffins.

43   BLUEBERRY OR OTHER FRUIT MUFFINS

Make like Plain Muffins (42), except fold in ⅔ cup washed, drained blueberries mixed with ¼ cup sugar and ¼ cup of the flour mixture with the last stirs of the batter. Other fruits may be added in the same way, such as raspberries, raisins, chopped dates or dried apricots, or sliced or quartered strawberries.

44   BACON MUFFINS

2 slices bacon	1 egg, beaten
2 cups all-purpose flour	1 cup milk or
½ teaspoon salt	⅓ cup evaporated milk and
2¼ teaspoons baking powder,	⅔ cup water
see p. 122	2 tablespoons melted bacon
2 tablespoons sugar	drippings

Chop bacon and pan-broil until done; drain thoroughly. Sift flour, measure, and resift twice with salt, baking powder and sugar; add crisp bacon and stir until well distributed. Beat egg and combine with milk and melted fat; add to dry ingredients all at once, and stir quickly until they are just dampened; then give 3 or 4 more stirs. *Do not* stir until smooth. Spoon into greased muffin pans, filling them ⅔ full. Bake in a hot oven (425° F.) 20 minutes or until nicely browned. Serve piping hot with butter. 12 medium-size muffins.

45   BRAN MUFFINS

1 cup all-purpose flour	¼ cup sugar
½ teaspoon salt	1 egg, beaten
1¾ teaspoons baking powder,	1 cup shredded whole bran
see p. 122	¾ cup milk
2 tablespoons butter or short-	
ening	

Sift flour, measure and resift 2 times with salt and baking powder. Cream butter and blend in sugar, add egg and beat until fluffy. Add bran and milk, stir until well mixed, then let stand a few minutes until bran takes up most of the liquid. Finally add flour mixture, stirring only until flour has disappeared. Fill buttered muffin pans ⅔ full. Bake in a moderately hot oven (400° F.) 30 minutes or until muffins are nicely browned. Serve piping hot with plenty of butter. 8 large or 12 small muffins.

46   CORN STICKS OR MUFFINS

¾ cup all-purpose flour   ¾ cup yellow or white corn
3 teaspoons baking powder,   meal
   see p. 122   1 egg
2 tablespoons sugar   1 cup milk
¾ teaspoon salt   ¼ cup melted shortening

Sift flour, measure and resift 2 times with next 4 ingredients, the last
time into mixing bowl. Beat egg well, stir in milk and melted shortening,
and pour all at once into center of dry ingredients. Stir quickly until dry
ingredients are just dampened, then give 3 or 4 more stirs. Batter should
not be smooth. Spoon quickly into greased, hot corn stick pans or muffin
pans, filling about ⅔ full. Bake in a hot oven (425° F.) about 25 minutes
or until golden brown. Remove from pans immediately and serve at once.
10 to 12 medium-sized muffins.

47   CRANBERRY MUFFINS

1 cup chopped raw cranberries   ¼ cup sugar
½ cup XXXX sugar   1 egg
2 cups all-purpose flour   1 cup milk
½ teaspoon salt   ¼ cup melted shortening
3 teaspoons baking powder,
   see p. 122

Combine chopped cranberries and ½ cup XXXX sugar. Sift flour,
measure and resift 2 times with next 3 ingredients. Beat egg, add milk
and beat well; add melted shortening and immediately add all at once
to dry ingredients, mixing until dry ingredients are just dampened, not
until smooth. Stir in cranberries until just distributed. Quickly spoon
batter into well-greased muffin pans. Bake in hot oven (400° F.) 20 to
25 minutes. 12 large or 16 medium muffins.

48   WHOLE WHEAT MUFFINS

1 cup all-purpose flour   2 to 4 tablespoons brown
3 teaspoons baking powder,   sugar, firmly packed
   see p. 122   ¾ cup chopped dates
1 teaspoon salt   1 cup milk
1 cup whole wheat flour   1 egg
    ¼ cup melted shortening

Sift flour, measure, and resift twice with baking powder and salt. Add whole wheat flour, brown sugar and dates and mix thoroughly. Combine and add milk, beaten egg and melted fat and mix quickly until dry ingredients are just dampened, then stir 3 or 4 times more. Spoon into buttered muffin pans, filling only ⅔ full. Bake in a moderately hot oven (425° F.) 15 to 20 minutes or until nicely browned. Dates may be omitted, if desired. 12 medium-sized muffins.

49   PINEAPPLE MUFFINS

2 cups all-purpose flour
3¾ teaspoons baking powder,
   see p. 122
½ teaspoon salt
¼ cup butter
¼ cup sugar

1 egg, beaten
1 cup milk
   8-oz. can pineapple chunks
2 tablespoons sugar mixed with
1 teaspoon cinnamon

Sift flour, measure and resift 3 times with baking powder and salt. Cream butter thoroughly, and blend in the ¼ cup sugar. Add egg and beat until smooth and fluffy. Add dry ingredients and milk alternately, beginning and ending with flour and beating well after each addition. Spoon batter into well-buttered muffin pans, filling about half full. Drain pineapple chunks and place one or two on top of each muffin and sprinkle with sugar-cinnamon mixture. Bake in a moderately hot oven (400° F.) about 20 minutes or until golden brown. Remove from pans and serve immediately. 15 medium-size muffins. (Use left-over juice in beverage or dessert.)

50   RICE MUFFINS

1 cup all-purpose flour
1 tablespoon sugar
½ teaspoon salt
1½ teaspoons baking powder,
   see p. 122

1 egg
⅔ cup milk
1 cup cold boiled rice (174)
2 tablespoons melted shortening

Sift flour, measure and resift 3 times with sugar, salt and baking powder, the last time into mixing bowl. Beat egg thoroughly, add milk and drained cooked rice; stir in shortening and immediately add the flour mixture, and stir until dry ingredients are just dampened; then stir 3 or 4 more times, but not until smooth. Spoon quickly into buttered muffin pans, filling ⅔ full. Bake in a moderately hot oven (425° F.) 20 minutes or until nicely browned. Serve hot. 8 to 10 medium-size muffins.

51 ROLLED OAT MUFFINS

1 cup milk or
⅓ cup evaporated milk and
⅔ cup water
1 cup quick-cooking rolled oats
2 tablespoons shortening
1 cup all-purpose flour

3 teaspoons baking powder, see p. 122
1 teaspoon salt
⅓ cup brown sugar, packed
½ cup raisins
1 egg, well beaten

Heat milk to scalding in top of double boiler; stir in rolled oats and shortening. Remove from heat to cool. Meanwhile sift flour and measure, then resift 3 times with baking powder and salt, the last time into mixing bowl. Stir in brown sugar and raisins, which have been washed and dried. When oatmeal mixture is lukewarm, add beaten egg, then stir into dry ingredients until just mixed, but not smooth. Spoon batter quickly into buttered muffin pans, filling ⅔ full. Bake in moderately hot oven (425° F.) 18 to 20 minutes. 8 to 10 large muffins.

52 TWIN MOUNTAIN MUFFINS

2 cups all-purpose flour
3¾ teaspoons baking powder, see p. 122
½ teaspoon salt
2 tablespoons butter

2 tablespoons other shortening
¼ cup sugar
1 egg, beaten
1 cup milk

Sift flour, measure and resift 3 times with baking powder and salt. Cream butter and shortening and blend in sugar gradually. Add beaten egg and beat until smooth and fluffy. Add flour mixture alternately with milk, beating well after each addition. Spoon into buttered muffin pans, filling about ⅔ full. Bake in a moderate oven (375° F.) about 25 minutes or until delicately browned. Serve hot. 18 small muffins.

53 POPOVERS

1¼ cups all-purpose flour
½ teaspoon salt
1 teaspoon sugar

1 cup milk
1 tablespoon melted butter
2 eggs, beaten

Combine all ingredients in mixing bowl and beat vigorously with rotary beater for 2 minutes. Have heavy muffin or popover pans, or pottery or glass custard cups thoroughly heated and lightly greased. Pour batter into hot cups, filling about half full. Bake 15 minutes in a hot oven (475° F.); then turn down to moderate (350° F.) and bake 15 to

20 minutes longer until very crisp and golden brown. Remove from oven, puncture with skewer to allow steam to escape. Serve immediately. 10 to 12 popovers, depending on size of pans.

54   QUICK APPLE STREUSEL COFFEE CAKE

1½ cups all-purpose flour
2¼ teaspoons baking powder, see p. 122
½ cup sugar
½ teaspoon salt
½ teaspoon cinnamon
1 egg
½ cup milk

¼ cup shortening
1½ cups chopped tart apples

Streusel topping:
¼ cup sugar
2 tablespoons flour
1 tablespoon butter
½ teaspoon cinnamon

Sift flour, measure and resift 3 times with baking powder, sugar, salt and cinnamon. Beat egg, add milk and melted shortening, and pour into dry ingredients; then add the raw apples and mix well. Turn into a well-buttered 8-inch square baking pan. Mix together ingredients for Streusel Topping to make a crumbly mixture, and sprinkle over top of batter. Bake in a moderately hot oven (400° F.) about 30 minutes or until done. 5 servings.

55   CINNAMON TOAST

Mix cinnamon with granulated sugar, using 1 teaspoon cinnamon to 3 tablespoons sugar. Sprinkle this mixture generously over hot buttered toast, and serve hot.

56   FRENCH TOAST

3 eggs
1½ cups milk, or ¾ cup evaporated milk and ¾ cup water
½ teaspoon salt
2 teaspoons sugar

10 slices stale bread cut in half
¼ cup butter or bacon drippings
XXXX sugar

Beat eggs thoroughly, add next 3 ingredients and beat well. Dip each slice of bread in milk mixture for a few seconds, then place in heated heavy skillet in which butter has been heated. Cook until golden brown on underside, turn and cook on other side. Add more fat as required. Sprinkle with XXXX sugar and serve at once with syrup. 5 servings.

57   HAWAIIAN FRENCH TOAST

  2 eggs   ⅔ cup pineapple juice
    Dash salt   6 slices white bread
  ½ teaspoon cinnamon   4 tablespoons butter
  2 tablespoons sugar   3 slices pineapple, heated

Beat eggs until light, then add salt, cinnamon, sugar and pineapple
juice and beat thoroughly. Soak the bread well in this mixture and sauté
in the butter heated in a heavy skillet until nicely browned on both sides.
Serve hot with a hot half-slice of pineapple (cut in halves to make 6 thin
slices) on each piece of toast. 3 to 5 servings.

58   MELBA TOAST

For true Melba toast, slice bread about ⅛-inch thick. Spread out on a
shallow baking pan and place in a very slow oven (250-300° F.) until
perfectly dry and crisp. The toast should be light brown and not curled.
Serve with butter. If desired, crusts may be removed before toasting.
     Ordinary sliced bread may be toasted in the same way to produce a
kind of zwieback. This will keep hard and crisp for several days in a
tightly covered tin container.

59   MILK TOAST

Allow at least 1 cup milk for 2 slices of toast. Toast and butter white,
whole wheat or rye bread and place in warm soup dishes. Heat milk to
scalding with a dash of salt and pepper, if desired. Pour the hot milk over
the buttered toast and serve immediately. A poached egg placed on the
toast makes this a heartier dish, but some prefer the plain milk toast with
a sprinkling of sugar.

60   GARLIC BREAD
                        (*Delicious with Salad*)

Mash 2 peeled cloves garlic to a paste. Stir garlic into ⅓ cup soft
butter. Slice a loaf of French bread 1″ thick not quite through to the
bottom. Spread slices apart slightly, but not enough to break apart,
spread one side of each slice thinly with garlic butter. If desired, sprinkle
generously with grated Parmesan cheese. Slide onto a baking sheet; place
in moderately hot oven (425° F.) 10 to 12 minutes or until blistering
hot and edges are toasted. Serve in a long basket lined with a napkin.
5 to 6 servings.

61 CROUTONS

If unsliced bread is used, cut in ¾-inch thick slices, then in ¾-inch strips; then cut the strips in ¾-inch lengths (cubes). If sliced bread is used, cut slices in strips ¾-inch wide, any length desired. Spread on a shallow baking pan or cookie sheet and brown in a moderate oven (350° F.) until of the desired color, turning occasionally. They will brown more quickly and have a delicious flavor if cubes are tossed in melted butter before browning. The cubes or strips may also be fried in deep fat or pan-fried with or without butter. Pan-frying with butter is more economical if the butter is spread on the bread itself; this may be done before cutting.

61a TOAST STICKS

Cut sliced white bread into ¾-inch strips. Lay on a shallow pan and brown in a moderately hot oven (400° F.) to desired color. Or whole slices of bread may be toasted in the oven, or in an electric toaster and the hot toasted slices cut into strips. Serve hot.

62 SWEET MILK WAFFLES

2 cups all-purpose flour
2 teaspoons baking powder, see p. 122
½ teaspoon salt
3 eggs, separated
1¼ cups sweet milk
⅓ cup melted shortening
2 teaspoons sugar

Sift flour, measure, and resift twice with baking powder and salt. Beat egg yolks, add milk and melted shortening, and immediately stir into flour mixture, beating until smooth. Beat egg whites until stiff, add sugar in 2 portions and again beat until stiff. Fold lightly but thoroughly into batter. Bake in a hot waffle iron, using ½ cup batter for each waffle, until golden brown. Serve immediately upon removing from iron with butter and syrup (924). 6 or 7 waffles.

Variation: For blueberry waffles, fold into the batter ⅔ cup blueberries.

63 BUTTERMILK WAFFLES

2½ cups all-purpose flour
2¼ teaspoons baking powder, see p. 122
½ teaspoon soda
1 teaspoon salt
3 eggs, separated
2 cups thick buttermilk
⅓ cup melted shortening
2 teaspoons sugar

Sift flour, measure, and resift twice with baking powder, soda and salt. Proceed as for Sweet Milk Waffles (62). 8 waffles.

64 BANANA WAFFLES

2 cups all-purpose flour	1½ cups milk or
2¼ teaspoons baking powder, see p. 122	½ cup evaporated milk and 1 cup water
1 tablespoon sugar	⅓ cup shortening
¾ teaspoon salt	1 cup mashed bananas
3 eggs	

Sift flour, measure, and resift twice with the other dry ingredients. Beat eggs, add liquid, and stir in sifted dry ingredients, melted shortening, and mashed banana. Continue beating all together with a rotary beater until the batter is free from lumps. Bake on hot waffle iron until golden brown. Serve with syrup (924). 6 servings.

65 CORN MEAL WAFFLES

1¾ cups all-purpose flour	1 teaspoon salt
1 cup yellow corn meal	2 eggs, separated
1½ teaspoons baking powder, see p. 122	2½ cups thick buttermilk
½ teaspoon soda	⅓ cup melted shortening
	3 tablespoons sugar

Sift flour, measure, and resift twice with corn meal, baking powder, soda and salt. Proceed as for Sweet Milk Waffles (62). 8 waffles.

YEAST BREADS

66 ICE BOX ROLLS

2 cakes compressed yeast or 2 packages granular yeast	4 teaspoons salt
¼ cup lukewarm water	2 eggs, well beaten
1 teaspoon sugar	8 cups sifted all-purpose flour, about
2 cups milk, scalded	⅓ cup melted shortening, cooled
⅓ cup sugar	

Soften yeast in the water with 1 teaspoon sugar. Scald milk, add the ⅓ cup sugar and salt and cool to lukewarm. Add softened yeast and the eggs and half the flour, beat with a wooden spoon until smooth. Add the melted shortening and most of the remaining flour, beat and stir thoroughly until smooth. Turn out onto floured board and knead in rest of flour until dough is smooth, elastic and no longer sticky. Place in a well-greased clean bowl, brush surface lightly with melted shortening, cover tightly (with waxed paper tied down with string, or plastic bowl cover). Place in refrigerator several hours or overnight. When ready to shape, remove from refrigerator, and turn out on a lightly floured board or pastry cloth. Divide dough for easy handling. Shape rolls and transfer to greased baking pans, brushing rolls with melted butter or shortening. Cover, let rise in a warm place (about 85° F.) until doubled in bulk (1 to 2 hours); then bake in a hot oven (425° F.) for 12 to 20 minutes until nicely browned. About 5 minutes before they are done, rolls may be brushed with 1 egg yolk beaten with 2 tablespoons cold water, and returned to oven to glaze. 3 to 4 dozen rolls.

Note: This dough may be kept in the refrigerator not longer than 2 days.

67   CINNAMON LOAF

Roll out ⅓ of the Ice Box Roll dough (66) into a 7 x 12-inch rectangle about ⅜-inch thick. Brush with melted butter and sprinkle with a mixture of 1 tablespoon cinnamon and ⅓ cup sugar. Roll up snugly like jelly roll, and place in greased loaf pan with sealed edge of roll underneath. Brush top with melted butter and let rise until double. Bake in a moderate oven (375° F.) about 40 minutes. 1 large loaf.

68   CINNAMON COFFEE CAKE

Prepare roll with cinnamon-sugar filling just as for Cinnamon Loaf (67), but instead of placing in bread pan, place the roll on a greased baking sheet. With scissors, cut about ¾ through roll, at 1-inch intervals. Lay the cut sections down flat, pulling one to the right, the next to the left, overlapping the sections on each side and leaving them attached in the center. Brush the entire surface with melted butter and let rise until double. Bake in a moderate oven (375° F.) about 30 minutes. Brush with confectioners' frosting (142). 1 large coffee cake.

69   RAISED DOUGHNUTS

Roll Ice Box Roll dough (66) or Sweet Roll Dough (85) out on lightly floured board to half an inch in thickness. Cut with floured doughnut cutter. Transfer to lightly floured board and cover. Let stand in warm place until double in bulk. Fry in deep fat heated to 365° F. to a golden brown. Drain on absorbent paper. While warm transfer a few at a time to a paper sack containing ½ cup granulated sugar. Shake to coat dough-

nuts. Eat while fresh. Split and toast any left over for a delicious breakfast bread.

70   BREAD STICKS

Use any desired yeast roll or bread dough (66, 83, 88 or 90). Pinch
off dough in uniform-sized balls, about 1½ inches in diameter. Lay on
lightly floured board. Grease fingers lightly and roll each ball lightly
back and forth until it becomes a cylinder 10 to 12 inches long and not
more than ⅜-inch thick. Lay on greased baking sheet. Cover and let rise
until double in bulk. Using very light pressure, brush with milk or cream
(use pastry brush). Leave plain, or with a razor sharp knife, make very
shallow diagonal cuts across the top. Sprinkle with poppy or sesame seed,
if desired. Bake in hot oven (425° F.) until golden brown, or from 8 to
10 minutes. Place a shallow pan of hot water on bottom of oven when
baking begins. This produces crisp crust and beautiful brown color. For
fancier bread sticks, make dough strips narrower and braid three together.
Cut off ends neatly—bake in the same way.

71   BUTTERHORN ROLLS

Use any desired yeast roll dough (66, 83, 88 or 90). Divide into
portions which may be rolled out into round sheets about 10 inches in
diameter and ⅜-inch thick. Brush with melted butter and cut each circle
into 12 pie-shaped pieces. Roll up each piece, beginning at the wide
end, stretching dough slightly as you roll. Lay straight or in crescent
shape on greased baking sheet with tip underneath to keep from un-
rolling. Cover, set in warm place to double in bulk. Brush with milk.
Bake in a hot oven (425° F.) 12 to 20 minutes, depending on size.

72   BUTTERFLY ROLLS

Use any desired yeast roll dough (66, 83, 88 or 90). After the first
rising, roll into rectangle about ¼-inch thick. Spread with softened
butter and sprinkle with a mixture of sugar and cinnamon (2 teaspoons
cinnamon to ⅓ cup sugar). Roll up tightly like a jelly roll and cut into
2-inch lengths. Lay handle of wooden spoon across center of each slice
parallel with the cut surfaces, and press down firmly. When pressure is
lifted, roll will take butterfly shape. Cover, let rise, bake like Butterhorn
Rolls (71).

73   CROOKED MILES

Use any desired yeast roll dough (66, 83, 88 or 90). After the first
rising, pinch off pieces of dough large enough to roll into cylinders 6

inches long and about ¾-inch in diameter. Tie a knot close to one end of the strip; then pull rest of strip through center of knot; repeat pulling dough through center until strip is used up. Place on greased baking sheet, brush with melted butter, and let rise until double. Bake like Butterhorn Rolls (71).

74   CINNAMON ROLLS

Use ⅓ of the Ice Box Dough (66) or ½ the Sweet Roll Dough (85). After first rising, roll into 8 x 14-inch rectangle, ¼-inch thick. Brush with melted butter and sprinkle with sugar-cinnamon mixture (2 teaspoons cinnamon to ¼ cup sugar) and raisins. Start at wide side, roll up like jelly roll, pinching edges to roll to seal. Cut into 1-inch lengths. Place close together in a greased pan, cut-side down. Cover and let rise until double. Brush tops with melted butter and sprinkle with more cinnamon-sugar mixture. Bake in a moderate oven (375° F.) 30 minutes.

75   BRAIDED ROLLS

Use any desired yeast roll dough (66, 83, 88 or 90). After the first rising, pinch off pieces of dough the size of large walnuts and place on floured board. Roll out with hands into 10-inch strings about ¼-inch in diameter. Place 3 strings side by side on the board, pressing the far ends firmly together, and braid in the usual way, making the braid moderately loose. Cut into 4-inch lengths, pressing cut ends firmly together. Place braids on greased baking sheet, brush with melted butter, cover and let rise in a warm place until double. Bake like Butterhorn Rolls (71).

76   CLOVERLEAF ROLLS

Use any desired yeast dough (66, 83, 88 or 90). After first rising, pinch off small pieces of dough and shape into smooth balls about the size of small walnuts or large marbles (size should be determined by size of muffin pans and size of roll desired). Dip balls into melted butter or shortening and place 3 in each greased muffin pan. Cover, let rise until double. Bake like Butterhorn Rolls (71).

Two larger balls or 4 small ones may be used for each roll if preferred. If both white and part whole wheat rolls are being made, make half the balls in each roll white and half whole wheat for variety. Or just before baking, sprinkle corn meal or bran over rolls moistened with milk.

77   CLOTHESPIN ROLLS

Use any desired yeast dough (66, 83, 88 or 90). After first rising, remove the desired amount of dough. Roll into a rectangular shape to ¼-inch thickness and about 8 inches long. Cut into strips ¼-inch wide. Dip clean, round, all-wood clothespins into melted shortening. Immediately wind a strip of dough around each clothespin, starting just below knob. Tuck both ends in to prevent unwinding. Place rolls on greased baking sheet; brush with melted shortening; cover, let rise until double. Bake like Butterhorn Rolls (71). While warm, slip clothespins carefully out of rolls.

78   KNOTS

Use any desired yeast dough (66, 83, 88 or 90). After first rising, cut off as much dough as is needed. Roll out like clothespin rolls, but cut strips ½ inch wide and 4 inches long. Hold strip by both ends, stretch lightly, tie into a loose knot. Lay on greased baking sheet, brush with melted butter, cover and let rise until double. Bake like Butterhorn Rolls (71).

79   PARKERHOUSE ROLLS

Use any desired yeast dough (66, 83, 88 or 90). After first rising, roll dough out on floured board to about ⅓-inch thickness. Cut with floured biscuit cutter. Lift out trimmings, roll and cut. Cover rolls with towel, let rest 15 minutes. With thin handled knife, make a deep crease across each roll a little off center. Brush surface with melted butter, fold rounds at the crease, pressing larger side over the smaller. Place 1-inch apart in a lightly greased baking pan. Brush tops with melted butter. Cover, let rise until double. Bake like Butterhorn Rolls (71).

80   PUFFBALLS

Use any desired yeast dough (66, 83, 88 or 90). After first rising, roll dough out about ¼-inch thick on a lightly floured board. Cut with a doughnut cutter dipped in flour. Transfer doughnut-shaped cut-outs to a greased baking sheet and brush with melted shortening. Take 2 of the cut-out "holes" and roll together in a ball; place these (or a ball of dough from trimmings of same size) in centers of doughnut-shaped cut-outs. Brush tops with melted butter. Let rise until double. Bake like Butterhorn Rolls (71).

81   VIENNA ROLLS

Use any desired yeast dough (66, 83, 88 or 90). After first rising, pinch
off pieces of dough and shape into smooth balls about 2 inches in
diameter. Place on board and roll with hands until ball becomes elon-
gated and pointed at the ends. Brush rolls with milk, and sprinkle with
caraway or poppy seeds. Place on greased baking sheet sprinkled with
corn meal. Cover and let rise until double. Bake like Butterhorn Rolls
(71).

82   ENGLISH MUFFINS

1¼ cups milk   ¼ cup lukewarm water
 ¾ teaspoon salt   4 cups sifted all-purpose flour
  1 cake compressed yeast or   3 tablespoons melted
  1 package granular yeast   shortening

Scald milk with salt, cool to lukewarm. Soak yeast in the water and
add to cooled milk. Add half the flour gradually, beating with wooden
spoon until flour is thoroughly mixed in. Add the cooled, melted shortening, beat until smooth. Mix in remaining flour to make a smooth,
soft dough. Put into clean greased bowl, brush top of dough with a little
water; cover with waxed paper and let stand in a warm place (about
85° F.) until dough is light (about 2 hours). Turn out on lightly floured
board and knead gently. Roll out ½-inch thick. Cut out in 3 to 4-inch
rounds. Place on board sprinkled with corn meal. Cover and let stand in
warm place until muffins begin to get light (about 45 minutes). Then
bake over low heat on a slightly greased, moderately hot griddle (300°
F.), about 10 minutes on each side. Cool. When ready to serve, split
muffins and toast each half on both sides in oven or broiler. Spread with
butter and serve piping hot. About 12 4-inch muffins.

83   QUICK YEAST BREAD

2 packages granular yeast   ⅓ cup sugar
  or 2 cakes compressed yeast   2 eggs, well beaten
1 cup lukewarm water   ⅓ cup melted shortening
1 teaspoon sugar   half butter
1 cup milk, scalded   6½ to 7 cups sifted all-purpose
2½ teaspoons salt   flour

Soften yeast in lukewarm water with 1 teaspoon sugar. Scald the milk,
stir in salt and sugar, and cool to lukewarm. When cooled, stir in the

yeast mixture combined with beaten eggs. Add about 4 cups of the flour and beat until smooth. Add cooled melted shortening and again beat smooth. Stir and knead in enough flour to make a smooth elastic, but not too stiff dough. Place in a lightly greased bowl, turn dough over. Cover, let rise in a cozy place (85° F.) about 1 hour, until just double. Then turn out onto lightly floured board and shape into rolls or into 3 loaves. Place in greased pans, cover, and let rise again in warm place until double, about 45 minutes. Bake rolls 15 to 20 minutes in a moderately hot oven (400° F.). Bake loaves 20 minutes at 400°, then reduce heat to moderate (350° F.) and bake 20 minutes longer. Serve rolls hot, but cool loaves before slicing. Makes about 2 dozen rolls or 3 small loaves.

84   PECAN ROLLS OR SCHNECKEN

2 cakes compressed yeast or	⅔ cup sugar
2 packages granular yeast	2 whole eggs or 4 egg yolks
1 cup lukewarm water	1½ teaspoons salt
1 teaspoon sugar	¼ teaspoon ground nutmeg
1 cup milk, scalded	About 7 cups sifted all-
½ cup shortening (half butter)	purpose flour

Soften yeast in lukewarm water with the 1 teaspoon sugar for 5 minutes. Cool scalded milk to lukewarm and combine with yeast. Cream shortening and blend in the ⅔ cup sugar; add eggs, salt and nutmeg, and beat until light. Measure 3 cups flour into large mixing bowl; add soaked yeast mixture and mix well. Next add the creamed mixture and beat until smooth. Add all but about ¾ cup of the remaining flour and mix into dough; then turn out onto floured board and knead until smooth, using remaining flour to prevent sticking, but keeping dough as soft as possible. Shape dough into ball and place in a greased clean bowl; grease top, cover, and let stand in a warm place (about 85° F.) until dough has doubled its bulk, about 2 hours. Divide dough in 2 portions and roll out one at a time into a 16 x 18-inch rectangle ¼-inch thick. Sprinkle with sugar and cinnamon, allowing ¼ cup sugar and ¼ teaspoon cinnamon for both portions of dough. Roll up snugly like a jelly roll and cut in 1-inch lengths. In the bottom of each buttered muffin pan place 1 tablespoon of the following mixture: 1 cup brown sugar, ¼ cup melted butter, 2 tablespoons white corn syrup and about ½ cup whole or broken pecans. Lay rolls cut-side down in pans. Set in warm place, cover, and let rolls rise until double about 45 minutes. Place in a moderate oven (375° F.). Bake about 25 minutes, until nicely browned. 2½ dozen rolls.

Note: Schnecken may be made from Ice Box Roll (66) dough if desired.

84a   PLUM KUCHEN
                            (*Canned Plums*)

⅓ Recipe Sweet Roll Dough   ⅛ teaspoon grated lemon
  (85)   rind, packed
  No. 2 can blue plums   ⅛ teaspoon cinnamon
1 tablespoon corn starch   ⅛ teaspoon salt
1 teaspoon lemon juice

Make dough and after 2nd rising, punch down and turn out on lightly
floured board or pastry cloth. Round up, cover with bowl and let rest
10 minutes. Roll into a circle to fit into bottom and up sides of a 9-inch
layer cake pan. Dough is about ¼-inch thick. Prick dough in bottom
with a fork. Lay drained plums, pitted and halved, cut-side up over
dough. Combine corn starch with a little of the plum juice to make a
smooth paste, stir in remaining juice and cook with constant stirring
until mixture thickens and is clear. Stir in remaining ingredients and
cool, then pour over plums. Let rise until double, about 1 hour. Bake in
a moderate oven (375° F.) 25 minutes or until rim is golden brown.
Cool 5 minutes then serve warm from pan. 4 servings.

85   STREUSEL COFFEE CAKE
                  (*Also use this Sweet Roll Dough for Raised
                   Doughnuts and all kinds of Sweet Rolls*)

1 package granular yeast   2 eggs, beaten
  or 1 cake compressed yeast   4 cups sifted all-purpose flour
¼ cup lukewarm water   ½ teaspoon mace or ground
⅓ cup sugar   cardamon
¾ cup milk, scalded   ½ cup butter, melted
1 teaspoon salt   ½ cup floured raisins

Soften yeast in the lukewarm water with ½ teaspoon of the sugar.
Scald milk, add remaining sugar and salt and cool to lukewarm. Combine softened yeast with cooled milk and beaten eggs; add half the
flour which has been resifted with the spice, and beat until smooth. Beat
in the cooled, melted butter; then add the remaining flour and the
floured raisins, and again beat until smooth. Turn out onto lightly
floured board and knead until smooth and elastic, adding not more than
½ cup additional flour. Shape into a smooth ball, place in a clean
greased bowl, and brush the surface lightly with melted fat. Cover with
clean towel and let rise in a warm place (about 85° F.) until double,
about 1½ to 2 hours. Divide dough in 2 portions and roll out each
portion to fit a rectangular pan about 7 x 11 x 2 inches; thoroughly grease
the 2 pans and fit the dough into them. Again cover and let rise in a

warm place until double. Sprinkle with Streusel Topping (86). Bake in a moderately hot oven (400° F.) 15 minutes, then reduce heat to moderate (350° F.) and bake 15 to 20 minutes longer. Serve warm. 2 coffee cakes.

To reheat coffee cake, place in pan, cover with dampened brown wrapping paper and place in moderate oven (350° F.) for about 10 minutes, or until hot through.

Variation: If desired, the above recipe may be adjusted so dough can be made up in the evening, stored in refrigerator overnight, and baked in the morning. Double the amount of yeast used, and make the dough in the same manner, allowing it to rise once. Then roll out dough and place in baking pans; rub the surface lightly with softened butter, cover with waxed paper and place in the refrigerator. In the morning, remove pans from the refrigerator, sprinkle the surface with streusel topping and let stand on top of the stove while the oven heats. Then bake as directed. Sufficient rising takes place in the refrigerator with the increased amount of yeast to make a coffee cake of excellent quality.

86   STREUSEL TOPPING FOR COFFEE CAKE

⅓ cup brown sugar, packed
¼ cup flour
1 teaspoon cinnamon or to suit taste

Few grains salt
3 tablespoons soft butter
⅓ cup chopped pecans, optional

Mix sugar, flour, cinnamon and salt together thoroughly. Work in the butter to produce a coarse, crumbly mixture. Stir in nuts until well distributed. Sprinkle over coffee cake before baking.

87   SWEDISH TEA BREAD
(*Jule Kake*)

1 package granular yeast or 1 cake compressed yeast
⅓ cup lukewarm water
1 cup scalded milk, cooled
3⅔ to 4 cups all-purpose flour

⅓ cup sugar
¾ teaspoon salt
⅓ cup melted butter cooled to lukewarm

Soften yeast in lukewarm water for 5 minutes, then add lukewarm milk and about half the flour, to make a soft batter and beat well. Cover and let rise in a warm place until double. Add sugar, salt, melted butter and remaining flour, and the following fruits and nuts:

½ cup seedless raisins
½ cup chopped dates
2 tablespoons shaved candied
    citron

6 candied cherries, chopped
½ cup chopped pecans

Mix lightly, then turn out onto lightly floured board or pastry cloth and knead for 10 minutes. Place dough in a clean buttered bowl, and let rise in a warm place (about 85° F.) until double. Shape into 1 large loaf or 2 small ones. Place in buttered pans and again let rise until double. Bake in a moderate oven (375° F.) about 15 minutes, reduce heat to moderate (350° F.) and bake 45 minutes longer, a total of 1 hour. 1 large or 2 small loaves.

87a   SWEDISH TEA RING

Use half the Swedish Tea Bread dough but omit fruit and nuts. Let rise as usual, then proceed as for Cinnamon Coffee Cake (68), except stretch the roll slightly and shape into a ring on a greased baking sheet, pinching the ends together before cutting. Cut through roll starting at outside of ring, so sections are joined at inner edge. Lay sections down flat, overlapping. Bake like Cinnamon Coffee Cake.

88   WHITE BREAD AND ROLLS

2 packages granular yeast
    or 2 cakes compressed yeast
1 cup lukewarm water
1 teaspoon sugar
2 cups scalded milk or milk
    and water

5 teaspoons salt
¼ cup sugar
10 to 12 cups sifted all-purpose
    flour
¼ cup melted butter or half
    other shortening

Soften yeast in lukewarm water with 1 teaspoon sugar for 5 minutes. Put scalded milk, salt and ¼ cup sugar into large mixing bowl. Cool to lukewarm. (If half water is used, this may be added cold to the scalded milk to hasten cooling.) Stir yeast mixture into lukewarm liquid. Add 4 cups of sifted flour and beat until smooth. Add cooled melted butter and enough more flour to form a medium firm dough. Turn out onto lightly floured board and knead until smooth and elastic. Place dough in a clean greased bowl, cover with clean towel and place in a cozy place (about 85° F.) to rise until double. When sufficiently risen, dough should not spring back but hold a dent when pressed with finger. Knead down and let rise again, about ¾ as much as the first time. Then turn dough onto lightly floured or greased board, divide into 4 portions and shape these in balls. Cover well, and let dough rest 20 minutes; then shape into loaves. Place loaves in greased pans, cover, and let rise again until double. Bake in a moderately hot oven (400° F.) 45 minutes. Bread when done should be well risen and golden brown, with a crisp crust which sounds hollow when tapped. Turn loaves out and cool thoroughly on cake coolers before slicing. 4 loaves.

This dough may also be used for making rolls (see recipes 72 to 81). Makes about 4 to 6 dozen, depending on size.

89   100% WHOLE WHEAT BREAD

2 cakes compressed yeast or	1 tablespoon salt
2 packages granular yeast	½ cup brown sugar
⅔ cup lukewarm water	6 cups unsifted whole wheat
1 tablespoon sugar	flour
2 cups milk, scalded	2 tablespoons melted butter

Soften yeast in lukewarm water with 1 tablespoon sugar. Scald milk, add salt and the ½ cup sugar and cool to lukewarm in a 4-qt. mixing bowl. Stir in softened yeast and half the flour, until thoroughly combined. Then stir in the melted butter, add the remaining flour and stir until thoroughly mixed. Dough will be very soft and sticky, but do not add more flour, for the softer the dough the more tender, light and moist the bread will be. Cover bowl and set in warm place (about 85° F.) to rise 1 hour. Leaving dough in bowl, knead it for 5 minutes until smooth and somewhat stiffened; do not use additional flour. Again cover and let rise for ½ hour. Divide dough into 2 portions and place in buttered pans 9 x 5 x 3-inches, pressing into corners and smoothing surface with buttered hands; dough will probably be too soft to shape into loaves before placing in pans. Cover pans with cloth and let loaves rise for ½ hour. Then bake in a moderately hot oven (400° F.) for 10 minutes; reduce heat to moderate (350° F.) and continue baking 50 minutes longer. Turn out immediately onto cake coolers and cool before slicing. 2 loaves.

90   PART WHOLE WHEAT BREAD

1 package granular yeast	4 teaspoons salt
or 1 cake compressed yeast	½ cup sugar or molasses
1 cup lukewarm water	4 cups unsifted whole wheat
1 teaspoon sugar	flour, about
3 cups scalded milk or half	7¾ cups sifted all-purpose flour
milk, half water	¼ cup melted shortening

Soften yeast in the lukewarm water with 1 teaspoon sugar for 5 minutes. Scald the 3 cups milk or milk and water, and add the salt and the ½ cup sugar or molasses. Cool to lukewarm. Combine the yeast with the luke-warm liquid and stir in two cups whole wheat flour and half the all-purpose flour. Add the cooled melted shortening and stir in; then stir in the remaining all-purpose flour and finally enough whole wheat flour to make dough barely stiff enough to knead. Turn out onto board lightly sprinkled with whole wheat flour and knead until smooth and elastic, keeping the dough just as soft as possible—somewhat softer than for white bread. Let rise until double in a warm place (about 85° F.) and shape into loaves at once. Set these to rise again until nearly double, and bake 50 to 60 minutes in a moderate oven (375-400° F.). 4 loaves.

This dough may also be used for making rolls. (See recipes 72 to 81.) About 3 dozen.

CAKE

WHY *is angel food cake almost always baked with a hole in the middle? What's the best way to prepare a cake pan so the cake won't stick in the bottom? Why do cake recipes always advise beginning and ending with flour, when you add dry ingredients and liquid ingredients alternately to a cake batter? If you're the kind of person who likes to know* WHY *before adopting a new technique, this chapter on cakes and cake making will have a special appeal to you.*

CAKE MAKING

There are only two big general classifications of cake: butter cakes, which contain shortening, and sponge or angel food cakes, which do not. A slight overlapping occurs in the case of the so-called "butter sponge" and chiffon cakes.

Butter cakes are the largest group, including most layer cakes as well as pound cakes and fruit cakes. They may be baked in any desired form: layers, loaves, sheets of various thicknesses, and individual cakes in muffin pans or molds. Custom determines in a few cases the form the cake shall take; for example, a pound cake is traditionally baked in a loaf pan. But in general, the form of the cake depends on the recipe used.

Sponge and angel food cakes are usually baked in tube pans, which have a hole in the center to give more uniform heat penetration in the slow baking they require. Sponge cakes are sometimes baked in layers, as for Boston cream pie, and frequently in thin sheets for use as jelly and cream rolls.

FACTORS OF SUCCESS IN CAKE MAKING

The homemaker who makes consistently good-quality cakes of all types has learned to take into account a great number of factors and to practice many different techniques. Most of them become more or less subconscious

116

as she becomes skilful, but the beginner or the woman who wants to improve her cake making will need to pay careful attention to these points:

1. Selection of the best quality of ingredients.
2. Assembling of both ingredients and mixing equipment before starting to work on the cake. This insures that all the necessary ingredients are on hand and that it will not be necessary to keep the batter waiting at a critical point to hunt for some missing piece of equipment or ingredient.
3. Accurate measurement of ingredients.
4. Good mixing technique.

SELECTION OF INGREDIENTS

Both sponge and butter cakes require careful choice of ingredients to produce the best possible quality.

Flour: Unless all-purpose flour is specified in a recipe, cake flour is used for all cake making. This is a soft wheat flour containing less gluten than all-purpose flour or bread flour, and has gone through a special milling process. It gives a much more delicate texture to the cake. If it is necessary to substitute all-purpose for cake flour, use 2 tablespoons less per cup than the recipe calls for, but do not expect identical results.

Sugar: A fine granulated sugar should be used for cake making. When brown sugar is used, it should be fresh and moist, and free from lumps.

Shortening: A good grade of butter gives a fine flavor to cakes, but any bland-flavored firm white shortening may be used with satisfaction, if the salt is increased slightly.

Eggs: Eggs should be fresh enough to have a good flavor and odor, and should be of medium size, unless otherwise specified. One medium egg white measures 2 tablespoons, and 1 medium egg yolk 1⅓ tablespoons. Egg whites at room temperature beat up to greater volume than egg whites just removed from the refrigerator.

Leavening: Baking powder, baking soda and beaten egg whites are the leavening agents used in cake making. In sponge and angel cakes, air incorporated into beaten eggs or egg whites is usually the only leavening. Soda is used when the liquid is sour cream, sour milk or buttermilk, and also when molasses appears in the recipe.

Flavoring: The best of flavoring extracts should always be used in cake, since an inferior flavoring will produce an inferior flavor in the finished product. The amount of flavoring required may be slightly greater when a shortening without flavor is used, than when butter is the shortening.

ACCURATE MEASUREMENT OF INGREDIENTS

Exact measurement of all ingredients is fundamental to success with all tested modern recipes, and even greater than usual care needs to be taken with cakes, because their texture depends largely on the balance between the various ingredients.

Flour: Sift the flour once *before* measuring. The flour in the bottom of the container is always more packed than that at the top, and this may make a difference of one or two tablespoons between the first cup taken from the box, and the last one. Sifting eliminates this packing. Measure the sifted flour by lifting it lightly into a standard measuring cup or fractional cups for *dry* measure—those having the mark level with the rim of the cup. Level it off with the edge of a spatula; never tap or shake the cup to level it, for this packs it again—as you can see by tapping down an already levelled cup of sifted flour.

Sugar: Granulated sugar packs slightly but not nearly so much as flour. It need not be sifted before measuring, but like flour, should be spooned into the cup and levelled off without tapping or shaking. Brown sugar, which is moist and packs readily, presents a quite different problem; to insure uniform measurement, unless the recipe directs otherwise, it should be packed firmly into the cup. All recipes in this book call for brown sugar to be packed for measuring.

Shortening: With butter which is divided into ¼-pound sticks, measurements may be estimated: ¼ pound equals ½ cup, etc. Other kinds of solid shortening should be packed into the cup, care being taken to avoid formation of air pockets. It can then be levelled off just like the dry ingredients. The method of measuring ½ cup of shortening by filling a measuring cup to the ½-cup mark with cold water and then adding shortening until the water reaches the 1-cup mark is not very accurate, due to the tendency of shortenings to enclose large air pockets.

Flavoring: In measuring flavoring, be careful not to hold the spoon over the mixing bowl while pouring from the bottle. If the bottle dribbles a few drops into the bowl as well as into the spoon, it may be enough to make the flavor of the cake stronger than is desirable. Hold it over a clean cup, and if there is any considerable overflow, it can be poured back into the bottle.

Measurement of all ingredients is simplified by the use of nested sets of measuring spoons and cups. These are available in heavy tin and in colored plastic. The tin or aluminum cups are most accurate and the difference in price is very small. The sets of cups contain a 1-cup, ½-cup, ⅓-cup and ¼-cup measure, each of which is accurate when filled to the brim and levelled off. For liquid measure, graduated glass measuring cups are convenient, because the 1-cup mark comes below the rim of the cup, thus helping to avoid overflow; but the nested cups are preferable for accurate measurement of dry ingredients.

Measuring spoons, desirable for both dry and liquid ingredients, are also nested, and also available both in metal and in plastic. Here too the metal spoons are more accurate. The sets contain a 1-tablespoon, 1-teaspoon, ½-teaspoon and ¼-teaspoon measure. These are absolutely essential to accurate measurement.

ASSEMBLING AND PREPARATION

Assembling ingredients and equipment: The first step in making a cake is to collect all the ingredients that will be needed, and all the mixing and measuring equipment.

Preparing cake pans: Sponge and angel food pans should never be greased; but the sides of pans for butter cakes require careful greasing (bottoms need not be greased if waxed paper liners are used). Butter is recommended for greasing pans, even if it is not used as shortening, because the crust gives the first taste-sensation in eating the cake, and the flavor of the crust is partly determined by the grease on the pan. Lining the bottoms of the pans with rounds of waxed paper, which have been cut with "ears" that protrude above opposite edges of the pans, will preclude any danger of the cake sticking to the bottom and insure a delicate crust; and the "ears" serve as handles by which the baked cake can be lifted from the pan onto the cake cooler. Always prepare the pans before starting work.

Lighting oven: Well-insulated ovens take from 4 to 10 minutes to heat to the desired temperature; one which is not very well insulated may take 20 minutes or even longer. Therefore it is safest to light and regulate the oven before starting to mix the cake, so it will be the correct temperature by the time the batter is mixed.

Sifting flour: The next step is usually sifting and measuring the flour, and resifting it with the salt, leavening, and spices, if any are used. (If there are fruits, nuts or chocolate to be cut up or otherwise prepared, this may be done before sifting the flour.) For convenience, the sifting may be done on sheets of waxed paper, so the sifted pile can be picked up and returned to the sifter easily. First sift the unmeasured flour onto one sheet of waxed paper; then measure the flour and turn into the sifter standing on a second sheet. Add the other measured ingredients, and sift them together. They should be sifted together three times. The pieces of waxed paper may be folded and put away with the sifter to be used another time.

STANDARD METHOD OF MIXING BUTTER CAKES

Certain techniques have been developed for the various steps of mixing a cake batter, because it has been found that they produce the best results in the finished cake. The standard method for cakes made with butter or vegetable shortening is given here. Some of the recipes in this book vary from this standard method; this is because, with the particular combination of ingredients used, a different method has been found to be more successful. For example, modern lard cakes require several techniques differing slightly from those which are standard for cakes made with other shortenings, in order to produce cakes equal in every respect to butter and vegetable shortening cakes.

The various steps in the standard method are described here in detail, together with the reasons for following them.

1.   Cream the shortening until it is soft and smooth. This is more easily done if the shortening is allowed to stand out of the refrigerator until it is at room temperature. Work it with a wooden spoon until smooth and free from lumps. This step is important to get the fat into a condition to blend smoothly and uniformly with the other ingredients, producing a smooth, uniform batter.

2.   Add the sugar and blend it thoroughly with the shortening. If the eggs are separated and the whites beaten and added to the batter at the end, some of the sugar (about 2 tablespoons to each egg white) may be saved and beaten into the whites.

3.   Add the egg yolks, beaten or unbeaten as the recipe requires, and beat the mixture vigorously with a wooden spoon until the mass is thick and fluffy, and quite pale in color. When this is done thoroughly, the finished batter will be much thicker and fluffier and the baked cake larger in volume and lighter than would otherwise be the case.

4.   Stir in the flavoring. The fat in the creamed mixture and the egg yolks seems to form a strong bond with the volatile part of the flavoring extract, so that the cake has a more pronounced flavor when the flavoring is added at this point.

5.   Add the sifted dry ingredients and liquid ingredients alternately in several portions, beginning and ending with a portion of the flour mixture, and beat until smooth after each addition. It is important to begin and end with the flour, for the addition of liquid tends to separate fat out from the creamed mixture and makes it more difficult to obtain a smooth, well-mixed batter, while the flour binds the ingredients. This can be readily observed as the ingredients are added. Ending with the addition of flour will produce a smoother, better-looking batter.

6.   Beat the egg whites until they are barely stiff, then add the sugar saved for that purpose, and beat it in thoroughly until it is very stiff and smooth, like a meringue. This treatment helps the whites to stand up and retain the air that is beaten in, and also makes it easier to fold them into the batter. Fold them in lightly but thoroughly, using a cutting and folding motion of the wooden spoon or rubber scraper.

7.   Pour the batter into the prepared cake pans, spreading it out quickly with a rubber scraper, spatula, or back of the mixing spoon, so it is slightly higher at the edges of the pans than it is in the middle; the rising will then tend to level the layer instead of causing it to round up in the center.

8.   Put the cakes into the oven which has been carefully regulated, and do not open the oven to look at the cake until the end of the first half of the baking time. Then note whether it is baking normally: rising should be nearly completed and browning begun. Near the end of the baking time,

check the progress of the baking again, and test the cake for doneness. Tests for doneness in common use are:

a. Noting whether the cake is beginning to loosen from the sides of the pan.

b. Sticking a clean toothpick or cake tester into the center and noting whether any uncooked or undercooked batter adheres. Tester should come out clean if cake is done.

c. Pressing with finger tips to see whether cake is springy, and therefore done.

Be careful not to permit the cake to overbake, for overbaking makes it dry and less delicate.

9. Remove cake from oven and let it stand on a wire cake rack about 5 minutes, then turn out onto rack, loosen paper and invert cake. If cake sticks around the edge, it may be loosened by running a sharp knife around it. Let cake barely cool, remove waxed paper, then frost.

STANDARD SPONGE CAKE RECIPE

In a sponge or angel food cake, the only leavening is the air incorporated into the beaten eggs or the whites. Therefore it is desirable to beat the maximum amount of air into the eggs or egg whites, and to handle them very lightly so that most of this air will be retained, to expand when the batter is heated in baking.

The mixing methods for the two types of cake are as follows:

1. *True sponge cake:* Sift and measure the flour and resift it with the salt. Beat egg yolks (or whole eggs) until they are very thick and lemon-yellow. Gradually beat in the sugar and flavoring. Add flour mixture alternately with liquid (usually water) beating in until well blended. If eggs have been separated, fold yolk mixture into the stiffly beaten egg whites carefully until well blended. Pour into ungreased tube pan, or jelly roll pan lined with waxed paper. Bake according to recipe.

2. *True angel food cake:* Sift and measure the flour, mix with about half the sifted sugar, and resift several times. Have egg whites at room temperature; sift salt and cream of tartar over them, and beat (preferably with a wire egg whip, which produces greater volume than a rotary beater) until just stiff, not dry. Add flavoring, and gradually beat in the rest of the sugar; then fold in the flour-sugar mixture carefully but thoroughly. Pour into ungreased tube pan and bake according to recipe.

Both sponge and angel food cakes should be cooled in the inverted pan. A good tube pan either can stand on the end of the tube (if it is taller than the sides of the pan), or will have supports to hold it off the table in an inverted position. This permits the delicate cells of the cake to become firm while the cake is suspended from the bottom and sides of the pan, so that when it is removed from the pan it will not collapse under its own weight.

TYPES OF BAKING POWDER

Two different types of baking powder are commonly used in the home, both containing baking soda and corn starch, plus certain acid reacting compounds which vary in nature and amount. The powders are named from the acid reaction ingredients. They are: (1) Sulfate-phosphate, so-called combination (or double-action) baking powder, containing sodium aluminum sulfate and calcium acid phosphate. (2) Tartrate baking powder, containing cream of tartar and tartaric acid, and phosphate baking powder containing calcium acid phosphate. Since food laws in general require that the ingredients be named on the label, you can readily determine which type of baking powder you are using.

The leavening gas given off by both types is the same, but the rate of formation and residue varies considerably. Baking soda is a chemical compound containing combined carbon dioxide. In the presence of water, soda reacts with the acid ingredient of the baking powder to liberate this carbon dioxide in gaseous form. In this reaction the batter or dough is permeated with very fine bubbles of the gas which make the batter light. The only function of the corn starch is to keep the active chemical ingredients separated and inactive while in the container. It has been found that a major portion of the corn starch formerly used in combination-type baking powders may be replaced with a specially precipitated calcium carbonate, which not only keeps the baking powder stable but also has the health advantage of enriching baked goods with substantial amounts of much needed calcium.

The rate of gas formation differs according to the type of baking powder. Sulfate-phosphate (combination type) baking powders have their lesser action in the cold batter, with the greatest action in the oven. That is why these baking powders can be sifted with the dry ingredients. Such batters or doughs, after being poured or rolled out and cut, may stand a short time without much effect on the leavening power. Tartrate and phosphate baking powders have the major portion of their action in the cold batter and the lesser action in the oven. For this reason, these baking powders are sprinkled over the batter the last minute of the beating, then beating is finished. Batter then is promptly poured into the pans and is promptly placed in the oven.

USE OF BAKING POWDER

In any batter or dough, the same amount of tartrate or phosphate baking powder is required, but ¼ less of a double action or S.A.S.-phosphate powder should be used. An excess of any baking powder tends to produce coarse texture, dryness and undesirable flavor.

When buttermilk or sour milk is used in a recipe, both baking powder and baking soda may be used. In this case, the soda serves to neutralize the acidity of the milk. (In this connection, it is safest to use buttermilk rather than naturally soured milk, as the latter may vary considerably in acidity.) But soda alone is not a balanced leavening agent.

Batters and doughs made with baking powder may be made a few hours in advance of baking if desired, then stored in the refrigerator. When this is done, cake batter should be poured into the pans and biscuits shaped before storing to avoid further manipulation. In waffle and griddle cake batter, which must be stirred and poured as it is baked, with the result that some of the leavening gas is lost, it is preferable to use a double action powder if the batter is to be stored for a time between mixing and baking.

Tartrate and calcium-phosphate baking powders are single-action; S.A.S.-phosphate baking powder is double-action.

91   ANGEL FOOD CAKE

1 cup cake flour	1¼ teaspoons cream of tartar
1½ cups fine granulated sugar	¼ teaspoon salt
1⅓ cups egg whites, 10 to 11	1 teaspoon vanilla
—at room temperature	¼ teaspoon almond extract

Sift flour, measure, and resift 6 times with half the sugar. Turn egg whites into 4 quart mixing bowl. Sprinkle the cream of tartar and salt over the surface. Beat with a wire whip until stiff but not dry, then gradually beat in the remaining sugar and the vanilla. (Whites may be beaten much more quickly with a rotary beater, but volume of cake will be slightly less.) Add sifted flour-sugar mixture in several portions, folding in gently but thoroughly with the wire whip. When completely blended, flow batter carefully into an ungreased 10-inch tube pan. Bake in a moderately slow oven (300° F.) for 60 to 70 minutes or until cake is delicately browned and springs back when lightly pressed with finger tip. Remove from oven and invert pan over funnel or tall bottle if pan does not stand on tube or side supports. Leave inverted until cake is thoroughly cooled. Then loosen sides with a thin bladed spatula and remove from pan. 10 to 12 servings.

92   MOCK ANGEL FOOD

1⅓ cups cake flour	1 cup sugar
2¼ teaspoons baking powder,	⅔ cup hot milk
see p. 122	1 teaspoon vanilla
¼ teaspoon salt	3 egg whites

Sift flour, measure and resift 3 times with baking powder, salt and ⅔ cup of the sugar, the last time into mixing bowl. Add milk slowly, beating until smooth; stir in flavoring. Beat egg whites until almost stiff, then gradually beat in remaining sugar until meringue is very thick and smooth. Fold thoroughly into batter. Pour into a 9-inch ungreased tube cake pan and bake in moderate oven (350° F.) 25-30 minutes or until it springs back when lightly touched. Remove from oven and invert until moderately cool, then remove from pan and set on cake rack to finish cooling. Serve unfrosted if desired, or spread with Raspberry Icing (148). 5-8 servings.

93   SPONGE CAKE

1 cup cake flour	½ teaspoon cream of tartar
6 eggs, separated	½ teaspoon salt
1 cup sugar	1 teaspoon vanilla
¼ cup water	½ teaspoon lemon extract

Sift flour, measure and resift 3 times. Put egg yolks into 4-qt. mixing bowl and beat with rotary beater 4 to 5 minutes or until so thick it is difficult to turn beater. Now gradually beat in ¾ cup of the sugar. Add flour and water alternately in 2 or 3 portions, beating until well blended after each. Now sift cream of tartar and salt over egg whites and beat until stiff, then beat in remaining ¼ cup sugar and flavorings. Now CUT AND FOLD yolk mixture lightly but thoroughly into egg whites. Turn into ungreased 10-inch tube pan. Bake in a moderately slow oven (325° F.) 1 hour or until cake springs back when lightly touched. Remove from oven and invert pan immediately over large funnel or long-neck bottle if pan does not stand on tube or side supports. Cool thoroughly, then remove from pan. 12 servings.

94   BOSTON CREAM PIE
(Sometimes Called Washington Pie)

Bake half the recipe for Sponge Cake (93) in one buttered 9-inch layer cake pan lined in the bottom with wax paper. Bake at 325° F. from 22 to 26 minutes. Cool in pan. Remove from pan, strip off paper, split cake in half so as to make two layers. Spread Cream (666) or Lemon Pie (670) Filling between layers. Sprinkle powdered sugar over the top. 5 servings.

95   COCOA BUTTER-SPONGE LAYER CAKE

1¾ cups cake flour	1½ teaspoons vanilla
1¼ teaspoons baking powder, see p. 122	1½ cups fine granulated sugar
	1½ tablespoons butter
3 eggs	¾ cup hot milk
½ teaspoon salt	½ pint whipping cream

Sift flour, measure and resift 3 times with baking powder. Beat eggs with salt and vanilla until thick and light in color, gradually adding the sugar. Add butter to the hot milk; when melted, stir quickly into egg mixture. Add flour mixture all at once and beat until batter is perfectly smooth. Turn into 2 well-buttered 8-inch cake pans lined in the bottom with waxed paper. Bake in a moderate oven (350° F.) 30 minutes or or until nicely browned. Turn out on cake racks and cool thoroughly. Then spread Cocoa Filling (149) between layers and on top of cake. Cover sides with stiffly whipped cream, and pipe rest of cream on top, or cover top entirely if desired. 10 servings.

96   DAFFODIL CAKE

1 cup cake flour	1 teaspoon cream of tartar
1½ cups granulated sugar	½ teaspoon vanilla
1 cup egg whites, 8 to 9	4 egg yolks
½ teaspoon salt	½ teaspoon orange extract

Sift flour, measure and resift 6 times with ¾ cup of the sugar. Turn egg whites into a large mixing bowl and beat with a wire whip until frothy; then sift salt and cream of tartar over them, and continue beating until just stiff enough to hold peaks, but not until dry. Fold in remaining ¾ cup sugar with the egg whip, adding about 2 tablespoons at a time. Now add the flour-sugar mixture in the same manner, cutting and folding while rotating the bowl slowly. When flour has all disappeared, continue cutting and folding 1 minute longer. Divide mixture gently into 2 equal parts. Fold vanilla into one portion, and into the other fold the egg yolks which have been beaten with the orange extract until very thick and light-colored. Now spoon the two batters into an ungreased tube cake pan, alternating a spoonful of the white batter with a spoonful of the yellow until all is used. Bake in a slow oven (275° F.) for 30 minutes, then in a moderately slow oven (325° F.) for 50 minutes. Invert pan and allow to cool thoroughly before removing cake from pan. 10 servings.

97   JELLY ROLL

¾ cup cake flour	¾ cup sugar
¾ teaspoon baking powder	½ teaspoon vanilla
¼ teaspoon salt	¼ cup XXXX sugar
2 tablespoons water	1 cup tart red jelly
4 eggs, separated	

Line a shallow jelly roll pan 15½" x 10½" x ⅝" with full width of waxed paper so it extends ½-inch all around over edge of pan—grease paper lightly. Prepare a towel by sprinkling evenly with XXXX sugar.

Start oven 10 minutes before baking; set to moderately hot (400° F.).

Sift flour, measure, resift 3 times with next 2 ingredients. Put water and egg yolks into a 3-qt. mixing bowl and place *over* hot water, then beat with a rotary beater until very thick and light colored. Add ½ of the sugar gradually and continue to beat until thick. Remove bowl from over hot water. Beat in vanilla. Remove beater, wash. Now sift flour in 4 or 5 portions over yolk mixture, folding it in with wire whip until smooth after each portion. Beat egg whites with clean rotary beater until they form soft shiny peaks, then gradually beat in remaining sugar until shiny peaks curve at tips. Fold whites lightly but thoroughly into batter with wire whip, using about 30 cut-and-fold-over strokes. Quickly flow batter gently down center of prepared pan from one end to other, then spread ever so lightly to edges. Bake on center rack of oven 7 to 8 minutes or until cake springs back when lightly touched with finger. Remove to cake rack and quickly loosen edges with thin-bladed knife. Turn out on prepared towel; immediately strip off paper. Roll up from *narrow-side* into an even roll, then roll up in the towel. Cool on cake rack. Unroll gently and spread evenly with jelly slightly broken up with a fork. Reroll and wrap in waxed paper, and place on a cardboard to keep straight. Store in a cool place. Slice with a saw-tooth knife. 8 servings.

98 LEMON JELLY ROLL

Make Jelly Roll exactly as in preceding recipe, except use Lemon Jelly Filling instead of the tart jelly. 10 to 12 servings.

98a CHOCOLATE BLANC MANGE ROLL

1 cup cake flour	4 eggs, separated
1 teaspoon baking powder	1 cup sugar
¼ teaspoon salt	1 teaspoon vanilla

Sift flour, measure and resift 3 times with baking powder and salt. Beat thoroughly together the egg yolks, ½ cup sugar and vanilla. Beat egg whites until stiff, add remaining sugar gradually and continue to beat until blended. Fold yolk mixture into whites and add dry ingredients, mixing lightly but thoroughly. Spread in a shallow baking pan (12 x 18 inches) which has been lined with waxed paper. Bake in a moderate oven (375° F.) 12 to 15 minutes. Loosen sides, turn out on a towel sprinkled generously with confectioners' (XXXX) sugar, immediately remove paper and trim off the crisp crusts. Cover cake with a sheet of waxed paper, quickly roll up cake, wrap in towel and set on a cake rack to cool. Unroll cooled cake and remove waxed paper; spread with chocolate filling and re-roll. Wrap filled roll in waxed paper and chill in refrigerator for at least an hour before serving. 8 to 10 servings.

Filling for Chocolate Blanc Mange Roll:

¾ tablespoon gelatine	Dash salt
3 tablespoons cold water	½ cup milk
1 square baking chocolate	¼ teaspoon vanilla
2 tablespoons water	¼ cup whipping cream
¼ cup sugar	

Soak gelatine in cold water. Melt chocolate (1124) over hot water. Add 2 tablespoons water, blend well and stir in sugar and salt. Add milk gradually to mixture and stir until smooth and thickened. Stir in softened gelatine until dissolved, remove from heat, add vanilla and chill until of consistency of a custard. Whip the cream until stiff and fold into chocolate mixture. Spread mixture on baked roll as directed above.

99   MOSS ROSE SPONGE CAKE

2 cups cake flour	2 cups sugar
*2 teaspoons baking powder, see p. 122	4 eggs
	1 cup milk, scalded
½ teaspoon salt	½ teaspoon almond extract

*Use 2 tsp double-action or 2½ tsp tartrate or phosphate baking powder. Line bottoms of two 8″ square pans with waxed paper; grease paper lightly. Start oven 10 min. before baking; set to mod. (350° F.). Sift flour, measure, resift 3 times with next 2 ingredients. Put sugar in deep 1-qt. bowl (small mixer bowl is best when using electric mixer) and turn eggs on top of sugar. A narrow bowl is needed to allow beater to dip deeply into egg-sugar mixture to thoroughly beat all the mixture at the same time. Beat with a rotary beater or with electric mixer at medium speed 10 min. or until mixture is very thick and fluffy. Now transfer batter to a larger bowl and thoroughly fold in dry ingredients in 3 portions. Add extract and the barely hot milk all at once, then beat vigorously with a spoon about ½ min. or until thoroughly blended. Batter is very thin. Pour immediately into prepared pans. Bake 25 to 30 min. or until cake springs back when lightly touched. Remove to cake racks to cool 10 min., then loosen sides and turn out on cake racks to finish cooling. Strip off paper. 12 to 14 servings.

Note: Cake may be baked in three 8″ layers or two 9″ layers.

100   JAM ÉCLAIR CAKES

½ cup cake flour
½ teaspoon baking powder
⅛ teaspoon salt
2 eggs, separated
¾ cup XXXX sugar

1 tablespoon cold water
¼ teaspoon vanilla
⅓ cup jam
Icing or unsweetened
whipped cream

Sift flour, measure, add baking powder and salt and resift 3 times. Beat yolks with sugar until thick and yellow. Add water and vanilla and beat well. Add to stiffly beaten egg whites and fold in well. Fold in the dry ingredients in 3 portions. Bake in buttered pan 7 x 7 x 1¼-inch in a moderately slow oven (325° F.) 35 to 40 minutes. Cut in pieces about the size of an éclair, make a slit in the side and insert jam. Top with Butter Cream Frosting (132) or whipped cream. 6 servings.

101   STRAWBERRY ICE-BOX CAKE

1 quart strawberries
½ cup butter
3 cups sifted XXXX sugar
1 whole egg, beaten
3 eggs, separated

3 to 4 tablespoons lemon juice
Pinch salt
Stale Sponge Cake (93) or
Golden Feather Cake (118),
using half the recipe

Wash and hull berries; select 12 to 18 perfect whole berries for garnishing, and mash rest to use in filling. Cream butter, add 1 cup of the sugar and blend well. Add whole beaten egg and about ½ cup sugar, and beat; then add 1 yolk, some of the crushed berries, lemon juice and more sugar; repeat until all are used, beating thoroughly after each addition until mixture is smooth and fluffy. Add salt to egg whites and beat until stiff; fold into first mixture. Line bottom and sides of spring-form pan with slices of stale cake and pour in half of the filling; add another layer of cake slices and rest of filling. Top with more cake slices. Place in refrigerator overnight, or for at least 3 or 4 hours. To serve, remove sides of pan. Garnish with whole strawberries or strawberry halves and whipped cream, if desired. 10 servings.

102   CHOCOLATE REFRIGERATOR CAKE

4 to 6 oz. sponge cake
2 teaspoons plain gelatin
¼ cup cold water
6 to 6½-oz. package semi-
sweet chocolate bits

½ cup milk
1 teaspoon vanilla
3 eggs, separated
1 cup whipping cream

Cut sponge cake into ¼-inch slices, then cut into lengths the height of loaf pan. Reserve a few even slices for top. Have ready a 5 x 9 x 3-inch loaf pan, and arrange cake lengths closely together around sides and bottom of pan. Soften gelatin in cold water. Heat chocolate and milk in top of double boiler over boiling water, stirring to a smooth paste. Stir in gelatin until dissolved. Remove from heat. Beat egg yolks well; stir into chocolate and beat until smooth. Beat egg whites until just stiff, then fold into chocolate mixture. Cool. Beat half the cream until stiff and fold into chocolate mixture. Now pour half the mixture into prepared pan. Add a layer of the leftover uneven cake slices, then pour in rest of chocolate. Top with reserved slices. Chill in refrigerator a few hours or overnight. To serve, unmold and garnish with remaining cream whipped stiff.

103 APPLE SAUCE CAKE

1¾ cups cake flour	1 cup sugar
1 teaspoon baking soda	1 egg
1 teaspoon cinnamon	1 cup unsweetened tart, stiff
½ teaspoon cloves	apple sauce (261)
½ teaspoon salt	1 cup seedless raisins
½ cup shortening	

Sift flour, measure and resift 3 times with soda, spices, and salt. Cream shortening well and gradually blend in sugar. Beat in egg, then apple sauce. Add flour mixture gradually, beating after each addition until well blended. Stir in raisins. Turn into a buttered 8-inch square cake pan lined with waxed paper in the bottom, bake in a moderate oven (350° F.) 45 minutes. Or bake in greased muffin tins 25 to 30 minutes. Cool before serving. Apple sauce cake improves with age, if kept in a breadbox. 6 servings.

104 COCOA BANANA CREAM SHORTCAKE

Filling:

¾ cup sugar	
6 tablespoons corn starch	
½ teaspoon salt	
2 cups milk, scalded	
2 eggs, slightly beaten	
2 tablespoons butter	
½ teaspoon vanilla	
2 or 3 bananas	

Cake:

½ cup sifted cake flour	
¼ cup cocoa	
¾ teaspoon baking powder	
¼ teaspoon salt	
2 tablespoons water	
½ teaspoon vanilla	
3 eggs, separated	
¾ cup sugar	

Filling: Mix sugar, corn starch, and salt. Gradually add milk and cook in double boiler until thick. Add small amount of hot mixture to beaten eggs; mix well and return to the remaining hot mixture. Cook, covered, over boiling water for about 15 minutes, stirring occasionally. Remove from heat; stir in butter and vanilla. Let cool.

Cake: Sift flour with cocoa, baking powder, and salt. Add water and vanilla to egg yolks and beat until thick, adding half of the sugar while beating. Beat whites until stiff; add remaining sugar gradually and continue beating until all is added. Fold yolk mixture into stiffly beaten whites, then fold in flour mixture lightly but thoroughly. Spread in a baking sheet (about 9 x 13 inches) lined with waxed paper in the bottom, and bake in a moderate oven (375° F.) for about 12 minutes. Loosen edges and turn out on a cake rack. When cool, cut in half. Spread one half with cream filling and slice bananas on it. Cover with other half and sprinkle with powdered sugar. Cut in desired sizes for serving. Top with whipped cream, if desired. 5 to 8 servings.

105   COCOA COCOANUT CAKE

2 cups all-purpose flour	1½ cups sugar
1½ teaspoons soda	2 eggs, beaten
¼ teaspoon salt	1 teaspoon vanilla
⅔ cup cocoa	½ cup buttermilk
⅔ cup shortening	½ cup boiling water

Sift flour, measure and resift 3 times with soda, salt and cocoa. Cream shortening until soft, add sugar, and blend thoroughly; add beaten eggs and beat vigorously until smooth and fluffy. Stir in vanilla. Add flour mixture alternately with buttermilk in 3 or 4 portions, beginning and ending with flour and beating well after each addition. Add boiling water all at once and stir until smooth. Turn into 2 buttered 8-inch cake pans that have bottoms lined with waxed paper. Bake in a moderate oven (350° F.) 30 minutes or until done. Turn out onto cake racks, cool, and lay together with Cocoanut Icing (147). 10 servings.

106   CHOCOLATE CREAM CHEESE CAKE

2½ cups cake flour	1¼ cups sugar
1 teaspoon soda	1 teaspoon vanilla
2½ teaspoons cream of tartar	2 eggs, separated
½ teaspoon salt	¾ cup milk
½ cup shortening	

Sift flour, measure and resift 3 times with soda, cream of tartar and salt. Cream shortening until smooth, add ¾ cup of the sugar and the vanilla, and continue creaming until blended. Separate eggs, beat yolks until light and lemon-colored, and combine with milk. Add egg-milk mixture to creamed shortening and sugar alternately with the sifted dry ingredients, beginning and ending with flour and beating thoroughly after each addition. Beat egg whites until stiff and gradually beat in remaining sugar. Fold meringue into batter. Turn batter into a buttered

7 x 11 x 1½-inch pan lined with waxed paper in the bottom, and bake in a moderate oven (350° F.) about 45 minutes or until golden brown and springy to the touch. Cool in pan about 10 minutes; then turn out onto cake rack and cool before spreading with Chocolate Cream Cheese Frosting (137). 8 servings.

Note: The above method produces a cake of fine texture and large volumn which compares very favorably with a cake made with all butter, and is considerably less expensive.

107   CINNAMON CAKE

2 cups cake flour	½ cup shortening, half butter
1 teaspoon soda	1¼ cups brown sugar, packed
½ teaspoon salt	2 eggs
2 teaspoons cinnamon	1 cup thick buttermilk

Sift flour, measure and resift 3 times with soda, salt and cinnamon. Combine butter and other shortening and cream thoroughly. Gradually blend in the sugar; then add eggs and beat vigorously until mixture is smooth and fluffy. Add flour mixture and buttermilk alternately in 3 or 4 portions, beginning and ending with flour, beating well after each addition. Turn batter into two 8-inch layer cake tins, buttered on sides and bottoms lined with waxed paper. Bake in a moderate oven (350° F.) about 25 minutes, or until springy when lightly pressed with fingertips. Turn out on cake racks, cool, sprinkle with powdered sugar or frost with Coffee Fruit Frosting (141). 10 servings.

107a   COTTAGE CHEESE CAKE

1 package zwieback (5¾ oz.)	½ teaspoon cinnamon
¼ cup sugar	½ cup butter, melted

Crush zwieback into fine crumbs with a rolling pin, and combine with remaining ingredients. Mix thoroughly and pat over bottom and sides of an 8-inch spring form pan. Chill while mixing the following filling:

9 eggs, separated	1 teaspoon vanilla
1 cup sugar	1½ teaspoons grated lemon rind
¼ cup all-purpose flour	1 cup (½ pint) whipping
1½ lbs. dry cottage cheese	cream

Beat egg yolks until thick and lemon-colored. Blend sugar and flour together; add to beaten yolks, mixing thoroughly. Rub cottage cheese through a sieve and add to yolk mixture, beating well. Stir in vanilla and lemon rind. Whip cream until stiff, lightly fold into cheese mixture, and finally fold in stiffly beaten egg whites. Turn mixture into crumb-lined spring form pan and bake for 1¼ hours in a slow oven (300° F.). Cool thoroughly on a cake rack before removing sides of pan. If desired, serve with sugared seedless grapes. 8 generous servings.

108   DOLLY VARDEN CAKE

3 cups cake flour
1½ teaspoons baking powder, see p. 122
½ teaspoon salt
¾ cup soft butter
2 cups sugar
4 eggs, separated
1 cup milk
½ teaspoon vanilla
½ cup currants, washed and plumped (1129)
½ cup finely chopped moist citron
2 teaspoons cinnamon
½ teaspoon cloves
½ teaspoon nutmeg

Sift flour, measure and resift 3 times with baking powder and salt. Cream butter, add sugar slowly and cream well. Add beaten egg yolks and beat until light and fluffy. Add sifted flour mixture alternately with milk in 4 or 5 portions, beginning and ending with flour and beating until smooth after each addition. Fold in stiffly beaten egg whites, then divide batter into two equal portions. Add vanilla to one portion, stirring just enough to mix. Turn into an 8-inch square baking pan, 1½ inches deep or a 9-inch round layer pan, 1¼ inches deep, bottom lined with waxed paper, and buttered on the sides. To the other portion add the fruits and spices, and stir just enough to distribute thoroughly. Turn into another similarly prepared pan of the same size and shape. Bake layers in a moderate oven (350° F.), the white about 30 minutes; the dark layer 35 minutes. Cool in pans on cake racks about 10 minutes, then turn out onto racks and cool thoroughly. Use spice layer for lower layer of cake, and spread Seven-Minute Icing (145) or Butter Cream Frosting (132) between layers and on top and sides. Cut with a very sharp knife. 10 servings.

109   RED DEVIL'S FOOD CAKE

2 cups cake flour
1 teaspoon soda
¼ teaspoon salt
1½ to 2 squares baking chocolate
½ cup soft butter or shortening
1½ cups sugar
2 eggs, beaten
1 teaspoon vanilla
½ cup thick buttermilk
½ cup boiling water

Sift flour, measure and resift 3 times with soda and salt. Melt chocolate over hot water (1124); cool. Cream butter until soft and smooth, then add sugar and blend thoroughly. Add beaten eggs and beat until smooth and fluffy. Stir in vanilla. Mix in cooled chocolate. Combine buttermilk and water. Add flour and liquid alternately in several portions, beginning and ending with flour and beating until smooth after each addition. Turn into two 8-inch cake pans, bottoms lined with waxed paper and buttered on the sides. Bake in a moderate oven (350° F.)27 to 30 minutes or until cake springs back when lightly pressed with finger tips. Turn out onto cake racks and cool. When barely cool spread with any desired frosting. 10 servings. (Note: One-half cup cocoa may be substituted for the chocolate. Sift cocoa with flour, soda and salt. Increase shortening to ⅔ cup, using half butter. Combine rest of ingredients in same way.)

110 LADY BALTIMORE CAKE

2¼ cups cake flour	1⅓ cups sugar
1½ teaspoons baking powder, see p. 122	1 teaspoon vanilla
	⅔ cup milk
½ teaspoon salt	4 egg whites
½ cup soft butter or other shortening	

Sift flour, measure and resift 3 times with baking powder and salt. Cream butter thoroughly, add sugar slowly and continue creaming until smooth. Stir in vanilla. Add sifted dry ingredients alternately with milk, in 3 or 4 portions, beginning and ending with flour and beating thoroughly after each addition. Fold in stiffly beaten egg whites. Turn batter into two 8-inch layer cake pans, buttered on the sides and bottoms lined with waxed paper. Bake in a moderate oven (375° F.) about 25 minutes, or until cake is springy when lightly pressed with finger tips. Turn out onto cake racks and cool. Frost the cooled cake with Lady Baltimore Icing (146). 10 to 12 servings.

111 OLD-FASHIONED MARBLE SPICE CAKE

Dark Part:

2¼ cups cake flour	¾ cup moist brown sugar, packed
1 teaspoon soda	
⅜ teaspoon salt	3 egg yolks, beaten
1½ teaspoons cinnamon	3 tablespoons molasses
1 teaspoon cloves	¾ cup buttermilk
¾ cup soft butter or shortening	

Light Part:

2 cups cake flour	1 teaspoon vanilla
1 teaspoon baking powder	¾ cup granulated sugar
¼ teaspoon soda	¾ cup buttermilk
⅜ teaspoon salt	3 egg whites
⅓ cup butter	

133

Grease a 3½-inch high 9-inch tube pan; line bottom with heavy waxed paper. Start oven 10 minutes before baking; set to moderately slow (325° F.). Mix cake as follows:

For Dark Part: Sift flour, measure, resift 3 times with soda, salt and spices.

For Light Part: Sift flour, measure, resift 3 times with baking powder, soda and salt.

Next: Measure, the ingredients for both parts, keeping them separate. Mix dark part first, then quickly mix light part so dark will not stand long.

Dark Part: Cream butter until smooth and shiny with a wooden spoon, add sieved brown sugar gradually, creaming thoroughly. Clean off and remove spoon. Beat in egg yolks with rotary beater, then molasses until fluffy. Remove beater. Add flour and buttermilk alternately in 4 or 5 portions, beginning and ending with flour and beating well with wooden spoon after each addition.

Light Part: Cream butter, add vanilla and sugar and cream thoroughly with wooden spoon. Scrape off spoon, remove. With rotary beater, beat in egg whites until smooth and fluffy. Remove beater and use spoon. Add flour mixture and buttermilk alternately in 4 or 5 portions, beginning and ending with flour and beating well after each portion. For marbled effect, dip alternate spoonfuls of light and dark batter into prepared pan. Bake 1 hour or until cake tests done. Cool in pan on cake rack 10 minutes, then loosen sides and around tube with thin-bladed knife. Turn out on rack and quickly turn top-side up and cool before cutting. Spread with frosting, if desired, but none is necessary.

112   HALF-A-POUND CAKE

½ lb. cake flour (2¼ cups sifted)	¼ teaspoon nutmeg
1 teaspoon baking powder, see p. 122	½ lb. soft butter (1 cup)
	½ lb. eggs (4 eggs)
¼ teaspoon salt	2 teaspoons rose water
	½ lb. sugar (1 cup)

Sift flour, measure or weigh and resift 3 times with baking powder, salt and nutmeg. Cream butter thoroughly and add the flour mixture in 3 portions, mixing until smooth after each addition. Beat eggs until thick and lemon-colored; add flavoring and sugar all at once, and beat until very light. Then beat the egg mixture thoroughly into the fat-flour mixture. Have a loaf pan 9 x 5 x 3 inches lined with 4 thicknesses of smooth brown wrapping paper; butter the inmost piece of paper thoroughly. Pour in the batter, pushing it well into the corners of the pan, so surface is level. Lay another piece of buttered brown paper across top of pan.

Bake in a moderate oven (350° F.) ½ hour, then remove paper from top and bake 1 hour longer. Cool a few minutes in pan before turning out onto wire cake rack to finish cooling. 1 loaf.

113   RICH LOAF CAKE

1¾ cups cake flour	¾ cup sugar
¾ teaspoon baking powder	3 eggs, separated
¼ teaspoon salt	½ teaspoon vanilla
⅛ teaspoon ginger	⅓ cup milk
½ cup soft butter	

Sift flour, measure and resift 3 times with baking powder, salt and ginger. Cream butter thoroughly, gradually blend in ½ cup of the sugar, add well-beaten egg yolks, and beat vigorously until smooth and fluffy (using egg beater if desired). Stir in vanilla. Add flour mixture and milk alternately in 3 or 4 portions, beginning and ending with flour and beating well after each addition. Beat egg whites until stiff, slowly adding remaining sugar. Carefully fold into batter. Turn into well-buttered 6-cup bread loaf pan, which has bottom lined with waxed paper. Bake in moderate oven (350° F.) 40 to 45 minutes or until center of cake springs back when lightly pressed with finger tips. Cool in pan on cake rack 5 minutes, then turn out onto cake rack. When cold, frost with Dark Chocolate Frosting (138) or any desired butter frosting. 10 to 12 servings.

114   SPICE CAKE

2 cups cake flour	Few grains cayenne, if
1 teaspoon soda	desired
½ teaspoon salt	1½ tablespoons boiling water
1 teaspoon cinnamon	½ cup shortening
½ teaspoon nutmeg	1½ cups sugar
½ teaspoon cloves	2 eggs, separated
	⅔ cup buttermilk

Sift flour, measure and resift 3 times with soda and salt. Combine spices and mix thoroughly with boiling water. Cream shortening until fluffy, then blend in sugar. Add beaten eggs and beat until smooth and fluffy. Stir in spice mixture. Then add flour mixture and buttermilk alternately in 3 or 4 portions, beginning and ending with flour and beating until smooth after each portion. Turn into two 9-inch layer pans, bottoms lined with waxed paper and sides buttered. Bake in moderate oven (375° F.) 25 minutes or until top springs back when LIGHTLY touched with finger tip. Cool in pan on cake rack 5 minutes, then remove to racks to cool right-side up. Frost with Orange Butter Frosting (135). 10 to 14 servings.

115   TWO-EGG CAKE

1¾ cups plus 1 tablespoon cake flour

1½ teaspoons baking powder, see p. 122

½ teaspoon salt

½ cup soft butter or other shortening

1 cup plus 2 tablespoons sugar

2 eggs, beaten

1 teaspoon vanilla

¾ cup milk

Sift flour, measure and resift 3 times with baking powder and salt. Cream butter until soft and smooth and gradually blend in the sugar, creaming until fluffy. Add beaten eggs and beat vigorously until light and fluffy. Add vanilla and stir in thoroughly. Add flour mixture and milk alternately in 3 or 4 portions, beginning and ending with flour and beating until smooth after each addition. Pour into two 8-inch layer cake pans, buttered on the sides and lined with waxed paper in the bottom. Bake in a moderate oven (350° F.) 25 to 30 minutes, until cake just begins to pull away from sides of pan and springs back when pressed lightly with finger tip. Cool in pan on cake rack 5 minutes, then turn out on rack right side up. When cool, frost between layers and on top and sides of cake with any desired frosting. 8 to 10 servings.

116   WHITE LAYER CAKE

2¼ cups cake flour

2¼ teaspoons baking powder, see p. 122

½ teaspoon salt

½ cup shortening

1⅓ cups sugar

¼ teaspoon lemon extract

1 teaspoon vanilla

½ cup egg whites

1 cup milk

Sift flour, measure and resift 3 times with baking powder and salt. Cream shortening until soft and smooth, then add 1 cup of the sugar and blend thoroughly. Add flavorings. Add half the egg whites, unbeaten, and beat vigorously until mixture is light and fluffy. Add flour mixture and milk alternately in 3 or 4 portions, beginning and ending with flour and beating well after each addition. Beat remaining egg whites until stiff, then gradually beat in remaining sugar and fold lightly but thoroughly into the batter. Turn into two 9-inch layer cake pans lined with waxed paper in the bottom and buttered on the sides. Bake in a moderate oven (350° F.) 28-30 minutes or until cake springs back when lightly pressed with finger tips. Cool in pans on cake racks 5 minutes, then turn out on racks to cool right side up. Spread any desired frosting between layers and on top and sides of cake. To make individual cup cakes, fill buttered muffin pans ½ full of batter, or place paper cups in muffin pan and fill ½ full. Bake at same temperature as layers, but about 5 minutes less. 8 to 10 servings.

117   WHOLE WHEAT CAKE

1¼ cups all-purpose flour
2¼ teaspoons baking powder, see p. 122
½ teaspoon salt
¾ cup whole wheat flour
½ cup shortening
¾ cup sugar
2 eggs, well beaten
½ teaspoon vanilla
1 cup milk (scant)

Sift the all-purpose flour, measure and resift three times with baking powder and salt, then add whole wheat flour and stir in thoroughly. Cream shortening, blend in sugar, and add beaten eggs; beat until smooth and fluffy. Stir in vanilla. Add flour mixture and milk alternately in 3 or 4 portions, beating well after each portion. Turn into two buttered 8-inch layer cake pans, lined with waxed paper in the bottom. Bake in a moderate oven (375° F.) about 25 minutes. Cool in pans on cake racks 5 minutes, then turn out on racks to cool. Leave plain or spread Date Filling (150) between layers. 10 servings.

118   GOLDEN FEATHER CAKE

1¾ cups cake flour
1½ teaspoons baking powder, see p. 122
½ teaspoon salt
½ cup soft butter or shortening
1 cup sugar
1 teaspoon vanilla
2 eggs, beaten
½ cup milk

Grease two 8-inch layer cake pans; line bottoms with waxed paper—grease paper. Start oven 10 minutes before baking; set to moderate (350° F.). Sift flour, measure, resift 3 times with baking powder and salt. Cream butter until soft and shiny with wooden spoon, gradually blend in sugar and cream until smooth and fluffy. Stir in vanilla. Scrape off spoon and remove. Add eggs, one at a time, and beat vigorously with rotary beater until smooth and fluffy. Remove beater. Add flour mixture and milk alternately in 3 or 4 portions, beginning and ending with flour and beating with wooden spoon until smooth after each portion. Turn batter into prepared pans. Bake 23 to 25 minutes or until cake barely begins to pull away from sides of pan. Don't overbake! Cool in pans on cake racks 5 minutes, then turn out on racks, loosen paper, invert and finish cooling. When barely cool, spread Lemon Filling between layers and top and sides with 7-Minute Icing. 8 to 10 servings.

NOTE: May be baked in muffin pans if cupcakes are desired. Bake at same temperature but about 5 minutes less.

119   APRICOT UPSIDE-DOWN CAKE

1 cup dried apricot halves
½ cup warm water
⅓ cup butter
½ cup brown sugar, packed
¾ cup granulated sugar
3 tablespoons white corn syrup
1 cup all-purpose flour
¼ teaspoon salt

2 teaspoons single action baking powder or 1½ teaspoons
  double-action baking powder
¼ cup shortening
½ cup granulated sugar
2 eggs
¼ teaspoon almond extract
¼ cup milk

Wash and soak apricots in the warm water for 30 minutes or longer. Melt butter in an 8-inch square pan, add the brown and ¼ cup granulated sugar, the corn syrup, and 2 tablespoons water from apricots. Boil 2 minutes; remove from heat. Sift flour, measure, and resift 3 times with salt and baking powder. Cream shortening, blend in the remaining ½ cup sugar, add eggs, and beat until fluffy. Add flavoring. Add flour mixture and milk alternately, beginning and ending with flour and beating well after each addition. Arrange apricot halves, rounded-side down in syrup in pan, and spread batter over them. Bake in moderate oven (350° F.) about 35 minutes. Cool several minutes; loosen sides of cake and turn out onto serving plate. Serve warm, with whipped cream if desired. 5 servings.

120   DUTCH CHERRY CAKE

2 cups all-purpose flour
2¼ teaspoons baking powder,
   see p. 122
½ teaspoon salt
1 cup sugar
2 eggs, separated

½ cup milk
⅓ cup melted butter
1 No. 2 can unsweetened
  red cherries
3 tablespoons brown sugar
1 teaspoon cinnamon

Sift flour, measure and resift 3 times with baking powder, salt and ¾ cup of the sugar. Beat egg yolks, add milk and melted butter and quickly stir into the flour mixture until batter is just smooth. Beat egg whites until stiff, then beat in remaining sugar until stiff and fold into batter along with 1 cup well-drained cherries. Turn into buttered baking pan which has been lined with waxed paper (7½ x 11 x 1½ inches), and sprinkle top with brown sugar and cinnamon mixed together. Bake in a moderately hot oven (400° F.) 35 minutes, or until browned on top. Serve hot or cold, with sauce made as follows: Heat cherry juice to boiling. Blend 1 tablespoon corn starch with 3 tablespoons sugar, add 3 tablespoons boiling water and mix to a smooth paste. Add to hot juice and stir over direct heat until sauce boils and thickens. Stir in a pinch of salt, 1 tablespoon butter, ⅛ teaspoon almond extract and remaining cherries. Serve warm or cold with whipped cream if desired. 6 to 8 servings.

121   PINEAPPLE UPSIDE-DOWN CAKE

1 cup sugar
3 tablespoons corn starch
  No. 303 can crushed
  pineapple
2 tablespoons melted butter
½ cup maraschino cherries
1⅔ cups all-purpose flour

½ teaspoon salt
2¼ teaspoons baking powder,
  see p. 122
⅓ cup shortening
2 eggs, beaten
½ teaspoon vanilla
½ cup milk

Mix ⅓ cup of the sugar with the corn starch, add juice drained from
the pineapple, and cook in heavy 10-inch skillet over direct heat stirring
constantly until sauce boils and becomes clear. Add drained pineapple
and butter. Drain cherries thoroughly and arrange in a pattern in the
pineapple mixture. Sift flour, measure and resift 3 times with salt and
baking powder. Cream the ⅓ cup shortening until soft, add the remaining ⅔ cups sugar and the eggs, and beat vigorously until smooth and
fluffy. Stir in the vanilla. Add flour mixture and milk alternately, beginning and ending with flour and beating well after each addition. Turn
batter into skillet over pineapple. Bake in a moderate oven (350° F.) 35
to 40 minutes or until center of cake is springy when lightly pressed with
finger tips. Cool in pan on cake rack about 10 minutes; then turn out
onto a serving plate. Serve warm, with or without whipped cream. 6 to 8
servings.

121a   PEACH UPSIDE-DOWN CAKE

½ cup butter
⅔ cup brown sugar, packed
1¼ lbs. peaches (4 peaches)
1½ cups cake flour
1¾ teaspoons baking powder,
  see p. 122

¼ teaspoon salt
½ cup granulated sugar
1 egg, beaten
¼ teaspoon almond extract
⅓ cup milk

Melt 3 tablespoons butter in a skillet with a handle which will not
burn in oven. Add brown sugar and heat slowly until sugar and butter are
blended. Peel peaches, cut in half, remove stones, and arrange cut side
down in the butter-sugar mixture in skillet. Sift flour, measure, and resift
3 times with baking powder and salt. Cream remaining butter; blend in
granulated sugar, creaming thoroughly. Add egg and beat until light and
fluffy. Stir in extract. Add sifted dry ingredients and milk alternately in
3 or 4 portions, beginning and ending with flour and beating well after
each addition. Pour batter over peaches and bake in a moderate oven
(350° F.) about 40 minutes or until cake springs back when touched
with finger. Cool 10 minutes in skillet, then turn out on large serving

plate. Serve warm with top milk or almond-flavored Hard Sauce (932). 6 to 8 servings.

122 GINGERBREAD

1½ cups all-purpose, or 1⅔ cups cake flour	½ teaspoon allspice
¼ teaspoon salt	⅓ cup soft margarine
½ teaspoon soda	½ cup sugar
½ teaspoon cinnamon	1 egg
¾ teaspoon ginger	½ cup light molasses
	½ cup buttermilk

Sift flour, measure and resift 3 times with salt, soda and spices. Cream margarine until smooth, add sugar and egg and cream until light and fluffy. Add molasses and beat vigorously for 2 minutes longer. Add flour mixture and buttermilk alternately in 3 or 4 portions, beginning and ending with flour and beating well after each portion. Turn batter into greased 11 x 7 x 1½-inch pan. Bake in a moderate oven (350° F.) 25 to 30 minutes. Cool in pan on cake rack 5 minutes, then turn out on rack and invert. Serve warm or cold with whipped cream, apple sauce or melted marshmallows. If glass baking dish is used, bake at 325° F.

NOTE: For best flavor, use light molasses or sorghum.

123 GINGERBREAD WITH WHIPPED CREAM AND ORANGE WEDGES

Bake Gingerbread (122) in greased muffin pans in a moderate oven (350° F.) for 20 to 22 minutes. Serve with whipped cream and garnish with orange sections.

124 HOLIDAY FRUIT CAKE
(Excellent cake that cuts into thin, whole slices. Expensive, but worth it.)

1 lb. moist candied pineapple	1½ teaspoons cinnamon
1 lb. moist candied citron	1 teaspoon allspice
½ lb. candied cherries	1 teaspoon cloves
11-oz. package moist currants	1 teaspoon soda
	2 teaspoons salt
1 lb. fresh dates, pitted	1 lb. butter or margarine
1 lb. moist light figs	½ lb. moist brown sugar, 1⅛ cups, packed
1 lb. pecans, cut coarsely	
1 cup medium syrup	1⅛ cups granulated sugar
3 tablespoons lemon juice	12 eggs, beaten
½ cup sherry or Port wine	½ cup light molasses
1 lb. all-purpose flour	

Use only the best of fruit and nuts. Cut pineapple and citron into thin, match-like strips. Cut the cherries into 8ths and the dates and figs into pieces about same size as cherry pieces. Put fruit and nuts into a large enamelware or glass bowl. Make the syrup by heating ½ cup sugar and 1 cup of water to boiling, then simmer 5 minutes. Add 1 tablespoon white corn syrup to hot syrup and pour over fruit with lemon juice and wine. Stir, cover and let stand overnight, stirring 2 or 3 times with wooden spoon to moisten fruit uniformly.

Meanwhile prepare baking pans by lining them neatly with 2 layers of parchment or smooth, brown wrapping paper. Have all ingredients at room temperature. Sift flour, measure, resift 3 times with next 5 ingredients. Cream butter, then add sugars gradually, creaming well. Stir in beaten eggs, then beat until smooth and fluffy. Now stir in molasses, then add flour mixture in 3 or 4 portions, beating well after each portion. Turn batter over fruit, scraping it all out with rubber scraper. Now mix with hands or wooden spoon, lifting fruit up through batter until well distributed. Fill prepared pans COMPACTLY with batter up to within ¼-inch of top. Press down and smooth top of batter with a spatula, then pat milk over top to cover with a thin film. Place pans in a jelly roll pan; set in oven on bottom shelf and pour water into jelly roll pan ¼-inch deep. Bake in very slow oven (250° F.) from 2 to 3 hours, time depending on size of pans, or until cakes test done. Be careful not to scorch. Cool cakes in pans on cake racks. Then remove cakes from pans but leave lining papers attached. Decorate and glaze cakes and let dry. Then wrap in moisture-proof cellophane paper and seal airtight. Store in covered box and let ripen a few weeks before serving. Chill in refrigerator 3 or 4 hours before slicing. 11 lbs.

125   **RICH FRUIT CAKE**

2 lbs. moist raisins	1 teaspoon cinnamon
2 lbs. moist currants	1 lb. soft butter
1 lb. citron, finely cut	1 lb. brown sugar
1 lb. pecans, chopped	12 eggs
1 lb. almonds, sliced	1 6-oz. glass blackberry jelly
4½ cups all-purpose flour	½ cup cream
2 teaspoons nutmeg	½ cup canned fruit juice
1 teaspoon mace	

Thoroughly wash and dry the raisins and currants; combine with citron and nuts. Sift flour, measure, and resift twice with spices; mix 2 cups of it with the fruits and nuts. Cream butter until soft and smooth, blend in sugar thoroughly, and add eggs one at a time, beating well after each egg is added. Add blackberry jelly which has been thoroughly beaten up. Add remaining flour mixture alternately with the cream and sherry, be-

ginning and ending with a portion of flour and mixing well after each
addition. Stir in floured fruits and nuts, and mix until well distributed
through the batter. Pack into loaf pans lined with 2 thicknesses of greased
brown paper or waxed paper. Bake the same as 124 for 2½ to 3 hours,
depending on size of pan. Cakes are done when they pull away from
sides of the pan and are firm to the touch in the center. 10 lbs. cake.

126   FRUIT CAKE BAKED IN CANDIED GRAPEFRUIT SHELLS

4 whole grapefruit	12 cups granulated sugar
3 quarts water	6 cups water
6 tablespoons salt	

The half-shells from breakfast grapefruit may be used; choose fruit with
thick skins. Remove dividing membranes from grapefruit shells. Cover
with 3 quarts water in which the salt has been dissolved, and let stand
24 hours. Pour off the salt water, cover with fresh cold water, and bring
to a boil. Pour off this water, cover with more fresh cold water, and again
bring to boil; repeat until water has been changed 6 times and grapefruit
is no longer bitter or salty. Simmer for 1 hour, or until shells are soft, in
the last water. Drain, and remove any loose white part of the rind; the
shells should be about ⅜-inch thick. Boil the sugar and 6 cups water
together until the syrup reaches (238° F.), keeping kettle covered during
the first 5 minutes to dissolve all sugar. Place grapefruit shells in the
boiling syrup and simmer for 20 minutes, until fruit is transparent and
well glazed. The beautiful transparent quality is obtained most readily if
peel is put in when the syrup reaches 238°. Let cool in the syrup for 12
hours. Then place to drain on wire cake racks set over cookie sheets.

When ready to bake fruit cake, fill the shells full of fruit cake batter
(124 or 125), heaping up slightly. Wrap a strip of unglazed wrapping
paper or cooking parchment around the edge to help hold shell in shape
and prevent the cake from cooking over; tie it firmly but not tightly with
twine. Place on trivets in a covered roasting pan containing about ¼-inch
of water. Cover and bake in a very slow oven (250° F.) 1¼ hours. Then
transfer cakes to a baking sheet and continue baking in the same slow
oven 30 minutes longer. Cool and store in tightly covered containers.
The cakes may be basted sparingly from time to time with fruit juice or
juice from pickled peaches, etc.

Just before using them, glaze (127) and decorate the cakes. A variety
of materials may be used for decorating (blanched almonds, candied
cherries, strips of angelica, cut-outs from thin slices of citron, etc.), but in
general the pieces should be kept small, in proportion to the small size
of the cakes. For gifts, wrap in moisture-proof cellophane, fastening it
with Scotch tape.

Note: The syrup in which the grapefruit shells are candied may be stored in a tightly covered jar in the refrigerator and used as a delicious and unusually flavored syrup for pancakes, waffles, French toast, etc.

127   APRICOT GLAZE FOR FRUIT CAKE

¼ cup dried apricots	1 cup white corn syrup
1½ cups cold water	

Wash apricots, cover with water and soak for several hours or overnight; then cook in the same water until tender, about 15 min. Drain off cooking water through a sieve or food mill, and rub only half the apricots through the sieve. (Use rest for fruit cup or sauce.) Measure juice and purée—there should be ½ cup. Add the corn syrup and boil rapidly 2 or 3 min. or until mixture is clear. Remove from heat. Use immediately by quickly applying to fruit cake with a pastry brush. If desired, decorations may be applied after the first coat of glaze, and a second coat applied over the decorations after first coat is set. Reheat glaze to boiling each time it is used. Allow glaze to dry thoroughly before wrapping or storing cakes. Enough to double coat 12 to 15 lb. fruit cake.

GLAZE FOR FRUIT CAKE

Combine ½ cup white corn syrup with ½ cup rum, brandy or fruit juice, stir thoroughly. Boil 2 or 3 min. with very little stirring. While hot, brush about 2 tbsp. over each cake.

127a   VANILLA CHIFFON CAKE
(A light fragile desert suitable with heavy meals and for children's parties)

2 cups cake flour	⅔ cup cold water
1⅓ cups sugar	2 teaspoons vanilla
*2½ teaspoons baking powder	1 teaspoon grated lemon rind, opt.
1 teaspoon salt	
½ cup less 1 tablespoon salad oil	1 cup egg whites, 7 large
	½ teaspoon cream of tartar
4 large or 5 small egg yolks, unbeaten	

*Sulfate-phosphate (double-action) type. Use 3¼ teaspoons tartrate or phosphate type. Have ready 10-inch tube pan—do not grease. Bake on *bottom rack* of oven. Start oven 10 minutes before baking; set to moderately slow (325° F.).

Sift flour, measure, resift 3 times with next 3 ingredients, the last time into a 3-qt. mixing bowl. Make a well in center of flour, pour in salad oil; add yolks, water, vanilla and rind to oil. Put whites into a 4-qt. mixing bowl, add cream of tartar, let stand while beating yolk mixture with wooden spoon until smooth and well-blended, 75 to 80 strokes. Clean off spoon and sides of bowl with rubber scrapper, leaving scraper in bowl. Beat whites with rotary beater until stiff enough for peaks to stand straight when beater is lifted up; whites are stiffer than for Angel Food or Meringue, but not stiff enough to look dry. Quickly shake whites from beater. Immediately pour yolk mixture in a steady stream over whites, cutting-and-folding-in with rubber scraper as you pour. When almost all yolk mixture is added, quickly scrape down sides of bowl and pour around over whites, continuing to cut-and-fold-in only until just well blended— no longer. NEVER STIR AND NEVER OVERMIX AS THIS TOUGHENS CAKE. Carefully flow batter at once into pan, quickly and lightly scraping out batter adhering to bowl. Place immediately in oven. Bake 55 minutes or until cake springs back when lightly touched with finger. When done, immediately invert over a large funnel or bottle heavy enough to support cake. Cool for at least an hour before removing from pan. Remove from pan like Angel Food, p. 123. Turn bottom-side-up on serving plate and spread with Vanilla, Lemon or Orange Confectioners' Frosting, p. 148. When serving cake unfrosted, place right-side up on serving plate. A sawtooth knife cuts this cake beautifully. 12 to 15 servings.

NOTE: Substitute 1 teaspoon lemon extract and ¼ teaspoon almond extract for the 2 teaspoons vanilla, if desired.

128 DOUGHNUTS

3½ cups all-purpose flour
4 teaspoons baking powder, see p. 122
1 teaspoon soda
½ teaspoon salt
¼ teaspoon nutmeg, optional

2 tablespoons shortening
1 cup sugar
2 eggs, beaten
½ teaspoon vanilla
1 cup buttermilk
Fat for deep frying

Sift flour, measure and resift 3 times with baking powder, soda, salt and nutmeg. Cream shortening, blend in sugar thoroughly, then add beaten eggs and vanilla. Add sifted dry ingredients alternately with buttermilk in 3 or 4 portions, stirring only until well mixed. Chill dough before rolling. Remove only part of dough from refrigerator at a time. Roll dough out on lightly floured board or pastry cloth from ¼ to ⅜-inch thick. Cut out doughnuts with floured cutter. Fry in deep fat heated to 375° F. Fry only until underside is golden brown, then turn and brown on other side. Lift doughnuts out with slotted spoon or in a wire basket.

Drain on paper toweling. Put granulated sugar, XXXX sugar or cinnamon and sugar into a paper bag, place doughnuts in while warm and shake to coat. 36 doughnuts.

129   BANANA DOUGHNUTS

5 cups all-purpose flour
3 teaspoons baking powder,
  see p. 122
1 teaspoon soda
2 teaspoons salt
1 teaspoon nutmeg
¼ cup shortening

1 cup sugar
3 eggs, well beaten
1½ teaspoons vanilla
¾ cup mashed bananas (about
  2 good-sized bananas)
½ cup buttermilk
½ cup flour for rolling

Sift flour, measure and resift 3 times with baking powder, soda, salt and nutmeg. Cream shortening, blend in sugar, add eggs, and beat until smooth and fluffy. Add combined vanilla, bananas and buttermilk and beat until well mixed. Add flour mixture and stir until smooth. Turn small portions of dough onto floured board, knead lightly, roll to ⅜-inch thickness, and cut with floured 2½-inch doughnut cutter. Fry in deep fat heated to 375° F. (see 128) until golden brown, then lift out and drain on absorbent paper. If desired, the dough may be covered tightly and kept in the refrigerator for 1 or 2 days, to be fried as needed. Makes about 3½ dozen.

CAKE ICINGS and FILLINGS

130   BAKED FROSTING

2 egg whites
¼ teaspoon salt

2 cups brown sugar, packed
¼ cup chopped nuts

Beat egg whites with salt to a stiff foam. Gradually add brown sugar and continue beating until blended. If turning the rotary beater becomes too difficult, rest of sugar may be mixed in with a spoon. Fold nuts into the frosting. Spread over cake batter in the pan just before placing in oven. If preferred, nuts may be sprinkled on top of frosting after spreading on cake. Bake for time and temperature required for cake recipe used (about 350° F., 25 to 35 minutes). Enough for two 8-inch layers or one layer 7 by 11 inches.

131   BROILED ICING

6 tablespoons butter, melted   ¼ cup cream or milk
⅔ cup brown sugar, packed   ½ cup moist grated cocoanut

Mix ingredients together thoroughly and spread on cake immediately after it comes out of oven. Then place cake in the broiler as far as possible from source of heat, with heat turned low. Broil until icing bubbles all over and becomes nicely toasted. Watch carefully to prevent scorching. Enough for a single layer 8 or 9 inches square or 7 by 11 inches.

132   BUTTER CREAM FROSTING

¼ cup soft butter   1 teaspoon vanilla
2 cups sifted XXXX sugar,   2 tablespoons cream
  packed   1 tablespoon white corn syrup
¼ teaspoon salt

Cream butter until very smooth; then add sugar gradually, creaming thoroughly. Add salt and vanilla. Gradually work in the cream, then the corn syrup to produce a smooth spreading consistency. Spread on cake. Sufficient for two 8-inch layers.

133   COFFEE BUTTER FROSTING

Make like Butter Cream Frosting (132), except substitute for the cream, 2 tablespoons of strong coffee infusion made as follows: Add ⅓ cup medium grind coffee to 1 cup water and heat just to boiling. Remove from heat immediately and let stand 2 minutes. Then strain through very fine strainer or through cheesecloth to remove all grounds. Cool before adding to frosting.

134   CHOCOLATE BUTTER FROSTING

To the Butter Cream Frosting (132), add ½ to 1 square baking chocolate which has been melted (1124) and cooled thoroughly.

135   ORANGE BUTTER FROSTING

Omit cream and vanilla from Butter Cream Frosting (132). Use instead about 1 tablespoon each of lemon and orange juice and 1 teaspoon grated orange rind.

136   THIN BUTTER ICING

2 tablespoons soft butter	1½ tablespoons milk
1 cup sifted XXXX sugar, packed	½ teaspoon vanilla
	1 teaspoon white corn syrup

Cream butter until smooth, then add sugar and milk alternately, a little at a time, stirring until smooth after each addition. Stir in vanilla and syrup. When smooth, pour over the cake and let stand until icing forms a glazy crust on top before cutting. Enough for one 8-inch layer.

137   CHOCOLATE CREAM CHEESE FROSTING

1 package (3 oz.) cream cheese	Pinch salt
1 square baking chocolate, melted (1124)	½ teaspoon vanilla
2 cups sifted XXXX sugar, packed	2 to 4 tablespoons milk or cream
	2 teaspoons white corn syrup

Work cream cheese with a spoon until very soft. Blend in the cooled melted chocolate and gradually add the sugar, beating until smooth after each addition. Add salt and vanilla, and stir in milk or cream and syrup to give a smooth spreading consistency. Spread on barely cooled cake. Enough for two 8-inch layers.

138   DARK CHOCOLATE FROSTING

¼ cup soft butter	About 3 tablespoons cream or milk
1½ cups sifted XXXX sugar, packed	½ teaspoon vanilla
¼ cup cocoa	

Cream butter until very smooth. Sift sugar and cocoa together and add to butter alternately with cream and vanilla, blending thoroughly. To darken color, place in saucepan and heat over very low heat, stirring constantly, until frosting is dark and glossy—about 5 minutes. Spread on cake immediately. Enough for two 8-inch layers. Also good on éclairs.

139   CHOCOLATE ORANGE FROSTING

2 teaspoons grated orange rind	1½ squares baking chocolate, melted (1124)
¼ cup soft butter	Pinch salt
2 cups sifted XXXX sugar, packed	3 tablespoons orange juice

Combine orange rind and butter and cream until smooth and soft. Add about half the sugar gradually, blending well. Then add cooled melted chocolate and salt, and mix thoroughly. Add remaining sugar alternately with enough orange juice to produce a smooth spreading consistency. Spread on cake. Makes frosting for two 8-inch layers or 24 cupcakes.

140 STRAWBERRY ICING

¼ cup soft butter
3 to 3½ cups sifted XXXX sugar, packed
Pinch of salt

4 tablespoons strained strawberry juice
2 tablespoons cream
Sliced berries

Cream butter until smooth, gradually blend in 3 cups of the sugar and salt, adding strawberry juice and cream from time to time to produce a smooth spreading consistency. Spread on cakes, saving out part of the icing. Add rest of sugar to make the mixture stiff enough to hold its shape. With pastry tube, pipe rosettes on top of cake and garnish with slices of strawberry. Enough icing for two 8-inch layers or 16 small cupcakes.

141 COFFEE FRUIT FROSTING

¼ cup soft butter
2 cups sifted XXXX sugar, packed
3 tablespoons strong coffee
1 to 2 tablespoons cream, or top milk

¼ teaspoon salt
2 tablespoons chopped candied cherries
2 tablespoons sliced blanched pistachios

Cream butter until smooth, then gradually blend in sugar, moistening with the coffee and cream as mixture becomes stiff. Blend in the salt and add cherries and pistachios, stirring until well distributed. Spread between layers and on top and sides of cake. Enough for two 8-inch layers.

142 CONFECTIONERS' FROSTING

1½ cups sifted XXXX sugar, packed
1½ tablespoons boiling water

1 teaspoon butter
½ teaspoon vanilla
1 teaspoon corn syrup

Turn sugar into mixing bowl. Combine boiling water with butter; when melted, add vanilla and syrup. Add to sugar and beat until smooth. Then add more boiling water, drop by drop, to produce spreading consistency. Beat 2 or 3 minutes, until very creamy, keeping sides of bowl scraped down. Spread immediately on warm cake. This frosting is frequently used for coffee cake, buns, doughnuts, and simple cakes.

Strained lemon juice or other fresh fruit juice may be substituted for water and vanilla in the recipe, if desired. Enough for two 8-inch layers.

143   FONDANT FROSTING

Use Fondant (161) that has ripened 3 or 4 days. Place 1 cup fondant in top of double boiler and place over hot water. Very gently work in enough hot water or cream to produce a smooth spreading consistency. Petits Fours and tiny cupcakes are coated with Fondant Frosting by dipping them into the frosting, then turning right-side up. This gives a shiny, perfectly smooth glazed surface.

144   FUDGE FROSTING

Make Chocolate Fudge (154). When fudge becomes stiff after beating, add cream a little at a time, beating in until the candy has a smooth spreading consistency. Spread on cake and let stand until set before cutting.

There are prepared fudge mixes on the market which make very satisfactory fudge frostings when directions on package are followed.

145   SEVEN-MINUTE ICING

1 egg white	¾ cup sugar
⅛ teaspoon cream of tartar	½ teaspoon vanilla
Pinch of salt	1 teaspoon white corn syrup
3 tablespoons cold water	

Put all ingredients, except vanilla, in top of double boiler, over boiling water. Beat with rotary beater for 7 minutes, or with an electric beater for 4 minutes, or until icing is stiff enough to stand in peaks. Remove from heat and add vanilla. If any graininess appears, add a few drops of lemon juice and continue beating until smooth. Spread on cake immediately. Makes enough for sides and top of two 8-inch layers. For a 3-layer cake, double the recipe.

146   LADY BALTIMORE ICING

Make a double recipe of the Seven-Minute Icing (145). Transfer about ⅓ of the icing to another bowl and quickly stir in the following ingredients:

12 maraschino cherries, well drained and chopped	½ cup chopped moist figs
	½ cup chopped pecans

Spread between layers of Lady Baltimore Cake (110). Frost top and sides with rest of plain Seven-Minute Icing. Enough for two 8-inch layers.

147   COCOANUT ICING

Frost cake with Seven-Minute Icing (145) and immediately sprinkle the fresh icing with fresh grated or moist-pack grated cocoanut, being sure to cover sides as well as top of the frosted cake.

Moss Rose Icing: Soak the cocoanut in 3 tablespoons of orange juice mixed with ¼ teaspoon of grated orange rind and 1 teaspoon of sugar. Squeeze moisture out of cocoanut before sprinkling over icing.

148   RASPBERRY ICING

¾ cup sugar	¼ cup raspberry preserves
2 tablespoons water	1 egg white
⅛ teaspoon salt	

Combine all ingredients in top of double boiler. Place over boiling water and beat constantly with rotary beater for 7 minutes or until frosting will stand in stiff peaks. Spread on cake immediately and let stand at least 2 hours before cutting. Enough for 1 Mock Angel Food cake (92) or two 8-inch layers.

149   COCOA FILLING

¼ cup cocoa	1½ cups milk
⅔ cup sugar	1 egg
½ teaspoon salt	1 tablespoon butter
3 tablespoons flour	½ teaspoon vanilla

Blend first 4 ingredients in top of double boiler, add milk and place over boiling water, stirring constantly until sauce thickens; then continue to cook 10 minutes with occasional stirring. Beat egg thoroughly and stir in a little of the hot mixture; then pour this into the rest of the hot sauce and cook 2 minutes longer, stirring all the time. Remove from heat, add butter and vanilla. Cool thoroughly before spreading between layers and on top of cake. Enough for two 8-inch layers.

150   DATE FILLING

1 cup seeded dates, chopped
¾ cup water
⅛ teaspoon salt

2 tablespoons lemon juice
1 tablespoon butter

Cook dates, water and salt in saucepan, stirring constantly until stiff and smooth, about 5 minutes. Add lemon juice and butter, stir well. Cool and spread between layers of cake. Makes filling for a 2-layer cake.

151   LEMON JELLY FILLING

½ cup butter
3 eggs or ⅔ cup egg yolks, beaten
2 cups sugar
2 tablespoons flour

½ cup plus 1 tablespoon strained lemon juice, 3 lemons
½ teaspoon grated lemon rind, packed

Melt butter in top of double boiler. Blend sugar and flour, add eggs and beat well, then stir this into the melted butter. Now stir in lemon juice. Cook OVER gently boiling water, stirring constantly until mixture is thick and clear, from 10 to 12 minutes. Remove from heat and stir in rind. Cool, then pour into a clean jar. Cover and store in refrigerator. Enough to spread between and over top of three 9-inch layers of cake or fills fourteen 3½-inch tarts. Spread 7-Minute Icing over the Filling on the cake, and spread whipped cream over tarts. Or fold whipped cream into the filling before spooning into tart shells. 2½ cups filling.

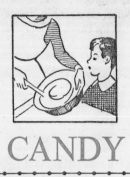

CANDY

THIS chapter is good news for the younger generation, for it not only contains many delicious candy recipes but also the information that under certain circumstances, candy is good for children! So long as it is perfectly wholesome and doesn't interfere with their regular meals, it's safe to give that "sweet tooth" something to work on. As for yourself, Mother—just take a good look in the mirror and make your own decision!

A sweet tooth is something which seems to be born in human beings. Almost everyone likes candy, especially in childhood. There is considerable evidence indicating a physiological reason for the craving for candy which many people, especially children, seem to feel. It is a source of quick energy which is valuable in times of great activity, and since children are almost always active and using up calories at a rapid rate, wholesome candy may be considered to have a real place in their diets.

There is nothing essentially objectionable about candy, if it is made with pure ingredients, is eaten in moderation, so as not to interfere with regular meals, and has some real food value. The ingredients of even the least expensive commercial candies must be pure, to conform to the pure food and drug laws, so there is no danger on this score. But it should be remembered that the habitual eating of even the purest candy is sure to put on pounds in the case of adults, and with children is equally sure to dull the appetite for the foods which they need for growth and health.

For that reason the candy which is eaten by both adults and children should generally have some nutritive value in addition to calories. Candies which consist of pure sugar with a little flavoring, such as plain fondant, should be used sparingly unless combined with fruits or nuts. Candies which contain a good proportion of dried fruits, whose sweetness is provided by natural sugar, are suitable for frequent use, because the dried fruits contain both minerals and vitamins. Between these two extremes are candies containing milk, nuts or fruits, and those made with brown sugar or molasses.

ABOVE—*Peach Upside-Down Cake* (121a), *luscious as it is with fresh peaches, can be an all-season favorite. You can make it with canned peaches, flavorful tart apple slices or with canned pineapple.*

ABOVE—*Nut Bread* (40) *is a tasty quick baking powder loaf. To make it still more intriguing, divide dough in 2 parts, add to one part ⅓ cup moist seedless raisins and ½ square baking chocolate, melted. Spread in layers in baking pan for an attractive Ribbon Loaf.*

This luscious streusel-flecked warm Plum Kuchen can play a double role with encores: (1) Serve warm with coffee for dessert. (2) A breakfast bread, doubling for both fruit and cereal.

Holiday time calls for lots of cookies, and all these tender fragile beauties are made from the same Butter Cookie Dough (221). Variety comes from the use of an assortment of various shaped cutters and different garnishes: Shaved toasted almonds, sliced candied cherries, chocolate shot, rock sugar crystals and tiny decorative candies were used to decorate these cookies.

This is a HOW-TO-DO-IT picture of Chocolate Pinwheel Cookies. Two kinds of dough—chocolate and plain cookie dough—are rolled out into rectangle shapes, then one rectangle of dough is carefully laid on top of the other, then both are carefully rolled up like a jelly roll. The roll then is wrapped neatly in waxed paper and chilled in refrigerator until firm enough to slice without misshaping the roll. A sharp, thin-bladed knife is required to slice cookies of uniform thickness. The cookies are then placed on baking sheet to bake like any other butter cookies.

These ingredients contain valuable nutrients as well as calories. This in-between group includes fudge, caramels, panocha, fondant bonbons with fruit or nut centers, and dried fruits stuffed with fondant.

In normal health, sugar is easily and quickly digested and assimilated. But it should be remembered that white sugar contains no protein, minerals or vitamins—only calories. Two scant tablespoons of sugar yield 100 calories. So candy should never take the place of *any* foods listed in the diet pattern (see page 3), but should be used only for extra fuel or energy value. In general, it is well to eat candy only at the end of a meal.

HINTS ON MAKING CANDY AT HOME

Choose a clear, dry day for making candy. An excess of humidity in the atmosphere will cause trouble with almost any kind of candy. So may excessively hot weather. This is especially true with products such as caramels and toffee, and with dipped chocolates.

In making all kinds of candy, a candy thermometer is a very valuable piece of equipment. Although there are traditional home tests for "doneness," involving dropping small amounts of the hot syrup into cold water and noting its behavior, the only way to be sure of getting identical results every time is to use a candy thermometer in addition to the cold water test. If the altitude of your locality is not more than 1000 feet above sea level, fudge cooked to 234° F.—the "soft ball stage" will always react to cooling and beating by becoming firm; and there will be no question about when it has reached that point, if a reliable candy thermometer is used, if the bulb is well below the surface of the boiling syrup, and if the reading is taken at eye level. See Table 22 "Cooking Temperatures for Candy," page 599.

Crystalline candies such as fudge and panocha require special handling. In all kinds of candy, sugar crystals should not be permitted to form on the sides of the pan, but should be wiped down with a damp cloth wrapped around the tines of a fork. This helps to prevent premature crystallization. To avoid graininess in candy, pour the hot syrup into a clean pan or bowl immediately on removal from the heat, with no scraping whatever. Then candy should be cooled sufficiently to hold pan on palm of hand without discomfort before it is beaten. Cooling may be hastened by setting the pan in a bowl of cold water, but no stirring should be done until it is cooled. After cooling, continuous beating will produce the very small crystals which give "velvetiness" to the candy.

Non-crystalline candies, such as caramels, should not be beaten except for stirring in the flavoring after removal from heat; then they should be poured directly into a buttered pan to become firm.

Flavoring of any kind should be added to candy at the end of cooking. This is because all flavorings are volatile and heat dissipates them rapidly.

With crystalline candies, the flavoring may be added after the candy is cooled and just before beating begins. Since flavoring is added to noncrystalline candies immediately after they are taken from the heat and while still hot, slightly more flavoring is used to compensate for the effect of the heat.

Nuts that are added to candy should be fresh and of good quality. Stale or withered nuts will spoil the flavor of any candy and defeat all your care to make it good.

Candy that is stored for any time or candy intended for a gift, should have each piece wrapped separately. Not only does this prevent pieces from sticking together, but it keeps them fresh and prevents drying out. Use a good grade of waxed paper (thin waxed paper may stick to the candy and make it difficult to eat) or moistureproof cellophane. Remember that ordinary cellophane used for wrapping gift packages is not moistureproof and will stick to candy.

152 CANDIED APPLES*

2½ lbs. Jonathan or Northern Spy apples

7 cups sugar
½ cup white corn syrup

Use very firm apples. Pare thinly, quarter, remove cores and cut quarters into ½-inch slices. Put fruit into 3-qt. saucepan and immediately barely cover with boiling water. Place over heat and as soon as water starts to boil, note time and boil EXACTLY 3 minutes. Drain, saving water. Now make syrup using 2 cups of drained off liquid and 2½ cups sugar. Heat syrup, and as soon as sugar is dissolved, add drained apples and again bring just to boil, because longer boiling tends to soften fruit. Now turn fruit and syrup into a clean glass or enamelware bowl and let stand uncovered 24 hours. Again drain syrup from fruit, and add ½ cup sugar and ½ cup white corn syrup to it and place over heat just long enough for sugar to dissolve, then return fruit to syrup and again heat just to boiling point. Then return syrup and fruit back to bowl and let stand uncovered another 24 hours. Again drain off syrup, add 1 cup sugar and heat until just dissolved, then return fruit to syrup and heat just to boiling, then return fruit and syrup back to bowl to stand 24 hours. Repeat draining and adding 1 cup of sugar, heating just to boiling, and letting stand 24 hours 3 more times. The fruit should stand in the syrup the last time for about a week, and at this time the syrup should be as thick as honey. Now drain fruit in a wire basket or colander, and after it drains well, dip basket or colander with fruit in it for a few seconds in gently boiling water to remove excess syrup. Now lay pieces of fruit on waxed paper to drain and dry.

After draining and drying 3 or 4 days, glaze fruit by dipping it in a hot syrup made by boiling 2½ cups sugar and ¾ cup water for 3 or 4 minutes. Then place pieces on clean waxed paper to harden. This glazing produces a non-sticky product. The leftover syrup may be used on pancakes or waffles.

°This method of candying fruit was developed by the New York State College of Agriculture at Cornell University and the N. Y. Experimental Station at Geneva.

153   CANDIED ORANGE AND GRAPEFRUIT PEEL

Prepare orange or grapefruit peel by pulling out all dividing membranes, and cutting into strips about ¼-inch wide. For a mild-flavored peel, thick-skinned oranges and grapefruit should be chosen. For a bitter-flavored peel, preferred by some people, choose thin-skinned fruit, or cut away the inner white portion of the rind. Cover the peel with cold water, bring to a boil, and drain. Repeat this, using fresh water each time, 4 times for orange peel and 6 times for grapefruit, or until peel is only slightly bitter. After last draining, add to the peel about an equal amount of granulated sugar. Place over low heat and gently toss around until the sugar is dissolved, then continue simmering until syrup reaches the soft ball stage (238° F.). Now turn into strainer to drain thoroughly, then roll each piece in granulated sugar. Spread on a plate to cool and dry. Store in a covered metal box.

154   CHOCOLATE FUDGE

2 squares baking chocolate	¼ teaspoon salt
2 cups sugar	2 tablespoons butter
1 cup milk	1 teaspoon vanilla
1 teaspoon white corn syrup	½ to 1 cup chopped nuts

Cut or break chocolate into small pieces, put into 3-qt. saucepan with sugar, milk, corn syrup, salt, and butter; stir until well mixed, and place over direct heat. Cook with occasional stirring to a soft ball (234° F.), being sure to remove the pan from the heat while making the test in cold water. When done, remove from heat, place in pan of cold water, and cool without further stirring or shaking of pan. When cool enough so hand may be held on bottom of pan comfortably, add vanilla and beat fudge vigorously until it begins to stiffen and loses its shine. Stir in nuts. Turn out into a buttered 8-inch square pan, pressing into a uniform layer. Mark in squares and cool thoroughly. 1¼ pounds.

155   MEXICAN ORANGE CANDY

1 cup sugar	1 cup evaporated milk
¼ cup boiling water	1 teaspoon grated orange rind
2 cups sugar	1 cup chopped nuts
Pinch salt	

Caramelize 1 cup sugar to a rich amber color (1121); add boiling water and boil, stirring occasionally until caramel is entirely dissolved. Turn into 3-qt. saucepan, add next 3 ingredients and cook to soft ball (236° F.). Just before candy is done, add orange rind. Remove from heat and cool as for Chocolate Fudge (154). Beat until candy begins to stiffen; then stir in nuts and drop from teaspoon onto buttered waxed paper. 1¾ pounds.

156   PANOCHA

1¾ cups brown sugar, packed	¾ cup evaporated milk
Few grains salt	¼ cup water
1 tablespoon corn syrup	1 teaspoon vanilla
1 tablespoon butter	⅔ cup chopped nuts

Combine first 6 ingredients in 3-qt. saucepan and cook to a soft ball (234° F.), stirring constantly. Cool and beat as for Chocolate Fudge (154), adding vanilla and nuts just before turning into buttered pan. 1⅛ pounds.

157   PLAIN CARAMELS

2 cups granulated sugar	2 cups evaporated milk
Dash salt	1 teaspoon vanilla or
2 cups white corn syrup	2 tablespoons rum flavoring
½ cup butter	

Put sugar, salt and corn syrup into 3-qt. heavy saucepan, bring to boil, and boil to a firm ball (245° F.), stirring occasionally. Gradually add the butter and milk, so slowly that mixture does not stop boiling at any time; continue to cook rapidly, with constant stirring, to a medium ball (242° F.). The candy sticks and scorches easily toward the last, so be careful about stirring. Remove from heat, add flavoring, and stir well; then pour into a buttered 9-inch square baking pan. Cool thoroughly before cutting. When cold, turn out onto a molding board covered with waxed paper and cut with a sharp, heavy knife, using a sawing motion. Wrap in waxed paper or in moisture-proof cellophane (ordinary cellophane will stick). 2 pounds.

Note: Use thin cream in place of evaporated milk, if desired.

158   CHOCOLATE CARAMELS

Add 3 squares baking chocolate to Plain Caramels (157). Melt the chocolate over hot water in saucepan in which candy is to be cooked; then add sugar, salt and corn syrup, and proceed as for Plain Caramels.

159   NUT CARAMELS

Just before pouring Plain Caramels (157) into pan, add ½ cup coarsely chopped pecans or walnuts.

160   DIVINITY

1 cup sugar	⅔ cup white corn syrup
½ cup water	¼ teaspoon salt
⅛ teaspoon cream of tartar	¼ cup water
3 egg whites	1 teaspoon vanilla
2 cups sugar	1 cup nuts

Put the 1 cup sugar, ½ cup water and cream of tartar into saucepan; stir to blend, then boil rapidly without stirring to 240° F., or until syrup will spin a thread 6 inches long when dropped from a metal spoon. Immediately remove from heat. Meanwhile beat egg whites until stiff. In another saucepan, have combined the 2 cups sugar, corn syrup, salt and ¼ cup water. When the first mixture is done, place the second mixture over the heat and boil with occasional stirring until syrup reaches 280° F. (medium crack stage). Meanwhile, pour the first syrup while hot over egg whites, adding slowly and beating continuously until stiff and smooth. Set aside until second syrup is done. Cool a minute or two, then pour it slowly over first mixture, continuing to beat until smooth and so stiff that it is hard to handle. Add flavoring and nuts, turn into buttered pan, and press out smooth. When set, cut into squares. Makes about 2 pounds.

Candied fruits, such as cherries and pineapple, may be cut fine and folded in for attractive color.

161   PLAIN FONDANT

3 cups sugar	1½ cups boiling water
⅓ teaspoon cream of tartar	

Put all ingredients into a 3-qt. saucepan and stir until sugar dissolves. Then bring to boil and boil briskly, without stirring, to soft ball stage (238° F.), or about 20 minutes. Have a wet cloth wrapped around the tines of a fork to wipe down any crystals that form around the sides of the pan while cooking. Remove from heat, cool just until bubbles disappear, and pour into a large shallow platter. *Do not* scrape the pan. Place the platter on cake rack, so syrup may cool from bottom as well as top; and cool until platter can be held on the palm of hand with comfort. Then beat with a wooden spoon until the mass loses its stickiness, becomes firm enough to handle and has a creamy appearance. Gather up in hands and knead until free from lumps and plastic. Place in a clean jar and cover, first with a damp cloth and then with lid of the jar. Let stand at least 24 hours to ripen before using. It will keep for weeks in the refrigerator if tightly covered. 1¼ pounds.

To melt fondant: If coloring is used, be careful to keep it very delicate. Both color and flavor may be kneaded into the cold fondant. Place 1 cup of the colored, flavored fondant in top of a double boiler and set over hot, not boiling, water. Turn the mass over occasionally, but do not stir as stirring starts crystallization. When lumps of solid fondant have disappeared and the candy has the consistency of corn syrup, it is ready for dipping bonbon centers or petits fours.

162   PEANUT BRITTLE

2 cups sugar	⅟₁₆ teaspoon salt
1 cup water	½ lb. shelled peanuts

Measure sugar, water and salt into a 3-qt. saucepan and stir until sugar is dissolved. Bring to boil, cover tightly and boil 3 minutes; remove cover and continue cooking until syrup takes on a rich caramel color (320° F.). Have peanuts spread out on a buttered shallow pan. Pour caramel syrup over the peanuts and let cool thoroughly before breaking in pieces. About 1½ pounds.

163   TAFFY (Swedish Style)

3⅓ cups granulated sugar	1 teaspoon peppermint extract
1⅓ cups cold water	Few drops red vegetable coloring
1 tablespoon vinegar	

Put sugar, water and vinegar into a 3-quart saucepan. Stir until sugar is partly dissolved, then wipe sides down with a damp cloth to remove any crystals. Heat rapidly to boiling and cook briskly without any stirring to 270° F. (soft crack stage). Immediately pour onto a lightly buttered marble slab, shallow platter or shallow enamel pan, reserving ½ cup. To the ½ cup add enough red coloring to give a red raspberry color. Pour this into a lightly buttered saucer and place over a pan of warm water to keep slightly soft; allow only a second or two for coloring it. Just as soon as the edges of the uncolored syrup begin to stiffen, draw the edges toward the center, using the buttered tines of a fork. As soon as candy is cool enough to be handled, add the peppermint extract and begin pulling with hands. While the candy is still hot, put it down frequently and butter the hands. Continue pulling candy until it is snowy white and fluffy in appearance. Lay candy down on slab and pull out into a piece of even thickness, about 18 inches long. Transfer the colored candy to a buttered platter or to the slab; divide into 4 equal portions, and draw each one out into a strip as long as the uncolored piece. Quickly press 2 of the strips into the surface of the uncolored candy; turn over and press the other 2 into the other side. Now draw out the whole piece about 6 feet long so it is of uniform thickness. With a pair of buttered kitchen shears, cut quickly into 1-inch pieces resembling puffy striped pillows. Let stand on buttered slab until hardened, then wrap in waxed paper or moistureproof cellophane squares, twisting ends together. 1½ pounds.

164   OLD-FASHIONED CANDIED FRUIT ROLL

½ lb. seedless raisins
¼ lb. dried figs
¼ lb. dried apricots
½ lb. dates
¼ lb. candied pineapple
½ lb. moist cocoanut

½ lb. pecans or walnuts
3 tablespoons butter, melted
2 cups sugar
¾ cup water
3 tablespoons vinegar

Wash raisins, figs and apricots and shake in a cloth to remove excess moisture. Remove seeds from dates and combine with washed fruits, pineapple and cocoanut. Put fruit-cocoanut mixture through a food grinder, using the coarse blade. Combine ground mixture with coarsely chopped nuts and spread out on a flat pan which has been spread with the melted butter. Put sugar, water and vinegar into 3-qt. saucepan, mix well, and wipe down sugar from sides of pan. Now boil without stirring to a soft ball (234° F.). Remove from heat and pour over the fruit. (Do not scrape any syrup out of the pan.) Let cool, then knead the mixture until well mixed. Form into two rolls about 2 inches in diameter. Wrap in waxed paper or a dampened, clean cloth and place in refrigerator for about 3 hours or until it slices well. Cut in ¼-inch slices. 3½ pounds.

165   PEANUT BUTTER PINWHEELS

1 egg white	2 cups sifted XXXX sugar,
½ teaspoon grated orange rind	packed
2 teaspoons lemon juice	2 tablespoons XXXX sugar
Pinch salt	¼ cup soft peanut butter

Beat egg white until stiff, then stir in orange rind, lemon juice, salt and 2 cups sugar until well blended. Sprinkle the 2 tablespoons sugar over a piece of waxed paper, and turn the mixture out onto this. Using a rolling pin rubbed with more sugar, roll out about ⅛-inch thick. Carefully spread the peanut butter over this sheet like jelly on a jelly roll. Roll the sheet up carefully like a jelly roll, and wrap it in the waxed paper. Lay the wrapped roll on a piece of cardboard to keep it straight and chill in the refrigerator. After 1 hour, transfer to a covered candy box. When ready to serve, cut in slices about ¼-inch thick. About ¾ pound.

166   POTATO KISSES

⅔ cup hot mashed potato	1 teaspoon vanilla
2 teaspoons butter, melted	Few grains salt
1 lb. XXXX sugar, sifted	½ lb. moist cocoanut
2½ tablespoons cocoa *or*	
1½ squares chocolate	

Put hot potatoes through a ricer to remove all lumps, then beat in melted butter. Put potatoes in a mixing bowl, add sugar and beat until thoroughly blended. Add cocoa, or melted chocolate which has been cooled, and beat thoroughly. Mix in vanilla, salt and cocoanut. Drop by teaspoons onto waxed paper. Keep the mounds of candy rather regular in shape and size. Place in refrigerator or other cool place for a short time to harden. Hardened candy should be kept in a tightly covered container. About 1½ pounds.

CEREALS

* * * * * * * * *

WHEN the word "cereal" is used, most Americans promptly think of breakfast foods; but properly speaking, any food made principally from cereal grains or flour is a cereal food. Thus spaghetti, rice and even popcorn are really cereals, just like your favorite packaged breakfast food.

* * * * * * * * *

All cereals are an inexpensive source of energy as they are composed chiefly of the carbohydrate—starch. All of them contain appreciable amounts of protein, some more than others. For example, 1 cup of cooked rolled oats contains 5.4 grams of protein, while 1 cup of cooked corn meal mush contains 2.6 grams, and 1 cup cooked rice contains 4.2 grams protein. The most important difference, however, is in the amount of vitamins and minerals they contain.

Whole grains, taken as a group, in their natural unrefined state are significant sources of the B vitamins, thiamine, riboflavin and niacin, and they also contain some phosphorus, copper and iron. These vitamins and minerals are concentrated in the embryo, (or germ) and in the outer covering of the grain—both of these parts are removed when the grain is refined. For this reason, refined cereals contain practically no vitamins or minerals, therefore, they are of little nutritive value except as a source of energy. Fortunately few of these cereals are now on the market.

In cooperation with the National Nutritional Program, leading manufacturers are making a contribution to better nutrition by "RESTORING" or "ENRICHING" processed or refined cereals, and it is done by these methods:

1.   A cereal is "RESTORED" by adding to it enough thiamine, niacin and iron to replace what is removed in the refining process.

2.   A cereal is "ENRICHED" by adding vitamins NOT naturally found in the grains, such as vitamin D, or the nutrients may be added in larger amounts than are found naturally in the grains.

Then there are whole grain cereals which are prepared without refining—they are preferred by many because of their natural color and flavor, and their interesting texture. The best known of the whole grain breakfast cereals are Rolled Oats, Rolled Wheat and Cracked Wheat. Also a few ready-to-eat cereals are made of the whole grains, as you can readily discover by reading the labels.

BREAKFAST CEREALS

There are 2 kinds of breakfast cereals—those that must be cooked and the ready-to-eat. The 5 types that must be cooked are FARINA, BROWN GRANULAR WHEAT CEREAL, ROLLED OATS, ROLLED WHEAT AND WHEAT-OAT CEREAL. They may be either type, quick-cooking or regular cooking.

There are 3 reasons for cooking cereal: (1) To improve flavor. (2) To improve digestibility. (3) To soften the cellulose which improves the texture. In cooking, the starch granules, which are of different sizes and shapes in different cereal plants, absorb water and become greatly enlarged. That is why cereal increases so much in bulk during cooking, and unless the cereal is cooked in sufficient water, the starch granules will not swell completely, and the cereal will not thicken like it should as it cooks.

The flavor of cereal is developed to the highest point when the starch grains swell to maximum size and the cellulose is softened just enough to make the texture pleasing. Longer cooking does not make the cereal more digestible, nor does it improve the flavor. Research also indicates that cereals cooked until the starch swells to its fullest and the cellulose softens sufficiently retain more thiamine than cereals that are cooked longer.

Cooking directions on modern cereal packages specify the cooking time which makes the product most enjoyable for eating and conserving thiamine. The cooking time for cooking the regular or old-fashioned type and the quick-cooking type cereals, of course differs. The quick-cooking cereals have been processed by various methods so only a few minutes of cooking is all that is needed. Some of the processes which make a cereal quick-cooking include further grinding or cutting, a special steam cooking, and in some instances, the addition of disodium phosphate. This disodium phosphate converts the cooking water to the alkaline side, which causes the starch granules to gelatinize more quickly.

167   GENERAL DIRECTIONS FOR COOKING CEREALS

It is well to become familiar with directions on cereal packages. They have been tested to produce the best possible product. The points to be remembered for the general cooking of all cereals are as follows:
(1) Measure the water and salt accurately.

(2) Heat the water to boiling point before adding cereal and salt.
(3) Measure cereal accurately by letting the cereal flow from package into cup, then level off with knife or spatula.
(4) Sprinkle the cereal from the cup slowly but steadily into the boiling water so boiling does not stop, and stir constantly while adding the cereal.
(5) Continue to stir cereal while it thickens to keep it from sticking to the pan.
(6) Now reduce heat and cook the specified time, according to directions on package; or cook the cereal from this point in a double boiler. Many cereals cook in a surprisingly short time.

168   HOW TO COOK BREAKFAST CEREAL
(*Rolled Oats or Rolled Wheat*)

3 cups boiling water   1½ cups rolled cereal
¾ teaspoon salt

169   GRANULAR CEREALS
(*Corn Meal and Farina*)

5 cups boiling water   1 teaspoon salt
1 cup cereal

DIRECT HEAT METHOD: To the measured amount of rapidly boiling salted water, slowly but steadily sprinkle in the measured cereal, stirring constantly. Now reduce heat and cook over direct heat, with frequent stirring, from 15 to 20 minutes. This method requires more attention than the double boiler method. Serves 4.

DOUBLE BOILER METHOD: (Direct Heat With Completion In Double Boiler.) Fill lower part of double boiler ⅓ full of water and heat to boiling. Place upper part of double boiler with the measured amount of boiling water and salt over direct heat, then heat to boiling point. Now slowly but steadily sprinkle the cereal into the water, stirring constantly. Cook over direct heat with constant stirring until cereal begins to thicken, then place over lower part of double boiler and cook for the time specified on the package, which ranges from 15 to 30 minutes, depending on the particular cereal.

There is no point in cooking cereals in a PRESSURE SAUCEPAN. The reason is that most cereals bought now belong to the quick-cooking variety, and pressure cooking has no advantage. And modern methods of cooking cereals have been so simplified that cooking the cereals by the DIRECT HEAT or DOUBLE BOILER methods takes less time than putting the cereal into the pressure saucepan and obtaining the required pressure.

REHEATING CEREALS

Reheating cereals seldom is necessary. It is easy to prepare just the amount of cooked cereal that will be consumed. And the packages of ready-to-eat cereals are sized to be suitable for any family so that re-crisping should be unnecessary. If reheating, however, is necessary, here are the ways to reheat cooked cereals such as FARINA, ROLLED OATS, ETC.:

(1)   Place cereal in saucepan and add a small amount of milk or water. Cook over low heat, stirring to prevent scorching. The amount of liquid to be added will depend upon the thickness of the cold cereal and the consistency desired when ready to serve.

(2)   Put cereal into top of double boiler, add a small amount of milk or water, cover and place over boiling water and cook without stirring until thoroughly heated.

When READY-TO-EAT cereals lose their freshness and crispness due to high humidity, freshen them in the following way:

(1)   Put cereal onto a cookie sheet, spread out evenly and place in a hot oven (425 to 450° F.) for only 2 or 3 minutes. On cooling, the cereal is fresh and crisp. Never put the package into the oven.

(2)   Pour the cereal into a shallow saucepan and place over low heat, stirring constantly for just a few minutes.

USES OF LEFTOVER CEREALS

Leftover cooked cereals may be used to make puddings, Polenta, Scrapple, Fried Cereal Slices such as corn meal mush. Small amounts of leftover ready-to-eat cereals may be mixed and served for an interesting new combination. Crushed ready-to-eat cereals tossed in melted butter make attractive and tasty casserole toppings instead of bread crumbs. Such cereal crumbs also make excellent coatings for croquettes, cutlets, fish or vegetable.

To reheated or freshly cooked granular cereals, fold in chopped moist cooked ham, chicken or pork. Heat thoroughly, then pour into loaf pans to become firm. Slice and fry just like Fried Mush.

SERVING SUGGESTIONS

Both hot and ready-to-eat cereals respond to a bit of edible garnish.

FOR HOT CEREAL:

(1)   Add thinly sliced or chopped moist dried apricots, moist dates, moist dried figs, prunes or raisins to the hot cereal the last few minutes of cooking.

(2)   Drop a teaspoon or so of bright red jelly or strawberry preserves into the center of light farina to replace the sugar.

(3)   Add a few tablespoons of honey or molasses to cereal the last few minutes of cooking for appealing new flavor.

(4)   Serve cereal with Vanilla Eggnog.

FOR READY-TO-EAT CEREAL:

(1)   Serve enough fresh fruits such as sliced peaches, raspberries and strawberries over the cereal to combine the breakfast fruit and the cereal.

(2)   Serve the cereal around a handsome baked apple.

(3)   Heat bite-size shredded wheat in a shallow pan with melted butter drizzled over it, then sprinkled with moist brown sugar. Heat in a moderate oven (375° F.) a few minutes.

(4)   Dip shredded wheat quickly in boiling salted water, remove from water and drain, then serve at once with hot or cold milk.

170   CRACKED WHEAT

1 cup cereal   1 teaspoon salt
4 cups boiling water

Cook according to General Directions (167). Various combinations of standard cereals are good for variety. To combine rolled oats and cracked wheat, use one-half the quantity suggested for each, that is: 1 cup rolled oats and ½ cup cracked wheat in 4 cups boiling water.

MACARONI, SPAGHETTI, NOODLES

Macaroni and spaghetti are made from durum wheat which is not only rich in protein but also in starch. In refining the wheat to produce the semolina, from which the macaroni and spaghetti are made, there is loss of minerals and vitamins. But manufacturers of macaroni and spaghetti do not consider it practical to enrich their products because the enrichment would be dissolved and lost in the cooking water. Sometimes dry spinach powder is added to spaghetti. This adds an attractive green color and increases the vitamin and mineral value.

Noodles are made from durum wheat flour and from hard wheat flour. They are enriched with egg, and sometimes have dried spinach powder added to them.

These cereal foods are used in the American diet chiefly as an alternate for potatoes. Although of less nutritive value than potatoes, they are usually served in combination with foods such as cheese, eggs, meat and tomato sauce, and the like—which, in combination with their carbohydrate and protein content make them highly nutritious and popular dishes.

All of these cereal foods require rapid cooking in a large amount of boiling water. They swell considerably—2 to 4 times in quantity, so 8 ounces of macaroni, spaghetti or noodles is usually sufficient to serve five. All of these foods should be cooked by dropping steadily into actively boiling salted water so boiling does not stop at any time. They should be cooked only until just tender—and no longer. The cooking time varies considerably, depending on the brand, and they should be drained as soon as tender. Rinsing is unnecessary except when macaroni is used in salads.

171   COOKING MACARONI, SPAGHETTI AND NOODLES

For a 7 or 8-ounce package, measure 3 quarts water into a 4-qt. saucepan, add 3 teaspoons salt and bring to a rapid boil, then drop in macaroni, spaghetti or noodles (left whole or broken into short lengths). Cook rapidly until tender. Time ranges from 8 to 10 minutes for noodles; 12 to 17 minutes for spaghetti; 7 to 20 minutes for macaroni. Different brands of all 3 products require different cooking times. Follow directions on package if any are given, or test frequently for tenderness by removing a little piece with a fork and tasting for raw starch. None of these products should be overcooked to a point where they are broken up and mushy. When done, drain in a colander. Rinse if desired by letting hot water run through it for a minute, then again drain thoroughly.

To serve buttered as an alternate for potatoes, add melted butter and toss until each piece is coated, allowing about ⅓ cup butter to a 7-ounce package.

To keep spaghetti strands whole, put ends into boiling water first, then as they soften, press rest of strands down into water.

172   FRIED CORN MEAL MUSH OR FARINA

Cook corn meal as directed (169). Pour the mush into a greased loaf pan or baking powder cans and cool thoroughly. Then cover and store in refrigerator for a day or two, if desired. When ready to cook, remove mush from the mold and cut into ¼ to ½-inch thick slices. The thinner the slice, the crisper will be the finished product. Dip slices in corn meal or flour. Have heated 1 to 2 tablespoons bacon fat or shortening in a heavy skillet. Lay in slices and pan-fry moderately fast until crisp and brown on both sides. Serve hot with butter and syrup (924) or jelly.

Note: Corn Meal Mush is delicious fried in butter, but a lower temperature and longer cooking time is required.

172a   POPPY SEED NOODLES

Drain fresh-cooked noodles quickly. Then turn into a heated bowl and drizzle with enough melted butter, or warmed sour cream, that when tossed gently, noodles will be thinly coated. Now sprinkle with poppy seed to add an interesting crunchiness and pleasing flavor. Serve at once.

173   SAUTÉED NOODLES

8-oz. package noodles   2 to 3 tablespoons bacon
                                       fat or butter

Cook noodles in plenty of boiling salted water until tender, about 8 minutes. Drain well. Heat fat in a skillet, add noodles and sauté, turning frequently until delicately browned. 5 to 7 servings.

173a   FRENCH-FRIED CRISP NOODLES

2 cups fine noodles (4 oz.)   2 tablespoons salt
2 quarts boiling water   Deep fat for frying

Drop noodles into the rapidly boiling water to which salt has been added. Cook briskly for 5 minutes, then drain noodles in colander and rinse by running hot water through them. Spread noodles out loosely on waxed paper or paper toweling and cover lightly with cheesecloth. Let stand several hours or until dried off but not hard. Or spread the noodles on a baking sheet and dry off for about 30 minutes in a slow oven (300-325° F.). Fry noodles a few at a time in a fine-meshed frying basket, in deep fat heated to 360° F., until they are a delicate golden brown. Lift out and drain thoroughly on paper toweling. Sprinkle with salt. Serve with chop suey, veal à la king, creamed fish, etc. 5 servings.

RICE

The FIRST STEP in the milling of rice is the removal of the husk or hull. This leaves natural brown rice—A GOOD SOURCE OF THIAMINE (B_1).

The SECOND STEP grinds away the outer layer of the grains and removes the "embryo." This leaves white polished rice. The by-products of this process are—RICE BRAN or RICE POLISHINGS—AND THEY CONTAIN THE VITAMINS AND MINERALS.

In the polishing process, some of the grains are broken, so the THIRD STEP is "screening". This removes the broken grains, as well as any foreign seeds and defective grains, leaving only the LONG GRAINS OF RICE. Years ago these grains were given a coating of talc or glucose. This coating is what made it necessary to wash the rice until the water was clear. Now with the discontinuance of this coating, it is unnecessary to wash rice. Many brands suggest *NOT TO WASH*, but a few RECOMMEND WASHING.

Converted Rice is a recent development. The UNHULLED RICE is first cleaned, then steeped in hot, circulating water 2 or 3 hours, time depending on variety of rice. The water is then drained off and the rice is steamed, then drained in a vacuum until a moisture content of 15% is attained. The last drying is done at atmospheric pressure, or air pressure at sea level. Now the rice is cooled by forcing air through the bins for about 8 hours, or until the moisture is equalized through the grains. Now the rice is ready to be milled in the usual way, by shelling, hulling and cleaning on a "pearling cone". By this process much smaller amounts of BRAN are removed, than from polished rice, and the final color of this rice is CREAMY, instead of PURE WHITE.

When CONVERTED RICE grains are examined under polarized light, they show the outer layer of starch to be gelatinized. These grains are much harder than UNCONVERTED RICE. When converted rice is cooked, it is practically as white as uncoverted rice. There are 3 modern methods of cooking CONVERTED OR UNCONVERTED RICE, which are as follows:

1. DOUBLE BOILER METHOD
2. DIRECT HEAT METHOD
3. BOILING METHOD

The first 2 methods give uniformly tender, fluffy grains of rice which stand apart—THESE 2 METHODS CONSERVE THE FOOD VALUE. The BOILING METHOD is the quickest, but it requires draining—THIS WASTES FOOD VALUE. After draining, the rice must be put in a colander over steam to fluff up.

174   THREE WAYS TO COOK RICE

(1) The oldest method which is still used to some extent is wasteful of food value. It is done by dropping 1 cup rice into 2 or 3 quarts of rapidly boiling salted water, then boiled rapidly uncovered until rice is just tender. Considerable water remains on the rice to be drained off and the wet rice left in the sieve is then placed over steam to dry off and become fluffy. Cooking takes from 15 to 22 minutes, time depending on rice.

(2) One cup of rice is dropped into 2¼ cups water with 1 teaspoon salt. Saucepan is covered tightly and placed over low heat to simmer about 25 minutes, or until tender. At the end of cooking, all the water is absorbed and rice is fluffy.

(3) One cup of rice is put into top of double boiler with 2½ cups boiling water and 1 teaspoon salt, then covered and placed over

boiling water to cook until tender, from 35 to 40 minutes. At the end of cooking, all water is absorbed and rice is dry and fluffy.

To make rice snowy-white, add 1 teaspoon lemon juice or ¼ teaspoon cream of tartar to the cooking water. One cup rice swells in cooking to make from 3 to 4 cups cooked rice.

175   RICE COOKED IN MILK

1 cup rice   1 teaspoon salt
3 cups scalded milk

Wash rice thoroughly in cold water. Place rice, milk and salt in top of double boiler and cook over boiling water about 40 minutes, or until rice is soft and all milk absorbed. This method of cooking rice is especially desirable for breakfast cereal for small children. 5 servings.

176   TOASTED RICE

4 cups cooked rice   ½ cup evaporated milk
1 egg   3 tablespoons butter

Cook rice by Methods (1) or (2). Beat egg, add milk and combine with rice. Return to heat and cook about 3 minutes, stirring constantly. Turn into a loaf pan lined with waxed paper and chill. When ready to serve, turn out of pan, strip off paper and slice about ½-inch thick. Pan-fry in butter until lightly browned on each side. 5 servings.

176a   POPPED CORN

1 cup fresh popcorn   ⅓ to ½ cup butter
¼ cup lard or vegetable   Salt to taste
  shortening

Pop ⅙ to ¼ cup of the corn at one time, the amount depending on the size of the container used for popping. If an old-fashioned wire popper is used, put in enough corn barely to cover the bottom. Shake slowly over moderately hot heat until corn starts popping; then shake faster until all the corn is popped. If a heavy kettle, skillet or metal popper, electric or not, is used, melt in the pan or popper 1 tablespoon of the lard for each ¼ cup corn. When hot, add corn, cover, and place over moderate heat. Shake the pan, or turn the crank of the popper until corn stops popping. Pour popped corn into a large bowl and pour melted butter over it, allowing about 2 tablespoons butter for each ¼ cup of corn used. Mix thoroughly and sprinkle generously with salt, tossing to distribute it. 5 to 6 servings.

Note: If dried out popcorn pops to only ⅓ the normal yield for the variety, add 2½ tablespoons water to 1 lb. shelled corn in a quart jar, then seal, and let stand 3 or 4 weeks. If yield is only ⅔ normal, add 1 tablespoon water to 1 lb. corn. This restores the corn to about its normal moisture content.

176b POLENTA
(An inexpensive, hearty Mexican 1-dish meal)

1 qt. boiling water	2 tablespoons milk
1 teaspoon salt	½ cup corn meal
1 cup yellow corn meal	½ cup shortening
1 cup fresh-grated Parmesan cheese	

Measure water into top of double boiler, add salt and slowly sift in the 1 cup of meal, stirring constantly to keep smooth. Cover, place over gently boiling water and cook 1 hour, stirring often. Now remove from heat and stir in cheese until melted. Pour immediately into 2 greased 9-inch cake or pie pans. Cool until firm enough to cut. Just before serving, cut into pie-shaped pieces; dip pieces in milk, then in corn meal to coat. Heat shortening in a heavy skillet until hot but not smoking, lay in Polenta and fry until brown and crisp, about 10 minutes on each side. Serve plain with crisp bacon or Tomato Sauce. 4 servings.

CHEESE

* * * * * * * *

ONE time when it doesn't matter much whether you're a mouse or a man is when cheese is served! Because a taste for cheese is something that most men have in common with all mice. Cheese is such a valuable food that the taste is one that should be encouraged by the homemaker, and the recipes in this chapter provide practical encouragement.

* * * * * * * *

Cheese is one of the most valuable of our foods. Besides being full of flavor which blends well with a great variety of other foods, it is very high in food value. Four ounces of American cheese contain almost the same amount of high-quality protein and of calcium as a full quart of whole milk.

The reason for this high food value is, of course, that cheese contains the solid parts of milk, including all its protein and minerals. In the cheese making process there is some loss in the vitamins of milk but ordinary American cheese is a better source of vitamin A than is milk.

The character of cheese, in both texture and flavor, depends to a considerable degree on its age as well as on its variety. Very young cheeses, such as cottage cheese and cream cheese, are very bland in flavor and very soft. These two types are both sour milk cheeses, which are not cured and are eaten as soon as they are produced. Most cured cheeses are aged, from a few weeks to several years, before they reach their full flavor. In general, the longer they are aged the sharper is their flavor and the dryer their texture. Domestic cheeses of the sort known as Brick, Longhorn, American Cheddar are young cheeses not more than 2 or 3 months old, and quite moist, soft and mild-flavored. Many European types, which are now being produced domestically, are considerably older, and may be "ripened" or aged under special conditions to produce their characteristic flavor and texture.

Some of the more familiar European types of cheese are Emmenthaler, more commonly known as Swiss; Roquefort, a French cheese originally made only from sheeps' milk; Gorgonzola and Stilton, an Italian and an English version of a cheese somewhat similar to Roquefort; Limburg (or Limburger), a strong-flavored cheese which originated in Belgium; Gouda, a Dutch specialty, as is the larger Edam cheese; and Camembert, another native of France.

Every one of these cheeses is now being produced in this country, and excellent quality is obtained in domestic reproductions. The name has been changed in some cases, as in the domestic Roquefort-type cheese, which is known as "blue cheese" from its typical blue veining. In other cases the size has been changed, as in the case of Gouda cheeses, which are being made in this country in 1- or 2-pound molds rather than the much larger sizes found in imported Goudas.

The most desirable cheeses for cooking are usually the American cheeses of which nearly 90 per cent are produced in Wisconsin and New York. Almost any degree of sharpness and gradation of flavor can be found in cheeses of the cheddar type. The mildest are the Wisconsin brick and Longhorn cheeses, and one of the sharpest is the variety known as Herkimer County cheese from a New York county where it originated. Some families prefer a mild-flavored cheese for cooking, but in general the sharp cheeses are most desirable for macaroni and cheese, cheese sauce, and similar dishes, while the milder varieties are good in sandwiches.

Cheese is being used more and more for dessert purposes as well as for cooking. A wedge of cheese, usually a sharp cheddar-type, is traditionally served with apple pie and recently we have come to enjoy it with cherry and other fruit pies. For eating with crackers, usually with an accompaniment of fresh fruit, various of the flavorful European-type cheeses are used, including Roquefort, or blue cheese, Liederkranz or Limburg, Camembert, and Brie (the last two both very soft, almost liquid inside a firm crust).

COOKING CHEESE

The protein of cheese is toughened by high temperatures and overcooking. In this it is similar to the protein of eggs. In general, cheese dishes should be cooked either at a low temperature or for a very short time at a high temperature.

Cheese that is cooked at too high a temperature in such a dish as baked macaroni and cheese, which requires a fairly long baking period, will become stringy and difficult to digest. Don't blame this "indigestibility" on the cheese, but on the cooking. If the oven temperature is cut down and the cooking time increased, the results will be not only more wholesome but more palatable too.

On the other hand, cheese that is grated and used for topping *au gratin* dishes may be browned when required, at quite a high temperature without ill effects, if it is subjected to this temperature for only a few minutes.

In other words, if the temperature is high, let the cooking time be short; if the cooking time must be prolonged, have the temperature low.

177   BAKED MACARONI AND CHEESE No. 1

7 or 8 ounces macaroni   Salt
    (1 package)   3 tablespoons butter
3 teaspoons salt   ½ pound sharp cheese, cubed
3 quarts boiling water   About 1¾ cups milk

Break macaroni into 1½ or 2-inch lengths. Add salt to rapidly boiling water in large saucepan; then drop macaroni in and boil from 8 to 20 minutes, or until macaroni is just tender, stirring occasionally to prevent sticking. Drain in colander. Run hot water through macaroni to rinse well. Arrange half the macaroni in a 6 cup buttered casserole, sprinkle with salt, and dot with half the butter. Cover with half the sliced cheese. Add another layer of drained macaroni and repeat with rest of ingredients. Add milk until it comes up to the top layer of macaroni. Set casserole in a shallow pan of water and bake in a moderately slow oven (325° F.) about 45 minutes, or until surface is a rich golden brown. 5 servings.

178   BAKED MACARONI AND CHEESE No. 2

7 or 8 ounces elbow macaroni   1 cup evaporated milk
3 quarts boiling water   1 cup water
3 teaspoons salt   1 egg, beaten
2 tablespoons butter   1 teaspoon salt
2 tablespoons flour   ½ pound sharp cheese, grated

Drop macaroni into the rapidly boiling water, add the 3 teaspoons salt, and cook rapidly from 8 to 20 minutes or until tender. Turn into colander to drain. Run hot water through to rinse well. Melt butter, blend in flour, and add milk and water. Stir over direct heat until sauce boils and thickens. Then stir in egg, salt and grated cheese, and stir until cheese is melted. Arrange macaroni and cheese sauce in layers in a buttered casserole, and bake in a moderate oven (400° F.) until toasted on top, 10 to 15 minutes. 5 servings.

179   MACARONI WITH CHEESE SAUCE

After combining cooked macaroni with cheese sauce (178), it need not be baked. Reheat if necessary over boiling water. This is a quick version of macaroni and cheese, especially desirable on a hot day.

180   BAKED MACARONI AND COTTAGE CHEESE

7 or 8 ounces macaroni	1 egg, beaten
3 tablespoons butter	1 jar cottage cheese
6 tablespoons flour	(12 ounces)
1 No. 2 can tomatoes	Pepper to suit taste
1 teaspoon salt	Buttered bread crumbs
1 onion, finely chopped	(1118) or grated dry cheese

Drop macaroni into 2 or 3 quarts rapidly boiling salted water, and cook until tender, from 8 to 20 minutes. Drain, rinse with hot or cold water and turn into buttered casserole. Meanwhile melt butter in saucepan and blend in flour; cook over low heat until mixture is brown. Remove from heat and stir in remaining ingredients, except crumbs or grated cheese. Pour over macaroni, stirring slightly to distribute, then sprinkle with bread crumbs or cheese. Bake in a moderate oven (350° F.) for 45 minutes. Serve immediately. 5 servings.

181   CHEESE EGG FLOAT

3 tablespoons butter	½ teaspoon celery salt
3 tablespoons flour	5 eggs
1½ cups milk	1 cup grated sharp cheese
½ teaspoon salt	(¼ pound)
1 tablespoon onion juice	5 slices toast

Melt butter in saucepan, blend in flour, add milk and seasonings, stirring constantly over low heat until sauce boils and thickens. Pour into shallow buttered baking dish. Break eggs and drop on surface; sprinkle with grated cheese. Bake in moderate oven (350° F.) for 15 to 20 minutes, or until eggs are done to desired firmness and cheese is nicely toasted. Serve on hot buttered toast. 5 servings.

182   CHEESE FONDUE

2 cups milk, scalded	Dash pepper
½ pound sharp cheese, grated or diced small	3 eggs, separated
	4 slices toasted white bread,
1 tablespoon butter	cut in dice
1 teaspoon salt	

Scald milk, add cheese, butter and seasonings, and mix well. Beat egg yolks until thick and lemon-colored, and slowly stir in hot milk mixture. Beat egg whites until stiff and fold into hot mixture lightly but thoroughly. Pour into glass baking dish (6 by 10 by 2 inches, or 8 inches square), and sprinkle toast dice on top. Bake in a shallow pan of hot water in a moderate oven (350° F.) for about 45 minutes, or until a sharp knife inserted in the center comes out clean. 5 servings.

183   **CHEESE SOUFFLÉ**

¼ cup butter	½ lb. sharp American cheese,
¼ cup flour	grated
1 teaspoon salt	4 eggs, separated
1 cup milk	Dash cayenne

Have ready 6-cup casserole—do not grease. Start oven 10 minutes before baking; set to slow (300° F.).

Melt butter in top of double boiler over boiling water. Blend in flour and salt until smooth. Add milk gradually and continue to cook and stir until mixture thickens. Add cheese, cover and cook, stirring frequently until cheese is melted and well blended. Beat egg yolks well, then gradually stir hot cheese sauce into them; stir in cayenne. Now cool slightly, then lightly but thoroughly fold into the egg whites, which have been beaten until stiff enough to form shiny peaks that curve at the tips. Turn carefully into casserole. Now use a teaspoon to make a track all around in the soufflé about 1-inch inside the casserole. This helps the crack to break in a more even line during baking. Place in oven with rack adjusted as near center as possible. Bake 1 hour or until puffed high and a rich golden brown. Serve at once. Creamed asparagus and broiled tomatoes go well with this souffle. 5 servings.

184   **CHEESE TOASTIES**

½ pound American cheese,	Dash salt
grated	6 hamburger buns
1 teaspoon prepared mustard	Butter
2 to 4 tablespoons milk	

Mix grated cheese with mustard, milk and salt. Split buns in half, toast or not as desired, and spread cut surfaces with butter and cheese mixture. Place under the broiler and toast until cheese is puffy and golden brown. Serve hot. 5 or 6 servings.

185   **CORN AND CHEESE RAREBIT**

¼ cup chopped green pepper	⅔ cup milk
½ teaspoon minced onion	1 12-oz. can cream style corn
1 tablespoon butter	½ pound cheese, diced
½ teaspoon salt	½ teaspoon Worcestershire
Dash of pepper	2 eggs, beaten
⅛ teaspoon paprika	Toast

Sauté green pepper and onion in butter until soft; add seasonings, milk and corn and simmer 10 minutes. Place over boiling water and stir in cheese and Worcestershire. When cheese is melted, stir in beaten eggs and cook 2 minutes longer. Serve on toast. 5 servings.

186 CORN AND TOMATO RAREBIT

3 tablespoons butter	½ pound American cheese
1 teaspoon chopped onion	1 No. 2 can cream style corn
¼ cup chopped green pepper	2 eggs, beaten
3 tablespoons flour	Salt and pepper to suit taste
1 No. 2 can tomatoes, puréed	½ teaspoon Worcestershire

Melt butter in top of 6-cup double boiler; add onion and green pepper, and sauté over direct heat until onion is soft and yellow. Stir in flour thoroughly; add tomatoes which have been rubbed through a sieve, and cook with constant stirring until mixture boils and thickens. Reduce heat. Add diced cheese and stir briskly until melted. Add corn and place over boiling water; when thoroughly heated, stir in beaten eggs and cook 2 minutes, stirring constantly. Remove from heat and add seasonings. Serve immediately, on hot toast or crackers. 5 or 6 servings.

187 HOMINY CHEESE CROQUETTES

¾ cup hominy grits	1½ tablespoons butter, melted
3 cups water	2 egg yolks
¾ teaspoon salt	1 egg, beaten with 1 table-
1½ cups grated sharp cheese	spoon water
(⅜ pound)	Cracker crumbs for rolling

Soak hominy in the water to which salt has been added for 3 or 4 hours; then cook over boiling water until tender, for about 30 minutes, stirring occasionally. Combine with grated cheese and melted butter. Beat egg yolks well and mix thoroughly. Chill. Shape in croquettes (balls, cones, or cylinders) and roll in beaten egg mixture and then in cracker crumbs. Fry until golden brown in deep fat heated to 375° F. Drain thoroughly and serve hot with Tomato Sauce (916). (An equal quantity of cooked whole hominy may be used in place of the cooked grits.) 5 servings.

188 JIFFY NOODLES

8 ounces broad noodles	⅓ cup chili sauce
1½ cups grated sharp cheese	¼ cup melted butter
(⅜ pound)	Salt to suit taste

Drop noodles into 2 quarts rapidly boiling water with 2 teaspoons salt, and boil rapidly until tender, from 8 to 10 minutes. Drain, then turn into mixing bowl. Add remaining ingredients, toss and serve immediately on hot platter. Spaghetti or macaroni may be used in place of the noodles. 5 servings.

189   PIMIENTO CHEESE

1 pound Wisconsin longhorn cheese   ½ cup Special Salad Dressing (847)
1 4-oz. can pimientos

Grate the cheese. Drain pimientos, chop, and add to cheese. Add dressing, and blend together thoroughly. Chill before using. Serve on lettuce or cabbage as a salad dressing, as a sandwich spread, or as stuffing for celery. About 1 quart.

190   RICE AND CHEESE CROQUETTES

1 cup rice   1½ teaspoons salt
1½ cups grated sharp cheese   Dash pepper
  (⅜ pound)   2 beaten eggs
1 egg, beaten   Dried bread crumbs

Wash rice or do not wash as package directs. Drop into 2 quarts rapidly boiling salted water, and cook rapidly until just tender (about 20 minutes). Drain and rinse by running hot water through it. Combine with cheese, egg, salt, and pepper. Chill. Shape mixture in balls, roll in crumbs, then in beaten eggs and again in crumbs. Fry until golden brown in deep fat heated to 375° F. Drain on absorbent paper and serve hot with any tart jelly or with Tomato Sauce (916). 5 servings.

191   TOMATO CHEESE FONDUE

1 cup tomato juice (719a)   1 tablespoon butter, melted
1 cup coarse soft bread crumbs   ½ teaspoon salt
¼ pound sharp cheese, grated   4 eggs, separated

Pour tomato juice over bread crumbs and let stand until well soaked. Stir in cheese, melted butter and salt. Beat egg yolks until thick and light colored, and stir into bread crumb mixture. Beat egg whites until stiff and fold in lightly but thoroughly. Turn into buttered casserole, set in a shallow pan of hot water, and bake in a moderate oven (350° F.) 45 minutes to 1 hour, or until a sharp knife inserted in the center comes out clean. 5 servings.

192   TOMATO RAREBIT

1 10½-oz. can tomatoes	1 teaspoon sugar
2 tablespoons butter	1 teaspoon salt
3 tablespoons flour	5 slices buttered toast
¾ cup milk	5 slices pan-broiled bacon
1 cup grated sharp cheese	(545)
(¼ pound)	

Put tomatoes through sieve and heat purée to boiling point. Melt butter, blend in flour, and stir constantly while adding milk; continue to stir over direct heat until sauce boils and thickens. Remove from heat and stir in grated cheese, sugar, salt, and hot tomatoes. Serve immediately on hot buttered toast. Garnish with bacon. 5 servings.

193   WELSH RAREBIT

¼ cup butter	¼ teaspoon Worcestershire
5 tablespoons flour	½ pound sharp cheese
½ teaspoon salt	1 egg, beaten
2 cups milk	5 slices hot toast

Make a white sauce of the first 4 ingredients (see directions 919). Place over boiling water. Add Worcestershire sauce and diced or grated cheese, and stir vigorously until cheese is melted. Pour in well-beaten egg, stirring constantly, and continue to stir while cooking about 1 minute longer. Serve immediately over the hot toast. Sprinkle with paprika, if desired. 5 servings.

COOKIES

JUST the mention of cookies brings back childhood memories to most folks, for cookies seem to have been invented especially for children. Grandma, as likely as not, made the reputation of her cookie jar with a single recipe; but today, even the novice cookie-maker can make a dozen different kinds of cookies that would have made Grandma gasp—especially if the novice studies this chapter carefully. These recipes will help your favorite small boys and girls build up a marvelous store of cookie memories.

Cookies, by definition, are small flat cakes. They may be crisp or soft, thick or thin, dark or light, smooth dough or full of fruits and nuts; and it goes without saying that they may be good or poor. However they are made, whatever kind they are, and whatever their cost, most people of all ages enjoy cookies—especially home-made cookies.

There are five principal types of cookies:

1. ROLLED: moderately soft dough, chilled, rolled thin and cut out.
2. DROP: softer dough, dropped from teaspoon.
3. ICE BOX: moderately soft dough, chilled until firm in refrigerator and sliced thin with sharp knife.
4. PRESSED: moderately soft dough, put through cookie press to form definite shapes.
5. BARS: dough baked in a sheet and cut in bars after baking.

All cookies require good ingredients, starting with a sweet-flavored shortening. Butter is desirable because of its flavor, but by increasing the salt and flavoring good results can be obtained with shortening or a bland lard. All-purpose flour is usually called for rather than cake flour.

The method of mixing cookies is very similar to that for cakes in most cases, except that less liquid or none at all in addition to the eggs, is usually used. To simplify the work, get all the ingredients ready before starting work, especially if there are nuts or chopped fruits to be added.

Whatever the type of cookie, a soft dough gives the tenderest product.

179

Of course a soft dough for a drop cookie is much softer than a soft dough for a rolled cookie, so no very definite statement about this can be made.

ROLLED COOKIES are the most difficult type to make. They take longer, use more equipment and more labor, and offer more difficulties than any of the others. It is easy to use too much flour in rolling them in the effort to keep them from sticking, and this will make the finished cookie less delicate. A good plan is to chill the dough in the refrigerator for half an hour before rolling and to use one of the new pastry cloths and rolling pin covers; if the weather is hot, roll the dough in small portions, leaving the rest of it in the refrigerator until ready to use. Chilled dough is both firmer and less sticky. If desired, part of the dough may be covered and left in the refrigerator overnight, so freshly baked cookies may·be had for two or three days from the same batch of dough.

DROP COOKIES are the easiest of all cookies. The only thing to be careful about is dropping the same amount of dough onto the baking sheet for each cookie (so all will bake done in the same time), and dropping the cookies far enough apart so they will not run together when they spread.

Dough for ICE BOX COOKIES is stiffer than for drop cookies, softer than for rolled ones. It needs to be just firm enough to be shaped in a roll and rolled up in waxed paper or packed into cookie molds for storage in the refrigerator until it becomes stiff enough to slice neatly into thin cookies. This will take several hours; and the well-wrapped rolls or molds can be kept for several days if desired. Have a very sharp knife for slicing them, and cut the cookies very thin—not more than 1/8 inch. Since ice box cookie dough is usually quite rich, it will make crisp, delicate cookies which must be thin to be at their best.

PINWHEEL, RIBBON and CHECKERBOARD COOKIES are all made with ICE BOX dough, part of which is colored with either chocolate or a food coloring.

Cookie dough for making various kinds of BARS is simply spread over a shallow greased baking pan; after baking the sheet is iced or left plain, and is cut, usually in squares, oblongs or diamonds. Brownies, some filled cookies, and many iced cookies are made in this manner.

PRESSED COOKIES are usually made from a special type of dough which is quite rich and very smooth, and stiff enough to hold the shape in which it comes from the press without spreading.

CARE OF COOKIES

It is frequently necessary to store cookies for several days, so it is important to have a suitable container for them. The tightly covered cookie jar, usually pottery, is the typical container. Never put more than one kind of cookie into the jar, or there will be an undesirable interchange of flavors; and for the same reason, have the jar thoroughly washed after each batch of cookies.

If crisp cookies become soft after storing, the crispness may be restored by placing the cookies on an ungreased baking sheet and letting them stand in a slow oven (300° F.) for 3 to 5 minutes.

194   BROWNIES

¾ cup all-purpose flour	2 eggs, beaten
¼ teaspoon salt	1 teaspoon vanilla
½ cup butter or other	2 squares baking chocolate,
shortening	melted and cooled (1124)
1 cup sugar	¾ cup chopped nuts

Sift flour, measure and resift with salt. Cream butter, gradually blend in sugar and add beaten eggs; beat until smooth and fluffy. Add vanilla and stir in melted chocolate. Add flour mixture alternately in 2 or 3 portions, stirring well after each addition. Add nuts with last few stirs. Spread in an 8-inch square cake pan which has been buttered, and bake in a moderate oven (350° F.) for 20 minutes. Remove pan to cake rack. Cut in pieces while still warm. Makes 16 to 20 brownies 1 x 2 inches.

195   COCOA INDIANS

1 cup all-purpose flour	1 cup sugar
¼ teaspoon baking powder	2 eggs
½ teaspoon salt, scant	1 teaspoon vanilla
¼ cup cocoa	¼ cup milk
½ cup shortening	⅔ cup raisins
(half butter)	

Sift flour, measure, and resift with baking powder, salt, and cocoa. Cream shortening; add sugar and continue creaming until thoroughly mixed. Add beaten eggs and vanilla and mix well. Add the sifted dry ingredients alternately with the milk, stirring well after each addition. Add raisins and pour into a 9 x 12-inch greased baking pan. Bake in a moderate oven (350° F.) for about 25 minutes. Allow to cool 10 or 15 minutes; then cut into cookies of desired size. Makes 15 to 18 depending on size.

196   CHOCOLATE DROP COOKIES

2 cups all-purpose flour	1 egg, beaten
½ teaspoon salt	1 teaspoon vanilla
½ teaspoon soda	2 squares baking chocolate,
½ cup shortening	melted (1124)
½ cup brown sugar, packed	¾ cup buttermilk
½ cup white sugar	½ cup chopped nuts

Sift flour, measure and resift 4 times with salt and soda. Cream shortening, add both sugars and cream until smooth. Add egg and beat until fluffy. Add vanilla. Stir in cooled melted chocolate. Add flour mixture and buttermilk alternately in 3 or 4 portions, beginning and ending with flour. Stir in nuts. Drop by heaping teaspoonfuls onto buttered cookie sheets, about 2 inches apart. Bake in a moderately hot oven (400° F.) for 10 minutes. Using broad spatula or pancake turner, transfer to cake racks and cool before storing or serving. Makes about 36.

196a   SOFT CHOCOLATE DROP COOKIES

Make exactly like Chocolate Sour Cream Drop Cookies, p. 181, except substitute 1⅓ cups moist brown sugar, packed, for the 1⅓ cups granulated sugar and reduce chocolate to 1½ squares.

197   CHOCOLATE SOUR CREAM DROP COOKIES
(*Good chocolate flavor, crisp and tender*)

2 squares chocolate	1⅓ cups sugar
1¾ cups all-purpose flour	1 teaspoon vanilla
½ teaspoon baking powder	1 egg
½ teaspoon soda	½ cup sour cream
½ teaspoon salt	½ cup broken nutmeats
⅔ cup soft butter or margarine	

Grease baking sheets lightly. Start oven 10 minutes before baking; set to moderately hot (425° F.). Put chocolate in a custard cup and set in a pan of hot water to melt; when melted, remove to cool. Sift flour, measure, resift 4 times with baking powder, soda and salt. In a 2-qt. mixing bowl, cream butter until smooth, add sugar in 2 portions, creaming well. Stir in vanilla, then beat in egg until fluffy. Stir in cooled chocolate until blended, then sour cream. Add flour mixture and mix well. Stir in nuts. Drop by heaping teaspoonfuls 2-inches apart onto prepared sheets. Bake 9 to 10 minutes or until barely done. Let stand on sheet on cake rack a minute or two, then remove to rack to cool. Store in box with tight-fitting cover with waxed paper between layers. 4 dozen.

197a   DATE PINWHEELS

1 lb. pitted dates, cut up	½ cup moist brown sugar, packed
½ cup water	
½ cup sugar	½ cup white sugar
2½ cups all-purpose flour	2 eggs, well beaten
½ teaspoon soda	½ teaspoon vanilla
¼ teaspoon salt	1 cup finely chopped nuts
¾ cup butter	

Put first 3 ingredients into saucepan and cook until thick, about 5 minutes, stirring constantly. Cool. Sift flour, measure, and resift twice with soda and salt. Cream butter until soft and smooth, blend in brown and white sugar, and add eggs; beat until light and fluffy. Stir in vanilla. Stir in flour and place dough in refrigerator to chill at least half an hour. Turn half of chilled dough out onto waxed paper and pat out with floured hands to form a rectangle; then roll carefully with a lightly floured rolling pin to a rectangle 10 x 14 inches and ⅛-inch thick. Combine cooled date mixture with the nuts, and spread half the mixture over the sheet of dough. Roll up like jelly roll, the long way of the sheet, removing the waxed paper as you roll. Then wrap the roll snugly in the waxed paper. It should be slender in proportion to its length. Repeat with remaining dough and filling. Chill wrapped rolls in refrigerator until firm; then slice thin, using a sharp, slender-bladed knife. Place on lightly greased cookie sheets and bake in a moderately hot oven (400° F.) for 7 minutes, or until lightly browned. Transfer to cake racks to cool. Makes 5 to 6 dozen cookies, depending on diameter of rolls and thickness of cookies.

Note: If daintier cookies are desired, divide dough into 4 portions instead of 2, and make 4 small rolls.

198   COCOA OATMEAL COOKIES

1¼ cups all-purpose flour	½ cup milk
½ teaspoon baking powder	1½ teaspoons vanilla
½ teaspoon salt	⅓ cup shortening, melted
⅓ cup cocoa	⅓ cup butter, melted
1¼ cups sugar	2 cups rolled oats
1 egg, well beaten	

Sift flour, measure, and resift twice with baking powder, salt, cocoa, and sugar. Combine beaten egg, milk and vanilla, and add melted butter and shortening. Mix thoroughly with the sifted dry ingredients. Then stir in the rolled oats and drop by teaspoonfuls onto a buttered cookie sheet. Bake in a moderate oven (350° F.) 15 to 20 minutes. Remove to cake racks to cool. About 5 dozen cookies.

199   GINGERSNAPS

2½ cups all-purpose flour   ¼ teaspoon cinnamon
½ cup shortening   ¼ teaspoon nutmeg
½ cup sugar   ⅛ teaspoon cloves
½ cup molasses   ½ teaspoon soda
1 egg, beaten   1 tablespoon hot water
1 teaspoon ginger   1 teaspoon vinegar

Sift flour, measure, and resift. Cream shortening, blend in sugar, and add molasses and beaten egg; beat until smooth. Mix spices thoroughly with soda and blend until smooth with hot water and vinegar; stir into creamed mixture. Add flour, mixing thoroughly until smooth. Drop from teaspoon onto buttered baking sheet, at least 2 inches apart. Bake 10 minutes in a moderate oven (375° F.). Remove to cake racks to cool. 4 to 5 dozen, depending on size.

200   THREE-WAY GINGER COOKIES

2 cups all-purpose flour   1 cup sugar
½ teaspoon salt   1 egg, beaten
1 teaspoon soda   ¼ cup dark molasses
1 teaspoon ground ginger   1 tablespoon vinegar
½ cup butter or other
  shortening

Sift flour, measure, and resift 4 times with salt, soda and ginger. Cream shortening until soft and smooth, and add the sugar gradually, creaming thoroughly. Add egg and beat until smooth and fluffy. Add molasses, beat hard, and then stir in vinegar. Add flour mixture and mix thoroughly. Drop by teaspoonfuls onto lightly greased cookie sheets, and bake in a moderate oven (375° F.) for 15 minutes, or until delicately browned. Remove to cake racks to cool. Makes about 4 dozen cookies.

Variation 1. Shape level dessert spoonfuls of the dough quickly into balls by rolling them lightly between buttered palms. Drop balls into ½ cup chopped nuts spread out on waxed paper. Transfer to greased cookie sheets, nut-side up, and bake as above.

Variation 2. Drop balls of the dough into a mixture of 3 tablespoons granulated sugar blended with 1 tablespoon grated orange rind. Transfer to cookie sheets, sugar-side up, and bake as above.

GUM DROP COOKIES

1 cup all-purpose flour	½ teaspoon vanilla
½ teaspoon baking powder	2 tablespoons milk
½ teaspoon salt	¾ cup spiced gum drops,
⅓ cup shortening, half butter	cut in small pieces
⅔ cup sugar	½ cup blanched almonds
1 egg, beaten	

Sift and measure flour; resift 3 times with baking powder and salt. Cream shortening; add sugar gradually and continue creaming. Add well-beaten egg and beat until fluffy. Stir in vanilla. Add flour mixture alternately with milk, beating well after each addition. Add gum drops and drop by rounded teaspoonfuls onto a greased baking sheet, about 2 inches apart. Stick 4 almond halves in top of each cookie. Bake in a moderately hot oven (400° F.) for about 10 minutes, or until cookies are lightly browned. Remove immediately to cake rack; they become crisp as they cool. About 24 cookies.

HERMITS
(Very palatable, tender and crunchy)

1 cup seedless raisins	1 teaspoon cinnamon
1 cup chopped nuts	½ teaspoon nutmeg
2¼ cups all-purpose flour	1 cup soft butter or margarine
¼ teaspoon salt	1 cup sugar
½ teaspoon soda	3 eggs

Grease baking sheets lightly. Start oven 10 minutes before baking; set to moderately hot (400° F.). Plump raisins (1129). Cool. Chop nuts. Sift flour, measure, resift 4 times with next 4 ingredients. Cream butter until shiny, add sugar in 2 portions, creaming well. Add eggs one at a time, beating until fluffy after each. Add flour in 2 or 3 portions, mixing until smooth after each. Stir in raisins and nuts until well distributed. Drop 2-inches apart by heaping teaspoonfuls onto baking sheet into neat mounds. Bake 10 minutes or until nicely browned. Remove at once from pan to cake racks to cool. Store in container with tight-fitting cover with sheets of waxed paper between layers. 3½ dozen.

202a   MOLASSES DROP COOKIES

(*Excellent! A moist fruit-nut filled cookie you will be proud to serve on any occasion, but serve them fresh*)

1 cup raisins, plumped (1129)	¼ cup moist brown sugar, packed
½ cup chopped nuts	
2 cups all-purpose flour	½ cup soft butter or margarine plus
1 teaspoon soda	
¼ teaspoon salt	2 tablespoons shortening
⅛ teaspoon ginger	1 egg
½ teaspoon cloves	½ cup dark molasses
½ teaspoon cinnamon	½ cup thick buttermilk

Grease baking sheets. Start oven 10 minutes before baking; set to moderately hot (400° F.). Wash raisins and plump, then cool. Chop nuts. Sift flour, measure, resift 4 times with next 5 ingredients. Press brown sugar through a coarse sieve to remove lumps. In a 3-qt. mixing bowl, cream butter and shortening with a wooden spoon until smooth, add sugar and cream well. Scrape spoon, remove. Beat in egg with rotary beater until fluffy, then beat in molasses until satiny. Remove beater and use spoon. Stir in flour mixture and milk alternately in 2 or 3 portions, beginning and ending with flour and mixing until smooth after each portion. Stir in raisins and nuts until well distributed. Drop by heaping teaspoonfuls onto prepared sheet. Bake about 10 minutes or until delicately browned. Remove at once from sheet to cake rack. When cool, store in jar or box with tight-fitting cover with sheet of waxed paper between layers. 3 dozen.

203   LEMON SUGAR COOKIES

2¼ cups all-purpose flour	¼ cup other shortening
¾ teaspoon baking powder, see p. 122	1 cup sugar
	1 egg
¼ teaspoon salt	½ teaspoon lemon extract
½ cup butter	

Sift flour, measure, and resift 3 times with baking powder and salt. Cream butter and shortening until smooth and soft; add sugar and blend well, then add egg and beat vigorously until fluffy and light-colored. Stir in lemon extract. Add flour mixture in 2 or 3 portions, stirring until smooth. Cover dough with waxed paper and chill in refrigerator for 1 hour. Shape dough into balls about the size of small walnuts, and place about 2½ inches apart on a buttered baking sheet. Cover a flat-bottomed glass tumbler with a piece of clean, smooth-textured white cloth which has been wrung out of cold water. Use this to press the cookies out flat, about ⅛ inch thick or slightly thicker. Bake in a moderately hot oven

(400° F.) for 6 to 8 minutes, or until delicately browned at edges. Remove to cake racks to cool before storing. About 4 dozen cookies.

204   OATMEAL DROP COOKIES

1½ cups all-purpose flour	1 egg
¼ teaspoon salt	1½ cups rolled oats
1 teaspoon soda	⅔ cup buttermilk
1 teaspoon cinnamon	½ cup chopped nuts
½ cup shortening	1 cup seedless raisins,
1 cup sugar	plumped

Sift flour, measure, and resift twice with salt, soda and cinnamon. Cream shortening, blend in sugar, and add slightly beaten egg; beat until smooth and light. Stir in half the flour; then add milk, rest of flour, oats, nuts, and raisins, stirring until well mixed. Drop from a teaspoon onto a buttered baking sheet, and bake in a moderately hot oven (400° F.) for 10 minutes, or until nicely browned. About 36 cookies.

205   OLD-FASHIONED LACE COOKIES

1 cup all-purpose flour	¾ teaspoon baking powder
1 teaspoon cinnamon	½ cup butter
Dash nutmeg	½ cup sugar
¼ teaspoon salt	½ cup light molasses
½ teaspoon soda	1 teaspoon lemon extract

Sift flour, measure, and resift 3 times with next 5 ingredients. Melt butter with sugar and molasses over boiling water and remove from heat. Add dry ingredients and lemon extract and beat until smooth; let stand over hot water for a few minutes. Drop by half-teaspoonfuls 3 inches apart onto a cookie sheet that has been greased and dusted with flour. Bake in a moderately slow oven (325° F.) for 12 to 15 minutes. Cool on pan 1 or 2 minutes before removing from pan to cake rack with a spatula. 5 dozen cookies.

The cookies are pliable when warm and can be shaped with the hands into cups or ruffles, or rolled around the handle of a wooden spoon.

206   PRALINE COOKIES

¾ cup butter	1 teaspoon vanilla
1½ cups brown sugar, packed	1½ cups sifted all-purpose flour
1 egg	1 cup chopped pecans

Cream butter until smooth, add sugar and egg, and beat until smooth and fluffy. Add vanilla. Sift in flour and blend thoroughly. Stir in nuts until well distributed. Shape level tablespoons of the dough in small balls and flatten out to about ⅛-inch thickness on a buttered baking sheet. They should be at least 1 inch apart when flattened. Bake in a moderate oven (375° F.) for 12 minutes, or until nicely browned. Cool on the pan for 2 or 3 minutes; then transfer to cake racks. Makes about 3 dozen cookies.

207 ROCKS

1½ cups all-purpose flour	1 cup sugar
¼ teaspoon allspice	2 eggs, beaten
½ teaspoon cinnamon	½ teaspoon soda dissolved in
½ teaspoon nutmeg	1 tablespoon hot water
¼ teaspoon salt	⅔ cup chopped nuts
½ cup shortening (half butter)	1 cup moist currants

Sift flour, measure, and resift 3 times with the spices and salt. Cream shortening till soft and smooth, gradually blend in sugar, and add beaten eggs; beat until fluffy and light-colored. Stir in soda and water mixture; then add flour mixture in 2 or 3 portions, and stir until well blended. Stir in chopped nuts and raisins or currants. Drop by teaspoonfuls, at least 2 inches apart, on lightly greased cookie sheet, and bake in a moderately hot oven (400° F.) for 10 minutes or until nicely browned. About 9 dozen cookies.

208 VANILLA CRISPS

1⅓ cups all-purpose flour	½ cup shortening (half butter)
1 teaspoon baking powder, see p. 122	1 cup sugar
	2 eggs, beaten
½ teaspoon salt	1½ teaspoons vanilla

Sift flour, measure and resift with baking powder and salt. Cream shortenings and blend in sugar well. Add eggs and beat until thoroughly combined. Stir in vanilla. Stir dry ingredients into creamed mixture. Drop small rounds on a cookie sheet dusted with flour. Bake in a moderately hot oven (400° F.) about 8 minutes, or until delicately browned. Makes 5 dozen 2-inch cookies.

209 BUTTERSCOTCH COOKIES

3½ cups all-purpose flour	1 egg, beaten
1 teaspoon cream of tartar	1 teaspoon vanilla
1 teaspoon soda	3 tablespoons cream
¾ cup shortening (half butter)	1 cup chopped nuts
2 cups moist brown sugar, packed	1 cup dates, chopped

Sift flour, measure and resift 4 times with cream of tartar and soda. Cream shortening, blend in sugar, and add egg, vanilla and cream; beat until smooth and fluffy. Add flour mixture and stir until flour disappears. Stir in nuts and dates. Shape in a roll, or divide in 2 or 3 portions and roll separately; wrap in waxed paper and chill in refrigerator overnight. Slice thin with a very sharp knife, and transfer to baking sheet. Bake in a moderately hot oven (400° F.) 7 minutes, or until nicely browned. Remove to cake racks to cool. About 60 cookies, depending on size and thickness.

210 CHECKERBOARD COOKIES

2½ cups all-purpose flour
1 teaspoon tartrate or calcium-phosphate baking powder, or ¾ teaspoon S.A.S.-phosphate baking powder
½ teaspoon salt

¾ cup butter (or half butter, half other shortening)
1 cup sugar
2 eggs, well beaten
1 teaspoon vanilla
1 square baking chocolate, melted (1124)

Sift flour, measure, and resift 3 times with baking powder and salt. Cream butter or shortening, blend in sugar thoroughly, and add eggs; beat until smooth and fluffy. Add vanilla, and stir in the flour mixture in several portions, until smooth. Divide the dough in two portions and mix the cooled melted chocolate with one portion. Line a small bread loaf pan or a refrigerator freezing tray with waxed paper, and pack half the chocolate dough into the bottom in a uniform layer. Place in refrigerator until very firm, then cover this with half the plain dough; then repeat chilling and adding another layer of chocolate, and finally the last of plain dough. Try to keep the layers uniform in thickness and smooth. Cover with waxed paper and chill overnight in the refrigerator.

Turn the layered loaf out onto waxed paper on a molding board and cut into uniform thick slices, using a thin sharp knife. To make checkerboard cookies, cut these slices ¼ inch thick, and lay four of them together so that, as viewed from the end, each chocolate strip lies above a white strip of dough. If dough has softened from handling, wrap these smaller loaves in waxed paper and again chill. Then slice thinly across the checkerboard pattern. Place cookies on baking sheet and bake in a moderate oven (400° F.) for 8 minutes, or until lightly browned. Transfer to cake racks to cool. Makes about 6 dozen cookies.

211   ICE-BOX COOKIES

1½ cups all-purpose flour	½ cup sugar
¼ teaspoon soda	⅓ cup brown sugar
½ teaspoon salt	1 egg
½ cup soft butter or shortening	1 teaspoon vanilla

Sift flour, measure, and resift 4 times with soda and salt. Cream butter until smooth; add sugars and beat until well blended. Add egg and beat until smooth and fluffy. Stir in vanilla. Gradually blend in the flour mixture, and turn dough into a small loaf pan which has been lined with waxed paper. Chill in refrigerator for several hours, until hard; then turn out onto cutting board, strip off waxed paper, and slice ⅛ inch thick or less, using a sharp thin-bladed knife. Transfer cookies to buttered baking sheet and bake in a moderately hot oven (400° F.) for 8 to 10 minutes, or until nicely browned. Cool on cake racks. About 20 cookies.

212   COCOANUT ICE-BOX COOKIES

To dough of Ice-Box Cookies (211), add 1 cup dry grated cocoanut firmly packed, before packing into the loaf pan for chilling. Bake as for Ice-Box Cookies.

213   GINGER ICE-BOX COOKIES

4 cups all-purpose flour	1 cup shortening (part butter)
1 teaspoon soda	1 cup sugar
2½ teaspoons ginger	½ cup sorghum molasses
½ teaspoon salt	2 eggs, unbeaten

Sift flour, measure and resift 3 times with soda, ginger and salt. Cream shortening, blend in sugar, add sorghum and eggs, and beat vigorously until smooth and fluffy. Then add flour mixture and stir until thoroughly combined. Pack into a refrigerator freezing tray lined with waxed paper, and place in refrigerator to chill until very firm; or shape in roll and wrap in waxed paper before chilling. Do not freeze. When ready to bake, slice ⅛ inch thick, place on buttered cookie sheet, and bake in a moderate oven (400° F.) for 10 minutes, or until nicely browned. The dough may be kept in the refrigerator several days, if well wrapped, and sliced and baked as cookies are needed. Makes about 6½ dozen cookies.

214   PECAN CRESCENT COOKIES

½ cup butter	¼ teaspoon almond extract
¼ cup unsifted XXXX sugar	1¼ cups sifted cake flour
¼ teaspoon vanilla	¾ cup coarsely chopped pecans

Cream butter until soft and smooth, add sugar and flavorings, and blend until smooth. Stir in flour gradually; finally stir in nuts. Shape in small crescent-shaped rolls, using about 1 teaspoon for each one. Place on a buttered cookie sheet and bake in a moderate oven (350° F.) for about 20 minutes. While still warm, roll in XXXX sugar. Makes about 3½ dozen.

215   CHOCOLATE PINWHEEL COOKIES

2¼ cups all-purpose flour
1 teaspoon tartrate or calcium-phosphate baking powder, or ¾ teaspoon S.A.S.-phosphate baking powder
½ teaspoon salt
⅔ cup butter (or half butter, half other shortening)
1 cup sugar minus 2 table-spoons
1 egg, beaten
¾ teaspoon vanilla
2 tablespoons milk
1 square baking chocolate, melted (1124)

Sift flour, measure, and resift 3 times with baking powder and salt. Cream butter or shortening, blend in sugar thoroughly and add egg; beat until smooth and fluffy. Stir in vanilla. Add flour mixture and milk alternately, beginning and ending with flour. Divide dough into 2 equal portions; stir cooled melted chocolate into one portion, and chill both in refrigerator for half an hour or longer. Place each portion between 2 sheets of waxed paper, and pat or roll out to an even thickness of about ⅛ inch; then remove the top sheets of waxed paper and lay the two doughs carefully together. Remove rest of waxed paper; roll up the double sheet of dough like a jelly roll, wrap snugly in a sheet of the waxed paper, and chill in refrigerator until very firm. When ready to bake, remove the paper wrapping and slice the roll thin, using a thin-bladed sharp knife. Place cookies on a lightly greased baking sheet, and bake in a moderate oven (375° F.) for about 10 minutes, or until very delicately browned. About 3 dozen cookies, number depending on thickness and size.

216   CHRISTMAS MERINGUE COOKIES

4 egg whites
1½ cups sugar
1 teaspoon cinnamon
1 lb. almonds, blanched and shaved
½ lb. moist candied citron, finely chopped

Beat egg whites until very stiff. Gradually add the sugar, continuing to beat with an egg whip. Turn mixture into top of double boiler, and stir constantly over boiling water until mixture is just warm. Remove from heat and fold in the cinnamon, almonds and citron carefully, until just blended. Drop by scant teaspoonfuls onto clean brown or white wrapping paper which has been greased with melted butter. Bake in a moderately slow oven (325° F.) for 25 minutes, or until very delicately browned. Brush underside of paper with water and remove cookies carefully by running a spatula under them. Makes about 5 dozen cookies.

217 CINNAMON STARS

1 lb. unblanched almonds	1 lb. XXXX sugar
Grated rind of 1 lemon	1 teaspoon cinnamon
6 egg whites	

Shake almonds in a clean dry cloth to rub off any loose material, but do not blanch. Grate almonds moderately fine in nut grater or in a food mill. Grate lemon rind, using only the yellow portion of the rind; fold the grated rind into waxed paper to avoid losing fragrance and moisture. Beat egg whites until very stiff, and gradually fold in the sugar which has been sifted to remove lumps. Then add lemon rind, folding in till well distributed. Remove ¼ of the mixture. To the remainder add the grated almonds and cinnamon, folding just until well blended. Roll out ¼ inch thick on a board or pastry cloth sprinkled generously with XXXX sugar. Cut out with a star cookie cutter, and on each cookie drop a portion of the reserved meringue, drawing it out into each point of the star. Transfer carefully to a cookie sheet rubbed very lightly with melted paraffin. Bake in a slow oven (300° F.) until lightly browned and crusty, from 40 to 50 minutes. Remove immediately from the pan and cool on cake racks. Makes 2 to 4 dozen cookies, depending on size of cutter.

218 COCOA MACAROONS

2 egg whites	¾ cup sugar
3 tablespoons cocoa	1½ cups cornflakes
¼ teaspoon salt	½ cup moist shredded cocoanut

Beat egg whites until stiff. Mix cocoa, sugar and salt together, and fold slowly into egg whites. Then fold in cornflakes and cocoanut. Drop from a teaspoon onto a baking sheet covered with waxed paper or buttered brown paper. Bake in a slow oven (300° F.) 20 to 30 minutes, or until well dried. Remove to cake racks to cool. About 2 dozen macaroons.

219 COCOANUT FINGERS

8 slices 2 or 3 day-old white bread	1½ cups moist shredded cocoanut
1 cup sweetened condensed milk	

Cut crusts from slices of bread and cut each slice into four strips. Dip each strip of bread into condensed milk and then into cocoanut, covering all four sides. Place on a greased cookie sheet and bake in a moderately slow oven (325° F.) 10 to 15 minutes, or until delicately browned. Remove from pan at once. They become crisp on cooling. (Ground nuts may be used with or in place of the cocoanut.) Makes 32 fingers.

220   CORNFLAKE KISSES

2 egg whites	½ cup chopped peanuts or
¼ teaspoon salt	walnuts
⅔ cup sugar	1½ cups crisp cornflakes

Beat egg whites and salt until just stiff enough to hold moist peaks; then add sugar gradually, about 1 heaping tablespoon at a time, continuing to beat after each addition until whites are very stiff. Mix in peanuts, using a fork; then fold in the cornflakes. Drop by teaspoonfuls onto ungreased, unglazed brown paper on a cookie sheet. Bake in a slow oven (300° F.) 30 minutes. Remove from paper to cake racks immediately. About 3 dozen kisses.

221   BUTTER COOKIES

1¾ cups all-purpose flour	½ cup sugar
½ teaspoon baking powder,	1 small egg, well beaten
see p. 122	½ teaspoon vanilla
⅔ cup soft butter	¾ square chocolate, if desired

Sift flour, measure and resift with baking powder. Cream butter thoroughly; add sugar and continue creaming until well mixed. Mix in the well beaten egg. Add vanilla. Stir in sifted dry ingredients in 2 or 3 portions until dough is just smooth. If some chocolate cookies are desired, add chocolate, which has been melted and cooled (1124), to half the dough. Roll out ⅛ inch thick on a floured board, and cut into desired shapes. A finish or topping may be made similar to that described in 224, using whole blanched almonds split in two, pieces of candied cherry, chocolate shot, etc. Bake on ungreased cookie sheet in a moderately hot oven (400° F.) for 6 to 8 minutes or until delicately browned. Cool on cake racks. Makes 3 to 4 dozen cookies.

Note: ½ teaspoon lemon extract and ¼ teaspoon of mace may be used in place of the vanilla.

222   PEANUT BUTTER COOKIES

2½ cups all-purpose flour	1 cup granulated sugar
½ teaspoon soda	1 cup moist brown sugar
1 teaspoon baking powder	2 eggs, beaten slightly
½ cup margarine	1 cup peanut butter
½ cup butter	2 teaspoons vanilla

Sift flour, measure and resift 3 times with soda and baking powder. Cream sugars until soft and well blended but not fluffy. Add eggs, margarine, butter and peanut butter. Mix thoroughly. Add flour. Knead in bowl only long enough to form a smooth dough. Divide into 4 parts and roll each part into a roll about 1 inch in diameter. Cut into 1 inch lengths. Roll pieces in palms of hands to form smooth balls. Lay on ungreased cookie sheets, 1 inch apart. Press with tines of fork to make criss-crosses. Bake in a moderate oven (375° F.) 10 to 12 minutes. Makes about 7 dozen cookies.

223   POPPY SEED COOKIES

3 cups all-purpose flour	1 egg, beaten—
¾ teaspoon soda	½ cup buttermilk
½ teaspoon salt	2 tablespoons lemon juice
½ cup butter	2 teaspoons grated lemon rind
¼ cup other shortening	¼ cup whole poppy seeds
1 cup sugar	

Sift flour, measure, and resift 3 times with soda and salt. Cream butter and shortening until smooth and soft; blend in sugar gradually. Add beaten egg and beat until fluffy. Add flour mixture alternately with buttermilk, beginning and ending with flour and beating well after each addition. Add lemon juice, rind, and poppy seeds, mixing thoroughly. Chill dough at least 1 hour; then roll out thin on a floured board, cut out, and transfer to lightly greased baking sheets. Bake in a moderately hot oven (425° F.) 6 to 8 minutes, or until delicately browned. Remove to cake racks to cool. Makes 4 to 6 dozen, depending on size.

223a   SPRITZ COOKIES

(This dough may also be used to make Rolled Butter Cookies)

1 cup butter	¼ teaspoon almond extract
¾ cup sifted granulated sugar	2½ cups all-purpose flour
2 egg yolks	

Cream butter thoroughly. Add sugar gradually. Blend in unbeaten egg yolks. Stir in flavoring, then flour and mix thoroughly. Pack into cookie press by taking dough up in hands and shaping into cylinder. Drop into tube. Force through cookie press onto cold, ungreased cookie sheets, about 1 inch apart. Bake in hot oven (425° F.) for 8 minutes or until a delicate brown. Remove cookies from pans onto cake racks while warm. If difficult to remove from pans return to oven for a minute. Cool thoroughly. Store in air-tight container. 4½ dozen medium cookies.

224   PRESSED SUGAR COOKIES

2 cups all-purpose flour	1 egg
¾ teaspoon baking powder	1 teaspoon vanilla
½ teaspoon salt	½ teaspoon almond extract
½ cup soft butter	1 egg white beaten with
½ cup sugar	1 teaspoon cold water

Sift flour, measure, and resift 3 times with baking powder and salt. Cream butter well, blend in sugar, and add egg, beating vigorously until smooth and fluffy. Stir in flavorings; then add flour and mix well until smooth. Chill dough; then shape in walnut-size balls and press out flat with tines of fork. (A flat bottomed glass covered with clean cheesecloth which has been wrung out in cold water may be used to flatten cookies.) Brush cookies with egg white mixture and sprinkle with granulated sugar, crushed rock candy, or chopped nuts. Bake in a moderately hot oven (400° F.) for 10 minutes, or until delicately browned. Makes 2 to 3 dozen cookies.

225   SPRINGERLIE

2 cups sugar, sifted	1 teaspoon grated lemon rind
4 eggs, separated	4 cups sifted all-purpose flour
1 cube ammonium carbonate	Anise seeds
20 drops oil of anise	

Stir sugar into beaten egg yolks. Beat whites until stiff, add to egg yolks and sugar, and stir vigorously for 10 minutes by hand or an electric beater on low speed. Crush ammonium carbonate thoroughly and add to mixture, along with anise oil and lemon rind. Add flour in several portions, combining well. Divide dough into 3 or 4 portions; turn one out onto floured board and place others in refrigerator. Roll out ¼ inch thick. Dust springerlie board with flour, by tying flour into a twist of cheesecloth and striking it lightly against the board. Stamp sheet of dough firmly with the floured springerlie board. Cut cookies apart between designs, transfer them to a lightly floured board or cookie sheet, cover with a dry towel, and let stand overnight. When ready to bake, brush flour from bottoms of cookies with a camel hair brush, and rub underside carefully with cold water. Place cookies on a buttered baking sheet sprinkled lightly with anise seeds. Bake in a slow oven (275° F.) until cookies are a delicate straw color, about 40 minutes. Cool on baking sheet; then store in covered jar or box. Springerlie may be eaten immediately, but they improve with age. They are a crisp, hard, but shell-like cookie. Makes about 6 to 8 dozen cookies, depending on size and thickness.

Note: Carved rolling pins for stamping springerlie are also available, but are seldom as satisfactory as the flat boards, of which the best are hand-carved.

DESSERTS

ONE function of desserts is to produce a sense of complete satisfaction at the end of the meal—which is a good enough reason for trying every one of the recipes in this chapter. But you'll probably need no coaxing to do that, for where is the hostess who doesn't love to hear the Oh's and Ah's that are sure to greet a particularly delectable dessert?

Dessert is one part of the meal which no member of the family has to be coaxed to like. Though many persons may forego dessert for one reason or another, this pleasing final course is something which almost everyone enjoys naturally and instinctively. That is one reason for serving dessert at the end of the meal: it produces a sense of complete satisfaction.

In planning menus, desserts require special attention from the homemaker. Many kinds are more or less rich and all are sweet, so they may contribute a high proportion of calories. Therefore it is important to fit them carefully into the particular menu being served. That is, if the meal has been fairly light, a heavy dessert, such as pie or cake or a rich pudding, will be not only suitable but welcome. On the other hand, after a hearty dinner, something light and less sweet and rich, such as fruit, gelatine desserts, sherbets and ices, will be more relished and better from a dietetic view.

There is nothing essentially "indigestible" about pie, steamed pudding, cake, or rich desserts of any kind. What gave them their bad reputation was the habit of many homemakers in the past of including these rich and well-liked dishes in every meal, regardless of what went before. The homemaker who balances her dessert against the rest of her menu can use even the richest kinds without hesitation, when they are suitable.

CUSTARDS

226   BAKED CUSTARD

3 cups milk or 1½ cups evaporated milk and 1½ cups
water
⅜ cup sugar (6 tablespoons)

¼ teaspoon salt
3 eggs, beaten slightly
1 teaspoon vanilla
Nutmeg

Scald milk with sugar and salt; stir slowly into beaten eggs, and add vanilla. Strain into custard cups which are set in a shallow pan of hot water. Sprinkle with nutmeg. Bake in a moderately slow oven (325° F.) until done, about 30 minutes. (This short baking time is possible only if the custard mixture is actually hot when poured into the cups and placed in the oven.) Just before baking time is up, begin to test for doneness,* and continue baking only until custard tests done. Be careful not to overbake, as baking too long or at too high a temperature results in wheying or "weeping." Cool and serve in the custard cups with a spoonful of jelly or any desired dessert sauce on top, if desired. 5 servings.

Custards may be unmolded onto a plate or saucer, if the cups are lightly greased with butter before the custard mixture is poured in.

Testing baked custard for doneness: Insert a sharp-pointed knife into one custard in two places: at center and half way between center and side of cup. First point may be slightly underdone, indicated by semi-liquid custard adhering to knife; second point should be done, indicated by knife coming out clean. Custard cup holds sufficient heat to complete cooking of custard after removal from oven.

227   BROWN SUGAR CUSTARD

1½ cups evaporated milk
1½ cups water
3 eggs, beaten slightly

¾ cup dark brown sugar,
firmly packed
¼ teaspoon salt

Combine evaporated milk and water and heat to scalding. Stir slowly into beaten eggs, add brown sugar and salt. Strain and pour into custard cups which have been set in a shallow pan of hot water. Bake in a moderately slow oven (325° F.) for 30 minutes, or until custard tests done (see Note to 226). Serve warm or cold, plain, or with a spoonful of tart jelly on top. 5 servings.

Note: One or two leftover egg yolks may be added to custard to make the product more nourishing. Either fresh or evaporated milk may be used to make any egg custard. For each cup of milk called for, use ½ cup of evaporated milk and ½ cup of water.

228 ## BUTTERSCOTCH CUSTARD

3 cups milk	3 eggs, beaten slightly
1/3 cup sugar	1 teaspoon vanilla
1/4 teaspoon salt	Butterscotch candy

Heat milk to scalding. Add sugar and salt, and stir slowly into the eggs. Add vanilla, strain, and pour into custard cups containing butterscotch candy (use 2 patties or about a heaping teaspoon of cracked butterscotch in each cup). Set cups in a shallow pan of hot water and bake in a moderately slow oven (325° F.) about 30 minutes, or until custard tests done (see Note to 226). Serve warm or chilled, unmolded if desired. 5 servings.

229 ## MINCEMEAT CUSTARD

3 cups milk	1/4 teaspoon salt
3 eggs, beaten slightly	5 tablespoons prepared
1/4 cup sugar	mincemeat

Scald milk and stir slowly into eggs. Stir in remaining ingredients and pour into greased custard cups. Set cups in a pan of hot water and bake in a moderately slow oven (325° F.) about 30 minutes or until custard tests done (see Note to 226). 5 servings.

230 ## ORANGE PUFF CUSTARD

2 tablespoons butter	1/4 cup orange juice
3/4 cup sugar	1 teaspoon lemon juice
2 tablespoons flour	1 1/2 teaspoons grated orange rind
2 eggs, separated	1/2 cup evaporated milk
1/4 teaspoon salt	1/2 cup boiling water

Cream the butter and mix thoroughly with the sugar and flour; add egg yolks and salt and beat until thick. Add orange and lemon juice, and orange rind; stir until smooth, then stir in the evaporated milk and water. Fold in beaten egg whites and pour into custard cups. Set in a shallow pan of hot water and bake in a moderately slow oven (325° F.) for 40 minutes, or until custard tests done (see Note to 226). Serve warm or cold. 5 servings.

231 ## PEANUT BUTTER CUSTARD

3 eggs, beaten slightly	1 cup evaporated milk
1/3 cup sugar	1 cup boiling water
1/4 teaspoon salt	1/2 teaspoon vanilla
1/4 cup peanut butter	

Combine eggs, sugar and salt. Combine the peanut butter very slowly with the evaporated milk. Add water and vanilla to this. Combine with first mixture and pour into custard cups. Set in a shallow pan of hot water and bake in a moderately slow oven (325° F.) 40 minutes, or until custard tests done (see Note to 226). 5 servings.

232 PUMPKIN CUSTARD

1 cup canned or fresh cooked pumpkin purée	½ teaspoon ginger
1 egg, beaten slightly	½ teaspoon cinnamon
½ cup brown sugar, packed	1 tablespoon hot water
½ teaspoon salt	1 cup evaporated milk

Mix pumpkin with egg, sugar, salt, and spices blended to a paste with the hot water. Stir in milk, then pour mixture into custard cups. Set cups in a shallow pan of hot water and bake in a moderately slow oven (325° F.) 40 minutes, or until custard tests done (see Note to 226). 5 servings.

233 SOFT OR "BOILED" CUSTARD

3 cups milk	3 eggs, beaten
⅓ cup sugar	1 teaspoon vanilla
¼ teaspoon salt	

Scald milk with sugar and salt in top of double boiler. Beat eggs well and slowly stir in the hot milk. Return to double boiler and cook over simmering water, stirring constantly, until mixture just coats a metal spoon. Custard will thicken somewhat on cooling, so do not try to cook it until thick, for this will cause it to curdle. Remove immediately from heat and set pan of custard in cold water; add vanilla, and chill before serving. Serve in sherbet glasses or sauce dishes, or as a sauce for cake or pudding. 5 servings.

Note: Custard which has begun to curdle can often be restored by placing it quickly over cold water (to stop cooking immediately) and beating vigorously with a rotary egg beater until smooth. Do not reheat.

233a SOFT MERINGUE

3 egg whites	¼ teaspoon vanilla extract, or
¼ teaspoon salt	1 teaspoon lemon juice
	6 tablespoons sugar

Have the egg whites warmed to room temperature for best results. Sprinkle salt and flavoring into the whites, and beat with a rotary beater until white but not stiff enough to hold peaks. Then start beating in sugar 1 tablespoon at a time until meringue is very thick and glossy, but not until dry. Sugar should be dissolved and meringue stiff enough to hold peaks.

For pie: Spread meringue lightly over cooled surface of pie, pushing it snugly against the edge of the crust all around; this will prevent it from pulling away from the crust. Do not smooth the surface out, but with a spoon or scraper swirl it around to form valleys and peaks; the peaks will take a deeper shade of brown and make attractive color and texture contrast. The meringue should be at least ¾-inch thick and may be thicker. Place the pie in a moderate oven (350° F.) and bake until the meringue is attractively browned, 12 to 15 minutes.

For puddings: The above meringue may be served on puddings, such as Floating Island (soft custard with a meringue "island") without cooking, in which case it should be made and dropped onto the custard just before serving. If preferred, the "islands" can be baked by dropping in mounds onto a buttered baking sheet and browning in the oven; or poached by dropping the mounds into simmering water in a covered pan. Poached meringues should be lifted out with a perforated spoon to allow them to drain.

The amount of the recipe makes sufficient meringue for 1 pie or to top 4 or 5 servings of pudding.

233b   MERINGUE SHELLS

3 egg whites	¾ teaspoon cream of tartar
⅜ teaspoon salt	¾ cup sugar

Have egg whites warmed to room temperature. Add salt and cream of tartar, and beat until mixture forms rounding peaks. Beat in sugar in portions of 1 tablespoon at a time, and continue beating until sugar is dissolved and mixture forms glossy pointed peaks. Shape into mounds, cups, or any other desired form on ungreased heavy wrapping paper or other unglazed paper on a baking sheet. A pastry bag is useful in shaping meringues. Bake in a very slow oven (250° F.) for 30 minutes for soft shells to 1 hour for dry, faintly browned shells. At the end of the baking period, turn off the heat and allow the meringues to remain in the oven until they cool. Press small meringue shells into scoops of ice cream, then spoon crushed sweetened berries over top for meringue glacé. Or serve individual meringues with berries and whipped cream. 5 servings.

234   FLOATING ISLAND

2 cups milk	4 eggs, separated
6 tablespoons sugar	1 teaspoon vanilla
¼ teaspoon salt	3 tablespoons lemon juice

Scald milk with 3 tablespoons of the sugar and the salt in top of double boiler. Beat egg yolks well, and slowly stir in the hot milk. Return to double boiler and cook over simmering water, stirring constantly until custard just coats a metal spoon. Remove immediately from heat, add vanilla and chill. Just before serving time, beat the egg whites until fluffy, add remaining sugar slowly and continue beating until mixed; then add the lemon juice and continue beating until very stiff. Drop meringue on top of chilled custard in individual serving dishes, and serve immediately. For cooked meringue, use only 2 egg whites and ⅓ cup sugar, then poach spoonfuls about 2 minutes in simmering water, covered. 5 servings.

Note: Two or three left-over egg yolks may be used in making this dessert, in which case smaller "islands" will result unless you can combine the smaller quantity of beaten whites with some whipped cream.

235   FRENCH CUSTARD

1 tablespoon butter	¼ teaspoon salt
1 tablespoon flour	5 egg yolks, beaten
3 cups milk	1 teaspoon vanilla
⅓ cup sugar	

Melt butter in top of double boiler, blend in flour and add milk slowly. Cook over direct heat, stirring constantly until boiling point is just reached. Stir in the sugar and salt. Stir slowly into the well-beaten egg yolks; then pour back into the double boiler and cook over simmering water, stirring constantly until custard just coats a metal spoon. Remove from heat, stir in the vanilla and chill before serving. 5 servings.

236   MERINGUE WITH CHOCOLATE CUSTARD

¼ cup cocoa	1 tablespoon butter
½ cup sugar	1 teaspoon vanilla
⅛ teaspoon salt	3 egg whites
¾ cup evaporated milk	⅛ teaspoon salt
1 cup water	⅓ cup sugar
3 egg yolks	

Sift first 3 ingredients together into top of double boiler. Stir in evaporated milk and water slowly to keep smooth. Cook over direct heat, stirring constantly until mixture boils; then place over boiling water. Beat egg yolks and slowly stir in a little of the hot mixture; add to rest of sauce in top of double boiler. Cook with constant stirring for 2 minutes. Remove from heat, stir in butter and vanilla and chill. When ready to serve, beat egg whites with ⅛ teaspoon salt until fluffy; then gradually add the ⅓ cup sugar, beating until smooth and stiff. To serve, pour the chilled custard over the meringue. 5 servings.

237   RHUBARB CUSTARD

1 pound rhubarb	⅛ teaspoon salt
1 tablespoon water	2 cups milk
1 cup sugar	3 eggs, beaten
3 tablespoons cornstarch	

Wash rhubarb; discard leaves and dice stems. Add water, cover, and cook slowly until rhubarb is soft. Mix together ½ cup of the sugar and 1 tablespoon of the cornstarch and stir into the rhubarb; stir constantly over low heat until sauce is thickened, then remove from heat. Mix remaining cornstarch, sugar and salt in saucepan, add milk and cook over direct heat with constant stirring, until mixture boils and thickens. Slowly stir into the beaten eggs and cook over hot water, stirring constantly for 2 minutes. When both custard and rhubarb sauce are cooled, stir the rhubarb into the custard. Serve chilled. 5 servings.

238   RICE CUSTARD

¼ cup uncooked rice	¼ teaspoon salt
2 cups milk	1 teaspoon vanilla
2 eggs, separated	3 tablespoons sugar
¼ cup sugar	

Wash rice or do not wash according to directions on package. Add to milk in top of double boiler and cook, covered, over boiling water until rice is tender, about 1 hour. Beat egg yolks thoroughly, add sugar and salt, and stir in some of the hot rice mixture; return to rest of hot rice and cook 2 minutes longer, stirring constantly. Remove from heat and cool partially. Then stir in vanilla. Beat egg whites until stiff, and gradually beat in the 3 tablespoons sugar until smooth. Fold into rice custard. Chill and serve with or without cream or milk with a garnish of jam or jelly on each serving, if desired. 5 or 6 servings.

239   APPLE RENNET-CUSTARD

1 medium-sized tart eating apple	⅛ teaspoon almond extract
1 pint milk*	1 package vanilla rennet powder

Pare and core apple and chop fine. Warm milk to just lukewarm (110° F.) in top of double boiler; remove from heat and add chopped apple and flavoring. Quickly stir in the rennet powder until dissolved, and pour immediately into 5 sherbet glasses; allow to stand at room temperature without moving for 10 minutes or until firm. Then chill in refrigerator. Serve with the following cinnamon hard sauce:

Cream 2 tablespoons butter until soft and blend in 1½ cups confectioners' (XXXX) sugar and 1½ teaspoons cinnamon. Add 1 teaspoon milk and beat vigorously until smooth. 5 servings.

239a   COCOA RENNET-CUSTARD

3 tablespoons cocoa	½ teaspoon vanilla
⅓ cup sugar	3 cups whole milk*
¼ cup water	1½ rennet tablets
¼ teaspoon salt	2 tablespoons cold water

Combine first 4 ingredients in a saucepan, blending until smooth. Bring to boil over direct heat, and simmer 3 to 5 minutes, or until perfectly smooth and slightly thickened. Stir vanilla into milk and add to syrup, heating slowly until lukewarm (110° F.). Meanwhile, dissolve rennet tablets in the 2 tablespoons cold water. When milk mixture is warm, stir in the dissolved rennet tablets quickly until mixed. Pour immediately into 5 or 6 sherbet glasses or custard cups, and let stand at room temperature without moving until firm (about 10 minutes). Then chill in refrigerator. Serve with Hard Sauce (932) or with whipped cream. Serves 5 or 6.

240   COTTAGE CHEESE RENNET-CUSTARD

1 jar (12-oz.) cottage cheese	1 package vanilla rennet powder
2 cups milk*	Strained honey

Distribute the cottage cheese among 5 sherbet glasses or custard cups. Warm the milk until just lukewarm (110° F.) in top of a double boiler.

---

*Do not use evaporated or soft curd milk in these rennet-custards, as it will not thicken.

Immediately remove from heat and stir in the rennet powder until dissolved. Quickly pour over the cottage cheese in the sherbet glasses and let stand without moving at room temperature for 10 minutes or until firm. Then chill in refrigerator. Just before serving, drizzle a spoonful of honey over each rennet-custard. 5 servings.

241   PEPPERMINT RENNET-CUSTARD

⅛ lb. peppermint stick candy   1 rennet tablet
2 cups milk*   1 tablespoon cold water

Crush candy into fine crumbs and let stand in milk in refrigerator for 1 hour. Dissolve rennet tablet in cold water. Turn milk and candy mixture into top of double boiler and heat until lukewarm (110° F.), stirring until candy is all dissolved. Remove from stove and stir in dissolved rennet tablet. Pour immediately into sherbet glasses or custard cups. Let stand 10 minutes at room temperature; then chill in refrigerator. Just before serving, garnish with a spoonful of thick Chocolate Sauce (926), or whipped cream. 5 servings.

FROZEN DESSERTS

Ice cream and its frozen relatives are among the most popular desserts which grace the American table, and are probably the most typically American of all foods with the possible exception of pie.

Theoretically, the term "ice cream" applies only to a frozen dessert with a custard base; "mousse" to any still-frozen dessert made with whipped cream. Nowadays, however, since most homes have mechanical refrigerators which make possible still-frozen desserts at any time, any sort of frozen dessert is called ice cream, except ices or sherbets which contain no cream and usually no milk.

Either the hand-turned freezer or the mechanical refrigerator gives a perfectly satisfactory ice cream when the right ingredients are used. Mechanical refrigerator ice creams are usually richer than those made in a freezer, since added richness helps to prevent formation of ice crystals when constant agitation, as in the freezer, is impossible. But freezer ice cream often tastes just as rich even though its ingredients are much lighter, due to the smoothness it acquires from the constant turning.

All ice cream mixtures have one requirement in common, and that is some ingredient to increase their viscosity. This used to be eggs or flour, producing the frozen custards common to our parents' youth; nowadays it may be eggs, flour, cornstarch, gelatine or marshmallows, which contain

*Do not use evaporated or soft curd milk in these rennet-custards, as it will not thicken.

gelatine. These substances all tend to discourage the formation of large ice crystals in refrigerator-frozen ice creams, and to increase the velvety smoothness of freezer ice creams.

The freezer ice cream recipes which have been family favorites may be adapted to the mechanical refrigerator by making a few simple alterations. The mixture must contain eggs or gelatine or marshmallows to be equally good when frozen in the refrigerator. If thin cream is called for, substitute whipping cream or evaporated milk, and whip until stiff before adding it. If the mixture contains any ingredient which may settle to the bottom (such as fruit, nuts, fruit purée, or chocolate), stir it well once or twice during the freezing process.

Freezer ice cream, because it is less rich than the still-frozen variety, is more economical. Also it can be consumed in larger quantities, because it is lighter, easier to digest, and also less fattening than richer mixtures.

Households which have both a freezer and a mechanical refrigerator can combine the two very conveniently. With a good-sized refrigerator, there will probably be enough ice in the freezing trays to freeze the cream in the freezer. Then, when it becomes too hard to turn, instead of packing the ice cream in ice and salt in the freezer, transfer it to the dry, chilled freezing trays and let it ripen and harden in the refrigerator's freezing compartment—with the cold control of course turned to the coldest point. It is easier to keep ice cream in this way than to pack it in the freezer, because ice must often be added to the freezer.

242   APRICOT ICE CREAM

1 cup dried apricots, 6 oz.	2 egg whites
1 cup hot water	⅔ cup whipping cream or
½ cup sugar	evaporated milk, chilled
¼ cup water	⅛ teaspoon almond flavoring

Wash apricots thoroughly in cold water. Pour hot water over them and allow to soak 3 hours; then cook in same water for 5 minutes. Rub through purée sieve; there should be 1 cup of pulp and liquid. If not, add water. Cool; then chill about 15 minutes. Boil sugar and ¼ cup water together until syrup threads; pour hot syrup over stiffly beaten egg whites, and beat until smooth and thick with rotary egg beater. Chill 15 minutes. Meanwhile, put chilled cream or milk in bowl surrounded by chipped ice and whip until very thick; then add almond flavoring, and continue whipping until stiff. Fold in chilled apricot purée; then fold in the egg white mixture lightly but thoroughly. Turn into freezing tray of mechanical refrigerator and freeze until firm. (If frozen in hand-turned ice cream freezer, the cream or evaporated milk need not be whipped.) 5 or 6 generous servings.

243 CARAMEL MOUSSE

½ cup sugar, caramelized   1 tablespoon butter
   (1121)   ⅟₁₆ teaspoon salt
½ cup boiling water   ¾ cup whipping cream or
3 egg yolks   evaporated milk, whipped
2 tablespoons evaporated milk   ½ teaspoon vanilla
2 tablespoons cold water

Caramelize the sugar to a rich amber color, and stir in the boiling water carefully, all at once. Increase the heat and continue stirring until the caramel is all melted and the syrup is slightly thickened. Beat yolks until thick and lemon-colored; add the 2 tablespoons evaporated milk and the cold water. Pour the slightly cooled syrup over the egg yolk mixture, stirring constantly. Then return the mixture to the skillet and cook for 2 minutes, over low direct heat, stirring constantly until the custard is smooth and slightly thickened. Add the butter and salt, and cool. Have the whipping cream or ¾ cup evaporated milk thoroughly chilled; then whip until stiff. Fold the cooled custard mixture and vanilla gently but thoroughly into the whipped cream or milk. Turn into freezing pans and place in the freezing compartment of a mechanical refrigerator, turning control to coldest point. Or if freezing with ice, place the mixture in the freezer can, close tightly, and surround with a mixture of 1 part salt to 4 parts cracked ice; let stand without turning until frozen hard, or for 2 to 3 hours. Do not remove from freezer until ready to serve. 5 servings.

244 CHOCOLATE ICE CREAM

1½ teaspoons gelatine   ¾ cup sugar
2 tablespoons cold water   ¼ teaspoon salt
1 cup milk   2 cups light cream
1 to 1½ squares bitter   1 teaspoon vanilla
   chocolate

Soften gelatine in cold water. Heat milk to scalding; then add finely cut chocolate, and reheat just to boiling point, stirring constantly. Add sugar, salt and gelatine, stirring until dissolved. Add cream and vanilla. Strain mixture into freezer can and allow to cool. When cool, cover and freeze until firm in a mixture of 8 parts cracked ice to 1 part salt; turn freezer slowly for first 3 or 4 minutes, then more rapidly until ice cream is firm. Remove dasher, replace cover, and cork hole; pack in an 8 to 1 ice-salt mixture and wrap with newspaper or sacking. Or pack in freezing tray of mechanical refrigerator and turn temperature control to coldest point possible until ready to serve. 5 servings.

245   RASPBERRY FRAPPE
(Economical and Surprisingly Good)

1 cup evaporated milk	Pinch of salt
1 tablespoon lemon juice	¾ cup seedless black raspberry
¼ teaspoon lemon rind	jam

Pour evaporated milk into a refrigerator tray and freeze to an icy mush. Transfer evaporated milk to a cold bowl, add lemon juice and beat with a rotary beater until stiff and light. Add remaining ingredients and continue beating until thoroughly blended. Pour mixture back into freezing tray and freeze 6 to 8 hours. 4 to 6 servings.

245a   LEMON CREAM FREEZE
(A Delicious Dessert)

1 14½-oz. can evaporated milk	¾ cup sugar
½ cup lemon juice	2½ teaspoons lemon rind
	1⁄16 teaspoon salt

Freeze milk in refrigerator tray to an icy mush; remove to a cold bowl, add lemon juice, beat until thick. Add sugar and salt gradually, then rind, beating until mixture is stiff and fluffy. Turn into tray and freeze. 6 servings.

246   FROZEN PEACH CREAM

¾ cup whipping cream or evaporated milk	1 cup XXXX sugar, packed
2 teaspoons lemon juice	⅛ teaspoon almond extract
	2 cups sliced fresh peaches

Thoroughly chill cream or milk and whip until stiff. Add the lemon juice and beat until very stiff. Beat in sugar and flavoring. Fold in peaches which have been mashed into very small pieces with a fork. Freeze in refrigerator tray for at least 2 hours. 5 servings.

247   PEPPERMINT STICK ICE CREAM

2 cups milk	½ pound peppermint stick candy
¼ teaspoon salt	
2 eggs, beaten	1 cup whipping cream or evaporated milk, chilled

Scald milk in top of double boiler. Add sugar and salt, then stir milk gradually into beaten eggs; then return to double boiler, and cook over hot water, stirring constantly until mixture just coats a metal spoon. Cool thoroughly. Stir in finely crushed candy. Beat chilled whipping cream or evaporated milk until stiff and fold into the peppermint custard. Freeze either in tray of mechanical refrigerator or in a hand-turned freezer packed with 8 to 1 ice-salt mixture. 5 servings.

248 RHUBARB MARLOW

1 cup sweetened stewed rhubarb (307)
24 marshmallows

1 cup whipping cream
Pink coloring, if desired

Heat rhubarb, add marshmallows, and stir over low heat until just melted. Cool. If mixture is very sweet, add lemon juice to give desired tartness. Chill until thick and syrupy; then whip cream until stiff and fold into the rhubarb mixture. Turn into freezing tray of mechanical refrigerator and freeze without stirring. If desired, the whipped cream may be tinted delicately pink before adding to the fruit mixture. 5 servings.

249 STRAWBERRY ICE CREAM

1 quart strawberries, washed and hulled
1 cup sugar
1 tablespoon lemon juice
¼ teaspoon salt

1 teaspoon gelatine
1 tablespoon cold water
1 cup whole milk
3 cups light cream

Crush berries and rub through a fine sieve to remove all seeds; there should be about 1¾ cups purée if berries of good quality are used. Add sugar, lemon juice and salt, stirring well; cover and place in refrigerator. Soften gelatine in the cold water and dissolve in milk heated to scalding. Cool. Combine with strawberry purée. Add cream. Turn into freezer can and freeze as for Old-Fashioned Vanilla Ice Cream (250). Serve plain or with sweetened sliced or crushed strawberries. Makes about 10 servings.

250 OLD-FASHIONED VANILLA ICE CREAM

1½ teaspoon cornstarch
3 cups milk
¾ cup sugar
2 eggs, beaten

¼ teaspoon salt
2 cups whipping cream
1½ teaspoons vanilla

Mix cornstarch to a thin, smooth paste with a little of the milk. Combine with 2 cups of the milk and the sugar, and cook over boiling water, with occasional stirring, for 20 minutes. Beat eggs until light, gradually stir in the hot cornstarch mixture, and return to the double boiler to cook 2 minutes longer, with constant stirring. Cool, put through strainer, stir in rest of milk, the salt, cream and vanilla. Pour into freezer can, and freeze until very firm with a mixture of 1 part salt to 8 parts cracked ice by measure. Remove dasher, press down cream, and replace cover, plugging hole with cork. Drain off all water from ice and repack can with salt-ice mixture, heaping up over top of can. Wrap whole freezer with newspapers or sacking. Or transfer ice cream to freezing tray of mechanical refrigerator and turn temperature to the coldest point until ready to serve. 8 to 10 servings.

251   CRANBERRY-APPLE MILK SHERBET

½ pound cranberries
1 cup water
1 cup thick tart applesauce
1 cup sugar

¼ cup orange juice
⅔ cup whipping cream or evaporated milk, chilled

Wash and pick over cranberries, add water and cook in covered pan until soft; put through sieve, cooking water and all, discarding skins. Combine cranberry purée with applesauce, sugar and orange juice. Beat chilled cream or evaporated milk until it is very thick and fluffy. Fold into fruit mixture thoroughly and freeze in mechanical refrigerator or in hand-turned freezer. (If frozen in hand-turned freezer, milk or cream need not be whipped.) 5 servings.

252   LEMON MILK SHERBET

⅔ cup strained lemon juice
   (3 or 4 lemons)
1½ cups sugar
2½ cups scalded milk

1 cup evaporated milk
¼ teaspoon salt
¼ teaspoon lemon rind, grated

Squeeze and strain lemon juice just before using; its flavor deteriorates on standing. Add sugar to scalded milk and stir until dissolved. Cool, then add chilled evaporated milk, salt and lemon rind. Freeze in a hand-turned freezer in an 8 to 1 ice-salt pack until mixture is mushy. Open freezer carefully to avoid entrance of any salt, and pour in lemon juice, stirring quickly. Replace dasher and lid and continue freezing until firm. Remove paddle, drain off water, and plug hole in lid; repack with an 8 to 1 ice-salt mixture. Wrap entire freezer with heavy paper, canvas or burlap and let stand 2 or 3 hours to ripen. 8 to 10 servings.

To freeze in mechanical refrigerator, use the same ingredients, except add to the scalded milk 2 teaspoons plain gelatine softened in 2 tablespoons cold water; and instead of adding liquid evaporated milk, chill thoroughly and whip until thick; then add 2 teaspoons of the lemon juice and continue whipping until stiff. Add remaining lemon juice to cooled milk-sugar mixture and freeze to a mush; then stir up and fold in whipped evaporated milk and grated lemon rind. Return to freezing tray and freeze until firm.

If both refrigerator and hand-turned freezer are available, a good plan is to freeze the sherbet in the freezer and then repack in a refrigerator tray to ripen.

253   PINEAPPLE BUTTERMILK SHERBET

1 quart thick buttermilk   1 cup sugar
1 9-oz. can crushed pineapple

Mix ingredients together thoroughly and pour into freezing trays of mechanical refrigerator. Set refrigerator for fast freezing and freeze mixture until mushy. Pour into chilled bowl and beat until smooth with rotary beater. Return to trays and continue freezing until firm. 8 to 10 servings.

254   PINEAPPLE ICE

1 cup sugar   ¼ cup lemon juice (1 large
3 cups water   lemon)
1 9-oz. can crushed pineapple   ⅛ teaspoon salt
1 small banana, mashed

Combine sugar and water and boil for 5 minutes. Cool thoroughly. Add remaining ingredients and mix well. Pour into refrigerator freezing trays, set refrigerator for fast freezing, and freeze to a mush. Stir and return to refrigerator to finish freezing until solid. Or, if desired, freeze in a hand freezer in an 8 to 1 ice-salt mixture. (See 252 for directions.) 5 servings.

255   PRUNE MARSHMALLOW FREEZE

1 cup prune juice   ¼ cup prune purée (285)
12 marshmallows (about ¼   2 tablespoons lemon juice
   pound), cut in quarters

Heat prune juice (use water in which dried prunes were cooked) to boiling. Add marshmallows and beat with rotary beater until they are melted and the mixture is smooth. Beat in prune purée and lemon juice, and turn into freezing tray of mechanical refrigerator; freeze about 1 hour, then remove and beat well, and continue freezing until firm. Or turn into the can of a hand freezer and freeze in an 8 to 1 ice-salt mixture until firm. (See 252 for directions.) 5 servings.

256   THREE-FRUIT ICE

1¼ cups water	Juice of 1 large orange
1 cup sugar	Juice of 1 lemon
Dash salt	2 ripe bananas, mashed

Bring half the water to a boil with the sugar and salt; remove from heat and add rest of water, fruit juices, and mashed bananas. Pour into freezing tray of mechanical refrigerator and freeze. When mixture is thick and mushy, turn out into a chilled bowl and beat thoroughly. Return to freezing tray and finish freezing until firm. (If frozen in a hand-turned freezer, this ice will be very smooth and fine-textured. Use an 8 to 1 ice-salt mixture. See 252 for directions.) 5 servings.

FRUIT DESSERTS

257   AMBROSIA

3 large bananas	Sugar to suit taste
3 large oranges, chilled	½ cup grated moist cocoanut

Peel and slice bananas and oranges and combine, adding sugar if desired. Place in serving dishes and sprinkle grated cocoanut over the top. Serve at once. 5 servings.

If preferred, the bananas may be sliced into the serving dishes and the oranges squeezed and juice poured over them. Then sprinkle with sugar and cocoanut. When prepared by this method, the sliced bananas and orange juice may stand in the refrigerator for half an hour or so, as the orange juice prevents the bananas from becoming discolored.

258   APPLE CRUMBLE

⅓ cup all-purpose flour	4 cups peeled, cored and
¾ cup brown sugar, packed	sliced tart apples
⅓ cup shortening (half butter)	

Combine flour and brown sugar and cut in shortening to make a crumbly mixture. Arrange pared, sliced apples in a shallow baking dish, sprinkle sugar mixture over top, and bake in moderate oven (375° F.) for about 30 minutes or until top is brown and crunchy and apples tender. 5 to 6 servings.

APPLE DUMPLINGS

5 large or 7 medium tart cooking apples	⅓ to ½ cup sugar
Plain pastry (631)	2 tablespoons butter

Peel, core and coarsely dice apples. Roll pastry out in a rectangle about 12 x 18 inches and ⅛-inch thick, and cut into 6-inch squares. Place one-sixth of apples in center of each square, sprinkle with sugar, dot with butter. Moisten edges of pastry, gather up and pinch together, sealing the apple in. Transfer to shallow baking pan and bake in a hot oven (450° F.) for 12 minutes, or until slightly browned; then reduce heat to 325° F. and continue baking 25 minutes longer or until apples are tender. Serve warm, with cream or Lemon Sauce (934). 6 servings.

260 ## APPLE DUMPLING PUDDING

1 cup all-purpose flour	1 egg, beaten
½ cup sugar	¼ cup milk
2 teaspoons tartrate or calcium-phosphate baking powder or 1½ teaspoons S.A.S.-phosphate baking powder	3½ cups thin fresh-cooked apple sauce (261) or No. 2½ can
½ teaspoon salt	¼ teaspoon cinnamon
1 tablespoon butter	1½ tablespoons lemon juice

Sift flour, measure, and resift with sugar, baking powder, and salt, into mixing bowl. Add butter and mix with finger tips. Combine beaten egg and milk and pour into dry ingredients; beat until thoroughly mixed. Heat the apple sauce, combine with cinnamon and lemon juice, and pour into a large baking dish (10 x 6½ x 2 inches). Drop batter by tablespoonfuls onto the hot apple sauce. Cover and bake in a hot oven (450° F.) for 10 minutes, then uncover and bake 15 minutes longer or until crust is golden brown. Serve with cream or top milk. 5 servings.

261 ## APPLE SAUCE

For a typically smooth, stiff apple sauce, choose apples which do not hold their shape in cooking, but cook quickly to a mush. Red Junes, Early Transparents and Duchess apples are some good varieties for this type of apple sauce. They should be cooked until mushy in water then the sugar should be added.

2 lbs. tart apples (6 to 8), pared and sliced	½ cup sugar, or to suit taste
½ cup water	Cinnamon, if desired

Put apples and water into a saucepan, cover tightly, and cook over moderate heat without stirring until apples are mushy. Add sugar (exact amount depends on taste and on tartness of apples), stir just to mix, and cook for a minute or two longer. Remove from heat and whip with spoon to a smooth stiff sauce. A little ground cinnamon may be added if desired to give the sauce a darker color and spicy flavor. Serve warm or cold. 4 to 6 servings.

Note: For an "applesauce" in which the apple slices keep their shape, see 272.

262   "DRESSING UP" CANNED APPLE SAUCE

Canned apple sauce has improved greatly in quality during the last few years, but it is purposely made bland in flavor and may therefore not be as pleasing to some palates as freshly made apple sauce from tart apples which is seasoned to suit the individual taste.

Canned apple sauce may be "dressed up" to order in a number of different ways. Add a little lemon juice and sugar to the sauce. Or combine a little lemon juice and grated lemon rind with 2 or 3 tablespoons of sugar and sprinkle it over the servings. Or sprinkle with cinnamon and sugar; or stir the cinnamon and sugar in. Half a cup of plumped raisins (306) may be folded into the sauce just before serving. A tablespoon of Orange (935) or Lemon Sauce (934) for each serving adds flavor and also eye appeal.

Many people like apple sauce best if it is thoroughly chilled before serving; some prefer it hot.

263   APPLECOT SAUCE

¼ lb. dried apricots   ½ cup sugar
1½ lbs. tart apples (5 or 6
    medium sized)

Wash apricots, soak for 4 hours in enough water to cover (about 1½ cups), then simmer for 10 minutes. Pare, core and slice washed apples. Put apple slices on top of the apricots, cover, and simmer until the apples are tender, from 10 to 15 minutes. Thoroughly mix the sugar with the fruits and simmer 2 minutes longer. Serve hot or cold, strained or unstrained, as desired. 5 or 6 servings.

264   ## APPLE SNOW

4 medium-size tart cooking   1 tablespoon lemon juice
  apples   Jelly
3 egg whites   Custard Sauce (930)
¾ cup sugar

Pare, core, and slice apples into saucepan; add ¼ cup cold water, cover tightly, and cook slowly until mushy. Mash and whip until smooth and fluffy; there should be ¾ to 1 cup stiff sauce. Chill. Beat egg whites until just fluffy, and gradually beat in the sugar and lemon juice until very stiff and smooth. Fold in the chilled apple sauce until thoroughly blended. Serve chilled, with Custard Sauce and a spoonful of red jelly on top. 5 servings.

265   ## APPLE AND CRANBERRY SAUCE

1 lb. tart cooking apples   ¾ cup water
½ lb. cranberries   1¼ cups sugar

Pare, core and slice apples. Pick over cranberries, discarding soft ones; wash and put into 3-quart saucepan with apples. Add water, cover tightly, and cook until both fruits are tender, 15 to 20 minutes. Add sugar, stirring just enough to distribute, and cook 2 or 3 minutes longer, until juice forms a syrup. Remove from heat and chill before serving. 5 or 6 servings.

266   ## BAKED APPLES No. 1

5 large baking apples   ¼ cup raisins or chopped nuts
½ cup brown sugar   2 tablespoons butter

Wash and core apples. Fill the cores with the brown sugar and raisins or nuts and dot with butter. Place in baking pan or casserole and pour enough water around them just to cover the bottom of the pan. Bake in a moderate (350° F.) oven 45 minutes to 1 hour, or until apples are tender when pierced with a fork. 5 servings.

Variation: Fill centers of the apples with ½ cup drained crushed pineapple and ¼ cup brown sugar. Dot with butter, pour water into pan, and bake as above.

267   ## BAKED APPLES No. 2

5 large tart red baking apples   ½ cup water
1 cup sugar   ½ lemon, cut in slices

Wash and core apples. Bring sugar and water to a boil. Add lemon slices. Cook apples in this syrup for 5 minutes, turning over and over. Transfer apples, lemon slices and syrup to a baking dish and bake in a moderate oven (375° F.), 15 minutes or until tender, basting apples frequently with the syrup. Serve apples with the cooking syrup and the lemon slices or with cream. This method cuts the cooking time for baked apples to less than half. 5 servings.

268   CINNAMON APPLES

5 tart cooking apples   ¼ cup cinnamon red-hot
2 cups sugar   candies
1 cup water

Wash, pare, and core apples. Make a syrup of sugar, water and red-hots. Place apples in the syrup and cook gently 15 to 20 minutes, until just tender, turning the apples frequently so all sides become colored. Cool and serve in the syrup as a dessert; or lift out, draining thoroughly, and serve on lettuce leaves with mayonnaise as a salad. Syrup may be saved and used again, adding more water and a few more red-hots as needed. 5 servings.

269   ESCALLOPED APPLES

2 lbs. tart cooking apples   3 tablespoons butter
½ cup sugar

Pare, core and thinly slice the apples. Arrange apples in 3 layers in a buttered casserole, sprinkling each layer with sugar and dotting with butter. Cover the casserole and bake in a 350° F. oven 30 to 40 minutes or until apples are tender. Serve hot or cold. 5 or 6 servings.

270   FRIED APPLES

Wash, core and slice into rings or quarters, but do not peel, 2 pounds of tart cooking apples. Place them in a heavy skillet in which 3 tablespoons fat have been melted. Butter, or bacon, ham or pork drippings, give the apples a good flavor. Cover and cook over moderate heat until soft (5 to 10 minutes); then uncover and sprinkle with sugar, and cook uncovered until apples are delicately browned on under side. If overcooked the apples will fall to pieces. Lift out carefully with a pancake turner. Serve hot. 5 servings.

271   POACHED APPLES

Combine 1 cup water, 2 cups sugar and the juice of 1 lemon in a small skillet and simmer five minutes. Wash and core 2 lbs. tart apples, cut in crosswise slices or rings ⅜ inch thick, and drop them into the hot syrup; simmer until tender. Lift out and serve hot. The syrup may be used again if a little more water and sugar are added each time. 5 servings.

271a   POACHED ORANGE SLICES

Choose seedless oranges and cut in slices about ⅜-inch thick. Cook in syrup just as for Poached Apples (271). These make an attractive garnish for baked ham.

272   STEWED APPLES

Fall apples tend to keep their shape when cooked and do not readily cook to a mush. Jonathans, Rhode Island Greenings, Northern Spies, Baldwins and many other varieties are more adaptable to stewing apples than to apple sauce. They should be cooked in a sugar syrup from the beginning, to aid in keeping their shape and color.

1 cup sugar	1 lemon, juice or slices
1 cup water	Cinnamon, if desired
1 quart pared, quartered apples	

Combine sugar and water and bring to a boil. Add apples, cover, and cook slowly until syrup boils; continue cooking gently, pressing the apples down occasionally with a spoon until they are tender and transparent-looking. If lemon slices are used, cut very thin and add to the hot syrup along with the apples. If lemon juice is preferred, add when apples are done. Add cinnamon to give desired color and flavor. Serve apples with the syrup warm or cold, with or without cream or top milk. 5 to 6 servings.

273   DANISH APPLE "CAKE"

¼ cup butter	2 tablespoons water
2 cups fine dry bread crumbs	2 cups hot sweetened tart
1 teaspoon cinnamon	apple sauce (261)
2 teaspoons sugar	Vanilla Sauce (938) or
2 tablespoons cornstarch	Lemon Sauce (934)

Melt butter, add bread crumbs, cinnamon and sugar and brown over low heat, stirring constantly. Mix cornstarch with water until smooth;

stir into apple sauce and boil 3 minutes, stirring constantly. Place crumb mixture and apple sauce in serving dish in alternate layers, beginning and ending with crumbs. Chill for 2 or 3 hours and serve with desired sauce. 5 servings.

274 STEWED DRIED APRICOTS

½ lb. dried apricots   ½ to ⅔ cup sugar
3 cups cold water

Wash the apricots thoroughly. Place in a saucepan, add the water, cover and let soak at least 4 hours or overnight. Put the soaked apricots to cook in the same water, cover and simmer very gently for 15 minutes. Just before removing from the heat, stir in the sugar. Serve warm or cold with or without top milk or cream. 5 servings.

275 APRICOT PURÉE

½ lb. dried apricots   2 cups cold water

Wash the apricots, soak and cook just as for Stewed Apricots (274). When done, rub through a food mill or a coarse sieve, using a wooden spoon to rub all purée through until only a dry mass of fiber remains in sieve. For a sweetened purée, stir in ½ to ⅔ cup sugar, according to taste; many recipes call for unsweetened purée. 2 cups.

276 APRICOT FRITTERS

1½ cups all-purpose flour
1½ teaspoons baking powder, see p. 122
¼ teaspoon salt
2 tablespoons granulated sugar
1 egg, well beaten
⅔ cup milk
1 cup drained canned apricots, chopped
2 tablespoons confectioners' sugar

Sift flour, measure and resift twice with baking powder, salt and granulated sugar. Add sifted dry ingredients to well-beaten egg mixed with milk and stir until smooth. Dip out spoonfuls of the apricots and coat with confectioners' sugar; then dip into batter so they are well covered. Drop from the spoon into deep fat heated to 375° F., and fry to a deep golden brown. Remove from fat, drain for a few moments on absorbent paper or paper toweling, and serve hot with syrup (924). 5 servings.

277   APRICOT WHIP

1½ teaspoons lemon juice   2 egg whites
½ cup evaporated milk, chilled   ¼ cup sugar
1 cup dried apricot purée
  (275)

Add lemon juice to thoroughly chilled evaporated milk and whip until stiff. Fold in the sweetened apricot purée. Beat egg whites, adding sugar gradually, until very stiff and smooth. Fold into apricot-milk mixture. Turn into a buttered casserole, set in a shallow pan of hot water and bake in a moderate oven (350° F.) 20 minutes; then reduce heat to a slow oven (300° F.) and bake 20 minutes longer. Serve immediately. This dessert may also be served uncooked and ½ cup whipping cream, whipped, may be used in place of the egg whites. 5 servings.

278   BAKED BANANAS

5 medium-sized green-tipped   About 1½ cups crushed corn-
  bananas   flakes
3 tablespoons lemon juice

Peel the bananas; roll first in lemon juice and then in the crushed cornflakes. They should be well coated. Lay in a buttered baking pan and bake 20-25 minutes in a moderate oven (350° F.). Serve hot, plain or with Lemon Sauce (934). 5 servings.

279   BANANA BUTTERSCOTCH PUDDING

1 cup brown sugar, firmly   ¼ cup butter
  packed   5 bananas, sliced
2 tablespoons milk

Combine the brown sugar, milk and butter in a saucepan and cook until sugar is melted and mixture bubbles up. Serve hot or cold over sliced bananas. For a more elaborate dessert, this may be served with a puff of whipped cream or whipped evaporated milk. 5 servings.

280   BANANA FRITTERS

¾ cup all-purpose flour   1 egg
¾ teaspoon baking powder,   ⅓ cup milk
  see p. 122   5 medium-sized bananas
⅛ teaspoon salt   (not too ripe)
¼ cup granulated sugar

Sift flour, measure and resift with baking powder, salt and sugar. Beat egg well, add milk and pour into dry ingredients, mixing thoroughly. Peel bananas and cut each in half lengthwise and once across. Dip pieces of banana into the batter and fry in deep fat heated to 375° F., until they are golden brown. Drain and serve hot with maple-flavored syrup (924) or Lemon Sauce (934). 5 servings.

280a   PAN-FRIED BANANAS

5 slightly under-ripe bananas	Juice of ½ lemon
⅓ cup butter	4 tablespoons tart jelly

Choose all-yellow or green-tipped bananas. Heat butter in a large skillet; peel bananas and cut in halves lengthwise. Lay cut side down in the bubbling butter and squeeze lemon juice over them. Cook until bananas are delicately browned on under side; then turn with a pancake turner or large spatula, being careful not to break them. Continue to cook till second side is delicately browned; then transfer carefully to a hot platter. Pour butter remaining in skillet over them and decorate by dropping a teaspoon of jelly in the center of each piece. 5 servings.

Note: Cooking may be continued until bananas are very soft and well-browned, if preferred. This gives a product sweeter and more delicate, but somewhat less attractive in appearance.

281   STEWED BLACKBERRIES

1 quart blackberries	Pinch of salt
½ cup water	½ cup sugar

Carefully wash berries, swishing them through cold water, then lift them into a saucepan. Remove any hulls. Add water, cover and heat slowly to a simmer and cook for about 15 minutes. Shake pan or stir gently during cooking to prevent berries sticking to the bottom. Add salt and sugar and heat 2 or 3 minutes longer. Remove from heat and chill. If the fruit is very ripe, add 1 or 2 tablespoons lemon juice. 5 servings.

281a   STEWED CHERRIES

1 quart sour red cherries	½ to ¾ cup sugar, according
½ cup water	to tartness of cherries

Wash and pit cherries; there will be about 2½ cups pitted. Turn into a saucepan, add water, cover and simmer until tender, about 10 minutes.

Stir in the sugar and continue heating for a minute or two or until sugar is entirely dissolved. Serve hot or cold as a dessert. 5 servings.

Variation: Stewed cherries make a pleasing sauce for cottage pudding and many people like them with pancakes or waffles. For this purpose the juice should be thickened as follows: Blend 1½ to 2 tablespoons cornstarch with a little of the cherry juice until smooth. Stir into rest of cherries and heat, stirring constantly until sauce is clear. Stir in 1 to 2 tablespoons butter and a few drops of almond extract, if desired.

282 CRANBERRY SAUCE OR JELLY

1 lb. cranberries (about 1 qt.)	2 cups sugar
1 cup boiling water	Pinch salt

Pick over berries, removing stems and discarding all soft ones. Wash and drain, put into saucepan with the water, cover and boil briskly for 10 minutes. If a smooth sauce or jelly is desired, rub berries and juice through a sieve. Add the sugar and salt to the purée or to the un-sieved berries and continue cooking until sugar is entirely dissolved. Serve either hot or cold. The puréed sauce will jell on cooling. 3¼ cups sauce or 3 cups jelly.

283 STEWED DRIED FRUIT

Wash dried prunes, apricots, peaches, pears, figs or raisins thoroughly but quickly in cold water. Barely cover with lukewarm water, cover and let stand 3 or 4 hours. Then heat fruit and simmer until tender (15 to 20 minutes) in same water in which it was soaked. Add sugar to suit taste, allowing from 2 tablespoons to ⅓ cup for each ½ pound of fruit. Amount will depend on tartness of fruit and on personal taste; many persons prefer to add no sugar at all, except to apricots (274).

For variation, a combination of dried fruits may be cooked together in the same manner.

284 DRIED FRUIT COMPOTE

½ cup moist dried apricots	½ cup dates
½ cup moist raisins	⅓ cup lemon juice
½ cup moist dried figs	¼ cup honey
½ cup moist dried prunes	

Wash apricots, raisins, figs, and prunes quickly through several cold waters. Dry on absorbent paper. Remove pits from prunes and dates and put all fruit through a food grinder. Turn fruit into a bowl and add lemon juice and honey, mixing well. Cover tightly and place fruit in refrigerator for a day or two to marinate. Serve in chilled sherbets with plain or whipped cream. 5 generous servings.

285   DRIED FRUIT PURÉE

1 lb. any dried fruit   ⅔ cup sugar, or to taste
2½ cups water

Wash fruit quickly but thoroughly in cold water, lifting out into saucepan. Add water, and let soak 3 or 4 hours. In same water, simmer gently over low heat until tender (15 to 20 minutes). During last 5 minutes of cooking, add sugar, stirring until dissolved. Cool and drain, saving juice. Pit if necessary and rub fruit through a sieve. If the purée is thicker than desired, add juice to bring to desired consistency. A very stiff purée may be preferred for fruit whips, medium stiff for cake filling. More sugar may be added if desired. Store in a tightly covered sterile jar in the refrigerator. Makes about 2½ cups. (Leftover juice may be used for breakfast, poured over fruit cup, etc.)

286   DRIED FRUIT WHIP

½ lb. mixed dried fruit   ½ cup sugar
1½ cups water   2 tablespoons lemon juice
¾ cup evaporated milk, chilled

Wash the dried fruits (peaches, apricots, prunes and pears) and put in a saucepan with the water. Soak 3 or 4 hours. Bring to boil, then simmer gently, covered, 15 to 20 minutes or until very tender. Put fruit and liquid through sieve. Whip the evaporated milk (1128). Stir sugar and lemon juice into fruit purée, and fold in the stiffly whipped evaporated milk. Serve chilled, or frozen if desired. 5 servings.

287   FRUIT CUP

Almost any combination of fruits, fresh or canned or both, may be used to make a delicious fruit cup. Here are some suggested combinations:
1. Bananas, seedless white grapes, diced peeled oranges
2. Bananas, strawberries, canned sliced peaches
3. Strawberries, fresh pineapple, bananas
4. Fresh peaches, raspberries
5. Oranges, bananas, diced raw apple

When canned fruit is used, a little lemon juice added to the juice gives a pleasing tartness. Maraschino cherries are always an attractive addition, one to a serving often being sufficient. A small amount of juice from the cherries adds color as well as flavor. If the fruits used are not sufficiently juicy, orange juice or left-over canned fruit juice may be added. Moist-pack grated cocoanut, or unsalted nuts like pecans and walnuts, are a nice addition to the fruit cup, and the cup may be topped with a little whipped cream, if desired.

288   GRAPEFRUIT SHORTCAKE

1¼ cups all-purpose flour	1½ tablespoons flour
1½ teaspoons baking powder, see p. 122	¼ cup sugar
	Pinch salt
½ teaspoon salt	½ teaspoon vanilla
3 tablespoons shortening	2 tablespoons chopped
⅜ cup milk (6 tablespoons)	Maraschino cherries or
3 small grapefruit	strawberries
¼ cup butter	

Sift the 1¼ cups flour, measure and resift twice with baking powder and salt. Cut in shortening, add milk and stir vigorously until dough thickens. Divide into 2 parts and roll out ⅜-inch thick on floured board. Place first portion in baking pan; brush with melted butter and cover with second portion. Bake in hot oven (425° F.) 20 minutes, or until nicely browned. Peel and section grapefruit and cut in small pieces; drain off juice (should be 1 cup; if not, add water). Melt the butter, stir in flour, and when smooth, add sugar, salt, and grapefruit juice. Cook until sauce boils and thickens. Remove from heat and add vanilla. Break short-cake open, cover with grapefruit, sprinkle with cherries or berries and serve warm with the sauce. 5 servings.

288a   BROILED GRAPEFRUIT

Cut grapefruit in halves. Remove core by clipping around it with kitchen shears; lift out. With grapefruit knife or sharp paring knife, cut sections loose around sides. Sprinkle each half with white or light brown sugar, using 1 to 3 teaspoons on each, according to sweetness desired, and dot with ½ teaspoon butter for each half. Place under broiler for about 10 minutes or until warmed through and browned around edges. Over-cooking tends to make the grapefruit slightly bitter; it should be heated just until warm and until sugar is well melted.

289   LIME FLUFF

5 tablespoons quick tapioca	½ teaspoon salt
2½ cups water	¼ cup lime juice
¾ cup sugar	½ teaspoon grated lime rind
1 tablespoon butter	2 egg whites

Mix tapioca, water, sugar, butter and salt in a saucepan and bring to a boil, stirring constantly. Remove from heat and add lime juice and rind. Beat egg whites until stiff. Pour hot tapioca mixture over them, beating well while pouring. Cool, then chill thoroughly. 5 servings.

290   BAKED PEACHES

Pare 5 large or 10 medium peaches and place whole in a casserole. Add 1 tablespoon water and sprinkle with ½ cup sugar. Cover casserole and bake in a moderate oven (375° F.) 20 to 30 minutes or until tender. Chill before serving. 5 servings.

291   STEWED PEACHES

1½ lbs. cling or freestone peaches	About ½ cup sugar

Pare and quarter peaches, and remove stones. Add a small amount of cold water (about ½ cup), cover and heat slowly, simmering until peaches are soft (5 to 15 minutes, the time depending on ripeness). Stir sugar into hot peaches, chill and serve. 5 servings.

292   PEACH MERINGUE

¼ teaspoon cream of tartar	½ cup granulated sugar
⅛ teaspoon almond extract	6 peaches, or 12 canned
⅛ teaspoon vanilla	peach halves
⅛ teaspoon salt	Whipping cream
2 egg whites	

Sprinkle cream of tartar, flavorings and salt over egg whites in a large mixing bowl, and beat until very foamy. Then gradually add the sugar, continuing to beat until meringue is very stiff and smooth, holds peaks well, and all sugar is dissolved. Prepare baking sheet by covering with well-buttered unglazed paper (smooth brown wrapping paper will do). Draw a 7-inch circle on the paper and spread or pipe meringue around this circle, filling in center and building sides up as high as possible; or line an 8- or 9-inch pie tin with buttered paper and spread meringue in this, heaping up sides. Place in a very slow oven (250° F.) and bake for 1½ to 2 hours, or until surface is dry and crisp. Carefully remove from paper and place on cake rack to cool and dry. Just before serving, pare and slice peaches, sprinkle with sugar and heap into meringue shell. Pile whipped cream on top. 5 servings.

293   SUGARED PEACHES

Pare and slice 5 large peaches; sprinkle with sugar and let stand at least half an hour or until most of the sugar is dissolved in the juice. Flavor will be more intense if they are allowed to stand at room temperature rather than in the refrigerator, but many persons prefer to sacrifice a small degree of flavor in order to have the peaches well chilled. 5 servings.

294   PEAR OR PEACH MERINGUES

1 egg white	2½ tablespoons cornstarch
¼ cup sugar	2 tablespoons sugar
½ teaspoon vinegar	½ cup orange juice
1 No. 2½ can pear or peach halves	2 egg yolks Juice of 1 lemon

Beat egg white until stiff. Add sugar gradually and continue beating until very stiff and smooth. Add vinegar and beat at least 1 minute longer. Pile meringue in hollows of pear or peach halves which have been placed in a buttered shallow baking pan and bake in a moderate oven (350° F.) for 12 to 15 minutes. Meanwhile, mix cornstarch with the 2 tablespoons sugar, add orange juice and juice drained from fruit and cook over direct heat, stirring constantly until sauce boils and thickens. Place over boiling water, cover and cook 10 minutes longer, stirring occasionally. Beat egg yolks thoroughly, add lemon juice and stir in a little of the hot mixture; then stir into rest of sauce in double boiler and cook 3 minutes longer, continuing to stir. Remove from heat immediately. Serve hot sauce over hot fruit meringues. 5 servings.

294a   STEWED PEARS

1 cup sugar	4 large or 5 medium cooking
1½ cups water	pears
1 lemon, sliced thin	

Put sugar and water in a saucepan and heat to boiling. Add lemon slices. Thinly pare pears, cut in half, remove cores and cut each pear half in four pieces. Drop sections immediately into the hot syrup, cover and simmer until tender, 15 to 20 minutes depending on hardness of pears. Remove and discard lemon slices, or serve them in syrup with pears. 5 servings.

295 BAKED FRESH PEARS

5 fresh pears, about 2 lbs.	¼ cup water
2 tablespoons sugar	2 teaspoons butter
2 tablespoons lemon juice	

Pare, halve and core the pears. Arrange cut side down in baking dish and sprinkle with sugar and lemon juice. Pour water around them and dot pears with butter. Cover and bake in a moderately slow oven (325° F.) until pears are soft, from ½ to 1 hour depending on type of pear. If preferred, the pears may be cored and left whole like baked apples. 5 servings.

296 BAKED PEARS WITH MARSHMALLOWS

1 No. 2 can Bartlett pear halves	1 lemon, sliced paper thin
3 teaspoons sugar	6 marshmallows
¼ teaspoon cinnamon	

Place drained pears in a baking dish with 6 tablespoons of their juice. Mix sugar and cinnamon together and sprinkle over pears. Place a paper-thin slice of lemon on each pear half and a marshmallow on top of the lemon slice. Place in a moderately hot oven (400° F.) for 5 minutes, or until marshmallows are delicately browned. Serve immediately, pouring the juice left in the baking pan over the pears. The leftover juice may be used in other foods (1135). 5 or 6 servings.

297 PLUM DUMPLINGS

Plain pastry for double crust (631)	½ cup sugar, scant
10 blue plums	Cinnamon, if desired

Roll out pastry in rectangular shape and about ⅛-inch thick. Then cut into 4-inch squares. Place a washed whole plum in the center of each square and sprinkle each with two teaspoons of sugar. Wet edges of crust with water or egg white. Bring corners up to center and pinch edges together firmly. Bake 25 to 30 minutes in a hot oven (425° F.). Serve with cinnamon combined with remaining sugar and cream, if desired. 5 servings.

298 STEWED FRESH PLUMS

2 lbs. blue plums *or* fresh prunes	1½ cups sugar
	½ cup water

Wash prunes and prick skins several times with a skewer. Put sugar and water into saucepan, cover and heat to boiling. Drop in the prunes, cover and simmer over low heat until prunes are tender, 5 to 8 minutes. Cool, then chill thoroughly before serving. 5 servings.

299   SUGARED FRESH PINEAPPLE

To determine whether a pineapple is ripe, pull out one of the spines. If it comes out easily, the fruit is sufficiently ripe. The easiest way to prepare the fruit is to cut it in crosswise slices and pare each slice. Cut out the centers of the "eyes" and the tough core and cut the rest of the slice into dice. Place in a mixing bowl in layers, sprinkling each layer with sugar. Cover and let stand several hours, so juice can flow out and sugar dissolve. The fruit may be placed in the refrigerator if desired, but the flavor will be more pronounced if fruit is not served too cold.

To eat from fingers: A convenient way to serve fresh pineapple is to cut away or to pull out the spines and remove cones of the flesh by cutting around the "eyes" with an apple corer or a sharp knife through to the center. The cones may then be taken in the fingers and dipped in sugar to eat. This eliminates the necessity for peeling.

300   PINEAPPLE DATE WHIP

½ cup evaporated milk	½ cup chopped pitted dates
1 tablespoon lemon juice	Dash salt
1 cup crushed pineapple	Sugar to suit taste

Have evaporated milk thoroughly chilled in refrigerator. Turn into chilled bowl and beat until thick; then add lemon juice and continue beating until quite stiff. Fold in pineapple, dates and salt; then fold in sugar, if any is required. Serve immediately. 5 servings.

301   STEWED PRUNES

Wash dried prunes thoroughly, place in saucepan, and barely cover with lukewarm water. Let soak 3 or 4 hours; then cook in the same water over low heat until fruit is tender—the slower the cooking, the better the product. Since prunes are very sweet, no sugar need be added when they are cooked plain. Chill before serving.

Variation 1: To ½ lb. dried prunes, allow 1 lemon. Slice very thin and add to prunes when they start to cook with 3 to 4 tablespoons sugar. Serve lemon slices with stewed prunes.

Variation 2: Instead of cooking the prunes, allow them to stand in the soaking water for a day or more until sufficiently softened. Keep closely covered.

Variation 3: Just before serving, add peeled and sliced or diced oranges to the prunes.

Variation 4: Serve the plain stewed prunes, or prunes stewed with lemon slices, with cream when the fruit is dessert.

302   PRUNE WHIP No. 1

3 egg whites   ¾ cup stiff prune purée (285)
Pinch salt   ¼ teaspoon grated lemon *or*
¼ cup sugar   orange rind, if desired

Beat egg whites until stiff; add salt and gradually beat in sugar until very stiff and smooth. Fold in the chilled prune purée and grated rind carefully, leaving the mixture streaked. Serve chilled, plain, or with cream, whipped cream or Soft Custard (233). Instead of the egg whites, 1 cup heavy cream, whipped, may be used. 5 servings.

303   PRUNE WHIP No. 2

½ lb. dried prunes   1 package orange-flavored
1 tablespoon lemon juice   gelatin

Wash prunes thoroughly. Barely cover them with water and soak 3 to 4 hours; then simmer until tender in the same water. Cool and drain off liquid. Add to this the lemon juice and enough water to make 2 cups; heat this to boiling, remove from heat and stir in the gelatin. Chill in refrigerator until syrupy; then whip until fluffy. Fold in the prunes which have been pitted and chopped or pressed through a colander or sieve, and return to refrigerator for an hour or two. Serve chilled with cream if desired. 5 servings.

304   STEWED QUINCE

2 lbs. quince   ½ to ¾ cup sugar

Pare quince. Cut in quarters and remove the core. Slice very thin, letting slices drop into 3 cups hot water. Cover closely and simmer until quince is tender, 30 to 45 minutes. More water may be needed. Add sugar to suit taste. Reheat to boiling. Cool before serving. 5 servings.

305   STEWED RAISINS

Wash ½ lb. seedless raisins thoroughly in cold water. Barely cover the raisins with water, cover saucepan and let stand one hour. Then simmer until tender about 15 minutes. Serve hot or cold. 5 servings.

306   PLUMPED OR PUFFED RAISINS

Wash raisins, put into colander or sieve and place over saucepan of simmering water. Cover and steam 10 minutes or until raisins are puffed. Puffed raisins give an unusual flavor to cake, pudding, and cookies.

307   STEWED RHUBARB

2 lbs. rhubarb   2 tablespoons water
1 cup sugar

Cut off leaves of rhubarb and wash stalks thoroughly. Do not peel unless the skin seems particularly tough, as the skin gives stewed rhubarb its attractive color. Cut stalks in 1-inch pieces, add the sugar and water. Cover kettle and cook slowly until rhubarb is tender. Chill and serve plain or with cream. 5 or 6 servings.

Variation: A combination of half rhubarb and half strawberries stewed together is delicious.

308   RHUBARB STRAWBERRY MERINGUE

3 cups cut rhubarb   1 pint strawberries, washed
2 tablespoons flour   and hulled
1¼ cups sugar   2 eggs, separated
2 tablespoons water

Trim off leaves and root end of rhubarb, and cut stems into ½-inch lengths. Turn into a saucepan with the flour and 1 cup of the sugar blended together, add water, and simmer for 10 minutes, stirring frequently. Add strawberries. Remove from heat and stir in the well-beaten egg yolks. Turn into an 8-inch square casserole and bake in a moderate oven (350° F.) for 10 minutes. Beat egg whites until stiff with remaining sugar, and spread over pudding; return to oven reduced to slow (300° F.) and bake 15 minutes longer, or until meringue is delicately browned. If preferred, meringue may be put onto the cooled pudding with a pastry tube or in puffs dropped from a spoon, then baked. 6 to 8 servings.

309　　　　　　　　STRAWBERRY SHORTCAKE

　　1 quart strawberries　　　　　1 recipe Shortcake (31)
　　⅔ cup sugar, or to suit taste　　Melted butter

Wash and hull strawberries and slice or crush them. Mix with the sugar; cover and let stand at least 30 minutes or until juice flows freely. Meanwhile, mix shortcake dough. Roll thin (about ⅓-inch thick) and cut out with biscuit cutter of desired size. If crusty shortcakes are desired, lay all biscuits out on baking sheet; if less crusty ones are preferred, transfer half of them to baking sheet, brush with melted butter, and lay rest of rounds on top. Bake as directed for Shortcake. To serve, place one biscuit (or lower half of biscuit) on serving dish, drizzle with melted butter and spoon strawberries and juice over it. Cover with another half biscuit and spoon more berries and juice over top. Serve immediately with whipped cream if desired. 5 generous servings.

Variation: Bake plain Sponge Cake (93) in a ring form. Cool and fill center to overflowing with fresh sugared strawberries and pineapple. Garnish with whole strawberries and whipped cream.

310　　　　　　　　FRESH PEACH SHORTCAKE

Make like Strawberry Shortcake (309), but substitute 2 pounds fresh peaches, pared and sliced, for the strawberries.

311　　　　　　　　FRUIT SHORTCAKE

Make shortcakes as for Strawberry Shortcake (309), and use sweetened fruit such as stewed rhubarb (307), stewed dried apricots (274) or any fresh or canned fruit with thickened juice instead of strawberries.

GELATIN DESSERTS

312　　　　　　　　APPLE DELIGHT

　　1 tablespoon gelatin　　　　⅛ teaspoon salt
　　¼ cup cold water　　　　　　1 lb. tart cooking apples
　　1 cup sugar　　　　　　　　3 tablespoons lemon juice
　　½ cup water　　　　　　　　¼ teaspoon grated lemon rind

Soak gelatin in cold water. Boil sugar and the ½ cup water for 3 minutes. Add salt and pared, sliced apples (should be 3 cups); cover, simmer until tender. Remove from heat, stir in gelatin. Add lemon juice and rind; cool. Pour into mold or bowl; chill until firm. Unmold (320) and serve with cold Custard Sauce (930) or cream. 4 servings.

Variation: To save sugar, substitute 1 cup sweet cider for the ½ cup water, reduce sugar to ½ cup and omit lemon juice and rind.

313   APPLES IN RASPBERRY GELATIN

1 package raspberry gelatin   5 good-flavored apples,
1¾ cups hot water   peeled and sliced or grated

Dissolve gelatin in the water. When it begins to set, fold in apples and pour the fruit-gelatin mixture into mold which has been rinsed in cold water. When set, unmold (320) on large serving plate, or serve sliced on small desert plates. 5 servings.

314   APRICOT BAVARIAN

2 teaspoons plain gelatin   ½ cup whipping cream or
⅓ cup cold water   evaporated milk, chilled
¾ cup apricot purée (275)   2 teaspoons lemon juice
¾ cup XXXX sugar

Soften gelatin in cold water. Heat apricot purée to boiling, add sugar and softened gelatin and stir until dissolved. Cool until mixture becomes thick and syrupy. Whip thoroughly chilled cream or evaporated milk, using chilled bowl and beater. When stiff, add lemon juice and continue beating until well blended. Fold into apricot mixture, turn into mold, and chill until firm. Unmold (320) onto chilled serving plate. 5 servings.

315   BANANA GRAPE MOLD

1 tablespoon gelatin   1 teaspoon lemon juice
¼ cup cold water   3 tablespoons sugar
1 cup hot water   3 bananas, sliced
1 cup grape juice (707)

Soften gelatin in cold water; then dissolve in the hot water. Combine with grape juice, lemon juice and sugar, stirring until sugar is dissolved. Pour a little of the mixture into bottom of mold in which one banana has been arranged in any desired pattern. Chill. When rest of mixture is cool and syrupy, add remainder of bananas. Pour into mold and chill in refrigerator until firm. Unmold (320) onto chilled serving plate. 5 servings. (If grape juice is bought, omit water and use 2 cups juice.)

316   GRAPE GELATIN

Omit bananas from Banana Grape Mold (315).

317   BUTTERSCOTCH MARSHMALLOW PUDDING

1 tablespoon gelatin	¾ cup sugar
¼ cup cold water	2 egg whites
½ cup boiling water	½ teaspoon vanilla

Soften gelatin in cold water; then dissolve in boiling water. Stir in sugar and cool. Beat egg whites until stiff and fold into cooled gelatin mixture. Add vanilla and chill in refrigerator until set, in an oiled square mold or baking pan. Cut in squares and serve with Butterscotch Sauce (925). 5 to 6 servings.

318   CARAMEL SPONGE

¾ cup sugar	2 eggs, separated
½ cup boiling water	¼ teaspoon salt
1 tablespoon gelatin	1 cup milk
¼ cup cold water	1 teaspoon vanilla

Put ½ cup of the sugar into a heavy metal saucepan or skillet, and stir constantly over direct heat until melted to an amber-colored liquid. Slowly add the boiling water and simmer until caramel is entirely dissolved, stirring occasionally. Cool for about 10 minutes. Soften gelatin in cold water. Beat egg yolks, add salt and milk and slowly stir in the caramel syrup. Return to saucepan and cook over low heat, stirring constantly until mixture just coats the spoon. Remove from heat and stir in the gelatin; add vanilla and chill. When mixture has become thick and syrupy, beat the egg whites until stiff, add rest of sugar, and beat until blended; then whip the gelatin mixture until fluffy, and add to the egg whites, beating until well mixed. Pour into mold, bowl, or sherbet glasses and chill until firm. Serve with whipped plain cream. 5 servings.

319   CHOCOLATE BAVARIAN

1 tablespoon gelatin	1½ cups whipping cream or
¾ cup cold water	evaporated milk
1 square (1 oz.) baking	½ cup sugar
chocolate	½ teaspoon vanilla

Soften gelatin in ¼ cup of the cold water. Melt chocolate over boiling water; add ½ cup of the cream or evaporated milk, sugar and rest of water and cook about 5 minutes, stirring until smooth. Pour over softened

gelatin, stirring until dissolved. Add vanilla and cool until mixture is
thick and syrupy. Have rest of cream or evaporated milk thoroughly
chilled and whip with rotary beater in chilled bowl until stiff. Whip
chocolate mixture until smooth and fold in the whipped cream or evaporated milk. Turn into mold which has been rinsed with cold water and
chill in refrigerator until set. 5 servings.

320   FRUIT-FLAVORED GELATIN

1 package fruit-flavored gelatin	2 cups boiling water

Turn the gelatin into a heat-proof mixing bowl, add the boiling water
and stir until gelatin is entirely dissolved. Pour into a mold or leave in
the bowl and chill in the refrigerator until congealed.

To hasten congealing: Dissolve the gelatin in 1 cup boiling water;
then stir in 1 cup cold water. This reduces the time required for cooling.

To whip the gelatin: Allow the gelatin to chill until it is thick and
syrupy, just on the verge of setting. Then whip with an egg beater until
smooth, fluffy and light colored. Return to refrigerator until firm.

To elaborate gelatin: Juice from canned or fresh fruit may be substituted for all or part of the water in making up the gelatin. If one cup
of drained diced fruit is added to the gelatin it will be necessary to reduce the liquid to 1½ cups. To arrange the fruit in a pattern which will
appear on the top of the mold as it comes to the table, pour in a little of
the liquid gelatin, arrange the fruit in this, and chill until set. Then pour
in rest of gelatin mixed with rest of fruit.

To unmold gelatin: Dip mold to the depth of the gelatin in lukewarm (not hot) water for a minute; run a sharp knife around the edge
and shake mold vigorously to loosen. Turn out onto chilled plate. Repeat
if it does not slip out readily. If the mold is rubbed with salad oil before
pouring in the gelatin, dipping in warm water will not be necessary, and
vigorous shaking alone will loosen the gelatin.

321   GRAPE BAVARIAN

1 tablespoon plain gelatin	¼ cup sugar
2 cups grape juice (707)	½ cup whipping cream or
⅓ cup orange juice	evaporated milk, chilled
1 tablespoon lemon juice	

Sprinkle gelatin over ¼ cup of the cold grape juice and let soak 5 minutes. Heat over hot water, stirring until gelatin dissolves. Meanwhile, combine rest of grape juice with orange juice, half the lemon juice, and the sugar, stirring until sugar is dissolved; then stir in the gelatin mixture. Chill until thick and syrupy; then beat with rotary beater until light and fluffy. Have cream or evaporated milk thoroughly chilled; beat until stiff, add rest of lemon juice and beat until very stiff. Fold thoroughly into grape gelatin and transfer to mold which has been rinsed with cold water. Chill until firm. Unmold (320) onto cold serving plate. 5 servings.

322   GRAPEFRUIT FLUFF

1 tablespoon gelatin	1 cup milk
¼ cup cold water	2 tablespoons sugar
1 No. 2 can grapefruit sections	1 teaspoon cornstarch
2 eggs, separated	Pinch salt
¼ cup sugar	1 tablespoon butter

Soften gelatin in the cold water; then dissolve in a little juice drained from the grapefruit which has been heated. Add to rest of juice and the grapefruit which may be diced or left whole as desired. Chill until liquid starts to congeal. Beat egg whites until stiff; then gradually beat in the ¼ cup sugar. Whip this meringue into the gelatin mixture. Chill until firm. Beat egg yolks, add milk, and stir in the 2 tablespoons of sugar combined with the cornstarch. Cook over boiling water, stirring constantly, until sauce thickens. Stir in salt and butter and cool. Serve over the grapefruit fluff. 5 or 6 servings.

323   LEMON PINEAPPLE FLUFF

1 package lemon-flavored gelatin	1 9-oz. can crushed pineapple
1¼ cups hot water	½ cup whipping cream or evaporated milk, chilled
3 to 4 tablespoons lemon juice (juice of 1 lemon)	Pinch salt

Dissolve gelatin in the hot water; add all but 1 teaspoon of the lemon juice, and the juice drained from the crushed pineapple. Chill until syrupy. Have the cream or evaporated milk ice cold; turn into a bowl surrounded by cracked ice, and beat until thick. Then add the remaining 1 teaspoon of lemon juice and salt and continue beating until mixture just holds its shape. Whip the gelatin mixture, stirring in the drained pineapple; then fold in the whipped cream or evaporated milk. Continue chilling at least 1 hour; it does not become very stiff. Serve in sherbet glasses. 5 servings.

324   OATMEAL JELLY DESSERT

⅓ cup rolled oats
¼ teaspoon salt
1½ cups boiling water
½ cup XXXX sugar

1 tablespoon gelatin
2 tablespoons cold water
½ cup whipping cream or
    evaporated milk

Add oats gradually to salted boiling water. Boil 2 minutes, then cover and cook over hot water 45 minutes to 1 hour. Remove from heat, add sugar and stir until dissolved; then rub through a strainer. Soften gelatin in the cold water and melt it over hot water. Stir into the first mixture. Fold in the whipped cream or whipped evaporated milk. Pour into small molds and chill until set. Unmold (320). Serve with fresh or canned berries, if desired. 5 servings.

325   FRESH ORANGE BAVARIAN

1 tablespoon plain gelatin
¼ cup cold water
1 cup orange juice
1½ tablespoons lemon juice

Pinch salt
½ cup sugar
¾ cup whipping cream or
    evaporated milk, chilled

Soften gelatin in the cold water; then place over hot water and heat until gelatin is melted. Combine orange juice with lemon juice (saving out 1 teaspoon lemon juice), salt, and sugar. Add gelatin, stir thoroughly, and chill until thick and syrupy. Then whip with egg beater until light and fluffy. Whip chilled cream or evaporated milk until thick; then add the 1 teaspoon lemon juice and continue beating until stiff. Fold whipped cream or milk thoroughly into gelatin and turn into a mold which has been rinsed with cold water. Chill until firm. To unmold, loosen around edges with a sharp knife, dip into warm water and shake until sides are loose. Turn out onto a chilled serving plate. Garnish with sections of peeled orange and whipped cream, if desired. 5 servings.

326   ORANGE JELLY

1½ tablespoons gelatin
1 cup cold water
1 cup boiling water
⅔ cup sugar
2 teaspoons grated orange rind

2 teaspoons grated lemon rind
1 cup orange juice
½ cup lemon juice
Pinch salt

Soften gelatin in the cold water; then add boiling water, stirring until gelatin dissolves. Add remaining ingredients and stir until well blended. Cool, turn into a 4-cup mold which has been rinsed in cold water, cover and place in refrigerator to congeal. Unmold (320). Serve plain, or with plain or whipped cream. Plan to serve gelatin soon after it has congealed so that vitamins will not be lost. 5 or 6 servings.

327   ORANGE BUTTERMILK JELLY

½ cup strained orange juice
1 tablespoon lemon juice
1½ cups thick buttermilk
  Pinch salt
  About ⅓ cup sugar (or to suit taste)

1 tablespoon gelatin
3 tablespoons cold water
2 oranges, peeled and sectioned
  Whipping cream

Combine orange and lemon juice with buttermilk and salt and sweeten to suit the taste (depending on sweetness of orange juice). Soften gelatin in cold water; then heat until melted over hot water. Stir into buttermilk mixture. Pour into a mold or bowl, and chill until firm. Unmold (320) and garnish with orange sections, and serve with whipped cream if desired. 5 servings.

328   PEACH GELATIN

1 package orange-flavored gelatin
1 cup hot water

About 4 medium peaches
Sugar to suit taste
Plain or whipping cream

Dissolve gelatin in the hot water; cool. Peel peaches, remove stones, and mash to a smooth pulp; stir in sugar to suit taste. There should be 1 cup of purée. Fold purée into gelatin mixture, turn into mold rinsed with cold water, and chill until firm. Unmold (320); slice and serve with cream. 5 servings.

329   PINEAPPLE BAVARIAN

1 tablespoon plain gelatin
¼ cup cold water
1 9-oz. can crushed pineapple
1 cup whipping cream or evaporated milk, chilled

Juice of 1 lemon (3 tablespoons)
¼ cup granulated sugar

Soften gelatin in the cold water. Drain juice from pineapple and heat to boiling; stir in gelatin until dissolved, then set aside to cool. Have the cream or evaporated milk thoroughly chilled, either by pouring into freezing tray of refrigerator for an hour or two, or by placing in a bowl of cracked ice and salt. When well chilled, beat in chilled bowl with rotary beater until fluffy; then add lemon juice and sugar, and beat until very stiff. Fold in gelatin mixture and crushed pineapple. Chill in refrigerator until firm, and serve cold. 5 servings.

330   PINEAPPLE SNOW

1 tablespoon plain gelatin	3 tablespoons lemon juice
¼ cup cold water	2 egg whites
1 9-oz. can crushed pineapple	Pinch salt
Water to make 1 cup liquid	¼ cup sugar

Soften gelatin in the cold water. Drain pineapple; measure juice and add enough water to make 1 cup liquid. Heat to boiling, add softened gelatin and stir until dissolved. Add drained pineapple and lemon juice. Chill in refrigerator until mixture begins to congeal. Beat egg whites until stiff; add salt and gradually beat in sugar until very stiff and smooth. Whip gelatin mixture and fold thoroughly into egg white mixture. Turn into mold rinsed with cold water, and chill in refrigerator until firm. Unmold (320). Serve with Custard Sauce (930), if desired. 5 servings.

331   MOLDED PLUM PUDDING

1 tablespoon gelatin	¾ cup steamed seedless raisins
¼ cup cold water	½ cup chopped nuts
1¾ cups hot water	½ cup chopped dates
¼ cup shredded candied citron	3 tablespoons lemon juice

Soften gelatin in the cold water; then add hot water and stir until dissolved. Cool; then add remaining ingredients and chill. When it begins to congeal, stir until fruit and nuts are well distributed, and pour into individual molds; chill until firm. Unmold (320). Serve with Orange Sauce (935). 5 servings.

332   PRUNE AND ORANGE JELLY

¼ lb. dried prunes	¾ cup cold water
1 package orange-flavored gelatin	2 oranges, peeled and sliced or diced
1 cup boiling water	

Soak prunes overnight in just enough cold water to cover; drain and remove stones. Cut in quarters, or smaller if prunes are quite large. Turn gelatin into mixing bowl, add boiling water, and stir until dissolved; add cold water (including water in which prunes were soaked) and stir in prunes. Cool until gelatin begins to congeal; then add oranges and chill until firm, either in a bowl or mold. Unmold (320). 5 servings.

333 RASPBERRY BAVARIAN

1½ cups boiling water	Pinch salt
1 package raspberry-flavored gelatin	½ cup whipping cream or evaporated milk, chilled
¼ cup sugar	1 teaspoon lemon juice

Pour boiling water over the raspberry gelatin and stir until dissolved. Add sugar and salt, and chill gelatin until thick and syrupy. Turn the well-chilled cream or evaporated milk into a chilled bowl and whip until stiff; add lemon juice and continue beating until very stiff. Using same beater, whip up gelatin until light and fluffy; then add the whipped milk or cream and fold in thoroughly. Turn into a mold which has been rinsed with cold water. Chill until firm. Unmold (320) onto a chilled serving plate. Garnish by piping with whipped cream, if desired. 5 servings.

This same method may be used for any fruit-flavored gelatin. A pleasing variation is to fold in the whipped cream or milk only partially to give a marbled appearance.

334 MOLDED RASPBERRY CREAM

1 package raspberry-flavored gelatin	½ cup boiling water
	1½ cups milk

Dissolve the gelatin thoroughly in the hot water, and cool. When completely cooled, but before thickening, stir in the milk. (Milk may curdle if combined while gelatin mixture is warm.) Pour into individual molds and chill in refrigerator until firm. Unmold and serve. Other fruit flavors may be used, and the mixture is also good if whipped with an egg beater when partially congealed, and again allowed to set. 5 servings.

335 RASPBERRY SPONGE

½ pint red raspberries	3 tablespoons cold water
⅔ cup sugar	½ cup hot water
3 tablespoons lemon juice	2 egg whites, beaten
1 tablespoon plain gelatin	Plain or whipping cream

Wash and crush berries; add sugar and lemon juice, and stir until sugar is dissolved. Soften gelatin in the cold water; add hot water and stir until dissolved. Add to raspberries and stir well; chill until mixture begins to congeal. Beat egg whites until stiff; add raspberry gelatin and continue beating until thoroughly mixed. Chill until firm. Serve in sherbets with cream. 5 servings.

336 SNOW PUDDING

1 tablespoon plain gelatin	6 tablespoons lemon juice
¼ cup cold water	(2 lemons)
1 cup boiling water	2 egg whites
⅔ cup sugar	

Soften gelatin in the cold water; pour boiling water over it and stir until dissolved. Add sugar and lemon juice; chill until mixture begins to congeal. Then whip. Beat egg whites until stiff and fold thoroughly into gelatin mixture. Cover bowl and chill in refrigerator until firm. Serve in sherbet glasses with Custard Sauce (930) spooned over top. 5 servings.

337 STRAWBERRY SPONGE

1 pint strawberries	3 tablespoons cold water
½ cup sugar	½ cup hot water
1 tablespoon lemon juice	2 egg whites or
1 tablespoon plain gelatin	¾ cup whipping cream

Wash, hull, and crush strawberries. Add sugar and lemon juice and stir until sugar is dissolved. Soften gelatin in the cold water; add hot water and stir until dissolved. Add to strawberries and stir well; chill until mixture begins to congeal. Beat egg whites or the cream until stiff with rotary beater; add strawberry mixture and beat with spoon until thoroughly mixed. Chill until firm. Serve in sherbet glasses with or without cream. 5 servings.

PUDDINGS

338 BLACKBERRY PUDDING

2 cups sifted all-purpose flour	2 eggs, beaten
3 teaspoons baking powder, see p. 122	2 tablespoons lemon juice
½ teaspoon salt	1 No. 2 can blackberries
¼ cup shortening	(1¾ cups berries and
⅔ cup granulated sugar	¾ cup juice)

Sift flour, measure and resift 3 times with baking powder and salt. Cream shortening until smooth and soft; add sugar, blending in thoroughly, then the eggs and beat until mixture is fluffy and light in color. Add flour mixture alternately in 3 or 4 portions with lemon and blackberry juice, beginning and ending with flour and beating until smooth after each addition. Fold in blackberries just enough to distribute them.

Turn into a well-buttered baking dish (7 x 11 x 2 inches) and bake in a moderate oven (350° F.) 35 minutes. Then increase heat to moderately hot (400° F.) and bake 10 minutes longer. Serve from baking dish, hot or warm, with Lemon Sauce (934). 10 servings.

339   BREAD PUDDING

5 slices day-old bread	½ cup sugar
2 tablespoons butter or margarine	3 eggs, beaten
	3 cups milk, scalded
½ cup moist raisins	¼ teaspoon cinnamon
¼ teaspoon salt	

Toast bread and spread with all the butter while hot. Arrange toast in a buttered baking pan (10½ x 6½ x 1¾ inches). Sprinkle with raisins. Stir salt and all but 2 tablespoons of the sugar into the eggs. Add milk and stir to mix well. Pour over the toast and let stand 10 minutes. Press toast lightly down into milk occasionally so it soaks up most of the milk mixture. Mix cinnamon with remaining 2 tablespoons sugar and sprinkle over top. Place dish directly on oven rack. Bake in a moderate oven (350° F.) about 25 minutes, or until knife inserted in center comes out clean and top is an appetizing brown. Serve warm or cold. 5 to 6 servings.

340   COCOA BREAD PUDDING

2 cups evaporated milk	½ cup sugar mixed with
2 cups water	¼ cup cocoa
2 tablespoons butter	½ teaspoon salt
2 cups sifted dry bread crumbs	1 teaspoon vanilla
2 eggs, slightly beaten	Cream

Combine evaporated milk with water, add butter and heat to scalding. Pour over bread crumbs, stir well and set aside. Beat eggs slightly and add remaining ingredients, continuing to beat until well mixed. Combine thoroughly with milk and crumb mixture and pour into buttered 6-cup baking dish. Bake in a moderate oven (350° F.) 45 minutes, or until custard tests done (see Note to 226). Serve hot or cold with plain cream. 6 to 8 servings.

341   ORANGE MARMALADE BREAD PUDDING

5 slices day-old bread, toasted	1¾ cups milk
3 tablespoons soft butter	3 teaspoons lemon juice
¾ cup orange marmalade	⅛ teaspoon nutmeg
3 eggs, slightly beaten	Cream

Spread each slice of toast (do not remove crusts) with butter and marmalade, using all the marmalade. Cut in cubes and turn into buttered casserole. Mix slightly beaten eggs with milk, lemon juice and nutmeg and pour over the toast cubes. Bake in a slow oven (300° F.) 45 minutes, or until custard tests done (see Note to 226). Serve warm or cold, with cream or Lemon Sauce (934). 5 servings.

342   BROWN BETTY

2 cups coarse stale bread crumbs	¼ teaspoon salt
6 cups sliced, pared, tart apples	3 tablespoons lemon juice
½ cup sugar	¼ cup water
¼ teaspoon cinnamon	2 tablespoons butter
	Cream

Put ⅓ of the crumbs into a buttered casserole and cover with half the apples. Mix the sugar, cinnamon and salt together and sprinkle half the mixture over the apples. Add another layer of crumbs and another of apples and sprinkle with rest of sugar mixture. Top with crumbs, pour lemon juice and water over all and dot with the butter. Cover and bake in a moderate oven (350° F.) 30 minutes; then uncover and bake 15 minutes longer. Serve hot or cold with or without cream. 5 servings.

343   CARAMEL BLANC MANGE

⅓ cup granulated sugar	¾ cup cold water
½ cup hot water	1⅔ cups evaporated milk, scalded
¼ cup corn starch	
½ cup granulated sugar	1 teaspoon vanilla
⅛ teaspoon salt	Cream

Turn the ⅓ cup sugar into a skillet and heat, stirring constantly until sugar melts to an amber-colored liquid. *Carefully* add the hot water and continue to stir over low heat until the caramel is entirely dissolved. Then remove from heat. Mix cornstarch with the ½ cup sugar and salt in top of double boiler; add cold water and blend until smooth, then stir in the caramel syrup. Cook over direct heat, stirring constantly, until mixture boils and thickens. Slowly stir in scalded milk; then place over boiling water, cover and cook 20 minutes, stirring occasionally. Remove from heat and stir in vanilla. Chill well and serve plain or with Chocolate Sauce (926) or cream. 5 servings.

344   CHOCOLATE BLANC MANGE

2 squares (2 oz.) baking chocolate
2 tablespoons butter
⅓ cup cornstarch
¾ cup sugar
¼ teaspoon salt

1½ cups evaporated milk, scalded
1½ cups hot water
1 teaspoon vanilla
Plain cream

Melt chocolate and butter over hot water in top of double boiler. Mix cornstarch, sugar, and salt together; stir in about ¼ cup of the milk, then add to melted chocolate and blend thoroughly. Stir in rest of milk and water and cook over direct heat, stirring constantly until mixture boils and thickens. Replace over boiling water, cover and cook 15 minutes longer with occasional stirring. Remove from heat, stir in vanilla and cool before serving. Serve plain or with cream. 5 servings.

345   CINNAMON BLANC MANGE

2½ cups milk
¼ cup cornstarch
⅓ cup brown sugar, packed
⅜ teaspoon salt

1 teaspoon cinnamon
⅟₁₆ teaspoon almond extract
1 tablespoon butter

Scald 2 cups of the milk in top of double boiler. Combine cornstarch, sugar, salt and cinnamon and mix until smooth with remaining cold milk. Stir carefully into the scalded milk and cook over boiling water about 15 minutes or until thick, stirring occasionally. Add flavoring and butter, mixing well. Serve warm or cold, with cream or top milk if desired. A spoonful of tart red jelly makes a colorful, tasty garnish. 5 servings.

346   CHOCOLATE EGG YOLK PUDDING

3 squares (3 oz.) baking chocolate
1 cup sugar
1 tablespoon flour

¼ teaspoon salt
2 cups milk, scalded
5 egg yolks, beaten
½ teaspoon vanilla

Melt chocolate over hot water (1124); mix sugar, flour and salt, and blend with melted chocolate. Stir in 1 cup of the hot milk until smooth; then cook over direct heat until it boils, stirring constantly. Stir rest of scalding hot milk slowly into beaten egg yolks; add to chocolate mixture and cook 2 or 3 minutes longer over boiling water, stirring constantly. Remove from heat and stir in vanilla. Cool and serve plain or with milk or cream. 5 servings.

This is an excellent way of using left-over egg yolks.

347   CHOCOLATE MARSHMALLOW PUDDING

2½ squares (2½ oz.) baking   1⅔ cups evaporated milk
   chocolate   ¾ cup water
½ cup sugar   12 marshmallows, quartered
6 tablespoons flour   1 egg, well beaten
¼ teaspoon salt   1 teaspoon vanilla

Melt chocolate over hot water in top of double boiler (1124). Thoroughly mix the sugar, flour and salt; add to chocolate and stir until well blended. Add about ¼ cup of the milk, stir to a smooth paste and stir in the rest of the milk and the water. Cook until thickened, stirring constantly. When thick, add the marshmallows, cover and continue cooking 15 minutes with occasional stirring. Stir a little of the hot mixture into the beaten egg and return to double boiler for 2 minutes, stirring all the time. Then remove from heat and add vanilla. Serve warm or cold, with milk or cream. 5 servings.

348   CHOCOLATE WHEAT PUDDING

½ cup cracked wheat cereal   2 tablespoons cocoa
1 cup water   ⅓ cup water
¾ cup evaporated milk   1 teaspoon vanilla
¾ teaspoon salt   2 tablespoons butter
⅓ cup sugar

Put cereal into top of double boiler, then stir in the 1 cup water, evaporated milk and salt; cover and cook over boiling water ½ hour, or until thickened, stirring occasionally to prevent lumping. Combine sugar and cocoa, mix with the ⅓ cup water and bring to boil; stir into cereal and cook 15 minutes longer. Remove from heat, add vanilla and butter. Serve hot or cold with cream or milk. 5 servings.

349   COCOA PUFF

3 egg whites   3 tablespoons cocoa
½ cup sugar   ½ teaspoon vanilla

Beat egg whites until stiff. Add one-half the sugar gradually, continuing to beat until very stiff and smooth. Sift cocoa with rest of sugar and add gradually, continuing to beat all the while. Finally beat in vanilla. Pile into dessert dishes and chill. Serve with cream. 5 servings.

350   CORNSTARCH PUDDING

⅓ cup cornstarch   4 cups milk
½ teaspoon salt   ¼ cup butter
¾ cup sugar   1 teaspoon vanilla

Mix cornstarch, salt and sugar, and blend until smooth with 1 cup of the milk. Scald rest of milk, add the cornstarch mixture, and stir constantly over direct heat until it boils and thickens. Place over boiling water, cover and cook 10 minutes longer, stirring occasionally. Remove from heat, stir in butter and vanilla, and pour into large bowl or individual molds (such as custard cups) to cool. Unmold and serve with any desired sauce or with preserves or fresh fruit, such as crushed sugared strawberries and cream. 5 servings.

351 BANANA CORNSTARCH PUDDING

Fold sliced bananas into the warm Cornstarch Pudding (350). Chill and serve with Custard Sauce (930) or with cream or milk.

352 BUTTERSCOTCH PUDDING

Make exactly like plain Cornstarch Pudding (350), except substitute 1 cup brown sugar packed into cup, for the granulated sugar. Serve with cream or milk. 5 servings.

353 COTTAGE PUDDING

1½ cups cake flour	¾ cup sugar
1½ teaspoons baking powder, see p. 122	1 egg
½ teaspoon salt	½ teaspoon vanilla
¼ cup shortening	½ cup milk

Sift and measure flour and resift 3 times with baking powder and salt. Cream shortening and blend in sugar. Add egg and beat until smooth and fluffy. Stir in vanilla. Add flour mixture alternately with milk in 2 or 3 portions beating well after each addition. Turn into buttered rectangular baking pan (7 x 11 x 1½ inches) and bake in a moderate oven (350° F.) 30 minutes. Cut into squares and serve with Lemon Sauce (934). 6 to 8 servings.

354 DATE CAKE DESSERT

1⅓ cups all-purpose flour	1 egg
1 teaspoon soda	½ lb. dates
1 tablespoon butter	1 cup boiling water
1 cup sugar	

Sift flour, measure and resift 3 times with soda. Cream butter and sugar well, then beat in the egg. Cover chopped, pitted dates with the boiling water. Add to the creamed mixture alternately with the flour mixture, beating well. Pour into a buttered pan (7 x 7 x 1½ inches) and bake in a moderate oven (375° F.) 25 minutes, or until it springs back to the touch. Serve warm or cold, with Lemon Sauce (934) if desired. 6 to 8 servings.

355   DATONA PUDDING

¾ cup whole wheat flour
1½ teaspoons baking powder, see p. 122
½ teaspoon salt
3 tablespoons butter

½ cup sugar
1 egg, slightly beaten
¾ cup milk
¼ cup chopped walnuts
¼ cup chopped dates

Sift flour, measure, resift 3 times with baking powder and salt; stir bran left in sifter into the sifted flour mixture. Cream butter, blend in sugar, add egg, and beat well until smooth and fluffy. Add dry ingredients alternately with milk, beginning and ending with flour and beating after each addition. Add nuts and dates, stirring just enough to distribute. Turn into a buttered baking pan (8 x 8 x 1 inch) and bake in a moderate oven (375° F.) 25 minutes, or until it begins to leave sides of pan. Serve hot or cold, with Lemon Sauce (934). 6 to 8 servings.

356   DUTCH APPLE CAKE

2 cups all-purpose flour
½ teaspoon salt
3 teaspoons baking powder, see p. 122
½ cup sugar
¼ cup melted shortening
1 egg, beaten

1 cup milk
3 large tart cooking apples, pared, quartered, cored and sliced
1 teaspoon cinnamon
1 tablespoon butter

Sift flour, measure and resift 3 times with salt, baking powder and ⅔ of the sugar. Stir cooled melted shortening into egg and milk which have been beaten together, and add all at once to the dry ingredients. Stir quickly until flour mixture is just dampened; then stir 3 or 4 times more, but not until smooth. Turn into buttered pan (7 x 11 x 1½ inches) and spread out in even layer. Arrange apple slices in rows over top pressing sharp edges lightly into dough and sprinkle with remaining sugar mixed with the cinnamon. Dot with butter. Bake in a moderately hot oven (425° F.) 25 minutes, or until golden brown. Serve warm with butter or with Lemon Sauce (934). 5 to 6 servings.

357 INDIAN PUDDING

3 cups milk	½ teaspoon cinnamon
⅓ cup cornmeal	1 tablespoon molasses
¼ cup sugar	½ cup raisins
½ teaspoon salt	

Scald the milk. Combine cornmeal with sugar, salt, and cinnamon; pour scalding hot milk over them and stir well. Mix in molasses and raisins. Pour into buttered baking dish and bake in moderate oven (350° F.) for 1¼ hours, stirring several times during baking. Serve hot or cold, plain or with cream or ice cream. 5 servings.

358 JAM MERINGUE PUFF

1 cup milk	¼ teaspoon vanilla
3 tablespoons sugar	¼ to ⅓ cup tart jam or jelly
⅛ teaspoon salt	Pinch salt
3 eggs, separated	

Scald milk in top of double boiler with sugar and salt. Beat egg yolks and stir in about half of the scalding hot milk; return to other half of milk in double boiler and cook over boiling water, stirring constantly, until custard coats a metal spoon. Remove immediately from heat; add vanilla. Cool and chill. When ready to serve, beat the egg whites until fairly stiff; add the jam or jelly and a pinch of salt, and continue beating until very stiff and smooth. Dip into individual serving dishes and serve with the custard sauce. 5 servings.

359 LEMON CHIFFON PUDDING

3½ tablespoons flour	2 eggs, separated
⅔ cup sugar	3 tablespoons lemon juice
2 tablespoons butter	⅔ cup milk

Mix flour and sugar together and add to creamed butter, blending thoroughly. Stir in beaten egg yolks, lemon juice, and milk; and fold in stiffly beaten egg whites. Fill individual custard cups ⅔ full and bake in a moderately hot oven (350° F.) 35 minutes, or until custard tests done (see Note to 226). Serve warm or cold. 5 servings.

360 ## LEMON CRACKER PUDDING

1 cup evaporated milk
1 cup water
⅔ cup coarse cracker crumbs
¾ cup sugar
½ teaspoon salt
2 tablespoons lemon juice

½ teaspoon grated lemon rind
2 tablespoons melted butter
2 eggs, separated
¼ cup sugar
1 tablespoon lemon juice

Add milk to water and scald in top of double boiler. Combine cracker crumbs, ¾ cup sugar, salt, 2 tablespoons lemon juice and the rind, and add slowly to scalded milk and water, stirring constantly. Stir in melted butter and beaten egg yolks. Pour into greased baking dish and bake in a moderately slow oven (325° F.) 45 minutes. Then remove from oven, cover with meringue made by beating whites of eggs until stiff, gradually adding ¼ cup sugar and 1 tablespoon lemon juice. Bake in a moderate oven (350° F.) until meringue is brown (12 to 15 minutes). Serve warm or cold. 5 servings.

361 ## LEMON CREAM PUDDING

1 cup sugar
⅛ teaspoon salt
¼ cup cornstarch
1 cup cold water
¾ cup milk

3 eggs, separated
½ cup lemon juice
½ teaspoon grated lemon rind
Currant jelly (705)

Thoroughly mix sugar, salt and cornstarch in top of double boiler. Stir in cold water and milk, and stirring constantly, cook over direct heat until mixture boils and has a transparent-look. Place over boiling water, cover and cook 15 minutes. Separate eggs and beat the yolks; stir in lemon juice and rind. Stir a little of the hot mixture into the egg yolks; then return to the double boiler and cook 2 minutes longer, stirring constantly. Remove from heat. When lukewarm, fold in the egg whites which have been beaten until just stiff. Chill, and serve in sherbet glasses with a currant jelly garnish. 5 servings.

362 ## LEMON GRAPE-NUT PUDDING

¼ cup soft butter
¾ cup sugar
2 eggs, separated
2 tablespoons flour

¾ cup milk
⅓ cup grape-nuts
Grated rind and juice of
½ lemon

Cream butter and blend with sugar. Add well-beaten egg yolks, flour, milk and grape-nuts, mix well and stir in lemon rind and juice. Beat egg whites until stiff and fold in lightly but thoroughly. Turn into a four-cup buttered casserole and bake in a moderately slow oven (325° F.) until pudding is a rich golden brown, from 40 to 45 minutes. Serve warm with milk or cream. 5 servings.

363   ORANGE FLOAT

½ cup sugar
¼ teaspoon salt
2 tablespoons cornstarch
1 cup water
1 egg, separated

½ cup orange juice
½ teaspoon grated orange rind
1½ tablespoons lemon juice
Orange sections

Mix sugar, salt and cornstarch thoroughly; add water and stir well. Cook over direct heat until mixture boils. Stir into beaten egg yolk; cook over hot water 10 minutes longer. Beat egg white until stiff; pour cooked mixture over it and stir carefully until well mixed. Combine orange juice and rind with lemon juice and stir in gradually. Pour into serving dishes and garnish with orange sections. 5 servings.

364   RICE CREAM

½ cup rice
1⅔ cups evaporated milk
1 cup water
½ teaspoon salt
¼ cup granulated sugar

1 teaspoon vanilla
¼ cup brown sugar, packed firmly
¼ teaspoon cinnamon

Wash rice and add to 1 cup of the evaporated milk, water, and salt. Cover and cook over boiling water 1 hour and 10 minutes or until the rice is tender. Stir frequently. Now remove from heat, add granulated sugar and chill thoroughly. Then beat in vanilla, brown sugar and cinnamon with a fork. Have remaining evaporated milk thoroughly chilled. Whip the milk (1128) until stiff. Fold into rice mixture thoroughly. Again chill, then serve. 5 generous servings.

Note: Just before rice is done, if desired, stir in well 1 or 2 well-beaten egg yolks.

365   GLORIFIED RICE

½ cup whipping cream
¼ cup sugar
16 marshmallows (¼ lb.)

1 No. 1 flat tin crushed pineapple, drained
2 cups cooked rice (174)

Eggs are delicious and wonderfully nourishing if poached in milk (393) just long enough for the whites to be like soft jelly and the yolks the consistency of thick cream. Hot buttered toast is a perfect accompaniment, and a blue casserole adds up to a perfect color scheme.

A luncheon mainstay that soothes and nourishes—A steaming bowl of Oyster Stew (971) with heated crisp crackers.

Here is the way a skillet full of eggs look when they are cooked according to the VARIATION RECIPE (390). *Cooking them covered, with a little water added to the fat in the skillet, coagulates the thin film of white over as well as around the yolks.*

Sizzling hot, lean-streaked bacon with corn fritters and syrup are a luncheon combination that can be quickly prepared, and will be enthusiastically received.

*Link Sausage and Little Griddle Cakes cooked to look like these are irresistible.
Precede these with fresh fruit, and add some good syrup and a cup of steaming
fragrant coffee and the total is a perfect breakfast.*

Whip cream, add sugar, quartered marshmallows, pineapple, and cooled rice; mix lightly. Chill 3 or 4 hours before serving. 5 servings.

366   OLD-FASHIONED RICE PUDDING

⅓ cup uncooked rice	¼ cup sugar
4 cups milk, scalded	2 tablespoons butter
¼ teaspoon salt	

Combine all ingredients in a flat baking dish (6½ x 10½ x 1¾ inches) and place in a slow oven (300° F.) and bake for 1½ hours, or until rice is perfectly tender and pudding is thick and creamy, not dry. Stir every 15 minutes with a fork, carefully turning under the brown top and scraping the edges down. Serve hot or cold. 5 servings.

367   TAPIOCA CREAM

1 egg, separated	⅜ cup (6 tablespoons) sugar
3 cups milk	¼ teaspoon salt
¼ cup quick tapioca	1 teaspoon vanilla

Beat egg yolk and combine with milk, tapioca, sugar and salt in top of double boiler. Place over boiling water and cook for 10 to 12 minutes after the water begins to boil again, stirring frequently. Remove from heat and cool about 10 minutes; mixture thickens as it cools. Add vanilla; beat egg white until stiff and fold into the tapioca mixture. Chill. Serve plain or with cream. Strawberry or raspberry jam or preserves, or orange marmalade is a pleasing garnish. 5 servings.

368   BUTTERSCOTCH TAPIOCA

To make Butterscotch Tapioca, substitute dark brown sugar for the granulated sugar in recipe 367.

369   FRUIT JUICE TAPIOCA

In recipe for Tapioca Cream (367), substitute fruit juice (pineapple, grape, or juice from canned fruit) for all or part of the milk. Omit the vanilla. Diced or crushed fruit may be added, if desired. When concentrated fruit juice such as grape juice is used, it may be diluted with water (about 1 cup water to 2 cups juice).

370   FRESH FRUIT TAPIOCA

2 cups sliced or crushed fresh fruit
Sugar to suit taste
Water
5 tablespoons quick tapioca
¼ teaspoon salt
2 tablespoons lemon juice, or to suit taste

Strawberries, sour red cherries, raspberries, peaches or any fresh fruit may be used with this recipe. When the fruit has been prepared, add the desired amount of sugar and let stand ½ hour. Drain off all juice, measure and add enough water to make 2½ cups of liquid. Add the tapioca and salt, and bring to a boil over direct heat. Remove from heat, add drained fruit and lemon juice, and chill, stirring occasionally as it cools. Serve with or without cream. 5 servings.

371   APPLE TAPIOCA

1 egg, separated
2 cups milk
3 tablespoons quick tapioca
⅓ cup sugar
Dash salt
2 apples, peeled and grated

Beat egg yolk in top of double boiler, then stir in milk, tapioca, sugar and salt, and cook over boiling water 10 minutes, stirring constantly. Add apples and cook 5 minutes longer. Cool, then fold in stiffly beaten egg white and chill. 5 servings.

372   CHERRY TAPIOCA

1 No. 2 can sour red cherries, packed in syrup
⅔ cup water
3 tablespoons quick tapioca
¼ cup sugar
Few grains salt
2 tablespoons lemon juice

Drain cherries; combine the juice with water, tapioca, sugar and salt. Bring to boil, stirring constantly; as soon as it boils vigorously, remove from heat and stir in lemon juice and drained cherries. Stir occasionally while cooling. As tapioca cools, it will thicken. Serve chilled, with top milk. 5 servings.

Note: If unsweetened cherries are used in the above recipe, ½ to ¾ cup of sugar will be required. Cooked fresh cherries may be used.

373   CANNED FRUIT TAPIOCA

The same method as for Cherry Tapioca (372) may be used with any other canned fruit, such as pineapple, peach, or pear. The fruit should be diced before adding to the tapioca, and sweetened to suit taste.

374   LOGANBERRY TAPIOCA

6 tablespoons quick tapioca	1 12-oz. tin loganberry juice
½ cup sugar	¾ cup water
¼ teaspoon salt	1½ tablespoons lemon juice

Mix tapioca, sugar, salt, loganberry juice and water; stir well and cook over direct heat, stirring constantly, until it reaches a full rolling boil. Remove from heat and stir in lemon juice. Cool and chill before serving. It becomes much thicker when cold. Serve with top milk or cream. 5 servings.

375   RAISIN DELICIOUS

½ cup brown sugar, packed	⅓ cup white sugar
½ cup white sugar	¾ cup all-purpose flour
1½ cups boiling water	1 teaspoon baking powder, see p. 122
1 tablespoon butter	
¼ teaspoon cinnamon	¼ teaspoon salt
¼ teaspoon salt	⅓ cup sweet milk
¾ cup raisins	⅓ cup coarsely chopped nutmeats
1 teaspoon vanilla	
2 tablespoons butter	

Mix first 7 ingredients in saucepan and boil to a medium syrup (about 15 minutes); remove from heat and add vanilla. Meanwhile prepare drop batter as follows: Cream butter, add sugar and cream until blended. Sift flour, measure and resift with baking powder and salt. Add to sugar-butter mixture and combine well. Add milk all at once and stir until dry ingredients are thoroughly blended. Drop batter from tablespoon into a well-buttered baking pan (7 x 11 x 1½ inches) and pour the raisin syrup over it. Sprinkle with nuts and bake in a moderate oven (350° F.) for about 30 minutes or until golden brown. Serve warm or cold with cream or top milk. 5 servings.

376   UPSIDE-DOWN CHERRY PUDDING

1½ cups all-purpose flour	1 teaspoon vanilla
1½ teaspoons baking powder, see p. 122	1 cup milk
¼ teaspoon salt	Sauce:
½ cup butter or other shortening	1 cup sugar
1 cup sugar	1 No. 2 can sour red pitted cherries
1 egg, unbeaten	½ cup boiling water

Sift flour, measure and resift twice with baking powder and salt. Cream butter, add sugar gradually and continue creaming until light and fluffy. Beat in whole egg. Stir in vanilla. Add sifted ingredients alternately with milk, beginning and ending with flour and beating well after each addition. Pour into a buttered 9-inch square pan. Prepare sauce by heating sugar, cherries, juice and boiling water and pour it over the batter. Place in a moderate oven (350° F.) and bake from 35 to 45 minutes, or until pudding begins to shrink from sides and top is golden brown. When baked, cherries and sauce will be on the bottom. Serve like any other pudding. 8 servings.

377 STEAMED FRUIT PUDDING

1 cup buttermilk	¼ cup butter
¾ cup fine, dry bread crumbs	½ cup brown sugar, packed
⅓ cup flour	2 tablespoons molasses
½ teaspoon cinnamon	1 egg
⅛ teaspoon cloves	1 cup raisins
1 teaspoon baking soda	

Pour the buttermilk over the bread crumbs and let soak 30 minutes. Sift flour, measure and resift with cinnamon, cloves and baking soda. Cream butter, add sugar and blend thoroughly. Add molasses and egg and beat until fluffy. Stir in sifted dry ingredients, soaked crumbs and washed raisins. Mix well. Turn the batter into a greased mold (4 to 5 cup size). Cover with brown or waxed paper and tie loosely with string; steam 1½ hours (1132). Serve with Orange Sauce (935) or Hard Sauce (932). 5 servings.

378 BAKED CARROT PUDDING

1½ cups all-purpose flour	½ cup shortening
1 teaspoon salt	1 cup brown sugar, packed
1¼ teaspoons cinnamon	1 cup grated raw carrot, packed
¼ teaspoon cloves	1½ cups finely chopped apple
½ teaspoon nutmeg	(3 medium-sized apples)
1½ teaspoons baking powder, see p. 122	¾ cup seedless raisins

Sift flour, measure, and resift 3 times with salt, spices and baking powder. Cream shortening thoroughly and gradually blend in sugar. Add carrot, apple, and raisins and mix thoroughly. Add flour mixture slowly, mixing until well blended. Turn into buttered individual molds; bake in a moderately slow oven (325° F.) 50 minutes, or steam for 1½ hours in covered molds. Serve hot with Lemon Sauce (934). 8 to 10 servings.

379   BAKED PRUNE PUDDING

¼ cup cracker crumbs   ¼ cup evaporated milk
  (4 crackers)   ¼ cup water
¾ teaspoon baking powder,   ½ cup sugar
  see p. 122   1 tablespoon melted butter
1 cup seeded cooked prunes   ¼ teaspoon salt
  (301), drained and chopped   1 teaspoon vanilla
¼ cup chopped walnuts or
  pecans

Mix cracker crumbs thoroughly with the baking powder; then combine all ingredients thoroughly, and turn into a buttered glass baking dish
(8½ x 4½ x 1¾ inches). Bake in a moderate oven (350° F.) for 30
minutes. Serve hot with milk or cream. 5 servings.

380   COTTAGE CHEESE AND HONEY

A delicious dessert combination consists of cottage cheese served with
cream and honey. Pour on the thin cream or top milk and drizzle honey
over the top. Fresh strawberries or raspberries are a pleasing addition to
this dish, and so is fresh pineapple. When fruit is added, the honey may
be combined with the cream (¼ cup honey to 1 cup cream).

EGGS

HAVE you ever wondered why slices of hard-cooked egg in food photographs have their yolks in the exact center, and why the pictured yolks are radiantly yellow from rim to rim? And does this make you wonder why yolks in your hard-cooked eggs list heavily to one side, and why they have dark circles around them? You will find the answers to these questions, and many others, in this chapter, as well as complete directions on how specialists in egg cookery cook eggs and egg dishes to make them attractive and to obtain the greatest nutritive value.

Eggs are one of the most important foods in cookery—they have many uses and are very valuable nutritionally. No housewife could very well get along without using eggs as eggs, eggs in custards, omelets, soufflés, sauces, cakes, etc. Eggs are not only rich in food value, but have flavor, color, leavening power and a dozen other characteristics which make them valuable to the cook as well as to the "eater".

There is one rule that should be followed in any type of egg cookery, and that is: Eggs should be cooked at a low to moderate temperature to assure appealing and uniformly tender eggs and egg dishes. HIGH TEMPERATURE and LONG COOKING makes the egg white tough, less digestible and darkens the surface of the yolk. A properly cooked egg is one of the most easily digested of all foods. A hard-cooked egg, if cooked at a low temperature for the right length of time, is no less digestible than a soft-cooked egg.

Foods made with eggs as the principal ingredient as in custards and soufflés, when cooked at a high temperature soon lose their eye and palate appeal because they soon droop and "weep", indicating that the protein coagulated too rapidly and too completely.

BOILING: A "boiled" egg should not be boiled at all, but SIMMERED. Simmering means cooking just below the boiling point. There are 2 types of boiled eggs: (1) Soft-cooked. (2) Hard-cooked.

254

SOFT-COOKED EGGS

COLD WATER METHOD: Place eggs in pan and cover them with cold or lukewarm water to come ½-inch above eggs. Bring rapidly just to boiling, then turn off heat, and if necessary set pan off burner to prevent further boiling. Cover and let stand 2 to 4 minutes, depending on individual preference. Cool eggs promptly in cold water for a few SECONDS to prevent further cooking, and to make them easy to handle.

BOILING WATER METHOD: Bring water in pan to just a rapid boil, using enough water to come ½-inch above eggs. Meanwhile warm very cold eggs slightly in warm water to avoid cracked shells. Transfer eggs to boiling water with a spoon, turn off heat, and if necessary set pan off burner to prevent further boiling. Cover and let stand 6 to 8 minutes. Cool as above.

COOKING MORE THAN 4 EGGS: Use either method. Do not turn off but reduce heat to keep water below SIMMERING. Hold 4 to 6 minutes. Cool as above.

HARD-COOKED EGGS

COLD WATER METHOD: Place eggs in pan, then add enough cold or lukewarm water to come ½-inch above eggs. Bring rapidly just to boiling. Then turn off heat, and if necessary set pan off burner to prevent further boiling. Cover and let stand 15 minutes. Cool promptly and thoroughly in cold water—this makes shells easier to remove and helps prevent dark surface on yolks.

BOILING WATER METHOD: Bring water in pan to just a rapid boil, using enough water to come ½-inch above eggs. Meanwhile warm very cold eggs slightly in warm water to avoid cracked shells. Transfer eggs to boiling water with a spoon. Now reduce heat to keep water BELOW SIMMERING. Cover and hold at SIMMERING 20 minutes. Cool promptly and thoroughly in cold water as above. Crack shells and remove.

TO REMOVE THE SHELL: When egg has cooled, crack the shell in many places, then roll between hands to loosen shell. Start the peeling at the large-end of the egg. Holding the egg under running water helps to ease off the shell.

CAUSES FOR DARK SURFACED EGG YOLKS: There are 4 ways to prevent formation of dark surface on hard-cooked egg yolks: (1) Use only fresh eggs. (2) Cook at a low temperature. (3) Do not overcook. (4) Be sure to chill the cooked eggs promptly and thoroughly, then crack shells immediately.

POACHING: Poaching eggs means cooking eggs removed from shell in SIMMERING water. To preserve the shape, the egg is sometimes broken into a metal poacher placed over, or in hot water. If poacher is not used, the egg should be broken into a saucer and carefully slipped into the hot water. When done to the desired firmness, usually when the white has just coagulated, the egg should be carefully lifted from water with a slotted spoon or pancake turner, letting it drain a moment. Poached eggs may be served on hot toast, buttered rice or noodles, mashed potatoes, buttered vegetables like spinach and asparagus and corned beef hash.

FRYING: Frying eggs means cooking them in very shallow fat. The fat should not be very hot for a tender, delicate fried egg. However, some like the crisp, lacy edge produced by fat that is quite hot. Eggs may be fried "Over or Up". "Over" means the egg is turned and cooked on both sides. "Up" or "sunny-side-up" means that it is fried on one side only. The film that remains over the yolk of an egg cooked "sunny-side-up" should be cooked by spooning hot fat over it. Butter, bacon or ham fat, lard and vegetable shortening are all used for frying eggs.

Another pleasing method of frying eggs is to use just enough fat to grease the bottom of the skillet. Cook the egg in this to set the bottom surface, then add ½ teaspoon water for 1 egg, and a little less for each additional egg in the skillet. Cover tightly and cook over low heat until eggs are cooked to desired doneness. Eggs cooked in this manner are somewhat like poached eggs.

Eggs occasionally are fried in deep fat heated to a moderate temperature, about 360° F. The egg should be broken into a saucer and slipped carefully into the hot fat. The French-fried egg should be cooked only until just brown, then removed immediately with a slotted spoon.

Frying is one of the least desirable ways of cooking eggs from a dietetic standpoint. Not only does the high temperature necessary for good frying toughen the white, but the coating of fat slows down the digestion rate. For this reason fried eggs are not recommended for children. However, so many adults like their eggs fried better than any other way, so on the principle that it is much better to eat fried eggs than not eat eggs at all, frying should not be ruled out.

SCRAMBLING: The most usual way of preparing scrambled eggs is to break them into a bowl, add seasonings and 1 tablespoon of milk or cream per egg, then beat them slightly. Then they are poured into a heated skillet containing a small amount of fat and gently folded over from bottom and sides as they coagulate. Or they may be cooked without fat, or with very little, over hot water in the top of a double boiler. Constant stirring should be avoided. Scrambled eggs may be either soft or firm. Another method of scrambling is to break the whole eggs into hot fat in a skillet, then stir lightly with a fork; this results in streaking the yellow part of the eggs interestingly with the white. Various chopped foods such as crisp bacon, ham, dried beef, grated Cheddar cheese, chopped cooked vegetables or flaky cottage cheese stirred into scrambled eggs when nearly done makes them delightful.

OMELETS: There are 2 types of omelets: (1) The French type similar to scrambled eggs. (2) The puffy or American type resembling a soufflé. In the French omelet, the yolks and whites are beaten together, poured into a hot skillet with fat, after cooking a few minutes, a spatula is used to gently lift (never stir) cooked portions to permit the uncooked mixture to flow underneath. In the puffy omelet, the whites are beaten separately until stiff, then the beaten seasoned yolks are folded into them. The mixture is cooked in a greased skillet without stirring or other manipulation, first on top of the stove until bottom is cooked and then in the oven until completely set.

CUSTARDS

Custards are baked or cooked on top of the stove. They consist of milk, eggs, sugar and flavoring. One egg will thicken 1 cup of milk, but more eggs may be used. Or 2 egg yolks may be substituted for 1 whole egg. True custard has no other thickening than eggs. However, a tiny amount of flour is sometimes added to give more body, or to replace 1 or more of the eggs required to make more custard with a given number of eggs.

BAKED CUSTARD: The eggs are beaten slightly and milk stirred into them. If the milk is scalding hot when added to eggs, the baking time is cut down considerably. This mixture is usually poured through a strainer (to remove stringy bits of egg white) into buttered custard cups placed in a pan almost as deep as custard cups. Then the pan is placed in oven and hot water is poured into it to come almost to top of cups. Custard is baked in a slow oven. Setting the cups in water tends to equalize the temperature and slow down the rate of cooking from underneath. The time required depends largely on size of custard cups. The usual test for doneness is to insert a sharp-pointed knife into center of one of the custards; if it comes out clean, the custard is done. However, custard baked in a heavy glass or pottery casserole or cup holds the heat and should be taken out a little sooner as cooking continues even after removal from oven. Cooking custard too long or at too high a temperature causes "weeping" or wheying in baked custard.

SOFT OR "BOILED" CUSTARD: Soft custard is cooked on top of the stove over SIMMERING water. It should never be actually boiled or cooked over direct heat. The cooking time may be reduced by scalding the milk before adding to the beaten eggs, sugar and salt. When the ingredients are combined, the mixture is poured into the top of a double boiler and cooked over SIMMERING water with constant stirring until custard just coats a metal spoon. This type of custard is often made with egg yolks only, using 2 or 3 yolks to 1 cup of milk, and this is an excellent way to use up leftover yolks.

Cooking should never be continued after mixture coats a spoon in an effort to make it thicker, as prolonged cooking will cause "curdling". Pour soft custard immediately into a chilled bowl to stop cooking quickly. Soft custard that has begun to separate or show signs of "curdling" as a result of over-cooking should be removed immediately from heat, placed over cold water and beaten vigorously with a rotary beater. This will restore its smoothness in most cases if the separation has not gone too far. The custard will thicken as it cools. If a still thicker custard is desired, the way to get it is to use additional eggs or yolks, or to start with milk just slightly thickened with a little flour.

SOUFFLÉS

Soufflé is a French word meaning "puffed up," and this is an exact description of what happens to a soufflé in cooking. Basically, a soufflé consists of a white sauce with egg yolks added which is then folded into the stiffly beaten egg whites. The mixture is baked at a low temperature until the air cells of the beaten egg whites expand and become set. Various ingredients may be added to the basic mixture, such as cheese, which is melted in the hot white sauce or chopped meat, fish or vegetables, which are stirred into the sauce before folding into the beaten whites. There are also sweet dessert soufflés of various flavors, such as lemon, orange, chocolate and rum.

The secret of a successful soufflé is threefold: first, careful manipulation; second, cooking very slowly; and third, serving promptly. The best soufflé is produced by baking in a moderately slow oven (325° F.) about 1 hour. It will have a rather soft golden crust and will be somewhat dry inside; and it may stand up for some minutes. Soufflés cooked in this manner may be held successfully for belated guests by turning the oven as low as possible. A browner, crustier soufflé with a more moist and creamy inside is produced by baking in a moderately hot oven (425° F.) for 25 to 30 minutes. This type must be served the moment it is taken from the oven as it falls rapidly.

EGG CARE

Eggs should spend their entire lives under refrigeration—both in the store and in the home. This not only keeps them fresh for a longer time, but aids in keeping the yolks in the center, which is so important for hard-cooked eggs to be devilled or sliced for use as a garnish. In summertime especially, the dealer should be as careful of his eggs as he has to be of his butter, and the consumer has a right to demand that they be kept in his refrigerator, at 40 to 45° F., until she buys them.

For many cooking purposes, however, it is a good plan to remove from the refrigerator the eggs that are to be used and let them warm up for half an hour. This helps prevent the shell from cracking when the eggs are put into hot water to boil. Egg whites at room temperature produce more volume, when beaten than do chilled whites. But since eggs separate more easily when chilled, try separating them immediately on removal from the refrigerator; then allow the whites to warm up for 15 or 20 minutes before beating. Yolks may be used cold.

EGG QUALITY

The position of the yolk, the condition of the thick and thin white and the size of the air cell determine interior quality. A high quality egg when broken out on a plate has a high curved yolk, well centered and banked in a thick white. There is a little thin white. These are the characteristics of a fresh egg. As the egg loses quality, the air cell becomes larger due to moisture loss. There is less thick white. The yolk floats to the side or top of the egg. The lower quality egg when broken out on a plate has a flattened yolk and the white is watery and thin.

Biological abnormalities sometimes appear in eggs as blood spots—bright or dark specks. They occur very infrequently. They may be lifted out of the egg before cooking. They do not alter the nutritive value or the cooking performance.

EGG GRADES

Eggs are graded on the basis of outside appearance, weight and interior quality. Interior quality is judged by candling. Candling consists of holding and turning the egg before a beam of light strong enough to observe the interior. Eggs may be graded according to federal, state or private standards. The federal standards use the letters A, B, C, for designation. Many fine graded eggs are sold under a brand or trademark name without a "letter" grade.

Graded eggs carry the grade, the size and in some cases the date of candling on the carton. Graded eggs are not always available in all markets.

The choice of quality should be determined by the use and the price. High quality eggs are ideal for cooking in the shell, poaching and frying. Lower qualities may be economically used for other cooking.

381   EGGS BAKED IN BACON RINGS
                           (*Shirred Eggs*)

> 5 slices enriched bread   5 eggs
> 8 slices bacon   Salt and pepper

Cut out rounds of bread to fit snugly in bottoms of muffin cups. Pan-broil bacon until half done and remove to a plate. Pour off all bacon fat except 1 teaspoon. Brown the bread rounds on both sides in the fat, then place in bottom of muffin cups. Line sides of cups neatly with 1½ strips of the partially cooked bacon. Break an egg into each cup and season with salt and pepper. Drop ¼ teaspoon bacon fat over each egg. Bake in a moderately slow oven (325° F.) 20 minutes, covered or uncovered, as desired. Remove carefully with spatula onto hot plate. 5 servings.

382   BAKED EGGS IN TOMATO CUPS

5 medium tomatoes   5 eggs
½ teaspoon salt   5 slices bacon
2 tablespoons butter   Parsley

Wash tomatoes, remove cores at stem end, then scoop out enough of the pulp to provide space for each egg. Save pulp. Sprinkle salt inside of tomatoes. Divide butter and put a portion into each tomato. Place in shallow greased baking pan and place in a moderately hot oven (400° F.) and bake 7 to 8 minutes. Remove from oven and quickly break an egg into each tomato cup. Pour removed tomato pulp around tomatoes. Return to oven and cook eggs to desired consistency, 5 to 10 minutes. Meanwhile pan-broil bacon until done (545). Arrange tomatoes on hot platter, garnish with bacon and parsley. 5 servings.

383   CREAMED EGGS

5 hard-cooked eggs (395)   5 slices hot buttered toast
2 cups medium white sauce
  (919)

Shell eggs and slice or dice, then fold them carefully into the hot white sauce so as not to break up eggs too much. Pour over toast and serve at once. 5 servings.

384   EGGS IN CHEESE SAUCE

Follow directions for Creamed Eggs (383), except add 1 cup grated sharp cheese to the hot white sauce (919). Stir until blended before adding eggs.

385   CREAMED EGGS AND ASPARAGUS ON TOAST

3 tablespoons butter or bacon   5 hard-cooked eggs (395)
  fat   No. 2 can green asparagus
3 tablespoons flour   or 1 lb. cooked fresh
1½ cups milk   5 slices buttered toast
1 teaspoon salt

Melt butter, blend in flour and gradually add milk (liquid drained from asparagus may be substituted for part of the milk), stirring constantly until sauce boils and thickens. Add salt, eggs which have been shelled and cut into sixths or sliced, and the drained asparagus. Heat over boiling water before serving on buttered toast. 5 servings.

386   EGGS BENEDICTINE

  6 ham slices, cut thin   6 eggs, poached (391)
    Butter or bacon fat   ⅔ cup Hollandaise sauce (910)
  3 large English muffins (82)

Pan-broil ham in fat until edges are curly. Split muffins in halves and
toast. Place hot ham slices on hot toasted muffins, then put hot poached
eggs on the ham and pour Hollandaise sauce over all. Serve hot. 6 servings.

387   DEVILED EGGS No. 1

  5 hard-cooked eggs, (395)   ¼ teaspoon dry mustard
  ½ teaspoon salt   1 teaspoon vinegar
  ⅛ teaspoon pepper   2 tablespoons melted butter

Cut shelled, cooled hard-cooked eggs in halves lengthwise. Remove
yolks and mash; add remaining ingredients and whip until smooth and
fluffy. Heap into whites and sprinkle with a little paprika or chopped
parsley. 5 servings.

388   DEVILED EGGS No. 2

A simpler method of preparing stuffed eggs is as follows: Halve eggs,
remove yolks and mash thoroughly with mayonnaise, allowing ¾ teaspoon mayonnaise to each egg, and salt and pepper to suit taste. Stuff
into whites and sprinkle lightly with paprika.

389   DEVILED EGGS No. 3

To either of the egg yolk mixtures (387 or 388), add chopped crisply
cooked bacon or mashed liver sausage in the amount desired. Anchovy or
other fish pastes or mashed sardines may be used in the same way. The
salt needed will be altered if the added ingredient is salty, so add salt
last.

390   FRIED EGGS

Break eggs one at a time into a saucer, and slide into a skillet in which
fat has been melted. Two tablespoons fat will be enough for 5 eggs. It
should be hot enough to sizzle when eggs are dropped in. Baste yolks
with hot fat, dipping it up with a spoon until there is a film over them,
then cook until whites are coagulated to desired stage. Some like eggs
well done, others prefer them "rare." If desired, turn the egg over and fry

top side for a minute or two; this is often done for a fried egg sandwich. Cook eggs slowly to avoid toughening the white.

Variation: For an exceptionally delicate fried egg, use just enough fat to grease the bottom of the skillet. Slide the eggs into the hot skillet and cook long enough to set the bottom; then add 1 teaspoon water for the first egg and from ½ to ¾ teaspoon for each additional egg. Then cover and simmer gently until eggs are done to desired firmness.

391   POACHED EGGS

Grease the bottom of a shallow pan, add water to a depth of at least 2 inches and heat to simmering. Break eggs one at a time into a saucer and slip into the hot water, reducing heat as low as possible, so water does not even simmer. Do not crowd the eggs. Cook very slowly until the white is firm and the yolk filmed over. Then lift the eggs out carefully, one at a time, with a slotted spoon or pancake turner, permitting them to drain thoroughly. Place each egg on a slice of hot buttered toast to serve. Regular egg poachers or muffin rings give the cooked eggs a rounder shape.

392   POACHED EGGS IN POTATO NESTS

For a supper dish, drop Poached Eggs (391) into nests made of hot seasoned mashed potatoes (1077). In individual servings of the mashed potatoes, make depressions large enough to hold the eggs. Garnish with strips of crisp bacon.

393   EGGS POACHED IN MILK

1 cup milk	5 eggs
1 tablespoon butter	Buttered toast
Salt to taste	

Scald milk in a 1-qt. saucepan, add butter and when melted, stir in a little salt. Drop eggs into hot milk, then place over low heat until firm enough to suit family preference. Then lift eggs out onto buttered toast, and pour remaining milk over them. Do not try to cook all 5 eggs at the same time. This is a hearty, satisfying breakfast dish. 5 servings.

394   SOFT-COOKED EGGS

Always cook eggs in a glass or enamelware pan; cooking eggs in an aluminum pan always turns it black. Add enough water to the eggs to come ½-inch above them. Place over high heat and bring water rapidly to the boiling point. The instant boiling starts, cover and remove from heat and let stand from 2 to 4 minutes, depending on individual preference. Time exactly. Then lift eggs out immediately and hold under running cold water or dip quickly in cold water for comfortable handling. Serve at once in the shell, or broken and spooned into egg cups.

Prepare eggs for babies or young children by placing in boiling water, then remove to back of stove, cover and let stand from 6 to 8 minutes. If eggs are removed from refrigerator ½ hour before cooking, there will be little danger of cracking when they are put into the hot water. See p. 255 for Boiling Water Method for soft-cooking eggs.

395   HARD-COOKED EGGS

Always cook eggs in a glass or enamelware pan. Add enough water to come ½-inch above the eggs. Place over high heat so water will come rapidly to boiling. As soon as boiling point is reached, turn off heat and remove pan to back of stove. Cover and let stand 15 to 20 minutes. Immediately lift eggs into a dish and let cold water run over them. As soon as they can be handled comfortably, crack the shell in numerous places, roll egg between palms, then start removing shell from the large-end. Hold under running water from time to time to aid in removing the shell quickly and smoothly. Preferably, eggs should be hard-cooked and shelled just before they are to be used, but if they are to be held a few hours, place in a dish containing a few folds of wet paper toweling, then cover tightly and store in refrigerator. See p. 255 for Boiling Water Method for hard-cooked eggs.

395a   EGGS à la GOLDENROD

5 hard-cooked eggs (395)   5 slices toast, buttered, if
2 cups medium white sauce   desired
    (919)

Cook eggs just in time to be ready for use. Then shell eggs and separate whites from yolks; chop the whites coarsely and add to the hot white sauce. Reheat until whites are hot, then pour over hot toast. Rub egg yolks through a sieve onto the creamed whites, and serve immediately. 5 servings.

A *Pretty Variation:* Put the hard-cooked egg whites through a ricer, combine with white sauce, and pour over toast arranged on a platter. Place a whole egg yolk in the center of each and add a dash of paprika for color. Garnish platter with a sprig of parsley at each end.

396   SCRAMBLED EGGS

Break 6 eggs into mixing bowl. Add 6 tablespoons milk or thin cream and 1 teaspoon salt with pepper to taste. Beat eggs just enough to break up yolks and whites; this may be done with a fork for slight beating, or with an egg beater if more beating is preferred. Or eggs may be left unbeaten. Have 3 tablespoons butter melted in skillet over low heat. Pour egg mixture into skillet and cook slowly without stirring until whites just begin to coagulate at bottom and sides of pan. Then start to lift up the mixture with a spatula, loosening sides and scraping bottom of pan so liquid portion can flow down; continue lifting and scraping gently until eggs are done to firmness desired. Leftover egg whites or yolks may be substituted for one or two of the whole eggs. Serve immediately. 5 servings.

397   HEARTY SCRAMBLED EGGS

To make a heartier dish of Scrambled Eggs (396), add ½ cup cottage cheese, chopped cooked ham, liver or shredded dried beef to the egg mixture just as it is beginning to coagulate. If a sufficient quantity is used, this makes a fine main dish for a simple family dinner.

398   PARSLEY SCRAMBLED EGGS

Add 1 tablespoon medium fine chopped parsley to the beaten eggs and proceed as for Scrambled Eggs (396). 5 servings.

399   BACON OMELET

Make a Puffy Omelet (402). Have ⅓ lb. bacon broiled (544) until crisp and a delicate brown; drain thoroughly and crumble. When omelet is done, sprinkle bacon over half of it, then cut omelet quickly in half, fold over and carefully slide onto hot platter. Serve immediately. 5 servings.

400   FRENCH OMELET

4 eggs	¼ cup water
½ teaspoon salt	2 tablespoons butter
Few grains pepper	

Beat eggs until mixed but not foamy; stir in seasonings and water. Melt butter in a heavy skillet and turn mixture into the hot skillet. Cook omelet slowly, pricking and lifting with a fork during cooking period.

Cook until firm to the touch of finger, 8 to 10 minutes. The omelet may be cooked entirely on top of range or put in oven part of the time to dry the top. Fold omelet, then slide onto a hot platter. Serve immediately. 5 servings.

Variations: Serve omelet with hot spinach, bacon, tomato sauce or hot broiled fruit such as peaches or apricots.

401   PARSLEY OMELET

Add 1 tablespoon coarsely chopped parsley to the beaten eggs and proceed as for French Omelet (400).

402   PUFFY OMELET

6 eggs, separated	2 to 4 tablespoons butter
1 teaspoon salt	

Beat egg whites until stiff. Beat yolks with salt until very thick and light in color, then fold them into the whites lightly but thoroughly. Heat a 10-inch skillet, add butter and when melted, pour in the egg mixture. Cook very slowly over low heat about 20 minutes or until bottom of omelet appears delicately browned and crisp when gently lifted from side with a knife or spatula. Do not stir at any time. Now slip skillet containing omelet into a moderate oven (350° F.) from 2 to 5 minutes, or until top is dry and slightly browned. Loosen quickly around edges; make a quick cut through the center; fold over and slide omelet onto hot serving plate. Serve immediately. 5 servings.

403   CELERY SOUFFLÉ

3 tablespoons butter	Dash pepper
½ cup flour	5 eggs, separated
2 cups milk	1 cup fine-diced celery
1 teaspoon salt	

Melt butter, remove from heat and blend in flour and a little of the cold milk until smooth. Add rest of milk and cook over direct heat, stirring constantly until sauce boils and thickens. Add seasonings. Beat egg yolks thoroughly, then gradually stir in the hot sauce and the celery. Beat egg whites until stiff and fold in lightly but thoroughly. Turn into a 6-cup buttered casserole. Bake in a moderately slow oven (325° F.) 50 minutes or until a rich brown. Serve immediately. 5 or 6 servings.

404   CHIPPED BEEF SOUFFLÉ

3 tablespoons butter   4 eggs, separated
¼ cup flour   1 cup canned peas
¾ cup liquid from peas   1 cup chopped dried beef,
1 cup evaporated milk   ¼ lb.

Melt butter, blend in flour and add pea liquid and evaporated milk; stir constantly over direct heat until sauce boils and thickens. Stir into the well-beaten egg yolks, then add peas and beef. Now fold into the stiffly beaten egg whites. Turn into a 6-cup buttered casserole. Bake in a moderately slow oven (325° F.) 1 hour. Serve immediately. 5 servings.

405   MEAT SOUFFLÉ

3 tablespoons butter   1 cup milk
3 tablespoons flour   3 eggs, separated
½ teaspoon salt   1 cup chopped cooked meat

Melt butter, blend in flour, add salt and milk and cook and stir over direct heat until sauce boils and thickens. Stir hot sauce slowly into the well-beaten egg yolks, then fold in chopped meat and cool a few minutes. Beat egg whites until stiff and fold meat mixture into whites. Turn into a well-buttered 6-cup casserole. Bake in a moderately slow oven (325° F.) about 1 hour or until nicely browned. Serve immediately. 5 servings.

406   OATMEAL SOUFFLÉ

2 tablespoons butter   2 tablespoons chopped
1 cup milk   pimiento
½ cup quick rolled oats   ½ teaspoon salt
½ cup grated cheese   2 slices bacon, cooked,
  Dash of dry mustard   crumbled
                                3 eggs, separated

Add butter to milk and heat to simmering over direct heat. Now add oats and cook 5 minutes, stirring constantly. Remove from heat and stir in cheese. When cheese melts, add mustard, pimiento, salt, bacon and beaten egg yolks. Beat whites until stiff, then fold oat mixture into whites. Turn into buttered casserole. Bake in a moderately slow oven (325° F.) 50 minutes. 5 servings.

407   POTATO FRANKFURTER SOUFFLÉ

5 medium potatoes   2 tablespoons butter
¾ teaspoon salt   3 eggs, separated
1 cup hot milk   ¼ lb. frankfurters, chopped

Pare potatoes and cook until tender in boiling salted water; drain and mash thoroughly or put through ricer. Add salt, hot milk and butter and whip until smooth, fluffy and white. Stir in beaten egg yolks and finely chopped frankfurters. Beat egg whites until stiff and fold in yolk mixture lightly. Turn into buttered baking dish. Bake in a moderate oven (350° F.) 30 minutes or until puffy and golden brown. 5 servings.

408   SPAGHETTI SOUFFLÉ WITH CREAMED HAM

  ¾ package spaghetti, 5-6 oz.   3 eggs, separated
  2 tablespoons butter   3 cups unseasoned medium
  3 tablespoons flour   white sauce (919)
  1 teaspoon salt   2½ cups diced cooked ham
1½ cups milk   Salt and pepper
    Dash pepper

Drop broken spaghetti into 1½ quarts boiling salted water and boil uncovered until just tender, about 20 minutes. Drain, rinse well with hot water and again drain. Melt butter, blend in flour and salt, add milk, and stir over direct heat until sauce boils and thickens. Cool and stir in pepper and beaten egg yolks; fold in spaghetti. Beat egg whites until stiff and fold in thoroughly. Turn into buttered casserole or ring mold and bake in a moderately slow oven (325° F.) 45 to 50 minutes or until a knife inserted in center comes out clean. Combine unseasoned white sauce with the ham and season to taste. Unmold spaghetti soufflé onto hot platter and serve with creamed ham. Macaroni may be used in place of spaghetti. 5 servings.

FISH

* * * * * * * *

OF COURSE, the ideal way to cook fish is to build a fire alongside a trout stream, and have the frying pan sizzling hot in readiness for the big ones that did not get away. But don't despair if you can't achieve this ultimate ideal, for you can still go to the market and catch your favorite fish whenever you like. In this chapter you'll learn to cook each fish in the way that suits him best, which is not always in a frying pan.

* * * * * * * *

Fish is a food which formerly could be enjoyed regularly only by people who lived close to the source of supply. For salt water fish, it was necessary to be near the coast; with fresh water fish, the supply had to be brought in by the amateur fisherman in the family. And even then there was no year-round supply of fish, for fresh varieties are produced in abundance and in good quality, only at certain seasons in certain localities.

During the past few years, however, vastly improved methods of refrigeration and refrigerated transportation have made fish in their season available to all parts of the country. And newly developed freezing processes have made it possible to obtain most of the popular varieties of fish even out of their season, during most of the year. Freezing makes no appreciable change in the appearance, quality or food value of the fresh fish. Frozen fish can be cooked by the same methods as fresh fish.

The increased distribution of all kinds of fish is an important contribution to the diet of all parts of the country, not only because it makes greater variety possible, but from a nutritional standpoint. Fish, like meat, is a complete protein food and contains both vitamins and minerals, though in different proportions than meat.

Salt-water fish are particularly valuable for their iodine content, for they

*Information in this chapter is adapted from *Fishery Market News*—August 1941 Supplement, issued by United States Department of the Interior, Fish and Wild Life Service.

supply 50 to 200 times as much iodine as foods from other sources. This makes salt-water fish an important addition to the diet of people who live in the "goiter belt" of the United States, which includes most of the country west of the Alleghenies and east of the Rockies. Fish also contain phosphorus, iron, copper and magnesium.

As for vitamins, the fatty salt-water fish such as salmon and mackerel, are the only important food sources of vitamin D, and are also rich in vitamin A. As everyone knows, fish liver oils are standard sources of both these vitamins; but in fatty fish the body oils also contain a good supply of them. Both fresh and frozen fish also contain some of the factors of vitamin B complex, and some fish contain vitamin C.

The fat content of fish and shellfish depends upon the variety (see Table 6), and the proportion of fat in the fattier varieties changes with the season. The percentage of fat in fin-fish varies from ½ to 20 per cent of the edible portion; all shellfish are low or fairly low in fat content, averaging 2½ per cent or less. The fat content of fatty fish is as easily and completely digested as fats found in other foods, and gives them high energy value.

PURCHASING FISH

Both fresh and frozen fish and shellfish may be purchased in a variety of cuts or forms, which are commercially standardized. By asking for one of the following forms when you buy fish, you may be sure of getting the same form every time. (See illustrations, page 270.)

Forms of fin-fish:		*Forms of shellfish:*
whole	fillets—	live in shell
drawn	single	shucked
dressed	butterfly	headless
pan-dressed	sticks	cooked meat
steaks	frozen	frozen
frozen		

FISH

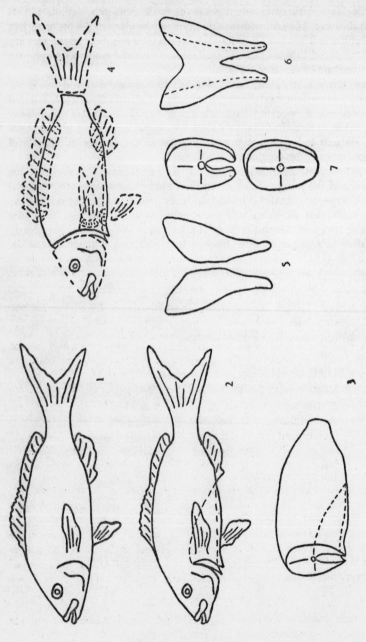

(1) *Whole;* (2) *Drawn;* (3) *Dressed;*
(4) *Pan-dressed;* (5) *Single Fillets;* (6) *Butterfly Fillets;* (7) *Steaks.*

Whole fish: Fish marketed whole are usually varieties that keep best without dressing. They are either naturally small fish, or small sizes of certain varieties. These fish must be scaled, drawn, washed and beheaded. The fins may be removed and the fish split or cut into serving portions. Small fish such as smelts or brook trout are usually cooked whole.

Drawn fish: Many varieties of fish are marketed with only the entrails removed. To prepare for cooking, they must be scaled, washed and the heads removed, if desired. The fins may be removed and the fish split or cut up. Small drawn fish or larger ones intended for baking are often cooked whole. Fish cooked with heads and fins on are juicier and more flavorful than those which are beheaded and de-finned.

Dressed fish: Dressed fish come scaled and drawn, and usually have the head, tail and fins removed. Very large dressed fish are sometimes marketed in chunks or pieces. Smaller sizes are ready for cooking as purchased, or they may be split open. Large dressed fish may be baked whole, but frequently are split or cut into steaks or fillets.

Pan-dressed fish have scales, entrails, head and fins, and sometimes the backbone removed. The fish may be split open either along belly or back. They are ready for cooking without further preparation, and are always smaller fish.

Steaks: A fish steak is a cross-section of a large dressed fish such as salmon or halibut. Each steak is at least ⅝-inch thick and equal to one or more serving portions. The cross-section of the backbone in the center of the steak is usually the only bone present; it may be easily removed in one piece after cooking. Steaks are ready to cook as purchased, except that very large ones should be divided into serving portions before cooking.

Fillets: Fillets are the meaty sides of the fish cut lengthwise away from the backbone. A single fillet is one side of a fish. It may weigh from several ounces to several pounds, depending on the size and thickness of fish. A butterfly fillet is the 2 sides of the fish, held together by the uncut belly of the fish. *Sticks* are pieces cut either crosswise or lengthwise from fillets of large fish. Fillets are practically boneless and require only cutting into serving portions before cooking.

Shellfish purchased alive in shells are crabs, lobsters, clams and oysters; and whenever they are purchased, be sure they are alive. Shucked shellfish consist of the meat removed from the shells; oysters, clams and scallops are marketed in this form. Fresh shrimp, green or cooked, are usually marketed with the heads removed, but in the shell. Cooked crab, shrimp or lobster meat is the edible portion removed from the cooked shellfish. This cooked meat is very perishable and should be used promptly after buying.

FISH PURCHASING HINTS

1. Fresh and frozen fish are equally good; use them both to provide more variety at reasonable prices.

2. Buy the various varieties of fresh fish when in season in your locality—that is when they are cheapest and best. Frozen fish is available the year around.

3. Try less familiar varieties when they are abundant and inexpensive. They may be just as desirable as the types you know which cost much more. The demand for favorite varieties may increase their price to a point where less known varieties are much better values.

4. Purchase the size of fish which is the best buy. Small or large fish of a given variety may be available in abundance only in certain seasons. Large sizes are not always best, though plump fish are usually preferable to thin fish of the same variety. But smaller sizes are cheaper, just as easy to prepare and more tasty.

5. If you need to save time and labor in preparing fish, buy steaks, fillets and sticks.

6. Buy fish that suits your cooking method. Dealers are glad to recommend varieties and suggest the most practical form for your needs.

7. Buy the right amount to serve. Usually ⅓ to ½ pound of fresh or frozen fish per person will provide adequate servings after cooking.

8. Beware of "bargains" in fish. It is never a good plan to buy heldover fish because fish is very perishable.

HINTS ON COOKING AND HANDLING FISH

1. Keep fresh fish chilled until ready to cook. It spoils quickly so cook promptly after buying.

2. To trim the fins off, cut into the flesh on each side of the base of the fin. This permits easy removal of fin and fin bone, either before or after cooking.

3. Keep frozen fish hard-frozen until ready to prepare for cooking. Once thawed, frozen fish should never be re-frozen, but cooked immediately.

4. If you buy packaged or wrapped fillets or steaks, note on the wrappers whether they have been salted. Light salting is the rule, and not much additional salt is needed.

5. To keep hands from smelling "fishy" after handling raw fish, chill them thoroughly in cold water before you touch the fish at all.

6. After handling fish, clean your hands with hot water and salt, and rinse the salt off thoroughly before using any soap.

7. "Fishy" dishes should be washed in a strong solution of salt and water to remove the fish odor before using soap.

TABLE 6. FAT CONTENTS, COOKING METHODS AND FUEL VALUE OF FISH

Variety of Fish	Fat Content of Edible Portion			Suggested Methods of Cooking					Fuel Value of Edible Portion in Calories per pound
	Very low	Fairly low	High but variable	Broil	Bake	Boil or Steam	Deep fat or Pan fry	Chow-der	
SALT-WATER FISH									
Alewife	–	x	–	x	–	x	x	–	550
Barracuda	–	–	x	x	x	x	–	–	510
Bluefish	–	x	–	x	x	–	x	–	535
Blue runner	–	x	–	x	x	–	x	–	445
Butterfish	–	–	x	x	–	–	x	–	745
Cod	x	–	–	x	x	x	–	x	315
Croaker	–	x	–	x	x	x	x	x	415
Cusk	x	–	–	x	x	x	x	x	315
Drum, red	–	x	–	–	x	x	–	x	345
Eel, common ...	–	–	x	x	–	–	x	–	710
Flounders:									
Blackback (Winter)	x	–	–	x	x	x	x	x	290
Fluke (Summer) ...	x	–	–	x	x	x	x	x	290
"Sole" (Pacific)	–	x	–	x	x	x	x	x	345
Southern	–	x	–	x	x	x	x	x	395
"California halibut"	–	x	–	x	x	x	x	x	415
Groupers	–	x	–	x	x	x	–	x	370–395
Haddock	x	–	–	x	x	x	–	x	325
Hake	x	–	–	–	x	x	–	x	340
Halibut	–	–	x	x	x	x	–	x	550
Herring, sea (AC & PC) ..	–	–	x	x	x	–	–	–	620–825
Horse mackerel (PC)	–	–	x	x	–	x	–	–	620
Kingfish (PC) ..	–	x	–	x	x	–	x	–	360
Kingfish (King mackerel) ...	–	–	x	x	x	–	–	–	900
King whiting (Kingfish) ...	–	x	–	x	–	x	x	x	455
"Lingcod"	–	x	–	x	x	x	–	–	355
Mackerel (AC & PC)	–	–	x	x	x	–	–	–	715–900
Mullet	–	x	–	x	x	x	–	x	530

x—indicates fat content or suitable cooking method.

TABLE 6. FAT CONTENTS, COOKING METHODS AND FUEL VALUE OF FISH
(Continued)

Variety of Fish	Fat Content of Edible Portion			Suggested Methods of Cooking					Fuel Value of Edible Portion in Calories per pound
	Very low	Fairly low	High but variable	Broil	Bake	Boil or Steam	Deep fat or Pan fry	Chow-der	
SALT-WATER FISH —Cont'd									
Pollock	–	x	–	x	x	x	–	x	425
Pompano	–	–	x	x	x	x	–	–	730
Rockfish (PC)	–	x	–	x	x	–	–	–	375
Rosefish	–	x	–	x	x	–	x	–	455
Sablefish	–	–	x	x	x	x	–	–	900
Salmon:									
Atlantic	–	–	x	x	x	x	–	–	955
Chinook (King)	–	–	x	x	x	x	–	–	990
Chum (Fall)	–	–	x	x	x	x	–	–	600
Pink	–	–	x	x	x	x	–	–	625
Silver	–	–	x	x	x	x	–	–	725
Scup (Porgy)	–	x	–	x	x	–	x	–	520
Sea bass:									
Black (AC)	–	x	–	x	x	x	x	x	395
White (PC)	–	–	x	x	x	–	x	–	410
Sea trout:									
Gray	–	x	–	x	x	–	x	–	390
Spotted	–	x	–	x	x	x	x	x	455
Shad	–	–	x	x	x	–	–	–	740
Sheepshead (AC)	–	x	–	x	x	–	x	–	490
Smelt:									
Atlantic	–	x	–	x	–	–	x	–	395
Pacific	–	–	x	x	–	–	x	–	900
Snapper, red	–	x	–	x	x	x	–	–	395
Spanish mackerel	–	–	x	x	x	–	x	–	900
Spot	–	x	–	x	–	–	x	–	455
Striped bass	–	x	–	x	x	–	x	–	455
Sturgeon	–	x	–	x	x	–	–	–	405
Swordfish	–	x	x	x	x	–	–	–	520
Tautog	–	x	–	x	x	–	x	–	380
Tilefish	–	x	–	x	x	x	–	–	340
Tomcod (AC)	–	x	–	x	x	–	x	–	330
Tuna (all kinds)	–	–	–	x	x	x	–	–	570–770

TABLE 6. FAT CONTENTS, COOKING METHODS AND FUEL VALUE OF FISH (Continued)

Variety of Fish	Fat Content of Edible Portion			Suggested Methods of Cooking					Fuel Value of Edible Portion in Calories per pound
	Very low	Fairly low	High but variable	Broil	Bake	Boil or Steam	Deep fat or Pan fry	Chow-der	
SALT-WATER FISH —Cont'd									
White perch (AC)	–	x	–	x	x	–	x	–	515
Whiting	–	x	–	x	x	–	x	–	340
Wolffish	–	x	–	x	x	x	x	x	455
Yellowtail (PC)	–	–	x	x	x	–	x	–	600
FRESH-WATER FISH									
Blue pike	–	x	–	x	x	–	x	–	360
Buffalofish	–	x	–	x	x	–	x	–	430
Carp	–	x	–	x	x	x	x	–	420
Catfish	–	–	x	–	–	x	x	x	445
Lake herring	–	x	–	x	x	–	x	–	615
Lake trout	–	–	x	x	x	x	x	–	745
Pickerel (Jacks)	–	x	–	x	x	–	x	x	360
Sauger	–	x	–	x	x	–	x	–	355
Sheepshead	–	x	–	x	x	x	–	–	445
Smelt	–	x	–	x	x	–	x	–	395
Suckers	–	x	–	x	x	–	x	–	420
Whitefish	–	–	x	x	x	–	x	–	680
Yellow perch	–	x	–	x	x	–	x	–	370
Yellow pike	–	x	–	x	x	–	x	–	360
SHELLFISH									
Clams (Hard & Soft)	x	–	–	x	x	x	x	x	345–355
Crabs (AC & PC)	x	–	–	x	x	x	x	–	370
Lobster, common	x	–	–	x	x	x	–	x	380
Oysters	x	–	–	x	x	x	x	x	365
Scallops	x	–	–	x	x	x	x	x	335
Shrimp	x	–	–	–	x	x	x	x	370

AC—Atlantic Coast. PC—Pacific Coast.

TABLE 7. METHODS OF COOKING FISH

Suggested Methods of Cooking Various Cuts of Fin-Fish

Method of Cooking	Fat Content		Drawn[1]	Dressed[1]	Pan Dressed	Steaks	Fillets
	High	Low					
Bake	x	([2])	x	x	x	x	x
Boil or Steam	([3])	x	x	x	−	x	x
Broil	x	x	x	x	x	x	x
Deep fat fry	x	x	x	x	x	x	x
Pan-fry	x	x	x	x	x	x	x
Chowder	−	x	x	x	−	−	x

[1] Drawn and dressed fish usually are baked in the form purchased, but are split or cut in portions for the other methods of cooking.

[2] Lean fish require more care in basting.

[3] Fat fish are more apt to fall apart.

Suggested Methods of Cooking Various Kinds of Shellfish

Method of Cooking	Live in Shell				Shucked	Headless	Cooked Meat
	Clams	Crabs	Lobsters	Oysters	Clams Oysters Scallops	Shrimp	Crab Lobster Shrimp
Raw	x	−	−	x	x*	−	x
Bake	x	−	x	x	x	x	x
Boil or Steam	x	x	x	x	x	x	x
Broil	x	x	x	x	−	−	−
Deep fat fry	−	x	−	−	x	x	x
Pan-fry	−	x	−	−	x	x	x
Chowder	−	−	−	−	x	x	x

* Except scallops.

409   HOW TO JUDGE QUALITY OF FISH

Fresh fish has firm, elastic flesh. Test it by pressing the flesh gently with the fingertips. If fresh, the flesh should spring back; if stale, the dent will remain. The eyes should be bright and full, not filmed or sunken. Gills should be reddish pink. Fresh fish has a characteristic "fresh" odor which is unmistakable.

Fish bought alive should be swimming actively in the tank, not resting sluggishly on the bottom.

Frozen fish should be frozen hard.

Fish in brine should be covered with brine, and should have firm flesh and a brine odor.

Dry salt fish should be clean, firm-fleshed, and show some salt grains on the surface.

Smoked fish should be firm, with a sweet, smoky odor.

410   CLEANING SCALE FISH

First remove the fins, cutting into the flesh on both sides at the base. Many kinds of fish have such stiff, sharp fins that there is danger of injuring the hands in scaling them if the fins are left on. Then, holding the fish by the tail and working toward the head, scrape off the scales with a blunt knife. If the knife is held at the correct angle the scales will not fly. Wash off clinging scales in cold water; then cut off the head just behind the gills, then the tail. Either a sharp knife or a pair of kitchen shears may be used. Slit the belly from end to end and remove entrails, being careful not to break the gall. Wash the whole fish inside and out under running cold water, to remove all clotted blood. Drain thoroughly. If fish is not to be cooked immediately, wrap loosely in waxed or cellophane paper or place in a plastic bag and store in the refrigerator.

411   CLEANING CATFISH AND EEL

These fish have a thin, sleek outer skin ranging in color from bluish to yellowish. This skin is easily removed by dipping the fish repeatedly into simmering water until it loosens and can be readily scraped off. Rinse in cold water. Then remove head, tail and entrails, and cut into serving portions.

412   SKINNING CARP

Carp is often sold alive, and must be dressed in the home; though it may also be purchased dressed and ready for cooking. First, to kill the fish and to permit free bleeding, stick a knife halfway through the body, back of the head and just behind the gills; a very sharp, thin, pointed knife is needed for this process. Then cut out the back fin and remove the scales and outer skin. Grasp the fish by the tail and shave off the scales and outer skin in strips, by working the knife toward the head without cutting into the flesh. Then split the belly from back to front, being careful not to cut into the entrails, which may then be removed as a whole. Cut off the head back of the front fins, cut away the tail and other fins, and wash the fish thoroughly in cold water. Drain thoroughly.

A simpler method of removing the entire skin is to plunge the fish (or its previously prepared fillets) into boiling water, allowing it to remain about half a minute after boiling starts again. The skin may then be easily rubbed off while the fish is hot, then the flesh should be quickly rinsed in cold water. Boiling, however, must not be prolonged beyond the point where the skin slips off easily, or the flesh will break up.

To improve the flavor of carp, prepare the following dressing: Mix ½ cup salt, ½ cup grated or ground onion (with its juice), 1 tablespoon vinegar, ½ teaspoon black pepper and a pinch of mace. Place the dressed carp in a deep dish and cover with the dressing. Let it stand for 1 hour and then rinse thoroughly, discarding the dressing. Wash the fish in a pan of cold water for about 1 minute to remove all salt from the surface. It may then be fried, broiled, baked or boiled like any other fish.

413　　　　　PREPARING FISH FILLETS

Place the knife between the flesh and the end of the first rib bone at the head end of the cleaned fish. Cut the flesh loose down to the back bone, leaving as little flesh as possible attached to the bone. Continue this process all down one side of the fish to the tail; then loosen the flesh from the back bone. Turn the fish around and repeat on the other side. Lift out the bones and cut the boned fish in serving size portions. The bones may be used for making fish stock.

414　　　　　FISH BAKED IN PARCHMENT

Choose small cleaned whole fish or fillets of large fish. Wash whole fish thoroughly in cold water, then drain; or clean fillets by wiping with a damp cloth. Cut parchment paper about 3 times as wide as the fish, and about 1½ to 2 inches longer. Rub paper well on inside with soft butter and sprinkle fish with salt (1 to 1¼ teaspoons to the pound). Place fish in center of paper and sprinkle generously with lemon juice, and paprika. Fold paper neatly over the fish, finishing with a "hem" around 3 edges which can be secured with wire paper clips or pins. Bake in a moderate oven (350° F.) 20 minutes. When done, slide the fish packets onto hot platter. With scissors, cut away parchment and remove, letting juices flow over the fish. Serve immediately with a garnish of lemon and cucumber slices and crisp watercress. 1½ to 2 lbs. cleaned fish serves 5.

415   QUICK BAKED FISH, SPENCER METHOD

2 lbs. fish	2 teaspoons salt
¼ cup evaporated milk	2 cups fine dry bread crumbs
¼ cup water	Salad oil

This method may be used for cleaned small whole fish, fillets or thick steaks cut from larger fish. When buying fish steaks, have them cut ½-inch thick. Dip fish into a mixture of evaporated milk, water and salt, and then roll it in bread crumbs until thickly coated with crumbs. Place in an oiled baking pan, sprinkling each piece lightly with oil. (Allow 2 tablespoons oil for the 2 lbs. of fish.) Heat oven very hot (500°-600° F.), put fish into hot oven and bake uncovered for 10 minutes. Never add water; do not turn fish while baking. When done, pieces of fish will be brown and dry on outside, tender and juicy on inside. 5 servings.

416   DELICIOUS BOILED FISH

2½ lbs. fish (pike, salmon, cod, perch, haddock, etc.)	2¼ teaspoons salt
	1 tablespoon lemon juice
2½ cups boiling water	2 teaspoons sugar
24 whole black peppers	2 tablespoons flour
1 teaspoon chopped parsley	2 tablespoons cold water
1 small bay leaf	1 egg yolk

Clean fish by removing all scales and wiping clean with a damp cloth. Cut into serving portions (small fish may be cleaned and left whole), and lay pieces in a heavy saucepan. Add the boiling water, peppers, parsley, bay leaf and salt. Cover, place over low heat and simmer for 30 minutes. Drain off liquid and strain it. There should be 1½ cups liquid. Put this into another saucepan and add the lemon juice and sugar and the flour mixed to a smooth paste with the cold water. Cook slowly, stirring constantly to keep smooth until mixture boils. Beat egg yolk, stir into it a little of the hot sauce and pour into the mixture in the saucepan. Continue cooking, stirring constantly for another minute. Serve fish in a hot shallow vegetable dish with the sauce poured over it, or on a small hot platter garnished with parsley and with the sauce in a gravy boat. 5 servings.

417 BROILED FISH

Either fat or lean fish may be broiled. Cuts most frequently used are fillets or steaks, pan-dressed fish, drawn or dressed fish, and split or cut portions.

Let fish stand from 1 to 8 minutes in a solution of 2 tablespoons salt to 1 cup of water, the time depending upon the thickness of the fish. Thin pieces should be left in the solution only 1 or 2 minutes; those of medium thickness for 3 minutes; very thick ones 5 to 8 minutes. Then drain thoroughly. Oil the heated broiler rack, place the fish on it (skin side up if split or whole fish is used), and brush with oil. The broiler rack should be about 2 inches below the source of heat. Cook until the skin is covered with dark brown bubbles, or steaks are golden brown, about 5 minutes. Turn and cook on the other side until nicely browned, from 3 to 7 minutes longer. The fish should be turned only once, but may be basted several times with melted butter or cooking oil. The total broiling time will be from 7 to 12 minutes, depending on the thickness of the fish. Fish should be nicely browned, but not cooked too thoroughly, or it will be dry and fall to pieces.

418 BROILED SALT MACKEREL

2 lbs. salt mackerel fillets	2 teaspoons chopped parsley
¼ cup melted butter	1 lemon, cut in wedges

Lay the fish in a flat pan, flesh side up and cover with cold water; let soak 12 hours. Drain and pat dry with clean cloth or paper toweling. Brush with melted butter and place on an oiled hot broiler rack, skin side up. Broil 5 to 10 minutes, or until skin is browned and full of bubbles, basting once or twice with melted butter. Turn and baste flesh side with butter; then broil to desired brownness. Slide carefully onto a hot platter, sprinkle sparingly with chopped parsley and drizzle with a little more melted butter. Serve piping hot, with lemon wedges and parsley for garnish. 5 servings.

419 FRENCH-FRIED FISH

½ cup yellow cornmeal	1⅓ tablespoons salt
½ cup flour	2 lbs. fish fillets or steak

Mix together thoroughly the cornmeal, flour and salt, and place in a shallow pan. Dip the serving-size portions of fish into cold water; then roll in the cornmeal mixture until covered on all sides. Put fish into a wire frying basket, just one layer deep. Lower basket into deep fat heated to 385-400° F. Fry until fish has an even golden brown crust (4 to 8 minutes, depending on variety of the fish). 5 servings.

420   PAN-FRIED FISH

Choose fillets or steaks, pan-dressed fish, or drawn or dressed fish split or cut into serving portions. Prepare just as for French-Fried Fish (419). Place enough shortening in a heavy skillet to make a ¼-inch layer when melted; heat to sizzling. Place the coated fish in the pan and cook 3 minutes or until nicely browned on the under side. Cover pan and remove from heat for about 2 minutes, permitting fish to cook in its own steam. Then remove cover, turn the fish and return pan to heat. Cook about 3 minutes longer. Fish less than ⅝-inch thick requires less cooking time; thicker fish requires longer. 5 servings.

421   TO FRESHEN CODFISH

Method 1. Let cold water run over the codfish for 15 minutes; then place in a saucepan, cover with cold water, heat slowly just to the boiling point, but do not boil. Pour off water. Repeat this process until the fish tastes fresh.

Method 2. Let cold water run over the codfish for 15 minutes; then let warm water run over it for 5 minutes. Drain, cover with cold water and let soak over night.

Method 3. Soak codfish in cold water for 3 or 4 hours, changing the water every hour.

421a   CREAMED CODFISH

½ lb. salt codfish   3 cups milk
4 tablespoons butter   Dash pepper
4 tablespoons flour

Freshen codfish (421). Drain and pull apart in coarse shreds. Melt butter in top of double boiler; blend in flour, add milk, and cook over direct heat, stirring constantly until sauce boils and thickens. Add fish, and pepper to suit taste, and place over boiling water. Cover and cook 20 to 30 minutes. Serve on toast or over boiled potatoes. 5 servings.

422   CODFISH au GRATIN

Prepare Creamed Codfish (421a) as described above. Add 1 cup grated cheese to the white sauce just before adding the codfish, stirring until blended. Instead of continued cooking in double boiler, pour creamed fish into shallow baking dish and sprinkle with buttered bread crumbs. Bake in moderate oven (350° F.) until nicely toasted, from 20 to 30 minutes. 5 servings.

423   CODFISH BALLS OR CAKES

½ lb. salt codfish	3 tablespoons milk
4 medium boiling potatoes	2 eggs, well beaten
1 tablespoon butter	

Freshen codfish (421), then drain and separate into shreds. Peel and quarter potatoes and put into a 3-qt. saucepan. Add fish, barely cover with boiling water. Cover and simmer until potatoes are tender, about 20 minutes. Drain thoroughly in a sieve or colander. Mash potatoes and codfish together, add butter and milk and whip vigorously until smooth and fluffy. Add well-beaten eggs and beat well. Shape with spoon into frazzled balls and fry until golden brown in deep fat heated to 375° F. Drain for a few moments on absorbent paper or paper toweling and serve hot. For Codfish Cakes, shape into patties and pan-fry in butter or bacon drippings. Serve with Tomato Sauce (916) if desired. 5 to 6 servings.

424   CODFISH CASSEROLE

½ lb. salt codfish	1 cup grated cheese
3 tablespoons butter	Salt and pepper to suit taste
3 tablespoons flour	⅓ cup fine dry bread crumbs
1 No. 1 8½-oz. can peas	2 tablespoons melted butter
Milk	

Freshen codfish (421). Drain and flake the fish. Melt butter, blend in flour and add liquid drained from peas, to which enough milk has been added to make 2 cups. Stir constantly over direct heat until thickened; then add grated cheese and seasonings. Salt may not be needed if fish retains enough salt. Fold in peas and codfish and turn into a buttered casserole. Mix crumbs with melted butter and sprinkle over top. Bake in a moderately slow oven (325° F.) 45 to 50 minutes. 5 servings.

425   CREAMED FINNAN HADDIE

2 cups medium-thin white sauce (919)	¾ lb. finnan haddie, cut up

In making white sauce, use 1½ tablespoons flour per cup of milk and omit salt. Place over boiling water. Cut up finnan haddie into small pieces, using kitchen shears for convenience. Stir into the hot white sauce, cover, and cook 20 to 30 minutes. Serve on toast or on boiled or baked potatoes. 5 servings.

426   FINNAN HADDIE AND POTATO CASSEROLE

¾ lb. finnan haddie
4 medium potatoes, pared and diced

2½ cups milk
2 tablespoons butter

Cut finnan haddie into serving-size pieces and put into saucepan with potatoes and milk. Heat slowly until milk begins to simmer. Turn into a shallow baking dish and dot with butter. Bake in a moderate oven (350° F.) until potatoes are tender, from 30 to 35 minutes. Serves 5.

427   FISH CAKES

3 medium potatoes
2 cups fish flakes (11½-oz. tin)
½ cup evaporated milk

¾ teaspoon salt
Dash pepper
Shallow fat for frying

Scrub potatoes and boil in jackets until tender. Remove skins and mash (cold boiled potatoes also may be used). Add fish, milk and seasonings, and mix thoroughly. Cool mixture. Shape into small flat cakes and pan-fry in hot fat until brown and crusty on both sides. May be served with Dill Sauce (906) or Tartar Sauce (915). 5 to 6 servings.

427a   FISH PIE

2½ cups fish stock
4 tablespoons butter or shortening
⅓ cup flour
¼ cup drained, cooked or canned peas
1 cup drained, cleaned cooked or canned shrimp

1 cup flaked baked or boiled fish, or canned salmon
1 teaspoon prepared horseradish, if desired
Plain pastry for single crust (631)

First prepare the fish stock as follows: Put the head and backbone of a raw fish into a saucepan with 1 cup diced celery, ½ cup thickly sliced carrot, 1½ teaspoons salt and 3 cups cold water; cover and simmer 20 minutes, then strain; there should be about 2½ cups stock. Pick out and save the pieces of celery and carrot for use in pie filling.

Melt butter, blend in flour and add the fish stock, stirring until sauce boils and thickens. Add the cooked carrots, celery, peas, shrimp and flaked fish. Stir in horseradish. Turn mixture into a 9-inch deep pie plate and cover with pastry which has been rolled about ⅛-inch thick and gashed in several places; crimp edge to rim of dish. Bake pie in a hot oven (450° F.) 20 to 25 minutes, until crust is nicely browned. Serve piping hot. 5 servings.

Note: When purchasing a fish steak or fillet, ask the dealer for a fish head and bones with which to make the fish stock. He will be glad to give you these without extra cost.

428   CREAMED SALMON

1 1-lb. can red or pink salmon	3 teaspoons minced parsley, or
2 cups medium white sauce (919)	2 tablespoons chopped sweet pickle, if desired

Drain salmon, remove skin and bones, then coarsely flake fish. Fold salmon and juice into white sauce in top of double boiler, and continue cooking over boiling water until thoroughly heated. Add minced parsley or pickle, if desired, just before serving. 5 servings.

Variation 1: Stir 1 cup grated cheese into white sauce before adding salmon.

Variation 2: Add 1 cup drained cooked or canned peas or asparagus to the creamed salmon.

429   SALMON AU GRATIN

1 1-lb. can pink or red salmon	½ cup drained cooked celery
1 tablespoon lemon juice	(1020)
1 tablespoon butter	Salt and pepper to suit taste
1 tablespoon flour	¼ cup fine dry bread crumbs
1 cup milk	¼ cup grated American cheese

Drain salmon, discarding bones and skin, then flake. Add lemon juice. Melt butter, blend in flour and fish juice, then milk; stir over direct heat until sauce boils and thickens. Add salmon, celery salt or cooked celery, salt and pepper as desired. Turn into buttered casserole and sprinkle bread crumbs and cheese mixed together over the top. Bake in a moderately hot oven (400° F.) about 20 minutes. 5 servings.

Note: Use boiled fresh or left-over fish instead of the salmon.

430   SALMON CROQUETTES

1 1-lb. can pink or red salmon	1 cup fine dry bread crumbs
1 cup thick white sauce (919)	1 egg, beaten
made with fish juice and milk	Deep fat for frying
1 tablespoon lemon juice	

Drain salmon, discard skin and bones, then flake coarsely. Add white sauce and lemon juice and mix thoroughly. Cool and shape into croquettes, roll in bread crumbs and dip in beaten egg; then roll again in bread crumbs. Fry in deep fat heated to 375° F. until croquettes are golden brown. Drain for a minute on absorbent paper or paper toweling. Serve with Egg Sauce, Tartar Sauce, or Tomato Sauce (909, 916, 915). 5 servings.

431   SALMON LOAF

1 1-lb. can pink or red salmon	1½ cups bread crumbs
1 tablespoon lemon juice	½ teaspoon baking powder
Dash of cayenne	½ cup evaporated milk
1 teaspoon salt	½ cup liquid (fish juice and
2 eggs, beaten	water)
⅔ cup chopped celery	

Drain salmon, discard skin and bones, save juice. Flake fish, add remaining ingredients, then mix well. Pack mixture firmly into a greased glass loaf pan. Bake in a moderate oven (350° F.) until brown and firm, from 30 to 40 minutes. Serve with Tomato (916) or Cheese Sauce (920). Salmon loaf mixture may be made into patties and pan-fried. 5 servings.

432   SALMON PATTIES

1 1-lb. can pink or red salmon	Salt and pepper to suit taste
2 eggs, slightly beaten	1 tablespoon lemon juice
1 cup seasoned mashed potato	¼ cup shortening
or ½ cup fine bread crumbs	

Drain salmon, discard skin and bones, save juice. Crush fish, stir in eggs, fish juice and potato or crumbs, blending well. Add seasonings and lemon juice, mixing well. Divide into ¼-cup portions and shape into flat patties, about ½-inch thick. Heat shortening sizzling hot in heavy skillet, lay in patties and brown on both sides to a rich golden color. Remove to a hot platter and garnish with parsley and lemon wedges, if desired. May be served with Tartar (915) or Celery Sauce (904). 5 servings.

433   SALMON SOUFFLÉ

¼ cup butter   2 cups milk
⅓ cup unsifted flour   4 eggs, separated
1½ teaspoons salt   1 1-lb. can pink or red salmon

Melt butter in top of double boiler, blend in flour, add salt and milk
and cook over direct heat, stirring constantly until sauce boils and thickens. Beat egg yolks until light, stir in a little of the hot sauce and pour
back into rest of sauce; cook over boiling water, stirring constantly, for
2 minutes. Remove from heat. Drain salmon, discard skin and bones,
save juice, then flake fish. Mix fish and juice with sauce. Beat egg whites
until stiff and fold lightly but thoroughly into the mixture. Pour into a
well-buttered 6-cup casserole and bake in a moderately slow oven (325°
F.) 1 hour. Serve immediately. 5 servings.

Note: Use any left-over cooked fresh fish in place of the salmon.

434   SALMON AND MACARONI CASSEROLE

7 oz. macaroni (2 cups,   ½ teaspoon salt
  broken)   Dash pepper
3 tablespoons butter   ¼ cup fine bread crumbs,
3 tablespoons flour   buttered
1 1-lb. can pink or red salmon   ¼ cup grated cheese
  Milk

Drop macaroni into 2 quarts boiling salted water (2 teaspoons salt)
and cook rapidly until barely tender (from 15 to 20 minutes). Drain and
rinse with hot water. Meanwhile, melt butter, blend in flour and add
juice drained from salmon plus enough milk to make 1½ cups liquid;
stir over direct heat until sauce boils and thickens. Add seasonings and
macaroni. Arrange macaroni and flaked salmon from which skin and
bones have been removed, in alternate layers in a buttered casserole, beginning and ending with macaroni. Mix bread crumbs with grated cheese
and sprinkle over top. Bake in moderate oven (375° F.) 20 to 25 minutes.
5 servings.

435   SALMON AND RICE CASSEROLE

½ cup uncooked rice   1 1-lb. can pink or red salmon
2 eggs, well beaten   2 tablespoons chopped parsley
½ cup milk   1½ teaspoons salt
¼ cup butter, melted   2 tablespoons lemon juice
½ cup fine dry bread crumbs

Wash rice or do not wash as directed on package; drop into 1 quart rapidly boiling salted water and cook briskly until tender (about 20 minutes). Drain and rinse in hot water. Beat eggs thoroughly and combine with milk and rice; toss butter and crumbs together and stir into mixture. Then fold in flaked salmon from which skin and bones have been removed and remaining ingredients. Turn into a buttered baking dish or into individual custard cups and bake in a moderately slow oven (325° F.) 30 to 40 minutes. Serve hot. 5 servings.

436   FISH PASTRY SHELL WITH SALMON-LOBSTER FILLING

Plain or cheese pastry
(631 or 632)
3 tablespoons butter
1 small onion, chopped
3 tablespoons flour
1 cup milk

1 1-lb. can red salmon, flaked
1 cup cooked fresh lobster
meat, or 1 6-oz. can, flaked
Salt to suit taste
2 tablespoons lemon juice

Roll out pastry into 2 11-inch circles ⅛-inch thick, and cut out 2 identical shell shapes, using a previously prepared paper shell pattern, which is approximately 11 inches long and 10½ wide at the widest part of the shell (see illustration). Place one shell on a buttered baking sheet, and the other on a piece of waxed paper; chill both in refrigerator. Melt butter in saucepan, add onion and sauté until yellow. Blend in flour and add milk; cook with constant stirring until sauce boils and thickens. Fold in remaining ingredients, then cool. Spread fish mixture over pastry shell on baking sheet, heaping slightly in the center and leaving about ½-inch free at edge all around. Wet edge with cold water and lay other shell over top; press edges firmly together to seal. Mark shell as in illustration, using handle of knife, and gash in several places along these markings. Bake in a hot oven (450° F.) 15 minutes, then reduce heat to moderate (350° F.) and bake 30 minutes longer or until delicately browned. Transfer to hot platter, garnish with parsley and serve at once. This may be baked as an ordinary double-crust pie if preferred. Serves 5 to 8.

437   CREAMED TUNA FISH

1 13-oz. can tuna fish

2 cups medium white sauce
(919)

Drain and flake fish coarsely. Combine with the hot white sauce and reheat over boiling water for 10 minutes. Serve on mashed potatoes, hot boiled rice or noodles or on toast. One tablespoon chopped pimiento and ½ cup sautéed mushrooms may be added for richer color and flavor. 5 servings.

438   TUNA AND CELERY FONDUE

1¼ cups milk	1 cup diced celery
1 tablespoon butter	1 7-oz. can tuna fish
1 cup soft bread crumbs	3 eggs, separated
½ teaspoon salt	1 tablespoon lemon juice

Scald milk, then add butter, crumbs, salt, celery and tuna which has been drained and flaked. Beat egg yolks well and stir in a little of the hot mixture; then return to saucepan and heat for 3 minutes or until thickened, stirring constantly. Remove from heat and fold in lemon juice and stiffly beaten egg whites. Turn into buttered casserole and bake in a moderately slow oven (325° F.) 1 hour, or until a knife inserted in the center comes out clean. If desired, the celery may be cooked in a small amount of boiling water for 5 minutes before combining with other ingredients; otherwise it will remain slightly crisp even after baking. 5 servings.

439   TUNA AND NOODLE CASSEROLE

1 7-oz. can tuna	8 oz. noodles
3 cups medium white sauce (919)	Buttered bread crumbs

Drain and flake tuna, add to white sauce, then heat over boiling water. Meanwhile, cook noodles in 2 quarts boiling salted water, until tender (171). Drain well. Arrange noodles in alternate layers with the creamed tuna in a buttered casserole. Sprinkle buttered bread crumbs on top and bake in a moderate oven (350° F.) about 20 minutes, or until golden brown. 5 servings.

Variation: Add 1 cup grated cheese to white sauce and proceed as above. Cooked sliced potatoes may be used in place of the noodles.

440   SPECIES OF CLAMS

1. Hard-shell or quahog clams from the Atlantic coast have the most general distribution. The large ones of this variety are used in making broths and chowders. The small ones, such as "Little Necks" and "Cherry Stones" are good served raw on the half shell, in cocktails and also steamed or broiled.

2. Soft-shell clams come from both the Atlantic and Pacific coasts. They are good for clam bakes, frying, steaming, roasting and broth.

3. Razor clams come from the Pacific coast and are used principally in making chowders.

Clams are bought alive in the shell and are sold by the dozen. To determine whether they are alive, try to open the shell with the fingers. A live clam holds its shell tightly closed.

441   CLEANING CLAMS

If time permits, lay the live clams one layer deep in a pan with enough cold water to cover them, and add ½ cup cornmeal for each dozen clams. Let them stand several hours or overnight. The clams absorb the cornmeal and work out the sand, which may be held in their shells. Scrub the clams and rinse thoroughly with cold water. To open live clams for serving on the half shell, insert a strong sharp slender knife between the shells and cut around the clam through the muscle. Twist the knife slightly to pry the shell open and loosen meat. Then drain, or drop both juice and meat into a bowl. If sand adheres to meat, rinse off quickly in cold water. If sand is in juice, let stand for sand to settle, then drain off juice and use with clam meat.

442   CLAMS ON THE HALF SHELL

Clean and open clams, (441). Discard empty half shells. Loosen meat in other half shells and remove shell particles. Place a small cup or glass of Cocktail Sauce (907) in center of serving plate. Surround with crushed ice, spreading it to rim of plate. Arrange 6 half shells with cleaned clam meat on ice. Garnish with parsley. Serve with lemon wedges, horseradish and crisp crackers. 30 clams serve 5.

443   STEAMING CLAMS

Choose Little Neck hard-shell clams and clean as described above (441). Place the unopened clams in a shallow pan in a steamer and steam until the shells open; then remove immediately. Remove one shell of each clam and discard. Serve the clams on the remaining shells on a hot plate. Provide melted butter for dipping the clams, also salt and pepper. The broth in the pan may be served along with the clams in separate cups. Allow 2½ to 3 dozen for 5 servings.

444   ROASTING CLAMS

Clean the clams thoroughly and place in a baking pan. Roast in a moderately hot oven (425° F.) until the shells open. Serve as for steamed clams. Allow 2½ to 3 dozen for 5 servings.

445 HOW TO BUY CRABS

The most common varieties are blue crabs from the Atlantic and Gulf coasts, and the larger Dungeness crabs from the Pacific coast. All varieties have both hard and soft shelled stages. Normally, crabs are hard shelled, but as they grow the shells must be enlarged, so the old shell is discarded from time to time and a new one forms. If the crab is caught just before the new shell hardens, it is called a soft shelled crab. Hard shelled crabs are available all year, but are most plentiful in the summer. Soft shelled crabs are in season from May to October. Crabs are purchased alive by the dozen, and should be kept alive in moist seaweed until they are cooked. Frozen crab meat in the shell and out of the shell, as well as fresh crab meat is now available at many fish markets.

446 COOKING HARD-SHELLED CRABS

Buy only live crabs. Have enough boiling salted water to cover the crabs. To each 2 quarts of boiling water, add ¼ cup vinegar, 2 tablespoons salt, and 1 tablespoon paprika. Drop the live crabs into this boiling solution. Cook rapidly for 5 minutes after active boiling starts, then reduce the heat and simmer 10 minutes longer. Or put the crabs into a steamer and steam for 25 minutes.

The sweet, edible meat is found in the claws, legs and body of the crab. After cooking, pull off the claws and legs, then crack the shells. Break off the segment that folds under the body at the rear. Holding the crab in the left hand with the back toward you, slip fingers of the right hand under the top shell and pull the body downward so as not to break it. (The top shell is sometimes used for baking deviled crabmeat.) Holding the crab under cold running water, remove the digestive tract. Then split the crab along the central crease. Hold half the body in the left hand, and with a sharp knife cut the hard membranous covering along the outside edge. With a nutpick, remove the tender sweet meat in each cavity, being careful not to break off pieces of shell into the meat. Pick the meat out carefully so it will not be necessary to wash it off, for washing results in a loss of both flavor and food value.

447 COOKING SOFT-SHELLED CRABS

Use only live crabs and dress them in this way, before cooking: Place the live crab with its back up on a board, and kill by cutting off the head ½ to ¾-inch back of the eyes. Turn back the tapered pointed ends of its back about half way, and scrape out the spongy material that is exposed. Then peel off the tail or "apron" which laps under the crab, together with the spongy mass under it. Wash the crab in cold water.

Soft-shelled crabs are cooked by frying. Have deep fat heated to 360° F. While it heats, let the crabs stand in a salt solution of 2 tablespoons salt to 1 cup water for about 2 minutes; then drain, dip into beaten egg, and roll in fine bread crumbs. Arrange crabs one layer deep in a wire frying basket and lower into the hot fat. Fry until golden brown, turning over once. Lift out onto absorbent paper or paper toweling to drain, and serve with Tartar Sauce (915). The entire soft-shelled crab is edible. 1 large, 2 medium or 3 small crabs serves 1.

448   CRABMEAT CAKES

3 tablespoons butter	¾ cup dry bread crumbs
1 clove garlic, peeled	6½-oz. can crabmeat (1⅔
4 tablespoons flour	cups flaked crabmeat)
1 cup milk	1 egg, beaten
¾ teaspoon salt	2 tablespoons butter
Dash pepper	1 hard-cooked egg (395)
½ teaspoon Worcestershire	

Melt butter in saucepan with clove of garlic sliced into several pieces. Remove pieces of garlic when butter is melted. Blend in flour and add the milk, stirring constantly until the sauce boils and thickens. Add salt, pepper, and Worcestershire, then remove from heat. There should be 1¼ cups sauce. To ½ of the sauce add ¼ cup bread crumbs and crabmeat from which cartilage has been removed. Mix well, cover tightly and put in refrigerator to chill. When thoroughly chilled shape the mixture into 10 small patties, then dip patties into remaining bread crumbs, beaten egg and again in crumbs. Pan-fry in melted butter in a hot skillet until browned on both sides, about 5 minutes. Serve hot with remaining white sauce which has been reheated with the chopped hard-cooked egg and thinned with about ¼ cup milk. 5 servings.

449   HOW TO BUY LOBSTERS

Lobsters are in season all year, but are most plentiful in summer. Only live lobsters or fresh-cooked lobster meat should ever be bought. Live lobsters have dark green shells with red specks; when cooked the shells become bright red. Two types are found on the market: the North Atlantic variety which have large claws, and the Florida or California variety which have no claws but have large antennae protruding from the head.

A lobster weighing a little less than 2 pounds and heavy for its size will be fullest of tender sweet meat. The white flesh of the claws, body and tail and the roe and liver, are the edible parts of a lobster. The female lobster's roe is called coral, and is considered a great delicacy by some people who therefore prefer the female; but the male has firmer flesh and a more brilliant red shell when cooked. The male lobster has a narrower tail than the female, and the two uppermost fins within his tail are stiff and hard. Female lobsters with the eggs attached are said to be "berried," and their sale is prohibited in most states because of conservation laws. One lobster serves 1 to 2 persons.

450   BOILING LOBSTERS

Only live lobsters should be used and they should be boiled as soon as they are delivered. Half-fill a large kettle (2½ gallon capacity) with boiling water. Cover and bring to a full rolling boil. Add ¼ cup salt; then put in the live lobster, grasping it by the middle of the back. (The lobster should have its claws pegged by the dealer for the protection of those who are less skilled in handling lobster and might otherwise get pinched.) Put it in head first; it will be instantly killed. Cover pot and boil rapidly 4 to 5 minutes, then reduce heat and simmer 20 to 30 minutes, the time depending on size. Then lift the lobster out and lay on its claws to drain.

To open boiled lobster: First twist off the 2 large claws, then the 4 pairs of small claws. With a hammer or a nutcracker, break each of the large claws and remove the meat from each in one piece. Separate tail from body at the joint by holding one part in each hand and pulling until they come apart. Hold the tail in the palm of the left hand, hard shell side down, and with kitchen shears, make a slit the full length of the tail. Pull apart and break the white meat loose in one large piece. Run a small sharp knife down the length of this piece of meat to the center, where a dark line will be found. This is the intestine and should be removed carefully. Then take the body shell in the left hand and draw out the body meat carefully with the right hand, so as not to remove the stomach or "lady," which should be discarded along with the spongy lungs at the sides of the body. The green liver is edible, and is used in preparation of sauce or to garnish the lobster platter. Break the body meat into several pieces and pick out the flesh around the bones. The eggs or roe ("coral") should be used for garnishing. Be careful not to let any of the tough feathery gill-like particles under the shell become mixed with the meat.

451   BROILED LOBSTER

Place the live lobster with pegged claws on its back on a cutting board, and kill by inserting a sharp knife between the body and tail segments, thus cutting the spinal cord. Cross the large claws. Start at the head and make a deep cut lengthwise through the body and tail, being careful not to cut the stomach or "lady," which is a sack lying just back of the head.

Pull the two halves apart without breaking. Remove the "lady", and also the intestines which run the length of the body and tail. Crack the large claws. Brush the meat with melted butter or other shortening and sprinkle with salt and pepper. Spread lobster, shell side down, on the thoroughly heated broiler rack and broil slowly for 20 minutes about 4 inches below the source of heat. Now remove to serving platter and drizzle over it melted butter made tart with lemon juice. Garnish with lemon slices and parsley, and serve immediately. Serves 1-2—depending on size of lobster.

452   LOBSTER NEWBURG

2 cups diced boiled lobster meat, fresh-cooked or canned	1 cup thin cream
2 tablespoons sherry	2 egg yolks, beaten
¼ cup melted butter	¼ teaspoon salt
1 tablespoon flour	1 teaspoon lemon juice
	Paprika

Heat the lobster thoroughly with the sherry and 3 tablespoons of the butter, being careful not to brown the butter. In another saucepan, combine the remaining butter with the flour, then add the cream. Now place over direct heat and stir constantly until the sauce boils. Remove from heat, stir into the beaten egg yolks, then return to the saucepan, cooking over low heat with constant stirring for about 2 minutes or until thickened. Add the heated lobster and seasonings and mix well, but do not heat again or the sauce may curdle. Serve immediately with toasted crackers or crisp toast. 5 servings.

453   HOW TO BUY OYSTERS

No food is of more consistently high quality than oysters because their cultivation, production, handling, transportation and marketing are subject to rigid government supervision. The oyster industry is carried on by every coastal state in the country. The best-known varieties are "Blue Points" and "Rockaways" from Long Island, "Cotuits" from Massachusetts, and "Lynnhavens" from Virginia. Pacific coast oysters, grown mostly in Puget Sound, are world-famous for their fine flavor.

The old idea that oysters can be eaten only in months with an "R"— that is, from September through April—is largely superstition. The belief arose from the fact that oysters are not desirable for food during the spawning season which was supposed to be from May 1st to September 1st. However, the spawning season differs in different localities and with different varieties, and oysters of prime quality are available from some source all year. The price is higher during the summer, due to their perishability. Some cities and localities prohibit their shipping and sale during the hot months.

Oysters may be purchased shucked by the pint, quart or gallon, or in the shell by the dozen. Oysters purchased in the shell are usually the small "Blue Point" oysters which are desirable for eating raw on the half shell.

454   HOW TO OPEN OYSTERS

Insert the point of a strong-bladed sharp knife between the shells just back of the hinge which is at the pointed side of the oyster. Cut through the large muscle that holds the shells tightly together. Separate the shells and loosen the oyster meat.

455   HOW TO CLEAN SHUCKED OYSTERS

Put the oysters into a sieve or colander over a saucepan, and pour cold water over them, allowing *not more* than ½ cup cold water to each quart of oysters. Then pick up each oyster separately and examine to remove bits of broken shell. Never let oysters stand in water. The water and liquor in the saucepan may be strained and used with the oysters if they are stewed or escalloped.

456   OYSTERS ON THE HALF SHELL

Clean and open oysters (454, 455). Discard the empty half shells. Loosen meat and remove any shell particles. Put 2 tablespoons Cocktail Sauce (907) in a small glass or cup in middle of a dinner plate. Surround with crushed ice to rim of plate, spreading ½-inch thick. Arrange 6 half shells containing oysters on the ice. Garnish with sprigs of parsley or cress and lemon wedges. Serve with grated horseradish, Tabasco Sauce and crisp crackers. Blue Point oysters are best for eating raw. Thirty oysters serve 5.

457   ESCALLOPED OYSTERS

1 pint oysters	½ teaspoon salt
2 cups coarse cracker crumbs	Pepper
¼ cup melted butter	½ cup milk

Look over oysters and remove any bits of shell. Chop the oysters coarsely (cutting in 3 or 4 pieces with kitchen shears is a convenient method) and combine with their liquor. Mix cracker crumbs and melted butter and arrange a layer of half the buttered crumbs in a shallow baking dish. Pour oysters over them in a uniform layer, then sprinkle with the salt and pepper. Cover with remaining crumbs and pour milk over all. Bake in a moderately hot oven (400° F.) 20 minutes. 5 servings.

Variation: To increase size of servings, substitute 4 cups toasted coarse bread crumbs for the cracker crumbs and increase the milk to 1 cup.

458   FRIED OYSTERS

Allow 1 quart large oysters for 5 servings. Drain the oysters thoroughly and dry lightly between two towels or sheets of paper toweling to remove as much moisture as possible. Sprinkle with salt, and pepper if desired; then dip into beaten egg and roll in fine cracker or bread crumbs. Place in a frying basket in a single layer and lower into deep fat heated to 360° F. Fry until of the desired brownness; then turn out onto absorbent paper or paper toweling to drain for a minute or two. Serve piping hot with Tartar Sauce (915) if desired.

459   PAN-FRIED OYSTERS

Prepare oysters just as for Fried Oysters (458), but fry in a skillet in hot fat about ¼-inch deep until as brown as desired.

460   HOW TO BUY SHRIMP

Shrimp are shellfish like lobster and crab. They come to the market with heads removed, packed in ice. They may be sold either in this green form or boiled, with or without the shells. The average length of shrimp is from 2 to 3 inches, and they come from 20 to 30 to the pound (3 to 4 servings in most cooked dishes). Shrimp are found in all coastal waters, but the most abundant shrimp fisheries are located in Puget Sound. Prawns are similar to shrimp but much larger, often attaining a length of 7 inches; they are also much less common.

The economical way to buy shrimp is "green"—uncooked and unshelled. They have little color before cooking, but become pink to bright red when boiled. Canned shrimp are available packed in either tin cans or glass jars. They are ready for use except that in some brands the dark sand vein down the back needs to be removed.

461   PREPARING FRESH SHRIMP

2 cups water	2 teaspoons salt
1 cup sliced celery	1½ tablespoons chopped onion
1½ teaspoons whole black peppers	2½ lbs. green shrimp
	2 slices lemon

Bring water to a boil and add celery, black peppers, salt and onion. Simmer 30 minutes while shrimp is being prepared. Shuck the shrimp by breaking the under shell and opening from front to back; remove the meat in one piece. Remove the dark sand vein from the center back of each shrimp by making a shallow cut from end to end along the back and only deep enough to reveal the dark vein, then gently pull it out all in one piece. Wash in clear cold water. Now add lemon slices to the boiling liquid, boil 5 minutes, then strain the liquid, discarding all the solids. Measure liquid, add water to make 1½ quarts and return to the kettle. Bring to a boil, add the shrimp and reheat to boiling, then reduce heat to simmering and cook 5 to 10 minutes, the time depending on the size, or until they are tender. Drain shrimp, discarding the liquid, 2½ lbs. green shrimp will make about 2½ cups after shucking and cooking.

Variation: Husk and clean shrimp as described above. Drop into enough boiling salted water to cover (1 teaspoon salt to a quart of water), then simmer from 5 to 10 minutes. Drain, and use in any desired way.

462   CREAMED SHRIMP

2 lbs. green shrimp or 2 5-oz. cans shrimp
2½ cups medium white sauce (919)

2 tablespoons finely chopped sweet pickle or capers

Clean and cook shrimp (461). Or clean canned shrimp by removing dark veins down backs, then rinse in cold water. Fold cooked or canned shrimp into hot white sauce in top of double boiler and continue heating over boiling water until they are hot through, about 15 minutes. Turn into serving dish and sprinkle pickles or capers over top. 5 servings.

463   FRENCH-FRIED SHRIMP

2 lbs. green shrimp, *or* two 5¾-oz. tins wet-pack shrimp, drained and cleaned
½ cup flour

1 teaspoon sugar
¼ teaspoon salt
1 egg
¼ cup water

Clean but do not cook shrimp. Sift flour, measure, and resift with sugar and salt into a mixing bowl. Beat egg, add water and add to flour mixture, stirring until smooth. Dip shrimps into batter one at a time, and drop into deep fat heated to 375° F.; fry to a delicate golden brown. Lift out onto absorbent paper to drain a few moments, then serve while piping hot with Tartar Sauce (915) or soy sauce. 5 or 6 servings.

464
SHRIMP COCKTAIL

1 lb. green shrimp, cleaned
  and cooked (461)
½ cup chili sauce
½ teaspoon prepared horseradish

¼ teaspoon Worcestershire
¼ teaspoon lemon juice
⅓ cup finely diced celery
  Heart leaves of lettuce

Chill cooked, cleaned shrimp thoroughly. Combine remaining ingredients except lettuce and mix with shrimp. Serve in small sherbet glasses
or cups lined with heart leaves of lettuce. 5 servings.

465
HOW TO BUY SCALLOPS

Scallops are mollusks like clams and oysters, but they are seldom seen
in their shells. The part which is marketed is the single large muscle that
opens and closes the shell; clams and oysters both have similar muscles,
but they are much smaller. Small "Long Island" scallops from the coastal
bays are about ¾-inch thick and pinkish white; they are in season from
September through April. The larger white deep sea scallop is in season
all year; it may be as large as 2 inches in diameter. The small scallops are
considered to have the sweetest flavor. Deep sea scallops are available
frozen as well as fresh.

466
FRIED SCALLOPS

1 quart scallops
  Fine dry bread crumbs
2 eggs, beaten

Pepper, if desired
Deep fat for frying

If scallops are large, split across the grain and cut into ¾-inch cubes.
Immerse scallops for 3 minutes in cold salted water (1 tablespoon salt to
each cup of water). Drain thoroughly. Roll in bread crumbs, then dip
into beaten egg seasoned with pepper, and again roll in crumbs. Place
one layer deep in a wire frying basket, and lower into deep fat heated to
375° F. Fry about 4 minutes or until richly browned and tender. Drain
and serve piping hot, with Tartar Sauce (915) if desired. 5 servings

467
PAN-FRIED SCALLOPS

For pan-frying, scallops may be dipped in crumbs, egg and crumbs as
for Fried Scallops (466), or may be cooked without any coating. Have
about ⅛-inch layer of butter or other fat heated in a skillet. Cook the
scallops for 4 minutes over low heat, turning when about half done. Serve
piping hot. A sauce may be made for the uncrumbed scallops, if desired,
by adding a couple of tablespoons of water to the residue in the skillet and
stirring over low heat until it is dissolved.

MEAT

* * * * * * *

MEAT is the hub of the meal for the average American family. In this chapter you will learn how to do justice to those occasional de luxe cuts which make a gala meal. Also, what is even more important, you will learn to make the modestly priced pot roasts, stews, braised meats and meat loaves taste so good that the folks will give three cheers for the cuts that make the budget budge!

* * * * * * *

There are only two basic ways of cooking meat—by dry heat and by moist heat. Each of these methods has modifications: under dry heat we have roasting, broiling and pan-broiling; under moist heat, braising and cooking in water. The method to be used depends on the kind and cut of meat to be cooked.

In general, dry heat cooking is successful with meats which have comparatively little connective tissue, and which readily become tender when cooked. Moist heat is required by meats with more connective tissue because this is tenderized by long, slow cooking. Meats of the first type cannot be cooked as satisfactorily by moist as by dry heat; and meats of the second class are never satisfactory when cooked by dry heat.

ROASTING

To roast meat is to cook it by dry heat in the oven. Therefore roast meat is never cooked in a covered roaster, since it would then steam, producing moist heat. The temperature of the oven is probably the most important factor in producing a satisfactory roast. The oven should be pre-heated to a temperature of 300-350° F. (300° F. to 325° F. for veal, beef, smoked pork and lamb; 350° F. for fresh pork) and maintained at this moderately low temperature throughout cooking. No water should be added at any time.

Searing, or putting the roast into a very hot oven for a few minutes and then lowering the temperature to finish cooking, was formerly thought to improve a roast by "sealing in the juices," but more modern experimental work has shown that instead of retaining the juices better, searing meat produces greater shrinkage and makes the meat dryer. However, persons who like a rich brown gravy with their roast meats continue to sear the meat, even at the expense of a little more loss in weight.

A roast may be salted either before or after cooking; this is the only preparation necessary; flouring is not necessary. Nor is basting necessary, for if the meat is placed in the roaster fat-side up, the fat which cooks out will gradually flow down and make the roast self-basting. (Very lean meat such as veal should be larded with fat bacon or salt pork before roasting.)

TABLE 8. CUTS COOKED BY ROASTING.°

Beef	Veal	Pork	Lamb
Rib	Leg	Ham	Leg
Standing	Loin	Fresh	Loin
Rolled	Shoulder	Smoked	Shoulder
Chuck ribs	Boned, rolled	Loin	Boned, rolled
(good quality)	Boned, stuffed	Picnic shoulder	Boned, stuffed
Tenderloin		Fresh	Ribs
Rump		Smoked	Crown roast
Top round		Boston butt	
(good quality)		Crown roast	

° TEN LESSONS ON MEAT FOR USE IN SCHOOLS, Seventh Edition, published by National Live Stock and Meat Board, Chicago, 1950.

TABLE 9. TIME-TABLE FOR ROASTING.*

ROAST	WEIGHT	OVEN TEMPERATURE CONSTANT	INTERIOR TEMPERATURE WHEN REMOVED FROM OVEN	APPROXIMATE TIME PER POUND
BEEF	*Pounds*	*Degrees F.*	*Degrees F.*	*Minutes*
Standing ribs	6–8	300	140	18–20
			160	22–25
			170	27–30
Standing ribs (1 rib)	2.0	350	140	33
			160	45
			170	50
Rolled ribs	5–7	300	140	32
			160	38
			170	48
Standing rump	5–8	300	150–170	25–30
Rump	5–7	300	150–170	25–30
PORK—FRESH				
Loin—Center	3–5	350	185	35–40
Half	5–7		185	40–45
Ends	2–3		185	45–50
Picnic Shoulder	4–6	350	185	30–35
Boned and rolled	3–5	350	185	40–45
Cushion	3–5	350	185	35–40
Boston butt	4–6	350	185	45–50
Fresh ham	10–12	350	185	30–35
PORK—SMOKED				
Ham—Whole, tendered ..	10–12	300	160	18–20
Half, tendered	6	300	160	22–25
Shank end	3	300	160	40
Butt end	3	300	160	45
Cottage butt	2–4	300	170	35
Picnic	5–7	300	170	35
LAMB				
Leg	5–8	300	175–180	30–35
Shoulder—Rolled	4–6	300	175–180	30–35
Shoulder	3–5	300	175–180	40–45
Cushion	3–5	300	175–180	30–35

TABLE 9. TIME-TABLE FOR ROASTING.*
(Continued)

VEAL				
Leg roast	5–8	300	170	25
Loin	4–6	300	170	30–35
Rack—4–6 ribs	3–5	300	170	30–35
Shoulder	5–8	300	170	25
Shoulder—Rolled	4–6	300	170	40–45

Oven temperatures for the constant temperature method were selected because they give results comparable to the searing method in browning, amount of shrinkage, and in roasting time per pound. This table serves as a guide, therefore, in roasting by either method.

* TEN LESSONS ON MEAT FOR USE IN SCHOOLS, Seventh Edition, published by National Live Stock and Meat Board, Chicago, 1950.

To check the doneness of roast meat, the use of a meat thermometer is recommended. During cooking, the roast becomes hot on the outside first, and gradually heats up to the center. When the center of the roast reaches a certain temperature, it can be depended upon to have reached a certain doneness. Most modern meat thermometers have a scale marked both in degrees and in doneness; that is, 185° will be marked well done for fresh pork, whereas 170° will be well done for beef (see 543 and 469).

In using a meat thermometer, be sure it is inserted so the bulb is in the center of the roast, but does not touch any bone or fat. Insert it before placing the roast in the oven.

BROILING

Broiling is a method of dry heat cookery which is done by direct heat, either over hot coals or, as in the modern range, under a gas flame or electric heating unit. In pan-broiling, the heat is transmitted by the hot metal of a skillet or frying pan which is greased only with the fat of the meat itself. Both methods are used only for very tender meats, such as fine steaks and lamb chops, and the object is the same, to produce a richly browned surface and plump juicy center which is done just to the desired point. This speedy method results in a product of superior flavor and appearance.

As in roasting, a moderately low temperature is now being advised for broiling. If the broiler has a regulator, or if it is regulated by the oven regulator, it should be set for 550° F. and pre-heated for 10 minutes. If there is no temperature regulator, the heat may be turned on full. The broiler rack should be placed so the top of the meat is 3 inches from the source of heat for 2-inch steaks or chops, or 2 inches from the source of heat for 1-inch steaks or chops. This will make the temperature at the surface of the meat about 350° F.

Steaks and chops are the cuts which are usually broiled and pan-broiled.

Steaks should be cut at least 1-inch thick, and chops at least ¾-inch thick. Thinner cuts cannot be broiled successfully, because the center will become done before the outside is sufficiently browned and this means that the meat will become dry. Pan-broiled steaks and chops may be somewhat thinner because browning occurs more rapidly by this method.

Fresh pork is never broiled. Pork requires thorough cooking to bring out its full flavor and also to make it safe for health; and it cannot be cooked long enough by broiling, though pork chops and steaks may be pan-broiled if it is done slowly. Veal contains so much connective tissue and so little fat that it requires pounding to break the tissues, and brushing with fat for it to be broiled successfully. Veal is better cooked with moist heat to make it tender.

The broiling method is extremely simple and very quick. Place the steak or chops on the pre-heated broiler rack and cook until the upper side is nicely browned. It may be necessary to slash the edge fat in several places to prevent curling. When one side is done, turn and broil until browned on the other side. The meat may be broiled until rare, medium or well-done, as preferred; but well-done steaks and chops are not very juicy, so they are seldom cooked more than medium-done. Doneness may be checked by means of a meat thermometer inserted horizontally into the center of the meat but this is less convenient than with roast meats.

Pan-broiled meats are cooked in much the same way, except that they are placed in a pre-heated heavy skillet instead of on the broiler rack. The skillet need not be greased, but may be rubbed with the edge fat on the meat itself for a few seconds before the meat is laid in; this will prevent sticking until the fat in the meat begins to cook out. If any additional fat is used for lean meat such as lamb patties, use only enough to grease the pan.

TABLE 10. CUTS COOKED BY BROILING AND PAN-BROILING.*

Beef	Lamb	Pork
Sirloin steaks	Shoulder chops	Ham slice
Pin-bone	Rib chops	Bacon
Round-bone	Loin chops	Sausage
Wedge-bone	English lamb chops	
Double-bone	Steaks from the leg	
Porterhouse steak	Ground lamb patties	
Club steak		
Rib steak		
Tenderloin (fillet mignon)		
Chuck steak (of good quality)		
Ground beef patties		

* TEN LESSONS ON MEAT FOR USE IN SCHOOLS, Seventh Edition, published by National Live Stock and Meat Board, Chicago, 1950.

TABLE 11. TIME-TABLE FOR BROILING.*

CUT	WEIGHT	APPROXIMATE COOKING TIME	
		Rare	Medium
	Pounds	*Minutes*	*Minutes*
BEEF			
Chuck steak—1 inch	2⅓	24	30
1½ inches	4	40	45
Rib steak—1 inch	1½	15	20
1½ inches	2	25	30
2 inches	2¼	35	45
Club steak—1 inch	1	15	20
1½ inches	1¼	25	30
2 inches	1½	35	45
Sirloin steak—1 inch	3	20	25
1½ inches	4¼	30	35
2 inches	5¾	40	45
Porterhouse steak—1 inch	2	20	25
1½ inches	2½	30	35
2 inches	3	40	45
Ground beef patties			
1 inch thick by 3 inches ...	4 ounces	15	25
LAMB			
Shoulder chops—1 inch	3 ounces	Lamb chops	12
1½ inches	6 ounces	are not served	18
2 inches	10 ounces	rare	22
Rib chops—1 inch	2 ounces		12
1½ inches	4 ounces		18
2 inches	5 ounces		22
Loin chops—1 inch	3		12
1½ inches	5		18
2 inches	6		22
Ground lamb patties			
1 inch by 3 inches	4 ounces		18
PORK			
Ham slice			
½ inch	¾–1	Ham always	20 (well done)
1 inch	1½–2	cooked well done	25–30
Ham slice—tendered			
½ inch	¾–1		10–12
1 inch	1½–2		16–20
Bacon			4–5

This time-table is based on broiling at a moderate temperature (350° F.). Rare steaks are broiled to an internal temperature of 130° F.; medium to 160° F. Lamb chops are broiled to 170° F. Ham is cooked well done. The time for broiling bacon is influenced by personal preference as to crispness.

* TEN LESSONS ON MEAT FOR USE IN SCHOOLS, Seventh Edition, published by National Live Stock and Meat Board, Chicago, 1950.

FRYING

Many persons confuse the terms "broiling," "frying," "pan-frying," and "pan-broiling." Plain broiling applies only to cooking in a broiler where the heat is applied directly—not through a pan. In true frying the food is cooked in hot fat, which may be either deep or shallow.

Pan-frying and pan-broiling, however, are quite similar operations, since both are done in a frying pan or skillet. The difference is chiefly in the amount of fat used. Pan-frying is done with enough added fat in the skillet so the meat definitely cooks in the shallow fat, while pan-broiling requires just enough added fat to prevent the lean meat from sticking. This may be just the fat that cooks out of the meat itself; with chops that have a rim of fat, it is usually possible to grease the pan after it is heated by piling the chops together, holding them by the bone ends, and rubbing the fatty rims over the hot surface. Then the chops are laid flat on the greased surface.

Both pan-frying and pan-broiling require that the meat be browned quickly in a hot skillet with the required amount of fat, and then cooked, uncovered, at a reduced temperature until done to the desired degree. Because both methods involve brief cooking, they are suited to tender meats only. They develop an attractive brown surface and an excellent flavor.

When water is added to pan-fried meat after browning and the cooking is continued in a covered pan until the water is nearly or entirely evaporated, the meat is actually braised or fricasseed rather than pan-fried.

BRAISING

Braising is a method of moist-heat cookery in which a very small amount of liquid is used to complete the cooking, after the meat has been browned in its own fat or in a small amount of added fat. Braised meat is always cooked in a tightly covered pan, or Dutch oven either on top of the stove or in the oven.

Types of meat dishes which are cooked by braising are pot roasts, Swiss steaks, sauerbraten, fricassees and meats cooked in a covered casserole. Pork and veal chops and steaks are most successfully cooked by braising.

The liquid used in braising meats may be water, meat stock, vegetable pot liquor, milk, cream or sour cream, tomato juice, diluted vinegar, cider, grape juice, or other fruit juices; or in some cases it may be simply the juice from the meat itself. When an acid, such as vinegar, tomato juice or fruit juice, is the liquid employed, it affects the flavor considerably and may have some tenderizing effect. In a very tightly covered kettle, such as a Dutch oven with a well-fitting lid, it is often possible to cook a pot roast without adding any liquid. The steam formed from the meat juices collects as liquid inside the lid and drops back to the bottom of the kettle. When water is used, it should be added in small portions as needed, using just enough to prevent the meat from cooking dry and scorching.

Some of the flavor of the meat is lost to the liquid in braising. Therefore it is important to use the liquid as gravy to be served with the meat. It may be poured over the meat just as it is, or extended by thickening with flour and adding more liquid (water, milk, cream or stock) after the meat has been removed. The flavor of the liquid or drippings from braised meat is so concentrated that it makes excellent gravy.

Braised meats require more cooking time per pound than roast meats. In fact the object of braising is to provide longer, slower cooking in moist heat to soften the connective tissue. The cooking temperature, whether braising is done in the oven or on top of the stove, should therefore be low, not above simmering.

All the less tender cuts of meat may be cooked by braising. This method not only makes them more tender but develops their natural rich flavor. Some of these beef cuts are treated by scoring or pounding before they are cooked; this treatment breaks the tough connective tissue. Meats which have been scored require a shorter cooking time, and pounding has some tenderizing effect but less than does scoring, because pounding may only bruise the tissues while scoring cuts them.

TABLE 12. CUTS COOKED BY BRAISING.*

Beef	Pork	Lamb	Veal
Neck	Rib chops	Breast	Breast
Fore shank	Loin chops	Neck slices	Steaks
Chuck	Shoulder steaks	Shank	Rib chops
Brisket	Tenderloin	Shoulder	Loin chops
Plate	Steaks from leg	Shoulder chops	Shoulder chops
Short ribs	Heart	Heart	Shoulder
Flank steak	Kidney	Kidney	Cuts from leg
Heel of round	Liver	Liver	Heart
Round steak			Kidney
Rump			Liver
Oxtails			
Heart			
Kidney			
Liver			

* TEN LESSONS ON MEAT FOR USE IN SCHOOLS, Seventh Edition, published by National Live Stock and Meat Board, Chicago, 1950.

TABLE 13. TIME-TABLE FOR BRAISING.*

CUT	AVERAGE WEIGHT OR THICKNESS	APPROXIMATE COOKING TIME
BEEF		
Pot-roast	3–5 pounds	3–4 hours
Swiss steak	1½–2½ inches	2–3 hours
Fricassee	2 inch cubes	1½–2½ hours
Beef birds	½ inch (x 2 in. x 4 in.)	1½–2½ hours
Short ribs	Pieces (2 in. x 2 in. x 4 in.)	1½–2½ hours
Round steak	¾ inch	45–60 minutes
Stuffed steak	½–¾ inch	1½ hours
PORK		
Chops	¾–1½ inches	45–60 minutes
Spareribs	2–3 pounds	1½ hours
Tenderloin		
Whole	¾–1 pound	45–60 minutes
Fillets	½ inch	30 minutes
Shoulder steak	¾ inch	45–60 minutes
LAMB		
Breast—stuffed	2–3 pounds	1½–2 hours
Breast—rolled	1½–2 pounds	1½–2 hours
Neck slices	¾ inch	1 hour
Shanks	½ pound each	1–1½ hours
VEAL		
Breast—stuffed	3–4 pounds	1½–2½ hours
Breast—rolled	2–3 pounds	1½–2½ hours
Birds	½ inch (x 2 in. x 4 in.)	45–60 minutes
Chops	½–¾ inch	45–60 minutes
Chops—breaded	½–¾ inch	45–60 minutes
Steaks or cutlets	½–¾ inch	45–60 minutes
Shoulder chops	½–¾ inch	45–60 minutes

* TEN LESSONS ON MEAT FOR USE IN SCHOOLS, Seventh Edition, published by National Live Stock and Meat Board, Chicago, 1950.

STEWING

Stewing is a method of cooking by moist heat in which considerably more water is used than is required for braising. It requires just enough water to cover the meat. Stewing is frequently used for less tender cuts, which, due to the bony structure, are usually cut up into small pieces, the whole piece being difficult to handle.

Stews are cooked covered either on top of the stove or in the oven; for top-of-stove cooking, a heavy kettle or Dutch oven is desirable; for oven cooking, an aluminum, iron or glass casserole may be used.

Stews may have a brown or light gravy, and may be cooked with potatoes only or with a combination of vegetables, and with or without an assortment of seasonings and spices. If dumplings are cooked with the stew, or if it is served with rice, macaroni, noodles, biscuits or the like, potatoes may well be omitted from the stew itself.

The difference between a brown stew and a light stew is that in the brown stew the meat is well browned in a little fat before water is added; in a light stew, the meat is not browned. If the meat is well browned, the stew takes on the richer color of the brown surface and this appeals to most people, although the flavor is not very different from that of unbrowned meat.

Another factor in determining the color of the stew is the kind of meat used. Beef stews will always have a richer color than stews made with the light meats, veal and lamb.

A large variety of vegetables may be used in stews. These include, to name only those most frequently used, potatoes, carrots, onions, green beans, turnips, celery, peas and tomatoes. The combination should be planned as carefully as though the vegetables were to be served separately, taking into consideration the flavor, color and texture. Vegetables are usually diced or sliced, or otherwise divided to make the pieces about the size of the pieces of meat. The vegetables will require less cooking time than the stew meat, and should be added to the stew when the meat is partially cooked, in order not to overcook them. To do this it is important to know the average time required to cook each vegetable, before beginning. (See recipes in chapter on Vegetables, pages 539 to 587.)

TABLE 14. CUTS USED IN STEWING.*

Beef	Lamb	Veal
Fore shank	Neck	Neck
Neck	Breast	Breast
Brisket	Shoulder	Shoulder
Plate	Flank	Flank
Short ribs	Kidney	Kidney
Chuck	Heart	Heart
Flank		
Heel of round		
Kidney		
Heart		

* TEN LESSONS ON MEAT FOR USE IN SCHOOLS, Seventh Edition, published by National Live Stock and Meat Board, Chicago, 1950.

Only certain cuts of fresh pork are suitable for stewing, such as pig hocks, spareribs and neck bones.

Cooking times for stewing cannot be recommended, as the time depends largely on the size of the pieces into which the meat is cut, as well as on the tenderness of the meat. The meat should be cooked at simmering temperature until it is perfectly tender.

SIMMERING OR "BOILING"

"Boiling" is a term frequently applied to the cooking of meat in a larger amount of water than is used in braising. This is an erroneous term, however, since the water should never be permitted to boil, but only to simmer gently, if the shape, flavor and food value of the meat are to be preserved. Simmering is the correct term.

The principal difference between simmering and stewing is that usually large pieces of meat are cooked by simmering, such as hams, picnic shoulders, tongue, and corned beef; whereas stewing usually applies to small pieces. Cured meats, such as those mentioned, are most frequently cooked by simmering, though this method is also applied to fresh meats, such as veal which is being pre-cooked for veal à la king. When fresh meats are cooked in this way, the cooking water makes an excellent stock or broth which may be used to add flavor to soups and gravies.

Simmering is also the method used to make soup stock. In this particular case the meat is cut up and simmered gently for several hours, to extract as much flavor as possible; it is then usually strained out, and may be chopped and returned to the soup, or used in a well-seasoned hash or croquette mixture. Cracked bones add to both flavor and food value of soup stock; these are of course strained out and discarded after cooking. Soup bones may be put on to cook in either hot or cold water.

Whether meat is being simmered to cook it or to obtain stock, the amount of water should be just enough to cover it. If an excess is used, the flavor of both the meat and the broth will suffer by dilution.

TABLE 15. CUTS FOR MAKING SOUP.*

Beef	Lamb	Veal
Neck	Neck	Neck
Fore shank	Shank	Shank
Knuckle bone	Breast	Breast
Hind shank		

* TEN LESSONS ON MEAT FOR USE IN SCHOOLS, Seventh Edition, published by National Live Stock and Meat Board, Chicago, 1950.

MEAT GRAVY

An important part of the meat course at any meal is the gravy served with it, for good gravy is not only delicious in itself, but it also enhances the flavor of the meat or the starchy food with which it is served.

Gravy usually accompanies roast and braised meats or poultry, some pan-broiled meats and fried chicken. When we speak of gravy, a thickened or cream gravy is usually meant; but the juices from the meat itself, perhaps with a little hot water added to extend the amount and dissolve all the rich-flavored residue in the pan, is another type which is called pan gravy and is preferred by many persons.

Good gravy should have the definite flavor of the meat with which it is served, not of some other meat. Beef gravy is delectable with roast beef, but with roast pork it is out of place. For this reason it is almost impossible to "fake" gravy. Every kind of meat gravy has its own typical flavor; and its color varies, influenced by the method of cooking, the cooking temperature, and the kind of liquid used for making the gravy. Most people like a rich brown gravy, except for chicken gravy, which is characteristically a pale tan.

The thickness of gravy should depend altogether on the preference of the family which is consuming it: some like it as thick as thick white sauce, others prefer a minimum of thickening or none at all. In some parts of the United States, a thickened gravy is regarded with contempt; and only the plain meat juices are served as gravy.

Whenever meat or poultry is roasted, there will be a considerable amount of flavorful juices and fat in the bottom of the roasting pan. Often there is too much fat for good gravy, and the excess should be skimmed off and saved for other cooking uses. Generally some of the most savory brown residue sticks to the pan. If the gravy is not to be thickened, add a small amount of hot water (not more than a few tablespoons) and place the pan over the heat, scraping lightly with a wooden spoon until the residue is loosened and dissolved. Cook this solution until it is sufficiently concentrated to have a good rich flavor; or if it should be already too strong in flavor, add more boiling water to dilute it slightly. This juicy gravy may be served just as it is, with suitable seasoning; or a few finely chopped, sautéed mushrooms or chestnuts are a pleasing, flavorful addition.

If the gravy is to be thickened, add flour directly to the fat and the brown residue in the roasting pan, in the proportion of about 1 tablespoon of flour to each tablespoon of fat, or enough to make a smooth paste with no free fat. Blend the fat and flour thoroughly together, then add water or milk gradually, stirring until the gravy boils and thickens. The thickness can easily be adjusted to suit the family's preference by adding more or less liquid. All the residue will dissolve as the gravy is stirred after the liquid is added. When the gravy has thickened, it should be simmered gently with occasional stirring for about 5 minutes—long enough to cook the flour thoroughly without impairing the flavor of the gravy. Straining will not be necessary if the gravy is kept smooth by stirring as it cooks; straining is never desirable for it removes all the bits of meat which give character to the gravy.

With braised meats or pot roasts the method of making gravy is different. When the meat has been dredged with flour before cooking, and a little water has been added to the pan, the gravy may already be thick enough when the meat is done. If a larger quantity of gravy is desired, more liquid and a flour-water paste will be needed to extend the amount. The liquid may be milk, cooking water from vegetables, meat stock or water flavored with a bouillon cube. But if the meat was not floured and a considerable amount of unthickened liquid remains in the pan, the gravy may be thickened with a thin paste of flour and water, stirring this into the boiling hot liquid until it reaches the desired thickness; then simmer five minutes longer to cook the flour.

Pan-fried or pan-broiled meats like lamb chops or braised pork chops, or fried chicken, call for the same method as roast meat. Pour off any excess fat and blend the flour with the fat and juices remaining in the pan; then slowly stir in liquid.

If an unusually large amount of gravy is needed, extra meat broth made in advance to be used in place of other liquid will insure a good rich flavor. If a boned roast is being cooked, secure the bones from the butcher and simmer these for several hours in water to obtain a good-flavored broth. Or if the roast is not boned, buy a soup bone along with the roast and do the same thing. With chicken, extra wing-tips, backs or feet may be bought and cooked along with the neck and giblets to make broth. By using such broth as the liquid, a much larger amount of flavorful gravy may be made than when plain water or milk is used.

Gravy should always go to the table piping hot. The gravy boat should be heated thoroughly before the gravy is poured into it by letting boiling water stand in it for a few minutes.

There are a few meat dishes (such as meat loaf) which yield no juices for gravy making, and in these cases the place of gravy must be taken by sauces. The sauce section of this book contains recipes for sauces which are good not only with the meats themselves, but with the vegetables which are served with them.

468   MEAT GRAVY

To each ¼ cup fat and savory brown juice in the roasting pan, add ¼ cup flour and blend until smooth. Add 2 cups cold water or cooking water from boiled potatoes, or milk; stir constantly over direct heat while heating until it boils and thickens. Season to taste. If a thinner gravy is desired, add more water. Gravy coloring or caramel (1121) gives a more attractive brown gravy, but usually does not improve the flavor.

Variation: To make gravy for braised meat or pot roast, which has a considerable amount of liquid in the pan, remove the meat and slowly stir into the simmering liquid enough flour-water paste (1125) to make gravy the right thickness. If it is too thick, add water, cooking water from potatoes or other vegetables, to give the desired consistency. Season to suit taste with salt and pepper.

BEEF

469   RIB ROAST OF BEEF

When purchasing a standing rib roast of beef, ask the butcher to cut off the rib ends, and cook these separately by braising (478a), as they are less tender than the rib-eye muscle. In the rolled type of rib roast, these ends are wrapped around the rib-eye and so cannot be cooked separately. Carving of the standing roast is simplified if the butcher will also separate the chine bone by sawing across the ribs where they meet the backbone, then tying the bone in place.

Place the standing rib roast fat side up in an open roasting pan so it rests on both ends of the ribs as on a rack. Season with salt and pepper and insert the meat thermometer so the bulb reaches the center of the large muscle without touching fat or bone. Roast in a moderately slow oven (300-325° F.) until meat reaches desired doneness. This will take 18 to 20 minutes to the pound for rare meat; 22 to 25 for medium; 27 to 30 for well done. The thermometer should read 140° F. for rare, 160° F. for medium, 170° F. for well done. Clip string and remove chine bone before transferring roast to platter. A 9- to 11-lb. roast serves 10 to 12.

470   ROLLED RIB ROAST

Purchase a 2-rib beef roast, and have the butcher roll it; ask him for the bones removed and have them cracked. The trimmed and rolled roast should weigh about 3¾ pounds. Rub salt and pepper, if desired, into the surface of the roast. Insert a meat thermometer so that the bulb will be in the center. Place the roast on a rack in an open roasting pan; it should lie on its side in order to have fat on top, making it self-basting. Cook to the desired doneness. The thermometer should read 140° F. for rare; 160° F. for medium; 175° F. for well done. This requires 18 to 20 minutes per pound for rare meat; 22 to 25 for medium; or 27 to 30 for well done. Make gravy (468) from drippings left in pan and serve with noodle mushroom mounds, made as follows:

Put the beef bones into a saucepan, cover with water and add a branch of celery and 1 teaspoon salt. Cover and simmer at least 2 hours while roast is cooking. Remove bones and celery and add salt to suit taste. Reheat to boiling, add 4 oz. noodles, or (½ of a 7- or 8-oz. package) and boil until they are tender, about 8 minutes. The last 2 or 3 minutes, add a small can of button mushrooms, juice and all, or ¼ lb. fresh mushrooms which have been cleaned and sautéed in butter (1043). When noodles are done, drain off cooking water and use in making meat gravy. Mold the hot noodles and mushrooms in small custard cups or ½ cup measures and turn out on platter around the roast. Servings of buttered vegetables may be placed on the platter between the noodle mounds. Garnish with parsley.

Roast serves 5 at first meal with enough left over for sandwiches the next day.

471   FRIED ROUND STEAK

For frying, have steak sliced from chuck or top of beef round. Allow 1½ lbs. cut ½-inch thick for 5 people. Pound with a wooden mallet or edge of heavy saucer until almost paper thin. Dredge in flour mixed with salt, allowing ¾ teaspoon salt for each pound of meat. Heat 2 tablespoons of shortening until sizzling hot in a heavy skillet; lay in steak and brown quickly on both sides. It should then be done. Transfer to hot platter and drizzle melted butter over it. Make gravy from the residue in the pan (468). Steak may be cooked in a large piece or cut in serving portions before cooking.

472   "BOILED" BEEF AND NOODLES

Choose beef plate, ribs or brisket. Three pounds will be sufficient for 5 servings. Wipe meat thoroughly with damp cloth; cut into large serving portions, cover with water and simmer gently in covered kettle until tender, 1½ to 2½ hours, depending on tenderness of meat. Add 4 ounces egg noodles and 2 teaspoons salt about 20 minutes before serving time; then increase heat so liquid boils gently and continue cooking until noodles are tender. 5 servings.

473   BOILED DINNER WITH CORNED BEEF

2 lbs. corned beef
3 carrots
6 small parsnips
6 medium potatoes
6 small onions
½ medium size head of cabbage
Salt

Cover corned beef with cold water and heat to boiling; then reduce heat, cover kettle and simmer until beef is tender, 2 to 2½ hours. Meanwhile scrape carrots and parsnips and split in half lengthwise; pare potatoes and cut in halves, peel onions and cut cabbage in wedges, after removing outer leaves. Add vegetables to kettle and cook 20 to 30 minutes longer or until vegetables are tender. Add salt if needed. 5 servings.

Nothing stirs the family appetite more than an announcement about a big juicy steak coming up on tonight's dinner menu. Broiled tomato slices not only point up the beauty of the steak, but they taste good with it.

Ham is just about the best buy in meat when you consider the number of serv-ings obtained. Three or 4 center slices can be removed for broiling, the butt end can be baked, scored and glazed, as shown here for company big meals. The shank end can be baked or used as the hub of a "boiled" dinner.

Chilled flavorful potato salad tumbled into the center of an attractive platter, then flanked with equally chilled cold cuts such as liver sausage, veal loaf and salami. Dot with cold edible garnishes such as pickles, olives and hard-cooked eggs. Then tuck in some crisp lettuce here and there for a very tempting hot weather fare.

You too can arrange a beautiful platter of cold cuts. Of course, you start with quality cuts and slices of uniform thickness. The shape of the slices and their color make it easy to do an attractive arrangement job, as you can see. But let your inner artistic self guide you in making your very own arrangement. Add a little parsley or cress, some slices of hard-cooked egg, olives or radishes for that "finished touch."

474   CORNED BEEF AND CABBAGE

Cover 2 lbs. corned beef with cold water; heat to boiling, reduce heat, cover kettle and simmer 2 to 2½ hours or until meat is tender. Chop 3 lbs. cabbage coarsely and place in a separate kettle; cover with boiling water, add 1 teaspoon salt and boil rapidly in an uncovered kettle 6 to 8 minutes or until just tender. Drain thoroughly. Arrange on platter. Slice corned beef thin across the grain and arrange slices over the cabbage. 5 servings.

Variation: If preferred, cabbage may be cooked in water drained from the corned beef when it is done. This will impart some flavor to the cabbage and no salt need be added.

475   BEEF BEAN POT

½ lb. dried kidney beans *or*
   1 No. 2 can kidney beans
⅛ lb. salt pork, sliced thin
¼ cup chopped onion
½ lb. diced or ground beef
1 No. 2½ can tomatoes

3 teaspoons salt
¼ cup chopped green pepper, if desired
1¼ cups water
Crackers or toast

If dried kidney beans are used, wash and soak them over night, then drain and cook in enough boiling salted water to cover for about 30 minutes. Heat pork until some fat is released. Add chopped onion and ground or diced beef and stir and cook until grey in color. Then stir in drained beans, tomatoes, salt, green pepper and water. Cover and simmer ½ hour or until the beans are thoroughly tender. Serve hot with crisp crackers or toast. 5 to 8 servings.

476   BEEF-TOMATO-MACARONI MEDLEY

1½ lbs. ground beef chuck
2 tablespoons butter or bacon fat
1 cup water

2¼ cups peeled fresh tomatoes, *or* 1 No. 2 can
8 oz. macaroni, cooked (171)
Salt to suit taste

Cook the meat in the butter in a heavy skillet, stirring frequently until grey in color. Do not scorch; or make patties of it and brown in the bacon fat. Add water, cover and simmer gently about 20 minutes; then add tomatoes and drained cooked macaroni. Season to suit taste and continue cooking at simmering temperature, a few minutes longer until liquid is reduced to consistency of gravy. 5 servings.

477 BEEF AND SPAGHETTI DINNER

7-oz. package spaghetti	Dash black pepper
2 teaspoons salt	10½-oz. can condensed
1 lb. ground beef	cream of tomato soup
1 tablespoon butter	1½ cups water
1 teaspoon salt	

Cook spaghetti in 3 quarts rapidly boiling water with the 3 teaspoons salt 20 minutes, or until perfectly tender. Drain and rinse in hot water. Cook meat in a hot skillet with the butter until grey in color. Then add salt, pepper, and spaghetti. Dilute the soup with the water and pour over the mixture; then cover and place skillet in a moderate oven (350° F.) to bake 30 minutes. Serve piping hot. 5 servings.

478 BRAISED BEEF BALLS

1¼ lbs. ground beef	½ teaspoon dry mustard
1 small onion, grated	1 tablespoon horseradish,
1 egg, beaten	if desired
1 teaspoon salt	2 tablespoons bacon fat
Few grains pepper	

Mix beef with onion, egg and seasonings. Shape into 5 or 6 balls and brown well in a heavy skillet containing hot bacon fat. Add 1 cup water, cover, and simmer about 30 minutes or until flavors are blended and meat done. Thicken liquid remaining in skillet, if desired, with 2 tablespoons flour blended with ¼ cup cold water. Add enough milk to make 1¼ cups gravy. Serve hot. 5 servings.

478a BRAISED MEAT

Cut of meat	Amount to make 5 servings	Thickness of cut	Approximate time required to cook
Lamb shanks	2½ lbs.		60 minutes
Lamb shoulder chops	2½ lbs.	¾ inch	50-60 minutes
Lamb neck slices	2 lbs.	¾ inch	60 minutes
Pork shoulder steaks	2½ lbs.	¾ inch	45-50 minutes
Veal shoulder steaks	2 lbs.	¾ inch	45-60 minutes
Shortribs	2½ lbs.		1½-2 hours
Chuck steak	1½ lbs.	¾ inch	45-60 minutes
Oxtails	2½ lbs.		60-120 minutes

Wipe meat with damp cloth. Dredge with flour and brown on both sides in 2 tablespoons fat in a heavy skillet or Dutch oven. Sprinkle with ¾ teaspoon salt for each pound meat and a dash of pepper if desired.

Add ½ cup water or any desired liquid, such as tomato juice; cover, and simmer over very low heat or in a slow oven (300° F.) until meat is tender. Vegetables may be cooked with the meat if desired. Peel or scrape the vegetables and add to the meat during the last 25 minutes of cooking. The following vegetables are suggested: 2 onions, 3 branches celery, 5 carrots, and 5 potatoes. Add more liquid during the cooking period if needed. To make gravy, make a paste of flour and water, using 2 table-spoons of flour for every cup of liquid. Add the flour-water paste to the liquid after removing meat from skillet (more water may be added to make enough gravy). Stir until gravy boils and thickens, season to taste. 5 servings.

479 CHILI CON CARNE

5 slices bacon	1 No. 2½ can tomatoes
1 medium onion, sliced	Salt to suit taste
1 lb. ground beef	Chili powder to suit taste
1 No. 2 can kidney beans	(1 to 2 tablespoons)

Pan-broil bacon until done. Remove bacon and sauté onion in the drip-pings until tender, 7 to 10 minutes. Add meat and cook and stir until grey in color. Chop bacon and return to mixture; add remaining ingredi-ents. Simmer until flavors are well blended, about 20 minutes, then serve hot. If desired, the meat mixture may be served over hot cooked rice (174). 5 servings.

479a GROUND BEEF IN GRAVY

1 lb. ground beef (round or chuck)	2½ cups water
	1 teaspoon salt
3 tablespoons butter	Dash black pepper
1 tablespoon grated onion	

Put meat into butter in a hot skillet with onion and cook with constant stirring to a light brown color. Add water and seasonings and simmer, covered, for 30 minutes. Thicken to desired thickness with a flour-water paste (1125). Serve hot on toast or on mashed (1077) or baked potatoes (1067). 5 servings.

480 DICED MEAT ROAST

½ lb. beef chuck	1 teaspoon salt
½ lb. veal shoulder	1 egg, beaten
½ lb. lean fresh pork	¾ cup cracker crumbs
1 bouillon cube	1 tablespoon lemon juice
½ cup hot water	¼ lb. salt pork

Cut beef, veal and pork into ½-inch dice. Dissolve bouillon cube in hot water. Combine all ingredients except salt pork, mixing thoroughly. Pat into a loaf pan. Slice salt pork thin and lay over top of loaf. Bake in a moderate oven (350° F.) for 1 hour. Turn out onto platter, then invert. Garnish with parsley and serve hot. 5 servings.

481   BROILED STEAK

Sirloin, porterhouse, club and tenderloin are the steaks usually cooked by broiling; so are all kinds of ground beef steaks when shaped into patties. If the butcher has not trimmed the fat off neatly, use a sharp knife to even off the edge and make it more attractive. Pre-heat the broiler 4 or 5 minutes with the heat turned up to the highest point. Place the steak on the broiler rack, shaping it compactly as you wish it to appear on the platter. Slide the rack under the heat so that the surface of the steak will be just 3 inches from the tip of the gas flame or the electric unit, if the steak is 2 inches thick, or 2 inches below if the steak is 1 inch thick. At this distance from the heat the temperature at the surface of the meat will be about 350° F., the ideal broiling temperature.

Broil the steak to the desired brownness on the top surface, turn over to brown on the other side and sprinkle top with salt, and pepper if desired. The time required for broiling steak depends on its thickness, its surface area (larger steaks take somewhat longer), and on the stage of doneness desired. The time table (page 303) gives broiling times for steaks and other broiled meats.

When done, lift steak onto a hot platter. Drain off the excess fat in the pan below the broiler, and if there is a rich brown residue, pour this over the steak. Garnish and serve immediately. French-Fried Onions (1050), Sautéed Mushrooms (1043) and French-Fried Potatoes (1076) are pleasing accompaniments for broiled steak.

482   HAMBURGER PATTIES

1½ lbs. ground beef chuck	Dash black pepper
1 egg, beaten	3 tablespoons butter or
1¼ teaspoons salt	bacon drippings

Have meat freshly cut and put through food chopper just once. Combine with egg, salt and pepper, mixing thoroughly but lightly. Shape into 10 patties, round, oval or square each about ½-inch thick. Heat fat until sizzling hot in skillet, lay patties in it and brown quickly on both sides, turning carefully with pancake turner. Reduce heat, cover and cook slowly about 8 to 10 minutes or until cooked through. Transfer patties to hot platter and pour over them the juice remaining in the pan. Garnish with parsley. 5 servings.

483   HAMBURGER NOODLE CASSEROLE

2 tablespoons butter or bacon fat	1 cup canned tomatoes
	1 teaspoon salt
¾ lb. ground beef chuck	1 No. 2 can peas
1 medium onion, sliced	8 oz. noodles, cooked until tender
1 cup water	

Heat butter or bacon fat in skillet, add meat and stir until very lightly browned. Add onion, water, tomatoes and salt; cover and simmer for 30 minutes, stirring occasionally. Add peas with their liquid, and cooked noodles; and cook uncovered, stirring frequently 10 or 15 minutes longer, or until as much of the liquid as desired has evaporated. Add more seasonings if desired, and serve hot. 5 servings.

484   HAMBURGER ROLLS WITH TOMATOES

1½ lbs. ground beef chuck	1 tablespoon milk
1 teaspoon salt	Fine dry bread crumbs
Dash pepper	1 No. 2 can tomatoes
2 tablespoons water	1 medium onion, sliced
1 egg, beaten	

Mix meat thoroughly with salt, pepper and water. Form into barrel-shaped croquettes. Dip into egg which has been beaten with the milk; then roll in crumbs. Brown in shallow fat in a hot skillet, turning to brown all sides. Rub the tomatoes through a sieve and pour over the croquettes; add the onion. Cover skillet and cook 20 to 25 minutes, turning the croquettes occasionally. Serve hot with the tomato sauce poured over them. 5 servings.

485   ITALIAN RICE

¾ cup uncooked rice	1 No. 1 can tomatoes (2 cups)
2 tablespoons bacon fat	½ cup water
¾ lb. ground beef chuck	1½ teaspoons salt
1 medium onion, chopped	Dash black pepper
½ green pepper, chopped	2 teaspoons sugar
⅓ cup chopped celery	

Wash rice or do not wash according to directions on package. Heat fat in a 10-inch heavy skillet; add rice, ground beef and onion and cook with frequent stirring until meat and rice are brown and onion is soft. Add green pepper and celery and cook slowly 5 minutes, stirring frequently. Then add remaining ingredients, cover and simmer gently for 30 minutes longer or until rice is perfectly tender. Stir occasionally. 5 servings.

486   ITALIAN SPAGHETTI WITH MEAT SAUCE

1½ tablespoons butter
1 medium onion or 1 clove garlic, chopped fine
1 lb. hamburger
1¼ teaspoons salt

1 No. 2½ can tomatoes
1 cup water
⅓ cup tomato paste or catsup
¾ pound spaghetti
¼ lb. Parmesan cheese, grated

Heat butter in heavy skillet or Dutch oven; add onion or garlic and brown lightly. Add hamburger, and stir constantly to keep well separated while browning lightly. Then add salt, and tomatoes which have been rubbed through a sieve and water. Cover and simmer 30 to 40 minutes. About 5 minutes before serving add tomato paste and stir until well blended. Meanwhile cook spaghetti in 4 quarts boiling salted water (4 teaspoons salt), dipping ends into boiling water and slowly pushing rest in as ends become softened. Cook until tender, about 20 minutes; drain, rinse with hot water and again drain. Heap onto hot platter, pour hot meat sauce over spaghetti, and sprinkle grated cheese on top. 5 servings.

487   KIDNEY BEAN AND BEEF CASSEROLE

1 tablespoon butter or drippings
1 lb. ground beef
1 teaspoon salt

1 No. 2 can tomatoes
1 No. 2 can red kidney beans, drained
½ cup buttered bread crumbs

Melt fat in skillet, add meat and stir frequently until lightly browned. Add salt and tomatoes. Arrange in a buttered casserole in alternate layers with the beans. Top with bread crumbs. Bake in a moderate oven (350° F.) 40 minutes. 5 servings.

488   MEAT BALLS WITH SAUERKRAUT

4 cups ground cooked meat, lightly packed
2 cups cold cooked cereal
3 tablespoons chopped onion
1 teaspoon salt
¼ teaspoon black pepper
½ teaspoon celery salt

1 egg or 2 yolks, unbeaten
2 tablespoons bacon fat
1 No. 2 can sauerkraut
⅓ cup brown sugar, packed
¼ cup water
2 tablespoons vinegar

Combine first 7 ingredients thoroughly and shape into small balls. Heat bacon fat in a skillet, add meat balls and brown on all sides. Pour sauerkraut and juice over meat balls. Add brown sugar, water and vinegar; cover and simmer 20 to 30 minutes, or until meat balls are done through. 5 generous servings.

489   MEAT LOAF No. 1

1 lb. ground veal	2½ teaspoons salt
1 lb. ground beef	¼ teaspoon dry mustard
1 lb. ground pork	⅛ teaspoon celery salt
1 cup fine dry bread crumbs	⅛ teaspoon paprika
2 eggs, beaten	¼ teaspoon black pepper
¼ to ⅓ cup chopped onion	

Combine the 3 meats thoroughly in a large mixing bowl, then work in the bread crumbs. Beat eggs well, add onion and other seasonings and mix well. Add to meat and stir or knead until blended. Pack firmly into a buttered loaf pan, then unmold onto a flat baking pan. Bake in a moderate oven (350° F.) 1½ hours or until well done. 10 servings.

Note: Unmolding the uncooked loaf and baking it on a flat pan produces more brown crusty surface. However, loaf may be baked in the loaf pan, without unmolding, if preferred, but let cooked meat loaf stand in pan 15 to 20 minutes before unmolding so meat can absorb all juice.

490   UPSIDE-DOWN MEAT LOAVES

Soak 10 dried apricots for half an hour in just enough lukewarm water to cover. Drain and place in bottoms of buttered muffin pans. Prepare Meat Loaf No. 1 (489), and pack mixture into muffin pans on top of apricots. Bake in a moderate oven (350° F.) 30 to 35 minutes. Turn out and serve upside down with apricot on top. 10 servings.

491   MEAT LOAF No. 2

1½ lbs. ground chuck	1 cup coarse soft bread crumbs
1 egg, beaten	1¼ teaspoons salt
1 cup milk	⅛ teaspoon black pepper

Combine all ingredients thoroughly and pack firmly into a bread loaf pan. Turn out onto a greased shallow baking pan. Bake in a moderate oven (350° F.) about 1 hour or until done. Serve hot with Tomato Sauce (916) and a parsley garnish. The meat loaf mixture may be baked in custard cups for individual loaves, in which case the baking time should be reduced to 30 or 35 minutes. 5 servings.

492   PIQUANT CHEESEBURGERS

1½ lbs. ground beef | 3 tablespoons pickle relish
¼ cup milk | 2 teaspoons prepared mustard
¾ teaspoon salt | *or* prepared horseradish
Dash pepper | ⅓ cup butter
½ lb. American cheese | 6 buttered buns, toasted
⅓ cup chili sauce

Mix ground beef with milk, salt and pepper. Form into 6 patties, about 3 inches in diameter. Cut 6 slices of cheese slightly smaller than meat patties. Mix the chili sauce, pickle relish and mustard or horseradish thoroughly. Melt butter in skillet and pan-fry the patties slowly 10 to 15 minutes, turning several times as they cook. Place on buttered toasted buns, spread with the piquant sauce, and top with a slice of cheese. Broil until cheese begins to melt. Serve with other half of hot buttered bun at the side, and with green onions, radishes, celery, olives, or other relishes. Serves 5.

493   SALISBURY STEAK

1½ lbs. ground beef chuck | 2 teaspoons grated onion
or rump | 1 egg, beaten
1¼ teaspoons salt | Melted butter
Pepper to suit taste

Purchase meat in the piece and have it ground once. Combine all ingredients except butter, mixing thoroughly but lightly. On a buttered shallow baking pan, mold the meat into the shape of an oblong or a sirloin or porterhouse steak, making it about 1¼-inches thick and pushing edges up so they will be square like a steak. Brush top and sides with melted butter and place in a hot oven (450° F.). Bake 10 minutes, then reduce heat to moderately slow (325° F.), to finish cooking, which will take about 25 minutes longer. Brush with butter once or twice during baking. Slide carefully onto hot platter, using pancake turner. Serve with Tomato Sauce (916) if desired or with more melted butter. 5 servings.

494   SPANISH RICE AND BEEF

4 slices bacon | 1 No. 2½ can tomatoes
1 medium onion, chopped | ¾ cup uncooked rice
1¼ lbs. ground beef | ½ teaspoon paprika
1½ teaspoons salt

Lay 4 slices of bacon together and with a knife or shears cut into small pieces. Sauté bacon in skillet until done; remove from skillet and pour off about half the fat. Brown onion in remaining bacon fat; add ground beef and salt, and cook until beef is just grey in color. Add tomatoes, cooked bacon and well-washed rice and turn into a greased casserole. Cover and bake in a moderate oven (350° F.) for 1½ hours or until rice is tender. Add hot water if needed during cooking. 5 servings.

495   STUFFED CABBAGE ROLLS

1 small head of cabbage	1 egg, beaten
1 lb. ground beef	½ cup milk
2 teaspoons chopped onion	1 teaspoon salt

Trim off soiled leaves of cabbage and remove core. Cover with boiling water and let stand 5 minutes or until cabbage leaves are limp. Separate leaves carefully reserving five of the largest leaves for the rolls. Combine meat thoroughly with onion, egg, milk and salt. Place ⅕ of the meat mixture on each leaf and fold up envelope fashion. Fasten with tooth pick. Lay, flap down, in Dutch oven or saucepan. Add ½ cup water, and cover rolls with rest of cabbage leaves. Simmer, covered, for 1 hour. Serve with Tomato Sauce (916). 5 servings.

Variation: The cabbage rolls may be browned delicately in butter or drippings before adding rest of cabbage leaves and the water.

496   TOMATO HAMBURGERS

1¼ lbs. ground beef	1 egg
⅓ cup tomato purée	2½ tablespoons flour
½ cup fine cracker crumbs	1 teaspoon salt
1 tablespoon chopped onion	¼ teaspoon pepper

Mix ingredients together thoroughly and drop rounded tablespoonfuls into hot skillet in which 2 tablespoons fat have been melted. Shape and flatten with pancake turner and cook until well browned on both sides. 5 servings.

497   BAKED POTATOES IN BLANKETS

1 lb. round steak, cut thin	⅓ cup flour
5 medium baking potatoes	1 teaspoon salt
(about 2 lbs.)	1 tablespoon fat

Pound the round steak with edge of heavy saucer or meat pounder and cut into pieces the proper size to wrap around the potatoes. Rub a small amount of salt on the peeled raw potatoes and wrap the pieces of steak around them, fastening them with toothpicks. Roll in the flour mixed with the salt and brown in hot fat. Place in a greased covered casserole, cover and bake in a moderately slow oven (325° F.) for 1 hour and 20 minutes or until potatoes are done. From time to time during the baking, pour on a small amount of hot water to prevent drying of the steak. If desired, catsup may be put over the meat a few minutes before serving, and if any liquid remains in the bottom of the casserole it may be served as gravy. 5 servings.

498   BEEF POT ROAST

4 lbs. beef chuck, round or rump	Pepper, if desired
3 teaspoons salt	3 tablespoons shortening
	½ cup hot water

Wipe meat with damp cloth. Rub with salt, and sprinkle with pepper if desired. Heat fat to sizzling in a heavy skillet or Dutch oven; put in the meat and brown slowly on all sides. Add water, cover tightly, and simmer until meat is perfectly tender, about 1½ to 2 hours. Add more water if needed to keep from going dry. After browning the meat and adding water, cook it in a slow oven (300° F.) if preferred. Serve the liquid remaining in the pan as a gravy, thickening if desired with a little flour mixed to a smooth paste with cold water (1125). 8 to 10 servings.

498a   BEEF POT ROAST WITH MACEDOINE OF VEGETABLES

2½ lbs. beef chuck or rump roast	3 branches celery
3 tablespoons bacon fat	1 medium onion, peeled
2 teaspoons salt	4 small turnips, peeled
4 medium potatoes, peeled	½ teaspoon salt
1 large carrot, scraped	1 teaspoon chopped parsley

Wipe meat with a damp cloth. Heat fat in a heavy skillet or Dutch oven and brown meat well but slowly on all sides. Add the 2 teaspoons salt and ¼ cup water, cover tightly and simmer for about 1½ hours or until almost done. Meanwhile prepare the vegetables and chop fine; heap the potatoes, carrot and celery on top of meat, cover and continue cooking 15 to 20 minutes or until tender. At the same time, cook the chopped onion and turnip uncovered in 1½ cups boiling water with the ½ teaspoon salt until both are tender. When done, drain off water and save. Add onion and turnip to the vegetables in the kettle, then add enough of the cooking water to make the desired amount of gravy. Stir to mix well; then remove meat and vegetables to a hot platter, and thicken liquid remaining in the kettle with a flour-water paste (1125) to desired thickness. Sprinkle meat and vegetables with chopped parsley and serve with the gravy in a separate dish. 5 servings.

499   SPANISH POT ROAST

Make Beef Pot Roast (498), but substitute a No. 2 can of tomatoes for the hot water, and add 1 small onion, chopped.

500   BEEF POT ROAST WITH VEGETABLES

When Beef Pot Roast (498) has simmered until tender, 1½ to 2 hours, add 8 small peeled onions, 8 carrots scraped and cut in halves and 8 small potatoes pared and cut in halves. Cook about 20 minutes longer; add more water if necessary. Remove meat and vegetables to hot platter and make gravy (468) if desired. 8 to 10 servings.

501   BEEF AND VEGETABLE PIE

1½ lbs. beef chuck or rump	1 medium onion
2 tablespoons bacon fat	Salt and pepper to suit taste
1 teaspoon salt	Plain pastry for single crust
4 medium potatoes	(631) or biscuit dough (26)
5 medium carrots	

Cut beef in 1-inch cubes, brown lightly in bacon fat and cover with boiling water; add salt and simmer, covered 30 to 40 minutes or until almost done. Wash, pare and dice potatoes; scrape and slice carrots and peel and slice onion; add to meat with more boiling water if needed, and simmer until all are tender. To thicken the gravy, stir in flour and water paste (1125) to give the desired thickness. Add salt and pepper to suit taste. Bring to boil and pour into a buttered casserole. Cover with pastry (631), which has been rolled thin and gashed in several places to allow escape of steam, or arrange biscuits over the top. Bake in a moderately hot oven (425° F.) about 15 minutes or until biscuits are golden brown. 5 servings.

502   BEEF STEW WITH VEGETABLES

1½ lbs. beef stew meat	1 large onion, sliced ½" thick
3 tablespoons butter or bacon fat	1 bunch carrots, scraped
	4 medium potatoes, pared and quartered
1 teaspoon salt	
Dash pepper	Chopped parsley

Purchase stew meat from shank, neck or flank of beef. Wipe each piece with a damp cloth, cut in 2-inch cubes, roll in flour and brown in butter until richly browned on all sides. Sprinkle with salt and pepper; add enough hot water to cover the meat, then cover kettle tightly and simmer gently until meat is perfectly tender, 1½ to 2 hours. Half an hour before serving time, add onion slices, carrots split lengthwise in quarters and the diced potatoes. Continue cooking until vegetables are tender. Remove meat and vegetables to serving dish, sprinkling them with chopped parsley if desired, and keep hot. Thicken liquid to desired consistency using 2 tablespoons flour blended to a smooth paste with ¼ cup cold water. Pour gravy over meat. 5 servings.

503   BRAISED BRISKET WITH SWEET-SOUR GRAVY

3 lbs. beef brisket
2 tablespoons butter
3 teaspoons salt
Pepper to suit taste

1 carrot, scraped and sliced
½ cup chopped celery
1 medium onion, sliced
¼ cup vinegar

Cut brisket into 2-inch thick slices. Melt butter and brown meat on both sides; add seasonings, vegetables and vinegar. Cover tightly and simmer 1½ to 2 hours or until very tender. Remove meat to hot platter. If unthickened gravy is desired, skim off excess fat and quickly evaporate liquid remaining in pan by boiling until the required amount remains. For thickened gravy, see 468. To intensify the sweet-sour flavor, add 1 tablespoon vinegar and 1 teaspoon sugar. 5 to 7 servings.

504   ROUND STEAK BIRDS

1½ lbs. round steak cut ½-inch thick
1 teaspoon salt
½ cup fine dry bread crumbs

1 slice cooked bacon cut in ½-inch lengths (545)
3 sprigs parsley, chopped
½ medium onion, chopped
2 tablespoons bacon fat

Pound steak with the edge of a saucer; cut into 5 pieces and salt each piece. Combine bread crumbs, bacon, parsley and onion, adding a little hot water or meat stock to bind. Place ⅕ of this dressing in center of each piece of meat, and roll up, fastening securely with string. Melt the 2 tablespoons fat in a skillet; brown the meat rolls well on all sides. Pour in 1 cup hot water, cover and simmer for 1 hour; add more water if necessary. Remove to hot platter and keep hot while making gravy (468). Serve gravy poured over the meat rolls. If desired, use meat stock instead of water for cooking birds and making gravy. 5 servings.

SAUERBRATEN

3 to 4 lb. pot roast, larded (1134)
Dash pepper
Dash nutmeg
2 teaspoons salt
1 medium onion, sliced
1 bay leaf
2 tablespoons parsley, finely chopped
¾ cup vinegar
¾ cup water
¼ cup sugar
2 tablespoons butter or bacon fat
2 tablespoons flour
¼ cup cream or evaporated milk
½ cup seedless raisins

Have butcher lard pot roast or do it yourself (1134). Rub meat with pepper, nutmeg and salt. Place in crock or enamel (not iron) pan. Add onion, bay leaf and parsley. Heat vinegar, water and sugar to boiling and pour over meat. Cover and set in cool place overnight. Drain meat, brown in butter or fat in heavy skillet, and add ½ cup of the liquid in which meat soaked and the onion. Cover and simmer very slowly for about 3 hours or until meat is very tender, adding more of the spiced sour liquor as liquid in pan evaporates. When done, remove meat and keep hot while making gravy. Blend flour with the cream or evaporated milk and add to liquid from cooked meat; add raisins and stir over direct heat until gravy is thickened. Serve over meat. 5 to 7 servings.

SPICED BEEF
                         (*Another Sauerbraten*)

½ cup water
½ cup cider vinegar
1 teaspoon salt
1 teaspoon whole allspice
1½ lb. slice beef chuck 1-inch thick
2 medium onions
2 tablespoons shortening
½ teaspoon salt
¼ teaspoon poultry seasoning

Combine and heat first 4 ingredients; pour over meat in a glass, enamelware or earthenware container and let stand 2 hours, turning frequently. Drain and save liquid. Slice onions and brown with meat in shortening in a heavy skillet, not iron. Sprinkle seasonings on both sides of meat, add drained liquid, cover tightly and simmer 1½ to 2 hours or until very tender. Remove meat to hot platter. Add water to make desired amount of gravy and thicken with flour-water paste (1125). Serve hot. 5 servings.

507   STEAK ROLL

1¼ lbs. round steak cut   2 teaspoons crushed dried
    ½-inch thick   celery leaves (1136) or ¼
¼ cup chopped onion   cup fresh celery, finely
¼ cup bacon fat   chopped
1 quart soft bread crumbs,   1 bouillon cube dissolved in
    packed   1¼ cups boiling water
½ teaspoon sage   1 egg, beaten
                                     Salt and pepper to taste

Wipe steak thoroughly with damp cloth and pound all over vigorously
with edge of heavy saucer. Sauté onion in fat until yellow; add to bread
crumbs and combine lightly with all remaining ingredients; if crumbs are
quite dry, more liquid may be added. Spread dressing over the steak and
roll up like a jelly roll; secure by tying at ends and center with string.
Brown on all sides in a small amount of fat in a skillet; add ½ cup hot
water, cover tightly and bake in a moderately slow oven (325° F.) 1 hour
or until meat is very tender. Remove meat roll to hot platter, remove
string and keep hot while making gravy from drippings in skillet (468).
5 servings.

508   SWISS STEAK

2 lbs. round steak   3 tablespoons shortening
⅓ cup flour   2 cups water or 1 No. 2 can
1 teaspoon salt   tomato juice
    Dash pepper

Wipe steak thoroughly with clean damp cloth. Mix flour with salt and
pepper and pound into steak with edge of heavy saucer. Melt shortening
in skillet and brown steak well on both sides. Then pour in the water or
tomato juice, cover tightly and bake in a slow oven (300° F.) about 1½
hours or until very tender. If preferred, cooking may be finished on top of
the stove over low heat rather than in the oven. Serve with the gravy. 5 or
6 servings.

Variation: Spanish Steak. Instead of the water or tomato juice, add
to the browned steak 1 No. 2 can tomatoes, ½ cup sliced celery, 2 tablespoons sliced onion, 2 tablespoons chopped green pepper. Finish cooking
in the same manner as for Swiss Steak.

BEEF TURNOVERS

1½ cups all-purpose flour
2¼ teaspoons baking powder,
    see p. 122
½ teaspoon salt
3 tablespoons shortening
½ cup milk

1½ cups ground cooked meat,
    packed
2 beef bouillon cubes dissolved
    in 3 cups boiling water
3 tablespoons corn starch
1 teaspoon Worcestershire

Sift flour, measure and resift with baking powder and salt. Cut in shortening with pastry blender until particles are size of rice grains. Stir in milk to make a soft dough. Turn out on floured board and pat out; fold and pat out again 4 or 5 times. Roll out ⅛-inch thick. Cut 5 strips 6 inches long and 3 inches wide. Moisten meat with ⅔ cup bouillon and heap ⅕ of the mixture on half of each strip of dough. Moisten edges and fold other half over the meat. Press edges together with tines of a fork. Place on a greased baking sheet. Bake in moderately hot oven (425° F.) 12 to 15 minutes. Make gravy by thickening rest of bouillon with corn starch mixed to a smooth paste with a little water; stir over direct heat until it boils, and season with Worcestershire sauce. Left-over gravy or meat stock left from cooking meat may be used instead of the bouillon for the gravy. Serve hot over the turnovers. 5 servings.

BEEF HASH No. 1

1 cup beef broth *or* 1 bouillon
    cube in 1 cup boiling water
2 cups grated raw potato
1 medium onion, grated

2½ cups diced cooked beef
1 teaspoon salt
2 tablespoons bacon fat

Use 1 cup broth made from bones left from beef roast or substitute bouillon. Combine broth, potato, onion, beef and salt, and put into hot fat in a heavy skillet. Cover and simmer 25 to 30 minutes or until potato and onion are well cooked and hash is slightly browned on under side. Add more water if hash becomes dry. Uncover skillet and place in a moderate oven (350° F.) 15 to 20 minutes longer. Remove from oven and fold hash over omelet-fashion. Place on a hot platter, using a wide spatula or turner. 5 servings.

BEEF HASH No. 2

2 medium onions, sliced
2 tablespoons bacon fat
4 medium potatoes, cooked,
    diced

2 cups diced left-over beef
    roast or pot roast
Milk
Salt and pepper to taste

Sauté onions in bacon fat until soft. Add potatoes and beef, then add just enough milk to moisten and the seasonings. Mix well, cover skillet and simmer until under side of hash is well browned. Slide hash onto a hot platter and garnish with parsley. 5 servings.

512 GOULASH

2 cups diced left-over roast beef or pot roast	1 No. 2 can tomatoes
1½ lbs. potatoes, 3 or 4	1 lb. small white onions
1 cup water	2 tablespoons butter
	Salt to suit taste

Combine meat with potatoes which have been pared and cut into 1-inch dice. Add water and tomatoes, cover and cook until potatoes are tender. Meanwhile, peel and slice onions and sauté in the butter until soft and yellow, or leave onions whole and boil in enough water to cover until just tender. Add to meat and vegetable mixture. Season to suit taste and serve piping hot. 5 servings.

513 MEAT, POULTRY OR FISH CROQUETTES

3 tablespoons butter	¾ teaspoon salt
¼ cup flour	¼ teaspoon celery salt
1 cup milk *or* ½ cup evaporated milk and ½ cup water	½ teaspoon grated onion
	Sifted dry bread crumbs
2 cups diced or ground cooked meat (any meat, poultry or flaked cooked fish)	1 egg, well beaten
	2 tablespoons milk

Melt butter, blend in flour, add 1 cup milk and stir constantly over moderate heat until sauce boils and thickens. Add meat, seasonings and onion and mix well. Chill, then shape into croquettes. Now roll in crumbs, then in beaten egg to which 2 tablespoons milk have been added, and again in crumbs. If convenient, chill at least an hour in refrigerator before frying, as crumbs adhere better. Place in wire basket and fry in deep fat (360° F.). About 10 croquettes.

514 FRIED CORNED BEEF

Chill two 12-oz. cans of corned beef thoroughly in the refrigerator. Open cans and remove the meat in one piece. Cut in ½-inch slices with a very sharp knife. Heat butter or bacon fat in a heavy skillet, lay in the corned beef slice and fry until hot through and slightly browned on both sides. 5 to 6 generous servings.

515   CHIPPED BEEF AND NOODLE CASSEROLE

7 oz. broad noodles
1½ quarts boiling water
1 teaspoon salt
3 tablespoons butter
3 tablespoons flour
1½ cups evaporated milk
1½ cups water

¼ lb. chipped beef rinsed in hot
water, then cut in inch pieces
1 cup grated sharp cheese
2 tablespoons fine bread
crumbs
1 tablespoon melted butter

Drop noodles into boiling water, add salt and cook rapidly until noodles are just tender, about 8 minutes; drain. Meanwhile make white sauce (919) with butter, flour, milk and water, stirring constantly until thickened. Add beef and all but 2 tablespoons of the cheese, and stir until cheese melts. Arrange noodles and sauce in layers in a buttered casserole. Mix remaining cheese with bread crumbs and melted butter, and sprinkle over top. Bake in a moderate oven (375° F.) about 20 minutes or until crumbs are nicely toasted. 5 servings.

516   CREAMED EGGS AND CHIPPED BEEF ON TOAST

3 tablespoons butter
6 tablespoons flour
2 cups milk *or* 1 cup evaporated milk and 1 cup water

3 hard-cooked eggs
¼ lb. chipped beef rinsed in hot
water, then cut fine
Salt if required

Melt butter, blend in flour, add milk and stir over direct heat until sauce boils and thickens. Add quartered hard-cooked eggs and chipped beef, then place over boiling water until heated thoroughly. Add salt if required. Serve on hot toast. 5 servings.

517   FRIZZLED CHIPPED BEEF

Melt 2 tablespoons butter or bacon fat in skillet, and lay in it ¼ pound chipped beef, which has been carefully separated into whole slices, then rinsed quickly in hot water. Fry until fat is absorbed and beef is curled up and slightly crisped. Serve hot. Serves 5.

518   CREAMED CHIPPED BEEF

Prepare 2 cups medium white sauce (919), omitting the salt. Add ¼ lb. dried beef which has been rinsed quickly in hot water, then cut up with scissors and frizzled (517). Place over hot water and continue heating 5 to 10 minutes. Serve on toast, boiled rice (174), mashed (1077) or baked potatoes (1067), hominy (1037), or noodles (171). 5 servings.

LAMB

519   ROAST LAMB SHOULDER WITH DRESSING

4 lbs. lamb shoulder	1 cup chopped celery
3 teaspoons salt	6 cups coarse dry bread
¼ teaspoon curry powder	crumbs
½ teaspoon paprika	2 egg yolks, beaten
1 teaspoon salt	1 cup milk
Pinch dry mustard	2 tablespoons melted butter
2 tablespoons chopped onion	

Wipe meat thoroughly with a damp cloth. If butcher has not made a pocket, split open and remove bones, cutting so meat can be rolled around the dressing. (Simmer the bones for 1 hour in enough water to cover, to make lamb broth for soup or gravy.) Rub meat inside and out with the 3 teaspoons salt. Combine the next 6 ingredients, and mix thoroughly with the dry crumbs. Beat egg yolks, add the milk and melted butter, and mix with the seasoned crumbs. Let stand until all the liquid has been soaked up. Pack dressing lightly into pocket of meat and fasten with skewers and string. Place in open roasting pan and bake in a slow oven (300° F.), allowing 35 minutes for each pound of meat. Make gravy (468), using broth from bones. 8 to 10 servings.

520   ROAST LEG OF LAMB

Wipe the leg of lamb clean with a damp cloth; do not remove the fell. Cut a clove of garlic into 4 pieces. Make 4 equally spaced gashes on fat side (under side) of leg, and insert the pieces of garlic in these gashes (garlic may be omitted). Rub the leg all over with salt and pepper. Place on a trivet or small rack in an open roasting pan, fat side up; in lamb, the fat layer is on the inside of the leg rather than on the outside or skin side. Insert meat thermometer in the thickest part of the leg so the bulb is at the center of the roast, touching neither bone nor fat. Place in moderately slow oven (325-350° F.) and cook 30 to 35 minutes to the pound, or until thermometer registers 180° F. Transfer to hot platter and cover to keep hot. Drain off excess fat from roasting pan and make gravy from savory brown residue (468). Lamb should be well-done and should be served very hot. Garnish with parsley or fresh mint and serve with Mint Jelly (709a) or Mint Sauce (913). A 6- to 6½-lb. leg of lamb will serve 5 at one meal with hot sliced roast lamb and with enough left over for Lamb Scallop (534) the following day.

521   LAMB AND SAUSAGE CASSEROLE

5 shoulder lamb chops	Butter, about 2 tablespoons
1 teaspoon bacon fat	¼ lb. mushrooms, cleaned
5 pineapple slices, drained	3 tomatoes, peeled and cut in
5 medium sweet potatoes,	halves, *or* 1½ cups canned
pared, sliced ½-inch thick	Salt and pepper
5 pork sausages	¾ cup pineapple juice ·

Brown chops on both sides in the fat in a skillet; transfer to shallow casserole or ovenware platter, and lay a slice of drained pineapple on each chop. Lay sliced potatoes around the chops and place sausages over the potatoes. Put a bit of butter in each mushroom cap and arrange tomatoes and mushrooms among the potatoes. Sprinkle salt and pepper over all, and pour pineapple juice into casserole. Cover and bake in a moderate oven (350° F.) 45 minutes or until chops and potatoes are tender. Serve very hot. 5 servings.

522   LAMB SHOULDER CHOPS WITH DRESSING

5 lamb shoulder chops	2 tablespoons chopped parsley
2 tablespoons bacon fat	½ to 1 teaspoon poultry
3 cups coarse stale bread	seasoning
crumbs	½ teaspoon salt
½ cup cold water	1 egg, beaten
1 medium onion, grated	5 slices bacon, half cooked

Brown chops in bacon fat. Meanwhile, soak crumbs in the water until they take it all up; squeeze out the excess. Sprinkle onion, parsley, and seasonings over crumbs, add beaten egg and mix lightly but enough to blend well. Put dressing in a buttered baking dish; cover with the browned chops. Cover dish and bake in a moderate oven (350° F.) about 1 hour. Remove cover, place a slice of bacon on each chop and bake 15 minutes longer to crisp bacon. 5 servings.

523   BROILED LAMB CHOPS

Broil rib, loin or shoulder lamb chops just as for Broiled Steak (481). Pleasing accompaniments for broiled lamb chops are sautéed pineapple slices or mint jelly. Fresh mint is an attractive garnish in place of parsley.

524   PAN-BROILED LAMB CHOPS

Have loin or rib lamb chops cut not more than ½-inch thick for pan-broiling. Stack the chops together and hold them with the fat edges down in a hot skillet. Then rock them back and forth until the surface is delicately browned and enough of the fat is fried out to grease the skillet and prevent the lean meat from sticking. Now separate the chops and lay them flat in the hot skillet. Turn every 30 seconds for the first 2 or 3 minutes; then lower the heat and continue cooking, allowing 12 minutes altogether for ½-inch chops. The last time of turning, sprinkle both sides with salt, and pepper if desired. Remove to a hot platter. The rich brown residue left sticking to the bottom of the skillet makes a flavorful gravy. Add about ⅓ cup water for 7 chops, place over low heat and loosen residue by stirring with a fork. Heat to boiling, season to suit taste and pour over chops or potatoes to be served with them. Garnish chops with fresh mint or parsley.

525   LAMB PATTIES

5 lamb patties *or* 1¼ lb. ground lamb and 5 strips bacon	½ teaspoon salt
	1 bouillon cube
	½ cup hot water
2 tablespoons bacon fat	

If lamb patties are not already shaped and wrapped with bacon, shape them from the ground lamb and surround each with a strip of bacon, fastening with a toothpick; sprinkle with salt. Heat fat in skillet, lay in patties and brown on both sides. Dissolve bouillon cube in hot water and pour around patties. Cover tightly and cook over moderate heat until thoroughly done, about 20 minutes. Serves 5.

526   LAMB AND PORK LOAF

1 lb. ground lamb	2 tablespoons chopped onion
½ lb. ground lean pork	2 eggs, beaten
1½ teaspoons salt	1 cup bouillon or meat stock
1½ cups sifted dry bread crumbs	Pepper
¼ cup finely chopped celery	¼ cup melted butter

Combine all ingredients except ½ cup of the bread crumbs and the butter. Mix thoroughly and press mixture into a loaf pan (8½ by 4½ by 2¾ inches). Mix together melted butter and the ½ cup of bread crumbs, and pat over top of the loaf. Bake in a moderate oven (350° F.) for 1½ hours. 5 servings.

527   BARBECUED LAMB RIBLETS

See Barbecued Spareribs (555). Substitute 3 lbs. lamb riblets for 3 lbs. spareribs.

528   CURRIED LAMB

1½ lb. lamb shoulder	2 cups lamb broth
3 tablespoons butter or bacon fat	1½ to 2 teaspoons curry powder
1 cup diced celery	2 tablespoons hot water
2 tart apples, pared and diced	2 tablespoons flour
½ cup sliced onions	3 or 4 cups cooked rice (174)

Wipe meat with damp cloth; barely cover with water and simmer until about tender. Drain, saving broth. Cut lamb into 1-inch dice. Melt the butter or bacon fat in a skillet, add celery, apples, and onions, and sauté until soft, then add lamb and lamb broth. Cover and simmer 20 to 30 minutes. Blend curry powder with hot water and let stand 5 minutes; then blend in the flour, adding cold water if necessary to make a smooth paste. If lamb mixture is nearly dry, add about 1 cup boiling water, then stir in the curry paste. Continue simmering for 5 minutes, stirring frequently. Serve on hot platter with border of fluffy boiled rice and garnish of parsley. 5 servings.

529   IRISH STEW

1½ lb. lamb shoulder, cut in pieces for stew	2 teaspoons salt
Flour	Dash pepper
3 tablespoons butter or bacon fat	5 medium potatoes, pared and cut in 1½-inch dice
Water	5 carrots, scraped and diced
	1 small onion, sliced

Wipe meat with damp cloth; dredge thoroughly with flour and brown on all sides in a skillet or Dutch oven in which the butter or fat has been heated. Add 1 cup water, cover and simmer 45 minutes; then add salt, pepper, potatoes, carrots and onion, and 1½ cups more boiling water. Continue simmering until both lamb and vegetables are tender, about 30 minutes. Serve piping hot. If desired, a little chopped parsley may be added just before serving. 5 servings.

530   LAMB AND LIMA BEAN CASSEROLE

¼ lb. dried lima beans	1 clove garlic, peeled
1½ lbs. lamb shoulder	1½ teaspoons salt
2 tablespoons shortening or bacon fat	Pepper, if desired
	1 cup boiling water

Wash lima beans and soak overnight in cold water. Drain. Wipe meat with damp cloth; cut into 1-inch dice and brown in the shortening with the chopped garlic. Add salt and pepper and turn into a casserole. Add lima beans and boiling water, cover and bake in a slow oven (300° F.) about 1 hour or until meat and beans are tender. 5 or 6 servings.

531   BAKED STUFFED BREAST OF LAMB

1 lamb breast, 2 to 2½ lb.	½ cup diced celery
2 teaspoons salt	1 tablespoon chopped onion
Pepper	2 tablespoons melted butter
2 cups soft bread crumbs	

Wipe lamb breast with damp cloth and split open to make a pocket. Rub inside of pocket with half the salt and pepper. Combine remaining ingredients and stuff loosely into the pocket. Fasten pocket together with skewers or tie securely. Place in baking pan, add ¼ cup water, cover and bake in a moderately slow oven (325° F.) until done, allowing 45 minutes per pound of meat. Make gravy from savory brown residue in pan (468). 5 servings.

532   BRAISED STUFFED LAMB BREAST

1 large lamb breast (about 3 lb.)	2 cups meat stock or bouillon (2 bouillon cubes to 2 cups hot water)
Salt and pepper	
1½ tablespoons chopped onion	1 teaspoon salt
1 tablespoon butter	½ teaspoon poultry seasoning
¾ cup uncooked rice	2 tablespoons bacon fat

Have pocket cut into lamb breast from large end. Wipe meat with damp cloth and sprinkle inside and out with salt and pepper. Cook onion in the butter until soft, add washed, drained rice and sauté until rice is golden, then add liquid and seasonings. Simmer 20 minutes or until rice is soft. Stuff into pocket of breast, fold over once and tie with string to hold in shape. Brown breast on all sides in fat in a heavy skillet or Dutch oven. Add ½ cup hot water, cover and simmer gently for 1½ hours or until meat is tender. 5 servings.

Note: Plain bread stuffing (697) may be used in place of the rice stuffing.

533   LAMB HASH

2 tablespoons bacon fat	1 cup gravy *or* chicken bouillon cube dissolved in
2 cups chopped cooked lamb	
3 cups mashed or chopped boiled potatoes	1 cup hot water
	Salt and pepper to taste

Heat fat in a heavy skillet, add meat and potatoes, stirring to mix well. Add liquid and seasonings and stir again. Cover and heat thoroughly over low heat with occasional stirring to prevent sticking. 5 servings.

534   LAMB SCALLOP

2½ to 3 cups diced leftover lamb   1 No. 2 can tomatoes
    1 tablespoon fat   1 cup fine dry bread crumbs
1¼ teaspoons salt   2 tablespoons butter

Brown meat in a skillet in the 1 tablespoon fat. Add salt. Arrange layers of browned meat, tomatoes and bread crumbs in a casserole, topping with crumbs. Dot all over with butter and bake in a moderate oven (350° F.) ½ hour or until thoroughly heated through. 5 servings.

PORK

535   BAKED HAM

Scrub the ham well, using cold water; then dry. Insert a meat thermometer into the center of the ham, through the fat side, making sure the bulb touches no bone or fat. Place ham fat-side-up on rack in open roasting pan, and cover ham with a piece of clean brown wrapping paper, or a large paper sack torn open, tucking it well down at the sides. Place in a moderately slow oven (300 to 325° F.) and bake uncovered, allowing 15 to 25 minutes to the pound. Regular hams will require the full 25 minutes, but the tenderized hams need only enough cooking to heat them well all the way through. Calculate the time required for your particular ham. The internal temperature registered by the meat thermometer should be 170° F. for regular hams, 150° F. for tender hams. Tender hams differ somewhat in the degree of tenderness; the directions which come with these hams should be studied carefully before cooking.

One-half hour before the ham is done, remove it from the oven, discard the paper, and carefully remove the skin (if any). Score the fat in squares, diamonds, or triangles, being careful not to cut through to the lean. Spread with a glaze made by patting sieved brown sugar all over the fat and drizzling honey over the top. Return to a moderate oven (375° F.) to glaze 30 to 40 minutes. If ham is cold when it is returned to oven, more time will be required for glazing.

536   BAKED PICNIC HAM

Remove wrapping from picnic, noting exact weight. Calculate baking time, allowing 24 minutes to the pound if tenderized and 30 minutes per pound if not. Wipe with damp cloth and place skin or fat side up in an open roaster; cover with brown wrapping paper or a brown paper sack torn open, and tuck around sides. Place in a moderately slow oven (325° F.) for the time calculated. When this time is up, remove from oven, discard paper wrapping and remove skin. Serve hot or cold.

If a glaze is desired, remove from oven half an hour before end of cooking time, remove skin and score fat in squares or diamonds. Sprinkle generously with brown sugar and strained honey; stick with whole cloves. Return to moderately hot oven (375°-400° F.) for at least half an hour or until surface is nicely glazed.

Note: If a meat thermometer is used, the internal temperature should register at least 150° F. for tender or 170° F. for regular picnic when the meat is done.

536a   BAKED HAM SLICE

Inch thick center ham slice   1 teaspoon dry mustard
¼ cup brown sugar   Milk to cover ham

Place ham slice in casserole or baking dish. Rub with mustard and sprinkle with sugar. Then pour milk over to just cover ham. Cover and bake in a moderate oven (350° F.) 1 hour or until tender. Serves 5.

537   BROILED HAM

Regulate heat for broiling (550° F.). The best ham for broiling is the tenderized type. Have steaks cut 1-inch thick. Place steaks on broiler rack about 3 inches below heat. As soon as surface of ham appears dry (about 1 minute), brush with melted butter and continue brushing with butter frequently. When top side is well browned, turn, brush other side with butter and broil until nicely browned. Allow about 5 minutes on each side for each inch of thickness. Remove ham to hot platter, and pour the drippings over it. Serve hot. A 1½-lb. ham steak serves 5 generously.

Note: Instead of butter, the ham fat which collects in the drip pan may be used for brushing.

538   PAN-FRIED HAM

Cut ham in ¼-inch thick slices. Heat 1 tablespoon bacon fat or butter in heavy skillet until sizzling hot, then lay in ham slices. Cook quickly until fat on edge is browned, turning from time to time to cook evenly. Ham is done when fat is browned. Serve on hot platter. Any kind of ham —raw, baked or boiled—cooked by this same method is delicious for hot sandwiches.

539   ESCALLOPED POTATOES AND HAM

¾ lb. ham   1 teaspoon salt, if required
 6 to 8 medium potatoes   2 cups milk

Cut ham in ½-inch cubes. Pare and slice potatoes. Heat milk to boiling, add ham and potatoes, and again heat to boiling—add salt if tenderized ham is used. Turn into a greased baking dish. Bake in a moderately
slow oven (325° F.) 30 to 45 minutes or until potatoes are tender. Ham
cubes may be pan-fried (538) before adding to potatoes. 5 servings.

540   HAM AND POTATO CASSEROLE

1 lb. ham slice ½-inch thick   Salt if needed
1 tablespoon bacon fat   Dash black pepper
2 tablespoons butter   6 to 8 medium potatoes,
2 tablespoons flour   sliced thin
1½ cups milk

Pan-fry ham in bacon fat until browned on both sides. Place in well-
buttered casserole. Melt butter, blend in flour, add milk and stir over direct heat until sauce boils and thickens. Add salt, if tenderized ham is
used, and pepper. Arrange sliced pared potatoes over ham, and pour hot
sauce over them. Bake in a moderately slow oven (325° F.) until potatoes
are tender, about 1 hour; cover casserole for first half hour, then remove
cover for remaining time. Either raw or cooked ham may be used for this
dish. 5 servings.

541   HAM AND SWEET POTATO CASSEROLE

1½ cups diced cooked ham   ½ cup milk
6 cups cooked sweet potatoes   1½ tablespoons lemon juice,
  (1084)   ½ lemon
2 eggs, beaten   ½ teaspoon salt or to taste

Brown ham slightly in 1 tablespoon butter or ham fat. Whip potatoes
until smooth and combine with beaten eggs, milk, lemon juice and salt;
again whip thoroughly. Mix with the browned ham and drippings, and
turn into a buttered casserole. Bake in a moderate oven (350° F.) 45
minutes. Serve hot. 5 servings.

542   ROAST FRESH BOSTON STYLE PORK BUTT

Wipe a 4- to 5-pound fresh pork butt with a damp cloth. Sprinkle meat
with salt and place on a rack in an open roasting pan with the fat side up.
Roast in a moderate oven (350° F.) until done, or about 3 hours. Allow

337

40 to 45 minutes to the pound. If meat thermometer is used it should register 185° F. when meat is done. Serves 5 people for 2 meals.

543   ROAST LOIN OF PORK

Have backbone loosened from ribs so carving will be easy. Sprinkle with salt and pepper, and place in open roasting pan, fat-side-up, rib-ends down. Place in a moderate oven (350° F.), uncovered. Bake until done, allowing 30 minutes to the pound. If meat thermometer is used, it should be inserted into the center of the roast, clear of bone or fat before meat is put into oven; when done, thermometer should register 185° F. Drain off excess clear fat, leaving rich brown drippings in pan, then make gravy of this flavorful residue (468). Gravy may be seasoned with sage if desired.

543a   CROWN ROAST OF PORK

Have butcher tie the rib sections of 2 pork loins together and shape them into a circle, and then French the ends of the bones. A crown roast prepared this way weighs from 5 to 7 pounds.

Sprinkle roast with salt and pepper as for Pork Loin Roast. Set crown upside down in a shallow roasting pan. Insert meat thermometer into center of meat so as not to touch fat or bone. Place in moderate oven (350° F.) and bake until done, 30 to 35 minutes to the pound, or until thermometer registers 185° F. When roast is two-thirds done, drain off some of the clear fat. Now turn roast right-side up and fill center with Bread Stuffing, p. 416, then finish roasting. When done, remove roast to hot platter and put frills on ends of bones for garnish . . . and for carver to take hold. Make gravy as for Roast Loin of Pork. About 10 servings.

544   BROILED BACON

Pre-heat broiler and lay slices of bacon flat on the rack, which is adjusted about 3 inches below source of heat. Broil slowly, watching carefully, and turn once or twice during cooking so it will be done evenly on both sides. This method requires more care than does baking, but bacon cooked by broiling has a particularly pleasing flavor and is free of greasiness. Save fat which collects below broiler for seasoning.

545   PAN-BROILED BACON

Put slices of bacon into a cold skillet, laying them out flat. Cook over low heat, turning 2 or 3 times so bacon will be done evenly. The fat may be poured off when cooking is about half done. Bacon cooked this way should be laid on a hot plate covered with absorbent paper to drain a few minutes before serving. Slow cooking gives the best flavor.

546   BAKED BACON

Separate slices of bacon and lay them slightly overlapping on a rack in a shallow baking pan. Place in a moderate oven (325°-350° F.) and cook until slightly browned and crisp. Bacon cooked in this way does not require turning and needs very little attention until nearly done. If cooked on a rack, it will be crisp and free of excess grease without further draining.

546a   PAN-FRIED CANADIAN BACON

Heat 1 teaspoon butter in heavy skillet for each half pound of sliced bacon. Brown richly on both sides. After removing bacon, add 2 or 3 tablespoons water to residue in pan, heat and pour over bacon, if desired.

547   SAUSAGE, BACON AND TOMATO GRILL

1 lb. pork sausage links	2 large tomatoes, sliced thick
⅓ lb. bacon	

Place sausages on broiler rack and broil *slowly* about 8 minutes, turning once or twice and watching carefully. Now place bacon on rack and continue to broil until sausages are nicely browned and bacon slightly crisped. When sausages are about half done, place tomato slices on rack and cook until just softened. As foods are done, place on hot serving platter. If preferred, all three foods may be pan-fried on top of the stove. 5 servings.

Note: Slow cooking, whether in broiler or on top of stove, results in less shrinkage and better flavor and appearance in both sausages and bacon.

548   BAKED PORK CHOPS WITH APPLES

5 thick pork shoulder chops	6 good-flavored tart apples
(1½ to 2 lbs.)	¼ cup water
Salt	¼ cup sugar

Wipe chops with a damp cloth. Brown slowly but well on both sides in a hot greased skillet. Sprinkle with salt. Core and slice unpared apples 1 inch thick. Arrange on top of pork chops. Add water, sprinkle lightly with salt and the sugar, cover and place in moderate oven (350° F.) for 45 minutes to 1 hour or until chops are tender. Apples may be poached separately, if desired.

549   BRAISED PORK CHOPS

Have chops cut about 1 inch thick. Wipe with damp cloth. For 5 chops weighing about 2 pounds, heat 1 teaspoon fat sizzling hot in a heavy skillet. Brown chops slowly on both sides. Sprinkle with 1 teaspoon salt, cover, reduce heat and cook 30 to 40 minutes or until tender, turning once or twice. Remove chops to hot platter and keep warm. Make gravy from fat and brown residue in pan, using about 1 cup boiling water or milk (468). Serve with chops. 5 servings.

550   PORK CHOPS EN CASSEROLE

5 thick loin or rib chops	1 No. 2 can cream style corn
1 tablespoon fat	⅓ cup diced green pepper
Salt and pepper	½ cup hot water

Brown pork chops slowly on both sides in the hot fat. Sprinkle with salt and pepper. Mix corn and green pepper and arrange in buttered casserole in alternate layers with browned chops. Add water, cover, and bake 45 minutes in a moderate oven (350° F.); then remove cover and bake 15 minutes longer. 5 servings.

551   SPANISH PORK CHOPS

5 thick pork chops, 2 lbs.	1 teaspoon salt
1 tablespoon fat	¼ teaspoon pepper
1 onion, sliced	2 tablespoons flour
2 cups canned tomatoes	3 to 4 cups boiled rice (174)

Brown chops slowly on both sides in the fat, then remove chops from pan. Now brown onions in same skillet, then add chops, tomatoes and seasonings. Cover and simmer 30 to 40 minutes. Remove meat and thicken the tomato mixture with the flour mixed to a smooth paste with ¼ cup cold water; boil 2 to 3 minutes, stirring constantly. Place rice in center of platter, arrange chops around rice, and pour tomato sauce over all. 5 servings.

552   STUFFED PORK CHOPS

5 double rib pork chops	½ cup finely diced celery
1½ cups soft bread crumbs	2 teaspoons melted butter
¼ teaspoon poultry seasoning	Flour
1½ teaspoons salt	Milk

Have butcher make a pocket for dressing on inside of each chop, with opening between the two bones. Wipe chops with damp cloth. Lightly mix together the crumbs, seasonings, celery and melted butter, then stuff into chops. Lay in a baking dish or skillet (not one with a wooden handle), and sprinkle with flour. Pour in milk to a depth of about ½-inch; do not cover chops with it. Cover and bake in a moderately slow oven (325° F.) about 2 hours or until chops are perfectly tender, removing cover the last half hour. If milk evaporates too much, add a little water once or twice during cooking. When done, there should be ample gravy to serve with the chops. 5 servings.

553   PORK SHOULDER CHOPS WITH SAUERKRAUT

5 pork shoulder chops (about 1½ lbs.)	2 tablespoons sugar if desired
1 teaspoon salt	½ teaspoon caraway seed, optional
1 No. 2½ can sauerkraut	

Wipe chops with damp cloth. Brown slowly on both sides in hot, lightly greased heavy skillet; sprinkle with salt. Turn sauerkraut over chops, and sprinkle sugar and caraway over top (sugar takes edge off sourness of kraut). If kraut is dry, add ½ cup water. Cover and simmer gently about 1 hour until chops are very tender. 5 servings.

554   PORK SHOULDER STEAK WITH SPANISH RICE

1½ lbs. pork shoulder steak	2 teaspoons salt
½ cup chopped onion	⅛ teaspoon black pepper
½ cup chopped green pepper	1 teaspoon paprika
½ cup chopped celery	2 to 3 teaspoons sugar
1 No. 2 can tomatoes	1 cup uncooked rice
1 cup water	

Wipe meat with damp cloth; brown slowly on both sides in heavy skillet. No additional fat will be needed if meat is well streaked with fat. Add all ingredients except rice, turn heat low, cover and simmer 30 minutes. Then add thoroughly washed rice and simmer 30 to 40 minutes longer or until rice and meat are tender. Serve hot. 5 servings.

555   BARBECUED SPARERIBS

3 lbs. spareribs	½ tablespoon prepared mustard
1 medium onion, chopped	
1 tablespoon butter or bacon fat	½ cup water
	½ cup chopped celery
1 tablespoon vinegar	2 teaspoons salt
1 tablespoon sugar	Dash cayenne
3 tablespoons lemon juice	1 to 2 tablespoons Worcestershire, if desired

Wipe spareribs with damp cloth; cut in serving-size pieces. Place in a shallow baking pan and bake in a moderate oven (350° F.) 30 minutes. Meanwhile, sauté onion in butter or fat for 5 minutes, then add remaining ingredients, mix well and simmer 5 minutes. Pour over the spareribs and continue baking for an hour longer, basting from time to time with the sauce. 5 servings.

556 BRAISED SPARERIBS

Wipe 3 pounds of spareribs with a damp cloth and cut into serving portions. Dip in flour seasoned with 1½ teaspoons salt and ⅛ teaspoon pepper. Then brown in hot bacon drippings. Reduce heat, add water (about ¼ cup), cover and simmer until tender, about 1 hour. If preferred, place browned spareribs in baking pan, add water, cover and bake in a moderately slow oven (325° F.). 5 servings.

557 FRUITED SPARERIBS

1 pound dried prunes	1½ teaspoons salt
3 pounds spareribs	2 or 3 apples, sliced

Soak prunes over night; remove pits. Wipe spareribs with damp cloth. Cut in serving portions. Lay half in baking dish; add half the salt. Cover with soaked and pitted prunes. Put apples on top of the prunes. Cover all with remaining spareribs and sprinkle on other half of salt. Cover and bake in a moderate oven (350° F.) until meat is tender or from 1½ to 2 hours. If desired, cover may be removed last half hour of baking to brown top. 5 servings.

558 SPARERIBS AND SAUERKRAUT

Cut 3 lbs. spareribs into serving-size portions. Wipe with damp cloth. Pack into kettle and barely cover with water; add 1½ teaspoons salt and simmer until very tender, about 1 hour. Add 1 No. 2½ can sauerkraut, pushing kraut down into meat stock. Cook 30 minutes longer or until most of liquid is evaporated. A tart apple, sliced, may be put in with the kraut. Some persons like the addition of a little sugar (about 1 tablespoon) to take the edge off the sourness. A teaspoon of caraway seeds may be sprinkled over the kraut when it is added to meat, if desired. 5 servings.

559   STUFFED SPARERIBS

3 lbs. spareribs   1½ tablespoons chopped onion
2 cups water   ½ teaspoon celery salt
2 teaspoons salt   1 teaspoon sage
6 cups fresh bread crumbs   1½ cups broth (cooking water
1 tablespoon parsley, chopped   from spareribs)

Wipe spareribs with damp cloth. Place in heavy saucepan or large
skillet, add water and 1½ teaspoons of the salt, cover and simmer gently
about 1 hour. Remove from heat, and if desired, cool and remove the
bones. Arrange a section of ribs in bottom of a greased casserole, then
spread with a layer of dressing, made by mixing together the remaining
ingredients with rest of salt. Add another layer of meat, another of dressing and top with remaining meat. Bake in a moderately slow oven (325°
F.) from 1 to 1¼ hours or until meat is tender. 5 servings.

560   BOILED DINNER WITH HAM HOCKS

2½ to 3 lbs. ham hock   5 medium onions
1 bunch carrots   2-pound head cabbage
5 medium potatoes

Wipe ham hock thoroughly with damp cloth. Cover with boiling water
and simmer, covered 1½ to 2½ hours or until meat is tender. Time will
depend on type of ham. Meanwhile, wash vegetables; scrape carrots and
cut in halves lengthwise; pare potatoes and peel onions and cut cabbage
in wedges after removing soiled outer leaves. Add vegetables to kettle
and increase heat so liquid boils gently; cook uncovered about 20 to 30
minutes longer until vegetables are tender. If preferred, cover the kettle,
but cook wedges of cabbage in a separate uncovered pan until just tender, then add to platter when ham hock and other vegetables are served.
5 servings.

561   BRAISED PIG HOCKS

2½ lbs. fresh pig hocks   Hot water
2 teaspoons salt

Wipe meat with a damp cloth, place in a 3-qt. saucepan, sprinkle with
salt and barely cover with hot water. Cover and heat until liquid boils,
then reduce heat and simmer 2 to 3 hours or until meat is tender enough
to slip off the bones. 5 servings.

Variation: One quart sauerkraut may be added the last half hour of
cooking.

562   PORK CHOP SUEY

1 lb. lean pork	1 tablespoon molasses
1 tablespoon bacon or pork fat	1 tablespoon soy sauce
2 cups diced celery	1½ tablespoons corn starch
3 medium onions, sliced	1 No. 2 can assorted chop suey
¾ teaspoon salt	vegetables
1 cup boiling water	3 cups cooked rice (174)

Cut pork into thin strips and sauté 5 minutes (not until browned) in the hot fat. Add celery and onions and cook 2 or 3 minutes longer or until slightly softened. Add salt and the boiling water; cover, and simmer 15 to 20 minutes. Add molasses, soy sauce and corn starch which has been blended until smooth with ½ cup water. Cook until mixture boils, stirring constantly, then add drained chop suey vegetables and continue cooking until thoroughly heated. Serve with hot fluffy rice and additional soy sauce if desired. 5 servings.

563   PORK SCRAPPLE

½ lb. fresh lean pork	¼ teaspoon pepper
2 quarts water	½ cup yellow corn meal
1½ teaspoons salt	

Simmer pork in water until very tender in a covered 3-qt. saucepan. Let cool. Skim off fat from surface of liquid. Remove meat and chop medium fine. Save broth. Combine 2½ cups strained broth with chopped meat, add seasonings and corn meal and cook over direct heat, stirring until thickened. Transfer to double boiler and cook over simmering water about 1 hour. Pour into a buttered bread pan and chill. Slice about ½-inch thick. Brown slices in a hot skillet with butter or bacon fat and serve piping hot. 5 servings. If desired, make a large quantity as it keeps in the refrigerator for a week or more.

563a   PAN-BROILED LINK SAUSAGES

Separate 1 lb. sausage links carefully so as not to break skin at each end. Put links in a cold heavy skillet; place over low heat and cook until well browned, turning frequently. It will take 12 to 15 minutes to cook well done. OR place links in skillet, add 2 tablespoons water for each half pound, cover and steam 5 minutes. Remove cover, drain off liquid that remains, then cook sausage slowly, turning frequently to brown evenly. Do not prick. Remove sausages to a hot platter. Drain off all fat. Add 3 tablespoons water to skillet, stir and reheat until brown residue dissolves. Pour pan-gravy over sausage. Serve promptly. 4 servings.

564   BAKED ACORN OR BUTTERNUT SQUASH WITH LINK SAUSAGE

3 medium-sized acorn squash   1 lb. pork link sausage
1 tablespoon butter

Cut squash in halves and remove seeds and fibers. Butter cut surfaces
and place cut-side-down on a baking sheet. Bake in a moderately hot
oven (400° F.) 30 to 40 minutes or until squash is tender when pierced
with fork. If desired, squash halves may have a mixture of brown sugar
and butter sprinkled over their rims; then returned to oven to toast to a
luscious brown. Just before serving, broil sausage (563a) until nicely
browned on both sides. Arrange sausages in cavities of squash halves to
serve. Sausage patties (565) may be used instead of the links. 5 or 6
servings.

565   PORK SAUSAGE PATTIES

Shape 1½ lbs. pork sausage meat into 10 patties ½-inch thick and
brown on both sides in a hot skillet. Cover and cook over low heat
15 to 20 minutes, depending on thickness of patties. Pour off excess fat
as it accumulates in the pan. 5 servings.

566   SPANISH SAUSAGE

1½ lbs. pork sausage, country   ½ cup finely chopped celery
  style   ½ teaspoon salt
No. 2 can tomato juice or   Dash of pepper
No. 2½ can tomatoes,   1½ teaspoons sugar
  strained   2 tablespoons flour
½ cup finely chopped onion   ¼ cup water
½ cup finely chopped green   Grated Parmesan cheese
  pepper

Shape sausage into 10 patties and brown in hot skillet. Now pour off
half the accumulated fat and add tomato, onion, green pepper, celery
and seasoning. Cover and simmer 1 hour. Remove sausage to a hot
platter. Blend flour and water and when smooth, add to tomato juice
in which sausage was cooked. Stir until it boils and thickens. Pour sauce
over meat; sprinkle with cheese. Serve hot. 5 servings.

567   CITY CHICKEN LEGS

1 lb. lean pork   ¼ cup milk
1 lb. boneless veal   ½ cup fine dry bread crumbs
1½ teaspoons salt   ¼ cup shortening
  Pepper   ½ cup meat broth or water
1 egg, beaten

345

Trim off excess fat from pork, then cut both pork and veal into 1½-inch cubes. Stick skewers through center of these cubes, alternating pork and veal, using enough to fill skewers a little more than half full. Sprinkle salt and pepper over meat, then press into chicken-leg shape. Dip in egg mixed with the milk. Then roll in crumbs until well coated. Heat shortening in a heavy skillet and brown "legs" slowly on all sides. Then add broth, reduce heat, cover and SIMMER about 1 hour or until tender. Make gravy from drippings to serve with the "legs" if desired. 5 to 6 servings.

568 SALT PORK AND CREAM GRAVY

¾ lb. salt pork sliced ⅛-inch thick
Flour
1 tablespoon bacon fat

3 cups milk
1 teaspoon finely chopped parsley

If salt pork is very salty, freshen in hot water 5 minutes. Drain and pat dry with paper toweling, then dip in flour and pan-fry in a skillet in the bacon fat. Cook until pork is brown and crisp, then remove to hot platter. Add 3 or 4 tablespoons flour to fat in skillet, blending until smooth; then pour in the milk and stir constantly until it boils and thickens. Simmer 5 minutes longer, stirring occasionally and add salt if needed. If gravy becomes too thick, thin it with additional milk. When ready to serve, stir in the parsley and serve with the crisp salt pork. 5 servings.

If preferred, the pork may be cut into ½-inch dice and cooked until crisp without dipping in flour. Then proceed as above. This gravy is excellent with mashed or baked potatoes.

569 PORK AND RICE CASSEROLE

2 eggs
3 cups ground cooked pork
½ cup uncooked rice
1 cup milk

1½ teaspoons salt
¼ teaspoon pepper
½ teaspoon Worcestershire

Beat eggs slightly and combine with remaining ingredients. Turn into a casserole, cover and bake in a moderate oven (350° F.) 1 hour or until rice is tender. Serve hot with Tomato Sauce (916), if desired. 5 servings.

570   CREAMED SPICED HAM IN BAKED HUBBARD SQUASH

½ Hubbard squash, about
2½ lbs.
12-oz. can pork luncheon
meat
¼ cup butter

6 tablespoons flour
1 cup evaporated milk
1 cup water
1 teaspoon salt
Dash pepper

Scrape seeds and fibrous material from cavity of squash and place upside down on a buttered baking pan. Bake in a moderately hot oven (400° F.) 45 minutes to 1 hour or until squash is very soft on inside when pricked with a fork. Meanwhile cut the pork luncheon meat into ½-inch dice. Melt butter in saucepan, blend in flour, add the milk and water and cook until mixture boils and thickens, stirring constantly to keep smooth. Add seasonings and meat, and place over very low heat or over boiling water until creamed meat is hot through. Remove baked squash to platter, pour creamed meat into cavity and serve immediately. In serving, scoop out the tender meat of the squash along with the creamed meat. Diced left-over chicken may be substituted for the meat. 5 servings.

VEAL

571   VEAL LOAF

2 lbs. ground veal
½ lb. ground fresh fat pork
½ cup fine dry bread crumbs
2 tablespoons evaporated milk
1 tablespoon melted butter

2 tablespoons finely chopped
onion
2 teaspoons salt
4 hard-cooked eggs (395)

Combine meat thoroughly with other ingredients, except eggs. Pack ¾ of meat mixture into a buttered bread loaf pan. Make a trench through center and place the shelled eggs in it, end to end; press rest of mixture over the eggs. Turn loaf out onto a buttered shallow baking pan, brush surface with melted butter and bake in a moderate oven (350° F.) about 1½ hours or until done through. Serve either hot or cold. 8 to 10 servings.

572   VEAL PATTIES

1¼ lbs. ground veal
1 teaspoon salt
Dash pepper
1 tablespoon chopped onion

1 egg, beaten
2 tablespoons margarine
1 chicken bouillon cube
1 cup water

Mix veal with seasonings, onion and beaten egg. Shape into patties ¾ to 1-inch thick and brown well in margarine in a heavy skillet. Dissolve bouillon cube in 1 cup hot water. Pour bouillon around patties in skillet, cover and cook at simmering temperature 45 to 60 minutes or until well done. 5 servings.

572a   VEAL ROAST

Low temperature cooking is as important in roasting veal as in cooking all other kinds of meat. To roast a veal rump roast or any other veal roast, sprinkle the meat well with salt and pepper. Place on a rack in an open pan, preferably one just a little larger than the roast. Insert a meat thermometer in the thickest muscle of the meat, being careful that it does not touch bone or fat. (To eliminate danger of breakage, be sure to make a hole in the meat with a skewer before inserting the thermometer.) Lay strips of fat over the top of the meat and roast in a 325° F. oven until meat thermometer registers 180° F. This will take about 35 to 40 minutes per pound. No basting of the meat is necessary. No water need be added, for at this low temperature the drippings will not scorch.

573   BRAISED VEAL SHOULDER STEAK

2 lbs. veal shoulder steak	1 teaspoon salt
Flour	¼ cup water
3 tablespoons margarine	

Wipe meat with a damp cloth and coat thoroughly in flour. Brown well on both sides in the margarine heated in a heavy skillet. Sprinkle meat with salt, add water, cover tightly and simmer gently until very tender, 1½ to 2 hours. Add more water from time to time if necessary. When meat is done, remove to a hot platter and make gravy from liquid remaining in skillet (468). 5 servings.

574   BREADED VEAL CHOPS

5 veal chops, about 2 lbs.	¼ cup margarine
1 egg, beaten	¼ cup boiling water
¼ cup milk	2 tablespoons chopped onion
Fine dry bread crumbs	2 tablespoons chopped green
Salt and pepper	pepper, if desired

Wipe chops with damp cloth. Dip first in beaten egg mixed with the milk, then in bread crumbs mixed with salt and pepper (¾ teaspoon salt to a pound of meat). Brown chops on both sides in hot margarine in a heavy frying pan. Add water, onion, and green pepper if desired. Cover tightly and cook very slowly for 1 hour, adding more water if needed. Uncover the last 10 minutes of cooking. 5 servings.

575 JELLIED VEAL LOAF

2 lbs. veal breast or shoulder
3 cups cold water
2 teaspoons salt
1 or 2 hard-cooked eggs, diced (395)
2 tablespoons chopped sweet pickle

3 tablespoons vinegar
6 tablespoons mayonnaise
Salt and pepper to taste
1 to 2 tablespoons gelatin
¼ cup cold water
Lettuce
Tomato wedges

Cut meat into 1-inch dice, removing fat and gristle. Simmer in a covered pan with water and salt for about 1 hour, or until very tender. Drain off broth and chill; there should be 2 cups—if not, add cold water. Combine meat with egg, pickle, vinegar, mayonnaise and seasonings. If broth forms a stiff jelly when cold, use 1 tablespoon gelatin, otherwise use 2 tablespoons. Soak the gelatin 5 minutes in the ¼ cup cold water; then melt over hot water. Heat broth just until liquid, add melted gelatin, and stir into meat mixture. Pour into loaf pan which has been rubbed with salad oil. Chill until firm. Turn out and slice. Garnish with lettuce and tomato wedges or radishes. 10 to 12 servings.

576 POT ROAST OF VEAL

2½ lbs. veal shoulder
3 tablespoons margarine
1 medium onion, chopped

⅓ cup chopped celery
1½ teaspoons salt

Wipe veal with a damp cloth. Brown on one side in the margarine in heavy kettle or Dutch oven. Turn meat over, add onion and celery, stirring vegetables occasionally until meat is well browned. Sprinkle meat with salt. Add about ½ cup hot water, cover tightly and simmer until meat is tender, about 1½ hours. Serve with gravy, which may be thickened if desired (468). 5 servings.

576a POT ROAST OF VEAL WITH APPLE DRESSING

2¾ lbs. veal shoulder
¼ cup butter or margarine
2 teaspoons salt
Dash pepper
1 chicken bouillon cube

1¼ cups hot water
2 tart apples
1 medium onion
2 tablespoons sugar
2 cups soft bread crumbs

349

Wipe veal with a damp cloth and cut so it will about cover the bottom of the casserole or skillet being used. Melt half the butter in a heavy skillet and brown the veal well on all sides. Leave meat in the skillet or transfer to a casserole, as preferred. Add 1½ teaspoons salt, pepper and the bouillon cube dissolved in the hot water. Peel and chop apples; also peel, chop, and slowly sauté onion in remaining fat. Add the apple, onion, sugar and rest of salt to bread crumbs and toss to mix ingredients well. Heap dressing on top of the veal, which should be well above surface of the liquid or dressing will become soggy. Rub inside of lid of skillet or casserole with butter and cover the meat. Place in a moderately slow oven (325° F.) for about 2½ hours or until veal is tender. Then remove cover and continue cooking about 15 minutes to brown dressing slightly. Carefully remove veal and dressing, then thicken gravy with a flour-water paste (1125). 5 servings.

577 STUFFED VEAL SHOULDER

3 lbs. veal shoulder	3 cups coarse bread crumbs
¼ cup shortening	1 cup meat stock or 1 bouillon
1 tablespoon chopped onion	cube in 1 cup hot water
2 teaspoons chopped parsley	1¼ teaspoons salt
½ teaspoon celery salt	

Have pocket cut in meat to hold dressing. Wipe meat with a damp cloth. Melt half the shortening in a heavy skillet, add onion and cook slowly until soft, then add parsley, celery salt and bread crumbs. Toss about until well mixed. Cool. Add half the liquid and mix; stuff lightly into the pocket of the roast; tie or sew up with twine. Rub outside of roast with the salt, then brown it on both sides in remaining shortening in the same heavy skillet or Dutch oven. Pour in rest of liquid, cover and bake in a moderately slow oven (325° F.) until meat is tender, 2 to 2½ hours, adding more boiling water if necessary. Liquid remaining in pan may be thickened for gravy (468). 5 to 6 servings.

578 STUFFED VEAL ROLLS

1½ lbs. boneless veal, sliced thin	1 chicken bouillon cube
1 cup diced celery	1 cup water
2 tablespoons chopped onion	½ teaspoon salt
¼ cup butter or margarine	Dash pepper
3 cups crumbs from 3 or 4-day old bread, packed	¼ cup flour
	1 teaspoon salt
	⅛ teaspoon pepper

Wipe veal with damp cloth and cut into 5 pieces and pound well. Sauté celery and onion in 2 tablespoons of the butter, add bread crumbs and toss until coated with the butter, then cool. Dissolve bouillon cube in water and add ¾ cup of it to stuffing, then add seasonings and mix well. Place a portion of stuffing on each piece of veal. Roll up and fasten securely with tooth picks. Now coat rolls in the flour mixed with salt and pepper. Brown rolls in hot skillet with rest of butter. Add remaining bouillon and ¼ cup water. Cover and simmer gently until meat is tender, about 1 hour. Gravy may be thickened if desired (468). 5 servings.

Variation No. 1: Prepare veal cutlets as in 578, but instead of the stuffing, place a scraped carrot and small peeled onion on each piece of veal. Roll up, fasten with tooth picks and brown rolls in hot skillet with 2 tablespoons butter. Add 1 cup tomato juice, cover and simmer until meat and vegetables are tender. 5 servings.

Variation No. 2: Use ½ cup evaporated milk and ½ cup water in place of tomato juice in Variation No. 1. Bake in slow oven (300° F.) about 1½ hours. 5 servings.

579   VEAL BAKED IN MILK

2 lbs. veal steak or veal cutlets	¼ cup butter or margarine
2 teaspoons salt	1 cup evaporated milk
1 egg, beaten	1 cup water
Flour for dipping	

Wipe meat with a damp cloth and cut into serving-size pieces. Sprinkle with salt; dip in beaten egg and then in flour. Heat butter in a skillet and brown the meat on both sides. Transfer meat and drippings to a casserole. Add evaporated milk mixed with water. Cover and bake in a slow oven (300-325° F.) 2 hours or until very tender. 5 servings.

580   VEAL BIRDS

2 lbs. veal shoulder steak cut about ⅜-inch thick	½ teaspoon poultry seasoning
2 cups coarse fresh bread crumbs	2 teaspoons salt
	Dash black pepper
1 tablespoon chopped onion	½ cup meat stock (or 1 bouillon cube in ½ cup hot water)
1 egg, beaten	

Wipe steak with damp cloth and cut into serving-size portions. Combine remaining ingredients thoroughly. Pile a portion of the dressing in center of each piece of veal, roll up, and tie securely with fine twine.

Brown rolls on all sides in hot fat in a heavy skillet; add 1 cup hot water, cover tightly and simmer about 1¼ hours or until meat is tender, adding more water if needed. Serve with liquid remaining in pan. 5 servings.

581   VEAL CHOP SUEY

¼ cup bacon fat
1 lb. veal, cut in narrow strips
1 cup sliced onions
2 cups diced celery
1½ cups boiling water
1 teaspoon salt

1 tablespoon molasses
2 tablespoons chop suey sauce
2 tablespoons cornstarch, mixed to paste with ¼ cup cold water
3 to 4 cups cooked rice (174)

Heat fat in large skillet or Dutch oven. Add veal and cook, stirring occasionally until nicely browned on all sides. Add onion, celery, boiling water and salt, cover, and simmer until veal is tender, about 30 minutes. Add remaining ingredients except rice and continue to cook, with constant stirring, until mixture boils and thickens. Serve with fluffy, hot boiled rice. 5 servings.

582   VEAL à la KING

1 lb. boneless veal
¾ teaspoon salt
1 cup celery, diced
2 tablespoons chopped green pepper
¼ cup butter or margarine
6 tablespoons flour

1 tall can evaporated milk
1½ cups veal stock
2 hard-cooked eggs, diced (395)
1 tablespoon chopped pimiento
Salt and pepper to suit taste

Wipe meat with damp cloth; place in saucepan, add salt and barely cover with boiling water. Cover kettle and simmer gently from 1 to 1½ hours or until meat is just tender. Drain, saving broth. Cut meat in ½-inch dice. Sauté celery and green pepper in the butter 5 minutes, or until just soft; then stir in flour until smooth. Measure veal stock, adding water if necessary to make 1½ cups, then add with evaporated milk to butter-flour mixture. Cook over moderate heat, stirring constantly until sauce boils and thickens. Add veal, eggs, pimiento and seasonings. Reheat thoroughly and serve on toast, in patty shells or on crisp fried noodles (173a). 5 servings.

583   VEAL AND SPAGHETTI

1½ lbs. boneless veal
Water to cover
1½ teaspoons salt

Leaves from 4 branches celery
8-oz. pkg. spaghetti
Few grains pepper

Wipe veal with damp cloth; cut into 1-inch dice. Place in a saucepan with water to cover; add salt and celery leaves, cover and simmer about 1 hour or until veal is tender. Add enough boiling water to make 4 cups liquid, add broken spaghetti and pepper, cover and cook 15 to 20 minutes or until spaghetti is tender. Thicken liquid with a flour-water paste (1125), if desired. Remove celery. Serve hot. 5 servings.

584   VEAL FRICASSEE DINNER

2 lbs. boneless veal	4 carrots, diced
2 tablespoons margarine	3 onions, sliced
1½ teaspoons salt	2 tablespoons finely cut parsley
Water	4 potatoes, sliced

Wipe meat with a damp cloth, cut in 1½-inch dice and brown in hot margarine. Sprinkle salt on meat and add water to cover. Cover skillet tightly and simmer until meat is tender, about 1½ hours. Prepare vegetables and add them ½ hour before end of cooking time. Just before serving, thicken gravy, if desired, with flour and water paste (1125), stirring over direct heat until it boils. 5 servings.

585   VEAL PAPRIKA

1½ lbs. boneless veal	1 cup thick sour cream
1 clove garlic, sliced	1 teaspoon paprika
¼ cup butter or margarine	Salt to suit taste
¼ cup water	

Wipe veal with a damp cloth and cut in 1-inch dice. Sauté veal and garlic in butter until brown. Add water, cover tightly and simmer gently until veal is perfectly tender, about 1 hour. Add sour cream, paprika and salt and reheat to boiling. Serve at once. 5 servings.

586   VEAL STEW

1½ lbs. veal for stew	5 small whole onions
3 cups water	3 medium potatoes, pared and
2 teaspoons salt	cut in 8ths
Dash of pepper	Flour
5 carrots, cut in 1-inch pieces	

Wipe veal with damp cloth, cut in dice and place in a 3-quart saucepan. Add water and salt. Cover, simmer 45 minutes, then add pepper, carrots and onions; again cover and cook 15 minutes. Add potatoes, and continue cooking until they are just tender, about 20 minutes longer.

Thicken liquid with flour mixed to a smooth paste with cold water, using 2 tablespoons flour to each cup of liquid and stirring until it boils. 5 servings.

Variation: Veal may be rolled in flour and browned in fat before adding the water to give a richer flavor and color to gravy.

587   VEAL AND VEGETABLE PIE

1 recipe Veal Stew (586)   ½ recipe Baking Powder Biscuits (26)

Turn hot veal stew into casserole. Lay unbaked small biscuits (cut around the edge with a knife to give the effect of a flower) close together over the surface and bake in a moderately hot oven (425° F.) 15 to 20 minutes or until biscuits are well browned and thoroughly baked. 5 servings.

SAUSAGES

588   BOILED FRANKFURTERS

Drop 8 to 10 frankfurters into 1 quart actively boiling water, turn off heat, cover and let stand on back of stove 5 minutes. Drain and serve immediately. 5 servings.

589   PAN-FRIED FRANKFURTERS

Heat 2 tablespoons fat in a heavy skillet and put 8 to 10 frankfurters in whole, or split in half lengthwise; brown moderately fast on all sides, cooking until heated through. Serve immediately. 5 servings.

Variation: To add interesting appearance and different flavor, make a shallow spiral cut—corkscrew fashion—the full length of frankfurter before pan-frying. The cut opens attractively in frying.

590   FRANKFURTERS ON BUNS

Heat 8 to 10 frankfurters either by simmering (588) or by pan-frying (589). Split long buns, toast and spread with butter, then place frankfurters inside. If desired, buttered side of buns may be spread lightly with prepared mustard, sweet pickle relish or catsup. 5 servings.

591   ## BARBECUED FRANKFURTERS

1 medium onion
2 tablespoons butter
2 tablespoons vinegar
2 tablespoons brown sugar
4 tablespoons lemon juice
1 cup catsup
1 tablespoon Worcestershire

½ tablespoon prepared mustard
½ cup chopped celery
Salt to taste
½ cup water
1½ lbs. frankfurters, 12-15

Brown onion in butter, add rest of ingredients, except frankfurters, and cook slowly for 20 minutes. Prick skins of frankfurters. Place in the sauce, cover and cook slowly until heated through and flavored by the sauce. 5 or 6 servings.

592   ## CREAMED FRANKFURTERS

8 frankfurters (about 1 lb.) sliced about ¼ inch thick
2½ tablespoons chopped onion
⅓ cup butter or bacon fat
5 tablespoons flour

2½ cups milk, or 1¼ cups evaporated milk and 1¼ cups water
1¼ teaspoons prepared mustard
¼ teaspoon salt or to taste

Sauté sliced frankfurters and onion in the butter until onion is soft, about 5 minutes. Blend in flour, then add liquid and cook with constant stirring until sauce boils and thickens. Stir in seasonings. Serve hot on crisp hot toast. 5 servings.

593   ## ESCALLOPED POTATOES AND FRANKFURTERS

4 large potatoes, 2½ lb.
½ lb. frankfurters
1 cup diced celery
2 tablespoons butter

2½ tablespoons flour
2 teaspoons prepared mustard
½ teaspoon salt
2 cups milk

Pare and slice potatoes. Cut frankfurters in ½-inch slices. Arrange alternate layers of potatoes, frankfurters and celery in a buttered baking dish. Melt butter in a saucepan and blend in flour, mustard, and salt; add milk and stir over direct heat until sauce boils. Pour over ingredients in casserole. Bake covered in a moderate oven (350° F.) 45 minutes to 1 hour or until potatoes are tender. 5 servings.

594   ## FRANKFURTER AND LIMA BEAN CASSEROLE

2 cups dried lima beans
2 tablespoons light molasses
2 tablespoons brown sugar

1 teaspoon salt
¼ lb. bacon
5 frankfurters about ½ lb.

Wash beans and soak overnight in cold water, then drain, cover with fresh water and simmer gently until tender, about 30 minutes. Drain, saving cooking water. Turn beans into buttered casserole. Combine molasses, brown sugar and salt and add enough of the cooking water to make 2 cups; pour over beans. Cover casserole and bake in a moderate oven (350° F.) 2 hours. Cover may be removed last 15 minutes of cooking to brown top. Just before beans are done, broil or pan-broil bacon (545) until crisp; cook frankfurters as in 588. Arrange drained frankfurters on top of beans and lay crisp bacon over frankfurters. Serve piping hot. 5 servings.

595   FRANKFURTERS IN BLANKETS

1 recipe baking powder   10 frankfurters about 1 lb.
  biscuits (26)

Roll dough into an 8 x 20-inch rectangle, about ¼-inch thick, then cut into 4-inch squares. Lay a frankfurter on each square, roll up and fasten by moistening edges of dough and pinching together. Place on baking sheet and bake in a moderately hot oven (425° F.) 15 minutes or until nicely browned. Serve with Mustard Sauce (922). 5 servings.

Note: Half-cooked little pork sausages may be used in place of the frankfurters.

596   SAUERKRAUT WITH FRANKFURTERS

1 No. 2½ can sauerkraut   ½ cup water
1 tart apple, sliced   10 frankfurters or 16 cooked
2 tablespoons sugar   pork sausages (563a)
2 tablespoons bacon or sausage
  drippings

Turn sauerkraut into large saucepan, add sliced apple, sugar, fat and water. Cover pan and simmer until apple is barely tender. Lay frankfurters or sausages on top of kraut; cover, and cook gently about 10 minutes longer or until frankfurters are heated through. 5 servings.

597   SAVORY FRANKFURTERS

8 to 10 frankfurters, 1 lb.   ½ cup sweet pickle relish
¼ lb. American cheese

Make a lengthwise gash in the frankfurters to form a long pocket, being careful not to cut clear through. Grate cheese, mix it with the pickle relish and stuff into the frankfurter pockets. Place in broiler about 3 inches below source of heat, and broil until frankfurters are hot through and cheese is melted and slightly toasted. Serve hot. 5 servings.

598   BOILED BOLOGNA

Cook a one-pound piece of bologna with the casing on. Cover with boiling water and simmer 15 minutes in a covered kettle. Lift out and remove casing. Serve on hot platter, cut in ¼-inch slices and overlapped. Garnish with parsley. 5 servings.

599   GRILLED BOLOGNA CUPS

Have ½ pound bologna sausage sliced thin. Brown quickly on both sides in hot fat—the slices curl to form cups. Serve with 5 hot poached (391) or pan-fried (390) eggs. Baking powder biscuits (26) and currant jelly (705) are a pleasing accompaniment for breakfast or luncheon. 5 servings.

MEAT SUNDRIES

THERE are a number of particularly valuable kinds of meat which do not fit into the usual classifications of regular meat cuts. Liver, heart, kidneys, sweetbreads, tripe, brains and tongue all fall into this group, and are called MEAT SUNDRIES *or* SPECIALTIES. *Some of them, especially liver, kidneys and heart, are exceptionally good sources of certain vitamins and minerals, and for this reason are valuable constituents of the diet; and all are important because they are a good way of introducing more variety in the meat course. Some of the sundries are most economical; others are rather expensive, owing to the limited supply or to their perishability. Some are very hearty, others very delicate.*

Like the regular cuts of meat, most of the sundries may come from any of the four meat animals: beef, veal, pork or lamb. In general, sundries from veal and lamb are the most delicate in flavor and texture; but if correctly prepared and cooked, all of them are delicious, and the differences in flavor, texture and color between the various types only add to the possible variety.

Heart, tongue and tripe are all muscular, and since all have been very active muscles, they require long slow cooking with moist heat, like the less tender regular cuts. Liver and sweetbreads are glandular organs and are considerably more tender muscle meats. Kidneys are also glands, and the small lamb, pork and veal kidneys may be broiled, but large beef kidneys require braising or simmering in water to make them equally tender. Brains are similar in appearance and in texture to sweetbreads, but are slightly less firm.

Liver. Liver is the most familiar of all the sundries. As the richest of all food sources of iron, and as a good source of vitamins, it is valuable nutritionally. Since its value was first discovered, only about thirty years ago, it has become well established as a part of the meat diet in many American homes. Calf or veal liver is the favored variety, because it is very tender and delicate in flavor; this popularity is reflected in its price, which is much higher than that of beef, pork or lamb liver. In food value, however, beef liver has one-third more iron per pound than calf or lamb liver, and pork liver has actually three times as much iron. Therefore, though somewhat less delicate in flavor and texture, pork and beef liver are much better buys than calf liver, and when carefully prepared are just as good eating. Lamb liver is also delicate like calf liver because it comes from a young animal. It is usually inexpensive wherever it is available.

The only tough part of liver is the membranous covering or "skin," and the veins which run through the whole organ. When sliced, this skin is found only on the outside edge of each slice; the veins may appear anywhere in the slice. It is easy to remove the skin from a slice by sticking the point of a paring knife under it at one point, tearing it back until it can be grasped in one hand and then gently pulling and loosening it from the meat with the knife if necessary until the whole strip is removed. To remove the veins, a pair of pointed shears is useful to cut around one end of the vein until it can be grasped in the fingers; after that, the flesh may be scraped away from the rest of the vein with the knife. Very much the same method is used in preparing a larger piece of liver, in which the veins are longer and the skin covers a larger area. Patience is required, but the housewife who persists will be rewarded by her family's increased enjoyment of this valuable meat.

Another factor in making liver more palatable is short cooking. Whatever the method used, liver should be cooked just long enough to lose the pink color at the center of the piece or slice. Overcooking makes it dry. In purchasing liver, caution the butcher to cut the slices so their thickness is uniform throughout each slice; for carelessly sliced liver may be ¼-inch thick at one end of the slice and ½-inch or more at the other end, and when this happens, the thin end is sure to be overcooked before the thick end is done. It requires from 2½ to 5 minutes' cooking on each side in a hot, well-greased skillet to pan-broil liver sliced from ¼ to ½-inch thick.

Kidneys. Kidneys are generally used for stew or in combination with beefsteak in steak and kidney pie. The tiny lamb kidneys are sometimes used in mixed grills, whole or split and stuck on skewers alternately with dice of other tender meat and broiled, or split, broiled and served with broiled lamb chops. Veal kidneys are also tender enough to be broiled, but beef and pork kidneys require moist heat.

Like liver, kidneys are covered with a thin tough membrane. This should be removed and the kidneys washed thoroughly. Then each kidney should be split and the fat and heavy veins which make up the core removed.

Heart. The most exercised muscle in the body is the heart, and for this reason heart is the least tender of the meat specialties. Calf, lamb and pork hearts are somewhat more tender than beef hearts, but all require moist-heat cookery. Beef hearts are much larger than the other kinds; one beef heart of good size will serve a family of five. Lamb hearts make nice individual servings; small pork hearts also serve one person, large ones two; the average calf heart will make two servings.

Split heart open about half way down on one side. Then cut away arteries and veins at the top and the stringy fibers and dividing membranes on the inside. Now wash thoroughly, both outside and in the cavity with plenty of warm water. Soaking in sour milk, buttermilk or a vinegar solution for 3 or 4 hours or overnight may or may not help to make the heart tender but we do know that such acids impart a good flavor. If this method is used, drain off the milk or vinegar solution, rinse in clear water, and then stew or braise the heart. TO STEW, cover the cleaned heart with salted water (1 teaspoon salt to each quart of water) and simmer until tender. Beef hearts require 3 to 3½ hours; veal, lamb and pork hearts about 2½ hours.

BRAISING of heart is done the same as for any other meat; that is, the heart is browned on all sides in a small amount of fat, and after adding seasonings and a very small amount of liquid, the skillet or Dutch oven is covered and the heart simmered very gently until tender. By this method, beef heart will need 2½ to 3½ hours, and the smaller varieties 1½ to 2½ hours. If desired, the hearts may be stuffed with a well-seasoned bread dressing and tied or sewed together before browning.

Tongue. Tongue is also a much exercised muscle like heart. Wash it thoroughly, scrubbing with a brush in warm water; smoked or pickled tongue should be soaked for several hours before cooking in clear water. Tongue is always cooked in simmering water, salted as for heart. A large beef tongue will take 3 to 4 hours to become tender when simmered with a cover. When done, put the tongue into cold water to loosen the skin and also to make it easier to handle; then remove the skin and cut away the roots. Return the skinned tongue to the cooking water and reheat if served hot; or if served cold, cool it in the water, then place in the refrigerator to keep it juicy.

Sweetbreads and brains. Brains and sweetbreads are white, very delicate in flavor and require special care in preparation. Because they are unusually perishable, they should never be stored without pre-cooking. To pre-cook sweetbreads or brains, soak them for a few minutes in cold water; then remove the thin membranous covering with care so as not to break the tissues. Cover with cold water to which 1 teaspoon salt and 1 tablespoon lemon juice or vinegar have been added for each quart of water, and simmer 15 minutes. Then drain and drop into cold water to chill quickly. The acid helps to keep the meat white. The meat is now thoroughly cooked and may be used as it is in salad; any further cooking is simply to make it more attractive.

Sweetbreads are often creamed with chicken or veal, or they may be used in salads or browned in butter by broiling or pan-broiling. Pre-cooked brains are often broken into pieces and scrambled with eggs, or dipped in egg and crumbs and fried in deep or shallow fat until delicately browned, or dipped in melted butter and broiled. They may also be reheated in a well-seasoned cream sauce or tomato sauce.

Tripe. Whether fresh, pickled or canned, tripe is always pre-cooked when purchased. That is, the butcher cleans and parboils it. However, further cooking in water is necessary before the tripe is tender enough to eat.

Two varieties of tripe are sold, the plain or smooth type, and the more popular honey-comb tripe, which is valued for its beautiful appearance. It is smooth on the outside, but the inside is deeply honey-combed. The method of preparation is the same for both kinds. They should be thoroughly washed, and then simmered in salted water for at least 1 hour. After the tripe is tender, it may be served in a variety of ways: dipped in egg and crumbs and fried in deep fat, brushed with melted butter and broiled, creamed, spread with bread dressing and baked, served with tomato sauce or combined with various ingredients in casserole dishes.

600   REMOVING SKIN AND VEINS FROM LIVER

To make liver pleasanter to eat, the tough membrane and veins should always be removed before cooking. The entire liver is covered with a tough membrane, so each slice cut from the liver has a strip of membrane all around its edge. This is easily removed by inserting a sharp knife just under it at one point and pulling and scraping it from the meat. If the slice is floured first this operation is easier, as the liver is less slippery. The veins may be cut out with sharp-pointed scissors. If liver is purchased in one piece, remove veins by loosening at one end until they can be gripped with one hand, and flesh can be scraped away with the knife. This leaves liver looking somewhat torn, but the tears will not be seen after cooking, and the liver will be tender and pleasant to eat. If liver is very slippery to handle, dip the hands occasionally into additional flour.

601   PAN-FRIED LIVER

Have liver sliced uniformly ¼ to ½-inch thick. Remove skin and veins, then coat with flour. Heat butter or bacon fat in a skillet, and brown the liver first on one side and then on the other. Sprinkle with salt—¾ teaspoon to each pound of liver—and pepper if desired. Reduce heat and continue cooking slowly until liver is done, from 5 to 10 minutes, turning once or twice. Overcooking should be avoided as it makes the liver tough and dry. Serve with pan-broiled bacon (545), if desired. Garnish with parsley or watercress. To serve 5, allow 1½ lbs. liver and ¼ lb. bacon.

602   PAN-FRIED LIVER AND ONIONS

1½ lbs. beef liver	1 lb. onions, peeled and sliced
2 tablespoons bacon fat	½ teaspoon salt

Remove skin and veins from liver. Heat the bacon fat in a skillet; add sliced onions, sprinkle with salt, cover and cook slowly until tender, 5 to 7 minutes. Remove onions to hot dish and keep warm while pan-frying liver in same skillet (601). Serve liver and onions on hot platter. Garnish with parsley or cress. 5 servings.

603   BRAISED LIVER

1½ lbs. liver in one piece
   Salt pork
1 small onion, chopped
   Hot meat broth or bouillon

   Salt to taste
1 teaspoon poultry seasoning
   Dash pepper
2 teaspoons chopped parsley

Wipe liver with a damp cloth, remove skin and veins (600). Lard rounded side with strips of salt pork (see directions for larding, 1134). Sauté onion slowly until soft and yellow in salt pork fat, then add liver and brown it on all sides. Half cover with hot broth or with bouillon made by dissolving 1 chicken bouillon cube in each cup of hot water required. Add seasonings. Cover closely and simmer about 45 minutes or until liver is no longer pink inside, basting frequently. Liquid may be made into gravy or it may be flavored with lemon juice and served without thickening. Serve with a sprinkling of chopped parsley. 5 or 6 servings.

604   BRAISED LIVER WITH RICE AND TOMATOES

Substitute a No. 2½ can tomatoes for the hot meat broth or bouillon in the above recipe (603). After the liver has cooked 25 minutes, add ¾ cup uncooked rice. Add water to the tomatoes if necessary to prevent rice from becoming too dry. Simmer 20 minutes longer or until rice is tender. Serves 5.

605   LIVER AND BACON WITH FRIED NOODLES

5 slices bacon
7 or 8 oz. noodles, cooked

1 lb. beef liver, sliced
1 teaspoon salt

Pan-broil bacon until as crisp as desired; drain and place on hot platter. Add well-drained cooked noodles (171) to bacon fat, turn carefully over and over to coat all noodles with fat without breaking them, and cook rapidly without further stirring until delicately browned. Turn and brown other side. While noodles are browning, remove skin and veins from liver (600) and pan-fry in a small amount of hot fat for 5 to 10 minutes or until just done through. Sprinkle noodles and liver with salt. Serve hot, surrounding noodles with liver and bacon. 5 servings.

606   BROILED LIVER STEAK

1½ lbs. beef liver sliced 1-inch thick
3 tablespoons butter, melted
1 teaspoon salt

Pepper, if desired
2 teaspoons chopped chives or parsley

Be sure liver slices are the same thickness all over; this is important for even cooking. Remove the skin and veins (600). Brush liver on both sides with melted butter and place on the pre-heated broiler rack. Adjust broiler rack so surface of liver is 3 inches below the source of heat (electric heating element or tip of gas flame). Cook 6 minutes on one side, then turn and cook about 6 minutes on other side or until just cooked through. Remove to a hot platter. Brush with more butter, and sprinkle with salt, pepper and chopped chives or parsley. Garnish and serve immediately. A pleasing accompaniment is French-fried onions (1050). 5 servings.

607   POOR MAN'S GOOSE

1¼ lbs. beef or pork liver, sliced
2 tablespoons bacon fat
Salt and pepper

5 medium onions, sliced
5 medium potatoes, sliced
5 slices bacon

Remove skin and veins from liver (600), then cut liver into serving pieces. Brown slices lightly on both sides in hot fat, about ½ minute on each side. Sprinkle with salt and pepper. Put liver and drippings into bottom of large (10-cup) casserole. Add onions, then potatoes, and sprinkle with more salt and pepper. Top with bacon slices. Cover casserole and bake in a moderate oven (350° F.) 1 hour. Then remove cover and bake 15 minutes longer to crisp bacon. Serve hot. 5 servings.

608   FRENCH-FRIED LIVER

1½ lbs. liver cut ½-inch thick
½ cup flour

1½ teaspoons salt
Fat for frying

Remove skin and veins from liver slices (600) and cut in strips ½-inch wide and about 4 inches long or longer. Mix flour and salt thoroughly and roll strips of liver in the mixture. Have deep fat heated to 360° F. Drop in floured pieces of liver and cook 1 to 2 minutes, no longer; they will be light brown in color. Drain quickly on absorbent paper and serve hot. 5 or 6 servings.

609   BAKED LIVER AND VEGETABLES

1½ lbs. beef liver in 1 piece	1 teaspoon salt
¼ cup flour	10 small new potatoes,
5 slices bacon	about 2 lbs.
1 large onion, sliced	⅛ teaspoon black pepper
2 cups diced celery	¾ cup hot water
1 cup canned tomatoes, strained	

Remove skin and veins from liver (600), then coat liver in flour. Pan-broil bacon in a heavy skillet until just done. Lift bacon out and drain. Sauté onion and celery in the bacon fat until soft and yellow. Add the flour that did not cling to the liver, and stir until smooth; then add tomatoes and salt and continue stirring over moderate heat until sauce boils and thickens. Lay floured liver in the gravy, and over it arrange the pared, halved potatoes. Cover with close-fitting cover and bake in a moderate oven (350° F.) until potatoes are soft, about 45 minutes. Remove cover and place cooked bacon over the liver. Return to oven and cook uncovered for about 5 minutes to reheat bacon. Remove liver and potatoes to a hot platter, arranging bacon over the liver. Pour gravy around them or serve it in a separate bowl. 5 servings.

610   ITALIAN STYLE LIVER, MACARONI AND TOMATOES

2 cups macaroni, broken	¼ cup bacon fat
1 lb. beef or pork liver	1 tablespoon chopped onion
¼ cup flour	¾ cup water
1 teaspoon salt	1 No. 2½ can tomatoes
⅛ teaspoon pepper	

Drop macaroni into rapidly boiling salted water (2 teaspoons salt to 2 quarts water) and boil until just tender, about 20 minutes. Drain. Meanwhile remove skin and veins from liver with a sharp knife (600). Cut liver in one-inch dice, roll in flour mixed with salt and pepper; brown in the bacon fat in a 10-inch heavy skillet along with the onion. Add water and tomatoes and heat to boiling. Add macaroni, cover and simmer 10 minutes. Serve hot. 5 or 6 servings.

611   SPANISH LIVER

1 lb. liver, sliced	2 large potatoes
½ medium onion	½ bay leaf
½ cup salad oil	1 teaspoon salt
3 tablespoons lemon juice	1 tablespoon catchup

Carefully remove skin and veins from liver (600). Rub each slice with onion; then cover with oil and lemon juice mixed together and let stand 1 hour. Pare and dice potatoes. Drain and cut liver into 1-inch dice, combine with potatoes and cover with boiling water; add bay leaf and salt, then simmer until potatoes are tender. Just before serving, remove bay leaf and add catchup and reheat. Then transfer to serving dish and sprinkle with paprika if desired. 5 servings.

612   LIVER à la GOURMET

2 tablespoons olive or
  salad oil
2 cloves garlic, peeled
2 medium onions
½ lb. mushrooms
1 No. 2 can tomatoes

1¼ lbs. calf or beef liver
3 tablespoons flour
1 teaspoon salt
  Dash black pepper
2 tablespoons butter

Heat oil in skillet, add sliced garlic and onions and cook slowly until soft and yellow. Add cleaned sliced mushrooms, cover tightly and simmer 3 or 4 minutes. Put the tomatoes through a sieve to remove seeds and add to skillet; continue simmering gently. Meanwhile remove skin and veins from liver (600) and coat thoroughly in flour which has been mixed with salt and pepper. Brown in butter in another skillet until just browned on both sides. Pour sauce over liver, cover and simmer 5 minutes longer. 5 or 6 servings.

613   LIVER LOAF

1¼ lb. beef or pork liver
1 cup milk
2 tablespoons melted butter
3 eggs, beaten
2 teaspoons salt
¼ teaspoon pepper

1 tablespoon grated onion
⅛ teaspoon nutmeg
1½ cups fine dry bread crumbs
1 teaspoon meat extract paste
  in ¼ cup water

Remove skin and veins from liver (600). Cover slices with boiling water, place over heat and boil 1 minute, then drain well. Cool. Put liver through food chopper. Add remaining ingredients and mix thoroughly. Turn into buttered loaf pan—4½ x 8½ x 2¾ inches. Bake in a moderate oven (325°-350° F.) 1 hour or until a knife inserted in the center comes out clean. Unmold onto serving platter and garnish with parsley. Serve hot with Sautéd Mushrooms (812) or cold with catchup or chili sauce. 10 servings.

614   LIVERBURGERS

¾ lb. ground beef or pork liver
¾ lb. ground beef chuck
1 cup fine cracker crumbs
2 eggs
1 teaspoon salt

1 teaspoon celery salt
Dash pepper
1 teaspoon grated onion
3 tablespoons bacon fat

Have liver and beef ground together and add cracker crumbs to it. Beat eggs—then stir in next 4 ingredients. Thoroughly mix egg mixture with meat and crumbs. Form into 10 flattened patties. Fry about 4 minutes on each side in hot bacon fat in a heavy skillet over low heat, turning only once. Serve hot. 5 servings.

615   GRILLED LIVER SAUSAGE

Have liver sausage sliced about ½-inch thick. Remove casing and brush both sides with melted butter. Place on broiler rack about 3 inches below source of heat and broil on one side only until hot through and slightly browned. Transfer to hot platter and serve with pan-fried tomatoes, onions or buttered cabbage. The slices may be pan-fried in butter or bacon drippings heated in a heavy skillet, turning to brown on both sides. 1¼ pounds liver sausage makes 5 servings.

616   LIVER SAUSAGE AND CREAMED CABBAGE

1 medium head green
    cabbage
2 teaspoons salt
¼ cup butter
¼ cup flour
2½ cups milk

Pepper to taste
1¼ lbs. liver sausage sliced
    about ½-inch thick
1 hard-cooked egg
Paprika

Remove and discard soiled outer leaves of cabbage; cut head into thin wedges. Lay carefully in large saucepan; sprinkle with 1 teaspoon of the salt. In another saucepan, melt butter, blend in flour and add milk and rest of salt; stir constantly over direct heat until sauce boils. Reduce heat as low as possible, cover and keep hot. Pour enough boiling water over cabbage to just cover it, then boil uncovered until tender. Meanwhile, remove casing from sausage slices and pan-broil in butter or bacon drippings until brown and hot through. Drain cabbage and transfer to hot platter or chop plate. Pour white sauce around or over it, arrange hot sausage over the cabbage. Garnish with hard-cooked egg and sprinkling of paprika in center. 5 servings.

617
KIDNEY STEW

3 large or 4 medium pork kidneys, about 1 lb.	2 tablespoons chopped onion
½ teaspoon salt	2 tablespoons butter
2 teaspoons lemon juice	3 tablespoons bacon fat
⅓ cup flour	1 teaspoon salt
	1 tablespoon chopped parsley

Wash kidneys thoroughly and remove membranous covering. Split kidneys through center and remove white fatty cores and large veins. Cut in ½-inch dice, cover with 2 cups cold water, add the ½ teaspoon salt and lemon juice and let soak at least half an hour. Drain and rinse well in cold water. Add 2 cups boiling water, cover, and simmer 30 minutes; then drain, saving liquid. Coat kidneys in the flour and brown them and the chopped onion in the butter and bacon fat heated together. Blend in rest of flour in which kidneys were coated. Add salt and gradually stir in 2½ cups water, using half fresh water and half cooking water from kidneys. For milder flavor, use all fresh water. Stir constantly while cooking until gravy boils and thickens. Serve piping hot with a sprinkling of chopped parsley, over mashed potatoes, fluffy rice or toast. 5 servings.

618
BRAISED KIDNEYS AND SHORTRIBS

1 lb. lamb or veal kidneys	1 teaspoon salt
1 lb. beef shortribs	3 tablespoons bacon fat
½ cup flour	1½ cups boiling water

Remove membranes, split each kidney through center, and remove fatty cores and tubes. Soak kidneys in cold water to cover with ½ teaspoon salt for 1 hour or more. Cut shortribs into serving portions and coat thoroughly in flour which has been mixed with the salt. Melt fat in heavy iron or aluminum skillet and brown shortribs on all sides. Now add the water, cover and simmer about two hours or until tender. Add kidneys the last half hour of cooking. Serve juices remaining in skillet as gravy. 5 servings.

619
DEVILED KIDNEYS

2 lbs. beef kidneys	1 tablespoon lemon juice
¼ cup butter	⅓ cup flour
1½ teaspoons dry mustard	¾ cup hot water
3 teaspoons salt	4 cups boiled rice (174)
¼ teaspoon paprika	6 slices broiled bacon (544)

Wash kidneys, split, and remove cores and tubes; scissors are convenient for this purpose. Wash again and cut each kidney in 6 pieces. Cover with cold water, add 1 teaspoon salt and soak half hour. Drain well. Melt half the butter, blend with mustard, rest of salt, paprika and lemon juice. Roll each piece of kidney in this sauce, then in the flour. Melt remaining butter in skillet, add kidneys and brown on all sides. Add hot water, cover and simmer until kidneys are tender, about 20 to 30 minutes. If sauce becomes too thick, add a little more hot water. Serve kidneys hot, in their own sauce with boiled rice and crisp broiled bacon. 5 servings.

620   STEAK AND KIDNEY PIE

1 pair beef kidneys	10 small white onions, ¼ lb.
2 tablespoons vinegar	1 lb. ground steak or chuck
¼ cup bacon fat	1 lb. diced pared potatoes
2 teaspoons salt	Pastry for single crust (631)

Split kidneys and remove cores, tubes and membranous covering. Soak 30 minutes in 1 quart cold water to which the vinegar has been added, then drain, dice and brown in 2 tablespoons of the fat. Barely cover with water, add 1 teaspoon salt and simmer slowly until tender, about 45 minutes. Add water from time to time as needed to keep meat covered with liquid. Cut onions in halves or quarters and sauté in remaining fat until slightly browned; add ground meat and rest of salt and continue cooking over moderate heat for 20 minutes, or until meat is nicely browned, stirring frequently. Meanwhile cook potatoes until tender in just enough boiling salted water to cover. Add the kidneys and potatoes with their cooking liquid to the ground meat. Thicken gravy (468) if desired. Turn into an 8-inch casserole, cover with Plain Pastry (631) gashed in several places to let steam escape. Bake in a moderately hot oven (425° F.) about 20 minutes or until crust is nicely browned. Serve hot. 5 servings.

621   BRAISED STUFFED HEART

1 beef heart, about 3 lbs.	Pepper to suit taste
1 teaspoon salt	1 egg, beaten
2 cups coarse soft bread	¾ cup milk
crumbs	¼ cup chopped celery
½ teaspoon poultry seasoning,	1 teaspoon chopped onion
if desired	2 tablespoons melted butter

Prepare the heart for cooking, see p. 357. Wash thoroughly inside and out. Drain and sprinkle inside with half the salt. Combine bread crumbs with rest of salt and other seasonings, then add beaten egg mixed with milk. Add remaining ingredients, mixing lightly, then stuff into heart. Tie or sew up heart. Place in buttered casserole or Dutch oven that can be covered and add ½ cup water. Cover and bake in a moderate oven (350° F.) 3 to 3½ hours or until tender, adding more water during cooking if necessary. Make gravy (468) from liquid remaining after heart is lifted out. 5 servings.

622   PAN-FRIED BEEF HEART

Select 1 young beef or 2 small calf hearts. Prepare heart as described on p. 359. Wash thoroughly. Cut heart crosswise into ½-inch thick slices. Coat slices in flour; sprinkle with salt and pan-fry in butter or bacon fat for about 10 minutes or until well browned on both sides. Serve immediately. 5 servings.

623   STEWED HEART

3 calf or 4 lamb or pork hearts	2 tablespoons flour
2 tablespoons minced onion	¼ cup cold water
¼ cup finely chopped celery or carrot	Gravy coloring—Kitchen Bouquet
1 teaspoon salt	Boiled rice (174) or mashed
Pepper to taste	potatoes (1077)

Wash hearts thoroughly in warm water, split and remove veins and arteries. Cut in small dice and cover with cold water for 15 minutes. Then drain and cover with boiling water. Add onion, celery or carrot and salt, cover and simmer 2½ hours; add water as needed. When heart is tender, add pepper and flour, which has been blended to a smooth paste with the cold water. Boil 5 minutes, stirring until thickened. Add gravy coloring to give the desired brown color. Turn out onto platter and arrange a border of hot boiled rice or mashed potatoes around meat. Garnish with parsley and paprika. 5 servings.

624   HEART CHOP SUEY

1 small beef or 2 veal hearts	¼ cup flour
¼ cup butter or bacon fat	½ cup cold water
4 medium onions, sliced	Salt and pepper to taste
1 small stalk celery, diced	2 tablespoons soy sauce
2 cups meat broth or	or Worcestershire
2 bouillon cubes in 2 cups water	3 or 4 cups boiled rice (174)

Split hearts open, remove arteries and veins, then wash thoroughly inside and out in warm water. Drain well. Cut into narrow strips and roll in flour. Brown lightly in melted butter or bacon fat in large heavy skillet or Dutch oven. Add onions and brown lightly, then add celery and enough meat broth or bouillon to cover. Cover tightly and simmer until meat is tender, about 1 hour. Blend flour and water to a smooth paste and stir into chop suey; if gravy is too thick, add a little boiling water. Add seasonings. A little dark molasses or caramel (1121) may be added for color, if desired. Serve with hot boiled rice. 5 servings.

Note: Add a No. 2 can chop suey vegetables along with the flour-water paste for a pleasing variation.

625   BOILED FRESH TONGUE

Scrub the tongue thoroughly and place in a kettle. Cover with fresh cold water to which ¾ teaspoon salt is added for each pound of meat. Heat to boiling, reduce heat, cover and simmer until tongue is so tender that skin can be removed easily. This requires 2 to 3 hours, depending on size of tongue. When tongue is done, remove from kettle and place in cold water for a few minutes; then drain and remove skin and roots at base of tongue. Return tongue to cooking water and let remain until serving time. Reheat in cooking water or serve cold. 8 to 10 servings.

626   COLD JELLIED TONGUE

1 medium-size tongue, about 3 lbs.	¼ cup cold water
2 tablespoons plain gelatin	2 cups broth from boiling tongue

Scrub tongue, and rinse well. Then fit tongue into a 3 or 4-qt. kettle. Add enough water to cover, then simmer until tender—2 to 3 hours for a beef tongue. Take from the kettle, place in cold water and as soon as it can be handled comfortably, remove skin and roots; then return to the cooking water to cool. Press cooled tongue into mold, either round glass casserole or loaf-shaped pan. Soak gelatin in the cold water for 5 minutes, then stir it into the tongue broth which has been re-heated to boiling. When dissolved, season to suit taste with salt and pepper, and pour over the tongue in the mold. Chill until firm. Slice tongue thin, leaving the gelatin adhering. Garnish with cress, lettuce or parsley and serve very cold. 8 to 10 servings.

627   CREAMED SWEETBREADS

2 pairs sweetbreads	2 cups milk
1 tablespoon vinegar	Salt and pepper to taste
¼ cup butter	Toast or crisp noodles (173a)
⅓ cup flour	Parsley or paprika

Soak sweetbreads in cold water ½ hour, then drain and carefully remove all loose fiber. Cover with cold salted water, add 1 tablespoon vinegar, heat to boiling, then reduce heat and simmer 15 minutes. Drain and cover with cold water. Again drain and remove any remaining surface membrane and cut into ½-inch cubes. Meanwhile make a white sauce (919) of the butter, flour, milk and seasonings. Add diced sweetbreads, heat and serve immediately on toast or crisp noodles. Garnish with chopped parsley or dash paprika. One or two diced hard-cooked eggs or ½ pound mushrooms, sautéed, may be added to the creamed sweetbreads. 5 servings.

628 SCRAMBLED BRAINS

1 lb. calf brains	Dash pepper
¼ cup butter	1 tablespoon Worcestershire
5 eggs, beaten	2 tablespoons tomato catchup
1 teaspoon salt	Parsley

Prepare brains as follows: Cover with cold water and let soak 30 minutes, then wash thoroughly and remove as much of the membrane as possible. Drain and simmer 15 to 20 minutes in vinegar water (1 tablespoon vinegar to each pint of water). Drain and cool in cold water, then handling carefully, remove any remaining membrane. Heat butter in heavy skillet, combine brains with next 5 ingredients and cook like Scrambled Eggs (396). Serve on hot platter with chopped parsley sprinkled over the top. 5 servings.

629 TRIPE à la CREOLE

1 lb. honey-comb tripe	1 tablespoon Worcestershire
6 tablespoons bacon fat	2 teaspoons salt
3 tablespoons chopped onion	½ teaspoon paprika
1 No. 2 can tomatoes	3 tablespoons chopped green
2 tablespoons flour	pepper
3 tablespoons cold water	3 or 4 cups cooked rice

Wash tripe thoroughly, then put it into a 3-qt. saucepan. Cover with fresh cold water, heat to boiling, then reduce heat and simmer gently 2 or 3 hours or until very tender. Then drain. Heat half the fat in a heavy skillet; add onions and cook until browned; add tomatoes put through a sieve and simmer 10 minutes. Now add flour which has been blended to a paste with the cold water and cook over direct heat, stirring constantly until mixture boils and thickens. Add seasonings and green pepper. Dry the parboiled tripe thoroughly, then coat in flour and brown on both sides in rest of hot fat. Place on hot platter and cover with the hot tomato sauce. Garnish with parsley and serve with hot fluffy steamed rice (174). 5 servings.

630 TRIPE DE LUXE

3 cups chopped celery
2 cups chopped onion
3 tablespoons chopped parsley
¼ cup olive oil or shortening
1½ lbs. parboiled honey-comb tripe (1133)

2½ cups tomato juice
1 teaspoon salt
Pepper
¼ cup grated Parmesan cheese
¼ cup fine dry bread crumbs

Sauté first 3 ingredients in olive oil until lightly browned. Cover with the tripe. Add tomato juice, salt and pepper, cover closely and bake in a moderately slow oven (325° F.) about 3 hours or until tender. Remove cover, sprinkle with Parmesan cheese mixed with the bread crumbs and return to oven with temperature increased to moderately hot (400° F.) until nicely toasted, about ½ hour. Serves 6 or 7.

PASTRY and PIES

IF there is any Great American Dessert, one which more Americans like better than any other, it's probably pie. Fruit pies, cream pies, custard pies, chiffon pies—all have their backers for first place in this big league of favorite desserts. There is every reason why modern pies should be even better than those (of tender memory) which Grandma used to make; and there's no reason why YOURS *shouldn't be better too, especially if you follow carefully the recipes in this chapter.*

One of the severest tests of a good cook is her ability to make good pastry, not just now and then, but every time. And one of the essentials of a good pastry maker is ability to recognize what good pie crust is.

The same pastry which is good when baked without a filling will be good when baked with a filling, so let us look at an unfilled baked pie shell to see what its characteristics should be.

Good baked pastry has a blistery, pebbly surface, indicating that it will be flaky when cut. It should be tender and easily cut with a fork, but not so tender that it crumbles. The color should be a delicate brown all over with a very little richer brown at the edge. And the crust should be fairly thin so the bottom as well as the rim will become crisp.

This kind of pastry is just as easy to make as tough, hard, compact pastry. The two kinds can be made with exactly the same kind and proportion of ingredients, the only difference being in the handling. Mixing must be done with a light hand, and the technique of handling pastry dough lightly once learned, is like swimming or bicycle riding—hard to forget.

INGREDIENTS

The correct types of ingredients naturally make the best pastry, and since only 4 ingredients are required—flour, shortening, water and salt—it is easy to have them just right.

Flour: ALL-PURPOSE FLOUR of good quality is best for making pastry. Bread flour tends to make a heavier, tougher crust, though by increasing the proportion of shortening to flour, it is possible for an expert to make good pastry with bread flour too. Cake flour is too expensive for economical pastry making and it is not very desirable, because it makes a crust tender to the crumbling point.

Shortening: A firm, bland-flavored shortening should be chosen, such as bland lard, a hydrogenated shortening or chicken fat. Butter may be used and will give an unusually pleasing flavor to the pastry, but it is more difficult to work with and will not give as tender a crust as other shortenings, due to the presence of quite a bit of water as well as some milk solids in the butter; remember that butter is not 100 per cent fat. Oil is sometimes used but always produces a crust which, though tender, is crumbly rather than flaky. The fat used for pastry should be firm, but need not be chilled unless the weather is warm.

Water: Water used in making pastry should always be ice cold.

Salt: Salt is necessary to give flavor to the pastry, since the other ingredients are bland in flavor. A slightly salty crust is pleasing with any pie filling.

METHOD OF MIXING

Given a good recipe, the mixing is the most important part of pastry making. A light hand is vital; with a light hand even the novice can make good pastry, and without it, even years of experience will not make a skilful pastry maker. Here are the 6 simple steps:

1.   Sift flour before measuring.

2.   Measure by lifting sifted flour into the cup heaped up, then level it off with a spatula or knife.

3.   Add salt and sift together with flour into the mixing bowl.

4.   Add firm shortening and cut into the flour, using 2 knives with a criss-cross motion or a wire pastry blender which can be bought in any five-and-ten-cent store. Continue cutting until the particles of fat with their coating of flour are the size of dried split peas.

5.   Slowly drip the ice water over the top, mixing very lightly with a fork, and tossing aside the part which has been moistened. The mixture should never appear like a dough, but should be *just* moist enough so the particles will stick together when pressed between the finger tips. Too much water makes the pastry tough because more flour is added in rolling; too little makes it crumbly. The exact amount of water needed in a given recipe depends on the dryness of the flour, the temperature of the room, the humidity of the atmosphere and other factors which are soon learned by experience.

6.   Gather the moistened fat-flour mixture into a ball, then press it quickly

and lightly together. Wrap it in waxed paper and chill in the refrigerator for 15 to 20 minutes before rolling.

ROLLING

Keep the LIGHT TOUCH in rolling pastry.

After the pastry has been chilled, divide it into the required number of portions; two for a double crust pie (631), making the portion for the lower crust a very little larger than the other portion. While working on one portion, put the rest back into the refrigerator.

Place the dough to be rolled on a lightly floured board or pastry cloth. A pastry cloth is especially good for beginners because it holds the flour more evenly and gives it up more slowly than does the uncovered board and there is less danger of sticking, or of rolling too much flour into the pastry. The rolling pin may be covered with stockinet and floured.

First flatten out the ball of dough with patting motions of rolling pin, keeping it circular in shape; then begin to roll, working always from the center out in all directions. This helps to keep the shape round, while it also tends to keep the handling light. If there is any sticking, loosen the pastry with the edge of a spatula and lift it with one hand while quickly sprinkling a little more flour under it with the other. If the edges fray (indicating that a little more water should have been used), pull edges of the cracks carefully together or patch them with pieces of the pastry.

Roll the pastry a little less than ⅛-inch thick, and at least 2 inches larger in diameter than the pie pan to be lined. Fold the sheet of pastry through the center and lift it carefully and quickly into the pie pan so the fold is across the center of the pan. Now unfold it and fit it down snugly into the angle of the pan, smoothing it by running a finger carefully around this angle.

FOR A SINGLE-CRUST PIE

If a single-crust pie, either pre-baked or baked with filling in it, is to be made, the excess dough around the edge should be trimmed off. To trim the pastry flush with the edge of the pie pan, run a sharp paring knife around the rim; or if a higher pastry rim is desired, cut the dough off with scissors evenly ½-inch beyond the rim of the pan. This extra half-inch of dough should then be turned back, either over or under, so the folded edge is flush with the edge of the pan's rim. This double thickness of dough at the edge is especially desirable when there is a runny or juicy filling, as the rim can be built up high enough to hold the filling in.

The edge may be fluted in many ways. The simplest (and flattest) is by pressing the tines of a fork down into the dough which lies on the rim. Most of the elaborate edges are done with the fingers, pressing, pushing or folding the dough into the desired shape.

If the filling is to be baked in the shell such as custard or pumpkin pie, pour it into the unpricked pastry shell, and bake according to the recipe.

If the crust is to be baked before putting in a pre-cooked filling, as for cream or chiffon pies, prick pastry all over the bottom and sides quite close together with the tines of a fork. These holes allow for escape of air from bubbles which might expand in the crust and push it up in big blisters as it bakes, spoiling the shape.

FOR A DOUBLE-CRUST PIE

If a double-crust pie is to be made, as for fruit or mince pies, roll out the upper crust after filling and trimming the lower crust. Roll top crust the same thickness as the lower crust, but not as large, and about ½ to 1-inch wider than the pan, depending on how much the filling is heaped up. While still on board, gash it in several places, preferably in a design to allow steam to escape.

Now put filling into the lower crust. For fruit pies, have the filling well heaped up as fruits shrink in cooking, and you want a well-filled pie when it is done. Mincemeat filling need not be heaped as it will not shrink. Add flour, sugar and other seasonings as directed in the individual recipes for the various pies.

Brush rim of the lower crust with water or slightly beaten egg white, then lay the upper crust over the filling, press pastry together gently at the rim to seal, then trim off the excess dough of both upper and lower crusts at the same time with a sharp knife. Flute the edges carefully, being sure the 2 layers are sealed together. (For a very juicy pie, the lower crust may be trimmed flush with the edge of the pan and the upper crust ¼ to ½-inch wider all around; then tuck the excess of the upper crust *under* the edge of the lower crust before fluting.)

BAKING

A pastry shell should be baked delicately brown in a moderately hot oven (425° F.) 12 to 15 minutes. At end of 5 minutes, prick and collapse any bubbles that appear. Double crust pies with raw filling in them are generally baked 12 to 15 minutes in a hot oven, (450° F.) then temperature is reduced to meet the requirements of the particular recipe used.

OTHER USES FOR PASTRY

Plain pastry is most frequently used in pies for dessert. However, many other dishes are made with the same type of pastry. Some of these are:

1. Meat or fish pies.
2. Tarts. Tiny pies baked in small or individual tart pans; or pastry baked in wafers and filled with jelly, sandwich-fashion.

Just as milk and butter have added to the flavor and food value of these foods, so has a cleverly incorporated garnish added to their eye appeal. In the top row, Cream of Vegetable Soup (961) is brightened by a sprinkling of peas, carrots and diced ham. Celery au Gratin (1023) needs no garnish besides its golden-brown crust. BE-LOW, the Meat Croquettes (513) are gayly capped with egg slices and flanked by colorful buttered asparagus and carrots.

Cooked vegetables make excellent salads provided they are cooked only until just done—not one second longer. Some "bite" must still be left in them. Another important factor is to choose vegetables that harmonize in color and flavor. The combination here includes peas, carrots, cauliflower and beets—with plenty of crisp hearts of lettuce for crunch.

Peach Pie **(653)** *or any other fresh fruit pie takes kindly to a lattice crust, which is really just a simple problem in weaving strips of plain pastry together on top of the pie.*

Nut Pie **(673)** *is a modification of a particularly rich and luscious Southern favorite. A little less rich than its Southern model, it is just as luscious.*

Nowadays we can enjoy Roast Turkey (695) any time of the year when the occasion demands a feast. And it's truly a festive occasion when the dinner table presents all at one time, a handsome turkey, Corn on the Cob (1024) and Strawberry Tarts or Pie (660). Other attractions on the menu are a Tossed Salad (825), a casserole of mashed potatoes sprinkled with toasted crumbs, Ice Box Rolls (66) and Apple Jelly (704a).

3. Dumplings. Usually fruits (whole or cut up and sweetened) enclosed in pastry and baked.

4. Turnovers. Squares of pastry dough filled with fruit or creamed meat or fish mixtures, folded and sealed envelope-fashion, then baked.

5. Cobblers and deep dish pies are fruit pies with or without a lower crust. Cobblers are usually baked in dishes at least 2½-inches deep. Deep dish pies, as the name implies, are baked in casseroles deeper than regular pie pans.

PASTRIES

631   PLAIN PASTRY

("*Makes one 9-inch double-crust pie, or two 8-inch pie shells, or ten 3½-inch tarts*)

2 cups all-purpose flour	½ to ⅔ cup shortening
1 teaspoon salt	6 tablespoons ice water, about

Sift flour, measure and resift twice with salt. If lard is the shortening, use ½ cup; if vegetable shortening, use ⅔ cup. Cut fat into flour with a pastry blender or 2 knives, or rub in with finger tips until fat-flour particles are about the size of split peas. Now add the water by teaspoons (or shake the water from a clothes-sprinkling bottle), mixing lightly with a fork and tossing aside the part of the mixture that is dampened. Gather these moistened fat-flour particles into a ball, press gently together; wrap in waxed paper and chill in the refrigerator a few minutes. (Chilling is not essential if the kitchen is cool, but in warm weather or in a warm kitchen it is always desirable.) When ready to roll pastry for double crust, divide dough into 2 portions, one only slightly larger than the other; for single crusts, divide in half. Shape larger part quickly into a thick disc and roll out for the lower crust, starting at center and rolling outward in all directions to a thickness of about ⅛-inch. For successful rolling, have the board lightly floured, and lift the dough and turn it around (not over) several times during rolling. A floured pastry cloth and rolling pin cover are helpful, especially to the inexperienced pastry maker.

To transfer pastry to pie pan, fold it through the center and lift into the pan; then unfold and pat carefully into pan, fitting into the angle all around the pan.

For *a pre-baked single crust*, trim off dough to within ½-inch of rim of pan, then turn dough under so folded edge is flush with rim of pan. Flute edge, then prick pastry closely all over with tines of fork. Bake in a moderately hot oven (425° F.) about 12 to 15 minutes, or until crust is a light golden brown. After 5 minutes, look at the crust and collapse any bubbles by pricking. Cool in the pan on a cake rack.

For a filled single-crust pie, trim and flute edge but do not prick. Put filling in and bake in a hot oven (450° F.) 12 minutes, then reduce heat to temperature required by filling and continue baking according to directions in recipe.

For a double-crust pie, leave edge of lower crust untrimmed. Put in filling, then trim. Roll out rest of pastry large enough to fit top of pie, and gash in several places to allow escape of steam. Lay upper crust over filling. Moisten edge of lower crust with water, then press upper and lower crusts together to seal them well. Then trim both together and flute edge. Bake in a hot oven (450° F.) 12 to 15 minutes, then reduce heat to temperature required for filling, and continue baking according to directions in recipe.

For tart shells, roll out for each shell about ⅓ as much pastry as is required for a single-crust pie, and fit into a small individual tart pan. Trim, prick, place on a wire cake rack, and bake like any single crust.

632   CHEESE PASTRY
(*Two Methods*)

In making cheese pastry, use Plain Pastry recipe (631), increasing shortening by 1 tablespoon. Add ⅓ cup grated sharp cheese; an aged dry cheese is best for this. Stir the grated cheese into the fat-flour mixture and continue mixing as for Plain Pastry. Another method of mixing is as follows: Roll out plain pastry; sprinkle half the surface with grated cheese, fold the other half over it, and roll out again. Repeat until all the cheese has been rolled in. The latter method is useful chiefly when left-over plain pastry is being made into Cheese Sticks, but this is not recommended for pie crust, as the repeated rollings tend to toughen the pastry. Bake cheese pastry as directed for Plain Pastry. Cheese pastry is excellent for apple or cherry pie.

633   CHEESE STICKS

Make Cheese Pastry by either of the two methods suggested (632). Roll ⅛-inch thick, then cut into strips about ⅜-inch wide and as long as desired. These strips may be laid on cookie sheet and baked as they are, or may be twisted or braided, transferred to a cookie sheet, then pressed down at both ends so they will stick to the cookie sheet and keep their shape. Bake in a moderately hot oven (425° F.) 8 to 10 minutes or until golden brown, watching carefully to prevent overbaking. Serve hot or cold.

A larger amount of cheese may be used if desired.

634   WHOLE WHEAT PASTRY

1 cup whole wheat flour	½ cup lard or ⅔ cup vegetable
1 cup sifted all-purpose flour	shortening
1 teaspoon salt	About ⅓ cup ice water

Mix just as for Plain Pastry (631), except resift the two kinds of flour and salt together, then stir the bran back into the sifted mixture. Makes 1 double-crust or 2 single-crust pies.

634a   BREAD CRUMB PIE CRUST

¼ cup butter	1 cup fine dry bread crumbs
¼ cup brown sugar	1 teaspoon cinnamon
1 tablespoon water	

Heat first 3 ingredients to boiling; turn heat low and stir in bread-crumbs and cinnamon until well mixed. Turn into 8-inch pie pan and press into uniform layer over bottom and up sides. Bake in a moderate oven (350° F.) 10 minutes. Chill and fill with any pre-cooked or chiffon pie filling. Makes one 8-inch pie crust.

634b   GINGERSNAP PIE CRUST

¼ lb. gingersnaps	¼ cup soft butter

Roll the gingersnaps with a rolling pin to make fine crumbs; there should be 1¼ cups of crumbs. Blend butter and crumbs thoroughly, then pat the mixture over bottom and up sides of an 8-inch pie pan into a uniform layer. Bake in a moderate oven (350° F.) 10 minutes, then cool thoroughly before filling with pre-cooked or chiffon pie filling. One 8-inch crust.

FRUIT PIES

635   APPLE PIE

Plain pastry (631)   ¼ teaspoon cinnamon
7 to 8 medium size tart apples   1 tablespoon butter
1 tablespoon flour blended   1 tablespoon lemon juice,
  with   if desired
⅔ to ¾ cup sugar, depending
  on tartness of apples

Make pastry and roll out for a double-crust pie. Line a 9-inch pie pan with one sheet of pastry, fitting carefully into angles. Cut pared, quartered, and cored apples into uniform slices about ¼-inch thick. Arrange half the apples over lower pastry, then sprinkle with half the flour-sugar mixture. Add remaining apples and sprinkle with remainder of flour-sugar mixture and spice. Dot top with the butter and sprinkle with lemon juice. Brush edges of lower crust with water or slightly beaten egg white. Lay pastry for upper crust, gashed for steam vents, over the apples and seal upper and lower edges together. Trim off dough ½ inch from edge, turn under and flute. Bake in a hot oven (450° F.) 15 minutes, then reduce heat to a moderately slow oven (325° F.) and bake about 35 minutes longer or until apples are well cooked. Cool to lukewarm before cutting. Serve plain or with cheese, or with vanilla ice cream. 5 or 6 servings.

Note: If apples are very tart, omit spice and lemon juice.

636   APPLESAUCE AND ORANGE PIE

1 recipe applesauce (261)   2 oranges, pared and sliced
Baked pastry shell (631)   or diced

Have applesauce chilled. Turn into cooled baked pie shell and arrange orange slices over top. If oranges are diced, they should be mixed with the applesauce before turning into the crust. Garnish with whipped cream if desired. 5 servings.

637   DUTCH APPLE PIE

Plain pastry single crust   ¾ cup sugar
  (631)   ½ teaspoon cinnamon, if
7 or 8 tart cooking apples   desired
3 tablespoons butter

Roll pastry about ⅛-inch thick and fit into 9-inch pie pan; trim off excess dough and flute edge as desired. Peel apples, quarter and remove core; cut each quarter into four slices, lengthwise. Melt butter in saucepan, add apples, and toss about until each slice is coated with butter. Add sugar, which may be mixed with cinnamon if desired, and again toss about to distribute through the apples. Arrange apples neatly in the pastry-lined pan, so slices fit together compactly; they should be slightly heaped in the center. Bake in a hot oven (450° F.) about 20 minutes, or until crust is well browned. Then cover the pie carefully with another pie pan, reduce heat to moderately slow (325° F.), and continue baking about 30 minutes more, or until apples are tender. Lift off top pie pan and remove to cake rack to cool before cutting. The apples may, if desired, be covered with Streusel Topping (638) before baking, in which case do not cover with a pie pan. 5 or 6 servings.

638   STREUSEL TOPPING FOR APPLE PIE

½ cup flour
½ teaspoon cinnamon

⅓ cup light brown sugar, packed
⅓ cup butter

Sift flour and cinnamon together twice to mix thoroughly. Stir in sugar, which should be sieved if there are any lumps in it. Cream butter until soft and smooth, then work into flour-cinnamon-sugar mixture until well blended. Sprinkle the crumbly mixture over top of a single-crust apple pie. Enough to top 1 pie.

639   APRICOT TARTS

Cook ½ lb. dried apricots as described under Stewed Apricots (274), but reduce water to 2 cups. Chill and serve in 5 cooled baked individual tart shells (631). Serves 5.

If preferred, make a meringue filling for the tart shells by folding 1 cup sweetened apricot purée (275) into a meringue made by beating 3 egg whites until stiff, then beating in ¼ cup sugar and 2 tablespoons lemon juice. Serve chilled, or place in a moderate oven (375° F.) 15 to 20 minutes, to brown to a golden color. Serve warm.

640   BLACKBERRY COBBLER

Plain pastry for double-crust pie (631)
½ cup sugar

1 tablespoon flour
1 quart blackberries
1 tablespoon lemon juice

Line a shallow 10-inch round casserole, or a baking pan 7 x 11 x 2 inches, with pastry rolled thin. Mix sugar and flour, and sprinkle half the mixture over the bottom of the pastry; then pour in the washed, drained berries and sift rest of sugar mixture over top. Sprinkle with lemon juice. Roll out pastry for top crust to fit the dish, gash, lay over berries, and trim; or if preferred, cut pastry for top crust into smaller fancy-shaped pieces, one to a serving and lay on top. Bake in a hot oven (450° F.) 15 minutes or until pastry is golden brown; then bake at 300° F. until berries are cooked through, about 20 minutes. Serve hot. 5 servings.

641   BLACK RASPBERRY COBBLER

1 quart black raspberries	½ teaspoon salt
½ cup sugar	1¼ teaspoons baking powder,
2 tablespoons flour	see p. 122
1 tablespoon lemon juice	¼ cup shortening
1 cup sifted all-purpose flour	About ½ cup milk

Wash and drain fruit. Combine sugar and 2 tablespoons flour and mix with berries. Add lemon juice and put in buttered deep pie dish. Sift flour, measure and resift with salt and baking powder. Cut in shortening, using a pastry blender, then gradually stir in milk until dough clings together. Pat or roll out dough ¼-inch thick and place it on top of fruit mixture. Trim edges and cut several gashes in center for steam to escape. Bake in a hot oven (450° F.) 20 minutes, then reduce heat to slow (300° F.) and continue baking until berries are cooked through. Plain Pastry (631) may be used instead of biscuit dough for crust. 5 servings.

642   BLACKBERRY TURNOVERS

Plain pastry (631)	½ cup sugar
1 quart blackberries	

Roll pastry ⅛-inch thick or a little less, keeping the shape rectangular, about 14 x 21 inches. Cut into six 7-inch squares. Divide washed and hulled berries in 6 portions and heap up near one corner of each square; sprinkle a portion of the sugar over each heap. Brush edge of pastry all around with water; then fold free pastry over berries and press edges together to form a triangle. Make one or two gashes in top of each turnover. Lift carefully to an ungreased baking pan and bake in a hot oven (450° F.) about 15 minutes or until lightly browned; then reduce heat to slow (300° F.) and continue baking about 15 minutes longer or until berries are soft. Serve warm. 6 servings.

Note: APPLE or PEACH turnovers may be made in same way.

643   BLUEBERRY PIE

Pastry double crust pie (631)   Dash salt
3 cups blueberries   2 tablespoons lemon juice
3 tablespoons flour   1 tablespoon butter
¾ cup sugar

Roll out a little more than half the pastry ⅛-inch thick and fit into an
8-inch pie pan. Sort and thoroughly wash blueberries. Mix flour, sugar
and salt together and sprinkle about half the mixture over the bottom of
the pastry; then pour in the blueberries and sprinkle rest of sugar and
flour over top. Sprinkle lemon juice over all. Dot with butter. Roll remaining pastry a little thinner than for lower crust and gash in any desired
design. Brush edge of lower crust with cold water; lay upper crust over
pie, press crusts together at rim and trim off excess dough. Turn under
edge of pastry and flute. Bake in a hot oven (450° F.) 12 to 15 minutes, or
until crust begins to brown; then reduce heat to 325° F. and continue
baking until blueberries are cooked thoroughly, from 20 to 25 minutes.
Remove to cake rack to cool before cutting. 5 servings.

644   CHERRY COBBLER

½ cup sugar   1 teaspoon baking powder,
1¼ cups sifted all-purpose flour   see p. 122
1 No. 2 can or 4 cups fresh sour   3 tablespoons shortening
  red cherries   ⅓ cup milk
¼ teaspoon salt

Blend sugar and ¼ cup of the flour together, add juice from canned
cherries and cook over direct heat, stirring constantly until thickened.
Add cherries and turn into a baking dish. If fresh cherries are used, increase sugar to 1 cup. Pit cherries, put in baking dish and sprinkle with a
mixture of the sugar and ¼ cup of the flour. Sift remaining flour 3 times
with salt and baking powder. Cut in shortening. Add milk all at once
and stir until dough stiffens slightly, then turn out on floured board and
knead 3 or 4 times. Roll ¼-inch thick and cut in ¼-inch strips. Arrange
strips lattice fashion over cherries. Bake in a moderately hot oven (425°
F.) 15 to 20 minutes or until crust is nicely browned. Canned cherries
will now be done. Continue baking the fresh cherry cobbler 10 to 15
minutes longer, reducing the heat to moderately slow (325° F.). Serve
warm. Serves 5.

Variation: Plain pastry (631) instead of the biscuit dough may be
used to cover the cobbler.

645   CANNED CHERRY PIE

Plain pastry (631)   No. 2 can sour red pitted
½ cup sugar or to taste   cherries
1 tablespoon corn starch   ⅛ teaspoon almond extract
                                 1 tablespoon butter

Line an 8-inch pie pan with plain pastry. Mix sugar and corn starch together in saucepan; blend in juice drained from cherries. Cook over direct heat, stirring constantly until mixture boils and thickens. Remove from heat. Add almond extract and cool. Turn cherries into pastry-lined pan and pour thickened juice over them. Dot with the butter. Roll out pastry for upper crust, gashing for steam vents; moisten edge of lower crust with water, lay upper crust over filling and press edges together; trim and elaborate edge as desired. Bake in a hot oven (450° F.) 15 minutes or until crust is lightly browned, then reduce heat to moderately slow (325° F.) and continue baking 20 minutes. Cool on cake rack before cutting. 5 servings.

646   FRESH CHERRY PIE

Plain pastry (631)   3 cups pitted sour red cherries
¼ cup flour   ⅛ teaspoon almond extract
1 cup sugar, or to suit taste   1 tablespoon butter

Make pastry for a double crust pie. Roll out slightly more than half of it ⅛-inch thick to line an 8-inch pie pan, fitting pastry smoothly into angles. Mix flour and sugar thoroughly and sprinkle over cherries, then toss to mix well. Now turn cherries into pastry lined pan, then sprinkle with extract and dot with butter. Brush edges of lower crust with water or slightly beaten egg white. Lay pastry for upper crust, rolled thin and gashed for steam vents over the cherries; seal upper and lower edges together. Trim off pastry to within ½-inch of rim of pie pan, then turn under so folded edge is flush with rim of pan. Flute. Bake in a hot oven (450° F.) 15 minutes, then reduce heat to (325° F.) moderately slow and bake 20 to 25 minutes longer, or until cherries are done. Remove to cake rack to cool before cutting. Serve plain or with a wedge of sharp cheese, or with a scoop of vanilla ice cream. 5 servings.

646a   OPEN-FACE FRESH CHERRY PIE

9-inch baked pie shell   1 tablespoon flour
3½ to 4 cups pitted sour   ¼ cup water
cherries   1 tablespoon butter
1 to 1¼ cups sugar   2 or 3 drops almond extract
2 tablespoons corn starch   Whipping cream

Bake and cool pie shell. Put cherries into a 3-qt. saucepan, add the sugar blended thoroughly with corn starch and flour. Add water, stir thoroughly and place over moderate direct heat. Heat to boiling, stirring constantly but carefully so as not to break up fruit, then reduce heat and simmer until cherries are barely tender and juice is thickened and clear. Remove from heat and stir in butter and extract. Cool slightly, then pour into pie shell. When cooled, set in refrigerator for filling to thicken. Serve within a few hours topped with whipped cream. 5 to 6 servings.

647 CHERRY TARTS

Cherry tarts may be made exactly like Canned or Fresh Cherry Pie (645 or 646), except they are baked in individual tart pans rather than full-size pie pans. If preferred, however, tart shells (631) may be baked and cooled before filling with the cherries and thickened juice as described for Canned Cherry Pie. Chill and serve with whipped cream. This is an open-face type of tart, and very quickly made if tart shells are ready.

648 GOOSEBERRY TARTS

Plain pastry (631)   1½ tablespoons flour
4 cups green gooseberries   ⅛ teaspoon salt
¾ to 1 cup sugar depending on   1½ tablespoons butter
    sourness of berries

Roll out slightly more than half the pastry and line 5 individual tart pans; chill in refrigerator. Pick over gooseberries, discarding any soft ones and removing stems and tails, then wash. Combine sugar, flour and salt. Sprinkle over berries, stirring to distribute. Turn into unbaked pastry-lined tart pans, dot with butter and brush edge of pastry with water. Cover with rest of pastry rolled slightly thinner than lower crust and gashed to form a design to let steam escape. Press edges together firmly, trim and flute. Bake in a hot oven (450° F.) 15 minutes or until crust is delicately browned. Then reduce heat to moderate (350° F.) and continue baking 20 to 30 minutes or until berries are tender. 5 servings.

Note: Make gooseberry pie the same way, except roll out the pastry to fit an 8-inch pie pan.

649 OLD-FASHIONED JELLY OR JAM TARTS

Lay left over trimmings from plain pastry (631) on top of each other. Do not knead them together, but roll out about ⅛-inch thick. Cut out with cookie cutter dipped in flour. Place on a baking sheet, prick and bake in a hot oven (425° F.) 10 to 15 minutes or until lightly browned.

Cool and spread with any jam or jelly. For a more elaborate tart, cut half the rounds with a biscuit cutter and the rest with a doughnut cutter the same size. In making up the tarts, lay the doughnut-shaped piece over the jam-spread plain piece.

650   MINCE PIE

There are a number of excellent packaged mincemeats on the market. Some require no preparation, others require addition of water and a little cooking to make them ready for use as pie filling. These packaged mincemeats are so inexpensive that it is more economical as well as more convenient for most housewives to use them rather than to prepare their own mincemeat.

Prepare mincemeat according to directions on package and turn into a pastry-lined pie pan (631). Cover with gashed pastry, moisten edge of crust with water, press edges together, trim off excess and flute edges as desired. Bake in a hot oven (450° F.) 15 minutes or until crust is nicely browned; then reduce heat to moderately slow (325° F.) and bake about 15 minutes longer. Remove to cake rack to cool. Serve warm or cold. One pie serves 6 to 7.

651   MINCEMEAT TARTS

Make just like Mince Pie (650), only turn mincemeat into pastry-lined individual tart pans. Cover and bake as for pie.

A different type of tart is made by turning prepared mincemeat into baked individual tart shells. These may be topped with baked pastry cut-outs, such as stars, Christmas trees, Santa Clauses, or other desired shapes cut out with cookie cutters and baked on cookie sheet. Serve warm.

652   CANNED PEACH TARTS

Plain pastry (631)	1 tablespoon lemon juice
1 No. 2 can sliced peaches	⅛ teaspoon almond extract
1 tablespoon corn starch	1 tablespoon butter

Roll out pastry and line individual tart pans, fitting well into angles. Trim off excess and elaborate edges as desired; prick all over with tines of a fork. Bake in a moderately hot oven (425° F.) 12 to 15 minutes or until nicely browned. Cool. Drain all juice from peaches. Blend a little of the juice with the corn starch to form a smooth paste; stir this into rest of juice and cook over direct heat, stirring constantly until sauce boils and becomes clear and thick. Some may desire to add a little sugar. Remove from heat and stir in lemon juice and almond extract. Add peaches and butter and cool. When ready to serve, remove cooled tart shells from pans and pour in the peach mixture. The tarts may be garnished with a puff of whipped cream. 5 servings.

653   FRESH PEACH PIE

Plain pastry (631)   ¾ cup sugar
2 to 2½ lbs. peaches   2 tablespoons butter
2 tablespoons flour   ⅛ teaspoon almond extract

Make pastry for a double-crust pie. Roll out slightly more than half the pastry and fit into bottom of a 9-inch pie pan. Pare and slice peaches and place in layers in the pastry-lined pie pan, sprinkling the flour and sugar, mixed together between the layers. Dot top layer with the butter and sprinkle the flavoring over all. Roll out rest of pastry ⅛-inch thick and cut in strips about ⅜-inch wide. Lay over peaches to form lattice crust, placing all the parallel strips across one way and folding back alternate strips as each of the remaining strips is laid in place to produce a woven lattice. Bake in a hot oven (450° F.) 15 minutes, then reduce heat to (325° F.) moderately slow and bake 20 to 25 minutes longer or until peaches are soft. 6 servings.

654   FRESH PEACH TARTS

Make exactly like Fresh Peach Pie, except bake in individual tart pans (631). If desired, a plain gashed crust may be substituted for the lattice top suggested for the large pie. 8 to 10 tarts, depending on size of pans.

655   CANNED PEACH COBBLER

1 No. 2½ can sliced peaches   2 teaspoons butter
2 tablespoons flour   1 tablespoon lemon juice
3 tablespoons sugar   Plain pastry for single crust
Pinch salt   (631)

Drain juice from peaches and combine with the 2 tablespoons flour, sugar, and the salt, which have been sifted together. Cook over direct heat, stirring constantly until mixture boils and thickens. Remove from heat and add butter and lemon juice. Combine with peaches and pour into a 6-cup casserole or baking dish. Roll out the chilled pastry on a floured board to fit top of casserole; gash in several places and lay over peaches, then crimp edges of pastry. Bake in a hot oven (450° F.) 20 to 25 minutes or until crust is browned. Serve warm with an almond-flavored Hard Sauce (932) or with cream. 5 servings.

656   FRESH PEACH COBBLER

Plain pastry for single crust   ¾ cup sugar
   (631)   ⅛ teaspoon almond extract
3 lbs. peaches, (4 cups sliced)   2 tablespoons butter

Roll out pastry and trim to fit top of baking dish, then gash in any desired design. Pare peaches or dip into boiling water for about a minute, then remove skins. Cut in half, discard seeds, then cut halves into 4 slices. Place in a 6-cup baking dish or casserole and sprinkle with sugar and almond extract. Dot with butter and cover with the pastry. Bake in a hot oven (450° F.) 20 to 25 minutes. Remove to cake rack to cool. Serve warm or cold. 5 servings.

657   FRESH PLUM PIE

2 lbs. fresh plums   2 tablespoons flour
Plain pastry double crust   ½ teaspoon cinnamon
   (631)   1 tablespoon butter
¾ cup sugar

Wash plums but do not peel. Cut in halves and remove pits. Roll out slightly more than half the pastry to line an 8-inch pie pan, and fit carefully into angles. Arrange plums in the pastry-lined pan. Blend sugar, flour and cinnamon and sprinkle over the plums. Dot with the butter. Roll out rest of pastry, gash in several places. Moisten edges of lower crust, then lay upper crust over the plums and press upper and lower edges of pastry together. Trim off excess pastry and flute edge as desired. Bake in a hot oven (450° F.) 12 minutes, then reduce heat to moderately slow (325° F.) and bake 25 minutes longer or until fruit is tender. Remove to cake rack to cool. Serve warm or cold. 5 or 6 servings.

658   PRUNE WHIP PIE

½ lb. cooked dried prunes   2 eggs, separated
   (301)   ½ cup milk
¼ cup juice from prunes   1 teaspoon gelatin
1½ tablespoons lemon juice   2 tablespoons cold water
½ cup sugar   Baked 8 or 9-inch pastry
Pinch salt   shell (631)

Remove stones from prunes and press pulp through food mill or coarse sieve. Add juices, sugar and salt. Beat egg yolks, add milk and cook over boiling water, stirring constantly until mixture coats spoon. Remove from heat at once and stir in gelatin which has been softened 5 minutes in the cold water. Add to prunes. When cool, fold in stiffly beaten egg whites

and pour into baked pastry shell. Chill in refrigerator until set. 5 or 6
servings.

658a   RASPBERRY PIE

Plain pastry for double crust   3 tablespoons flour
(631)   Pinch salt
⅔ to ¾ cup sugar, depending   3 cups red or black raspberries
on tartness of berries   1 tablespoon butter

Line a 9-inch pie pan with plain pastry. Mix sugar, flour and salt,
and sprinkle over washed, drained berries. Toss to mix well, then turn
berries into pastry-lined pan. Moisten edge of lower crust and lay gashed
upper crust over berries. Trim off excess dough and crimp edges of the
2 crusts together, fluting as desired. Bake in a moderately hot oven (425°
F.) 15 minutes, then reduce heat to moderate (350° F.) and bake 20
minutes longer. Remove to cake rack to cool. Serve warm or cold. 6 servings.

659   RHUBARB PIE

1½ lbs. rhubarb, 3 to 4 cups cut   Plain pastry for double crust
1 cup sugar   (631)
2 to 3 tablespoons flour   1 tablespoon butter
⅛ teaspoon salt

Wash rhubarb thoroughly and trim off leaf and stem-ends. Cut into
¾-inch lengths. Combine sugar, flour and salt, add to rhubarb and mix
thoroughly. Roll out a little more than half the pastry and fit into an
8-inch pie pan. Turn rhubarb mixture into pastry-lined pan. Dot with
butter. Roll out rest of pastry for upper crust and gash to form a design
for steam vents. Brush edge of lower crust with cold water or slightly
beaten egg white. Lay upper crust over filling and seal edges together,
trim off excess dough, then finish rim. Bake in a hot oven (450° F.) 15
minutes, then reduce heat to moderate (350° F.) and bake 30 minutes
longer or until rhubarb is done. Remove to cake rack to cool. Serve warm
or cold. 5 servings.

660   FRESH STRAWBERRY PIE

1 quart strawberries   ⅓ cup corn starch
1 cup sugar   1 tablespoon lemon juice
Water   Baked 8-inch pie shell (631)

Wash and hull strawberries, picking over carefully to remove any imperfect ones. Add sugar and let stand overnight or at least 2 hours, cov-

ered. Drain off juice and add enough water to make up 1¾ cups liquid. Blend cornstarch to a paste with about ¼ cup of the liquid in top of double boiler, add rest of liquid and cook over direct heat with constant stirring until sauce boils and is clear. Place over boiling water, cover and cook 15 minutes longer. Remove from heat, add lemon juice, and fold in strawberries. Cool to lukewarm before pouring into baked pastry shell. Top may be decorated with cut-out pieces of pastry baked separately from the shells, or garnished with whipped cream. 5 servings.

661   STRAWBERRY WHIP PIE

1 pint strawberries	½ cup sugar
1 cup chilled whipping cream	Pinch salt
1½ tablespoons lemon juice	Baked 8-inch pie shell (631)

Wash and hull the strawberries then slice or cut in quarters. Save several perfect berries for garnish if desired. Just before serving, whip the cream in a chilled bowl with a chilled beater until stiff; add lemon juice, then beat in the sugar. Fold in the strawberries lightly and turn into the pie shell. Top with the selected whole berries. Serve at once. 5 servings.

CREAM PIES

662   BANANA CREAM PIE

5 tablespoons flour	½ teaspoon vanilla
½ cup sugar	2 or 3 well-ripened bananas
½ teaspoon salt	Baked 8-inch pie shell (631)
2 cups milk, scalded	¼ cup sugar
2 eggs, separated	

Mix flour, ½ cup sugar and salt in top of double boiler; slowly stir in hot milk and cook over direct heat until mixture boils and thickens, stirring constantly. Stir a little of the hot mixture into well-beaten egg yolks and pour back into double boiler. Place over boiling water and cook 2 minutes, stirring constantly. Remove from heat, add vanilla and cool until just warm. Peel bananas and slice into pie shell; pour cream mixture over them. Beat egg whites until stiff, gradually beat in the ¼ cup sugar until smooth and very stiff. Spread over pie to touch crust all around and place in a moderately hot oven (400° F.) about 8 minutes or until golden brown. Remove to cake rack to cool before cutting. 5 or 6 servings.

663
BUTTERMILK RAISIN PIE

¼ cup corn starch
1 cup sugar
¼ teaspoon salt
2 cups buttermilk
¼ cup moist raisins

2 tablespoons lemon juice
2 eggs, separated
1 tablespoon butter
Baked 8-inch pie shell (631)
¼ cup sugar

Mix corn starch, 1 cup sugar and salt in top of double boiler; add buttermilk, raisins and lemon juice and cook over direct heat, stirring constantly until mixture boils and thickens. Beat egg yolks until thick, stir in a little of the hot mixture, then pour back into top of double boiler. Place over boiling water and cook 2 minutes longer, continuing to stir. Remove from heat and stir in butter until melted. Cool slightly, then pour into cooled baked pie shell. Beat egg whites until stiff, then gradually beat in the ¼ cup sugar until meringue is very thick and smooth. Swirl meringue over pie filling, being sure it touches crust all around. Place in a moderate oven (350° F.) 12 to 15 minutes or until meringue is nicely toasted. Remove to cake rack to cool thoroughly before cutting. 5 or 6 servings.

664
BUTTERSCOTCH PIE

1 cup brown sugar, packed
3 tablespoons flour
1½ tablespoons corn starch
½ teaspoon salt
1½ cups scalded milk

3 eggs, separated
3 tablespoons butter
¾ teaspoon vanilla
Baked 8-inch pie shell (631)
½ cup whipping cream

Mix sugar, flour, cornstarch and salt thoroughly in top of double boiler. Add milk and stir until smooth; then place over boiling water and cook with frequent stirring for 15 minutes. Beat egg yolks thoroughly; stir in a little of the hot mixture, and pour back into double boiler. Cook 2 minutes longer, stirring constantly. Remove from heat, add butter and vanilla and stir until mixed. Cool. Beat egg whites until stiff, then fold into cooled mixture. Pour into cooled pie shell. Serve with whipped cream if desired. 5 or 6 servings.

665
CHOCOLATE PIE

2 squares baking chocolate
2 tablespoons butter
⅓ cup flour
1 cup sugar
¼ teaspoon salt
2½ cups milk, scalded

3 eggs, separated
¾ teaspoon vanilla
Baked 8-inch pie shell (631)
⅓ cup sugar
Chopped nuts, if desired

Melt chocolate and butter over hot water in top of double boiler. Mix flour, sugar and salt and stir into chocolate; add milk slowly and stir constantly until mixture is fully thickened, about 15 minutes. Beat egg yolks well, stir in a little of the chocolate mixture, then pour into rest of hot mixture and cook 2 minutes, stirring constantly. Remove from heat, cool partially and stir in vanilla. Pour into pie shell. Beat egg whites until stiff, then slowly beat in the ⅓ cup sugar until stiff. Swirl meringue over pie filling so it touches edges of crust all around. Sprinkle with chopped nuts, and place in a moderate oven (350° F.) 12 to 15 minutes, or until golden brown. Remove to cake rack to cool before cutting. 5 or 6 servings.

666   CREAM PIE

¼ cup flour	2 tablespoons butter
½ cup sugar	½ teaspoon vanilla
¼ teaspoon salt	6 tablespoons sugar
1½ cups scalded milk	Baked 8-inch pie shell (631)
3 eggs, separated	

Mix flour, ½ cup sugar and salt in top of double boiler; add scalded milk and stir well. Cook over direct heat until thick and smooth, stirring constantly. Beat egg yolks well, stir in a little of the hot mixture and pour back into double boiler; cook over boiling water 2 minutes, stirring constantly. Remove from heat and add butter and vanilla. Beat egg whites until light, and gradually beat in the 6 tablespoons sugar until stiff. Fold about ⅓ of the meringue into the cooled filling. Pour filling into cooled pie shell and spread remaining meringue over filling, so as to touch the edges of the crust all around. Place in a moderate oven (350° F.) and bake 12 to 15 minutes or until golden brown. Remove to cake rack to cool before cutting. 5 or 6 servings.

666a   COCOANUT CREAM PIE

Use recipe 666, folding ½ cup moist shredded cocoanut into the cooled filling just before folding in ⅓ of the meringue.

667   MERINGUE FOR ALL CREAM PIES

3 egg whites	6 tablespoons sugar
⅛ teaspoon salt	

Beat egg whites with salt until stiff enough to form soft, rounded peaks. Now add sugar gradually in portions of 1 tablespoon at a time, beating well after each addition. Continue beating until meringue is very thick and glossy. Spread meringue on the pie, so as to leave deep swirls on the top and to touch the rim of the crust all around. This prevents shrinking of the meringue. Bake in a moderate oven (350° F.) 12 to 15 minutes or a moderately hot oven (400° F.) 8 minutes, or until a delicate golden brown. Cool before cutting. This amount is sufficient for a 9-inch pie. For an 8-inch pie, 2 egg whites with a pinch of salt and 4 tablespoons sugar will be sufficient.

668 CREAM PUFFS

½ cup boiling water   ½ cup all-purpose flour
¼ cup butter   2 eggs

Pour boiling water over butter in a saucepan; bring to a boil and stir until butter melts. Now add flour all at once and stir constantly with a wooden spoon until the mixture leaves the sides of the pan and forms a ball. Remove from heat. Immediately add unbeaten eggs one at a time, beating to a smooth paste after each one. Then beat the mixture until smooth and velvety. Drop by heaping tablespoonfuls onto a greased baking sheet, keeping mounds uniform in shape and height, about 3 inches apart. Bake in a hot oven (450° F.) 15 minutes or until well puffed and delicately browned. Then reduce heat to slow (300° F.) and bake 30 to 40 minutes longer; this will bake the centers thoroughly, but puffs should become no browner. Remove to a cake rack to cool. When cold, cut off tops with a sharp knife. Fill with Cream Filling (669), thick Soft Custard (233), whipped cream or ice cream, and replace tops. 6 to 7 cream puffs.

Swan cream puffs: To make the swan neck and head, pipe the chou paste (cream puff mixture) through a large pastry tube, using a large star tube, onto the greased baking sheet in the shape of an S; for the tail, pipe a comma-shaped piece. Make one for each cream puff and remove from the oven after the first 15 minutes of baking. After filling the cream puffs, insert a head and a tail in each swan, cutting holes if necessary. The tops cut off to put in filling may be cut in half and stuck into the cream filling at an angle to simulate lifted wings.

668a ÉCLAIRS

Make just like Cream Puffs (668), except draw out the heaping tablespoonfuls of dough dropped onto the baking sheet into finger lengths. Bake, cool and fill as for Cream Puffs. Frost tops of filled éclairs with Dark Chocolate Frosting (138).

669   CREAM FILLING FOR CREAM PUFFS

½ cup sugar
¼ cup flour
½ teaspoon salt
1½ cups milk, scalded

1 egg, beaten
1½ tablespoons butter
¾ teaspoon vanilla *or* ½
teaspoon lemon extract

Mix sugar, flour and salt in top of double boiler. Gradually stir in the hot milk and cook over direct heat until thickened, stirring constantly. Stir a little of the hot mixture into the beaten egg; return this to rest of mixture and place over boiling water, stirring constantly for 2 minutes. Remove from heat, stir in flavoring and cool. Fill into cream puffs or éclairs. For best flavor and crispness, filled cream puffs or éclairs should be served the same day they are baked, and the filled puffs should be kept in refrigerator. Enough filling for 5 good-sized cream puffs.

670   LEMON PIE

⅓ cup corn starch
1¼ cups sugar
¼ teaspoon salt
1½ cups boiling water
3 eggs, separated

⅓ cup strained lemon juice
2 tablespoons butter
½ teaspoon grated lemon rind
Baked 8-inch pie shell (631)
6 tablespoons sugar

Mix corn starch, sugar and salt in top of double boiler; add boiling water and blend thoroughly. Cook over direct heat, stirring constantly until mixture is thick and clear. Beat egg yolks and stir in a little of the hot mixture; pour back into double boiler and cook 2 minutes longer with constant stirring. Remove from heat; add lemon juice, butter and lemon rind, mixing well. Cool and pour into cooled pie shell. Beat egg whites until barely stiff, add the 6 tablespoons sugar gradually and again beat until stiff. Swirl over pie filling so as to touch edges of crust all around. Place in a moderate oven (350° F.) 12 to 15 minutes or until golden brown. Remove to cake rack to cool before cutting. 5 or 6 servings.

671   LEMON CREAM TARTS

1 cup sugar
⅓ cup flour
¼ teaspoon salt
1½ cups milk
2 eggs, separated

1 tablespoon butter
⅓ cup lemon juice
1 teaspoon grated lemon rind
5 baked tart shells (631)

Mix 1 cup of the sugar with flour and salt; stir in milk until smooth. Cook over direct heat, stirring constantly until mixture boils and thickens. Slowly stir some of the hot mixture into beaten egg yolks, then return to pan; cook 2 minutes longer, stirring constantly. Remove from heat and stir in butter, lemon juice and rind. Cool and pour into cooled tart shells. Beat egg whites until stiff and gradually beat in remaining sugar. Spread over tarts and brown in a moderate oven (350° F.) 12 to 15 minutes or until golden brown. 5 servings.

672   LEMON GINGER CRUSTED PIE

¼ lb. gingersnaps, rolled   1½ cups cold water
  (1¼ cups fine crumbs)   3 eggs, separated
¼ cup soft butter   ¼ cup lemon juice
1 cup sugar   1 teaspoon grated lemon rind
½ cup all-purpose flour   1 tablespoon butter
⅛ teaspoon salt   ⅓ cup sugar

Mix the gingersnap crumbs and butter well, then pat them over bottom and sides of an 8-inch pie pan in a uniform thick layer. Chill. Combine 1 cup sugar, flour and salt in top of double boiler; add water and stir until blended, then cook over direct heat, stirring constantly until mixture boils and thickens. Remove from heat and stir a little of this mixture into the well-beaten egg yolks; add lemon juice, then stir into hot mixture, add lemon rind and replace over boiling water and cook 2 minutes, stirring constantly. Remove from heat, add the 1 tablespoon butter. Cool and pour into chilled crust. Beat egg whites until stiff, then slowly beat in the ⅓ cup sugar until meringue is stiff. Spread over top of pie, touching edges all around. Place in a moderate oven (350° F.) 12 to 15 minutes, or until meringue is nicely browned. Remove to cake rack to cool before cutting. 5 or 6 servings.

673   NUT PIE

1 cup brown sugar, packed   ½ teaspoon vanilla
⅓ cup flour   ½ cup chopped nuts
2 cups milk, scalded   Baked 8-inch pie shell (631)
2 tablespoons butter   ¼ cup granulated sugar
¼ teaspoon salt   Pinch salt
2 eggs, separated

Blend brown sugar and flour in a 3-qt. saucepan, then stir in scalded milk, butter and salt. Bring to boil, then cook slowly over direct heat 5 minutes, stirring constantly. Remove from heat and stir some of the hot mixture into the well-beaten egg yolks, then return to heat and cook 2 minutes longer, stirring constantly. Remove from heat, stir in vanilla and nuts. Cool slightly, then turn into cooled baked pie shell. Beat egg whites until stiff, then beat in granulated sugar and salt until stiff. Pipe this meringue over filling in lattice-fashion, or spread it on so it touches sides of crust all around. Place in a moderate oven (350° F.) 12 to 15 minutes or until meringue is nicely browned. Remove to cake rack to cool before serving. 5 to 6 servings.

674   DRIED PEACH CREAM PIE

½ lb. dried peaches	1½ cups milk
1¼ cups water	2 eggs, beaten
2 tablespoons corn starch	⅛ teaspoon almond extract
½ cup sugar	Baked 8-inch pie shell (631)
¼ teaspoon salt	

Wash peaches thoroughly, barely cover with water and simmer until perfectly tender, about 45 minutes. Drain, saving water. Mash peaches and cool. Mix corn starch, sugar and salt in top of double boiler; add milk and ½ cup of the cooking water, place over boiling water and stir until mixture is thickened; cover and continue cooking for 20 minutes. Stir a little of the hot mixture into the beaten eggs, then return to remainder of mixture in double boiler; cook about 2 minutes longer, stirring constantly. Fold in peach pulp and let cool. Stir in almond extract. Turn mixture into the cooled baked pie shell. Cool on a cake rack. Serve cold. If desired, eggs may be separated and whites beaten with 4 tablespoons sugar for a meringue. 5 servings.

675   SOUR CREAM PRUNE PIE

½ lb. dried prunes	2 eggs
1 cup boiling water	1 cup sour cream
¾ cup sugar	2 tablespoons lemon juice
2 tablespoons corn starch	Baked 8-inch pie shell (631)

Cut prunes from stones in small pieces, using scissors. Put into top of double boiler with the boiling water and heat until prunes are softened, 10 to 15 minutes. Mix sugar and corn starch and add to prunes; cook over boiling water 15 minutes, stirring frequently. Beat eggs, add sour cream and beat just enough to blend well. Pour into prune mixture and cook 6 to 8 minutes longer, stirring constantly. Remove from heat and stir in lemon juice. Pour into baked pie shell and cool before cutting. 5 or 6 servings.

676   CHESS PIE

1 cup soft butter	⅛ teaspoon salt
2 cups sugar	½ teaspoon vanilla
5 eggs, separated	Plain pastry (631)

Cream butter until smooth, add sugar and cream well. Add egg yolks and mix well. Fold in 2 egg whites beaten until stiff with salt and vanilla. Turn into an 8-inch pie pan lined with plain pastry. Bake in a moderately hot oven (425° F.) 12 minutes; now decrease heat to slow (300° F.) and bake about 20 minutes longer. Spread with meringue made from the 3 remaining egg whites beaten stiff then 6 tablespoons sugar gradually beaten into them. Bake in a moderate oven (350° F.) 12 to 15 minutes or until meringue is delicately browned. This is a very rich and a very delicious pie. 6 to 8 servings.

CUSTARD PIES

677   **CUSTARD PIE**

Plain pastry for single crust (631)
3 eggs
6 to 8 tablespoons sugar
¼ teaspoon salt
3 cups milk, scalded
½ teaspoon vanilla
Nutmeg

Roll pastry a little less than ⅛-inch thick and fit carefully into an 8-inch pie pan. Trim and flute edges; do not prick. Beat eggs slightly, just enough to mix yolks and whites; add sugar and salt. Stir in milk, then add flavoring. Pour immediately into the pastry-lined pan. Bake in a moderately hot oven (425° F.) 12 to 15 minutes or until crust browns; then reduce heat to slow (300° F.) and bake 25 to 30 minutes longer or until pie is coagulated to within ½-inch from center. Test this by gently shaking pie. You can see how much of the center is still liquid. An inch of liquid area in center will finish cooking after pie is removed from oven. Remove to cake rack to cool before serving. 5 or 6 servings.

Note: Correctly baked custard pie is never "weepy" but has a perfectly coagulated, jelly-like consistency.

678   **PEACH BLOSSOM PIE**

3 or 4 peaches, depending on size
Unbaked 9-inch pastry shell (631), chilled
2 eggs, beaten
1 cup milk
¾ cup sugar
1 tablespoon flour
Pinch salt
Few drops almond extract, if desired

Pare peaches, cut in halves and remove pits. Arrange, cut-side-up, in the unbaked pie shell. Beat eggs well, add milk and stir in sugar, flour and salt which have been mixed together; add the almond extract if it is used. Pour over the peach halves. Bake in a moderately hot (400° F.) oven 10 minutes; then reduce heat to moderately slow (325° F.) and continue baking 30 to 40 minutes longer or until a sharp knife inserted in the custard comes out clean. Remove to cake rack to cool. Serve warm or cold, with whipped cream if desired. 5 or 6 servings.

679 PUMPKIN PIE No. 1

1¾ cups canned pumpkin
¾ cup granulated sugar
½ teaspoon salt
1 teaspoon cinnamon
½ teaspoon ginger

2 eggs
1 cup evaporated milk
½ cup water
Unbaked 9-inch pastry shell (631)

Turn pumpkin into saucepan and cook over direct heat 10 minutes, until somewhat dry and slightly caramelized, stirring constantly. Remove from heat. Blend the sugar, salt and spices and stir into hot pumpkin. Beat eggs, add evaporated milk and water, and beat into pumpkin mixture until smooth. Pour into pastry-lined pie pan and bake in a hot oven (450° F.) 15 minutes; then reduce heat to slow (300° F.) and continue baking about 45 minutes longer, or until pie tests done. See test for custard pie. Cool before serving. 6 servings.

Note: Perfectly baked pumpkin pie has no wrinkles or cracks on its surface. Long slow baking produces a smooth, shiny surface with the true golden pumpkin color.

680 PUMPKIN PIE No. 2

1 No. 2 can pumpkin
4 eggs
1½ cups brown sugar, packed
1⅔ cups evaporated milk
1½ teaspoons ginger
1½ teaspoons cinnamon

2 tablespoons boiling water
¼ cup orange juice
1 teaspoon salt
2 unbaked 8-inch pie shells (631)

Turn pumpkin into saucepan and stir over direct heat until pumpkin is somewhat dried out and has a slightly caramelized appearance, 10 minutes. Beat eggs in mixing bowl, blend in sugar, and add evaporated milk and spices which have been mixed to a paste with the boiling water. Stir well. Add pumpkin, orange juice and salt and mix thoroughly. Pour into the unbaked pastry shells. Bake in a hot oven (450° F.) about 15 minutes until pastry edges are lightly browned, then reduce heat to 300° F. (slow) and continue baking until custard tests done, about 45 minutes longer. See test for custard pie. Remove to cake rack to cool before cutting. 2 pies—12 servings.

681   LIME PIE

1¼ cups granulated sugar   Grated rind of 1½ limes
⅓ cup corn starch   1 tablespoon butter
1½ cups boiling water   1 drop green food color
3 eggs, separated   6 tablespoons granulated sugar
⅓ cup lime juice and pulp,   8″ baked pie shell, cooled
   about 2 medium limes

Mix sugar and corn starch together in saucepan. Add water, stirring constantly to prevent lumps. Cook until mixture is thick and clear, about 1 minute, stirring constantly. Blend part of hot mixture into beaten egg yolks, then return to hot mixture in pan and cook a minute longer over low heat, stirring well. Remove from heat, add juice, rind, butter and coloring. Cool thoroughly, stirring occasionally. Then turn into pie shell. Beat whites until stiff, but not dry, add the 6 tablespoons sugar gradually, beating well after each addition. Swirl over pie filling being sure to touch crust all around. Bake at 375° F. 12 minutes. Remove to cake rack to cool. 6 servings.

CHIFFON PIES

682   APRICOT CHIFFON PIE

½ lb. dried apricots   2 tablespoons lemon juice
1½ cups water   ⅛ teaspoon salt
2 teaspoons gelatin   4 drops almond extract, if
4 eggs, separated   desired
¾ cup sugar   9-inch baked pastry shell

Soak washed apricots in the water for 1 hour, then cover and simmer in the same water for about 10 minutes or until very tender. Rub apricots and juice through a sieve, using a wooden spoon. Soften gelatin in 2 tablespoons cold water. Beat egg yolks in top of double boiler, add ¼ cup of the sugar, the lemon juice, salt and apricot purée. Cook over boiling water, stirring constantly until mixture just thickens, about 5 minutes. Add softened gelatin and stir until dissolved. Cool until thick and syrupy. Beat egg whites until stiff, then gradually beat in remaining ½ cup sugar, and the flavoring. Fold meringue thoroughly into cooled apricot mixture and pour into cooled baked pastry shell. Chill in refrigerator until set before serving. Serve with whipped cream, if desired. 6 servings.

683   CHERRY CHIFFON PIE

1 No. 2 can red cherries, packed in syrup	1 tablespoon lemon juice
1 tablespoon gelatin	½ cup sugar
4 eggs, separated	⅛ teaspoon salt
	Baked 8-inch pie shell (631)

Drain cherries, saving juice. Soften gelatin in ¼ cup of the juice. Chop the cherries fine. Beat egg yolks and add rest of cherry juice, lemon juice and half the sugar. Cook over boiling water, stirring constantly until just thickened. Remove from heat, add gelatin and stir until dissolved. Stir in cherries. Chill until mixture begins to set. Beat egg whites with salt until foamy, add remaining sugar and beat until very stiff and smooth. Fold into cherry mixture and turn into cooled pastry shell. Chill in refrigerator until firm. Serve with whipped cream, if desired. Serves 5 or 6.

684   LEMON CHIFFON PIE

1½ teaspoons gelatin	Dash salt
⅓ cup cold water	4 eggs, separated
1 cup sugar	Cooled baked 8-inch pastry shell (631)
3 tablespoons lemon juice	
Grated rind of 1 lemon	

Soften gelatin in 2 tablespoons of the cold water. Add rest of water, ½ cup of the sugar, lemon juice, rind and salt to the beaten egg yolks, and cook over boiling water, stirring constantly until just thickened. Stir in gelatin until dissolved. Cool until syrupy. Beat egg whites until stiff, gradually beat in rest of sugar until thick and smooth, then fold into cooled lemon mixture. Turn into pie shell and chill until firm. Spread with whipped cream, if desired. Serves 5 to 6.

POLTRY

HOW long do you need to cook the Thanksgiving turkey this year? Here's a way to find out for yourself, with no ifs or buts: Just simmer the giblets a day ahead of time, note how long the gizzard takes to become tender and add one hour—and that's the length of time your turkey should be roasted! After learning this and becoming familiar with other information in this chapter, you'll feel as much at home with a chicken or a turkey as though you had spent your life on a poultry farm, and your poultry dealer will regard you with new respect.

When turkey, goose, duck or chicken appears on the dinner table, it usually marks a special occasion or a special guest in most American homes. Because something extra is expected of poultry in the way of appearance and flavor, it is important to know how to choose, prepare and serve it in a way that will give maximum satisfaction.

Choosing the poultry is of first importance. The quality of the bird that comes to the table depends on the quality of the bird purchased, as well as on the homemaker's skill in preparing it. In buying a bird, the homemaker should insist on prime quality, and should know how to recognize this quality; only in this way can she avoid the disappointments which result from choosing inferior grade poultry.

High quality in poultry is easily detected: (1) The birds should be well-shaped with broad, full-fleshed breasts. (2) They should have creamy white or yellowish skin which is soft and slightly waxy to the touch. (3) There should be few, if any, bruises. (4) There should be no tears in the skin on the breast. (5) There should be no tears in the skin on the back that are not sewed up. (6) There should be no broken wings or legs. (7) There should be practically no pinfeathers. The highest grade poultry, U. S. Special or U. S. Grade AA, permits absolutely no pinfeathers or down to be left on the bird, and no tears nor bruises anywhere. If a bird falls short of these standards, it may still make good eating, but its quality is less dependable.

The quality of the dressed bird is largely the result of the care and feeding of the live bird. To develop a tender, meaty, sweet-flavored bird, a good diet and regular feeding are important. Poultry raisers and packers are becoming more and more careful to feed their birds all their lives a diet which will insure good flavor in the meat. In addition, the practice of confining the birds a week before slaughter to finish-feed them is becoming common. The effect of this is the same as that of "finishing" steers and other meat animals by a similar method; it improves flavor and results in a "marbling" of fat through the lean meat of the poultry. Prime quality poultry is always fed in this manner.

Poultry may be purchased in several ways: NEW YORK DRESSED poultry have the feathers removed but are not drawn. They are then frozen and are sent to the dealer frozen. Before being sold to the consumer, the dealer will defrost the bird under sanitary conditions, and it may or may not be drawn before it is sold.

FRESH FROZEN FULL-DRAWN poultry is fully drawn before freezing. It requires no further preparation by the dealer before selling it to the consumer other than defrosting it under sanitary conditions. This form of poultry is desirable because it makes possible the careful inspection of viscera before freezing. However, if evisceration is carelessly done, there is danger of contamination.

LIVE POULTRY also is sold in many communities. The consumer may choose her chicken "on the hoof" and have it dressed and drawn or not according to the practice of the dealer or the preference of the consumer. When purchasing live poultry, it should be remembered that the finest flavor and tenderness are produced by ageing the birds 48 hours after slaughter, including at least 36 hours of chilling. For these reasons poultry should never be cooked until at least 8 hours after slaughter.

It is now possible to buy cut-up chicken or turkey instead of purchasing a whole chicken, homemakers can go to many meat markets and buy a pound of chicken breasts or a pound of drumsticks, or even a pound of necks or backs, from which chicken soup or stock may be made. These pieces in almost all cases are from chickens of prime quality, and the price per pound varies according to the pieces selected. In this way it is possible to serve just the parts of the bird which the family likes, without waste and with the utmost convenience. Although chicken in this form is not available everywhere, the supply is growing rapidly with the growing demand.

The homemaker who wishes to draw (eviscerate) poultry at home should make a point to see it done by some skilled person, for this is the best way of learning good technique. Subsequently, practice will increase her own skill. There are several important points to remember in drawing any kind of poultry:

1.   If possible have the neck cut just below the head; then slit the neck skin down the *back*, and cut the neck out close to the body. The crop and windpipe should be removed from this end. Slitting the skin in the back rather than the front leaves the skin of the upper breast intact. The neck

skin may then be drawn back after stuffing and trussing, and tucked firmly under the folded wingtips.

2. Remove the viscera from the other end, and endeavor to remove them intact. This avoids the necessity of much washing to clean out the cavity. The incision should be made as small as possible, along the line from just below the end of the breast-bone to the vent, and should penetrate the body fat without cutting the intestinal tract. The vent should not be cut. After the intestines have been lifted out through this incision, cut *around* the vent. Then locate the gizzard at the right side of the body cavity and grasping it firmly, pull steadily until all the entrails come out intact.

3. Remove the oil sac at the base of the tail in the back by cutting under it toward the point of the tail.

4. Wash the bird inside and out with warm water. Soapy water may be used on the outside if desired, but must be thoroughly rinsed off. Rubbing with soda and then rinsing thoroughly is a good practice if the skin is much soiled, or if the viscera have broken in the process of removal. Drain the cavities well before stuffing. A chicken which is to be fried, stewed or braised should be washed thoroughly inside and out *before* disjointing or cutting up, and *not* afterwards, as flavor is lost through the many cut surfaces.

DIRECTIONS FOR TRUSSING POULTRY FOR ROASTING

A sturdy needle and a strong slender cord about a yard long are the only equipment required for trussing. A heavy darning needle may be used, but an upholsterer's needle, 6 to 8 inches long, is even more convenient. Special trussing needles are also available at most department stores.

1. Lay the unstuffed bird on its back with the tail to your right. Lift the legs so the drumsticks make right angles with the body, and insert the needle, guiding it to come out at the corresponding place on the opposite side. Leave an end of string several inches long.

2. Fold the wings so the tips lie under the back, turn the bird around. Insert the threaded needle down through the angle formed by the wing at your right; then across the back and up through the angle of the other wing. Cut the cord, leaving a long end.

3. Tie to other end of string at the side of the bird; draw the cord up snugly so as to bring the thighs close to the breast, and tie a secure knot. The body cavity may be stuffed at this point, if a stuffing is being used. Lace opening together using strong tooth picks or small skewers and twine.

4. Next insert the threaded needle between the tendons at the ends of the drumsticks, and continue with the same cord. . . .

5.   Through the flesh behind the tail, at the point where the oil sac was removed. Remove the needle and draw the cord up tight so the drumsticks fit snugly against the body and the ends of the bones close to the tail, thus closing the vent opening.

6.   Now insert more dressing (if stuffing is used) through the neck opening, using enough to round out the breast nicely.

7.   Fold neck skin to the back and tuck it under the cord and the wing tips. Fasten it securely to the back with small skewers.

8.   The stuffed and trussed bird, ready for the oven, makes a neat, compact parcel with a minimum of protruding parts to become overbrowned.

For quick removal of the trussing cords before the bird is served, cut the cord opposite the knot and pull it out by the knot.

KINDS OF POULTRY

Poultry, though it is one of the most luxurious of meats, is rapidly getting out of the luxury class as to price, because it is being produced in increasingly large quantities and on a highly scientific and economical basis. Ducks and geese are the least expensive kinds of poultry with turkey next, and chicken most expensive in proportion to the yield in edible meat.

TURKEY was formerly considered expensive because only large birds were available, and these only at certain seasons, which meant that the initial cost was high. Now turkey is available all the year around, which is one reason why it is becoming more and more inexpensive. Another reason is that producers are developing smaller birds, suitable for smaller families with less money to lay out on a single item. A small (10-pound) bird will serve a family of 5 generously at two meals—with hot sliced roast turkey one day and turkey hash or turnovers the next—and the carcass will still remain to make a delicious turkey soup. A hen turkey has more meat in proportion to its weight than does a tom, because of its thick plump breast. But hen turkeys seldom weigh more than 13 or 14 pounds, so for a large group, a tom turkey or 2 small hen turkeys should be purchased.

In families where turkey is served but once or twice a year, Thanksgiving often brings a flurry of trying to remember how long to cook the holiday bird. It is difficult to state the time exactly, because that depends not only on the size but on the age of the turkey. The simplest and most dependable way of determining the correct roasting time for your particular bird is to do a little experimental work of your own.

At the time when the turkey is being prepared for roasting, probably the day before the great day, clean the giblets (neck, liver, heart and gizzard) and put the neck, gizzard and heart into a saucepan. Cover it with cold water, heat to boiling, then cover pan closely and reduce to a simmer. Cook until gizzard is so tender it can be pierced with a fork as easily as cold mush; this usually takes 3 to 4 hours. The liver cooks done in 10 minutes or less, so it should be put in when the gizzard is nearly done. Note how long it took to cook the gizzard thoroughly tender, and add one hour to this time to determine the correct roasting time for your turkey. Transfer the cooled giblets and cooking water to a bowl, cover and place in refrigerator. Use the broth to make gravy, and chop the giblets to add to the gravy when it is ready to serve.

Turkey should be put into the roasting pan breast-side-down, and cooked in that position for half the time allowed, then turned and finished on its back. It should be cooked uncovered, with no water, in a moderate to slow oven (350-300° F.); the larger the bird, the lower the oven temperature should be. Occasional basting will prevent the skin from becoming too dry and will improve the texture and quality of the meat as well as the appearance of the bird. Basting poultry means brushing with melted fat from time to time. If browning is too rapid, cover the breast with several folds of brown paper, paper toweling, or better still, a piece of aluminum foil fastened down with one or two tooth picks or pins stuck through into the crop stuffing; paper may also be laid over the breast bone, and finally the crop, breast and thighs may all be covered with pieces of paper or foil, then with a cloth dipped in melted fat. Basting may be done through paper coverings but foil must be removed for basting.

TABLE 16. TIME FOR ROASTING TURKEY

Weight ready for oven*	Oven temp.	Cooking time minutes per lb.	Total cooking time
8 to 10 lbs.	325° F.	25 to 20	3 to 3½ hrs.
10 to 14 lbs.	325° F.	20 to 18	3½ to 4 hrs.
14 to 18 lbs.	300° F.	18 to 15	4 to 4½ hrs.
18 lbs.	300° F.	15 to 13	4½ to 5 hrs.
20 lbs.	300° F.	15 to 13	5 to 6 hrs.

*If the stuffed weight cannot be ascertained, the Dressed weight (feathers removed but not drawn) may be used instead, in calculating the roasting time.

Turkey (also other poultry) may be roasted without stuffing, in which case the cooking time will be a little less per pound than that suggested in the above table.

When the turkey is nearly done, according to your time calculation, test it for doneness by this method: Move the leg by grasping the end bone; if the joint moves easily, the ligaments are tender and the meat is done. Another way of testing whether the bird is done is with a roast meat thermometer. If the thermometer is inserted in the thickest part of the thigh muscle, it should register 190° F. when the turkey is done; if inserted in the center of the stuffing, 180°.

Any meat which remains on the carcass after the first meal should be stripped off immediately, cooled, then placed in a covered dish in the refrigerator. Bones should be cracked and placed in another covered container. If the whole carcass, uncovered, is left in the refrigerator overnight or longer, the flavor may be impaired by the absorption of flavor from other foods.

CHICKENS of various ages fall into various types, and each type responds best to certain ways of cooking. It is important to know these types in order to obtain the best results and the greatest value for your money.

A chicken which makes a delicious fricassee is almost sure to be very unsatisfactory for roasting.

TABLE 17. PURCHASING AND COOKING GUIDE FOR CHICKEN

Market types	Approximate size—sex	Characteristics	Quantity to buy per person	Method of cooking
broiler	1 to 2½ lbs. (either sex)	Young, soft-meated, tender. 8 to 12 weeks old.	¼ to ½ bird	roasting frying broiling
fryer	2½ to 3½ lbs. (male)	Differs from above only in size and age. 14 to 20 weeks.	¾ to 1 lb.	roasting frying
roaster	Over 3½ lbs. (male)	Tender, soft-meated, keel bone flexible. 5 to 9 months.	½ to ¾ lb.	roasting frying fricasseeing à la king
capon	4 lbs. and over (unsexed male)	Tender, soft-meated, usually 7 to 10 months.	½ to ¾ lb.	roasting
pullet	2½ to 5½ lbs. (young hen)	Tender, keel bone flexible. 4 to 9 months.	¼ to 1 lb. (depending on method of cooking)	frying roasting braising
fowl	2½ lbs. and over (female —"old hen")	Less tender, keel bone hard. 1 year or over.	¼ to ¾ lb.	fricasseeing soup making steaming stewing
cock	3 to 6 lbs. (male)	Darkened and toughened flesh. 1 year or over.	¼ to ¾ lb.	simmering chiefly soup

It is never wise to order a chicken by the common market term—"fryer," "roaster," etc.—and accept sight unseen the bird the dealer supplies. For complete satisfaction, the homemaker should make it a habit to pick out her bird according to the suggestions at the beginning of this chapter.

For roasting, chicken is stuffed, trussed and cooked much like turkey. The oven temperature should be moderately low (325-350° F.), and the time will be about 45 minutes per pound for small or up to 3½-pound birds and 30 to 40 minutes for 4 to 6-pound birds. The weight referred to is the weight of the stuffed, trussed bird; but if no kitchen scale is available, the drawn weight plus the estimated weight of the stuffing may be used for the calculation. Good-sized, young chickens (under one year) may be roasted throughout in an uncovered pan, but small birds (1½ to 3½ pounds) are best if cooked covered during the first half of the cooking time. For all sizes, it is recommended that the bird be placed breast side down during half the total cooking time; then turned on the back to finish roasting. Like turkey, chicken should be basted, and this may be done through a cloth laid over the breast and drumsticks to prevent too much or too rapid browning.

TABLE 18. TIME-TABLE FOR ROASTING CHICKEN

Weight ready for oven	Oven temp.	Cooking time minutes per lb.	Total cooking time
3½ to 4 lbs.	350° F.	45 to 40*	2 to 2¾ hrs.
4 to 5 lbs.	350° F.	40 to 35*	2½ to 3 hrs.
Over 5 lbs.	325° F.	35 to 30*	3 to 3½ hrs.

*Shorter time per lb. for the larger size in each case.

Chicken in contrast with other poultry is cooked in many ways other than roasting. Other favored methods are frying, fricasseeing (braising), broiling and stewing.

For frying, the cleaned chicken is cut into serving-size pieces. For very small chickens (1 to 1½ pounds), this may mean splitting once lengthwise; larger birds (up to 5 pounds) are usually disjointed and divided into a number of pieces.† The pieces should be thoroughly dried to avoid spattering when they are placed in the hot fat, and then coated with any desired coating

†Chicken for frying is usually cut into 11 pieces: 2 drumsticks; 2 thighs or second joints; 2 wings; 2 pieces of back—the tail piece, familiarly known as "the part that went over the fence last," and the rib piece, or "straw bonnet"; 2 pieces of breast— one containing the wish bone and the other the keel bone; and the neck, which for frying should be cut off with the skin attached. (If more pieces of breast meat are desired, the two large breast pieces may be cut in two with kitchen shears *after* frying.) In cutting up the frying chicken, be sure the skin belonging to each piece is left attached to that piece, both for better appearance when fried, and in order that the layer of fat immediately under the skin may be present to give flavor to the meat.

(flour, cracker crumbs, bread crumbs, corn meal and flour, etc., mixed with salt). This is easily done by putting the flour or other material into a clean paper bag, dropping the pieces in one by one and shaking thoroughly. Occasionally a family will prefer to prepare the chicken by dipping into a fritter batter before frying; this gives quite a different product. The pieces may be fried with no coating if preferred.

Have a thin layer of fat—butter, margarine or shortening, or a combination of two of them—heated in a heavy skillet. For butter flavor about ⅓ of the fat should be butter. Start cooking the thick meaty pieces first with the fat fairly hot, as the fat is absorbed, more may be added. When all the pieces are golden brown on all sides, reduce heat to moderately low, then continue cooking until the meat is well done, 20 minutes to 1 hour, depending on size and age of chicken.

When good-sized chickens are fried, the pan may be covered tightly after browning the pieces. Some prefer to add a small amount of water after browning, cover the skillet, and let the chicken simmer until the water has evaporated. Then uncover the pan and continue cooking until the crust is again crisp. This is really a form of fricasseeing, since no liquid is used in true frying or pan-frying.

By definition, fricasseeing means browning the meat in a small quantity of fat, then cooking slowly until tender in the meat juice or in some added liquid, such as milk, cream, vegetable juice or water, with the pan tightly covered. This may be done in a moderate oven rather than on top of the stove. Fricasseeing, like stewing and simmering, is a moist-heat method suitable for larger and less tender chickens.

Stewing differs from fricasseeing in that the chicken is cooked in water throughout, and not previously browned in fat. A large or small amount of water may be used according to the way of serving, and the chicken may be disjointed or left whole. The entire cooking should be done at simmering temperature, and cooking prolonged until the meat is so tender that it begins to fall away from the bones. The meat will be juicier and more flavorful if, when it is to be served cold (as for salad or sandwiches), the meat is removed from the broth so both may cool quickly, and then returned to the cooled broth and stored in the refrigerator until ready to use it. If more white meat is desired, as for chicken á la king, wrap the bird in 2 or 3 thicknesses of clean cheesecloth when it is put on to simmer; this will make the meat of thighs and drumsticks almost as light as breast meat.

Broiling is another dry-heat method, and used only for very young, small birds. To broil is to cook by direct radiant heat from hot coals, or under a gas flame or electric heating element. For broiling, the cleaned chicken is usually split in halves lengthwise. The time for a split chicken will be 45 minutes to 1 hour altogether: 10 to 12 minutes on each side to brown delicately, repeated until well browned on both sides, and perfectly tender. The broiling rack should be about 5 inches below the flame or heating ele-

Did you know that turkey is fast scrambling down out of the luxury class? Now-adays almost everyone can manage it for Thanksgiving, and if you want it for cold-slicing in the middle of summer, it's available then too. Here is the holiday bird (695) with homemade frills made out of small paper doilies. Corn-on-the-cob, fresh or frozen, adds a glamour touch to the meal.

© Poultry and Egg National Board.

Roast Chicken **(687)** *makes any day a holiday, and like turkey, it's becoming steadily less of a luxury. Small, whole white turnips, cooked, then scooped out to make nests for buttered green peas make a fetching garnish and a pleasing vegetable dish.*

Some ham sandwiches are just that, but these are four ham sandwiches (859, 860, 861 and 862) with imagination. Substantial and full of flavor, they combine ham with sliced bananas, big flakes of tuna, sliced cranberry jelly and cheese, and Swiss cheese, tomato, and bacon.

All of these tantalizing appetizers are made with cream cheese or sieved dry cottage cheese moistened with sweet or sour cream or salad dressing. Try these variations:

1. *Moisten either kind of cheese with cream, season with salt, sugar and cinnamon. Form into tiny balls, then toss in fine-chopped mint or nuts.*
2. *Moisten with salad dressing, season with salt and onion juice. Form into balls and roll in chopped parsley or fine-shredded carrot. Chill balls, then stick on picks and stick in chick.*
3. *Instead of making balls, spread mixture on neat slices of dried beef, roll up and fasten with picks. Or pile mixture in light heaps in center of big potato chips. Or stuff a sweet mixture into pitted dates or half-cooked dried pitted prunes. Or use as a filling for Ribbon Sandwiches* **(900a)**, *or pile on crisp wafers or toast squares.*

ment, and the chicken should be brushed several times during the broiling process with melted butter.

Duck and goose differ considerably from both turkey and chicken, not only in shape but in fatness. They may be stuffed or not as desired. Plain fruit stuffings, such as pared sliced apples, soaked dried prunes, or a combination of the two; plain rice or mashed potatoes; celery or plain sauerkraut, are often used for duck and goose, as well as bread stuffings.

Because the birds are very fat, they are efficient self-basters and no extra basting is necessary in roasting them. The fat should be poured out of the roasting pan once or twice as it collects to keep it clear and light-colored. Goose and duck fat are very desirable for pan-frying or sautéing foods, such as potatoes and onions, and goose fat is sometimes used for cookies.

The oven temperature for goose and duck, as for turkey and chicken, should be moderate, about 325-350° F. Place the stuffed bird breast-side-up on a rack in an open roaster (because of their fatness it is not necessary to cook them breast-side-down), and cook until tender, allowing 20 minutes per pound for duck and 25 to 30 minutes for goose.

Both duck and goose are occasionally cooked by fricasseeing or braising, but are not fried, and are seldom stewed.

Guineas have been something of a rarity in the past, and breast of guinea hen was considered to be a great delicacy. Now the distinctive wild flavor of this small, compact bird is becoming more popular and the supply is increasing. The breast is the meatiest part of the bird, and since the hen has the plumpest breast, the guinea hen is most prized for cooking.

Young guinea hen may be roasted like chicken. The cavity should be rubbed with butter, salt and pepper and filled with stuffing; or with one onion, one carrot and one branch of celery. Then the bird is trussed and placed breast down on a rack in an open roaster, with strips of fat salt pork or bacon over the back. When half done, the bird is turned over and the salt pork transferred to the breast. The oven temperature should be moderate (350° F.) and 20 minutes per pound should be allowed if the bird has only the vegetable stuffing; if a bread stuffing is used, increase the time about 5 minutes per pound.

The breast alone may be dipped in seasoned flour and pan-fried in chicken or bacon fat or butter; then served with a cream gravy. When this is done, the rest of the guinea may be simmered in a small amount of water and served as stew with drop dumplings or noodles.

685   BRAISED CHICKEN

4 to 5-lb. roasting chicken	¼ to ⅓ cup butter or
½ cup flour	shortening
2½ teaspoons salt	½ cup water
Dash pepper	

Clean chicken by singeing, then rub with soda, wash thoroughly and draw (page 402). Cut into serving pieces, drain well. Roll in flour seasoned with salt and pepper. Brown chicken well in hot fat, in a heavy skillet or Dutch oven which may be tightly covered. Add ½ cup water, cover and simmer gently until chicken is tender, from 45 to 60 minutes depending on age of fowl. If any steam escapes during cooking period water should be added as necessary. 5 generous servings.

686   FRIED CHICKEN

Select a 3 to 4-pound frying chicken. Clean, draw (page 402), cut into serving pieces (see Note, page 407), and coat with salted flour (1 teaspoon salt to ⅓ cup flour). In a heavy deep skillet or chicken fryer, heat enough shortening to make a layer ¼-inch deep. If a butter flavor is desired, at least ⅓ should be butter. Start cooking in fairly hot fat, placing the thick meaty pieces in first, then the bonier pieces. Fry moderately fast until browned on both sides, then reduce to low heat and continue frying very slowly until done, turning once or twice. If gizzard and heart are to be fried, they should be simmered in water until almost tender before frying; liver will fry in a few minutes without previous cooking. Make gravy (468) from fat left in pan. 5 servings.

Some prefer to cover the skillet, sometimes adding water after the first browning. This method is especially good with larger chickens which may be less tender, but it is actually fricasseeing (690) rather than true frying.

687   ROAST CHICKEN

Choose a nice plump 4½ to 5½-pound roasting chicken. Singe; then thoroughly clean and wash the bird inside and out, rubbing the skin with baking soda and washing this off well with cold water. Drain and dry thoroughly; then truss (see page 403) and stuff. Place breast-side-down on a trivet or wire rack in an open roasting pan, brush with melted butter or rendered chicken fat (1123). Bake in a moderate oven (325-350° F.), allowing 40 to 45 minutes to the pound (the larger the bird, the shorter is the time per lb.). When cooking time is half over, turn chicken on its back and brush again with melted fat. As breast, crop and thighs brown, cover with brown wrapping paper which may be fastened with a toothpick inserted into the crop stuffing, or with pieces of aluminum foil, then cover with 2 or 3 layers of cheesecloth. Baste through the paper and cheesecloth from time to time with melted fat. Remove trussing twine before placing chicken on platter to serve. 5 servings.

688   STEWED CHICKEN AND DUMPLINGS

3½ to 4-lb. stewing or roasting   3 teaspoons baking powder
   chicken   ½ teaspoon salt
  2 teaspoons salt   ¾ cup milk
                                    1 teaspoon minced parsley,
DUMPLINGS: optional

1½ cups all-purpose flour

Clean chicken by removing all pinfeathers with a strawberry huller or scraping them out with a paring knife, then singe. Rub skin well with baking soda and wash off carefully. After draining well, cut up chicken and peel off excess fat. Chicken should not be washed after cutting up; if washing is necessary, do it quickly in cold water. Keep in covered bowl in refrigerator until ready to cook. Drain off water that collects in bowl. Fit pieces of chicken compactly into kettle, sprinkle with 2 teaspoons salt, then barely cover with cold water. Cover closely, heat to boiling, then reduce heat to simmering and cook until tender, 1½ to 3 hours depending on age of fowl. Fifteen minutes before chicken is done, add dumplings prepared as follows:

Sift flour, measure, and resift 3 times with baking powder and salt. Add milk and stir just until dry ingredients are dampened; then add parsley and stir until well distributed. Remove cover from stewing kettle. There should be enough liquid in kettle to barely cover the chicken. Dip a teaspoon into the liquid, then into the dumpling batter, and drop a spoonful onto the chicken. Dipping spoon in the hot liquid prevents dough from sticking to spoon. Drop all dumplings in quickly; then replace cover and boil gently 12 minutes. Remove dumplings to platter, and arrange pieces of chicken around them. Pour the thickened liquid into gravy boat and serve at table. 5 or 6 servings.

Variation: Seven oz. noodles may be cooked in the chicken stock in place of the dumplings.

689   CHICKEN à la KING

  2 tablespoons butter   1⅓ cups chicken broth
  ⅓ green pepper, cut in strips   Salt and pepper to suit taste
  ¼ lb. fresh mushrooms, sliced   2 cups cold diced chicken
  ⅓ cup flour   ½ pimiento, cut in strips
1⅓ cups thin cream *or*
   evaporated milk

Melt butter in top of double boiler over direct heat, add green pepper and mushrooms, cover and simmer 5 minutes. Lift out pepper and mushrooms. Blend flour into the fat, add cream or milk, broth and seasonings and cook with constant stirring, still over direct heat until sauce boils and thickens. Add chicken, pimiento, green pepper and mushrooms; place over boiling water, cover and cook until chicken is heated through. Serve hot over toast, baking powder biscuits (26), crisp noodles (173a) or fluffy boiled rice (174). 5 servings.

690   CHICKEN FRICASSEE

Choose a young hen or roasting chicken for fricasseeing; this is a method for cooking less tender chickens. Cut the cleaned chicken into the usual number of serving pieces, see Note, page 407. Coat thoroughly with flour and brown pieces in melted fat, 1 tablespoon butter and 2 table-spoons other shortening. Add ½ cup of any desired liquid—water, milk or chicken broth—and salt, allowing ½ teaspoon to each pound of chicken. Cover tightly and simmer until perfectly tender, adding more liquid as required during cooking. Time required will be ½ to 2 hours, depending on age and size of chicken. If preferred, the covered pan may be placed in a moderately slow oven (300-325° F.) to complete cooking after the chicken is browned.

691   CHICKEN PIE

FILLING   *PASTRY*

½ cup cold chicken broth   1 cup all-purpose flour
⅓ cup flour   1½ teaspoons baking powder,
1½ cups hot chicken broth   see p. 122
2½ cups stewed chicken cut in   ¼ teaspoon salt
    large dice   3 tablespoons butter
¾ cup drained canned peas   ⅓ cup milk
¾ cup sliced celery
1 teaspoon salt

Make a paste by blending cold chicken broth and flour until smooth. Add paste to the hot chicken broth and cook over direct heat, stirring constantly until sauce boils and thickens. Combine with chicken, peas, celery and 1 teaspoon salt, and pour into a 6-cup buttered casserole. Sift the 1 cup flour, measure and resift 3 times with baking powder and ¼ teaspoon salt. Cut in butter with a pastry blender or 2 knives, then add milk, all at once, stirring quickly with a fork until dough just stiffens. Turn dough out onto floured board, knead half a dozen times, then roll out to make a circle about 8½ inches in diameter, or to fit top of casse-role, and about ¼-inch thick. Make several gashes near the center to allow steam to escape, then lay on top of the chicken filling. Crimp edge of dough, pressing it firmly against edge of casserole. Bake in a moder-ately hot oven (425° F.) from 20 to 25 minutes or until nicely browned. 5 servings.

ROAST DUCK

Choose a young 4 to 6-pound duck for roasting. Clean thoroughly first by singeing, then removing all down and pin feathers which must be done thoroughly by using a strawberry huller, then scraping with a paring knife. Next wash inside and out with cold water. Drain thoroughly. Duck may be stuffed or not, as desired. When stuffing is not used, one or two cored and quartered apples may be placed inside the duck to absorb any strong flavor; or celery and onions may be used to help season it. Mashed potatoes and seasoned boiled rice are popular stuffings for duck. Truss the duck like a chicken (see page 403) or leave untrussed, sprinkle with salt and pepper, and place breast-side-up on a rack in an open roasting pan. Do not prick the skin because this can release juices, leaving the meat dry and the skin a grey cast, but roast uncovered in a moderately slow oven (325° F.) until tender, allowing 20 minutes to the pound. No basting is required. Drain off excess fat in roasting pan, and use brown residue and a small amount of the fat to make gravy (468).

ROAST GOOSE

Have neck of goose cut off close to the head. To dress a goose, dip up and down in scalding water several times, then wrap in a piece of wet, hot canvas or a heavy cloth bag. Let steam 10 minutes, then remove feathers and down with a rubbing motion toward head of the bird. Singe, then pat over skin 2 or 3 tablespoons baking soda, rubbing thoroughly to remove all soil. Remove entrails (see p. 402). Wash thoroughly inside and out with clear water, then drain well for 2 or 3 hours. Goose may or may not be stuffed. It will cook more quickly without stuffing. Rub inside with 1½ teaspoons salt. If stuffing is desired, Fluffy Dressing (698) may be used, but butter should be omitted because of fatness of goose. Truss by folding the wings back and tying them so cord is drawn tightly across the back; tuck neck skin under the cord; tie legs together. Rub 1 teaspoon salt over the skin. Lay breast-side-up in open baking pan. Bake in moderate oven (325° to 350° F.) for 1 hour. Do not prick the skin. Pour off fat from time to time. (Goose fat makes excellent cookies and pie crust.) Cook until very tender, 3 to 4 hours for a 10 to 12 pound goose. Make gravy with the brown juice and a little of the fat in the bottom of baking pan, using 1½ to 2 tablespoons flour to each 2 tablespoons fat and juice in pan. Blend fat and flour thoroughly. Add water or milk, 1 cup to each 2 tablespoons flour used; cook gravy thoroughly. More water or milk may be used to thin to desired consistency.

Potato Dumplings (1078) are a good accompaniment for goose, if stuffing is not used.

One-half hour before goose is done, drain off most of the fat and drop

the dumpling dough by heaping tablespoons around the goose and bake
at the same temperature.

694   BRAISED DUCKLING

  4 lb. duckling cleaned weight   2 to 3 teaspoons salt

Duck may be cooked whole or disjointed, according to size of kettle
available. Preparation is the same in both cases: Singe duck and be extra
careful to remove all the down and pinfeathers. Wash thoroughly inside
and out, and drain. Pull fat out of duck and render (1123) in a Dutch
oven or any heavy saucepan with tight-fitting cover. Lay duck in hot
kettle and brown on all sides in its own fat. Sprinkle salt inside and out
and add a little water if pot is dry. Cover tightly and let cook very slowly
for 2 hours, turning occasionally and adding more water if needed. Pour
off liquid and serve "as is" for gravy, or thicken if desired (468). Continue cooking the duck, uncovered until the skin is browned and crisp.
5 servings.

695   ROAST TURKEY

Buy right size turkey—1¼ to 1½ lb. per person if for one meal, 2 lb.
per person if 2 leftover meals are the aim. Select turkey ahead of time,
but don't bring it home until the day before. Clean immediately. Remove pinfeathers with care, then singe and wash thoroughly. Drain well.
Remove fat from gizzard; render (1123). Cook giblets until tender, cool
and store in refrigerator. Meanwhile, pull neck skin of turkey back as
far as possible, rub ⅓ of the salt (a 14-lb. bird requires 2 tablespoons)
into breast flesh, then rub remaining salt inside bird. Rub outside with
rendered turkey fat. Cover with waxed paper, then with a cloth and store
in refrigerator.

The day before, prepare and combine all stuffing ingredients except
onions, celery and liquids. See Stuffings (697-700). Put dry stuffing ingredients in plastic bag, close and leave at room temperature. When
ready to stuff bird, prepare by adding onion, celery and liquids to stuffing.
Remove bird from refrigerator. Pack stuffing into neck and body cavities
lightly, then truss. See p. 403. Be sure to wrap the bony ends of drumsticks with 2 or 3 folds of cheesecloth and tie to prevent overbrowning.

Do not return turkey to refrigerator. Start roasting within an hour or so
after stuffing. Place bird on rack, breast-side-down in a pan large enough
for bird to fit in comfortably; one too large lets juice spread out over
exposed pan to burn and give gravy a scorched flavor; one too small
lets juice drip into oven to burn and "smell" up the house. Now fold
enough cheesecloth 4 times to cover bird completely. Dip folded cloth

into melted shortening (not bacon fat) and lay over bird, tucking snugly around it. Roast according to Chart, p. 405. Baste with ½ cup rendered turkey fat or butter and ½ cup hot water. When cooking time is half done, turn bird on back, re-arrange cheesecloth to cover well and baste again. To baste, remove turkey to top of stove, closing oven so it won't cool. Spoon basting liquid over cloth to coat skin of bird. Return to oven. Repeat basting every 20 to 30 minutes. Cover breast and thighs browning too fast with brown paper or aluminum foil. To baste, lift paper or foil up, then replace. When done, lift bird to hot platter, cover to keep hot while making gravy (695a). Letting bird stand half an hour before serving, makes it more easy to carve. To serve, remove trussing cords neatly. Garnish platter simply with loose bouquets of crisp parsley, leaving plenty of room for the carver. A 10-lb. turkey serves 6 to 7, a 14-lb. 12.

695a   TURKEY GRAVY

You can make only so much really fine flavored gravy. The amount depends on size of bird and amount of savory juices left in roasting pan. First, drain all fat and juice from roasting pan into a large glass measuring cup. Let stand for fat to float on top, then pour off all but ⅓ cup of the fat if turkey weighed 14 pounds, and a correspondingly less amount for a smaller turkey. Return fat and juice to roasting pan. Add ⅓ cup flour and stir and scrape until flour is blended in smoothly and the residue on bottom of pan is loosened. Add 2½ cups giblet broth or 2½ cups broth and milk. Place over low heat, stir constantly, shifting pan back-and-forth so gravy cooks evenly. Boil 5 minutes. If gravy becomes too thick, add more liquid to obtain right consistency. Season with salt and pepper. If unthickened pan-gravy is preferred, skim all but 2 tablespoons of fat from pan juices, add 1½ cups of broth, place over heat and stir and scrape until residue dissolves. Add ½ cup cooked, mashed chestnuts to pan gravy for delicious variation. Serve gravy in a very hot bowl. Makes 2½ cups thickened gravy or 1½ cups pan gravy.

Note: For Giblet Gravy, add ground or finely chopped cooked giblets to the thickened gravy and reheat.

696   TURKEY HASH

1½ cups chopped leftover turkey	1 tablespoon chopped parsley
	Salt and pepper to taste
2½ cups diced boiled potatoes	1½ cups turkey broth
2 tablespoons butter	

Remove turkey meat from bones in as large pieces as possible and wrap in waxed paper to keep moist. Put the broken bones into a 3-qt.

saucepan, add 1 branch celery and 2 slices onion, add barely enough
water to cover, then cover and simmer 1½ hours. Combine chopped
meat with the diced potatoes and brown in the butter heated in a skillet.
Add parsley, seasonings, and the broth obtained by simmering bones.
Cook slowly for 20 minutes, stirring occasionally, until flavors are blended
and moisture is evaporated to desired point. Serve hot. 5 servings.

697   BREAD STUFFING FOR ROAST TURKEY

1½-lb. loaf stale white bread   1½ teaspoons salt
1 cup diced celery   ⅛ teaspoon black pepper
¼ cup chopped onion   ¾ cup broth from cooking
¼ cup butter   giblets or milk
2 teaspoons poultry seasoning

Remove crust from bread and cut in 1-inch dice. Place in a 4-qt. bowl.
Sauté celery and onion in butter until soft and yellow: then turn over
bread; add seasonings and toss together until well mixed. Cool. Add broth
last and again toss until mixed. Stuff lightly into turkey. Sufficient for a
10-lb. turkey.

698   FLUFFY DRESSING FOR ROAST CHICKEN

6 cups bread crumbs   ½ teaspoon salt
6 tablespoons butter   1¼ teaspoons poultry seasoning
½ cup chopped celery   ⅛ teaspoon black pepper

Pull crumb from crusts of 3 or 4 day-old white bread and crumble
lightly between palms of hands; do not use crusts. Crumbs should be fine
—about twice the size of rice grains. Melt butter in large skillet, when
hot, stir in the crumbs. Continue heating over low heat, turning crumbs
constantly until all are coated with butter and slightly brown. Remove
from heat and add other ingredients, mixing thoroughly but lightly. Stuff
into chicken lightly to keep fluffy. Makes about 4 cups stuffing, enough
for a 4 to 4½-pound bird. Make at least twice this amount for a turkey.

699   CELERY STUFFING

¾ lb. 3-day old white bread   1 teaspoon salt
3 tablespoons butter   ⅛ teaspoon black pepper
1½ cups diced celery   ½ cup broth from cooking
1 tablespoon chopped onion   giblets, or ½ cup milk
½ teaspoon poultry seasoning

Tear bread into small pieces after removing crusts; there should be
about 6 cups of coarse crumbs. Melt butter in saucepan, add celery and

onion and cook with frequent stirring until soft and yellow. Add bread and seasonings and toss together until well mixed. Cool. Drizzle the cold broth over crumbs, then mix lightly with a fork and stuff lightly into the dressed chicken. Enough for a 4-pound chicken.

700   OYSTER DRESSING

3½ qts. coarse white bread crumbs, loosely packed	¼ lb. butter
	¾ cup finely chopped celery
1 teaspoon salt	½ medium onion, chopped
1 teaspoon poultry seasoning	1¼ cups chopped oysters
¼ teaspoon white pepper	

Pull crumb from crusts of 3 or 4-day-old bread, discarding crusts. Add salt, poultry seasoning and pepper, and toss to distribute seasonings. Melt butter in saucepan, add celery and onion, and sauté until just softened, then stir in oysters. Pour over bread crumbs and mix lightly with fork or hands. Stuff lightly into turkey. Enough for 12-lb. fowl.

PRESERVING
and CANNING

* * * * * * * *

IT'S a proud moment when you open the first jar of your very own peach pickles, strawberry jam or luscious red tomato juice! The following information on putting up your own jams, jellies, preserves, pickles and all kinds of fruit, will help you make sure of the maximum amount of applause from your family and friends.

* * * * * * * *

Rows of colorful home-canned fruits and vegetables, all neatly labeled, are an achievement of which any housewife may be justly proud. Yet home canning is a task which most inexperienced women are afraid to tackle, because the results are so impressive that the novice can hardly believe how simple the process is.

It pays to take special pains in putting up foods that are stored over a long period and are to be a source of pride and pleasure as long as they last, both to the cook and to her family and guests. An inferior product, on the other hand, or one which has been handled carelessly, will be a continual reproach. Like most other tasks in life, this is one which should be done well if it is undertaken at all.

Tomatoes and acid fruits are the best foods to start with if you are new at the job. They require no special equipment besides jars, rubbers, lids and a boiler deep enough to permit the jars to be covered to a depth of 1-inch with water. Non-acid vegetables and meats must be processed in a pressure cooker in order to destroy all organisms which might menace health; but the acidity of fruits and tomatoes makes it possible to destroy organisms at a much lower temperature, and the "boiling water bath" method is perfectly reliable for these foods.

The process of canning is the same for tomatoes as for acid fruits, except that no liquid whatever is added to tomatoes, whereas fruits usually have a boiling sugar syrup added, although it is possible to water-pack fruits without sugar if desired.

STEPS IN CANNING FRUIT AND TOMATOES

1.   Assemble all necessary equipment: Jars, *new* rubber rings, lids and a wash boiler or deep kettle; a large mouth funnel, heavy canvas gloves, tongs, and some type of jar-cap tightener (a piece of inner tube enables one to grasp the lid firmly) are desirable.

2.   Choose only choice, sound food for canning; the fresher the better. Blemished, very juicy fruit or tomatoes should not be used for canning even with the blemishes cut out, as they may still harbor spoilage organisms.

3.   Pare the fruit, add syrup and heat just to boiling. Put jars fitted with new rubber rings, or jars with vacuum seal lids into hot water and let stand 15 minutes. Now pack the hot fruit, not too tightly, into the hot jars to within 1-inch from top. Add boiling syrup to come ½-inch from top. Press tomatoes down in jars to release enough juice to fill jars.

4.   Run a spatula down the inside of the jar to dislodge any air bubbles. Wipe off ring and neck carefully with a clean, damp cloth. Bits of food interfere with a perfect seal. Make sure before putting on lid that syrup or juice comes to within ½-inch of top.

5.   Turn screw-type lids down tight; then turn *back* ¼-inch so air can escape as it expands with heating. For bail-type lids, raise the long bail into position over the lid and leave the short bail up. Screw vacuum seal lids down firmly.

6.   Place the partially sealed jars in boiling water deep enough to come 1-inch over tops of lids. A stout pair of tongs and a pair of heavy canvas gloves will protect your hands. An accident not only wastes food but may injure you seriously. Start counting the processing time the moment active boiling begins.

7.   When time is up, carefully remove jars using gloves and tongs.

8.   Vacuum seal lids should not be screwed down nor should the jar be turned upside down. Immediately complete the seal of other jars, either by screwing lid down firmly or by lowering short bail. Prove seal by inverting each jar (not vacuum seal) for a few moments. If liquid escapes, the lid or ring is defective. They can be replaced, and processing repeated; or better still, serve the food within a day or so.

9.   Set jars on wire cake racks with enough space between so they can cool rapidly. Avoid draughts. Do not delay cooling by covering jars or crowding them together, for as long as they stay hot cooking continues in the jar, resulting in a soft, less attractive product.

TABLE 19. HOME CANNING OF FRUITS AND VEGETABLES

ACID FOODS—FRUITS AND TOMATOES

Food: Fruits, tomatoes, pickled vegetables	Preparation	Time to process in boiling water bath at 212° F.	
		Pints Minutes	Quarts Minutes
Apples	Pare, quarter, core. Boil in thin syrup 5 minutes. Pack hot, cover with hot syrup. Adjust lids. Process for	15	15
	Or make apple sauce, sweetened or unsweetened. Pack hot. Adjust lids. Process for	10	10
Apricots	Same as peaches		
Berries (except strawberries)	Discard imperfect ones, wash, drain well. For firm berries, add ½ cup sugar to each qt. fruit, bring to boil, shake pan to keep from sticking. Pack hot, cover with hot syrup. Adjust lids. Process for	15	15
	For red raspberries and other soft berries, fill jars with raw fruit and shake down for full pack. Cover with boiling thin syrup made with berry juice. Adjust lids. Process	20	20
Cherries	For pitted cherries, follow directions for firm berries. For cherries with pits, follow directions for firm berries, but add a little water to prevent sticking. Adjust lids. Process for	15	15
Peaches	For easy peeling, put peaches in a wire basket or cheesecloth pouch and dip for a minute or two in boiling water, then quickly into cold. Slip off skins, take out pits. Slice or cut in halves. To keep from darkening, dip in a gallon of water containing 2 tablespoons salt and 2 of vinegar. If fruit is juicy, add ½ cup sugar to each quart raw fruit. Heat to boiling. For less juicy fruit, drop into thin to medium syrup, boiling hot and just heat through. Pack hot, cover with boiling syrup. Adjust lids. Process for	20	20
Pears	Pare, cut in halves, core. Same as less juicy peaches.		

TABLE 19. HOME CANNING OF FRUITS AND VEGETABLES (Continued)

Food: Fruits, tomatoes, pickled vegetables	Preparation	Time to process in boiling water bath at 212° F.	
		Pints Minutes	Quarts Minutes
Plums, prunes	To can whole, prick skin. Heat to boiling in plum juice or thin to medium syrup. Pack hot, cover with boiling syrup. Adjust lids. Process for	15	15
Rhubarb	Cut in ½ inch lengths. Add ½ cup sugar to each quart rhubarb and let stand to draw out juice. Bring to boil. Pack hot, cover with hot juice. Adjust lids. Process for	10	10
Sauerkraut	Heat well fermented sauerkraut to simmering, do not boil. Pack into jars, cover well with hot juice. Adjust lids. Process for	25	30
Strawberries	Wash berries, stem and add ½ cup sugar to each quart fruit. Bring slowly to boil. Remove from stove, cover, let stand over night. Bring quickly to boil, pack hot, cover with hot juice. Adjust lids. Process for	15	15
Tomatoes	Use only perfect ripe tomatoes. Scald, remove all of core, peel and quarter. Bring to rolling boil, stir as tomatoes heat. Pack hot, add 1 teaspoon salt to each quart. Adjust lids. Process for	10	10
Tomato juice	Use soft but perfect tomatoes. Remove all core, cut into pieces. Simmer until softened. Put through a fine sieve. Add 1 teaspoon salt to each quart. Reheat at once just to boiling. Fill into hot jars at once. Leave ¼ inch head space in jars, ½ inch in bottles. Adjust lids. Process for	15	15
Fruit juices	Berries, red cherries, plums or blends of these—remove pits; crush the fruit. Heat to simmering. Strain through a cloth bag. Add sugar, if desired—from ½ to 1 cup sugar to 1 gallon of juice. Heat again to simmering. Fill into hot jars or bottles. Leave ¼ inch head space in jars, ½ inch in bottles. Adjust lids. Process for	5	5

TABLE 19. HOME CANNING OF FRUITS AND VEGETABLES (Continued)

Food: Fruits, tomatoes, pickled vegetables	Preparation	Time to process in boiling water bath at 212° F.	
		Pints Minutes	Quarts Minutes
Fruit purées	Use soft, but sound fruit. Put cooked fruit through a fine sieve or food mill. Proceed as for fruit juices. Adjust lids. Process for	20	20

NON-ACID FOODS—VEGETABLES

Food: Non-acid vegetables	Preparation	Time to process in pressure canner at 10 pounds (240° F.)	
		Pints Minutes	Quarts Minutes
Asparagus	Trim off scales; cut into inch pieces. Cover with boiling water, boil 2 or 3 minutes. Pack hot; cover with hot cooking liquid. Adjust lids. Process for	35	40
Beans	*Fresh lima, shelled.* Can only young tender beans. Cover with boiling water, bring to boil. Pack hot, cover with freshly boiling water. Adjust lids. Process for	45	55
	Snap. Cut into pieces, cover with boiling water; boil 5 minutes. Pack hot; cover with hot cooking liquid. Adjust lids. Process for	30	40
	Green soy beans, shelled. Cover with boiling water; boil 3 or 4 minutes. Pack hot; cover with fresh boiling water. Adjust lids. Process for	60	70
Beets	*Baby beets.* Before washing, trim off tops leaving 1 inch of stems. Boil until skins slip easily, about 15 minutes. Skin and trim. Pack hot; cover with fresh boiling water. Adjust lids. Process for	40	45
Carrots	Scrape, slice. Cover with boiling water; boil 5 minutes. Pack hot; cover with hot cooking liquid. Adjust lids. Process for	40	45

TABLE 19. HOME CANNING OF FRUITS AND VEGETABLES (Continued)

Food: Non-acid vegetables	Preparation	Time to process in pressure canner at 10 pounds (240° F.)	
		Pints Minutes	Quarts Minutes
Corn	*Whole grain.* Cut corn from cob so as to get most of kernel but not husk. To each quart corn add 1 teaspoon salt and 1 pint boiling water. Heat to boiling and pack hot. Add no more salt and no extra water. Adjust lids. Process for *Cream style.* Too hard to process. Don't recommend	65	75
Greens	Can only fresh picked, tender greens. Pick over; wash thoroughly. Cut out tough stems and midribs. Boil in small amount water until wilted. Pack hot and loosely. Cover with hot cooking liquid. Add boiling water if needed. Adjust lids. Process for	95	105
Okra	Can only tender pods. Cover with boiling water; bring to boil. Pack hot; cover with hot cooking liquid. Adjust lids. Process for	35	40
Peas	*Green, shelled.* Cover with boiling water; boil 5 minutes. Pack hot; cover with fresh boiling water. Adjust lids. Process for	45	—
Pumpkin	Pare and cut into 1-inch cubes. Add a little water and bring to boil. Pack hot; cover with hot cooking liquid. Adjust lids. Process for	85	105
Squash	*Summer.* Do not pare. Otherwise same as pumpkin *Winter.* Same as pumpkin		
Sweet potatoes	Boil or steam until skins slip easily. Skin; cut into pieces. Pack hot; cover with fresh boiling water. Adjust lids. Process for	100	110

10. Label jars with name of contents and date of canning; gummed paper labels are most useful for this purpose. Use the oldest foods first. Store the jars in a cool, dark, moderately dry place. Coolness discourages development of organisms; darkness preserves food colors that fade readily when exposed to light. A heavy tan window shade drawn over the storage shelves is a good protection against light. Air that is too dry will crack rubber rings after several months of storage.

SYRUP FOR PACKING FRUITS

The thick, medium and thin syrups referred to in the time table for acid fruits are made in the following proportions:

Thin . . . . three times as much water as sugar
Medium . . . . twice as much water as sugar
Thick . . . . equal amounts sugar and water

Fruit juice, when available, may be used instead of water to produce a more intense flavor. To prepare syrup, cook sugar and water, or juice, together just until the sugar is dissolved. Use boiling hot.

JELLIES

Jelly is made by combining the concentrated juice of barely ripe fresh fruit with sugar, and if the fruit is lacking in natural pectin, with added commercial pectin. Good jelly can always be bought, the various brands varying in both price and quality. Generally, however, home-made jelly has a superior flavor and often a superior, more delicate texture; and if it is made when the fruit is most abundant, it is considerably more economical. Juice may be canned in season, if preferred, and the jelly can be made up from the juice as it is needed.

Grapes, plums and apples are fruits which are especially good for the inexperienced jelly maker to start with, because they have enough pectin and acid for successful jelly and have good flavor besides.

JAMS

Jam may be made from both pulp and juice of the fruit, or from the pulp only, or from pulp which has had part of the juice extracted. The fruit is never found whole in jam. Jam is most frequently made from berries, and the seeds are left in the fruit; but when fruits such as peaches and plums are used, the seeds are removed.

MARMALADE

Marmalade is a special type of jam in which oranges, grapefruit and lemons are the fruits most frequently used. Here the seeds are discarded but all the rest of the fruit including the finely cut rind is used.

PRESERVES

In preserves the fruit is kept whole as in small fruits like berries and cherries, or in pieces of definite shape for larger fruits; such as peaches or pears. The form is preserved by cooking the fruit in a sugar syrup; this may be done either by sugaring the prepared fruit and allowing it to stand until the sugar and fruit juice form a syrup, or by cooking it from the beginning in a heavy sugar-water syrup. The former method gives a somewhat better flavor and a less intensely sweet product, but the latter is useful for fruits that are very ripe. By either method this is one of the simplest ways of preserving fruit.

Preserves are good not only with yeast or hot breads and as a relish with meat, but make an attractive filling for cake and a delicious sauce for ice cream and puddings.

PICKLES AND RELISHES

If a tart or piquant relish is preferred to a sweet one, pickles are the answer. They are easily made, especially such simple ones as beet pickles, cucumber pickles, fruit pickles and piccalilli; they are not expensive to make, they store easily and keep well. The flavor of good home-made pickles is hard to match in the commerical variety. Chilling any pickle before serving improves its eating quality 100 per cent.

Pickling requires no special equipment other than a good-sized preserving kettle. The kettle may be of enamelware, aluminum, or any material other than copper. The use of a copper kettle for pickling gives the pickles a vivid green color which indicates the presence of copper salts. Since copper in this form is definitely harmful to the body, this vivid color is to be avoided rather than sought after by the housewife.

A feature much prized in some kinds of cucumber pickles is crispness. In some pickles this is produced by prolonged soaking in cold salt water. In others, alum is suggested to produce crispness. The use of alum is perfectly harmless, and such a small quantity is required that the flavor of the pickles is not affected by it.

TABLE 20. PRESERVING AND CANNING BUDGET FOR A FAMILY OF FIVE FOR ONE YEAR

Food	Approx. No. times served	No. containers to be filled*	Size of containers	Varieties suggested most often†
Jelly 110		135	4-oz. glasses	Crabapple Apple Grape Strawberry
Preserves .... 90 (jams, marmalades, fruit butters)		55	pt. jars	Peach butter Plum butter Apple butter Orange marmalade
Pickles 30		30	pt. jars	Crabapple Dill
Tomatoes 60		90	qt. jars	
Tomato juice 60		100	qt. jars	
Cherries 15		20	qt. jars	
Grape juice 10		30	qt. jars or bottles	
Peaches 30		45	qt. jars	
Pears 25		35	qt. jars	
Plums 15		20	qt. jars	

*It is suggested that considerably larger amounts of most of these foods be put up than are actually mentioned in the menus, if the supply is ample. This permits larger servings when desired, and also provides for guests and for between-meal refreshment, as with grape or tomato juice in hot weather, or jelly sandwiches for after-school lunches for children.

†The varieties mentioned are suggested most often in the menus, but the individual homemaker will of course use the preferences of her family as her guide in planning her own canning and preserving budget.

701   APPLE BUTTER

20 pounds apples
2 quarts sweet cider
4 cups sugar

1 tablespoon fresh ground cinnamon or preferably
3 large sticks cinnamon and
½ teaspoon ground anise or preferably 1 teaspoon anise seeds

Use fine-flavored tart apples, such as Jonathan, Northern Spy, Baldwin or Rhode Island Greening. Pare them thinly, quarter, core and slice; there should be about 11 quarts of sliced apples. Put into four 4-qt. saucepans, add 1 pint cider to each. Heat to boiling, then reduce heat, cover and cook to a sauce, shaking pans occasionally to prevent sticking.

If a fine-textured butter is desired, rub sauce through a sieve or food mill. Turn sauce into a flat pan; an ordinary enamelware roasting pan is satisfactory. Place in a moderately slow oven (325° F.) and cook about 1 hour, or until sauce is reduced about half; stir occasionally. Now add sugar, stirring thoroughly and cook about 1½ hours longer or until butter is a rich reddish amber color. If ground spices are used, stir them in when butter is removed from the oven; if whole cinnamon and anise seeds are used, tie them in a loose cheesecloth bag and add them about 30 minutes before the butter is done. Mixture should be stirred frequently after sugar is added to prevent sticking. When done, remove bag of spices and turn hot butter into sterilized jars; seal. About 3 quarts.

702   PEACH BUTTER

12 quarts sliced peaches   2 quarts granulated sugar
4 cups water

Use fully ripe, fine-flavored peaches, white or yellow, freestone or cling-stone. A full half-bushel of perfect peaches will make 12 quarts sliced. If peaches are Elbertas scald them in boiling water one or two minutes, then strip off the skins; pare other varieties thinly. Divide peaches among 3 pans holding 5 or 6 quarts each. Put 1⅓ cups water in each pan and cook about 20 minutes, until peaches are soft. Shake pans occasionally to prevent sticking. Peaches are less apt to stick if the pan is shaken rather than stirred. When fruit is tender, press through a sieve or put through a food mill, the latter method is easier. There should be 7 quarts of purée. Put into large enamel roasting pan and cook in a moderate oven (375° F.) 1 hour, stirring frequently and thoroughly to prevent sticking and scorching. Then add sugar, stirring in well, and reduce temperature to slow (300° F.). Continue cooking and stirring thoroughly every 15 or 20 minutes until butter is thick, fine textured and a rich reddish amber color. This requires 3 to 3½ hours of cooking. Pour into hot sterilized jars, then seal, cool and label. About 9 pints.

703   PLUM BUTTER

3 quarts red or blue plums   9 cups sugar
½ cup water

Wash plums carefully and put into a large preserving kettle with the water. Cover and heat over low heat just to simmering point; simmer gently until plums are burst and juice flows freely. Rub plums and juice through a purée sieve; there will be about 9 cups purée. Return purée to preserving kettle, heat to simmering, add sugar and stir until well mixed. Bring to boil, then boil vigorously, stirring almost continuously

427

until mixture gives jelly test—2 drops sheeting from edge of metal spoon, see 704. This requires 20 to 30 minutes of cooking. Pour into hot sterilized glasses. Cover at once with melted paraffin. About 2 quarts.

704   CRABAPPLE JELLY

Use barely ripe crabapples. Wash and remove stem and blossom ends. Cut apples in quarters, remove blemishes and put into a 4-qt. kettle with just enough water to cover, about 6 cups. Simmer covered until very soft, about 1 hour. Turn into jelly bag or pouch made of 2 or 3 thicknesses of cheesecloth and let drip for 2 or 3 hours. Do not squeeze bag. Measure juice and add an equal amount of sugar. Stir well. Boil rapidly in a wide, 4-qt. kettle until jelly sheets from a metal spoon—2 drops run together on edge of spoon and form a thin sheet which quickly breaks away. This requires about 15 minutes of boiling. Remove from heat; quickly skim and pour into hot sterilized jelly glasses. Cover with hot melted paraffin. About 8 cups.

CRABAPPLE JAM

Rub the pulp left in jelly bag through a sieve or food mill. Measure and add an equal amount of sugar. Cook with frequent stirring to a thick jam-like consistency, about 10 minutes. Pour into hot sterilized glasses, seal and store like jelly. This makes a pleasing spread similar to apple butter.

704a   APPLE JELLY

3 lbs. firm tart apples
3 to 5 cups water
Sugar

2 to 3 tablespoons lemon juice, if needed
Rose geranium leaves, if desired

Use any variety of tart, juicy cooking apple which is barely ripe. Fully ripe and overripe fruit lacks sufficient pectin for good jelling. Wash apples thoroughly, remove and discard stem and blossom ends; cut apples in quarters. Then slice quarters, skins, cores and all into a 4-qt. saucepan or preserving kettle. Add cold water to barely cover, the amount will depend on the size and shape of the pan. Cover pan, bring to a boil and *simmer* without stirring until apples are soft, 10 to 15 minutes. Crush apples with a potato masher, then cook 5 minutes longer. Then remove from heat and turn into a jelly bag or pouch made by gathering up several thicknesses of cheesecloth. Suspend over a bowl and let drip 2 hours. Do not squeeze bag. There will be 3 to 5 cups of clear juice, depending on juiciness of apples and on amount of water used. Put aside the pulp remaining in jelly bag. Measure juice into the washed saucepan, bring to a boil and cook rapidly 10 minutes. Taste the juice and if flavor is not tart enough, add lemon juice. Measure ¾ cup sugar for every cup of juice originally measured; add to boiling concentrated juice and continue boiling rapidly until 2 drops run together to form a sheet when dropped from edge of metal spoon. Remove from heat at once, skim jelly and pour immediately into hot, sterile jelly glasses, in each of which, if desired, a washed rose geranium leaf has been placed. Cover hot jelly with a thin layer of melted paraffin and set aside to cool; add another layer of paraffin when cooled to complete the seal. 5 to 6 glasses jelly.

704b   APPLE JAM

Apple pulp (left from 704a)   ½ teaspoon grated lemon rind
1½ cups sugar   1 stick cinnamon
3 tablespoons lemon juice   1 drop oil of anise, if desired

Turn apple pulp remaining in jelly bag after dripping juice for apple jelly into a food mill and rub through to remove skin and cores. Combine the apple purée (there should be 2 cups), sugar, lemon juice, rind and cinnamon in a 3-qt. saucepan. Bring to boil and boil briskly until thick, about 15 minutes, stirring constantly to prevent sticking. Remove from heat, discard cinnamon and stir in oil of anise. Pour into hot sterile jelly glasses and seal with melted paraffin. 3 glasses.

705   RED CURRANT JELLY

2 quarts red currants   2 cups sugar
1 cup water

Wash and sterilize jelly glasses. Wash currants in 2 cold waters, swishing them through water carefully so as not to break the fruit. Lift into a colander to drain, then strip currants from stems. There should be 7 cups of fruit. Turn into a 4-qt. saucepan, add water, heat slowly to boiling, then cook briskly about 5 minutes, or until fruit has a whitish color. Turn into jelly bag and let juice drip until there is 2½ cups of juice; do not squeeze bag or jelly will not be clear. Save pulp and rest of juice, if any, for jam. Heat juice to boiling in washed saucepan, add the sugar and boil rapidly from 3 to 5 minutes or until juice gives the jelly test—2 drops flow in sheet from metal spoon. Quickly skim and pour into hot, sterilized jelly glasses. Cover immediately with a thin film of melted paraffin; when cold, add another layer of paraffin. 4 to 5 glasses jelly.

706   RED CURRANT JAM

Turn into a saucepan the fruit pulp and whatever juice remains after dripping the juice for making jelly (705). Add ½ cup water and simmer gently for 5 minutes. Turn into a fine-meshed sieve and press the pulp through so nothing but the skins and seeds remain in the sieve. There should be 1½ cups purée. Add 1 cup sugar and mix well. Place over moderate heat and cook with constant stirring until mixture gives jelly test (see 704), from 4 to 5 minutes. Pour into hot sterilized jelly glasses and cover with paraffin as for the jelly. 2 glasses.

707   GRAPE JUICE

10 lbs. Concord grapes

Wash and stem grapes. Place in a 5 or 6-qt. preserving kettle, add ¼ cup water, and heat very slowly until juice can be seen on bottom of kettle when grapes are lifted aside. Now increase heat and simmer gently until juice flows freely, about 20 minutes. Shake pan occasionally to prevent sticking. Do not boil. Turn into jelly bag; suspend over large bowl and let drip 1 hour. Do not squeeze. Heat juice just to simmering, pour into sterilized glass jars and seal partially. Process in water bath at 170°, just below simmering, for 5 minutes. Remove jars from water bath and complete seal. Cool and store. Makes 3½ pints concentrated juice. For drinking, dilute and sweeten to suit taste.

708   GRAPE JAM

After extracting juice from grapes (707), put pulp from jelly bag into a fine sieve or colander and rub through as much as possible. To each quart of purée, add 3 cups granulated sugar and 2 tablespoons lemon juice. Place into a 4-qt. preserving kettle. Boil rapidly with constant stirring 20 minutes or until mixture gives the jelly test—2 drops sheeting from edge of metal spoon. Pour into sterilized glass jars and seal while hot with melted paraffin. 2 pints jam from each 2 pints purée.

709   GRAPE JELLY

To make jelly from grape juice prepared from well-ripened grapes as above (707), measure the juice, and to each cup of juice allow ¾ cup sugar. If grapes were barely ripe, use 1 cup sugar. Bring juice to rapid boil, add sugar all at once and stir until just dissolved. Then boil rapidly without stirring until mixture gives jelly test—2 drops sheeting from edge of metal spoon. Pour into hot sterilized jelly glasses and seal with melted paraffin. Makes the same amount of jelly as the amount of sugar used.

Jelly made from freshly extracted grape juice may crystallize after it stands several weeks. To be sure jelly will not contain crystals, can the extracted juice as described above. Let it stand a few weeks until the acid potassium tartrate forms deposits in the bottom of the jar. This is a purplish rock-like mass called argol. (Cream of tartar is made from argol.) Pour juice off carefully from argol deposit. Make jelly in the usual way.

709a   MINT JELLY

Prepare apple juice as for Apple Jelly (704a). Bring it to a boil and add 4 to 5 drops green vegetable coloring, and ¼ cup bruised fresh mint leaves tied in 2 thicknesses of cheesecloth. Cook and add sugar and lemon juice just as for apple jelly. When ready to pour, remove bag of mint leaves. 3 to 4 glasses.

710   STRAWBERRY JELLY

2½ quarts strawberries   1 tablespoon lemon juice
5¾ cups sugar   ⅔ cup liquid pectin

Wash berries thoroughly in cold water (see page 60), then hull and remove any blemishes or soft spots. Place berries in a 4-qt. saucepan or preserving kettle and stir in ¼ cup of the sugar. Cover and place over very low heat until juice begins to flow; then bring to simmer and remove from heat. Place fruit in a jelly bag or pouch made of double layer of cheesecloth and let drip, without squeezing or pressing until the extracted juice measures about 2¾ cups. Save pulp and any additional juice for jam. Put measured juice, lemon juice and rest of sugar into the washed kettle over moderate heat, stirring until sugar dissolves. Then bring to a full boil and quickly stir in the liquid pectin. Again bring to a full rapid boil, and boil hard without stirring ½ minute. Remove from heat and skim quickly. Pour into hot sterilized jelly glasses and cover with a thin film of melted paraffin. Cool, then add another layer of melted paraffin. About 8 glasses jelly.

711   STRAWBERRY JAM

Strawberry juice and pulp   1 tablespoon lemon juice
left from making jelly (710)   3 cups sugar
Water   ¼ cup liquid pectin

Measure any juice remaining after jelly has been made, and add enough water to make ½ cup of liquid. Place in preserving kettle together with the strawberry pulp. Crush thoroughly. Add lemon juice and sugar, and bring to a full boil over high heat, stirring constantly. Boil hard for 3 minutes; then stir in the pectin and remove from heat. Pour into hot sterilized jelly glasses and cover with melted paraffin while hot. About 6 glasses jam.

712　　QUICK ORANGE MARMALADE

3 large oranges, about 1¾ lbs.　　5 cups water
2 lemons　　6 cups granulated sugar
3 tablespoons lemon juice

Use sound, juicy oranges. They may be any size, but a large size is easier to prepare. Cut oranges and lemons into 8 sections each; scoop out pulp, discarding all seeds, then cut up and put into kettle. Now slice the rind paper-thin and add to kettle. Stir in additional lemon juice and water; bring to boil, simmer 1 hour, uncovered. Then add sugar, stir until dissolved and return to heat; again bring to boil and simmer about 50 minutes longer. Remove pan from heat. Test for doneness by dropping a teaspoonful of the hot liquid onto a thoroughly chilled plate and place in refrigerator for 5 minutes; if jellied by the end of this time, the marmalade is done; if not, continue cooking for a few minutes longer and again test for doneness. When done, pour into hot sterilized jelly glasses or jars and cover immediately with paraffin. When cool, add another thin layer of paraffin. About 4 pints marmalade.

713　　QUINCE HONEY
(California Quince is best quality)

3¾ lb. quinces or　　8 cups sugar
　7 cups shredded　　⅛ teaspoon salt
8 cups water

OVEN METHOD

Pare quince thinly, then shred rapidly so as not to discolor, and as each cup is prepared, put it into the water. Boil for 15 minutes, then add sugar and turn into a medium-size roasting pan. Place in moderately hot oven (425° F.) 1 hour, stirring every 5 minutes to keep fruit from settling and sticking. Roaster should stand flat on bottom of oven. After 1 hour, reduce temperature to moderate (350° F.) and continue cooking, stirring occasionally, until mixture is thickened and ruby-red in color.

TOP-OF-STOVE METHOD

Prepare quince as above and cook on top of stove for entire time. Cook until mixture has a reddish tinge and a honey-like consistency. If it becomes too thick before color is right, add a little more water and continue cooking. Stir frequently.

When done, pour into hot sterilized jars and seal with melted paraffin. When cold, add another thin layer of paraffin to complete seal. About 5½ pints.

714   STRAWBERRY ELECTRIC LIGHT PRESERVES

Wash berries carefully, drain well, then hull enough to make 1 quart. Place in colander, stand in bowl and pour boiling water over them; drain immediately. Turn into a 3-qt. saucepan, add 1 cup sugar and boil gently for 2 minutes. Then add 2 cups sugar and boil 5 minutes longer. Skim. Pour into clean, shallow glass or enamelware pan, cover with clean pane of glass, slightly raised at one end. Place under 100-watt electric light—goose-neck lamp is convenient. Let stand 36 to 48 hours, turning berries occasionally. Pack in sterile jars, seal with paraffin, then cover with lids. About 1¼ pints.

715   SEVEN-MINUTE STRAWBERRY PRESERVES

3 pints strawberries	3 tablespoons lemon juice
⅓ cup sugar	2½ cups sugar

Use only perfect, solid, ripe strawberries. Wash carefully, drain well, then hull. Leave whole. Place in a 3-qt. saucepan. Sift the ⅓ cup sugar over berries, add lemon juice and let stand overnight. Next morning, add the 2½ cups sugar. Heat to boiling, then boil 7 minutes, counting time from moment boiling starts. Pour immediately into hot, sterile jars and seal. About 1½ pints.

716   PEACH PRESERVES

8 quarts pared, halved peaches	7 cups sugar

Use fine-flavored perfect peaches which are ripe but not over-ripe. To have well-shaped peach halves, do not use peaches with soft bruised spots that have to be cut out. White peaches produce preserves with a rich reddish color; yellow peaches make an amber-colored preserve. Clingstone peaches are more trouble to prepare, but they produce a preserve of superior flavor and color. Lay the pared peach halves in layers in an enamel pan, sprinkling each layer with sugar. Cover pan and let stand overnight. Next morning drain off syrup and heat it to boiling. Then add the peaches carefully. If they are quite soft, preserve their shape by lifting them with the hands rather than with a spoon. Boil rather rapidly for about 30 minutes, shaking pan frequently to prevent sticking—stirring with a spoon may damage the shape. Then reduce heat and simmer slowly until peaches are transparent and have acquired the desired color, and syrup is thick and waxy. With average-size peaches this will require about 2 hours. Be sure to cook preserves to the right consistency. Pour into hot sterile jars and seal. About 8 pints.

717   CANNED PEACHES

Clingstone peaches are excellent for canning, but any good-flavored, firm-fleshed freestone variety may be used if preferred. They should be fully ripe but not over-ripe, though one or two over-ripe ones may be used in the syrup. For 8 pounds of peaches, prepare the following syrup: Put 1½ cups sugar, 1½ cups water, 1 or 2 peeled, halved over-ripe peaches, and 3 or 4 peach stones into a large preserving kettle. Boil about 10 minutes, then strain. Discard stones; peach pulp may be chilled and used as a fruit sauce. Pare the peaches thinly. If Elbertas are used, dip them quickly into boiling water to loosen skins, then cool and strip off skins. Now cut in halves, remove seeds, then drop the halves in the boiling syrup and simmer them 5 minutes. Then lift out and drop them hollow-side-down into wide-mouth jars, so the halves fit together not too compactly. When all the peaches are packed, pour the hot syrup into the jars to fill all spaces to within ½-inch of top. Wipe off jar rubbers and put on lids, sealing partially (see page 419). Process in boiling water bath 20 minutes, counting time from moment active boiling resumes; or in a pressure cooker under 2 pounds pressure for 15 minutes. Remove jars and complete seal. Cool at room temperature out of drafts before storing. 3 quarts. To can a bushel of peaches, divide them into 6 equal portions and proceed as above for each portion; do not attempt to do them all in one batch.

Variation: To save sugar, make syrup for 8 pounds peaches from 2 cups white corn syrup, 1 cup sugar, ½ cup water and ⅛ teaspoon salt. Cook peaches in this syrup before canning as above.

717a   CANNED PEARS

See Table 19, page 420. Also, see Steps in Canning, page 419.

718   CANNED ITALIAN PRUNES OR BLUE PLUMS

Use ripe but firm prunes. Wash thoroughly, drain, then prick them with skewer or needle. For each 5 pounds of prunes, heat 2 cups sugar and 2 cups water to boiling; add the prunes and boil gently 5 minutes in the syrup. Now lift prunes into clean hot jars and pour syrup over them to within ½-inch of top. Seal partially and proceed just as for Canned Peaches (717). 3 quarts.

Variation: To save sugar, make syrup for 5 pounds prunes from 1½ cups white corn syrup, 1½ cups sugar and ¼ teaspoon salt. Cook prunes in this syrup before canning as above.

718a   BLUE DAMSON PRESERVES

4 lbs. plums	8 cups granulated sugar
½ cup water	

Wash plums, discarding any imperfect ones. Leave plums whole or cut in half and remove the seeds. The seeds and skins contribute flavor to the preserves. There should be 3 quarts plums. Put plums and water into a heavy 6-qt. preserving kettle and pour sugar over the top. Heat slowly at first and stir gently every few minutes until the sugar dissolves, then increase heat and cook rather briskly for about 10 minutes. Again reduce heat, just simmering until the syrup gives jelly test—2 drops sheet from edge of metal spoon. The entire cooking requires from 40 to 50 minutes to really obtain jelly test. Pour in hot sterile jars and seal. 5 pints.

719   COLD PACK CANNED TOMATOES

Use fully ripe sound tomatoes, discarding any with blemishes or soft spots. Wash tomatoes perfectly clean. Place in wire basket and dip into boiling water a minute or two, or until skins slip. Then dip in cold water. Now remove all the cores and strip off skins. Pack into jars whole or cut in half, pressing down until juice fills spaces between tomatoes and comes up to within ½-inch from top of jar. Add 1 teaspoon salt to each quart of tomatoes. Wipe outside of jar with a clean, damp cloth. Adjust lids, see p. 419. Place jars in boiling water bath with water coming 1-inch above lids. When water begins to boil again, start counting the time and boil 45 minutes. Then lift out jars and immediately complete seal. See p. 419. Set jars on wire cake racks out of a draft to cool thoroughly. Label and store in a cool, dark, not too dry place. 1 bushel of sound tomatoes makes 22 quarts. Tomatoes heated to boiling before placing in jars, require only 10 minutes of processing.

One bushel of tomatoes is a practical amount to make up at one time. Use sound, fully ripe tomatoes for the reddest, richest juice; be sure they are free from soft spots and fresh cracks. Wash well, then remove cores and cut out any sun-healed scars or blemishes, discarding fruit which has even small soft spots, as these harbor spoilage organisms which may cause all juice to spoil after canning. Cut tomatoes in quarters, place in a large kettle. Heat to boiling, stirring occasionally to prevent sticking, then reduce heat and simmer about 10 minutes or until soft. Turn into a sieve fine enough to hold back seeds and skins. Rub juice and pulp through; discard skins and seeds. To conserve vitamin C, avoid exposing dripping juice to air as much as possible. Reheat juice to boiling point, then pour into hot sterilized glass jars, filling them to ¼-inch from top. Add 1 teaspoon salt to each quart, then carefully wipe off rim of each jar. Put on new rubber rings and new lids (if screw type), and seal partially (screw top down tight and unscrew ¼-turn; or fasten upper bail only). Place in a boiling water bath with water which covers jar tops to a depth of at least 1-inch and process 15 minutes. Count processing time the moment active boiling of the water starts. Remove jars to a wire rack, finish sealing and invert to test the seal; if there is leakage, the jar should have its rubber replaced and be re-processed. Set the jars far enough apart so that air can circulate between them to cool rapidly. When cool, store in a cool, dry, dark place. Jars should be wrapped in brown paper to prevent loss of color in the juice. On standing, the thick purée settles to bottom, so juice should be shaken or stirred before serving. About 18 quarts juice.

PICKLES

(Use only pure granulated salt to make pickles)

720   BEET PICKLES

6½ lbs. beets   4 to 5 cups sugar
  3 cups cider vinegar

Use bright red beets as nearly the same size as possible. If some are much larger than others, the larger ones may be cut in halves after cooking and peeling. Cut off tops of beets to leave about 1 inch of stems. Wash carefully through 2 or 3 waters to remove all soil from beets and stems; rub with hands, never with a brush which might break the skin and tap root and permit loss of color through "bleeding." Place beets in a 6-qt. kettle. Cover with boiling water, cover kettle and boil slowly until tender, 20 minutes to 1 hour, depending on size and tenderness of the beets. When done, drain and cool just enough so they can be handled; slip off skins and stems. Return while still warm to the washed kettle and add vinegar and sugar. If vinegar is stronger than 4% acidity, more sugar may be added to give the desired flavor. Heat just to simmering. The pickling syrup should barely cover the beets, and should have an oily appearance. Pack the hot beets into hot sterile jars, then pour the hot syrup over them to just cover the beets in each jar. Seal immediately. 6 pints. Chill before serving.

721   CRABAPPLE PICKLES

10 pounds Siberian crabapples	1 tablespoon whole cloves
3½ quarts sugar	2 teaspoons cassia buds
2¾ cups cider vinegar	1 stick cinnamon

Wash crabapples thoroughly in warm soapy water, then rinse well in clear water. Prick apples in several places with a skewer. Do not remove stems. Place in roasting pan. Put sugar and vinegar into 3-qt. saucepan, heat to boiling, stirring until sugar is dissolved. Pour over apples, add spices and cover pan. Place in a moderate oven (350° F.) and cook 1½ hours, pushing apples below surface of liquid every now and then. Uncover and continue cooking for about ¾ hour, or until apples are almost tender and about half have burst skins. Lift carefully into wide-mouth jars and cover with syrup. Seal and process in a hot water bath 10 minutes, counting time after water starts to boil again. 6 quarts. Chill before serving.

Note: The highest quality of pickles are made from crabapples when they are first in season, late August or early September. As the season advances, the crabapples become mellow, lose much of their fine flavor and firm texture which make good pickles.

722   CELERY CUCUMBER PICKLES

20 cucumbers from 3½ to 4 inches long	2 cups sugar
⅓ cup salt	1 pint chopped celery, loosely packed
Cold water to cover	½ pod hot red pepper
3 cups cider vinegar	½ pod sweet red pepper

Wash cucumbers thoroughly, split in half lengthwise and place in an enamelware or glass bowl, sprinkle with salt and add cold water to cover. Let stand overnight. Drain. Put vinegar and sugar into kettle and heat to simmering; add celery and peppers, then put in cucumbers and SIMMER 3 or 4 minutes only. Pack into hot sterile jars, fill jars up with syrup to within ½ inch of top and seal. 4 to 5 pints, depending on size of cucumbers. Chill before serving.

723   THUNDER AND LIGHTNING PICKLES
                        (*Senf Gurken*)

6½ lbs. yellow cucumbers,   1 tablespoon fresh grated
   4 to 5 large   horseradish
3 pints water   2 pods hot red pepper,
⅔ cup pure granulated salt   medium size
2 to 4 sprigs fresh green dill   2½ cups cider vinegar
   blossoms   ⅔ cup water
                                   ¾ cup sugar

Wash and pare cucumbers thinly. Cut in half lengthwise and scrape
out seedy portion. Cut halves in thirds lengthwise, then cut in half crosswise. Put into glass or enamelware bowl and cover with brine made with
the 3 pints of water and the salt. Cover and let stand overnight. Drain
well. Divide next 3 ingredients between 2 sterilized quart jars. Heat rest
of ingredients to boiling, add cucumbers and simmer 5 minutes. Pack
pickles into jars up to 1-inch from top. Add boiling solution to come
within ½-inch of top. Seal with glass or enamel-lined lids. 2 quarts.

724   DILL PICKLES

7 lbs. cucumbers about   ¾ cup pure granulated salt
   3½ inches long   2¼ quarts water
12 stalks fresh dill   12 green grape leaves
2½ cups cider vinegar

Wash cucumbers thoroughly in 2 or 3 cold waters then chill in cold
water 4 hours, then drain. Do not split cucumbers, but pierce each with
knife or fork, then pack vertically in clean, sterile quart or half-gallon
jars, leaving enough space in the top of jar for dill. Wash the dill quickly
through cold water to remove dust. Fold up compactly and stuff one
stalk down between pickles and one in top of each jar to fill up the
space above pickles. Heat vinegar, salt and water just to boiling; immediately pour over pickles, filling jars to ¼-inch from top. Stuff in
folded grape leaves. Seal, store in cool dark place. Pickles will be good to
eat in 3 to 4 weeks. 6 to 7 quarts.

725   TOMATO CATCHUP

7 lbs. tomatoes   1 teaspoon dry mustard
⅓ cup brown sugar   2 teaspoons celery seed
2½ teaspoons pure granulated   ½ stick cinnamon
   salt   1 teaspoon whole black
1 cup cider vinegar   peppers

438

Use firm, red-ripe tomatoes for a good-colored catchup. Wash, core and cut tomatoes into quarters. Boil tomatoes vigorously for ½ hour in a 6-qt. uncovered kettle, stirring occasionally. Then rub through a sieve pushing all of pulp through. Then return to washed kettle add sugar, salt, vinegar and mustard. Tie celery seed, cinnamon and black peppers in a cheesecloth bag and add to kettle. Heat to boiling and boil gently 45 to 60 minutes or to desired consistency, stirring frequently. Remove spice bag, squeezing thoroughly between 2 spoons. Pour hot catchup into clean, sterile bottles and seal immediately. About 1½ pints.

725a   HOT CHILI SAUCE

14 lbs. tomatoes, 1 peck	2 tablespoons pure granulated
2 hot red peppers, ½ cup chopped	salt
2 large white onions, 3 cups finely chopped	1 tablespoon celery seed
	¾ cup light brown sugar
	1 quart cider vinegar

Use firm, red-ripe tomatoes for good color in chili sauce. Wash tomatoes, dip in boiling water just long enough to loosen skins, then remove cores and skins. Cut fine and place in a colander to drain. Save the drained juice. Wash peppers, split lengthwise, remove and discard seeds and chop fine. Add peppers and peeled, chopped onions to tomatoes. Put the drained juice in an 8-qt. preserving kettle and boil rapidly about 30 minutes, or until reduced half in quantity. Add the tomato mixture and heat to boiling, then add remaining ingredients and cook moderately fast, stirring frequently until chili sauce is of desired consistency, or about 2½ hours. Pour into clean, hot glass jars and seal immediately. Half-pint jars are the best size. This chili sauce may also be served as a cocktail sauce on shrimp or oysters. 5 pints.

726   BREAD AND BUTTER PICKLES
(Green Tomato or Cucumber)

3 lbs. green tomatoes, 10 medium size or 3 lbs. cucumbers 1½" diameter	1⅔ cups sugar
⅓ cup pure granulated salt	1 teaspoon celery seed
5 cups cold water	2 teaspoons prepared mustard
½ lb. onions	1 teaspoon ginger
2 cups cider vinegar	¼ teaspoon turmeric
	⅛ teaspoon mace
	Few dashes red pepper

Use smooth, even-sized tomatoes that have acquired a whitish color which appears just before ripening, or green cucumbers. Wash. Remove stem-end and blossom scar neatly, then cut into ¼-inch crosswise slices.

Put into an enamelware or glass bowl. Sprinkle with salt and add water. Cover and let stand overnight. Next morning, turn into a colander and drain 10 to 15 minutes. Now put into a preserving kettle, add onions, peeled and sliced thinly, then vinegar, sugar and spices. Heat to simmering, then simmer only 3 or 4 minutes. Pack into hot sterile jars. Seal. 3 pints.

727   PICKLED PEACHES OR PEARS

12 to 16 medium-sized peaches   2 cups granulated sugar
  Whole cloves   6 sticks cinnamon
2 cups cider vinegar

Use firm but ripe peaches. Clingstones are best for pickles, but if Elbertas are used, dip in boiling water to loosen skins, then remove skins and leave fruit whole. Pare any other variety thinly. Stick each peach with 4 to 5 cloves and drop immediately into boiling hot syrup, made of the vinegar, sugar and stick cinnamon. Boil gently until peaches are tender, 8 to 10 minutes. Pack into hot sterile jars. Add hot syrup to come to within ¼-inch of top, then seal. Use same method for peeled Seckel pears. 2 quarts. Chill before serving.

728   CASSIA BUD PICKLES

4 pints water   3 cups cider vinegar
1 cup pure granulated salt   4 cups sugar
3 dozen 3-inch cucumbers   ½ oz. celery seed, 2 tbsp.
½ teaspoon powdered alum   ½ oz. cassia buds, 2 tbsp.

Heat water and salt just to boiling, then cool and add to washed cucumbers, cut in half lengthwise. Cover; let stand 1 week. Now drain, cover with boiling water, add alum. Let stand 24 hours. Again drain and cover with hot syrup, made by heating vinegar and 2½ cups of the sugar, the celery seed and cassia buds tied in a bag. For 3 successive days drain off syrup, add ½ cup sugar, heat, pour over pickles. On third day pack in jars, add boiling syrup. Seal. 2 quarts.

729   PICCALILLI

2 quarts green tomatoes   1 pint sliced green peppers
2 tablespoons pure granulated   1 pint sliced sweet red peppers
  salt   2 hot peppers, chopped
½ head cabbage, finely   1 tablespoon white mustard
  chopped   seed
4 medium onions, chopped   2½ cups cider vinegar
1 quart celery, finely diced   1¼ cups sugar

Mix chopped tomatoes with salt and let stand 3 to 4 hours. Squeeze out and discard water. Combine pulp with other vegetables; add mustard seed, vinegar and sugar. Heat just to boiling, then pack into hot sterilized jars. Seal. 3½ to 4 quarts, depending on firmness of vegetables.

730   VAN'S Turn-a-day PICKLES

2 quarts cucumbers 2½ to 3 inches long, 2¾ lb.	⅔ cup sugar
3 cups cider vinegar	2 teaspoons pure granulated salt
3 tablespoons prepared mustard	1½ teaspoons horseradish

Wash cucumbers thoroughly. Crisp 2 or 3 hours in ice water. Pack closely in quart jars to 1-inch from top. Blend remaining ingredients and pour over cucumbers. Remove air bubbles (p. 419) and add more liquid to come to within ¼-inch of top. Seal. Turn jars upside-down each day for a week. 2 quarts.

730a   INDIA RELISH

2 lbs. cucumbers	1½ cups sugar
2 lbs. green tomatoes	2 cups cider vinegar
4½ teaspoons pure granulated salt	2¼ teaspoons pure granulated salt
1 pint fine-cut celery or cabbage	¼ cup white mustard seed
1 cup ground onion	2 teaspoons celery seed
1½ cups ground green or red bell peppers	¼ teaspoon turmeric
2 tablespoons fine-chopped hot red pepper	⅛ teaspoon each mace and cloves

Use firm, green cucumbers about 6 inches long and 1¼ inches in diameter, and tomatoes that have the whitish color acquired just before ripening. Wash vegetables, remove stems, cores and blemishes. Put quartered tomatoes and cucumbers through a food chopper, using coarse blade. Put into a glass or enamel bowl, add salt, let stand overnight. Next morning squeeze out and discard liquid; add next 4 vegetables measured lightly, then other ingredients. Heat just to simmering and cook slowly 8 to 10 minutes, stirring occasionally. Pack in sterile jars with glass or enamel-lined lids. Seal. 4½ pints.

730b   CORN RELISH

8 cups raw corn cut from cob
1 quart chopped cabbage
1 cup diced celery
1 sweet red pepper, chopped
1 quart cider vinegar

2 cups brown sugar, packed
4 tablespoons dry mustard
2 tablespoons pure granulated salt
1 teaspoon turmeric

Cut corn from cob deep enough to get full kernels, but no bits of cob. Combine all ingredients except turmeric in a saucepan and bring to a boil; then simmer uncovered 30 minutes, stirring occasionally. Add turmeric and cook 5 minutes. Pour hot relish into sterilized jars and seal. About 5 pints.

731   WATERMELON PICKLES

9 lbs. prepared rind
3¼ quarts water
½ cup pure granulated salt
3 quarts sugar
3½ cups cider vinegar

1½ lemons, thinly sliced
1 tablespoon whole cloves
2 sticks cinnamon
1 teaspoon cassia buds

First cut rind into 1½-inch wide strips. Now cut away the green skin and remaining pink flesh on the strips. Cut the white rind into 2-inch lengths. Cover with water and salt, and soak overnight. Next morning, rinse thoroughly with several changes of fresh water. Then barely cover with fresh water and cook until tender about 1¼ hours. Drain off water and put rind into syrup made by heating sugar and vinegar to boiling, add lemon slices and spices tied in a cheesecloth bag. Cook until rind is transparent, about 1¾ hours, simmering rather than boiling rapidly. Pack in clean, hot sterile jars, cover with syrup and seal. About 3½ quarts. Chill before serving.

Note: Your druggist can get the cassia buds for you.

SALADS

NOWADAYS it's considered perfectly good etiquette to eat every bit of food on the salad plate, and to use both knife and fork if that seems most efficient. Your family will be glad of it when you begin using the recipes in this chapter, for there are so many appetite-tickling new combinations, both simple and elaborate, that you can serve a different one every day. Remember that nowhere else than in salad greens and other raw salad ingredients can folks get so many precious vitamins.

Once upon a time, people who talked about salad meant only lettuce or endive served with a plain oil dressing. Then salads were somewhat vaguely supposed to be good for one, but their principal function was as an appetizer. Since vitamins were discovered, we have learned that they exist in their fullest potency in uncooked foods, and that raw salad greens and other raw vegetables are chock-full of them.

As a result, the salad classification has expanded enormously. Not only a great variety of green salads, but salads of every description now are served in American homes every day. These salads are served as: (1) Simple relishes or appetizers. (2) A whole vegetable course, or a main course. (3) A dessert course made with fruit. (4) A full meal salad containing vegetables, meat, fish, eggs, cheese and gelatin. (5) Frozen fruit salads that look like ice cream, served either as a salad or a dessert. In fact, any combination of foods served on lettuce or other salad greens is now classified as a salad, especially when a salad dressing of some type is present.

There are a few hot salads, but the great majority are cold, and it is important to the success of a cold salad to have all the ingredients well chilled. Raw vegetables should be very fresh and crisp, not only because they are more attractive and appetizing that way, but because the fresher the foods are, the greater is their vitamin content. Keep salad greens and other vegetables in a hydrator in the refrigerator if possible. If there is no hydrator, the cleaned vegetables may be placed in plastic bags or wrapped in waxed paper before placing in the refrigerator; or they may be placed on a tray and covered with a clean damp towel to prevent them from drying out during a short period of storage.

SALAD GREENS

Salad greens are seldom perfect when brought home from the grocery store, but wilted greens definitely should never be bought, as they have lost much of their vitamin content. If only the outer leaves are wilted or bruised, or the leaf tips sunburned or nipped by frost, the greens can still be made into perfect salads. Just discard the soiled outer leaves, cut away blemished tips and other imperfections, and freshen the heads by cutting off the root and standing head cut-end down in cold water for half an hour. Then wrap the head in a clean, dry towel and shake gently to remove excess moisture.

If some leaves after this treatment do not look handsome enough for the salad plate, save them to combine with other foods in a chopped salad next day or to cook with spinach for a pleasing variation. If a variety of different crisp salad greens are cut up or broken neatly and uniformly, and lightly combined, a very attractive salad may be made of them.

A considerable variety of salad greens is now available on the market. The most frequently used and the most abundant is head lettuce, which can be used in a number of ways. The leaves may be separated, using the cupped heart leaves as a foundation for the salad; outer leaves may be shredded. The head, after trimming, may be cut into wedges or slices. For use in the salad bowl, breaking rather than cutting the head into chunks produces the best flavored salad. Head lettuce has a very mild flavor of its own.

Other greens in common use are leaf lettuce, Boston and Bibb lettuce, romaine, escarole, curly and French endive and watercress. All these varities are much more seasonal than head lettuce, and are available for a fairly short period each year. Raw spinach is also becoming more and more popular as a salad green.

MIXING SALADS

Mixing of salad ingredients and arrangement on the plates should be done casually and lightly to avoid breaking up the pieces. Fruit and vegetable salads especially are more attractive and more pleasing to eat if care is taken to keep the pieces whole and fairly good-sized, and the foods fresh and of good color.

With a very few exceptions, such as potato salad, which should stand in the refrigerator long enough for the potatoes to absorb flavor from the dressing, and molded salads, which must be made several hours ahead of time in order to congeal, salads should be served promptly after they are made and eaten as soon as they are served. A tired-looking salad, which has been standing on the table for some time awaiting arrival of the diners, is not appetizing. This applies particularly to the green part of the salad; a fruit, vegetable, meat or fish mixture may often be made up a little in advance and kept in a covered container in the refrigerator, ready to be dropped into the lettuce cups just before serving.

Salad dressing should not be added to any crisp green salad until just before serving, as it soon destroys the crispness. This is the reason why dressings are often served at the table. The amount of dressing used should be just sufficient to coat all the ingredients with a thin film. If the individual diner wishes more, he can help himself at the table.

Arrangement of the salad materials on the plate should be done with a sort of careful carelessness, to avoid the appearance of having been handled. Once a salad has been placed on a plate it should never be rearranged, or it will look messy and unattractive. Determine beforehand how much will be required for each serving, and put that amount and no more on each plate. It is desirable to use a good-sized salad plate, both to avoid the necessity of crowding the ingredients and to make it possible to cut the greens without danger of overflow.

Various garnishes add to the attractive appearance of individual salads. If other relishes are to be served, such as olives, pickles or radishes, they may often be placed on the salad plate rather than on a separate plate or relish dish. If the plate is fairly large for the salad, cheese sticks or salty crackers may be placed on the rim as a garnish. A bit of mayonnaise on top of the salad with a dash of paprika on top of the mayonnaise, adds pleasing color to many mixed salads.

SERVING AND EATING SALADS

Salads used to be served only following the main course, and this is still the custom at most formal dinners. More and more, however, they have come to be served informally either at the beginning of the meal as an appetizer course or along with the main course as a relish. In any case it is desirable to supply an extra fork for the salad, preferably a salad fork. If the salad is served as a separate course, the extra fork is, of course, a necessity.

The etiquette of salad eating used to dictate that no knife should ever be used on a salad, all cutting being done as best it could with the salad fork. The reason for this was that the salad consisted of ingredients that could easily be cut with a fork. With the advent of head lettuce, which is often served in wedges, the fork is no longer adequate and the use of the knife is both practical and safe. Many people with the habit of leaving the lettuce on their plates because it is too difficult to cut with a fork, are now learning to eat and enjoy it. It is perfectly proper, and highly desirable from a nutritional standpoint, to eat every bit of the food on the salad plate.

Small children will learn to enjoy salads more quickly and to eat them more easily if all the ingredients, including the lettuce, are broken or cut up quite small. This may be done either in the kitchen or at the table.

SALAD DRESSINGS

Nutritionally, the salad dressing is the least important part of the salad; but for eating pleasure it is perhaps the most important part. It not only lubricates the greens and makes them easier to eat, but also adds flavor, usually piquant. There are three principal types of salad dressing, each of the three having numerous variations.

Mayonnaise. True mayonnaise is an emulsion of salad oil and vinegar, with seasonings, and egg yolk as the emulsifying agent. Any commercial product which is labeled "mayonnaise" must contain these ingredients and these only. When a vegetable oil is used, or when some thickening agent is added, the product must be designated as "salad dressing" or "mayonnaise dressing," though it may be very similar in character and in flavor to true mayonnaise. Salad dressing is usually less expensive than real mayonnaise, and many prefer it because it tends to have a less oily flavor; it is also frequently more highly seasoned.

It is easy to make mayonnaise at home if you have a good rotary beater, electric mixer or an electric food blender. Home-made mayonnaise has the advantage that it can be seasoned to suit the family taste. But good mayonnaise may be bought commercially, and by trying various brands it is usually possible to find one similar to what the family prefers in the home-made variety. In buying mayonnaise or salad dressing, remember that a quart jar is always more economical than any smaller size.

Boiled salad dressing. This is usually a home-made dressing. It contains whole eggs or egg yolks, seasonings, vinegar or lemon juice and sometimes milk or cream. Frequently no oil or other fat is used, but butter may be added for flavor and richness.

French dressing. French dressing is a combination of salad oil (olive, corn, or cottonseed), lemon juice or vinegar, paprika to give color and other seasonings. It is temporarily emulsified by shaking in a bottle or beating vigorously just before using, and this must be repeated every time it is used if a quantity is made at one time. By adding a half teaspoon of egg yolk or egg white, the dressing becomes a much better emulsion when shaken. This, however, changes the typical French dressing consistency.

Some commercially made French dressings are very satisfactory, but few are as good as home-made. They generally are well emulsified which makes shaking unnecessary.

Various interesting flavors may be introduced into the home-made French dressing. One way is by the use of flavored vinegars such as tarragon, nasturtium, mint and marjoram. These are prepared by adding those herbs to plain vinegar, usually the cider or wine type, and letting them stand until a definite flavor is imparted to the vinegar. A little chopped onion may sometimes be added to the dressing itself; and some like the flavor given by storing it with a clove of garlic in the bottle. Crumbled blue cheese or grated snappy cheese may be added and will be especially good with plain green salads.

For the average family, it is not practical to make more than a quart of dressing at one time. It should be stored in an air-tight container, and mayonnaise as well as French and boiled dressing should be kept in the refrigerator. (When the container is emptied, be sure every trace of oil is washed out before it is used again.) A cold salad is always desirable. If the dressing is warm, the salad cannot be as fresh and crisp as it should be.

FRUIT SALADS

732 APPLE AND PEANUT SALAD

5 medium-size good flavored apples
Juice of 1 lemon
4 branches tender Pascal celery, diced

½ cup mayonnaise (843)
½ cup coarsely chopped peanuts
Lettuce

Quarter and core crisp unpared apples with tender skins. Cut into ½-inch dice and sprinkle with lemon juice to prevent discoloration. Cut celery into thin crosswise slices. Add the apples and mayonnaise and toss lightly. Just before serving, add the peanuts and serve on lettuce leaves, or as a stuffing for peeled whole tomatoes. Garnish with a dash of paprika. 5 servings.

733 RAW APPLE AND RAISIN SALAD

5 red tender-skinned apples
½ cup raisins, plumped (306)

⅓ cup mayonnaise (843)
Crisp lettuce

Wash but do not pare apples; core and dice. Combine lightly with washed, steamed raisins and mayonnaise. Pile lightly into lettuce cups on individual salad plates. 5 servings.

733a CINNAMON APPLE SALAD

Prepare Cinnamon Apples (268), allowing 1 apple per serving. Chill, drain and arrange on crisp lettuce. Top with a spoonfull of mayonnaise and a dash of paprika (843).

734   APRICOT-COTTAGE CHEESE SALAD

No. 2 can apricots, drained or	Crisp lettuce
¼ lb. dried apricots	Mayonnaise (843)
1 pint cottage cheese	

Drain apricots well, saving juice for beverage. If dried apricots are used, soak them in water overnight, then simmer 15 minutes or until almost tender, then chill and drain. Put a mound of cheese on each apricot, or put several apricots around a mound of cottage cheese on a bed of lettuce. Serve chilled with mayonnaise. 5 servings.

735   BANANA SALAD

3 bananas, well ripened	Crisp lettuce
¼ cup orange juice	Fruit salad dressing (842) or
Chopped peanuts—or other	mayonnaise (843)
nuts	

Peel bananas and cut in half crosswise. To prevent them from discoloring, prepare salads just before serving or coat bananas with lemon or orange juice. Then roll in chopped nuts. Drop into lettuce cups. Serve at once with fruit salad dressing or mayonnaise. 5 servings.

736   BANANA, APPLE AND CRANBERRY SALAD

1 cup cranberry jelly	Crisp lettuce
1 cup sliced ripe banana	3 tablespoons mayonnaise
¾ cup diced apple, unpeeled	(843)

Have cranberry jelly and apples chilled. Cut the jelly into ½-inch cubes. Combine with the banana and apple, add mayonnaise, then toss very lightly. Drop lightly into lettuce cups. Serve at once. 5 servings.

737   BANANA, MARSHMALLOW AND NUT SALAD

5 bananas, well ripened	¼ cup salad dressing (840)
Crisp lettuce	2 tablespoons cream
¼ lb. marshmallows, quartered	½ cup chopped peanuts

Peel bananas and cut in half lengthwise, then in half crosswise. Arrange lettuce leaves on salad plates. (If desired, bananas may be dipped a little while in lemon juice to prevent discoloration. This is desirable for salads that must stand before serving.) Fold marshmallows into salad dressing, add cream and pile lightly on top of banana quarters. Sprinkle peanuts over top. 5 servings.

738 CABBAGE AND APPLE SALAD

2 cups shredded cabbage	¼ cup mayonnaise (843)
1 cup cut tart apple	Salt to taste
1 teaspoon sugar	Crisp lettuce

Combine cabbage and apple, pared or not, cut in match-like strips. Add mayonnaise and salt and toss together. Add a little lemon juice and sugar, if needed. Heap lightly on lettuce. 5 servings.

739 CABBAGE, CELERY, APPLE AND GRAPE SALAD

2 cups shredded cabbage	1 cup white seedless grapes
1 cup sliced Pascal celery	⅓ to ½ cup mayonnaise (843)
1 cup diced pared apples	Crisp lettuce

Combine cabbage, celery, apples and washed, stemmed grapes. Toss lightly with the mayonnaise. Heap lightly on lettuce leaves for individual salads. 5 servings.

740 CABBAGE AND RAISIN SLAW

3 cups shredded cabbage	¼ cup mayonnaise (843)
½ cup seedless raisins, plumped (306)	Crisp lettuce

Combine first 3 ingredients and toss gently. Heap lightly into crisp lettuce cups. 5 servings.

741 CANTALOUPE AND BLACKBERRY SALAD

1 medium cantaloupe, chilled	Crisp lettuce
1 pint fresh blackberries, chilled	

Cut cantaloupe in wedges or rings, scoop out seeds and fiber from center, and pare off rind. Wash and drain blackberries. Arrange wedges or rings of melon on lettuce and fill center with berries. Serve with mayonnaise. 5 servings.

741a CANTALOUPE AND CHERRY SALAD

With a French vegetable cutter, scoop out balls of cantaloupe. Combine with an equal quantity of pitted sweet black cherries, or drained canned sweet cherries. Heap fruit lightly in cups of lettuce. Serve with French Dressing (841).

742   SHREDDED CARROT SALAD

5 medium-size carrots	1 teaspoon sugar
½ green pepper	Dash of salt
⅓ cup mayonnaise (843)	Crisp lettuce

Wash, scrape and shred carrots coarsely by rubbing on shredder only in one direction. Then shred green pepper in same way. Combine carrots and pepper lightly with mayonnaise, sugar and salt. Heap lightly on lettuce on individual salad plates. Chill before serving. 5 servings.

Note: Replace half the shredded carrot with finely chopped cabbage.

743   SHREDDED CARROT AND RAISIN SALAD

Add ½ cup raisins, which have been plumped (306) to the carrot mixture for Shredded Carrot Salad (742). Omit the green pepper. 5 servings.

744   SHREDDED CARROT AND PINEAPPLE SALAD

Add drained contents of a 9-oz. can crushed pineapple to Shredded Carrot Salad (742) and toss just enough to mix. 5 servings.

745   SHREDDED CARROT, APPLE AND ORANGE SALAD

3 medium-size carrots	cup mayonnaise (843)
2 juicy eating apples	Crisp lettuce
2 seedless oranges	

Wash, scrape and shred carrots. Wash and core apples; pare if desired, then cut in dice. Peel and dice or slice oranges. Combine carrots, apples and oranges with the mayonnaise, tossing gently. Chill. When ready to serve, heap lightly in lettuce cups on individual salad plates. 5 servings.

745a   CRANBERRY RELISH

1 quart cranberries	1 cup sugar
1 large seedless orange	

Pick over cranberries, discarding any soft ones, then wash in cold water and drain. Pare orange with a knife and pull out the white inner portion of the skin. Separate the orange into sections, removing the membrane. Put cranberries, orange sections and yellow part of orange peel through food chopper, using the coarsest blade. Stir in sugar. Turn mixture into a clean glass jar or bowl, cover tightly and let stand overnight or longer in the refrigerator or any cool place to blend the flavors. Serve as a relish with chicken, turkey or roast meat. About 2½ cups.

746   CRANBERRY BANANA SALAD

2 cups cranberries	2 well ripened bananas, diced
½ cup water	Crisp lettuce
1 cup sugar	Mayonnaise (843)

Wash and pick over cranberries, discarding soft ones. Add water, cover and cook slowly until berries are tender, about 20 minutes. Stir in sugar and cook 2 minutes longer, until liquid forms a syrup. Remove from heat and rub berries through a sieve; then carefully stir in diced bananas. Cool, then chill in refrigerator until jellied. Cut in squares and lift into lettuce cups. Serve with mayonnaise. 5 servings.

747   DATE, CREAM CHEESE AND LETTUCE SALAD

½ lb. dates	3 tablespoons mayonnaise
3-oz. pkg. cream cheese	(843)
	1 head lettuce

Pit dates and cut into 4 pieces. Cream the cheese, then blend with mayonnaise and mix in dates. Shred outer leaves of lettuce and mix lightly with cheese and date mixture. Serve on remaining heart leaves of lettuce. 5 servings.

748   FRESH FRUIT AND DATE SALAD

1 small fresh pineapple, chilled	¼ lb. dates, pitted, chopped
2 well-ripened bananas	5 tablespoons mayonnaise (843)
2 oranges	Crisp lettuce

Slice pineapple, pare slices and cut in small dice, discarding core of each slice. Peel and slice bananas and oranges; cut orange slices in quarters. Combine all fruits in mixing bowl, add mayonnaise and toss gently. Cover mixture and chill for at least an hour. When ready to serve, heap lightly into lettuce cups on individual salad plates. 5 generous servings.

749   COLD FRUIT PLATE

1 small head lettuce	Paprika
No. 2½ can fruits for salad	French dressing (841)
½ lb. cottage cheese	15 fresh dates, pitted

451

Arrange crisp lettuce cups on 5 luncheon plates. Drain chilled fruits, heap lightly on lettuce. (Save juice for beverage, gelatin dessert, etc.) Put a mound of cottage cheese on each plate beside the fruit mound. Sprinkle cheese with paprika. Chill and serve with French dressing. Garnish each plate with 3 dates. 5 servings.

750   FRUIT SALAD

Use any combination of drained canned or fresh fruits, including orange or grapefruit, diced or cut in wedges as desired. Chill and serve on lettuce with mayonnaise (843) or with boiled salad dressing (840).

751   FRUIT SALAD WITH MARSHMALLOWS

2 seedless oranges
2 well-ripened bananas
½ lb. seedless or seeded grapes
¼ lb. marshmallows, quartered

5 tablespoons mayonnaise
(843)
Crisp lettuce

Peel and dice oranges and bananas; add well washed grapes, quartered marshmallows and mayonnaise and toss gently. Cover and chill for an hour. When ready to serve, again toss gently and heap lightly into lettuce cups on individual salad plates. 5 servings.

752   GRAPEFRUIT, AVOCADO AND CREAM CHEESE SALAD

2 grapefruit
1 avocado
½ cup French dressing (841)

Crisp lettuce
3-oz. pkg. cream cheese
Paprika

Pare whole grapefruit, removing white membrane as well as skin. Cut out the sections, using a very sharp knife. Peel avocado, remove seed and slice ½-inch thick. Marinate both fruits in French dressing. Chill thoroughly. Just before serving, arrange drained fruits on lettuce leaves, with a ball of cream cheese in the center of each plate, then add a dash of paprika to the cream cheese. 5 servings.

Note: Cream cheese may be omitted or cottage cheese substituted.

753   GRAPEFRUIT SALAD

3 small grapefruit or No. 2
   can grapefruit sections

Crisp lettuce
⅓ cup French dressing (841)

To use fresh grapefruit, pare like an apple and remove sections whole. Canned sections should be drained, use juice as beverage. Arrange chilled sections in lettuce cups. Serve with French dressing. 5 servings.

Variation: A slice of tomato or avocado may be added to each serving of this salad for color and flavor. Watercress or curly endive is a pleasant change from lettuce.

754   ORANGE-COCOANUT SALAD

3 oranges, pared and sliced   ½ cup moist cocoanut
Crisp lettuce   French dressing (841)

Arrange orange slices to overlap on a bed of lettuce. Put a fluff of cocoanut in center. Serve with French dressing. 5 servings.

Variation: A little grated or very thinly sliced onion combined with the orange is a daring but pleasing addition, and a few slivers of green pepper, a pretty garnish.

755   ORANGE-RAISIN SALAD

3 seedless oranges   ⅓ cup mayonnaise (843)
½ cup raisins, plumped (306)   1 head lettuce

Pare oranges and dice or separate into sections. Combine with raisins, add mayonnaise and toss gently. Pile lightly on lettuce slices made by cutting head into five crosswise slices. Place on individual salad plates. 5 servings.

756   ORANGE WALDORF SALAD

1 large seedless orange   ⅓ cup chopped walnuts
Lettuce   Salt to taste
1 cup peeled and diced apples 3 tablespoons mayonnaise
1 cup chopped celery   (843)

Pare orange, cut into 5 slices and place in each crisp lettuce cup. Combine other ingredients, tossing gently together, then pile lightly on orange slices. 5 servings.

757   CANNED PEACH SALAD

No. 2 can peach halves   ½ cup chopped dates
¼ cup chopped nuts   ⅓ cup mayonnaise (843)
½ cup sliced Pascal celery   Crisp lettuce

Chill peaches in can. When preparing salad, drain peaches. (Juice may be used in a fruit juice beverage or as part of the liquid in a fruit gelatin dessert.) Mix chopped nuts, celery and dates with mayonnaise. Place a spoonful of this mixture in center of each peach half. Serve on crisp lettuce. 5 servings.

758   FRESH PEACH SALAD

5 freestone peaches	5 tablespoons mayonnaise or
Crisp lettuce or endive	French dressing
	Sugar if peaches are tart

Pare peaches, cut in halves and remove stones. If not to be served immediately, peaches should be sprinkled with lemon juice to prevent discoloration. Place on lettuce leaves on individual salad plates. Serve with mayonnaise or French dressing to which a little sugar may be added if desired. 5 servings.

Variation: Centers of peach halves may be filled with cottage cheese, or cream cheese combined with mayonnaise. Ripe olives make a pleasing garnish. Canned peach halves may be substituted when fresh peaches are out of season.

759   MOLDED PEACH SALAD

No. 2 can peach halves	Crisp lettuce or endive
1 package lemon-flavored	Mayonnaise (843)
gelatin	

Drain peaches and measure peach juice, adding enough water to make 1¾ cups of liquid. Heat liquid to boiling, add gelatin, stirring until dissolved. Pour a layer of gelatin about ¼-inch thick into a 9 x 5-inch pan. When congealed, place drained peach halves rounded-side-down on firm gelatin. Pour in another thin layer of gelatin, being careful that peaches do not slip around; when this layer is set, pour in the remaining gelatin and allow to set. To serve, cut the salad into sections, allowing one peach half to each serving. Serve on crisp lettuce with mayonnaise. 5 or 6 servings.

Variation: A few chopped toasted almonds make a tasty and attractive garnish.

760   PEACH, PRUNE AND COTTAGE CHEESE SALAD

¼ lb. dried prunes	½ lb. cottage cheese
No. 2 can peach halves	Crisp lettuce or endive

Soak prunes overnight in just enough water to cover. Drain (no cooking is necessary), split on one side and remove pits. Drain peaches. Stuff pitted prunes with cottage cheese, and arrange in hollows of peach halves on lettuce leaves on individual salad plates. Pile any excess cottage cheese in center of arrangement. Serve with or without mayonnaise (843), as desired. 5 servings.

761   **PEAR SALAD**

No. 2 can pear halves,   ⅓ cup mayonnaise or
drained   French dressing
Small head lettuce or
bunch watercress

Put chilled, drained pears on crisp lettuce or watercress. Serve with dressing. 5 servings.

Variation: 2 tablespoons whipped currant jelly may be folded into mayonnaise, or placed in hollows of pears for a pleasant change.

762   **PEAR AND CELERY SALAD**

5 fresh pears   1 cup finely diced celery
3 tablespoons lemon juice   Crisp lettuce or endive
¼ lb. sharp cheese, grated   5 tablespoons mayonnaise
                                     or French dressing

Pare pears, cut in halves lengthwise and remove cores. Dip in lemon juice to prevent discoloration. Mix grated cheese and celery together and heap in hollows of pear halves. Cover and chill. When ready to serve, arrange on crisp lettuce leaves and add dressing. 5 servings.

763   **PEAR AND COTTAGE CHEESE SALAD**

No. 2 can pear halves,   ½ lb. cottage cheese
drained   Mayonnaise (843)
Crisp lettuce or endive   Pimiento

Arrange pear halves hollow-side-up in lettuce cups. Spoon cottage cheese into each pear half and top with mayonnaise. Garnish with pimiento strip. Serve chilled. 5 servings.

Variation: Grate ¼ lb. American cheese and mix with enough mayonnaise to hold together. Make fluffy balls and drop into hollow of pear. Add ¼ cup very finely chopped celery to mayonnaise to be served over the top.

764   PINEAPPLE AND COTTAGE CHEESE SALAD No. 1

Crisp lettuce or endive   Paprika
5 slices pineapple, chilled   French dressing (841)
½ lb. cottage cheese, chilled

Arrange crisp lettuce cups on salad plates. Drain pineapple slices (saving juice for beverage or gelatin dessert) and place a slice in each lettuce cup. Heap cottage cheese in center of each slice of pineapple. Sprinkle with paprika. Serve with French dressing. 5 servings.

765   PINEAPPLE AND COTTAGE CHEESE SALAD No. 2

8 slices pineapple (No. 2 can),   ½ head lettuce
    chilled   ⅓ cup mayonnaise (843)
12-oz. jar cottage cheese,   1 tablespoon chopped
    chilled   parsley or chives

Drain pineapple thoroughly and cut slices in wedges. Combine lightly with the cottage cheese. Arrange lettuce cups on individual salad plates and heap pineapple mixture lightly into cups. Top with mayonnaise. Sprinkle with chives. 5 servings.

766   PINEAPPLE-DATE SALAD No. 1

No. 2 can sliced pineapple   Crisp lettuce or endive
1 cup pitted chopped dates   Pecan halves
Mayonnaise (843)

Drain pineapple, cut slices in wedges and mix with dates and mayonnaise. Cover and chill. Serve in lettuce cups garnished with a nut. 5 servings.

Note: Use 1½ cups fresh sugared pineapple when in season in place of canned.

767   PINEAPPLE-DATE SALAD No. 2

½ cup finely chopped dates   4 slices pineapple, diced
½ cup finely diced celery   ¼ cup mayonnaise (843)
½ cup diced apple   Crisp lettuce or endive

Combine dates, celery, apple, pineapple and mayonnaise and toss together gently to give a moist consistency. Cover and chill for at least an hour. Toss again and heap lightly in lettuce cups. 5 servings.

768   PINEAPPLE AND TOMATO SALAD

1 medium head lettuce
9-oz. can crushed pineapple, drained

1 firm tomato, diced
¼ cup mayonnaise (843)
Strips pimiento

Arrange lettuce cups on salad plates. Combine pineapple, tomato and mayonnaise, and toss together very gently. Heap lightly in lettuce cups. Garnish with pimiento. 5 servings.

769   PINEAPPLE, CABBAGE AND DATE SALAD

9-oz. can crushed pineapple, drained
3 cups shredded cabbage

½ cup pitted dates, chopped
½ cup mayonnaise (843)
Crisp lettuce or endive

Combine pineapple, cabbage, dates and mayonnaise, and toss together gently until mayonnaise coats all the ingredients. Then heap lightly into crisp lettuce cups. 5 servings.

770   STUFFED PRUNE SALAD

15 dried prunes
⅓ lb. cottage cheese

Crisp lettuce or endive
French dressing (841)

Wash prunes thoroughly, add water to cover and soak several hours. Simmer gently 10 to 15 minutes or until barely tender. Remove prunes from liquid, saving prune juice to drink; remove pits carefully and stuff cavities full with cottage cheese. Cover and chill. Arrange three prunes in a lettuce cup or beside a lettuce wedge on each plate. Serve with French dressing. 5 servings.

Variation: Serve stuffed prunes on pineapple slices on lettuce.

771   RED RASPBERRY AND COTTAGE CHEESE SALAD

½ pint red raspberries, chilled
1 lb. cottage cheese, chilled
1 tablespoon sugar

Crisp lettuce
½ cup sour cream (843)

Wash raspberries; drain. Combine lightly with cottage cheese and sugar. Pile lightly in lettuce cups on individual salad plates. Serve immediately with blob of sour cream. 5 servings.

772   WALDORF SALAD

3 large tart eating apples	½ cup coarsely chopped
1 tablespoon lemon juice	walnuts
1 cup julienned Pascal celery	½ cup mayonnaise (843)
	Crisp lettuce or endive

Pare apples, cut in quarters, remove cores; cut quarters in ¼-inch wedges. Sprinkle with lemon juice. Cut celery in slender lengthwise strips; hold together and cut crosswise into ½-inch lengths. Add to apples and toss together. Cover and chill. Just before serving time, add nuts and mayonnaise to mixture and toss gently to distribute dressing. Pile lightly into lettuce cups on individual salad plates. (If apples have red, tender skins, leave skins on for color.) 5 or 6 servings.

773   WHOLE MEAL FRUIT SALAD

Pare, then partially separate the sections of 5 small oranges, that is, pull sections apart only ¾ of the way down so as to form 5 orange cups. Place "orange-section-cups" in the center of salad plates. Fill each with 3 or 4 avocado dice. Peel and section 5 large oranges, arranging the sections of each orange in 3 groups around each orange cup. Between the orange sections arrange: in one space, 3 walnut bon-bons, made by pressing balls of cream cheese between 2 walnut halves; in second space, 3 pitted dates, each stuffed with 3 blanched almonds; in third space, 3 cooked, pitted prunes stuffed with peanut butter. Garnish fruits with curly endive or crisp lettuce. Serve with a French dressing made by beating or shaking together thoroughly the following ingredients: ¼ cup lemon juice, ¼ cup salad oil, ½ teaspoon salt, ½ teaspoon paprika and 1 tablespoon honey or sugar. 5 servings.

VEGETABLE SALADS

774   PICKLED BEETS AND ONIONS

Cook beets as directed (1005). Remove skins and slice beets ¼-inch thick, and measure slices, then slice thinly half as many Bermuda onions and add to beets. Sprinkle lightly with salt. Heat to boiling enough sweetened vinegar (half as much sugar as vinegar) to cover them; pour over beets and onions and let stand at least an hour or until cold before serving. If a spicy pickle is desired, add any desired spices to the vinegar while heating such as cloves, cinnamon, allspice, whole peppers, etc. One medium bunch of beets and 2 medium onions make 5 servings.

775 PICKLED BEET SALAD

Omit onions from the recipe for Pickled Beets and Onions (774). Serve the pickled beets with mayonnaise or dice the pickled beets and add to them chilled cooked green beans or peas, or diced cucumbers or celery. Add mayonnaise and toss together gently.

775a BEET RELISH

No. 2 can beets
1 cup sliced, pared cucumber
1 small onion, finely diced
¼ cup vinegar
¼ cup juice drained from beets
1 tablespoon sugar

¼ teaspoon salt
Dash black pepper
1 teaspoon finely chopped parsley or 2 teaspoons chopped dill

Drain beets, saving juice. Slice beets into mixing bowl and add remaining ingredients. Toss well. Cover tightly and chill in the refrigerator for at least 1 hour before serving to blend flavors. Serve instead of salad with cold meat or fish dishes. Rest of beet juice should be saved to combine with other vegetable juices and pot liquors for vegetable cocktail. 5 servings.

776 BEET, CHEESE AND ONION SALAD

2 cups cooked beets (1005)
¾ cup grated cheddar cheese
1 tablespoon chopped onion, or to taste

½ cup mayonnaise (843)
Crisp lettuce or endive
Chopped parsley

Combine sliced beets with cheese, onion and mayonnaise, tossing all together lightly. Heap into lettuce cups and sprinkle with chopped parsley. For a more tart mixture, the beets may be marinated an hour or two in diluted cider vinegar (½ cup vinegar and ½ cup water). 5 servings.

777 BEET AND PEA SALAD

2 cups diced or sliced cooked beets (1005)
1 cup cooked fresh peas (1060)

⅓ cup French dressing (841) or mayonnaise (843)
Crisp lettuce or endive

Combine chilled beets and peas with French dressing or mayonnaise and pile into lettuce cups. Serve at once. Beets may be marinated in the French dressing about 20 minutes before combining with peas. 5 servings.

778   CABBAGE SALAD

2 cups shredded cabbage	1 to 2 teaspoons sugar
1 cup shredded lettuce	French dressing (841)
1 tablespoon chopped onion	Crisp lettuce or endive
2 radishes sliced	

Combine first 5 ingredients in a mixing bowl. Add dressing slowly, tossing together gently until all ingredients are coated with dressing. Serve lightly piled into lettuce cups or from salad bowl. 5 servings.

779   SHREDDED CABBAGE AND CELERY SALAD

2 cups shredded cabbage	1 teaspoon sugar
1 cup sliced Pascal celery	1½ tablespoons chili sauce
⅓ cup mayonnaise (843)	Crisp lettuce
Dash salt	

Combine first 6 ingredients in a mixing bowl and toss to mix. Pile lightly into lettuce cups on individual salad plates. 5 servings.

780   CARROT AND CABBAGE SALAD

5 medium carrots	Dash salt
2 cups shredded cabbage, packed	2 tablespoons sweet pickle relish or chopped sweet pickles
½ green pepper, slivered	
⅓ cup mayonnaise (843)	Crisp lettuce
1 teaspoon sugar	

Wash, scrape and shred carrots. Combine with cabbage and pepper. Mix mayonnaise with next 3 ingredients, add to vegetable mixture, and toss lightly. Serve in lettuce cups. 5 servings.

781   CARROT AND PEANUT SALAD

5 medium carrots	⅓ cup mayonnaise (843)
¼ lb. salted peanuts (½ cup)	Crisp lettuce

Wash and scrape carrots; shred coarsely. Chop peanuts and combine with carrots and mayonnaise. Pile lightly in lettuce cups on individual salad plates. 5 servings.

782   COOKED CAULIFLOWER SALAD

1 small head cauliflower	½ cup grated sharp cheese
½ cup French dressing (841)	Crisp lettuce or endive

Separate cauliflower into flowerets and soak about 1 hour in cold water to which 1 teaspoon salt has been added. Drain, and cook in rapidly boiling salted water, uncovered, 6 to 8 minutes or until barely tender. Drain, cool and pour French dressing over cauliflower; let stand half an hour in refrigerator. Then add cheese; toss together thoroughly. Serve chilled, on crisp lettuce leaves. 5 servings.

783   RAW CAULIFLOWER SALAD

1 small head cauliflower	¼ lb. grated sharp cheese
⅔ cup French dressing (841)	1 small head lettuce

Soak cauliflower in cold salted water for 1 hour. Wash, separate into flowerets, slice large flowerets into thin fan-shaped pieces, and marinate in French dressing for an hour or more, in a covered bowl in the refrigerator. Then drain and add grated cheese and toss to mix. Serve chilled in lettuce cups. 5 servings.

784   CELERY CABBAGE SALAD

Wash one small head of celery cabbage well in cold water, but do not separate leaves. Dry thoroughly by rolling in a towel and shaking. Holding head firmly together, cut through it crosswise in ¼-inch thin slices. Serve these wheel-like slices with French Dressing (841) or Thousand Island Dressing (848). 5 servings.

785   CELERY STUFFED WITH CHEESE

¼ lb. sharp cheese, grated	1 whole stalk celery
Mayonnaise (843)	

Blend the grated cheese with enough mayonnaise to make a stiff paste and chill. Separate celery into individual branches, trimming off tough, coarse leaves. Scrape away all discolorations and wash thoroughly with cold water. Trim and cut neatly into 6-inch lengths. Roll up in towel and shake to remove moisture, then chill. Stuff cheese mixture into celery and serve on relish dish. For more elaborate service, press stuffed branches together in original celery stalk form and chill in refrigerator until cheese is firm. Then slice crosswise about ½-inch thick. These slices make an attractive salad, served on lettuce with French Dressing (841). 5 servings.

786   COLE SLAW No. 1

3 cups shredded cabbage	2 teaspoons sugar
¼ cup mayonnaise (843)	2 or 3 tablespoons sweet or
¼ teaspoon salt	sour cream

Choose crisp, tender cabbage for cole slaw. Have it chilled. Trim head, cut in quarters, and just before serving, shred with a very sharp knife. Measure cabbage well packed into the cup. Combine mayonnaise with salt, sugar and cream. Add to cabbage and toss until it is well coated with dressing. One tomato or ½ green or sweet red pepper cut fine, or ¼ cup chopped sweet pickles, may be added to cabbage along with dressing for variation in color and flavor. 5 servings.

786a   COLE SLAW No. 2

For old-fashioned cole slaw, combine the shredded cabbage with Sour Cream Salad Dressing (846a), instead of the above dressing.

786b   COLE SLAW No. 3—FARM STYLE

Substitute 1 tablespoon cider vinegar for the mayonnaise and cream, and add 3 thinly sliced radishes. Toss well.

787   PINEAPPLE COLE SLAW

A pleasing variation of Cole Slaw (786) is produced by the addition of ⅓ to ½ cup drained crushed or diced pineapple.

788   COTTAGE CHEESE AND CHIVES

Select fresh green spears of chives; wash and shake off moisture. Hold spears together and cut up small with kitchen shears. Add to cottage cheese in the proportion of about 2 teaspoons to 1 lb. cheese. Mix thoroughly and let stand in refrigerator at least half an hour before serving. Serve on lettuce with French Dressing (841), if desired. 4 to 5 servings.

789   COTTAGE CHEESE SALAD

1 lb. cottage cheese	Crisp lettuce or endive
1 teaspoon grated onion or	¼ cup mayonnaise (843)
1 tablespoon chopped stuffed olives	

Combine cottage cheese with grated onion or olives. Cover and let stand in refrigerator at least 30 minutes to blend flavors. Heap lightly into lettuce cups on individual salad plates and serve with mayonnaise, if desired. 5 servings. Onion may be omitted, or chopped chives may be substituted.

790   SLICED CUCUMBER SALAD

Wash, pare and slice 1 large cucumber and 1 walnut sized onion. Sprinkle with salt and pepper and 2 teaspoons sugar, barely cover with vinegar diluted with half as much water. Chill at least an hour. Serve as is, or drain and serve on lettuce with mayonnaise (843) or French Dressing (841). Peeled, thinly sliced tomatoes or red radishes also combine well with cucumber in seasoned vinegar. 5 servings.

790a   CUCUMBER COCKTAIL

1¼ cups finely diced, pared cucumber	Dash pepper
1¼ teaspoons sugar	2 teaspoons lemon juice
¾ teaspoon salt	½ cup sour cream
	Crisp lettuce or endive

Sprinkle cucumber with sugar, salt, pepper and lemon juice. Fold cucumber mixture into sour cream and chill thoroughly before serving. Serve in lettuce cups, or in sherbet glasses lined with heart leaves of lettuce. 5 servings.

791   CUCUMBER AND RADISH SALAD

Slice 1 bunch cleaned radishes and 1 medium pared or unpared cucumber quite thin and arrange slices in lettuce cups. Serve with French Dressing (841) to which grated onion has been added in the proportion of 1 tablespoon to ⅓ cup dressing. 5 servings.

792   STUFFED CUCUMBER SALAD

2 medium-size cucumbers	Crisp lettuce or endive
Pimiento cheese (189)	⅓ cup French dressing (841)

Wash cucumbers. They may or may not be pared. Cut in halves lengthwise, scoop out center portion containing large seeds. Fill centers with pimiento cheese, then press 2 halves together. Chill in refrigerator for an hour or more. To serve, slice cucumbers crosswise and arrange slices on lettuce leaves on individual salad plates. Serve with French dressing. 5 servings.

793   CUCUMBER AND ONION SALAD

1 large cucumber	2 bunches green onions
Crisp lettuce	1/3 cup French dressing (841)

Wash, pare and slice cucumber. Trim onions, wash and slice crosswise, then add to cucumbers and toss. Serve in lettuce cups. 5 servings.

If preferred, cucumber slices may be marinated in vinegar diluted with water, drained, then combined with onion and served with Mayonnaise, (843) or Russian Dressing, instead of French dressing.

794   EGG SALAD

6 hard-cooked eggs (395)	1/4 teaspoon salt
1/4 cup diced sour pickle	1/3 cup mayonnaise (843)
1/2 cup finely diced celery	1 small head lettuce

Shell eggs, then dice. Add pickle, celery, salt and mayonnaise and toss gently. Cover, chill in refrigerator. When ready to serve heap lightly in lettuce cups on salad plates. 5 servings.

795   GARDEN SALAD

1/2 cup French dressing (841)	1 lb. tomatoes peeled and quartered
1 head lettuce broken in chunks	1 bunch green onions, sliced
1 cucumber, sliced	

Pour half the dressing into the salad bowl, and add the other ingredients in the order named. Pour the rest of the dressing over all, toss together lightly, and serve from the salad bowl. 5 servings.

796   GREEN BEAN SALAD

1/2 lb. green beans *or* No. 2 can green beans	1/2 cup sliced radishes
1/4 cup sliced onions, dry or green	1/2 cup French dressing *or* mayonnaise
1 cup sliced celery *or*	Lettuce

If fresh beans are used, wash and cut into 1-inch lengths. Drop into boiling salted water and cook until barely tender, 20 to 30 minutes. Cool, then chill beans in their liquid. If canned beans are used, chill in the can and drain. When ready to serve, combine drained beans and other vegetables, add French dressing or mayonnaise and toss together. Heap lightly into lettuce cups. 5 servings.

797   KIDNEY BEAN SALAD

No. 2 can red kidney beans   ¼ teaspoon chili powder
1 cup sliced celery   ½ teaspoon prepared mustard
1 tablespoon chopped onion   Crisp lettuce
¼ cup sweet pickle relish   Mayonnaise (843)
1 teaspoon salt

Drain beans discarding juice. Add celery, onion, pickle relish and
seasonings to beans and mix thoroughly, being careful not to mash
beans. Chill and serve on crisp lettuce with mayonnaise. This salad may
also be used to stuff tomatoes. Serves 3 to 5.

798   PEA AND CHEESE SALAD

2 cups fresh cooked peas *or*   ½ cup sliced celery
  No. 2 can peas, drained   ⅓ cup mayonnaise (843)
¼ lb. American cheese   Crisp lettuce
3 tablespoons chopped sweet
  pickles

Chill the peas thoroughly in their liquid, then drain off juice. Dice
cheese about the same size as the peas. Combine peas with next 4 ingredients and toss gently. Serve in lettuce cups. 5 servings.

799   PEA MAYONNAISE SALAD

2 cups drained cooked or   ¼ to ½ teaspoon salt
  canned peas (No. 2 can)   Crisp lettuce
½ cup mayonnaise

Chill peas thoroughly; drain and mix lightly with mayonnaise, season
to suit taste. Heap in lettuce cups as an accompaniment for sliced cold
cuts or leftover meat. 5 servings.

800   SWEET POTATO SALAD

3 cups diced cooked sweet   1 teaspoon salt
  potatoes, about 2 lbs.   3 tablespoons French dressing
  (1084)   (841) *or* mayonnaise (843)
1½ cups diced celery   Crisp lettuce

Combine sweet potatoes, celery and salt. Add dressing and toss together lightly until all the potato is coated. Either kind of dressing is
good. If mayonnaise is used, marinate the potatoes and celery half an
hour in French dressing in a covered bowl in the refrigerator, then drain
and add mayonnaise. Serve in lettuce cups. 5 servings.

801   STUFFED TOMATO SALAD No. 1

5 large tomatoes	½ teaspoon salt
2 cups cooked fresh green beans (985)	1 teaspoon sugar
	Dash pepper
¼ lb. American cheese, diced	½ cup French dressing (841)
1 cup diced crisp cucumber	Crisp lettuce

Wash tomatoes, cut out cores and carefully scoop out centers; dice the scooped-out pulp. Cut beans in short lengths and mix with tomato, cheese, cucumber, salt, sugar and pepper. Add the French dressing and toss together. Heap this mixture into the tomato cups, cover and chill thoroughly in refrigerator. Serve each stuffed tomato in lettuce cups, with additional French dressing or with Mayonnaise (843). 5 servings.

802   STUFFED TOMATO SALAD No. 2

5 good-size tomatoes, chilled	7-oz. can tuna (½ lb.)
1 cup chopped celery	½ cup mayonnaise (843)
½ cup chopped sweet pickle	Crisp lettuce
2 hard-cooked eggs, diced (395)	

Wash tomatoes, then cut each almost to bottom in 6 even wedges. Now gently press apart to look like a half-opened flower. Now combine celery, pickle, eggs and drained flaked tuna. Add mayonnaise and toss together lightly. Heap salad mixture in center of tomatoes. Now place in lettuce cups. 5 servings.

803   STUFFED TOMATO SALAD No. 3

5 good-size tomatoes, chilled	Dash salt
1 cup sliced celery	⅓ cup mayonnaise (843)
1 cucumber, pared and diced	Crisp lettuce or endive
1 teaspoon sugar	

Wash tomatoes, cut each into 6 vertical sections, but don't cut sections apart at the base. Press sections slightly apart to make tomato look like a lily. Combine celery, cucumber, sugar, salt and mayonnaise. Heap mixture in center of tomatoes. Serve in crisp lettuce. 5 servings.

804   STUFFED TOMATO SALAD No. 4

5 good-size tomatoes, chilled	1 tablespoon chopped chives
Crisp lettuce	or ½ teaspoon grated onion
1 lb. creamed cottage cheese	Paprika
	Mayonnaise (843)

Wash tomatoes and remove core from stem ends. Cut into 6 sections, leaving attached at bottom, then open sections out like petals. Place on salad plates in nests of lettuce. Mix cottage cheese with chives. If dry cottage cheese is used, moisten with a little cream or milk. Pile into centers of tomatoes and sprinkle tops lightly with paprika. Serve with mayonnaise. 5 servings.

Variation: Add ¼ cup chopped stuffed olives to the cottage cheese.

805   TOMATO AND CUCUMBER SALAD

3 medium tomatoes   ⅓ cup mayonnaise (843) or
2 medium cucumbers, chilled   French dressing (841)
  Crisp lettuce or endive

Pour boiling water over tomatoes and let stand about 1 minute, then drain and dip in cold water. Then cut out cores, remove skins and cut into 5 or 6 wedges. Cover and chill. Pare and slice cucumbers. Arrange tomatoes and cucumbers in lettuce cups on individual salad plates. Serve with mayonnaise or French dressing. 5 servings.

806   TOMATO AND LETTUCE SALAD

3 medium tomatoes   ½ cup French dressing (841)
  Leaf or head lettuce

Scald, then peel tomatoes and chill. Arrange lettuce cups on individual salad plates, then cut tomatoes in thick slices, overlapping slices on lettuce. Pour dressing over salads and serve at once. 5 servings.

806a   TOMATO AND ONION SALAD

4 medium tomatoes   French dressing (841) or
1 medium onion   Blue Cheese dressing (841b)
  Crisp lettuce

Dip tomatoes into boiling water; then run cold water over them and peel. Peel and wash onion. Slice tomatoes about ½-inch thick and onions paper-thin. Arrange alternate slices overlapping on beds of lettuce on individual salad plates. Serve with either French or Blue Cheese Dressing. 5 servings.

807   VEGETABLE SLAW

½ cup mayonnaise (843)   1 cup shredded carrots
1 tablespoon prepared mustard   ½ cup thin sliced celery
2 teaspoons peanut butter   2 tablespoons minced onion
3 cups finely shredded cabbage   Crisp lettuce

Thoroughly blend mayonnaise, mustard, and peanut butter; add to vegetables, except lettuce, and toss lightly until well mixed. Chill before serving. Arrange lightly in heaps on lettuce. 5 servings.

MOLDED SALADS

808   BEET RING WITH COLE SLAW

1 tablespoon gelatin
3 tablespoons cold water
1½ cups hot water *or* water and juice from canned beets
½ cup vinegar

2 cups cooked beets (1005) *or* No. 2 can beets drained and riced
½ cup sugar
1 recipe Cole Slaw (786)

Soak gelatin in cold water 5 minutes, then add to hot liquid and stir until dissolved. Add vinegar, beets and sugar and pour into 5-cup ring mold. Chill until firm. When ready to serve, dip into warm water to loosen and unmold onto serving plate. Heap cole slaw in center of ring. 5 to 6 servings.

809   PERFECTION SALAD

1½ cups hot water
1 package lemon-flavored gelatin
3 tablespoons lemon juice
1 tablespoon sugar
½ teaspoon salt
9-oz. can crushed pineapple and juice

1½ cups finely shredded red or green cabbage
Crisp lettuce or endive
Mayonnaise (843) or boiled salad dressing (839)
Paprika

Add the hot water to gelatin, stirring until dissolved. Add lemon juice, sugar, salt and pineapple juice, and chill until gelatin begins to set. Shred cabbage, combine with pineapple and fold into gelatin mixture. Turn into a 4-cup mold which has been rinsed in cold water. Chill until firm. When ready to serve, unmold (320) the salad on a bed of lettuce or curly endive. Serve with mayonnaise or boiled salad dressing and a dash of paprika on top. 5 to 6 servings.

810   COOKED CRANBERRY APPLE SALAD

3 cups cranberries
1¾ cups water
1½ cups sugar
1 tablespoon plain gelatin
¼ cup cold water

2 apples, pared and diced
1 cup diced celery
Crisp lettuce
Mayonnaise (843)

Wash and pick over cranberries and cook until soft in the 1¾ cups water, then add sugar. Strain and rub pulp through sieve. Reheat to boiling and stir in gelatin which has been soaked in the ¼ cup cold water until gelatin dissolves. Pour a thin layer of cranberry gelatin into bottoms of individual molds and chill until set; then arrange apple wedges in an attractive design and pour in a little more gelatin to hold them in place; chill until set. Add rest of apples and celery to rest of gelatin mixture, pour into molds and chill until firm. Unmold (320) on lettuce leaves and serve with mayonnaise dressing. 5 servings.

811   RAW CRANBERRY APPLE SALAD

1 package strawberry-flavored gelatin	1 cup sugar
1½ cups hot water	1 cup diced, pared tart apple
1 cup chopped raw cranberries	1 cup diced celery
	Mayonnaise (843)

Dissolve gelatin in hot water. Combine cranberries and sugar and stir into the hot gelatin mixture. When cool, add apple and celery. Pour into a large mold or into individual molds and place in refrigerator until congealed. Unmold (320) and serve with mayonnaise and a garnish of lettuce leaves if desired. 5 servings.

812   MOLDED FRUIT AND VEGETABLE SALAD

1 package lime-flavored gelatin	1 cup diced, cooked carrots (1012)
1 cup boiling water	Crisp lettuce
9-oz. can crushed pineapple	Mayonnaise (843)

Dissolve gelatin in boiling water; add pineapple and cool until thick and syrupy. Add carrots and pour into one large mold or 5 individual ones. Chill until firm. Unmold (320) on lettuce, and serve with mayonnaise. 5 servings.

813   MOLDED GINGER ALE SALAD

5 teaspoons gelatin	No. 2 can crushed pineapple
3 tablespoons cold water	1 medium orange, peeled and
1 cup gingerale	diced (⅓ cup)
1 tablespoon lemon juice	Mayonnaise (843)

Soften gelatin in cold water; then place over hot water until gelatin melts. Add to gingerale and lemon juice. Stir in the pineapple (with juice) and orange dice. Turn into mold which has been rinsed with cold water. Chill in refrigerator until firm. Unmold (320) and serve with mayonnaise. 5 servings.

814   TOMATO ASPIC SALAD

2 tablespoons gelatin	½ teaspoon salt
½ cup cold water	½ teaspoon celery salt
No. 2 can tomatoes	1 teaspoon sugar
1 teaspoon chopped onion	2 tablespoons vinegar

Soften gelatin in cold water. Heat other ingredients to boiling, add gelatin, stir until dissolved, then rub mixture through sieve. Cool. Pour into a mold which has been rinsed with cold water and place in refrigerator to set. Serve with Mayonnaise (843) or sour cream. 5 or 6 servings.

815   SUNSHINE SALAD

1 package lemon-flavored gelatin	9-oz. can crushed pineapple
1¼ cups hot water	1 cup shredded raw carrots
1 tablespoon cider vinegar	Crisp lettuce
½ teaspoon salt	Mayonnaise (843)

Dissolve gelatin by stirring into the hot water. Add vinegar and salt, stir to mix well, then chill until syrupy. Add crushed pineapple with its juice and the carrots. Pour mixture into a mold that has been rubbed with salad oil and chill until firm. Unmold by loosening edges with paring knife and shaking loose onto chilled serving plate. Serve on lettuce with mayonnaise. 5 servings.

816   MOLDED VEGETABLE SALAD No. 1

1 package lemon-flavored gelatin	½ cup grated raw carrot
2 cups boiling water	1 teaspoon grated onion
2 cups shredded cabbage	Crisp lettuce
	Mayonnaise (843)

Dissolve gelatin in the boiling water, cool, then chill until syrupy. Meanwhile prepare vegetables. When gelatin is just about to congeal, fold in cabbage, carrot and onion. Pour into lightly oiled large mold or individual molds and place in refrigerator until firm. Unmold (see 815) and serve in lettuce cups on individual salad plates with mayonnaise. 5 servings.

817 MOLDED VEGETABLE SALAD No. 2

No. 2 can peas | ½ cup sliced celery
Water | 1 cup diced American cheese,
1 package lemon-flavored | about ⅓ lb.
gelatin | Lettuce
1 teaspoon salt | Mayonnaise (843)

Drain liquid from peas and add water to make 2 cups liquid. Heat to boiling and pour over gelatin, stirring until dissolved. Add salt and chill until thick and syrupy; then fold in drained peas, celery, and cheese. Turn mixture into oiled mold and chill until firm. When ready to serve, unmold (see 815) onto plate lined with crisp lettuce and serve with mayonnaise. 5 servings.

BOWL SALADS

818 FRENCH BOWL SALAD

1 large crisp head lettuce | 2 small tomatoes, peeled
1 small cucumber, pared | 1 clove garlic
2 branches tender celery | 1 slice very stale bread
1 small bunch green onions | ⅓ cup French dressing (841)
1 small bunch radishes

Wash vegetables thoroughly, drain and remove tops, stems, blemished parts, etc. Chill until just before serving time. Then cut clove of garlic in half and rub thoroughly over bread; drop bread into bottom of salad bowl. Pour in French dressing. Break lettuce in chunks (flavor is better when broken than when separated leaf by leaf); slice cucumber and cut celery in 1-inch lengths and combine in bowl. Push salad fork and spoon under mixture on opposite sides and lift up, repeating this tossing motion until ingredients are well coated with dressing. Remove slice of bread, garnish bowl with green onions, sliced radishes and wedges of tomato. Serve immediately. 5 servings.

819 FRUIT SALAD BOWL

1 crisp head lettuce | 1 medium size cantaloupe
2 avocados | ½ cup ripe olives
4 tomatoes, peeled | 4 medium oranges
3 heads French endive | 1 onion

Line a salad bowl with crisp lettuce leaves and in it arrange, alternately, slices of avocado, quarters of tomato and quartered heads of French endive. Garnish with melon balls, ripe olives, thin slices of orange and paper-thin slices of onion separated into rings. Drizzle French dressing (841) over all at table and toss (818) until every piece is coated with the dressing. Be sure bowl and all fruits are chilled. Serve on chilled plates with sprigs of watercress or mint. 10 servings.

820   MACARONI SALAD

7-oz. package elbow macaroni	½ cup chopped sweet pickle
½ cup mayonnaise (843) or boiled salad dressing (839)	⅓ cup chopped pimiento
	1 tablespoon prepared mustard
2 tablespoons chopped onion	1 teaspoon celery seed

Drop macaroni into 3 quarts rapidly boiling salted water (about 1 tablespoon salt) and boil until tender, 15 to 20 minutes. Drain and rinse with cold water; chill thoroughly in refrigerator. Mix remaining ingredients. If dressing is too thick, thin it with 1 or 2 tablespoons of juice from the pickles. Add dressing to chilled macaroni and toss together until each piece of macaroni is well coated with dressing. Serves 5.

MACARONI CHEESE SALAD

The ingredients in macaroni salad may be put into a salad bowl lined with lettuce, romaine or endive, and tossed at the table. Then grated Parmesan cheese may be sprinkled generously over salad.

821   POTATO SALAD

2½ lbs. new or boiling potatoes (8 to 10)	2 tablespoons juice from pickles
½ cup chopped sweet pickles	1 tablespoon prepared mustard
½ cup chopped onion	
1 bunch radishes, sliced	2 teaspoons salt
½ large cucumber, diced	¼ teaspoon celery seed
½ cup mayonnaise (843)	3 hard-cooked eggs, diced (395)

Scrub potatoes and boil them in their jackets until they are just barely tender. Drain and cool thoroughly; then peel and dice. There should be about 5 cups. Add all ingredients, except eggs and mix together until each piece of potato is coated with dressing and seasonings are well distributed. Then add diced eggs and toss together very lightly so as not to break up the pieces. Chill before serving. 5 to 8 servings.

822 ## HOT POTATO SALAD

8 boiling potatoes, 2½ lbs.	2 teaspoons salt
5 slices bacon	¾ teaspoon sugar
1 tablespoon flour	1 onion, sliced thin
½ cup water	2 teaspoons chopped parsley
½ cup vinegar	

Scrub potatoes but do not pare; cook until just tender in boiling salted water. Meanwhile, pan-broil bacon (545) until done; remove from fat and crumble. To fat remaining in pan, add the flour and blend well; then gradually stir in the water and vinegar. Cook over direct heat, stirring constantly until mixture boils and thickens. Add salt, sugar and thinly sliced onion. Peel and dice the hot potatoes, add bacon to them, and pour on the hot dressing. Mix lightly, add parsley, serve hot. 5 servings.

823 ## POTATO CARROT SALAD

3 cups diced cooked potatoes	3 tablespoons pickle juice
2¼ cups diced cooked carrots	½ teaspoon celery salt
⅔ cup chopped dill pickle	1 teaspoon grated onion
½ cup mayonnaise (843)	

Combine diced, cooked potatoes with carrots and pickle. Mix mayonnaise with pickle juice and add celery salt and grated onion, blending well. Add seasoned dressing to vegetable mixture, toss lightly and chill to blend flavors. Serve on lettuce arranged on individual plates or turn into a lettuce-lined salad bowl. 5 servings.

824 ## RAW SPINACH SALAD

½ lb. tender spinach	French dressing (841)
2 tomatoes, diced	Lettuce, if desired
5 green onions, sliced	1 hard-cooked egg, sliced
½ cup sliced celery	(395)
½ teaspoon salt	

Carefully wash spinach leaves through 3 or 4 waters. Drain well, shred coarsely and combine with tomatoes, green onions, celery, salt and French dressing. Serve in a salad bowl lined with lettuce leaves and garnish with slices of hard-cooked egg. 5 servings.

825   TOSSED VEGETABLE SALAD

1 small head lettuce, broken into bite-size pieces	Few sprigs parsley, cut fine
	1 bunch radishes, sliced
2 tomatoes, peeled and cut in 6 wedges	1 cucumber, pared, sliced
	½ cup French dressing (841)

Put ingredients into a salad bowl in the order given, then toss with salad fork and spoon until every ingredient is well coated with dressing. Serve immediately on salad plates or from salad bowl at table. 5 servings.

Any kind of raw vegetable may be used in this type of salad as well as those mentioned in the recipe. Thinly sliced carrots, diced celery, sliced green onions or onion rings, or any other vegetable which your family likes to eat raw, may be added either to this salad or substituted for the ingredients listed.

826   WATERCRESS SALAD

1 bunch crisp watercress	2 slices crisp bacon, crumbled (545)
1 hard-cooked egg, chopped (395)	½ cup French dressing (841)
1 teaspoon chopped onion	

Swish cress through cold water, then pull sprigs apart, discarding any damaged leaves and heavy stems. Add chopped egg, onion and bacon; pour dressing over all, and toss together until cress is coated with dressing and ingredients are well mixed. Serve immediately. 5 servings.

827   WILTED LETTUCE

1 lb. leaf lettuce or 1 head lettuce	2 tablespoons bacon fat
	½ teaspoon salt
1 bunch radishes (may be omitted)	1 teaspoon sugar
	1 tablespoon vinegar

Separate lettuce leaves and wash thoroughly; drain well, then lay in a folded towel and shake off as much water as possible. Tear leaves into 3 or 4 pieces. Wash radishes and slice over lettuce in a salad bowl. Heat bacon fat with salt, sugar and vinegar until mixture sizzles. Pour over lettuce and radishes and toss together until thoroughly combined. Serve immediately while warm. 5 servings.

MAIN DISH SALADS

828   **CHICKEN OR VEAL SALAD**

3 cups diced cooked chicken   ¾ cup mayonnaise (843)
  or cold boiled veal   2 teaspoons lemon juice
1½ cups diced celery   Crisp lettuce
½ teaspoon salt   Pimiento

Combine chicken or veal, celery and salt. Mix mayonnaise with the
lemon juice, add to the meat mixture, and toss lightly. Chill thoroughly
before serving. Serve in crisp lettuce cups on individual salad plates.
Garnish with pimiento strips. 5 to 8 servings.

829   **COLD MEAT SALAD**

2 cups diced cooked meat   1 tablespoon prepared
1 cup sliced Pascal celery   mustard
1 cup diced pared tart apple   ½ teaspoon salt
¼ cup mayonnaise (843)   Crisp lettuce

Combine meat, celery and apple. Mix mayonnaise thoroughly with
mustard and salt; add to meat mixture and toss lightly until all pieces
are well coated with dressing. Serve in lettuce cups. 5 servings.

830   **CORNED BEEF AND POTATO SALAD**

4 medium potatoes, boiled   2 tablespoons chopped sweet
  (1068)   pickle
  12-oz. can corned beef,   ¾ cup mayonnaise (843)
  chilled   Crisp lettuce
2 tablespoons chopped onion

Cool and dice the peeled boiled potatoes. Remove corned beef from
can and dice. Combine potatoes and corned beef with onion, pickles and
mayonnaise, mixing together lightly. Cover and let stand at least 2 or 3
hours in refrigerator to blend flavors. Serve on lettuce leaves. 5 servings.

Diced corned beef may be added to the regular Potato Salad (821) if
preferred. In either recipe, diced or chopped ham, tongue, bacon, or
frankfurters or other sausage may be substituted for the corned beef.

831   EGG AND SARDINE SALAD

5 hard-cooked eggs (395)   ¼ cup mayonnaise (843)
3¼-oz. can sardines   Salt
½ cup sliced celery   Lettuce

Shell and chop the cooled eggs. Drain sardines, remove bones and tails and add celery, eggs, mayonnaise, and salt to taste, mixing lightly. Serve in lettuce cups on individual salad plates or use as a sandwich filling. 5 servings.

832   SALMON SALAD

1-lb. can red or pink salmon,   ½ cup chopped sweet pickle
  chilled   1 tablespoon lemon juice
1 cup sliced celery, chilled   Lettuce
½ cup mayonnaise (843)

Drain salmon, remove skin and bones, then flake fish. Add celery, mayonnaise, pickle and lemon juice and mix together lightly. Heap in lettuce cups on individual salad plates and serve. 5 servings.

Diced cucumber may be substituted for the celery, if desired.

833   SALMON AND MACARONI SALAD

Add 4 ounces macaroni, cooked and chilled to Salmon Salad (832), increasing amount of dressing, if desired.

834   JELLIED SALMON SALAD

½ teaspoon salt   1 tablespoon gelatin
½ teaspoon mustard   ¼ cup cold water
1 tablespoon flour   1-lb. can red or pink salmon
1 tablespoon sugar   ½ cup diced celery
¼ cup evaporated milk   ½ cup diced cucumber
¼ cup water   Lettuce
1 egg, beaten   Mayonnaise (843)
3 tablespoons vinegar

Combine first 4 ingredients in top of double boiler; add milk, ¼ cup water, egg and vinegar. Cook over boiling water until thickened, stirring constantly. Soften gelatin in ¼ cup cold water; add to hot mixture and stir until dissolved. Cool until thick and syrupy. Flake salmon after removing skin and large bones; fold into cooled mixture along with celery and cucumber. Pour into a lightly oiled mold and chill until firm. Unmold (815) on lettuce-lined plate and serve with mayonnaise. 5 servings.

835 SARDINE SALAD

2 3¼-oz. cans sardines
1½ cups diced celery
¼ cup diced pickle
1 teaspoon vinegar

¼ cup mayonnaise (843)
1 tablespoon prepared mustard
Crisp lettuce

Remove tails and bones from sardines. Combine sardines with celery and pickle. Sprinkle vinegar over mixture; let stand 5 minutes. Add mustard to mayonnaise and mix well with other ingredients. Chill and serve in crisp lettuce cups. 5 servings.

836 SHRIMP SALAD

2 cups cleaned cooked shrimp (461), chilled
½ cup sliced celery, chilled
1 teaspoon minced onion
⅓ cup mayonnaise (843)

¼ cup chili sauce
3 tablespoons lemon juice
2 or 3 hard-cooked eggs, chilled (395)
Crisp lettuce

Combine first 6 ingredients. Slice eggs and arrange in a ring on lettuce-lined individual salad plates. Pile salad mixture in the center of the ring. 5 servings.

837 TUNA FISH SALAD

7-oz. can tuna fish
½ cup chopped celery
1 tablespoon lemon juice
1½ teaspoons capers, if desired

¼ cup chopped sweet pickles
⅓ cup mayonnaise (843) or boiled salad dressing (840)
Crisp lettuce

Drain tuna, then flake fish. Add remaining ingredients and toss lightly. Cover tightly and chill. Serve in lettuce cups. 5 servings.

SALAD DRESSINGS

838 AVOCADO SALAD DRESSING

1 medium-size avocado, ripe but firm
½ cup orange juice

1 tablespoon lemon juice
½ teaspoon salt

Peel avocado, cut in half and discard pit. Press avocado through sieve, add other ingredients and beat with a rotary egg beater until perfectly smooth. Serve as dressing for fruit or tomato salad, or head lettuce. About 1 cup dressing.

839   BOILED SALAD DRESSING No. 1

2 eggs
½ cup sugar
2 tablespoons flour
½ teaspoon salt
¾ teaspoon dry mustard

½ cup cider vinegar
2 tablespoons butter
½ cup evaporated milk
Few grains red pepper

Beat eggs until light in top of double boiler. Mix dry ingredients together and blend thoroughly with beaten eggs. Stir in vinegar and cook over boiling water, stirring constantly until mixture thickens. Remove from heat and stir in butter, evaporated milk and red pepper. Cool, then store in covered jar in refrigerator. About 1½ cups.

840   BOILED SALAD DRESSING No. 2

⅔ cup sugar
1¼ teaspoons salt
1 tablespoon flour
⅔ cup cider vinegar

⅔ cup egg yolks, slightly
beaten
4 teaspoons prepared mustard
Dash cayenne
¾ cup evaporated milk

Mix sugar, salt and flour in top of double boiler; stir in vinegar and mix until smooth. Cook over direct heat, stirring constantly until mixture boils and thickens. Slowly stir into beaten egg yolks; add mustard and cayenne and return to top of double boiler. Now cook over boiling water for 3 minutes, stirring constantly. Remove from heat and stir in the evaporated milk. Chill before serving. Delicious with fruit salad or head lettuce salad. About 2 cups.

Variation: If preferred, omit the evaporated milk and just before serving, fold in ½ cup whipping cream, whipped until stiff.

841   FRENCH DRESSING

⅔ cup salad oil
⅓ cup cider vinegar
¾ teaspoon salt
4 teaspoons sugar, or to taste
1/16 teaspoon dry mustard

1/16 teaspoon black pepper
1 teaspoon paprika
½ teaspoon onion juice,
(omit for fruit salad)

Combine all ingredients by beating thoroughly with rotary beater. Beat or shake well just before serving. About 1 cup.

841a ## LEMON FRENCH DRESSING

⅓ cup lemon juice
½ cup salad oil
1 teaspoon salt
1 teaspoon paprika

2 tablespoons sugar or honey
½ teaspoon celery seed,
if desired
Clove of garlic, if desired

Combine all ingredients and shake well before serving. Makes 1 cup. This dressing is an excellent marinade for cooked vegetables, meat and fish. Let them stand in the dressing until well seasoned. Drain, and serve with any additional dressing.

Variation: To make a sweet French dressing for fruit salads, omit the garlic and add ½ cup red jelly or ½ cup honey to the above ingredients.

841b ## BLUE CHEESE DRESSING

¼ cup blue cheese, 2 oz.
⅓ cup evaporated milk
½ teaspoon dry mustard
¼ teaspoon salt

⅛ teaspoon pepper
1 teaspoon paprika
⅓ cup salad oil
3 tablespoons lemon juice

Mash cheese with a fork; add milk, dry mustard, seasonings and paprika and mix well. Stir in salad oil 1 tablespoon at a time. Add lemon juice. Serve on green vegetable salads. About 1¼ cups dressing.

842 ## FRUIT SALAD DRESSING

3 tablespoons butter
2 tablespoons flour
½ cup milk
¼ cup egg yolks, about
3 yolks

¼ cup orange juice
1½ tablespoons lemon juice
2 or 3 tablespoons sugar
¼ teaspoon salt
¼ teaspoon prepared mustard

Melt butter, blend in flour, add milk and cook over direct heat, stirring constantly until mixture boils and thickens. Stir in beaten egg yolks and cook one minute longer, continuing to stir. Remove from heat; stir in fruit juices, sugar, salt and mustard. Chill thoroughly before using. About 1 cup.

843 ## MAYONNAISE

¼ teaspoon paprika
1 teaspoon dry mustard
1 teaspoon salt
2 teaspoons XXXX sugar
Dash cayenne pepper

2 egg yolks
¼ cup cider vinegar or lemon juice, chilled
1¾ cups olive or salad oil, chilled

479

Mix dry ingredients in mixing bowl. Add unbeaten egg yolks and mix well; then add ½ teaspoon vinegar or lemon juice. Add a few drops of oil, beating in with a rotary egg beater or electric mixer. Continue adding oil by drops, beating thoroughly after each addition until about 2 tablespoons oil have been added and the mixture has thickened. Beat in a little vinegar, then continue adding oil by teaspoons until 2 more tablespoons have been used. As mixture thickens, oil may be added in larger quantities, beating well after each addition. Add vinegar to thin the mixture whenever it becomes very stiff. Continue adding oil and vinegar, beating continuously until all has been used. 1 pint.

Note: If oil is added too rapidly at first, mayonnaise will not thicken; but this thin mixture may be beaten into another egg yolk, a little at a time, and the rest of the oil and vinegar added when the new mixture has thickened up.

843a   CRANBERRY MAYONNAISE

½ cup mayonnaise (843)   ¼ cup cream, whipped
½ cup cranberry jelly (282)

Blend mayonnaise and cranberry jelly well; fold in stiffly whipped cream. Serve with chicken (828) or banana salad (735). About 1½ cups dressing.

843b   RASPBERRY MAYONNAISE

2 tablespoons raspberry jelly   Dash salt
½ cup mayonnaise (843)   ¼ cup cream, whipped
2 tablespoons lemon juice

Break up raspberry jelly with a silver fork. Stir in mayonnaise, lemon juice and salt and fold in whipped cream. Serve with fruit salads. About 1 cup dressing.

843c   PEPPER-ONION MAYONNAISE

1 clove of garlic, cut   2 teaspoons lemon juice
1 tablespoon chopped parsley   ⅛ teaspoon paprika
1 tablespoon chopped green   ¼ teaspoon salt
   pepper   ⅛ teaspoon pepper
1 tablespoon chopped onion   1 cup mayonnaise (843)
1 tablespoon chopped
   pimiento

Rub bowl in which dressing is to be mixed with cut side of clove of garlic. Add parsley, green pepper, onion, pimiento, lemon juice and seasonings to mayonnaise and mix well. Serve with tossed green salads. About 1¼ cups dressing.

844   PEANUT MAYONNAISE

Combine mayonnaise (843) with coarsely chopped salted peanuts in any desired proportion. This dressing is especially good with plain head lettuce, or with banana or apple salad.

845   PEANUT BUTTER DRESSING

Add peanut butter to mayonnaise (843), using about 1 tablespoon peanut butter to ¼ cup mayonnaise. Blend thoroughly. This is popular with children.

846   RUSSIAN DRESSING

To make a quick, simple version of Russian dressing, combine 4 parts mayonnaise (843) with 1 part chili sauce, mixing thoroughly.

846a   SOUR CREAM SALAD DRESSING

1 egg yolk	¼ teaspoon salt
2 teaspoons vinegar	Pepper to taste
½ teaspoon dry mustard	½ cup sour cream
4 teaspoons sugar	

Beat egg yolk until thick, stir in vinegar, mustard, sugar and seasonings, and turn into the top of a double boiler. Place over simmering water and cook with constant stirring until slightly thickened. Cool and stir in sour cream. Chill thoroughly before serving. Serve with any cabbage or other vegetable salad. Makes ⅔ cup.

847   SPECIAL SALAD DRESSING

3 tablespoons flour	½ teaspoon celery seed, if
3 tablespoons sugar	desired
1 teaspoon salt	½ cup evaporated milk
¼ teaspoon dry mustard	½ cup water
½ teaspoon paprika	1 egg, beaten
⅛ teaspoon black pepper	⅔ cup cider vinegar

Mix all dry ingredients and celery seed in a saucepan; add evaporated milk and water and bring to boil; boil 3 minutes, stirring constantly. Remove from heat and stir hot mixture into well-beaten egg which has been combined with vinegar. Chill. This dressing is good for potato or macaroni salad, or wherever an oil dressing is not desired. About 1½ cups.

848   THOUSAND ISLAND DRESSING

Thousand Island Dressing is a term which is used to describe mayonnaise (843) with various additions. Sweet pickle relish, chopped green pepper, sweet red pepper or canned pimiento, chopped stuffed or ripe olives, or chopped hard-cooked eggs are the most usual additions. Any or all of these ingredients may be used in the proportion of 1 part to 2 or 3 parts mayonnaise.

848a   QUICK SOUR CREAM DRESSING

½ cup sour cream
2 or 3 dashes black pepper
1½ teaspoons sugar
½ teaspoon salt

1 teaspoon cider vinegar
⅛ teaspoon prepared mustard, optional

Put all ingredients into a mixing bowl and stir until well blended. Delicious on sliced cucumbers and onions, or sliced cucumbers, onions and tomatoes, or cole slaw. Makes ⅓ cup.

SANDWICHES

• • • • • • •

TAKE women's funny hats and fussy party sandwiches out of this world and what would men have to laugh about? But they have a sneaking admiration for giddy hats after all; and there's nothing secret about the gusto with which they go for sandwiches, even the fancy ones. Men, children, and womenfolks too, will find sandwiches they specially like in this varied collection of sandwich recipes for every occasion.

• • • • • • • • • •

Probably there is not an American who does not know the story of how the Earl of Sandwich, nearly two hundred years ago, called for a piece of meat between two slices of bread so he could eat without leaving the gaming table. Pleased with his invention, he called it a "sandwich." The inventive Earl would not recognize his brain-child in many of the sandwiches of today, which have long ceased to conform even in general to the pattern of a simple filling between two slices of bread. Only the schoolchild's or the working man's "lunch box" sandwich bears any marked resemblance to its first ancestor. Here are some common types of sandwiches that are popular today:

1. *"LUNCH BOX" SANDWICH:* 2 slices of buttered bread (enriched white, whole wheat, rye or a combination of any two) laid together with any desired filling, then the sandwich is usually cut in half for convenience in eating.

2. *HOT SANDWICH:* 2 whole slices of bread or toast placed side by side on a plate, then covered with hot sliced meat (sometimes fish), and gravy or sauce spooned over it. Eaten with fork.

3. *GRILLED OR TOASTED SANDWICH:* 2 untrimmed or trimmed (crusts removed) slices of bread spread with any desired filling, then put together and toasted on both sides under the broiler, in a buttered skillet or in a sandwich grill. Serve hot.

4. *OPEN-FACE SANDWICH:* 1 slice of bread or toast, untrimmed or trimmed, or 2 slices placed side by side, spread with butter and any

desired filling, or covered with sliced meat, cheese, tomato, etc. Sometimes grilled or toasted, especially when cheese is used.

5. *CLUB SANDWICH:* 3 or more slices of bread or toast, spread with butter and put together with a different filling in each layer; crusts usually trimmed off and sandwich cut in triangles.

6. *CANAPÉS:* Small open-face sandwiches, made of bread or toast cut out with fancy cookie cutters, then spread with butter and filling (865, 882 or 889) and garnished attractively. Usually served as appetizers.

7. *FANCY SANDWICHES* such as rolled, ribbon, checkerboard and mosaic will be found in the following recipe section.

8. *SANDWICH LOAF:* 3 or more slices of bread, cut either crosswise or lengthwise of a sandwich loaf, then spread with butter and a different filling spread on each layer, such as 850, 882, and 889. Crusts are trimmed off and loaf "iced" with a cream cheese mixture. Crosswise slices of bread make an individual loaf; lengthwise slices make a loaf which is sliced like cake for individual servings.

SANDWICH FILLINGS

There are even more kinds of fillings than sandwiches, ranging from the famous Earl's simple slab of meat to the most elaborate combination of fancy ingredients. But they are still divided into 3 main classes:

1. *"MAIN DISH" FILLINGS:* include sliced meat and cheese, potted meat, fish, chopped meat, hard-cooked, scrambled and fried eggs, peanut butter, and any definitely protein food mixture. May be combined with lettuce, sliced tomatoes, chopped pickles, chopped vegetables of various kinds.

2. *SWEET FILLINGS:* include jams, jellies, preserves, honey and spreads made by combining creamed butter or cream cheese with any of these ingredients, or with fruit, such as date paste, grated orange rind or lemon juice.

3. *RELISH FILLINGS:* include chopped vegetables mixed with mayonnaise dressing.

Most of these fillings can be used in most types of sandwich, and a good deal of overlapping is likely to occur. There is plenty of room for originality.

MAKING SANDWICHES

The best foundation for sandwiches is 2-day-old bread, which is fresh enough to be palatable but not so fresh that it tears when spread. The only exception to this is that the freshest of bread is required for rolled sandwiches. For thin, dainty sandwiches, buy unsliced bread and be sure you have a razor-sharp knife to slice it. The knife will need frequent sharpening if you have many sandwiches to make. Bread for dainty sandwiches should never be sliced more than ⅜-inch thick. Sliced bread is usually at least

½-inch thick, sometimes a little more, and a sandwich of these proportions is quite a mouthful; good for lunch boxes but not for teas.

The loaf may be sliced either crosswise for regular sandwiches, or lengthwise for rolled sandwiches or a sandwich loaf. In either case it is important to slice it uniformly thick. Crusts can be cut from the loaf before slicing the bread if preferred. It is a little more work and also a little more waste, but it is generally more satisfactory to trim the crusts off after the sandwich is made. It is easier to spread the bread before trimming, and the sandwich will look neater with filling that goes right to the edge of the bread if trimming is done after spreading the filling. The crusts will have a little butter and filling on them, but these make tasty after-school snacks for youngsters.

In making sandwiches, be sure to spread the bread well with a uniform thin layer of soft butter (about 1½ teaspoons of creamed butter per slice), or mayonnaise, whichever you are using. This is especially important with a moist or soft filling such as preserves, for it prevents excessive soaking of the bread. Of course each slice of bread must be buttered on the side next to the filling.

Spread the filling generously, especially if it is mild-flavored. The thickness should vary according to the thickness of the bread; slices ⅝-inch thick will require more filling to be tasty than slices ⅜-inch thick.

If sandwiches are to be kept a while or carried in a lunch box, they should be wrapped in waxed paper as soon as they are made. If different fillings are used, each sandwich should be wrapped separately, to prevent an interchange of flavors. Ribbon and checkerboard sandwiches and others which need to be chilled for a time, should always be snugly wrapped in waxed paper before storing in refrigerator. It not only preserves flavor but prevents drying out.

SERVING SANDWICHES

Regular sandwiches, for luncheons or for lunch boxes, present no particular problem of serving beyond that of making them as easy to eat as possible. This is done by cutting the whole sandwich into halves or quarters, so it can be handled conveniently. But if everyone is hungry and the sandwiches are good, no one will worry about the arrangement.

Party sandwiches—finger, ribbon, rolled, checkerboard, mosaic—lend themselves to arrangement. Flat trays, platters and large chop plates are ideal. Sandwiches of the same kind should be grouped together. Several kinds may be put on the same plate, but may be separated by sprigs of parsley, olives, or small pickles, which make an edible garnish. Such a tray of carefully made sandwiches is appealing to the eye as well as to the palate, and most women enjoy the little stir of admiration which they are bound to create.

MEAT SANDWICHES

849   BACON SANDWICHES

10 slices whole wheat bread   10 slices bacon, ½ lb.
⅓ cup soft butter   Radish slices or lettuce

Toast bread, spread immediately with soft butter. Put 2 slices each of broiled (544) or pan-broiled bacon (545) on 5 slices of toast. Add radish slices or lettuce and top with remaining slices of toast. Cut as desired. Serve hot. 5 servings.

850   BACON AND PICKLE SANDWICHES

10 slices bacon   ¼ cup mayonnaise (843)
⅓ cup chopped dill pickle   10 slices buttered bread

Pan-broil bacon until done (545); drain thoroughly and crumble. Combine with pickles and mayonnaise. Spread between slices of buttered bread. 5 sandwiches.

851   BACON AND TOMATO SANDWICHES

10 slices bacon   ¼ cup mayonnaise (843)
3 medium-size tomatoes,   10 slices buttered bread or toast
  peeled   5 leaves lettuce

Pan-broil bacon (545) until done. Slice tomatoes rather thick. Spread mayonnaise on the buttered bread. Place a leaf of lettuce on half the slices. On remaining slices arrange tomato and bacon slices. Lay together and serve. For convenience in eating, cut sandwiches in two diagonally. 5 sandwiches.

851a   BACON AND PEANUT BUTTER SANDWICHES

½ cup peanut butter   10 slices buttered bread
10 slices bacon, ½ lb.   5 leaves lettuce
5 stuffed olives, chopped

Mix the peanut butter well with its oil before measuring. Pan-broil bacon (545) until done, then drain on absorbent paper. Crumble bacon and mix well with olives and peanut butter. Spread on half the buttered bread slices, cover with a leaf of lettuce and top with remaining slices of bread. Cut each sandwich in half diagonally. Serve with radishes, pickles or more olives. 5 sandwiches.

852   GRILLED CHEESE AND BACON SANDWICHES

10 slices enriched bread
10 thin slices American cheese

3 tablespoons prepared mustard
10 slices bacon, ½ lb.

Toast bread lightly. Cover each slice with a slice of cheese, then spread cheese with mustard. Cut each slice of bacon in half and lay 2 half-slices on top of the cheese. Grill in broiler under low heat until bacon is crisp and cheese is melted and slightly browned. Serve hot with sweet or dill pickles. 10 open-face sandwiches.

853   CHIPPED BEEF SANDWICHES

¼ lb. chipped beef
1 teaspoon prepared mustard

5 tablespoons soft butter
10 slices enriched bread

Rinse beef quickly in hot water. Leave pieces whole or shred. Mix mustard and butter, spread on bread; lay beef on half the slices, then cover with remaining slices. A pleasing variation is to chop the beef fine and mix thoroughly with cream cheese to make a sandwich spread. 5 sandwiches.

854   BOLOGNA SANDWICHES

1 lb. bologna   10 slices buttered bread

Slice bologna thin, remove casing and place between slices of bread. If desired, sausage slices may be broiled or pan-fried in a little butter until brown. Or the sausage may be chopped and mixed to a spreading consistency with a little mayonnaise. 5 sandwiches.

855   CLUB SANDWICHES

15 slices toasted bread, buttered
5 leaves lettuce
5 slices roast or steamed chicken

10 slices bacon, cooked done (545)
2 tomatoes
1 small cucumber, sliced
¼ cup mayonnaise

On 5 slices of buttered toast, place lettuce leaves, and over this arrange chicken and bacon slices. Cover with 5 more slices of buttered toast, buttered-side down. Spread top of these slices with mayonnaise, and on them arrange slices of tomato and cucumber. Top with remaining slices of buttered toast buttered-side down. Stick toothpicks through opposite corners of each sandwich to prevent slipping, and cut each

sandwich in 2, 3 or 4 pieces before serving, using a very sharp knife. 5
sandwiches.

856   FRANKFURTER SANDWICHES

5 frankfurters	5 leaves lettuce
Mustard, sweet pickle relish or catchup, if desired	10 slices buttered bread

Split frankfurters lengthwise and pan-fry (589) in a little butter or
other fat. Place 2 halves on each of 5 slices bread, and spread with mustard, relish or catchup, as desired. Cover with a lettuce leaf and another
slice of buttered bread. 5 sandwiches.

857   HAM SALAD SANDWICHES

1 cup ground cooked ham	1½ teaspoons prepared mustard
¼ cup finely chopped sweet pickles	¼ cup mayonnaise
	10 slices buttered bread

Combine ham and pickles thoroughly, then mix with mustard and
mayonnaise to bind them together. Spread between slices of buttered
bread. 5 sandwiches.

858   MINCED HAM AND CHEESE SPREAD

2 cups ground cooked ham, 1 lb.	½ cup finely chopped pickles
2 cups grated American cheese, ½ lb.	Mayonnaise

Combine ham and cheese; blend with pickle and enough mayonnaise
to give a spreading consistency. Enough for 10 to 15 sandwiches.

859   HAM AND BANANA SANDWICHES

3 cups ground cooked ham, 1½ lbs.	2 tablespoons lemon juice
1 cup fine-diced celery	Salt to taste
1 teaspoon fine-chopped onion	10 slices buttered bread or toast
2 tablespoons prepared mustard	10 crisp lettuce leaves
Mayonnaise to moisten	2 ripe bananas, sliced
	Maraschino cherries

Combine the first 6 ingredients, mixing thoroughly; season to suit
taste. On each slice of buttered bread or toast, place a leaf of lettuce.

On the lettuce spread a generous amount of the ham salad mixture. Garnish with slices of banana and with pieces of maraschino cherry. 10 to 12 open-face sandwiches.

860   HAM AND CRANBERRY SANDWICHES

10 thin slices boiled ham	½ lb. sharp American cheese,
1½ tablespoons bacon fat	grated
10 slices buttered toast	Parsley
No. 2 can cranberry jelly	Sweet pickles

Brown the ham slightly in the bacon fat, in a skillet. Drain ham and place a slice on each slice of buttered toast. On top of ham, place a slice of firm cranberry jelly, and top with a portion of the grated cheese. Place sandwiches under a broiler to melt and brown the cheese quickly. Serve immediately with a garnish of parsley and sweet pickles. 10 open-faced sandwiches.

861   HAM AND TUNA FISH SANDWICHES

10 slices buttered toast or bread	2 tomatoes, peeled and sliced
10 crisp lettuce leaves	13-oz. can tuna fish
10 slices boiled ham	Mayonnaise (843)
Prepared mustard	Parsley

On each slice of buttered toast, place a lettuce leaf, and on the lettuce a slice of ham. Spread ham very lightly with mustard. Top the ham with 1 or 2 slices of tomato. Drain tuna and separate into large thin flakes. Divide it among the sandwiches. Garnish with a spoonful of mayonnaise and a tiny sprig of parsley. Serve immediately. 10 open-face sandwiches.

861a   HOT ROAST MEAT SANDWICHES

For each sandwich, butter lightly 2 slices of bread. Place 1 slice in the center of the serving plate; cut the other slice into 2 triangles and place one on each side of the whole slice. Arrange sliced hot roast meat on the whole bread slice and pour hot meat gravy over the meat and the rest of the bread. For a full luncheon plate, serve mashed potato on the same plate, and a serving of jelly or fruit pickles either on the plate or in a side dish. Apple sauce is good with a hot pork sandwich; mint jelly with lamb; or apple jelly with roast beef.

861b   COLD ROAST MEAT SANDWICHES

10 slices bread   Cold roast meat
⅓ cup soft butter or ⅓ cup   Lettuce
   Mayonnaise (843)

Spread slices of bread with butter or mayonnaise. Slice meat thinly just before serving sandwiches. Place slices of meat on half the slices of buttered bread; lay clean, dry, crisp lettuce on meat and top with another slice of buttered bread. Cut in desired shape and serve at once, or wrap lunch-box sandwiches in waxed paper. If the piece of cold roast is too small to slice, run meat through a food chopper or chop finely in a wooden bowl. Add mayonnaise to meat to obtain a spreading consistency. A little finely chopped celery or pickle may be added to the mixture to give a piquant flavor; then proceed as for sliced meat sandwiches. 5 servings.

862   SWISS HAM AND TOMATO SANDWICHES
(A famous sandwich)

10 slices buttered toast   3 medium size tomatoes,
10 lettuce leaves   peeled, sliced
10 slices boiled ham   10 slices broiled bacon (544)
10 slices Swiss cheese   ¾ cup 1000 Island Dressing

On each slice of buttered toast, place a crisp lettuce leaf; then a slice of ham, a slice of cheese, and one or two tomato slices, depending on size. Top with a slice of broiled bacon and serve with dressing poured over sandwich or in little paper cups at the side. 10 open-faced sandwiches.

863   LIVER SAUSAGE SANDWICHES

¾ lb. liver sausage   Lettuce, if desired
10 slices buttered rye bread   Crisp pickle slices

Sausage should be sliced about ⅜-inch thick and casing removed. Arrange between slices of buttered bread, with lettuce if desired. For hot liver sausage sandwiches, brown sausage slices (615) in a little butter or other fat, and toast the bread. Serve with pickles. 5 full-size sandwiches.

864   LIVER SAUSAGE SPREAD

Mash ¾ lb. liver sausage and mix with ⅓ cup chopped sweet pickle and a little mayonnaise to give a good spreading consistency. Grated sharp cheese makes a pleasing addition. After spreading on buttered bread, the sandwich may be left open-face or toasted under broiler, if desired. Enough for 5 sandwiches.

865 LIVER SAUSAGE MUSHROOM SPREAD

1 cup liver sausage, ½ lb.
½ cup finely chopped mushrooms
1 tablespoon butter
½ teaspoon Worcestershire
Salt if desired
Mayonnaise (843)

Combine mashed liver sausage with mushrooms which have been sautéed (1043) in the butter until tender. Add seasonings and mix in enough mayonnaise to bind the ingredients together. This mixture is a good sandwich spread, or when spread on potato chips, it makes unusual hors d'oeuvres. About 1½ cups.

866 SAUSAGE TOAST

¾ lb. pork sausage meat
2 teaspoons chopped parsley
⅓ cup grated American cheese
1 tablespoon prepared mustard
10 slices hot buttered toast

Turn sausage into hot skillet and cook with frequent stirring until well done, 15 to 20 minutes. Now drain off fat. Put meat into mixing bowl and add remaining ingredients, mixing thoroughly. Spread on hot buttered toast. 10 open-face sandwiches.

867 SQUARE-MEAL BISCUIT SANDWICHES

1 recipe biscuits (26)
1 lb. ground beef
1 teaspoon salt
3 tablespoons butter or bacon fat
¼ cup flour
No. 2 can cut green beans
Milk
¾ teaspoon salt
¾ cup grated sharp cheese

Turn biscuit dough onto floured board and roll into a rectangle 12½ x 5 inches and ¼-inch thick; cut into ten 2½-inch squares. Transfer to slightly greased baking sheet and bake in a hot oven (425° F.) 8 to 10 minutes. Meanwhile combine meat with the 1 teaspoon salt; shape in 5 thin patties and pan-broil in hot, slightly greased skillet until done. Melt butter in top of double boiler, blend in flour and add liquid drained from beans plus enough milk to make 1½ cups; stir constantly over direct heat until sauce boils and thickens. Add ¾ teaspoon salt and stir in cheese until melted. Add the beans and keep hot over boiling water. To serve, place a meat patty between 2 biscuits and spoon the hot sauce over all. Serve immediately. 5 servings.

868   POTTED MEAT

1 lb. beef for stew	¼ teaspoon mace
1 qt. water	¼ teaspoon dry mustard
1 onion, sliced	½ teaspoon salt
2 teaspoons salt	Meat broth to moisten
Dash cayenne pepper	

Cut beef into inch-dice; put into saucepan with water, onion and the 2 teaspoons salt. Cover and simmer until meat is tender, about 1 hour. Lift meat out of broth and cool. Then put through meat grinder. Blend well with remaining ingredients, using just enough broth to moisten and hold meat together. Press firmly into cups or other molds; cover and store in refrigerator. When ready to serve, unmold and slice thin. Makes 4 cups. Any remaining broth may be used in soup or gravy.

VEGETABLE SANDWICHES

869   BAKED BEAN SANDWICHES

No. 300 can pork and beans	Catchup or chili sauce
1 tablespoon grated onion	10 slices buttered bread

Drain and mash beans and mix with onion and a little catchup or chili sauce, if desired. Spread between slices of buttered bread. Serve with crisp pickle slices, radishes or cole slaw. 5 full-size sandwiches.

870   CHOPPED CABBAGE AND BACON SANDWICHES

1 cup finely chopped cabbage	¼ cup mayonnaise (843)
3 slices cooked bacon (545)	¼ teaspoon sugar
¼ teaspoon salt	10 slices buttered bread

Use only crisp green cabbage for sandwich fillings; about ⅛ of a medium-size head makes 1 cup chopped. Chop, do not shred. Combine with the crumbled bacon, salt, mayonnaise and sugar, mixing thoroughly. Spread between slices of buttered bread. Cut sandwiches in half from corner to corner. Serve immediately, or wrap securely in waxed paper if sandwiches must be prepared ahead of time. 5 sandwiches.

871   CARROT BUTTER

1 medium carrot	¼ teaspoon sugar
½ cup soft butter	1 tablespoon mayonnaise
⅛ teaspoon celery salt	

Scrape carrot clean, rinse, then shred; mix to a spreading consistency with the butter, which has been creamed until smooth. Add celery salt, sugar and mayonnaise. With this sandwich spread, the bread for sandwiches need not be buttered. Enough for 5 sandwiches.

872   CARROT-RAISIN SPREAD

2 medium carrots	¼ cup moist seedless raisins
½ cup soft butter	⅛ teaspoon salt

Scrape carrots clean, rinse off in water, then shred. Cream butter until smooth, then blend with carrots, chopped raisins and salt. A little mayonnaise may be added if needed to produce a spreading consistency. Enough for 6 to 8 sandwiches.

873   CUCUMBER, ONION, AND PICKLE SANDWICHES

1 small cucumber	¼ cup mayonnaise (843)
1 small onion	10 slices buttered bread
¼ cup chopped sweet pickles	

Pare cucumber and peel onion, and chop them together with the pickles. Mix with mayonnaise and spread on half the slices of buttered bread; top with remaining slices. Good with salmon or tuna salad. Enough for 5 sandwiches.

874   KIDNEY BEAN SANDWICH FILLING

No. 2 can red kidney beans	¼ teaspoon salt
½ cup finely chopped celery	2 tablespoons pickle juice
¼ cup chopped sweet pickle	Dash pepper

Drain beans and mash thoroughly with potato masher; there will be about 1½ cups. Add remaining ingredients and mix thoroughly. Make sandwiches with buttered bread or toast, and serve with sliced tomatoes or pickled beets. Enough for 8 to 10 sandwiches.

875   LETTUCE SANDWICHES

Head or leaf lettuce	3 tablespoons mayonnaise
10 slices buttered bread	(843)

Separate washed drained lettuce into leaves, or shred. Arrange leaves or shredded lettuce generously on half the slices of buttered bread, then spread rest of slices with mayonnaise. Lay together. If desired, both slices of bread may be spread with mayonnaise instead of butter. Good with chicken, meat or fish salads. Enough for 5 sandwiches.

876   PARSLEY BUTTER

Wash parsley, drain well, then strip leaves from stems and put leaves into a small glass and snip up fine in the glass with kitchen shears. Combine 3 tablespoonfuls chopped parsley with ½ cup of creamed butter. Add salt to suit taste, and blend in a little mayonnaise if needed to give a spreading consistency. Enough for 5 sandwiches.

877   MIXED VEGETABLE SPREAD

Shred 1-pared, medium size cucumber or chop it very fine; place in a piece of cheesecloth and squeeze out the juice. Juice may be combined with tomato juice for cocktail. Combine cucumber with ½ cup of very finely chopped cabbage or lettuce and mix with just enough mayonnaise to bind together. Add salt to suit taste. Enough for 5 sandwiches.

878   WATERCRESS SANDWICHES

1 bunch watercress	10 slices buttered bread
Salt	

Wash cress thoroughly; discard damaged leaves and white roots. Shake water from cress. Arrange between slices of buttered bread, sprinkling lightly with salt before covering. 5 sandwiches.

Note: Heart leaves of spinach may be used in place of watercress. And thin slices of roast turkey or chicken may be laid over the cress.

879   WATERCRESS AND BACON SANDWICHES

5 slices bacon	10 slices buttered bread
1 bunch watercress	

Pan-broil bacon (545) until done; drain thoroughly and crumble. Wash watercress and shake water out; remove white roots and any discolored leaves. Arrange cress over 5 slices buttered bread, sprinkle with chopped crisp bacon and cover with remaining bread slices. 5 sandwiches.

FISH SANDWICHES

880   SARDINE SANDWICHES

3¼-oz. can sardines	½ teaspoon prepared mustard
2 hard-cooked eggs, fine-chopped (395)	Salt to taste
	10 slices buttered bread
1 teaspoon lemon juice	

Drain sardines thoroughly and remove tails, also bones if desired. Mash sardines and combine with eggs, lemon juice, mustard and salt. Spread between slices of buttered bread. A leaf of lettuce in each sandwich gives crisp texture. 5 sandwiches.

881   **BROILED SARDINE SANDWICHES**

2 3¼-oz. cans sardines   1½ tablespoons prepared
1½ tablespoons catchup   mustard
                              10 slices buttered bread

Drain sardines, remove tails and bones. Chop or mash the fish fine. Add catchup and mustard, blending thoroughly. Spread on untoasted bread and place under broiler from 5 to 10 minutes, or until hot and slightly browned. If desired, bread may be toasted on one side and sardine mixture spread on the untoasted side before broiling. 10 open-face sandwiches.

882   **SHRIMP BUTTER**

5-oz. can shrimp or ¾   ½ cup soft butter
cup cooked fresh shrimp   2 tablespoons lemon juice
(461)

Clean canned shrimp by removing dark vein down back and rinsing with cold water. Pound to a paste in a wooden bowl. Cream butter until very smooth, add shrimp paste and lemon juice and mix thoroughly. 1¼ cups.

CHEESE, EGG AND NUT SANDWICHES

883   **CHEESE AND TOMATO SANDWICHES**

4 medium-sized tomatoes,   10 slices buttered toast
peeled   10 thin slices American cheese

Cut tomatoes in thick slices and arrange on buttered toast. Lay slices of cheese over the tomatoes and place under broiler until cheese is lightly toasted and tomatoes hot. 10 open-face sandwiches.

884   PAN-BROILED CHEESE SANDWICHES

½ lb. American cheese, sliced   ⅓ cup soft butter
10 slices bread

Place slices of cheese between slices of unbuttered bread; spread outside of sandwiches lightly and evenly with butter. Place sandwiches in moderately hot skillet and brown both sides to the desired golden-brown color, watching carefully. When done, cheese will be slightly melted. Serve piping hot. 5 sandwiches.

885   TOASTED CHEESE-HAM SANDWICHES

½ lb. American cheese, grated   10 slices buttered bread
   or sliced   5 thin slices boiled ham

Place grated or sliced cheese on 5 slices of the buttered bread; cover each with a ham slice and top with another slice of bread. If desired, spread ham with a little mustard before covering. Toast on both sides in broiler; or if desired, sandwiches may be put together buttered-sides-out and pan-broiled as in 884. 5 sandwiches.

885a   CHEESE PUFFS

1¼ cups grated sharp cheese,   3 tablespoons milk
   about ⅓ lb.   Dash salt
1 egg, beaten   10 slices bread

Thoroughly mix cheese, egg, milk and salt. Cut slices of bread in half and toast on one side. Spread untoasted side with the cheese mixture and place under broiler until cheese is puffy and toasted. Serve hot. 5 servings.

886   DENVER SANDWICHES

5 eggs   2 tablespoons chopped cooked
2 tablespoons chopped onion   ham
⅓ cup chopped green pepper   Salt and pepper to taste
                                   10 slices buttered bread or toast

Slightly beat eggs, add onion, green pepper and ham, and pour into hot, buttered 9 or 10-inch skillet. Cook over low heat until eggs are just firm. Sprinkle with salt and pepper. Cut into 5 pieces and place between slices of bread or toast. Two egg yolks may be substituted for one whole egg. 5 sandwiches.

887   **DEVILED EGG SANDWICHES**

5 hard-cooked eggs (395)   10 slices buttered bread,
2 tablespoons mayonnaise   using ⅓ cup butter
Salt to taste   5 leaves lettuce or 1 bunch
Prepared mustard, if desired   watercress

Shell the eggs and put them through a ricer or sieve. Mix thoroughly
with mayonnaise, salt and mustard, then spread on 5 of the bread slices.
Cover with lettuce or cress and lay remaining slices of bread on top. 5
sandwiches.

888   **EGG AND BACON SANDWICHES**

4 hard-cooked eggs (395)   ¼ cup mayonnaise (843)
4 slices pan broiled bacon   10 slices bread, buttered
   (545)   5 leaves lettuce

Shell eggs and chop rather fine; mix with the crumbled bacon and
mayonnaise. Spread on half the slices of buttered bread; cover each with
lettuce leaf and place another slice of bread on top. Cut each sandwich
in fingers. 5 sandwiches.

889   **EGG SALAD SANDWICHES**

5 hard-cooked eggs (395)   Salt to taste
¼ cup chopped pickles   10 slices buttered bread
1 teaspoon prepared mustard

Shell eggs and chop rather fine. Mix with pickles, mustard and salt.
Spread on half the slices of buttered bread; top with remaining slices.
Cut sandwiches diagonally in halves. 5 sandwiches.

890   **CUCUMBER AND EGG SALAD SANDWICH FILLING**

2 hard-cooked eggs (395)   Dash pepper
¾ cup diced cucumber   1½ tablespoons mayonnaise,
1 or 2 teaspoons minced onion   (843) mixed with
⅜ teaspoon salt   ⅛ teaspoon prepared mustard

Combine all ingredients lightly but thoroughly. Use immediately as
filling for sandwiches. About 1 cup filling, enough for 5 sandwiches.

891   **OLIVE AND EGG SANDWICHES**

3 hard-cooked eggs (395)   10 slices buttered bread
¼ cup chopped stuffed olives   5 leaves lettuce
⅓ cup mayonnaise (843)

497

Shell eggs and chop quite fine. Combine with olives and mayonnaise. Spread on 5 of the bread slices, cover each with a lettuce leaf, and lay another slice of bread on top. Cut each sandwich in 4 triangles. 5 sandwiches.

892 DATE NUT SPREAD

Mix ½ cup finely chopped walnuts, pecans or almonds with ¾ cup finely chopped pitted dates. Add a little lemon juice, if desired, and enough mayonnaise to give a spreading consistency. Add salt to suit taste. About 1½ cups.

893 FRUIT AND CREAM CHEESE SPREAD

Cream a 3-oz. package of cream cheese until soft and smooth; blend in 1 to 2 tablespoons of orange marmalade, strawberry or raspberry jam, or strawberry or raspberry purée, adding sugar to suit taste. Spread on toast or crackers or use as sandwich filling. About ½ cup.

894 OLIVE NUT SPREAD

Combine ¼ cup finely chopped walnuts or pecans and ½ cup finely chopped stuffed olives. Mix with just enough mayonnaise to bind together. Enough for 5 sandwiches.

MISCELLANEOUS

894a BREAD-AND-BUTTER SANDWICHES

Use day-old unsliced bread, and cut it ¼-inch thick. Use the best of fresh butter and let it warm to room temperature so it can be easily creamed before spreading. Use a generous amount of butter in proportion to the bread—1½ to 2 teaspoons creamed butter per slice. Bread-and butter-sandwiches usually have the crusts trimmed off and are cut into finger lengths for serving with tea. The bread should be buttered and the 2 slices laid together before the crusts are removed in order to have the butter coming to the very edge.

Variations: Instead of using plain butter, add seasonings to the butter as it is being creamed. Lemon juice and a small amount of grated lemon rind, orange juice, onion juice, horseradish, mustard—these are all possibilities for butter seasoning. Butter seasoned in this manner is also good for sandwiches which have other fillings; for example, lemon butter with a date-nut filling, or mustard butter with a ham filling. Instead of one kind of bread, a slice each of 2 kinds may be used to give an attractive ribbon effect.

895 PEANUT BUTTER SANDWICHES

Plain peanut butter is a sandwich spread in great favor with children and most grown-ups. To make it spread more easily, it may be mixed with milk, cream, mayonnaise or water as desired. Use as a filling between slices of buttered bread. A leaf of lettuce in the sandwich adds fresh crispness.

Variation: Thin slices of banana may be arranged over the peanut butter spread on the bread. A blend of 4 tablespoons butter, 4 tablespoons peanut butter and 2 to 3 tablespoons strained honey is also a delicious spread.

896 PEANUT BUTTER, BANANA AND JELLY SPREAD

¼ cup peanut butter   1 tablespoon currant jelly
1 very ripe banana, mashed

Mix all ingredients together just enough to blend. Use immediately. About ¾ cup.

896a JELLY SANDWICHES

Bread for jelly sandwiches should be generously buttered on the sides facing the jelly, in order to prevent soaking as much as possible. Therefore the butter needs to be thoroughly creamed and softened for spreading. Jelly for sandwiches may be whipped up with a fork in order to spread smoothly. Cream cheese may be used instead of butter, if desired.

897 PEANUT BUTTER-JELLY SANDWICHES

⅓ cup peanut butter   10 slices buttered bread
¼ cup tart jelly

Blend peanut butter thoroughly with the jelly. If filling is too stiff to spread, thin with cream, milk or mayonnaise. Spread on half the slices of bread; top with remaining slices. 5 sandwiches.

898   PEANUT BUTTER AND WATERCRESS SANDWICHES

½ cup peanut butter   Salt to taste
1 bunch watercress   10 slices buttered bread

Thin peanut butter with water, milk, cream or mayonnaise, if desired. Spread on half the buttered bread. Wash watercress, remove white roots and shake off the water. Place sprigs over peanut butter and sprinkle lightly with salt. Cover with rest of bread. 5 sandwiches.

899   HONEY BUTTER

Cream ½ cup butter thoroughly and gradually beat in ½ cup of strained honey until mixture is light and fluffy. This spread is delicious on hot biscuits, toast or crackers. About ¾ cup.

900   SANDWICH BAR

This is a new idea for summer refreshments or Sunday night supper. Supply a plateful or a trayful of open-face sandwiches with another plate or platter of buttered bread or toast on the side, then let your guests help themselves according to taste and appetite. Those with dainty appetites may cover the open-face sandwich of their choice with a slice of plain buttered bread; heartier eaters may put two open-face sandwiches together for an interesting flavor combination; and the hungriest of all may put a slice of buttered bread between two of the open-face sandwiches, making a three-decker or club sandwich.

An appetizing variety of sandwich fillings are:

1. Creamed cheese mixed with chopped chives and chopped bacon (545), overlaid with slices of crisp red radish.

2. Butter creamed with a little prepared mustard, then a leaf of lettuce cut to fit the bread, a slice of ham, and 2 lengthwise slices of sweet pickled gherkin.

3. Mayonnaise mixed with finely chopped chipped beef or ham (used instead of butter), with a crisp lettuce leaf, topped with slices of hard-cooked egg (395).

4. Creamed butter blended with grated cheese, topped with a trimmed lettuce leaf and 2 slices of crisp broiled bacon (544).

5. Mayonnaise blended with ground ham, topped with a lettuce leaf and a slice of Swiss cheese.

6. Mayonnaise as the spread (or use mayonnaise with added mustard); then a thin layer of finely cut Cole Slaw (786); top with a lettuce leaf and a slice of corned beef.

7. Plain mayonnaise spread, then a lettuce leaf, and a mound of avocado paste (mashed avocado seasoned with salt and lemon juice).

8. Butter creamed with a little grated onion, topped with a lettuce leaf and 2 slices of liver sausage.

9. Cream cheese softened with a little mayonnaise and mixed with chopped chives is the spread; topped with a lettuce leaf, a slice or two of ripe tomato and mayonnaise.

900a   ROLLED AND RIBBON SANDWICHES

Rolled—With very sharp knife, cut top crust from a loaf of fresh white or whole wheat bread, lengthwise. Spread cut surface thinly with creamed butter; then spread ⅓ of buttered surface with Ham and Cheese Spread (858), next ⅓ with Carrot Butter (871), and last ⅓ with Parsley Butter (876). Cut off a thin slice, keeping it uniform in thickness the length of the loaf. Trim off edge crusts and roll up tightly like jelly roll. Wrap in waxed paper and store in refrigerator; repeat with rest of loaf. Chill several hours, then just before serving, slice thin like jelly roll.

Ribbon—Spread Ham and Cheese Spread (858) on slice of buttered white bread; cover with slice of whole wheat bread and spread this with Parsley Butter (876). Top with another slice of white bread. Press together gently, wrap in waxed paper and chill in refrigerator for several hours. When ready to serve, trim off crusts neatly and slice "loaf" ¼-inch thick to make ribbon sandwiches.

SAUCES

＊ ＊ ＊ ＊ ＊ ＊ ＊ ＊ ＊

AN appropriate, well made sauce works wonders. In this chapter you will find recipes for all kinds of sauces to lend flavor and importance to all kinds of foods.

＊ ＊ ＊ ＊ ＊ ＊ ＊ ＊ ＊

Sauces are of so many different kinds that it is difficult to lump them together under one heading. We have sauces for meat, for vegetables, for fish and for desserts of all kinds.

All these varied types of sauce have the same fundamental purpose: to enhance the flavor and appearance, and add nutritive value to the foods they accompany. Therefore the sauce should present a pleasing contrast in flavor and color with the food. It should in most cases be thin enough to flow readily but thick enough not to soak into the food and be lost; although there are exceptions to this rule.

Hot sauces are usually more satisfactory if made just before they are to be used, although some can be made ahead of time and re-heated. One of the most frequently used of all sauces is white sauce; if this is properly cooked, so as to be perfectly smooth, and if it is stirred as it cools and then stored in a tightly covered container to prevent formation of a skin, it can be kept and warmed up when needed. Mock Hollandaise sauce, which is of the white sauce type, though differing by the addition of eggs, can be treated in the same manner; but true Hollandaise sauce should not be re-heated.

Cold sauces are always made ahead of time and permitted to chill, but there is a limit to the time during which they can be stored successfully, the rate of deterioration depending on the type of sauce.

901   BARBECUE SAUCE No. 1

1 medium onion, chopped ½ cup catchup
1 green pepper, chopped   2 tablespoons sugar
⅓ cup chopped sweet pickle 2 teaspoons prepared mustard
⅓ cup cider vinegar

Combine all ingredients, bring to boiling point and simmer gently for 5 minutes. Serve with boiled tongue, pork chops or ham. Makes about 1¾ cups.

901a   **BARBECUE SAUCE No. 2**

1 cup catchup—good commercial brand
1 onion, egg-size, chopped
½ clove garlic, cut fine
2 teaspoons pickled or fresh chili peppers, chopped
½ teaspoon dry mustard
½ small bay leaf

¼ teaspoon black pepper
1 teaspoon Worcestershire
⅓ cup fresh lime juice, 2 medium
½ teaspoon salt
½ cup water
1 teaspoon sugar

Measure all ingredients into a 2-qt. saucepan. Heat to boiling, cover, reduce heat and simmer 40 minutes, stirring frequently. Strain sauce through a coarse strainer forcing pulp through into sauce. Turn into bowl and serve warm over lamb, beef, pork, chicken or fish. 1½ cups.

Note: Cover and chill left-over sauce. Reheat for an excellent booster for chops or fish.

902   **BROWN SAUCE**

2 tablespoons butter
¼ cup browned flour (1131)

1 cup meat broth, good strength
¼ teaspoon salt

Melt butter in saucepan, add flour and blend thoroughly. Add broth and cook over direct heat, stirring constantly until sauce boils and thickens; add salt, reduce heat and simmer about 5 minutes. Serve with green beans or spinach. Makes about 1 cup.

903   **CARROT SAUCE**

1 chicken bouillon cube
1 cup grated raw carrots, packed, 4 medium carrots
1 cup boiling water

½ cup catchup
1 tablespoon flour
¼ cup cold water

Add bouillon cube and grated carrot to the boiling water and simmer with frequent stirring until carrot is soft, about 4 minutes. Add catchup and the flour and water mixed to a smooth paste; stir constantly until sauce again boils up well. Serve with Meat Loaf (489), Pea Loaf (1062) or Pan-Fried Liver (601). About 2 cups sauce.

904   CELERY SAUCE

¼ cup butter   2 cups milk
¾ cup fine-diced celery   Salt and pepper to taste
¼ cup flour

Melt butter in saucepan and add celery; simmer over low heat, stirring occasionally, for 5 minutes. Stir in flour until smooth; then add milk and cook over direct heat, stirring constantly until sauce boils and thickens. Season to suit taste. Makes about 2½ cups. This sauce is good as an accompaniment for fish, eggs, meat loaves or croquettes.

905   CIDER RAISIN SAUCE

2 tablespoons brown sugar   1 teaspoon ham fat
2 tablespoons cornstarch   ¼ cup seedless raisins
1½ cups sweet cider

Mix together sugar and cornstarch. Add cider and bring mixture to a boil, stirring constantly. Add ham fat and raisins and continue to simmer over low heat for 5 minutes, stirring occasionally. Serve with baked ham. Where no ham fat is available, bacon fat or butter may be substituted. About 1¼ cups sauce.

906   DILL SAUCE No. 1
                              (*For Fish or Beans*)

2 tablespoons butter   Dash pepper
3 tablespoons flour   1½ teaspoons finely chopped
1½ cups milk   fresh dill leaves
½ teaspoon salt

Melt butter, blend in flour, then add milk slowly; stir constantly over low direct heat until sauce boils and thickens. Add seasonings and dill, and place over boiling water for 2 or 3 minutes, stirring occasionally. Serve hot with cooked green beans or boiled fish. Makes about 1¾ cups.

906a   DILL SAUCE No. 2
                                 (*For Stew*)

2 tablespoons butter   1 teaspoon sugar
3 tablespoons flour   2 teaspoons finely chopped
2 cups meat broth, or broth   fresh dill leaves (or more)
   and water   1 egg yolk
1 to 2 tablespoons cider   2 cups diced fresh boiled veal
   vinegar   or lamb

Melt butter, blend in flour and slowly stir in the broth from boiled lamb or veal or from stew. Cook with constant stirring until sauce boils and thickens. Add vinegar, sugar and dill, and place over boiling water for 3 or 4 minutes, stirring occasionally. Beat egg yolk and stir in a little of the hot sauce; then pour it into the rest of the sauce and stir about 2 minutes longer over the hot water. Pour over meat for stew. 5 servings.

907   COCKTAIL SAUCE FOR SEAFOOD

½ cup chili sauce
⅓ cup catchup
⅓ cup prepared horseradish
1½ teaspoons Worcestershire

¼ teaspoon salt
2 tablespoons lemon juice
Dash black pepper
¼ cup very finely diced celery

Combine ingredients in the order given. Place in a clean glass container, cover and keep in refrigerator until ready to serve. This sauce is good for oysters or cherrystone clams on the half shell, or for crabmeat or shrimp cocktail. If a milder sauce is desired, substitute ¼ cup puréed canned tomatoes for half of the chili sauce. 1½ cups sauce.

908   DRAWN BUTTER SAUCE

¼ cup butter
2 tablespoons flour
1 cup boiling water

¼ teaspoon salt
Dash pepper

Melt half the butter in a saucepan, blend in the flour and gradually add the boiling water, stirring constantly until smooth. Continue stirring until the sauce boils and thickens. Add salt and pepper and remove from heat. Add remaining butter by teaspoonfuls, beating after each addition. Serve with boiled or baked fish. About 1¼ cups.

909   EGG SAUCE

3 tablespoons butter
3 tablespoons flour
2 cups milk
½ teaspoon salt
⅛ teaspoon pepper

Few drops Worcestershire
1 teaspoon lemon juice
4 hard-cooked eggs (395),
diced or sieved

Melt butter, blend in flour and add milk slowly, stirring constantly over direct heat until sauce boils and thickens. Add seasonings; then fold in eggs. Serve with fish loaf or fish patties. Makes about 2½ cups.

910   HOLLANDAISE SAUCE

¼ cup butter	1 tablespoon lemon juice
¼ cup cream (sweet or sour)	Salt to taste
2 egg yolks, beaten	Dash cayenne

Melt butter in top of double boiler; add cream and beaten egg yolks, stirring well. Add lemon juice and salt, and cook over boiling water, stirring constantly, until thick. Remove from heat and beat until light. Stir in cayenne if desired. Makes about ⅔ cup.

911   MOCK HOLLANDAISE SAUCE

3 tablespoons butter	⅔ cup milk
2 tablespoons flour	1 tablespoon lemon juice
½ teaspoon salt	2 egg yolks, beaten

Melt butter in saucepan, blend in flour and salt, then stir in milk; cook with constant stirring over direct heat until sauce boils and thickens. Remove from heat, add lemon juice and stir into beaten egg yolks. Place over boiling water and cook with constant stirring for 2 minutes, or until sauce is smooth and thick. Serve with cooked vegetables such as asparagus, broccoli, green beans or green onions, which have been thoroughly drained. About 1 cup.

912   MAÎTRE d'HOTEL SAUCE

¼ cup butter	4 teaspoons lemon juice
4 teaspoons fine-chopped parsley	¼ teaspoon salt, or to taste
	⅛ teaspoon pepper

Cream butter until soft and smooth, and add other ingredients in order named. Spread quickly over broiled fish, chops or steaks as soon as they are removed from the broiler or skillet and serve immediately. Do not return to the oven to keep hot after applying the sauce or the parsley will lose its fresh green color. This sauce may be made ahead of time and stored in the refrigerator, but will have to be re-creamed to make it soft enough to spread. This sauce is an attractive garnish as well as a pleasing flavor accent. 5 servings.

913   MINT SAUCE

¼ cup chopped mint	4 tablespoons sugar
⅓ cup cider vinegar	Pinch of baking soda

Chop mint finely by putting leaves in glass and snipping with scissors. Heat vinegar and sugar to boiling and pour over the chopped mint. Mix in soda, let cool and serve with any cut of lamb. 5 servings.

914   SPANISH SAUCE

No. 2 can tomatoes
1 onion, chopped or sliced thin
1 green pepper, chopped
½ cup chopped celery
Salt and pepper to taste

Combine tomatoes, onion, green pepper and celery in saucepan, bring to boiling point and cook slowly 20 to 30 minutes, or until somewhat thickened. Season to suit taste. About 2 cups.

If preferred, tomatoes may be rubbed through a sieve before combining with other ingredients; the sauce may then be thickened, if desired, by adding 1 tablespoon flour blended to a smooth paste with 3 tablespoons cold water and again bringing to boil.

915   TARTAR SAUCE

⅔ cup mayonnaise (843)
1 teaspoon grated onion
2 teaspoons chopped chives
1 teaspoon chopped parsley
2 drops tabasco sauce, if desired
1 teaspoon chopped sweet or dill crisp pickle
1 teaspoon capers, if desired

Mix all ingredients just enough to blend. This is an excellent sauce for fish, and is also good on corned beef hash. Makes about ¾ cup sauce.

916   TOMATO SAUCE

No. 2 can tomatoes
1 teaspoon grated onion
½ teaspoon salt
½ teaspoon sugar
2 tablespoons butter
2 teaspoons flour
¼ teaspoon Worcestershire

Combine first 4 ingredients and simmer for 15 minutes. Put through a strainer to remove seeds. Melt butter, blend in flour and add tomatoes and Worcestershire, stirring until sauce boils and thickens. Serve with fish, meat loaf, liver or cooked cabbage. Makes about 2 cups.

917   VEGETABLE CREOLE SAUCE

3 slices bacon
1 medium onion, sliced
3 tablespoons flour
½ teaspoon salt
1 cup chopped celery
1 bay leaf
2 tablespoons chopped parsley
No. 303 can tomatoes, 2 cups
1 cup canned peas

Pan fry bacon until done; then remove bacon and sauté onion in the fat until soft and yellow. Add flour and salt, and blend until smooth. Add celery, bay leaf, parsley and tomatoes, stirring constantly until sauce boils and thickens. Reduce heat and simmer gently about 15 minutes. Remove bay leaf. Now add peas and continue cooking until they are just heated through; then stir in the crumbled crisp bacon. Serve hot with Puffy Omelet (402) or Scrambled Eggs (396). 5 servings.

918   VINAIGRETTE SAUCE

1 teaspoon grated onion	1 teaspoon fine-chopped
2 tablespoons vinegar	pimiento
⅓ cup olive or salad oil	⅛ teaspoon salt
1 teaspoon fine-chopped	Dash pepper
parsley	¼ teaspoon prepared mustard
1 teaspoon fine-chopped	
green pepper	

Combine ingredients in order given and beat well. Excellent for asparagus, lettuce or any other vegetable salad. About ½ cup.

919   WHITE SAUCE

Thin white sauce:

1 tablespoon butter
1 tablespoon flour
¾ teaspoon salt
1 cup milk or ½ cup evaporated milk and ½ cup water

Medium white sauce:

2 tablespoons butter
2 tablespoons flour
½ teaspoon salt
1 cup milk or ½ cup evaporated milk and ½ cup water

Thick white sauce:

3 or 4 tablespoons butter
3 tablespoons flour
½ teaspoon salt
1 cup milk or ½ cup evaporated milk and ½ cup water

Melt butter in saucepan, blend in flour and salt until smooth. Now stir in cold milk gradually and cook over direct heat, stirring constantly until sauce boils and becomes thick and smooth. If stirring is done carefully, there will be no lumping, but white sauce that has lumped may often be restored by beating with a rotary beater or by rubbing through a sieve and then beating if lumping is considerable. If it is necessary to keep white sauce more than a few minutes before using, place over boiling water and keep it covered, stirring occasionally. About 1 cup sauce.

920   CHEESE SAUCE

To the White Sauce (919), after it is thickened, add from ¼ to 1 cup of grated sharp cheese, according to the flavor desired. Stir quickly until blended. If diced or sliced cheese is added to the sauce, it is advisable to place the sauce over boiling water while the cheese melts, stirring occasionally. One-fourth cup diced cheese is about equal to ½ cup grated.

921   HORSERADISH SAUCE

To 1 cup of thin White Sauce (919), add 4 teaspoons prepared horse-radish, mixing well. Good with ham or other meat loaves and with meat patties and croquettes.

922   MUSTARD SAUCE No. 1

To 1 cup of thin White Sauce (919), add 1 teaspoon prepared mustard, mixing thoroughly. Excellent with ham or meat loaf.

922a   MUSTARD SAUCE No. 2

*2 hard-cooked egg yolks	1½ tablespoons lemon juice,
1 raw egg yolk	½ lemon
¼ cup salad oil	1 tablespoon prepared brown
1 tablespoon sugar	Bahaiman mustard
¼ teaspoon salt	1 tablespoon thick cream
Dash of pepper	

Hard cook eggs in usual way (395). Shell immediately and remove yolks. (Use whites in sandwich filling or 1000 Island Dressing.) Rub yolks through a fine sieve, then blend in raw yolk to a very smooth paste. Add oil, a few drops at a time, beating to a smooth emulsion. Stir in rest of ingredients in order given, beating thoroughly. Excellent for Ham Loaf, Frankfurters, Tongue, Corned Beef, Veal, Pork, Fish and for spreading on bread for sandwiches. Makes ¾ cup.

*Note: Left-over egg yolks that are in good condition may be used. Turn 2 into a buttered custard cup. Cover and place over (not in) boiling water and cook 20 to 25 minutes, or until firm and mealy.

923   ONION SAUCE

To 1 cup of thin White Sauce (919), add 2 to 3 teaspoons grated onion, and reheat just to boiling. Good with any meat loaf, also with salmon loaf or salmon croquettes.

924   BROWN SUGAR SYRUP

2 cups brown sugar, packed   Dash salt
1 cup water   ¼ cup white corn syrup

Combine sugar, water and salt in a saucepan and bring to boil. Cover and boil gently 10 minutes, or until a thin syrup is formed. Keeping the pan covered prevents formation of crystals around sides of pan. Stir in corn syrup. Cool and put into covered jar. If more syrup is made than is needed immediately, the corn syrup may be cooked along with the sugar and water; this will prevent crystallization during the storage period. Keep in a tightly covered jar either in or out of refrigerator. About 2 cups.

A maple-flavored syrup may be made using white sugar instead of brown in the same proportion. When cooking is done, add maple flavoring a little at a time until desired flavor is obtained.

925   BUTTERSCOTCH SAUCE

1½ cups brown sugar, packed   ⅔ cup evaporated milk
⅔ cup white corn syrup   Dash salt
⅓ cup water   ½ teaspoon vanilla
¼ cup butter   ½ cup chopped nuts, if desired

Put sugar, corn syrup, water and butter into a saucepan and boil to the soft ball stage (236° F.). Cool, then beat in the evaporated milk, a little salt and vanilla. Stir in nuts and serve on ice cream, bananas, or any desired pudding. Makes about 2 cups.

926   CHOCOLATE SAUCE

5 squares (5 oz.) baking   ½ teaspoon salt
   chocolate   ¼ cup white corn syrup
1½ cups water   2 tablespoons butter
1¾ cups sugar

Add chocolate to water, bring to boil and cook 4 minutes, stirring constantly. Add sugar, salt and corn syrup and boil 4 minutes longer, continuing to stir. Remove from heat, add butter and beat until blended. Serve hot or cold as a sauce for ice cream, puddings or cake; or use as a base for hot or cold chocolate drinks, allowing 2 tablespoons for each cup of hot or cold milk. About 2¾ cups.

927   COCOA SAUCE No. 1

½ cup sugar
⅓ cup cocoa
⅛ teaspoon salt
¾ cup water

¾ cup evaporated milk,
    scalded
½ teaspoon vanilla

Blend sugar, cocoa and salt in a 1-qt. saucepan. Add water and stir until smooth, then stir in scalded milk and beat until smooth with rotary beater. Bring to boiling point and simmer gently for about 8 minutes or until syrup-like in consistency. Remove from heat and add vanilla. Chill thoroughly and serve with caramel blanc mange, cornstarch pudding, ice cream, cottage pudding or whenever a chocolate sauce or syrup is desired. About 1¼ cups sauce.

928   COCOA SAUCE No. 2

1 cup cocoa
1¼ cups sugar
½ cup white corn syrup
1½ cups water

¼ teaspoon salt
1 teaspoon vinegar
1 teaspoon vanilla

Blend the first 6 ingredients in a 1-qt. saucepan. Bring to the boiling point over direct heat and simmer gently for 5 minutes, stirring occasionally. Remove from heat and add vanilla. Cool, then store in covered container in refrigerator. This mixture may be used as a sauce for ice cream, cottage pudding or bananas; or 1 to 2 tablespoons stirred into 1 cup of hot or cold milk makes a quick, delicious chocolate milk drink. About 2½ cups.

929   COFFEE SAUCE

¾ cup boiling water
⅓ cup medium grind coffee
1 tablespoon butter
1½ tablespoons flour
½ cup milk

2 egg yolks, beaten
Pinch salt
½ cup sugar
½ teaspoon vanilla
½ cup whipping cream

Add the boiling water to the coffee in a saucepan, heat it just to the boiling point, then remove to a warm place to stand 5 minutes. Strain through four thicknesses of cheesecloth or through firm muslin. Melt butter, blend in flour and add milk slowly, stirring constantly over direct heat until sauce boils and thickens and is smooth. Stir some of the hot mixture into the beaten yolks; then add the yolk mixture to the hot sauce. Place over boiling water and cook 2 minutes, stirring constantly. Remove from heat and add ¼ cup of the strained coffee, salt and sugar; stir well. Chill, then stir in the vanilla and fold into the stiffly whipped cream. Serve immediately or store in a tightly covered jar in the refrigerator; it may be kept 2 or 3 days. This is a delicious sauce for chocolate blanc mange, cornstarch pudding, ice cream or steamed fruit pudding. About 2 cups.

930   CUSTARD SAUCE

2 cups milk	¼ cup sugar
2 egg yolks and 2 whole eggs or 5 egg yolks	⅛ teaspoon salt
	½ teaspoon vanilla

Scald milk in top of double boiler. Beat eggs slightly, add sugar and salt and slowly stir in the scalded milk. Return to double boiler and cook over boiling water until mixture just coats a metal spoon. Remove from heat immediately, then stir in vanilla and chill. If overcooked, custard will curdle. Curdled custard may often be restored by cooling immediately and beating with a rotary egg beater, but it will not be so thick. About 2¼ cups.

931   FOAMY SAUCE

⅓ cup butter	1 egg, beaten
1 cup XXXX sugar, packed in cup	1 egg yolk, beaten
Pinch salt	½ teaspoon brandy flavoring

Put butter into top of double boiler, but do not place over heat, cream butter until soft and smooth. Gradually work in the sugar and salt. Add beaten egg and yolk, place over boiling water, and continue beating with rotary beater until sauce is very foamy, from 3 to 4 minutes. Remove from heat, stir in brandy and serve warm or cold over steamed fruit puddings. Other flavoring, such as vanilla or a combination of vanilla and lemon extract, may be substituted for the brandy. Makes about 1 cup.

932   HARD SAUCE

½ cup butter	1 teaspoon vanilla or ¼ teaspoon almond extract or
1⅔ cups XXXX sugar, packed in cup	1½ teaspoons sherry or
Pinch salt	brandy flavoring

Cream the butter until soft and smooth. Stir in sugar mixed with salt, alternately with the flavoring. The mixture should be fairly stiff when finished. Press into a shallow mold or a 5-inch cake tin. Chill until hard. Serve in slices, or use a small fancy cutter to cut serving portions from the hard layer of sauce. 5 servings.

933   LEMON HARD SAUCE

⅓ cup butter
1¼ cups XXXX sugar, packed

Pinch salt
½ teaspoon grated lemon rind
4 teaspoons lemon juice

Cream butter until soft and smooth. Stir in sugar mixed with salt, mixing until smooth and stiff. Add lemon rind and juice and again beat well. Press into a mold or cup and chill in refrigerator until hardened. Unmold and cut into serving portions. Or serve without chilling in fluffy mounds. 5 servings.

934   LEMON SAUCE

1 tablespoon cornstarch
¾ cup sugar
Dash salt
¾ cup water

1 egg, separated
1 tablespoon butter
2 tablespoons lemon juice
⅛ teaspoon grated lemon rind

Mix the cornstarch, sugar and salt in top of double boiler; add water and cook over direct heat, stirring constantly until mixture boils and thickens. Stir into beaten egg yolk; return to pan, place over boiling water and cook 2 minutes longer, stirring constantly. Remove from heat and add butter and lemon juice and rind. Cool. Beat egg white until stiff and fold into the sauce. Serve hot or cold as sauce for cottage pudding. 5 servings.

935   ORANGE SAUCE

¾ cup sugar
2 tablespoons cornstarch
¼ teaspoon salt
1⅓ cups water
⅓ cup orange juice

1 teaspoon grated orange rind
4 teaspoons lemon juice
1 tablespoon butter

Combine sugar, cornstarch and salt in top of double boiler; add water and blend until smooth. Cook over direct heat, stirring constantly until mixture boils and thickens; then place over boiling water, cover, and cook 15 minutes with occasional stirring. Remove from heat and stir in remaining ingredients. Serve warm or cold as pudding sauce. Makes about 2 cups.

936   PINEAPPLE SAUCE

1 tablespoon cornstarch	No. 211 can pineapple juice
1/8 teaspoon cinnamon	2 tablespoons butter
1/4 cup sugar	

Mix together the cornstarch, cinnamon and sugar in top of double boiler, add a little of the pineapple juice and stir until smooth. Then add rest of juice and cook over direct heat until mixture boils and thickens, stirring constantly. Cover and cook over boiling water for 15 minutes, stirring occasionally. Remove from heat and add butter. Chill and serve over unfrosted plain cake or sponge cake, either fresh or stale. If stale cake is used, combine and allow to stand about 15 minutes before serving, so cake may become moist through. About 1½ cups.

937   SAUCE FOR FRESH FRUIT

Foundation recipe for sauce:

1 tablespoon cornstarch
1 tablespoon sugar
Dash salt
½ cup evaporated milk
½ cup water

Blend dry ingredients in top of double boiler, add a little of the milk, and blend to a smooth paste; then add rest of milk and water and cook over direct heat, stirring constantly until sauce boils and thickens. Cover and cook over boiling water for 15 minutes, stirring occasionally. Remove from heat and flavor according to any of the following variations:

1. Add ¼ teaspoon almond extract and serve with sliced fresh peaches or apricots.

2. Add 3 tablespoons orange juice, ¼ teaspoon grated orange rind, and ½ teaspoon lemon juice; beat up with egg beater. Serve with bananas.

3. Add 2 tablespoons lemon juice, 1/8 teaspoon grated lemon rind, and a dash of salt; beat well. Serve with sliced bananas, peaches or berries.

4. Add 1/8 teaspoon ginger, 1/8 teaspoon cinnamon, and a dash of salt. Beat with egg beater. Serve with sliced peaches or bananas.

Makes enough sauce for 5 servings of fruit, about 1 cup.

938   VANILLA SAUCE

⅓ cup sugar   ⅓ cup white corn syrup
½ teaspoon cornstarch   1 teaspoon vanilla
¼ teaspoon salt   1 tablespoon butter
⅓ cup milk

Combine sugar, cornstarch and salt in top of double boiler; add the milk and blend until smooth. Then add syrup and cook over direct heat, stirring constantly until sauce boils and thickens. Now remove from heat and stir in vanilla and butter. Serve warm as pudding sauce. Makes about 2½ cups.

SOUP

* * * * * * *

A THING of the past is the old-fashioned soup kettle which often stood on the back of the wood or coal kitchen range ready to receive meat trimmings and bones, and broth left from cooking meats and vegetables. It simmered and seethed day and night, and from it emerged the most savory of soups.

* * * * * * *

Modern kitchens have no room for such a "pot au feu," but it is possible to reproduce the old-fashioned soups without its help, and since soup is such an important item in the diet, every housewife should develop her soup repertoire. One of the important functions of soup is as an appetizer, and that is why it is served at the beginning of the meal. The hot, savory liquid puts the stomach in a good humor immediately. But the majority of soups are much more than just appetizers, they are rich in food value.

The soups which are most nutritious are the *cream soups*. These contain both milk and butter in addition to the vegetable which usually gives them their flavor. Therefore they are an important part of the meal in which they are served. Cream soups are especially useful in getting more milk into the diet, not only of children, but of adults who are reluctant to drink it. Since most cream soups are easily and quickly made, they have become very popular.

Chowder is a special kind of cream soup containing a large proportion of solid food, cut rather coarsely. Fish and clam chowders were the original members of this group, but modern chowders are often made with vegetables such as corn, potatoes and even spinach. They are, as a rule, so substantial that a good-sized bowlful is a hearty luncheon main dish.

Clear soups contain no milk. They may be made with meat or vegetable stock for flavor or with tomato juice. Vegetable soups often have a meat stock base, but their chief food value is determined by the amount of vegetables they contain. Such soup most closely resembles the old-time "pot au feu" and is simple to make though the cooking time is longer than for the average cream soup. Still, it is no great chore for the homemaker to put a soup bone into the kettle and slowly simmer out the essences of bone and meat, perhaps using the water saved from yesterday's potatoes and other vegetables to add flavor and some vitamin and mineral value. After the soup bone is removed, the meat remaining on it may be shredded and returned to the soup along with finely diced vegetables and seasonings.

For the housewife who likes to serve soup often for its warming, appetite-stimulating and nutritious qualities, but has no time to make even the quickest cream soup, there are the many varieties of canned soup. The quality of canned soups has improved so much in recent years that no one need hesitate to serve them. Both clear and cream soups are available in most of the leading brands. They may be the type which are ready to serve after heating just as they come from the can, or the condensed type, requiring the addition of water or milk before heating.

ACCOMPANIMENTS AND GARNISHES

Most people like some sort of crisp accompaniment with soup. This may be plain crisp toasted bread, or toast in the form of croutons, fingers or rings. Cheese pastry sticks or bread sticks are especially suitable for a festive occasion. And the many kinds of crackers—plain salted soda crackers, oyster crackers, butter wafers, cheese crackers and whole grain wafers—are always in favor. These are most appetizing when freshened in the oven just before serving, and served very hot. Many enjoy butter with the crackers.

If other relishes are being served, such as celery, radishes or olives, they should be served along with the soup, as the contrast of their crisp, cool textures with the soup increases the enjoyment of both soup and relish.

Soups may be garnished in a variety of attractive ways, and this garnishing is too often neglected. The garnish may be just a few crisp croutons floating on top of the bowlful, a sprinkling of chopped parsley, a few kernels of puffy popcorn or one of the puffed cereals, some gratings of raw carrot, or a puff of whipped or thick sour cream. Whatever the garnish, it should be put on just before the soup is served in order to be at its freshest and best when eaten.

SOUPS CONTAINING MEAT

939   BEEF BROTH WITH NOODLES OR RICE

Have butcher crack a 2½ to 3-lb. beef soup bone in several places. Wipe thoroughly with a damp cloth and put into soup kettle. Barely cover with cold or hot water. Heat to boiling, then reduce heat, cover and SIMMER gently at least 2 hours. This will produce a concentrated beef broth. Drain off or strain broth, then add enough water to make 6 cups. Season to taste with salt and pepper. Reheat broth, add 4 ounces of noodles and boil gently uncovered about 8 minutes, or until tender. Or add ½ cup raw rice and boil gently uncovered about 20 minutes. Add more salt if needed. 5 servings.

Note: Meat on the bone may be removed, chopped, and added to the soup.

940   CHICKEN BROTH WITH RICE

Use at least 2 lbs. of bony pieces of stewing chicken, such as wings, rib pieces, neck and feet for making soup. Chicken feet which have been scalded, skinned and trimmed make excellent stock. Cover the pieces with 2 quarts cold or hot water and heat to boiling. Then reduce heat, remove any scum, cover and simmer about 1½ hours or until meat slips easily from bones and broth has good strong chicken flavor. One carrot, 1 medium onion and 2 branches of celery may be added last half hour of cooking. Strain soup into another kettle. Return meat removed from bones to soup. Season with salt and pepper to taste. Add 1½ cups boiled rice (174) and reheat to boiling. Serve piping hot with crackers. Chopped parsley may be sprinkled on top of each serving as a garnish. 5 servings.

941   DUCK SOUP

Use bones of 1 large or 2 small roast ducks. Break into pieces; cover with cold water, about 7 cups and add 2 or 3 branches of celery and 1 carrot, sliced. Heat to boiling, reduce heat and remove scum. Cover and simmer until a rich-flavored broth is obtained, about 2 hours. Strain soup into another kettle and return meat left on bones to broth. Add 2 cups cooked rice (174). Reheat and season with salt and pepper. 5 servings.

942   LAMB BROTH

2½ lbs. lamb shoulder	1 green onion or 1 tablespoon
1½ teaspoons salt	chopped onion
1 branch celery	¼ bay leaf
	Pinch thyme

Have butcher cut meat in 4 to 6 pieces. Wipe with damp cloth. Cover meat with hot or cold water; add remaining ingredients and bring to a boil, then skim. Now reduce heat as low as possible, cover and simmer 1 to 1½ hours. Now remove from heat and cool until fat on surface is congealed, then skim fat off. Strain if desired. Reheat and serve with crackers or croutons (61). Meat may be removed from bone, chopped and added to broth for additional flavor and nutritive value. 5 servings.

Variation: ½ cup barley may be simmered in 1-qt. water with 1 teaspoon salt in a covered pan for 1½ hours until tender and added to the soup at the last with more salt and pepper if needed.

943   **OXTAIL SOUP**

2 oxtails, about 3½ lbs.
¼ cup barley
½ cup chopped onion
½ cup diced carrot
1 tablespoon salt

¼ teaspoon pepper
1 cup diced potatoes
1 tablespoon chopped parsley
1 tablespoon caramel (1121), or kitchen bouquet

Wipe oxtails with damp cloth. Chop at joints, making pieces 1 to 2 inches long. Put on to cook in 2½ quarts cold water, add barley when water boils; reduce heat and simmer gently for 2 hours. Then add onion, carrot, salt and pepper, and continue cooking 20 minutes. Add potatoes and cook until just tender. Remove oxtail, separate meat from bone and return meat to soup. Add parsley and caramel or other coloring. Serve hot. 5 or 6 servings.

944   **TURKEY SOUP**

Bones left from roast turkey
7 cups water
3 branches celery with leaves
½ cup raw rice

1 tablespoon salt
1 cup evaporated milk, if desired
2 sprigs parsley, chopped

Crack turkey bones and put into a 4-qt. saucepan. Add water and celery and heat to boiling, then reduce heat, cover and simmer 1½ hours. Remove from heat and strain out bones and celery. Reheat soup to boiling, add rice and salt. Simmer 30 minutes longer or until rice is tender. If desired, add evaporated milk and heat. Sprinkle with chopped parsley. 5 servings.

945   **VEGETABLE SOUP**

2½ lb. meaty soup bone
2 tablespoons bacon fat
5 cups water
½ bay leaf, if desired
¼ teaspoon marjoram, optional
6 whole black peppers

¼ cup sliced onions
¼ cup chopped celery, some leaves
3 teaspoons salt
2 cups fresh vegetables, finely chopped

Have butcher crack soup bone. Cut meat in small cubes and brown half of it in bacon fat. Add remaining meat, bone, water, spices tied in a cheesecloth bag, onion, celery and salt; cover and simmer 2½ to 3 hours. Strain through cheesecloth, reserving the meat; season broth to suit taste. Skim excess fat from top of broth, add vegetables and boil gently until tender. Serve soup hot with crisp crackers. Carrots, celery, green beans, peas, lima beans and potatoes are all excellent soup vegetables. If desired, some of the meat may be chopped and served in the soup, or all of it may be saved for croquettes or hash at another meal. 5 servings.

CREAM SOUPS

946   CREAM OF ASPARAGUS SOUP

1½ lbs. fresh asparagus	2 to 2½ teaspoons salt
3½ cups boiling water	½ cup cold water
1⅔ cups evaporated milk	2 tablespoons butter
3 tablespoons flour	½ teaspoon onion juice

Remove paper-like scales on asparagus with paring knife. Wash thoroughly. Break off the tough ends from tips, trim off the tough part of these ends, then slice trimmed ends thinly and drop into 2 cups of the boiling water and cook until tender, about 20 minutes. Meanwhile, cut tips into ¼-inch lengths and cook in a 3-quart saucepan in remaining water, 6 to 8 minutes. Now add the milk, and a thin paste made by blending flour and salt in ½ cup cold water. Continue cooking, stirring constantly until mixture boils and thickens. Turn the cooked asparagus ends into a sieve, straining directly into soup and rubbing through as much of pulp as possible. Reheat to boiling, add butter and onion juice. Serve at once.

Variation: Use chicken or veal broth in place of water to cook the tips for an unusually delicious soup. Use less salt when using broth.

947   CREAM OF BEET SOUP

3 tablespoons butter	2 teaspoons grated onion
3 tablespoons flour	1 tablespoon pickle relish
3 cups milk	¼ cup cider vinegar or to
No. 2 can beets	taste
1½ teaspoons salt	

Melt butter, blend in flour and gradually stir in milk; cook over direct heat, stirring constantly until sauce boils and thickens. Drain beets (save juice) and put beets through ricer or food mill into the hot sauce. Add salt, onion, beet juice and pickle relish, and heat again to boiling. Remove from heat, add vinegar and serve immediately. 5 servings.

948   CREAM OF CARROT SOUP

1 bunch carrots	¼ cup flour
2 tablespoons butter	1⅔ cups evaporated milk
1 tablespoon chopped onion	1 teaspoon salt

Scrape carrots, slice and cook in 2½ cups boiling water until perfectly tender; drain, saving water. There should be about 2¼ cups, if less, add fresh water. Put carrots through a ricer or food mill. There should be 1¼ cups riced carrots. Melt butter, add onion and cook until soft. Blend in flour, then add evaporated milk and water from carrots; stir over direct heat until mixture boils and thickens. Now stir in riced carrots and salt and reheat. Serve piping hot with crisp crackers or croutons (61). 5 servings.

949   CREAM OF CELERY SOUP No. 1

2 cups sliced celery	¼ cup flour
1 small onion, chopped	4 cups milk
1½ cups boiling water	1¼ teaspoons salt
½ teaspoon salt	1 teaspoon chopped parsley
¼ cup butter	

Cut both leaves and stems of celery. Put celery and onion into a 3-qt. saucepan, add water and salt, cover and simmer until tender about 10 minutes. Melt butter in another saucepan, blend in flour, add milk and cook with constant stirring until sauce boils and thickens. Now stir in the 1¼ teaspoons salt and the cooked vegetables with their liquid. Garnish individual servings with chopped parsley. Chopped or riced hard-cooked egg is also an attractive and nutritious garnish. 5 servings.

950   CREAM OF CELERY SOUP No. 2

2¼ cups chopped celery	1⅔ cups evaporated milk
3 thin slices onion	1 cup water
2 cups boiling water	1 cup chicken broth or 1
1 tablespoon butter	chicken bouillon cube dissolved in 1 cup water
1 tablespoon flour	
1½ teaspoons salt	1 egg, well beaten
Dash pepper	

Chop both leaves and stems of celery. Put celery and onion into a 3-qt. saucepan, add the water and boil gently until soft, about 10 minutes. Now rub through food mill or leave vegetables as is. Prepare white sauce (919) with butter, flour, salt, pepper, evaporated milk, water and chicken broth. Stir celery and onion slowly into well-beaten egg; pour into hot white sauce and cook 2 minutes longer, stirring constantly. Serve at once. 5 servings.

951   CREAM OF CORN SOUP

¼ cup finely chopped celery
2 cups boiling water
1 No. 2 can cream style corn

1 cup evaporated milk
2 tablespoons butter
Salt and pepper to suit taste

Measure celery into a 3-qt. saucepan, add water, cover and boil gently until soft. Now add remaining ingredients and heat thoroughly. The soup may be rubbed through a sieve, or it may be served without straining. Garnish with a sprinkling of popped corn (176a) if desired or serve with croutons (61), crackers or crisp toast. 5 servings.

952   CREAM OF LIMA BEAN AND CARROT SOUP

1 cup dried lima beans
1 quart cold water
1 medium carrot, sliced
2 slices medium onion
4 sprigs parsley
1⅔ cups evaporated milk

1 teaspoon Worcestershire
Few drops tabasco, if desired
2 teaspoons salt
¹⁄₁₆ to ⅛ teaspoon black pepper

Wash beans, add enough water to cover 2 inches deep and let soak overnight. Then drain and add the cold water, cover and simmer until tender, about 30 minutes. Then add vegetables and cook until tender, about 20 minutes longer. Now rub through a food mill or sieve; there should be 3 cups purée and liquid. If not, add water to make that amount. Combine purée with milk and seasonings and reheat to boiling just before serving. 5 servings.

953   CREAM OF MUSHROOM SOUP

½ lb. fresh mushrooms
2 small slices onion, chopped
4 cups milk

1 cup evaporated milk
1 teaspoon salt
2 tablespoons butter

Wash mushrooms and chop fine. Place mushrooms and onion in top of double boiler, add milk and cook over boiling water, stirring occasionally until mushrooms are tender, about 45 minutes. Add evaporated milk and salt and stir in butter. Serve piping hot. 5 servings.

954   CREAM OF NAVY BEAN SOUP

1 cup dried navy beans	½ teaspoon celery salt
4 cups cold water	Dash pepper
2 tablespoons diced onion	2 tablespoons grated carrot,
1 cup evaporated milk	optional
1 teaspoon salt	

Wash beans, cover with water and let stand overnight. Next morning drain, cover with the cold water, add onion, cover and simmer about 1½ to 2 hours or until beans are soft. Remove from heat and put through ricer or food mill into a saucepan. Add milk, seasonings and carrot and reheat. Serve hot. 5 servings.

955   CREAM OF ONION SOUP

2 slices bacon	1⅔ cups evaporated milk
1 cup sliced onions	1 teaspoon salt or to taste
2 tablespoons flour	Pepper to taste
3 cups water	5 slices buttered crisp toast

Cut bacon with shears into 1-inch lengths and drop into a 3-qt. saucepan. Fry until just done, then add onion and flour and stir until flour is blended with bacon fat. Add water, cover and simmer until onion is tender, about 15 minutes. Now add milk, salt and pepper and reheat to boiling. Place a slice of toast in the bottom of each soup bowl and pour hot soup over it. Serve immediately. 5 servings.

956   CREAM OF PEA SOUP

1 No. 2 can peas	1½ teaspoons sugar
Cold water	1 teaspoon salt
1 slice onion	2 cups thin white sauce (919)

Drain liquid from peas, measure and add cold water to make 2 cups liquid. Return to peas; add onion, sugar and salt. Place over heat and simmer 5 minutes, then rub through a sieve or food mill. There should be 2½ cups pulp and liquid. Combine with hot white sauce and serve hot. Float 2 or 3 croutons (61) on each portion just before serving. 5 servings.

957   CREAM OF POTATO SOUP

5 cups thinly sliced potatoes   1⅔ cups evaporated milk
1 medium onion, sliced   1 cup water
2 teaspoons salt   1 tablespoon finely chopped
3 tablespoons butter   parsley

Put potatoes and onion into a 3-qt. saucepan and barely cover with cold water. Add salt, cover and bring to boil, reduce heat and simmer 10 minutes or until potatoes are perfectly tender. Mash potatoes in their liquid. Add butter, evaporated milk and water. Stir and add a little more water if soup is too thick. Reheat to scalding, remove from heat, stir in chopped parsley. Serve immediately. 5 servings.

958   CREAM OF SALMON SOUP

2 slices onion   2 tablespoons butter
1⅔ cups evaporated milk   ½ teaspoon salt
2¼ cups water   ¼ teaspoon celery salt
   7¾-oz. can salmon   Dash black pepper
2 tablespoons flour

Heat onion, evaporated milk and 2 cups of the water to scalding point in top of double boiler; remove onion. Remove skin from salmon. Mash salmon and bones well with a fork and add to hot milk; cover and heat at least 5 minutes. Meanwhile, blend flour with the remaining ¼ cup water until smooth, then stir this paste slowly into hot mixture and continue stirring over boiling water until slightly thickened. Add butter and seasonings, cover and cook 15 to 20 minutes longer. Serve hot with crisp crackers or croutons (61). 5 servings.

959   CREAM OF SPINACH SOUP

2 tablespoons butter   Pepper
1 medium onion, sliced   1½ teaspoons flour
3 cups meat broth or 3   3 tablespoons cold water
   bouillon cubes in 3 cups   2 cups drained cooked spinach
   hot water   1¼ cups evaporated milk
¾ teaspoon salt

Heat butter in a 3-qt. saucepan, add onion and sauté slowly until soft. Now add broth, seasonings and flour blended to a smooth paste with the cold water. Cook over direct heat, stirring constantly until mixture boils. Add spinach which has been finely chopped or rubbed through a sieve, then add milk. Reheat to scalding and serve piping hot with croutons (61) or crisp crackers. 5 servings.

CORN CHOWDER

2 slices bacon
2 slices onion, chopped
1½ cups diced potatoes
2 cups fresh corn cut from cob,
  or No. 2 can cream-style
  corn

3 cups hot water
3 tablespoons butter
1 cup evaporated milk
2½ teaspoons salt
Dash black pepper

Cut bacon into inch lengths with shears into soup kettle, add onion and cook until onion is soft and bacon done. Now add potatoes, corn and water and cook until potatoes are tender. Add butter, milk and seasonings, reheat to boiling and serve piping hot. 5 servings.

MANHATTAN CLAM CHOWDER

2 oz. salt pork
1 medium onion, chopped
1 branch celery, chopped
1 medium carrot, grated
2 potatoes, diced (2 cups)
1½ cups tomatoes, fresh or
  canned
  10½-oz. can clams

1½ cups water
½ small bay leaf
1/16 teaspoon thyme, if desired
  Dash pepper
1½ teaspoons salt
1 tablespoon flour
1 tablespoon chopped parsley

Cut pork in small dice and put into a 3 to 4-quart pan. Fry until slightly browned, then add the vegetables, juice drained from the clams, water, bay leaf and thyme. Heat to boiling, then reduce heat, cover and simmer ½ hour. Then add the chopped clams, salt and pepper, and flour blended to a smooth paste with 2 tablespoons of water, stirring gently until mixture boils and thickens slightly. Serve with chopped parsley sprinkled over each serving. 5 servings.

FISH CHOWDER

3 oz. salt pork, diced small
1/3 cup sliced onions
1½ cups sliced potatoes
½ teaspoon salt
1/8 teaspoon pepper

½ cup water
1 lb. boned lean fish
3 cups milk *or* No. 2½ can
  tomatoes, sieved

Place diced pork in a heavy kettle or Dutch oven and fry until golden brown. Add onions and cook until soft and light yellow in color, 5 to 7 minutes. Now add potatoes, sprinkle with salt and pepper and add water; cook at moderate rate until potatoes are half done, about 5 minutes.

Then add the fish, placing in the kettle flesh-side down. Again cover and continue cooking until potatoes are done and fish is tender enough to fall apart, from 10 to 12 minutes. Remove skin from fish and discard. Now break fish into coarse flakes. For New England style chowder, add milk; for Manhattan style chowder, add tomatoes. Heat thoroughly but do not boil. Serve hot with crisp crackers. 5 servings.

966   LENTIL SOUP

1 cup dried lentils	1⅔ cups evaporated milk
6 cups water	⅛ teaspoon black pepper
1½ teaspoons salt	Salt to taste
¼ cup sliced onion	2 tablespoons chopped parsley
¾ cup chopped fresh celery tops	

Wash lentils in cold water; put into a 3-qt. saucepan and cover with cold water. Soak overnight. Then drain, add the 6 cups water, 1½ teaspoons salt, onion and celery tops, cover and simmer ½ hour or until very soft. Turn into a colander or food mill and rub lentils and onions through into another saucepan. Add milk and seasonings and reheat to simmering. Serve with chopped parsley sprinkled over top. 5 or 6 servings.

967   NAVY BEAN SOUP

½ lb. dried navy beans	1½ cups hot water or scalded milk
2 oz. salt pork, sliced	
1 qt. water	Salt and pepper to taste
1 medium onion, sliced	Chopped chives or parsley

Wash beans thoroughly and put them into cold water to come 2 inches over them and let soak several hours or overnight. Drain and put into kettle; add salt pork and 1-qt. fresh water. Heat to boiling, reduce heat, cover tightly and simmer until beans are mushy, about 1½ hours. Add onion the last half hour of cooking. Press soup through sieve, add water or milk and season and reheat. Garnish by sprinkling chopped chives or parsley over each serving. 5 servings.

968   ONION SOUP

2½ cups sliced onions	2 cups milk
2 cups vegetable or meat broth	Salt to taste
Water	5 tablespoons grated cheese

Put onions into a 3 to 4-quart pan. Add the vegetable or meat broth, and additional water if needed to cover onions. Simmer, covered until onions are tender, about 10 minutes. There should be about 2 cups of liquid left on the onions, if not, add more hot water. Then add the milk, and salt to taste; heat to scalding. Serve steaming hot with a tablespoon of grated sharp cheese sprinkled over each serving and with an accompaniment of hot crisp crackers, croutons (61) or Melba toast (58). If vegetable or meat broth is not available, two chicken bouillon cubes dissolved in 2 cups water will enrich the flavor, in which case little or no salt will be needed. 5 servings.

969   FRENCH ONION SOUP

2 cups sliced onions	1 cup diced celery
2 tablespoons butter	Salt to suit taste
1½ quarts boiling water	5 slices bread
1 veal knuckle	Grated Parmesan cheese

Sauté onions in butter until lightly browned. Pour boiling water on veal knuckle, add browned onions and celery and simmer until tender, about 1 hour. Remove bone and season soup to taste. If desired, kitchen bouquet or a little caramel (1121) may be added for more color. Toast bread, trim off crusts, cut in strips and float on top of bowlfuls of soup. Sprinkle grated cheese generously over toast strips. 5 servings.

970   OYSTER BISQUE
(A tasty oyster soup easy to swallow)

½ pint oysters with liquor	2 cups water
2 tablespoons butter	⅛ teaspoon celery salt
2 tablespoons flour	¾ teaspoon salt
2 cups evaporated milk	

Drain oysters, saving the liquor. Chop very fine either in a chopping bowl or with kitchen shears. Melt butter, blend in flour, add oysters and liquor and heat just to boiling, stirring constantly. Now add evaporated milk, water and seasonings and reheat. Serve immediately with hot crackers. 5 servings.

971   OYSTER STEW

1⅔ cups evaporated milk	¼ bay leaf
2 cups water	¼ cup cracker crumbs
1 slice onion	1 pint oysters
2 branches celery	3 tablespoons butter
2 sprigs parsley	Salt and pepper to taste

Heat milk, water, onion, celery, parsley and bay leaf over boiling water for 20 minutes. Remove vegetables and bay leaf and add cracker crumbs. Meanwhile, heat oysters in their own liquor until edges curl. Combine with milk; add butter, salt and pepper and serve at once. 5 servings.

972   POTATO CARROT SOUP

4 medium potatoes, pared	1¾ cups cooking water from
3 medium carrots, scraped	vegetables
2 medium onions	1⅔ cups evaporated milk
3 cups boiling water	Dash cayenne
2 teaspoons salt	Dash celery salt

Dice potatoes, carrots and onions and cook in the boiling water, with salt until tender, about 15 minutes. Drain, saving the water, then rice or mash the vegetables thoroughly. There should be 1¾ cups of cooking water, if not, add fresh water. Combine with milk, scald and slowly stir in mashed vegetables. Add cayenne and celery salt, reheat and serve. Dash each serving with paprika for color. 5 servings.

973   SOY BEAN SOUP

½ lb. dried soy beans	No. 2 can tomato juice
1 small onion, sliced	1 tablespoon sugar
1 quart water	2½ teaspoons salt or to taste

Wash soy beans thoroughly, put into a bowl, cover with water and let soak overnight. Drain beans and run through food chopper using coarse blade. Put into a 3-qt. saucepan with the onion and 1 quart water, cover and simmer gently 1½ to 2 hours or until soy beans are tender. Add remaining ingredients and reheat before serving. Shavings of shredded carrot make an attractive garnish. 5 servings.

974   SPINACH CHOWDER

No. 2 can spinach or 2 cups cooked fresh spinach	⅓ to ½ cup sliced white onions
3 medium potatoes	3 tablespoons flour
3 slices bacon	1 cup evaporated milk
	Salt to taste

Drain spinach, saving liquid, then chop spinach. Pare and dice potatoes and boil until tender in salted water to cover. Drain, saving water. Sauté bacon until done; then remove bacon from pan, add onions to fat and cook until soft and yellow. Blend in flour, add evaporated milk, ¾ cup of spinach liquid, and 1 cup water drained from potatoes. Then cook over direct heat, stirring constantly until sauce boils and thickens.

Add spinach, potatoes and salt, again bring to boiling and simmer 5 minutes. Serve hot with drained crumbled crisp bacon dropped on top of each serving as a garnish. 5 or 6 servings.

974a   SPLIT PEA SOUP

1 cup split peas	½ cup chopped celery
1 quart water	2 tablespoons butter
¼ teaspoon dried dill seeds or small spray of fresh dill	2 frankfurters cut crosswise into ¼-inch pieces
1½ teaspoon salt	Croutons
¼ cup sliced green onion	

Pick over peas and wash thoroughly through 2 or 3 waters. Put water into soup kettle, heat to boiling, then add peas, dill seed and salt. Cover and cook over low heat 1 hour, stirring from time to time with a fork to prevent sticking. Add onions and celery and continue cooking until peas are soft, about ½ hour. Melt butter in saucepan, add frankfurters and brown slightly. Press vegetable mixture through a sieve or food mill over frankfurters in saucepan. Simmer 10 to 15 minutes longer. Serve with croutons or a few slices of toasted rye bread cooked in the soup the last 10 minutes. 4 servings.

975   TOMATO AND CABBAGE SOUP

¼ cup butter	1 tablespoon sugar
⅓ cup flour	1½ cups evaporated milk
No. 211 can tomato juice	2¼ cups finely chopped cooked cabbage (1008)
½ bay leaf	1 cup water
1 slice onion	
1 teaspoon salt	

Melt butter and blend in flour; add tomato juice and stir over low heat until mixture boils and thickens. Add bay leaf, onion, salt and sugar to evaporated milk, and heat separately in top of double boiler over hot water. Just before serving, strain out the bay leaf and onion and add cabbage and water in which cabbage was cooked. Slowly stir the tomato mixture into the milk and cabbage. Serve immediately. 5 servings.

976   WATERCRESS OR SPINACH AND POTATO SOUP

3 cups meat broth or 2 chicken bouillon cubes in 3 cups water	¾ cup washed chopped watercress or raw spinach
4 medium potatoes, grated	1½ teaspoons salt
1 cup milk	Dash pepper
	¼ cup grated cheese

531

Heat broth or bouillon to boiling, add grated raw potato and simmer gently 10 to 15 minutes, stirring occasionally. About 5 minutes before serving, add milk, cress or spinach and seasonings. Serve hot with a sprinkling of grated cheese on each serving. 5 servings.

BOUILLONS

977   HOT TOMATO BOUILLON

No. 2½ can tomatoes
1 cup water
2 chicken bouillon cubes
Salt to taste

Dash pepper
Croutons
1 teaspoon chopped parsley

Rub tomatoes through a sieve fine enough to hold back the seeds but let all the pulp through. Heat purée with water and bouillon cubes until boiling. Season and serve hot with croutons (61), sprinkling a little chopped parsley over each serving. 5 servings.

977a   BEEF BOUILLON

Place 1 bouillon cube in each cup and pour boiling water over it, stirring until dissolved. Strength of bouillon will depend on size of cup and amount of water used. Canned beef bouillon requires only heating and, if condensed, the addition of water to prepare for serving. A pleasing drink, which is not a true bouillon, is prepared by substituting hot milk for water with either the bouillon cube or canned bouillon.

977b   COLD BORSHT
(*A delicious "quickie" summer soup*)

No. 2 can of beets
1⅓ cups chicken broth *or*
1⅓ chicken bouillon cubes dissolved in 1⅓ cups cold water

1 cup sour cream
¾ teaspoon salt
⅛ teaspoon pepper
1½ teaspoons lemon juice
2 tablespoons chopped chives

Use only half the beets and juice in the can. (Serve rest at another meal in a salad.) Drain beets; save juice. Put drained beets through food mill or potato ricer. Add beet juice and all ingredients, except chives. Stir well. Cover and chill thoroughly. To serve, stir well, then turn into chilled soup dishes. Sprinkle with chives. Accompany with Melba rye toast. 4 servings.

978   JELLIED TOMATO BOUILLON

To the Hot Tomato Bouillon (977), while boiling hot, add 1 tablespoon plain gelatin which has been soaked 5 minutes in ¼ cup cold
water. Cool and place in refrigerator to congeal. Serve in cold dishes
with a wedge of lemon or spoonfuls of sour cream. 5 servings.

979   TOMATO NOODLE SOUP

1-qt. 14-oz. can tomato juice	Dash pepper
2 teaspoons grated onion	3 tablespoons butter
1 teaspoon salt	1 chicken bouillon cube
½ of 7-oz. package narrow noodles	1 cup boiling water
1 to 2 teaspoons sugar	1 to 2 tablespoons chopped parsley

Put tomato juice, onion and salt into a 3 to 4-quart pan and heat to
boiling. Add noodles and simmer uncovered for about 15 minutes, or
until noodles are tender, lifting them from time to time with a fork. Add
sugar, pepper and butter. Dissolve bouillon cube in the boiling water
and add to soup. Just before serving, stir in the chopped parsley. Serve
with a sprinkling of grated sharp cheese or chopped crisp bacon on each
bowlful. 5 servings.

VEGETABLES

WHY *should a few tart apples be cooked along with red cabbage? How can you preserve both the vitamin content and the color of green vegetables when they are cooked? Why is the odor of cooking cabbage stronger when you cover it? What is pot liquor and why is it important? These are just a few of the questions you will be able to answer, to the benefit of your family's health and your own reputation as a cook, when you have finished this fundamental chapter.*

Cooking vegetables well may be as dramatic as making good angel food cake; it is just as rare an accomplishment and a much more practical one. From a health standpoint it is most important to your family that you should be a good vegetable cook, since vegetables supply a large proportion of the vitamins and minerals needed for health, and well-cooked vegetables will be eaten and enjoyed where poorly cooked ones will be left on the plate, doing no one any good.

Vegetable cookery is a matter of remembering a few simple facts about vegetables, most of which have to do with their color.

GREEN VEGETABLES

The green color of vegetable leaves and stems is given by a substance called chlorophyll, the same substance that makes grass green. Chlorophyll is affected by acids, alkalies and minerals, in the presence of heat. If acids or minerals are present in the water in which green foods are cooked, the green gradually changes to an unattractive greenish brown. If alkali is present, the green gradually becomes more intense.

Both of these changes are undesirable, because the natural color of green vegetables is the most appetizing color they can have. To keep this natural color, green vegetables should be cooked quickly and for as short a time as possible. They should be cooked uncovered, so the volatile part of the acids present in the vegetables themselves can pass off with the steam instead of condensing with it on the lid, then dropping back on the vegetables to come in contact with the chlorophyll. Vegetables cooked until just barely tender have a better flavor, better appearance and retain more food value than when cooked longer.

The addition of a small amount of soda to the cooking water intensifies the green color. This is not recommended, however, for even a slight excess will make the vegetable slippery and unpleasant to eat; and soda destroys a considerable proportion of the vitamin content. This applies to all green vegetables—spinach, chard, asparagus, Brussels sprouts, green cabbage, green beans, peas, etc.

RED VEGETABLES

The reaction of red vegetables to acids and alkalis is very different to that of green ones. They turn redder and more attractive-looking when there is acid in the cooking water, while the presence of alkali causes them to turn bluish. The pigments which color red vegetables, such as beets and red cabbage, are called anthocyanins.

To give red vegetables the benefit of all their own acid, the kettle in which they are cooked should be tightly covered. Addition of a little vinegar or lemon juice, or of tart apples, helps to keep the color brilliant. Vinegar or lemon juice is often added to beets toward the end of cooking, and improves flavor as well as color. Red cabbage is improved by cooking a few tart apples with it.

Red color in beets is also influenced greatly by care in preparation. About 3 inches of the stem should be left on, and care should be taken to avoid breaking the skin in washing, and to keep the tap root intact. Any break in the skin or the tap root results in "bleeding" into the cooking water, and this makes the cooked beets pale in spite of an acid water.

YELLOW VEGETABLES

Yellow vegetables are the least susceptible to color changes of all the vegetables. The yellow pigment, carotin, is not affected by either acid or alkali. Overcooking, however, often results in a gradual leaking of the pigment into the water, so the water becomes bright yellow and the food pale.

Yellow vegetables, which include carrots, yellow squash, sweet potatoes and yellow corn, may be steamed or boiled, either covered or uncovered. Covering the kettle, if they are boiled, will hasten cooking, and this is desirable to conserve the vitamin content.

WHITE VEGETABLES

Most white vegetables show no color, but they contain substances called flavones, which change to an unattractive brownish gray if there is an excess of iron in the water, or if the vegetable is overcooked. Therefore they should be cooked rapidly, until just tender, in order to expose them as briefly as possible to any iron that may be present in the water. Iron cooking utensils should be avoided.

Members of this group are white potatoes, white onions, white turnips and cauliflower. Potatoes may be cooked covered, but the others belong to the strong-juiced class and should be cooked in an uncovered pan.

STRONG-JUICED VEGETABLES

The class of strong-juiced vegetables includes representatives of most of the color groups: broccoli, Brussels sprouts, cabbage, cauliflower, kohlrabi, onions and turnips. They all contain volatile substances which if retained in the kettle by covering it, react on the sulphur content of the vegetables to produce compounds that are not only disagreeable in odor and flavor, but difficult to digest. The unpleasant cabbage smell which pervades some houses when cabbage is cooked is caused not by the cabbage itself, but by these unsavory sulphur compounds resulting from prolonged cooking in a covered kettle.

Therefore it is desirable to cook strong-juiced vegetables quickly, until they are just tender, and always in an open pan. Enough water to cover the vegetable is usually recommended, too, for this dilutes the substances which cause the difficulty.

QUICK COOKING

Under several of the color classifications of vegetables quick cooking has been specially advised. This is important enough to have a paragraph to itself. The briefer the cooking, the more of the food value of the raw food is retained in the cooked product, and the less will be lost to the cooking water or destroyed completely. Vitamin C is readily destroyed at high temperatures, and the longer a vegetable is cooked, the more vitamin content it will lose. In order to get the fullest possible food value out of foods, they should be cooked so as to lose a minimum of their vitamin content; and in the case of vegetables, this means quick cooking.

Use enough water to prevent the kettle from boiling dry, and let it boil rapidly until the vegetables are *just* tender.

POT LIQUOR

When a small enough amount of water is used so that all or most of it evaporates during cooking, there is danger of boiling dry. When a larger amount is used, there is danger of wasting some valuable minerals and vitamins which dissolve into the cooking water, since many housewives still discard the excess cooking water after the vegetable is done.

When more than the minimum amount of water is used for cooking, it should never be poured down the sink. This "pot liquor," as it is called, not

Red, yellow and green vegetables add beauty to the meal and elements essential in the diet for radiant good health. They are delicious plain-cooked and served with melted butter or variations of creamy white sauce. LOWER LEFT—*Parsley Sauce, which is plain white sauce with fine-chopped fresh parsley folded into it* **(919)**. *Or substitute sour cream for the milk to make Sour Cream Sauce, which is excellent on boiled cabbage.* LOWER RIGHT—*Catchup Sauce is made by folding ⅓ cup catchup into 2 cups of white sauce. Good on Fried Egg Plant* **(1036)** *or boiled cauliflower.*

It's really surprising what an imposing platter can be arranged with an assortment of vegetables, and no meat at all except a garnish of crisp broiled bacon. A cauliflower cooked whole, served with cheese sauce poured over it, makes a handsome rallying point for any vegetable platter. The tarts? Lemon Cream Tarts (671) with a garnish of whipped cream and a few sliced blanched pistachios.

To make these delightful luncheon plates, spread sliced bread, crusts trimmed off, with salad dressing. Put together with a slice of American Cheese. Cut sandwich into quarters diagonally. Place 2 peach halves in a nest of lettuce on plate. Fill one peach with raspberries, the other with blueberries. Add the quartered sandwiches and a lettuce cup of salad dressing in center.

Vegetables have beauty that's more than skin deep. Vegetable Plates can be made beautiful and valuable—if the color, shape, fragrance and nutrients of the vegetables are preserved. Here are 2 examples: TOP PLATE *is plain cooked buttered vegetables around a Tomato Cup of potato salad.* LOWER PLATE *adds Hollandaise Sauce to the broccoli with a center slice of Pan-broiled Tomato.*

only contains valuable food elements, but has a delicious flavor. It makes an unusual and very appealing broth while hot, or a good chilled cocktail. It may be added to tomato juice, or to any kind of soup, to improve the flavor and increase the food value.

The water from potatoes cooked without their skins should also be saved. It may be used immediately or poured into a clean jar, tightly covered and kept in the refrigerator until needed for making meat gravy or to dilute evaporated milk in making white sauces for other creamed vegetables.

To avoid further loss of vitamins, the pot liquor should be used as soon as possible after cooking.

OTHER METHODS OF COOKING VEGETABLES

The only cooking method which has been discussed so far is boiling, and this is in fact the most common method of cooking all vegetables. However, baking, braising, frying and steaming are all used for various vegetables. Suitable methods for the different vegetables are shown on page 538.

It will be noted that for green vegetables no other method than boiling is advised. All the other methods will bring about the discoloration which it is so desirable to avoid or at least to reduce to a minimum.

The other methods, however, conserve the mineral content of the food better than boiling, and are highly desirable for vegetables to which they are suited. Baking whole in the skin is the best of these methods for conserving minerals, since there is no loss whatever in the cooking process, assuming that there is no overbaking or scorching to necessitate discarding part of the food itself. White and sweet potatoes, squash and onions are excellent cooked in this manner, and may be eaten to the thinnest layer of outer skin. Wherever possible, the skin may be eaten too, as with baked white potatoes.

Casserole dishes made with pared and sliced raw foods also come under this heading, for here the only loss of minerals occurs in the paring and may be reduced to a minimum by those who learn how to pare vegetables thin.

In braising, which is a method of cooking with very little water or with the steam formed from the vegetable's own juices, the liquid used becomes a part of the flavorful gravy which is always served with the vegetable. So any minerals and vitamins dissolved in the cooking water are still consumed along with the food itself. Here again thin paring is important for the minerals are most abundant in layers of tissue just under the thin skin. In frying and sautéing there is no danger of mineral loss, but vitamins are destroyed if the cooking temperature is too high, or if cooking time is too long.

Steaming produces little loss in either minerals or vitamins, except in juices that leak out and drip down into the water in the bottom of the steamer. This is small compared with the loss that is possible in boiling.

TABLE 21. COOKING METHODS SUITABLE TO VARIOUS VEGETABLES

Boiling	Baking	Braising	Frying or Sautéing	Steaming
Asparagus	Eggplant	Celery	Eggplant	Beets
Beans, green	Onions	Onions	Corn	Carrots
and wax	Potatoes, white	Lettuce	Onions	Corn
Beets	and sweet		Parsnips	Parsnips
Broccoli	Squash		(after	Potatoes, white
Cabbage	Tomatoes		boiling)	and sweet
Carrots			Potatoes, white	Squash
Celery			and sweet	
Corn			Tomatoes	
Eggplant				
Kohlrabi				
Okra				
Onions				
Parsnips				
Peas				
Potatoes, white				
and sweet				
Spinach				
Squash				
Tomatoes				
Turnips				

It should also be pointed out that boiling produces no loss if the vegetables are cooked without paring, as may be done with new potatoes, sweet potatoes, beets and onions. The skin is easily removed after cooking.

SERVING CANNED VEGETABLES

Canned vegetables are of increasingly fine quality, and there are few homes where they are not served frequently. Remember that high quality canned vegetables are picked at the peak of their goodness, and are prepared and processed within a few hours of harvesting. Therefore they are, in a sense, even fresher than the fresh vegetables which we buy at the grocery store, which are seldom less and often more than twenty-four hours from the field or garden.

To serve canned vegetables with the utmost of flavor and food value, the liquid in which they are packed should not be discarded. Sometimes, as for whole kernel corn which has only a small amount of liquid, the vegetable may be heated and served in the juice. For some other vegetables, such as peas, which are packed with more liquid than it is desirable to serve on them, the liquid may be drained off and quickly boiled down to ⅓ the original quantity; then the peas may be put into the concentrated liquid to heat them, and served with whatever remains.

This liquid in which canned vegetables are packed consists of pure water, sometimes with a small amount of seasoning, plus the vegetable juice which cooks out in processing. It therefore contains some of the flavor of the canned product, and when concentrated by boiling down, adds to the flavor of the food.

Butter and some additional salt are usually required to bring out the full flavor of any canned vegetable.

COOKING FROZEN VEGETABLES

Frozen or frosted vegetables, commercially packed, are becoming so widely distributed that they are available in all cities and in many small towns. Families in rural and small town areas, often freeze and store their vegetables in home freezers or in community lockers, and the results compare favorably with the commercial product. A number of freezing processes are in commercial use, and some seem to give superior results; however, the principal difference seems to lie in the quality of the fresh foods chosen for freezing. Foods of excellent quality, quick-frozen within a few hours of picking, are similar in flavor, texture and appearance to the fresh product.

In general, frozen vegetables require a shorter cooking time than do fresh ones, even though they are put into boiling water while still frozen hard. Dry-packed vegetables, including almost all commercially frozen vegetables, are not usually thawed before cooking. Most packers give detailed directions for cooking them, including exact cooking times, and these should be followed carefully, since even slight overcooking affects the quality.

Vegetables should be cooked very soon after thawing has taken place, they should never be re-frozen. After cooking, their keeping quality is just like that of the fresh product; that is, they should be used up promptly or there will be loss of food value and some deterioration in flavor.

980   ARTICHOKES—FRENCH

Choose fresh artichokes. Swish each vigorously upside down through plenty of warm water to clean. Cut thin slice from end of stem. Trim off any brown tips of the petals, using kitchen shears. Cover with boiling salted water (1 teaspoon salt to each quart of water). Weight down with a heavy plate about 2 inches smaller in diameter than the saucepan to allow the escape of steam. Cook 35 to 40 minutes or until the petals will pull out easily; then remove and turn the artichoke upside down to drain thoroughly. Place on hot serving plate. Serve with hot melted butter or Hollandaise Sauce (910).

To eat the artichoke, pull the petals off one by one, dip the fleshy ends into butter or sauce, and slip flesh off between the lips, discarding the rest of the petals. When all the petals have been removed, only the hairy choke on top of the heart remains. Scrape the choke off neatly with a spoon or fork and discard. Eat the heart by cutting apart with a fork and dipping the pieces in butter or sauce.

981   BUTTERED OR CREAMED ASPARAGUS

Clean asparagus by snipping off the paper-like scales at sides of spears and the woody fiber at the bottom of the spears. Wash thoroughly in cold water. Break off the tough ends; these may be cooked separately for soup. Stalks may be left whole or cut in pieces 1 to 1½ inches in length. Barely cover with boiling salted water (1 teaspoon salt to each quart of water) and cook rapidly until tender. In general, asparagus gets tender in about 20 minutes, but very tender asparagus may be done in less time. Test by piercing with metal skewer or tines of fork. Add more hot water if it boils away during cooking; at end of cooking period water should be practically all evaporated. If any needs to be drained off, save it for soup or a beverage. Pour melted butter or a medium white sauce (919) or cheese sauce (920) over the drained asparagus, which may, if desired, be arranged on toast. Serve immediately. 2 to 2½ pounds asparagus serves 5.

982   ASPARAGUS AND EGG CASSEROLE

1½ lbs. asparagus	5 hard-cooked eggs (395)
1½ cups thin white sauce	Buttered bread crumbs

Clean and cook asparagus as directed (981). Drain, saving liquid. Make White Sauce (919), using evaporated milk diluted with asparagus liquid. Combine with cooked asparagus. Arrange layers of creamed asparagus in buttered casserole with shelled, sliced eggs between layers. Cover with buttered crumbs (1118) and bake in a moderately hot oven (400° F.) until sauce bubbles through toasted crumbs, about 20 minutes. 5 servings.

983   ASPARAGUS IN EGG SAUCE

1½ lbs. asparagus	Few drops Worcestershire
3 tablespoons butter	1 teaspoon lemon juice, if
3 tablespoons flour	desired
1 teaspoon salt	¼ teaspoon onion juice
2 cups milk	4 hard-cooked eggs (395)

Prepare and cook asparagus as directed (981). Meanwhile, melt butter, blend in flour and salt, and add milk; stir over direct heat until sauce boils and thickens. Add Worcestershire, lemon juice and onion juice.

Just before serving, fold in shelled and coarsely chopped eggs. Serve over hot, freshly cooked drained asparagus. 5 servings.

984   ASPARAGUS TOAST ROLLS

Trim crusts from large slices of fresh white bread, roll so opposite edges of the slice come together, and fasten with toothpicks. Toast on all sides in broiler or hot oven, watching carefully. Fill toast rolls with drained hot asparagus, canned or fresh cooked, and arrange on platter. Serve with Cheese Sauce (920) in which asparagus liquor or cooking water has been substituted for part of the milk. Garnish with crisp broiled bacon (544) and parsley. Two asparagus rolls make 1 serving.

985   BUTTERED OR CREAMED GREEN BEANS

Wash 1½ to 2 lbs. beans and snip off ends. Leave whole or cut in pieces and put into a 3-qt. saucepan. Cover well with boiling salted water, cook, uncovered, until tender, about 30 minutes, adding more boiling water if needed. Drain, saving any liquid for vegetable juice cocktail; add 1 teaspoon sugar, pour melted butter or a medium White or Brown Sauce (919 or 902), over the hot beans and reheat. Serve immediately. 5 servings.

Note: Half this amount of beans may be half-cooked, combined with an equal quantity of diced potatoes, and cooked until both are tender; then drained and buttered.

986   GREEN BEANS au GRATIN

5 slices bacon	½ cup milk
2 tablespoons flour	¾ cup grated sharp cheese
1 No. 2 can green beans *or* 2½ cups cooked fresh green beans	½ cup rolled cornflakes *or* bread crumbs mixed with 2 tablespoons melted butter

Pan-broil the bacon (545) until done; drain off fat, remove bacon to absorbent paper. Measure 3 tablespoons of fat and return to skillet. Add flour and stir until blended; then add liquid drained from beans—there should be about ⅞ cup—and the milk, and stir constantly over direct heat until sauce boils and thickens. Add beans and grated cheese, and turn into a buttered 6-cup casserole. Sprinkle with cornflake crumbs or bread crumbs and bake in a moderately slow oven (325° F.) about 20 minutes or until crumbs brown. Two minutes before removing from oven, sprinkle with the chopped crisp bacon. 5 servings.

987 GREEN BEANS WITH ONIONS AND BACON

1½ lbs. green beans	½ teaspoon salt
3 slices bacon, cut fine	Pepper
1 cup chopped onion	Paprika

Wash beans and snip off ends, then cut lengthwise in three or four strips and then once crosswise. Cook rapidly until just tender in barely enough boiling salted water to cover, about 20 minutes. The liquid should be practically all evaporated by the time the beans are tender and will require no draining. Meanwhile, pan-broil bacon over low heat, adding onions when bacon is half done. Heat together until bacon is done and the onions transparent. Add the beans, season with salt, pepper, and paprika and serve hot. 5 servings.

988 GREEN BEANS IN TOMATO SAUCE

2 tablespoons butter	1 tablespoon sugar
¼ cup flour	1¼ teaspoons salt
2 cups tomato juice	⅛ teaspoon dry mustard
No. 2 can green or wax beans	¼ teaspoon celery salt
1 egg, beaten	Pepper

Melt the butter and blend in the flour until smooth. Then add tomato juice and liquid drained from beans, and cook over direct heat, stirring constantly until thickened. Slowly stir hot sauce into the beaten egg, then return to pan and cook over very low heat, stirring constantly for about 2 minutes. Now add seasonings, and the beans, then reheat and serve. 5 servings.

989 CREOLE WAX BEANS

2 tablespoons butter	10½-oz. can tomatoes, or 1⅓
1 medium onion, chopped	cups fresh-cooked or home-
1 branch celery, chopped	canned
1 small carrot, grated	No. 2 can wax beans
	Salt and pepper to taste

Melt butter in a 3-qt. saucepan. Add onion, celery and carrot. Stirring frequently, cook slowly about 5 minutes, or until vegetables are softened. Now add tomatoes and cook rapidly for 10 minutes; then add beans, reduce heat, and simmer until the sauce has the consistency of a thin gravy, about 10 minutes longer. Add seasonings and serve. 5 servings.

990 **WAX OR GREEN BEANS WITH DILL SAUCE**

No. 2 can wax or green beans,   1½ teaspoons finely chopped
  or 2½ cups fresh cooked   fresh dill
2   tablespoons butter   Pepper
2   tablespoons flour   ½ to 1 tablespoon vinegar

Drain beans and measure juice or cooking water; add water if necessary to make 1⅓ cups of liquid. Melt butter, blend in flour and add the liquid gradually, stirring constantly over direct heat until sauce boils and thickens. Add dill and beans, stirring just enough to distribute dill through sauce. Heat slowly to boiling point, then add pepper and vinegar to suit taste and serve piping hot. If fresh dill is not available, substitute 1½ tablespoons chopped stuffed olives or pickles for the dill and omit the vinegar. 5 servings.

991 **HARVARD GREEN OR WAX BEANS**

3 to 4 cups water   3 teaspoons cornstarch
¾ teaspoon salt   3 tablespoons cider vinegar
1½ lbs. green or wax beans   Pimiento
3 to 4 tablespoons sugar

Heat water to boiling, add salt and beans which have been washed, trimmed and cut into 1-inch lengths; cook rapidly uncovered, until tender, 20 to 30 minutes. Drain, saving the cooking water. Mix the sugar and cornstarch. Measure ¾ cup of cooking water, add to cornstarch mixture and cook, stirring constantly until sauce boils and becomes clear. Now add vinegar and pour sauce over beans and let stand in warm place about 20 minutes to blend flavors. Add a few strips of pimiento and reheat before serving. 5 servings.

992 **BUTTERED KIDNEY BEANS**

Wash ½ lb. dried kidney beans thoroughly; put into a 3-qt. saucepan, add cold water to come 2 inches above beans and let stand several hours or overnight. Drain, and again cover with fresh cold water; bring to a boil, cover and simmer gently about 1 hour, or until beans are tender. There should be just enough water left so the beans will not be dry. Add a generous amount of butter and salt to suit the taste. A garnish of chopped parsley or green pepper adds to the flavor as well as the appearance of the dish. Bacon fat may be used in place of butter for seasoning. 5 servings.

993   KIDNEY BEANS WITH ONIONS

½ lb. dried kidney beans
1 cup sliced onions

3 tablespoons butter
Salt and pepper to suit taste

Prepare kidney beans as described under Buttered Kidney Beans (992). Then sauté the sliced onions until soft and slightly browned in the butter. Drain the beans and add to the onions, tossing together until beans are coated with butter. Add seasonings and serve hot. 5 servings.

994   KIDNEY BEANS WITH SALT PORK

3 oz. salt pork
2 medium-sized onions, chopped

1 tablespoon flour
No. 2 can red kidney beans
2 tablespoons cooking sherry

Cut salt pork into ½-inch dice; turn into skillet and pan-broil slowly until crisp. Add finely chopped onion and cook slowly until onion is soft and yellow, stirring to prevent scorching. Blend in the flour to a smooth paste, then stir in beans and sherry thoroughly, then simmer gently 10 minutes. 5 servings.

995   KIDNEY BEAN LOAF

No. 2 can red kidney beans
1 cup boiled rice (174)
2 eggs, beaten
½ teaspoon salt
½ teaspoon sugar

1 teaspoon grated onion
2 tablespoons melted butter
2 tablespoons chopped parsley, if desired

Drain and mash beans and mix well with other ingredients. Turn into buttered 3-cup loaf pan or casserole, and press down firmly. Bake in a moderate oven (350° F.) 1 to 1½ hours, or until a sharp knife inserted in center comes out clean. Unmold on to a hot plate and serve with Tomato Sauce (916) or Chili Sauce (725a). 5 servings.

996   BUTTERED DRIED LIMA BEANS

1½ cups dried lima beans
1½ teaspoons salt
3 tablespoons butter

Pepper
Parsley or pimiento

Wash beans and soak overnight in cold water. Drain; add 3 cups cold water and salt, and bring to boiling. Then reduce heat, cover and simmer gently until soft, 30 to 40 minutes. Liquid should be evaporated to a thin gravy-like consistency. Add butter to hot beans, more salt, if desired, and pepper. Serve hot. A sprinkling of chopped parsley, a few strips of pimiento, or a dash of paprika adds attractive color to these delicious beans. 5 servings.

997   BUTTERED NEW LIMA BEANS

3 cups freshly shelled limas   3 tablespoons butter
2 cups boiling water   Salt and pepper to taste

Wash the beans thoroughly and drop into the boiling water. Cover and simmer until tender, from 20 to 30 minutes, depending on size of beans. Add butter, salt and pepper to taste last 15 minutes of cooking. From ½ to ⅔ cup cooking liquid should still remain on beans after cooking. Again check seasoning, then serve immediately. 5 servings.

998   BAKED LIMA BEANS

2 cups dried lima beans   ¼ lb. salt pork, sliced thin

Wash beans, put into a 3-qt. saucepan. Add water to come 2 inches above beans and let soak overnight. Next morning drain, add 3 cups fresh water and sliced pork. Heat to boiling, then reduce heat, cover and simmer gently until soft, about ½ hour. Remove the pork, add salt if needed. Now turn beans with their liquid into a buttered casserole. Arrange pork over top of beans and place in a moderately hot oven (425° F.) until pork is browned. Serve hot. 5 servings.

999   LIMA BEAN CASSEROLE

2 cups dried lima beans   3 tablespoons molasses
1 medium onion, sliced thin   3 tablespoons granulated sugar
1½ teaspoons salt   1 teaspoon salt
2 oz. salt pork, sliced

Wash beans and put them into a 3-qt. saucepan. Then add water to come 2 inches above beans and soak overnight. Next morning, drain beans, add 4 cups water and the salt. Bring to boiling point, reduce heat, cover and simmer gently until soft, about 25 minutes, being careful not to boil hard enough to break beans. Now drain, saving cooking water, and pour half the beans into a casserole or bean pot; lay onion slices over them. Add rest of beans and bury salt pork in them, leaving rind exposed. Combine molasses, sugar, salt and 1½ cups cooking water and pour over beans. Cover, bake in a moderately slow oven (325° F.) 1½ hours. If beans get too dry, add boiling water to bring liquid almost to the top. Uncover and bake 2 to 2½ hours longer or to a rich golden brown on top. This dish may be reheated successfully, so it is practical to make twice the quantity, if desired. 5 servings.

1000   BAKED BEANS WITH TOMATOES

2½ cups dried navy beans	1 teaspoon salt
1 medium onion, sliced	⅛ teaspoon dry mustard
3 oz. salt pork, sliced	Few grains cayenne
No. 2 can tomatoes, sieved	⅓ cup brown sugar, packed,
2 cups water	or ⅓ cup molasses

Wash beans thoroughly and put them into a 3-qt. bowl. Add enough water to come 2 inches above beans and soak overnight. Next morning drain and combine with the next 7 ingredients in a saucepan; bring to boil, reduce heat, cover, and simmer 1 hour or until beans are soft enough to break open. Turn into a buttered casserole or baking dish and add brown sugar or molasses. Pull slices of salt pork to the top and bake, covered in a very slow oven (250° F.) 2 hours. Remove cover and bake another hour. Serve hot, with catchup or chili sauce if desired. 5 servings.

1001   OLD-FASHIONED BAKED BEANS

2 lbs. dried navy beans	¼ cup brown sugar
1 teaspoon soda	½ cup molasses
1 medium onion, sliced	¼ cup tomato catchup
1 tablespoon salt	¹⁄₁₆ teaspoon black pepper
4 teaspoons cider vinegar	¾ lb. salt pork, sliced
1 teaspoon prepared mustard	

Wash beans thoroughly and put them in a 4-qt. saucepan. Add enough water to come 2 inches above beans and soak overnight. Next morning drain. Then cover with fresh cold water, add soda and bring to boil. Again drain, rinse, cover with cold water and bring to boil. Put the onion in bottom of bean pot or deep casserole with all the rest of the seasonings. Add the hot beans and liquid with boiling water to barely cover. Lay strips of salt pork over top, cover and bake in a very slow oven (250° F.) until beans are tender, 9 to 10 hours, adding more boiling water as liquid evaporates. Remove cover and bake one hour longer to let salt pork become crisp and brown. Serve piping hot, plain or with catsup (725) or chili sauce (725a). 10 to 12 servings.

Variation: If sweeter baked beans are desired, add ¼ cup more of both brown sugar and molasses along with the seasonings. This also gives a richer brown color, which is preferred by many people.

1002   NAVY BEAN AND APPLE CASSEROLE

2 cups dried navy beans
1½ teaspoons salt
3 large tart apples, peeled and sliced

⅓ cup brown sugar
¼ lb. salt pork, sliced

Wash beans and put them in a 3-qt. saucepan. Add enough cold water to come 2 inches above beans and soak overnight. Next morning drain, add 4 cups fresh water and salt, bring to boil and simmer gently, covered, about 2 hours. Now drain, saving cooking water. Arrange beans and apple slices in alternate layers in a greased casserole, sprinkling sugar over each layer. Pour in 2 cups of the cooking liquid and top with slices of salt pork. Bake, covered, in a very slow oven (250° F.) about 1½ hours or until beans are light brown and thoroughly cooked. If they become dry in cooking, add more cooking liquid or hot water. 5 to 7 servings.

1003   BAKED BEANS IN TOMATO CUPS

5 large tomatoes
Celery salt

2 teaspoons sugar
No. 2 can baked beans

Wash but do not peel tomatoes. Cut out stem end and scoop out centers leaving thick walls. Sprinkle inside of tomato cups with celery salt and sugar and fill with baked beans. Butter a shallow baking pan and set the tomatoes in it. Bake in a moderate oven (350° F.) until tomatoes are soft and beans are hot through, about 20 minutes. If desired, a slice of bacon may be laid across each filled tomato and baking continued until the bacon is crisp. The scooped-out centers of the tomatoes may be quickly stewed, seasoned with salt, prepared mustard, and a little sugar, and strained to serve as a sauce around the baked tomatoes. 5 servings.

1004   NAVY BEAN STEW

2 cups dried navy beans
6 oz. salt pork, diced

1 pod dried hot red pepper
Salt to taste

Wash beans thoroughly and put them in a 3-qt. saucepan. Add enough cold water to come 2 inches above beans and let soak overnight. Next morning drain and cover well with cold water. Heat to boiling and simmer 15 minutes; then add diced salt pork, cover and continue cooking slowly until beans and pork are both very tender, from 1½ to 2 hours. Add hot water to beans during cooking to keep them stew-like in consistency. About 15 minutes before they are done, add red pepper. Season to suit taste. 5 servings. 1 lb. navy beans equals 2½ cups. Makes 5 cups boiled.

1005   BUTTERED BEETS

Cut off tops about 3 inches from the beets. If the leaves and stems are tender they may be cooked like spinach (1094) and served as greens. Do not cut off the main or tap root. Wash beets thoroughly, but carefully, taking care not to break the skin or the tap root, as broken skin or root permits the beet to "bleed." Cover the beets with water, either hot or cold and boil gently in covered kettle until tender—from 30 to 45 minutes, depending on size. Drain, cool and slip off stems and skins. Slice, dice or rice beets and re-heat, adding melted butter. A little chopped chives or parsley adds to the attractiveness of beets, and many persons prefer them served with vinegar or lemon juice. Allow 2 bunches of beets for 5 servings. Stems may be buttered and served with the beets, or served separately at another meal. We like buttered beets unsalted, you may want salt.

1006   HARVARD BEETS

No. 2 can beets	2 tablespoons cider vinegar
2 tablespoons butter	¼ teaspoon salt
1 tablespoon corn starch	Pepper
¼ teaspoon onion juice	1½ teaspoons sugar

Drain beets, saving liquid. Melt butter, blend in corn starch, add beet liquid and stir constantly over dircet heat until sauce boils and thickens. Add remaining ingredients and the beets and continue heating slowly until beets are hot through. 5 servings.

Cooked fresh beets may be used, substituting water for the beet juice.

1007   BUTTERED BROCCOLI

Select compact heads of broccoli, not too mature. Put heads down into cold, salted water for about half an hour to dislodge any insects. Then drain. Remove leaves, then strip off woody peeling from the stalks up to the heads. Slash heavy stalks into halves or quarters lengthwise, but do not cut into heads. Place in large kettle and cover with boiling salted water (1 teaspoon salt to 1 quart water). Boil briskly, uncovered, until just tender, 8 to 10 minutes. Drain and pour melted butter or cheese sauce (920) over it. Serve immediately. Broccoli is also good served with Hollandaise Sauce (910). 2 lbs. serves 5.

1008   BUTTERED OR CREAMED CABBAGE

The green cabbage of spring and summer is the most attractive to
the eye when cooked, but white winter cabbage tastes just as good and
has about the same food value, when properly cooked. If cabbage is old
or poor in quality, due to drouth or other conditions, trim off outside
leaves and end of stalk, and let the head soak at least 1 hour in ice water.
Then drain. Cut in quarters and remove the central stalk, then slice
or chop cabbage coarsely. Drop into boiling salted water and boil
rapidly, uncovered until just tender, 6 to 9 minutes. Drain thoroughly
and pour melted butter or medium White Sauce (919) over the hot
cabbage. Serve immediately. A 2 lb. head serves 5.

1008a   BUTTERED OR CREAMED BRUSSELS SPROUTS

    1 quart box Brussels sprouts   3 tablespoons butter *or* 1½
    2 teaspoons salt   cups medium white sauce
    1 teaspoon sugar

Choose bright green firm headed sprouts. Remove soiled outer leaves,
cut a thin slice from stem ends and remove any discoloration. Wash
well and soak 20 minutes in 1 qt. cold water to which 1 teaspoon of the
salt has been added. Then drain. Add rest of salt, sugar and sprouts to
1 quart boiling water and cook in an uncovered 3-qt. saucepan, boiling
vigorously until just tender, from 10 to 12 minutes, depending on size.
Drain well and add butter or cream sauce. Turn into a hot serving dish
and serve immediately. 4 servings.

Note: Cooking time may be shortened to 8 minutes if quarter-inch crosswise slashes are made in the stem end of each sprout.

1009   CABBAGE au GRATIN

    2 to 2½ lb. head cabbage   Salt to suit taste
    3 tablespoons butter   1½ cups grated cheese
    3 tablespoons flour   ½ cup fine dry bread crumbs
    ¾ cup evaporated milk   2 tablespoons butter, melted
    ¾ cup water from cabbage

Discard soiled outside leaves of cabbage. Cut head in quarters and
slice, rather coarsely. Cook in boiling salted water, uncovered until just
tender, about 7 minutes. Drain, saving water. Melt butter, blend in flour
and add evaporated milk and water drained from cabbage; stir constantly until sauce boils and thickens. Add salt, if needed. Place a layer
of cooked cabbage in bottom of a buttered casserole, pour part of the
sauce over it, sprinkle with part of the cheese. Repeat until all ingredients

are used, ending with cheese on top. Sprinkle with crumbs which have been blended with the 2 tablespoons butter. Bake in a moderate oven (350° F.) 20 minutes or until nicely browned. 5 servings.

1010 ESCALLOPED CABBAGE

2 to 2½ lb. head cabbage
2 cups thin white sauce (919)
½ green pepper, chopped

1 cup grated sharp cheese
½ cup buttered crumbs (1118)
3 slices half-cooked bacon

Cut trimmed cabbage into eighths, remove core and cook, uncovered, for 8 minutes in boiling salted water, 1 teaspoon salt to 1 quart water. Then drain. Place a layer of cabbage in a buttered baking dish or casserole, then a layer of white sauce, half the green pepper and half the cheese. Repeat. Sprinkle top with buttered crumbs and chopped bacon and bake in moderate oven (375° F.) until toasted, about 15 minutes. Serve immediately. 5 servings.

1011 RED CABBAGE WITH APPLES

2 to 3 lb. head red cabbage
3 tablespoons butter or bacon fat
1 small onion, chopped
2 tart apples, quartered and cored

1 tablespoon sugar
½ teaspoon salt, or to taste
⅓ cup vinegar
½ teaspoon caraway seed

Trim off soiled outer leaves of cabbage; cut cabbage in quarters and remove the core. Now shred rather coarsely. Melt butter or drippings in saucepan, add the onion and simmer 2 or 3 minutes; then add cabbage and apples and barely cover with boiling water. Cover pan and simmer gently for 45 minutes. Uncover pan, add sugar and salt and stir well. At this point the water should be practically evaporated; if not, increase heat and continue to cook, watching carefully until water evaporates. No liquid should be drained off. Add vinegar and caraway, stir well, and continue heating until vinegar is well distributed. Serve immediately. 5 servings.

Note: Do not substitute green or white cabbage for the red, as the vinegar which intensifies the red color will destroy the green.

1012 BUTTERED CARROTS

Wash carrots clean and scrape them to remove only the outer layer of skin. Tiny young carrots may be left whole for cooking, but older carrots should be split lengthwise in halves or quarters, or sliced crosswise. Cover with boiling salted water, 1 teaspoon salt to 1 quart water, and cook rapidly until tender in covered pan. This may take from 10 to 20 minutes, depending on size and age of carrots and how thick they are cut. Evaporate liquid, watching carefully; add 2 tablespoons butter and sprinkle a little chopped parsley on top. One large bunch carrots serves 5.

1013 CREAMED CARROTS

For creamed carrots, add to cooked carrots (1012) 2 cups medium white sauce (919) instead of melted butter.

1014 CREAMED CARROTS AND CELERY

2 cups sliced carrots
1 cup diced celery
2 tablespoons butter
3 tablespoons flour
1 cup evaporated milk

1 cup cooking water from vegetables
Salt to taste
Croutons (61)

Put carrots and celery into a 3-qt. saucepan, cover with boiling salted water, 1 teaspoon salt to 1 quart water, cover pan and boil gently until tender. Drain, saving water. Meanwhile melt butter in saucepan, blend in flour, add milk and 1 cup water drained from the vegetables, stirring constantly over low heat until sauce boils and thickens. Add salt if needed. Add cooked vegetables and reheat thoroughly. Serve the creamed vegetables poured over crisp croutons (61). 5 servings.

1015 CREAMED CARROTS AND SPINACH

1 lb. fresh spinach
1½ cups diced carrots
3 tablespoons butter
3 tablespoons flour
1 cup evaporated milk

½ cup cooking water from carrots
½ to 1 teaspoon grated onion, if desired
Salt

Pick over spinach carefully, discarding bad leaves and trimming off ends of stalks. Wash thoroughly through several cold waters. Place in a 3-qt. saucepan, add 1 cup boiling water and ½ teaspoon salt and cook uncovered until just tender, 5 to 10 minutes, turning the spinach over two or three times. Then drain well. Meanwhile, boil carrots gently in a small amount of salted water until tender; drain, saving the water. Melt butter in saucepan, blend in flour and add evaporated milk and ½ cup water from carrots; stir over direct heat until sauce boils. Stir in onion; add drained spinach and carrots, and fold in just enough to mix. Add salt to suit taste. Reheat if necessary and serve immediately. 5 servings.

1016   ESCALLOPED CARROTS AND POTATOES

1 tablespoon flour	5 or 6 medium carrots, sliced
1 cup evaporated milk	1 small onion, sliced
1 cup water	1 lb. boiling potatoes, pared, sliced
2 teaspoons salt	
Pepper	2 tablespoons butter

Blend flour to a smooth paste with a little of the milk; add remaining milk and water, stir until smooth and cook over direct heat, stirring constantly until sauce boils and thickens. Add seasonings and vegetables, and bring to boil again. Turn into a buttered 8-cup casserole, dot with the butter, cover and bake in a moderate oven (350° F.) for 30 minutes or until both vegetables are tender. 5 servings.

1017   GLAZED CARROTS

10 medium carrots	
½ cup brown sugar, packed	1 tablespoon butter
¼ cup water from carrots	⅛ teaspoon salt

Wash carrots and scrape clean, then split in half, lengthwise; barely cover with boiling salted water and boil uncovered for 10 minutes. Drain carrots, saving cooking water. Meanwhile, combine remaining ingredients in another saucepan and boil 5 minutes. Now turn carrots into buttered baking dish. Pour hot syrup over them, then bake in a moderate oven (350° F.) 15 minutes or until carrots are tender, occasionally dipping the syrup over the carrots. 5 servings.

1018   CARROT SOUFFLÉ

2 tablespoons butter	
2 tablespoons flour	3 eggs, separated
½ cup milk	2 cups shredded half-cooked carrots, 5 medium
1 teaspoon salt	

Make a white sauce (919) of the butter, flour, milk and salt. Pour hot sauce over the beaten egg yolks, stirring vigorously. Fold in carrots, then the stiffly beaten egg whites. Turn into a buttered 4-cup casserole and bake in a moderately slow oven (325° F.) about 1 hour. Serve at once. 5 servings.

1019   BUTTERED OR CREAMED CAULIFLOWER

Soak cauliflower in enough cold salt water to cover, 1 teaspoon salt to each quart water used, for half an hour. Drain. Now rinse head in cold water and trim by cutting off base of stalk and discarding all large leaves. The tiny leaves that cling to the outer flowerets may be left on. Break flowerets apart, removing large main stem. The main stem is a delicious tidbit to eat raw. Cover with a generous amount of boiling salted water, 1 teaspoon salt to each quart of water, and cook rapidly in uncovered pan until barely tender, from 6 to 8 minutes. Test by piercing with fork. Drain thoroughly and pour over the hot cauliflower melted butter, White Sauce (919), or Cheese Sauce (920). The cooking water makes good pot liquor. Sprinkle with paprika. One large head—2 lbs. Serves 5.

1019a   CAULIFLOWER IN CHIPPED BEEF CHEESE SAUCE

1½ to 2 lb. head cauliflower
2 cups unseasoned medium
White Sauce (919)

1 cup grated sharp cheese
2 oz. chipped beef

Let cauliflower stand in cold salted water for about 1 hour, 1 teaspoon salt to each quart water. Drain, rinse in cold water and separate cauliflower into flowerets. Cook, uncovered, in 6 cups boiling water, until just tender, or from 6 to 8 minutes. Meanwhile, make the white sauce and stir in the cheese until melted. Add chipped beef snipped into small pieces and serve hot sauce over drained hot cauliflower. If chipped beef is very salty, rinse it quickly in cold water before adding to sauce, if not salty, add salt to sauce to suit taste. 5 servings.

1020   BUTTERED CELERY

Outside branches of celery left after the hearts have been eaten raw may be cooked very successfully. Scrub them, scrape away blemishes and cut lengthwise in 2 or 3 strips; then cut into ½-inch lengths. Barely cover with boiling salted water and boil gently until tender, from 10 to 15 minutes. Drain and add melted butter. Celery cooking water should be saved for use in soup or vegetable juice cocktail. 2½ cups cut celery. Serves 5.

1021   CREAMED CELERY

For creamed celery, add to cooked celery (1020) 2 cups thin or medium White Sauce (919) instead of butter.

1022   ## BRAISED CELERY
                        (*Delicious and handsome*)

3 good-sized stalks celery   1½ cups chicken broth or 1
¼ cup butter   chicken bouillon cube in
2 teaspoons flour   1½ cups hot water
                          Salt

Trim off leaves and root ends of celery stalks, so that remaining stalks are 5 or 6 inches long, wash thoroughly by swishing vigorously through cold water several times to remove all soil. Do not separate branches. Cut stalks in half lengthwise. Melt butter in large heavy skillet, lay celery in cut-side down and cook slowly until celery is barely soft. Lift celery out carefully and blend flour with the butter; then add broth and stir briskly until sauce boils. Add salt to suit taste. Return celery to sauce, cover skillet and simmer gently 5 minutes longer. 5 servings.

1023   ## CELERY au GRATIN

4 cups diced celery   ¾ cup celery water
3 tablespoons butter   1 cup grated sharp cheese
3 tablespoons flour   Salt
¾ cup evaporated milk   ¼ cup buttered crumbs (1118)

Put celery into a 3-qt. saucepan and cook until barely tender in just enough boiling salted water to cover (1 teaspoon salt to 1-qt. water). Drain, saving water. Meanwhile, melt butter in saucepan, blend in flour, add milk and cooking water and stir until sauce boils and thickens. Remove from heat, add cheese and stir until smooth; add cooked celery and salt. Turn into buttered baking dish and sprinkle buttered crumbs over top. Bake uncovered in a moderate oven (350° F.) 20 to 30 minutes, or until crumbs are toasted. 5 servings.

1023a   ## BUTTERED CHAYOTE

Choose 2 medium-size chayotes each weighing about ¾ lb., to serve 5. They should be tender enough to be easily pierced with the thumbnail; otherwise they must be thinly pared. Wash and remove any blemishes on the skin, then cut in quarters, lengthwise, through flesh and seed; the seed is a special delicacy. Slice the quarters crosswise ⅛-inch thick. Put into a 3-qt. saucepan and add 1⅓ cups boiling water and ¾ teaspoon salt. Cover and boil briskly until tender, from 12 to 15 minutes; by this time most of the water should have evaporated. Add 4 tablespoons butter and pepper to suit the taste. Reheat to melt butter and evaporate remaining liquid watching carefully to prevent scorching. Serve immediately. 5 servings.

Variation: Sautéed mushrooms (1043) combined with buttered chayote are delicious.

1024   CORN ON THE COB

Choose the freshest corn possible. To test freshness and tenderness of corn, break a kernel with your fingernail. If the milk spurts out, the ear is young, tender and at least fairly fresh. Corn is best when cooked immediately after picking. Husk the corn and remove the silks. Have plenty of boiling water ready. Put the ears of corn into a kettle and pour on enough boiling water to cover. Boil 4 to 6 minutes, depending on age and tenderness of ears. Drain thoroughly and serve immediately with salt and plenty of butter.

1025   BUTTERED CORN

Fresh corn. Cut corn from the ears as directed for Fried Corn (1028), to make 3 cups. Barely cover with water, heat to the boiling point and simmer 5 to 8 minutes. Add salt to suit taste, and 2 to 3 tablespoons butter. Heat until butter is melted and most of water is evaporated. Two tablespoons diced green peppers may also be added. 5 servings.

Cream style corn. Put 2 tablespoons butter into a saucepan and heat slowly until melted. Tilt the pan from side to side until about an inch of the sides is coated with butter. Turn corn into the pan, cover and heat slowly to the boiling point. Serve immediately in small individual vegetable dishes with a sprinkling of paprika or finely chopped parsley, green pepper or pimiento on top. Ham or bacon fat may be substituted for butter if desired. A No. 2 can serves 5.

Whole kernel corn. Proceed as for cream style corn, stirring occasionally while heating thoroughly. Turn hot corn into a hot serving dish, add a dash of paprika and serve immediately. Two 12-oz. cans serve 5.

1026   CORN FRITTERS

1½ cups flour
¾ teaspoon baking powder, see p. 122
1½ teaspoons salt
2 eggs, beaten

½ cup milk
2 cups whole kernel corn, canned (drained) or fresh cooked

Sift flour, measure and resift with baking powder and salt. Combine beaten eggs and milk, mixing well; add to flour mixture all at once and stir until smooth. Fold in corn thoroughly. Drop from a teaspoon into deep fat heated to 375° F. and fry until golden brown on all sides. Lift out and drain for a minute or two on absorbent paper or paper toweling. Serve hot, with syrup (924) if desired. 5 servings.

1027   ESCALLOPED CORN AND CHEESE

1 egg, beaten	¾ teaspoon salt
No. 2 can cream style corn	1 cup fresh bread crumbs
1 cup milk	¼ cup grated sharp cheese

Pour egg into a 6-cup buttered casserole. Heat corn and liquids and gradually stir into beaten egg. Add salt, bread crumbs, and cheese and mix thoroughly. Bake uncovered in a moderately slow oven (325° F.) for 30 minutes or until custard tests done (see Note to 226). 5 servings.

1028   FRIED CORN

Husk and silk 8 to 12 ears of corn, then cut corn from the cob, using a very sharp knife and cutting off only about half the depth of the kernels. After cutting all around the ear, use the back of the knife to scrape out the remaining juice and pulp, scraping downward only, not back and forth. For 5 cups of corn, heat ⅓ cup butter or half butter and half bacon fat sizzling hot in skillet. Add corn and enough water to give consistency of thin gravy, season with salt and cook with constant stirring for five minutes, then reduce heat to simmering, cover tightly and cook about 20 minutes longer, stirring occasionally. The corn at this point should be quite thick. Good hot or cold and one of the best accompaniments for fried chicken. 5 servings.

1029   STEWED CORN

Cut corn from cob as directed for Fried Corn (1028). To 3 cups corn, add 1 cup water; cover and simmer gently for 10 minutes. Add 1 cup milk and 3 tablespoons butter, and simmer 10 minutes longer. Season to suit taste with salt and pepper. Serve immediately with a sprinkling of chopped parsley or a dash of paprika. 5 servings.

1030
SUCCOTASH No. 1

½ cup diced celery
2 tablespoons chopped onion
No. 2 can cut green beans
No. 2 can cream style corn

2 tablespoons chopped
pimiento
½ cup milk
1 tablespoon butter
¾ teaspoon salt or to taste

Simmer celery and chopped onion until tender in the liquid drained from beans. The liquid by this time should be almost evaporated. Now add corn, drained beans, pimiento, milk and butter, simmer until thoroughly heated and season to suit taste. 5 servings.

1031
SUCCOTASH No. 2

1 cup green lima beans
10 ears corn, boiled (1024)

3 tablespoons butter
Salt and pepper to taste

Cook lima beans (997). Drain, saving the liquid. Cut corn from the cob and combine with lima beans. Add enough of the bean liquid just to be seen through the mixture. Simmer until most of water is evaporated. Add butter, stir until melted, then add salt and pepper to suit taste. Serve immediately. 5 servings.

Dried lima beans cooked according to directions (996) may be substituted for the green limas, and canned corn may be used instead of fresh. If dried limas are used, cooking a piece of salt pork and a little onion with them adds to the flavor.

1032
FRESH CORN AND TOMATO CASSEROLE

8 to 10 ears fresh corn
¼ cup butter or bacon fat
4 slices crisp bacon

1 teaspoon salt, or to taste
2 large tomatoes, 1½ lbs.,
peeled, sliced

Cut corn from cob as directed for Fried Corn (1028). There should be 4 to 5 cups of corn. Melt butter or fat in skillet, add corn and sauté quickly, about 5 minutes. Add crumbled bacon and salt and arrange in buttered casserole in alternate layers with the sliced tomatoes. Place in a moderate oven (350° F.) and bake 30 minutes, or until corn is tender. Serve hot. 5 to 6 servings.

1032a   BRAISED CUCUMBERS

2 large or 3 medium-size cucumbers	1 teaspoon cornstarch
2 tablespoons butter	¼ cup cold water
½ cup boiling water	¼ teaspoon salt
1 chicken bouillon cube	Dash black pepper
	Chopped parsley or chives

Pare cucumbers and slice crosswise about ½-inch thick. Melt butter in skillet, add cucumbers and brown pieces delicately on both sides. Add the boiling water, cover tightly and simmer about 10 minutes or until the cucumbers are transparent-looking and fairly tender. Add bouillon cube and cornstarch which has been blended until smooth with the cold water. Stir gently until sauce again boils. Continue simmering 5 minutes longer; then add salt and pepper and serve hot. A sprinkling of chopped parsley or chives makes an attractive, flavorful garnish. 5 servings.

1032b   CUCUMBERS au GRATIN

2½ tablespoons bacon fat	¼ teaspoon onion juice
2½ tablespoons flour	1 cup grated sharp cheese
1¼ cups milk	⅓ cup fine dry bread crumbs
1 chicken bouillon cube	1½ tablespoons butter, melted
Dash pepper	2 medium cucumbers, peeled

Blend melted bacon fat and flour together well, add milk and stir constantly over direct heat until sauce boils and thickens. Stir in bouillon cube, pepper and onion juice, then remove from heat. Add grated cheese, stirring until cheese is melted. Stir bread crumbs in the melted butter to coat them well. Slice peeled cucumbers about ⅛-inch thick. Into a 6-cup buttered casserole, put alternate layers of cucumber slices and hot, seasoned cheese sauce. Top with buttered crumbs, cover and bake in a moderately slow oven (325° F.), for 30 minutes; then remove cover and continue baking about 10 minutes longer or until cucumbers are tender and surface browned. Serve piping hot. 5 servings.

1033   BAKED STUFFED EGGPLANT

1 large eggplant	2 tablespoons butter
2 cups chopped cooked meat	1 cup cooked rice (174)
1 cup fresh or canned tomatoes	1 teaspoon salt
2 tablespoons chopped onion	Paprika and black pepper
1 egg, beaten	½ cup buttered crumbs (1118)
1 teaspoon sugar	

Cut eggplant in halves lengthwise and scoop out pulp, leaving shells about ¼-inch thick. Place shells in cold water. Combine chopped eggplant pulp with meat, tomato, onion, egg, sugar, rice, butter and seasonings. Heat until boiling hot. Drain shells and fill with hot mixture. Sprinkle bread crumbs over top and bake 1 hour in a moderate oven (350° F.). 5 servings.

1034   FRENCH-FRIED EGGPLANT

Prepare eggplant just as for frying (1036), except cut the slices into strips like French-fried potatoes. Coat with egg and crumbs immediately. Have deep fat heated to 375° F. Place a single layer of eggplant strips in a frying basket and lower into the hot fat until they are just covered; cook until golden brown, from 1⅓ to 3 minutes according to color preferred. Drain on absorbent paper or paper toweling, sprinkle with salt and serve piping hot.

1035   EGGPLANT EN CASSEROLE

1½ lb. eggplant	1 cup grated cheese
6 tablespoons butter	1 teaspoon salt
2 onions, sliced	Pepper
3 tomatoes, peeled and diced or 1½ cups canned tomatoes	1 cup fine dry bread crumbs

Slice eggplant ½-inch thick, pare off skin and cut into dice to make about 5 cups of dice. Melt 3 tablespoons butter in a skillet and sauté the eggplant slowly for 5 minutes. Place in a buttered casserole with alternate layers of sliced onions, diced tomatoes and with ¾ cup of the grated cheese; season each layer with the salt and pepper. Top with crumbs which have been mixed with remaining cheese and dot with remaining butter. Bake in a moderate oven (375° F.) until vegetables are tender and top is nicely browned, about 35 minutes. 5 generous servings.

1036   FRIED EGGPLANT

A medium-sized eggplant, 1½ lbs., will serve 5 persons. Wash it and cut in slices about ¾-inch thick. Pare each slice and sprinkle with salt, allowing about 1 teaspoon for the whole eggplant. Pile slices on top of each other in a saucepan or baking dish, then place a weighted dish on top, and let stand for 1 hour. Then drain off the liquid that flows out.

Now dip the drained slices into a mixture of 1 beaten egg and ¼ cup milk; then coat well with sifted dry bread crumbs or flour; or coat with flour only. Melt ¼ cup fat, bacon fat, or half butter and half shortening in a large skillet; lay the eggplant slices in the melted fat and cook over moderate heat until brown on both sides and thoroughly tender, from 4 to 6 minutes. Well done eggplant is very soft all the way through. Serve from the eggplant shells. 5 servings.

1036a   FRIED EGGPLANT AND ONION WITH CHEESE SAUCE

2 tablespoons butter	¼ lb. sharp cheese, diced
¼ cup flour	1 medium eggplant
1 cup evaporated milk	2 small onions
1 cup water	6 tablespoons butter
¼ teaspoon salt	Salt to taste

Melt butter, blend in flour and add liquids, stirring constantly while heating until sauce thickens. Add the ¼ teaspoon salt and cheese, stir until cheese melts. Cover and keep hot over boiling water while preparing eggplant and onion. Slice eggplant ⅜-inch thick and remove skin. Peel onion and cut in about ¼-inch slices. Fry eggplant and onion in butter, using moderately low heat. Sprinkle with salt and cook slices from 4 or 5 minutes on one side or until delicately browned, turn, sprinkle with salt and brown the other side. Place eggplant and onion slices on a hot platter and pour hot cheese sauce over vegetables. 5 servings.

1037   SAUTÉED HOMINY WITH POTATOES AND ONION

¼ cup bacon fat	2 cups diced cooked potatoes
⅓ cup coarsely chopped dry or green onion	No. 2½ can hominy, drained
	1 teaspoon salt

Heat fat in a heavy skillet and cook onions slowly until transparent but not brown. Add potatoes and hominy, season with salt and cook over moderate heat, stirring occasionally until vegetables are light brown and crusty. 5 servings.

1038   KALE OR OTHER GREENS

2 to 3 oz. salt pork	2 lbs. kale or mustard, turnip, or dandelion greens

Choose pork with strips of lean and cut into ¼-inch slices. Put into a 4-qt. kettle and add 1 quart cold water. Heat to boiling, then reduce heat, cover and simmer 30 minutes. Then add the well-washed greens, cover and reheat to boiling. When greens have wilted down, turn over and press down until they are below the surface of the liquid. Continue cooking, uncovered, until they are very tender, 30 to 45 minutes, depending on age and tenderness. If more water is needed during cooking, add boiling water to keep the greens just covered. When done, drain off liquid and serve with slices of pork laid over the top. If more salt is needed, add at end of cooking. 5 servings.

1039   BUTTERED KOHLRABI

Choose young tender kohlrabi; it should be sufficiently tender so the skin can be readily pierced with the thumbnail. Strip off stems and leaves, then wash and peel, don't pare. Cut in crosswise slices about ¼-inch thick. Drop into just enough boiling water to cover and cook uncovered until just tender, about 10 minutes. Enough water should have evaporated so it will not be necessary to drain. Add 3 to 4 tablespoons butter, reheat and add salt to suit taste. Allow 2 lbs. for 5 servings.

1040   LENTIL STEW WITH HAM

½ lb. dried lentils	2 cups canned tomatoes
2 teaspoons salt	½ lb. boiled ham, diced
½ cup chopped onion	Dash pepper
2 tablespoons butter	3 tablespoons chopped parsley

Wash lentils, put into a 3-qt. saucepan. Add water to come 1-inch over lentils and let soak overnight. Next morning drain, cover with fresh cold water, about 2 cups, add salt and boil gently for 15 minutes or until tender. Sauté onion in the butter in a large skillet. Add lentils with their cooking water, tomatoes, ham and pepper; cook at moderate rate another 15 minutes. Serve hot, with a sprinkling of chopped parsley on each serving. 5 servings.

1041   BAKED LENTILS WITH BACON

1½ cups dried lentils	¾ cup evaporated milk
3 cups water	1½ tablespoons bacon fat
1 teaspoon salt	¾ cup sifted dry bread crumbs
6 or 7 slices cooked bacon (544)	3 tablespoons melted butter

Wash lentils thoroughly and put into a 3-qt. saucepan. Add water to come 1-inch over lentils and soak overnight. Next morning drain and rinse; then add the 3 cups water and salt. Cover, bring to simmering and simmer until tender, about 15 minutes. Do not drain. Add crumbled crisp bacon, evaporated milk, and bacon fat and mix well. Turn into a casserole and sprinkle with the bread crumbs which have been mixed with the melted butter. Bake, uncovered, in a moderate oven (350° F.) until crumbs are nicely browned, about 20 minutes. 5 servings.

1042   BRAISED LETTUCE

3 tablespoons butter   ½ teaspoon salt
2 medium solid heads lettuce

Melt butter in a 9-inch iron skillet. Trim lettuce without removing core; cut in halves and place in the butter cut-side down and cook until delicately browned. Then turn gently so as not to spoil shape of halves. Sprinkle lettuce with the salt, cover pan and turn heat very low; let simmer until tender, about 15 minutes. Serve hot with the juice which collects in the pan. 4 servings.

1043   SAUTÉED MUSHROOMS

½ lb. fresh mushrooms   Salt if desired
¼ cup butter

Clean the mushrooms by washing quickly in cold water and trimming a slice from the stem end. If skin is tough, strip off skin from caps, then slice mushrooms about ¼-inch thick, cutting vertically through stem and cap. Heat butter until bubbling hot but not browned. Add mushrooms and cover tightly, shaking the pan every few seconds to prevent sticking. After 2 minutes, turn the mushrooms with a fork. Cover and cook 2 or 3 minutes longer or until they are swimming in their own juice and have just started to boil. In this juicy stage they are most attractive in appearance and for eating. Add salt to suit taste, if required. Serve immediately with broiled steak, chops or hamburger patties. Serves 5 sparingly.

1044   CREAMED MUSHROOMS

½ lb. mushrooms   1 cup milk
¼ cup butter   1 cup evaporated milk
¼ cup water   1 to 2 tablespoons flour
½ teaspoon salt   Cold water

Prepare mushrooms just as for Sautéed Mushrooms (1043), and sauté in the butter for 5 minutes. Then add water and salt, cover, and simmer gently for 15 minutes. Just before serving, add milk and evaporated milk, and again heat to simmering. Blend flour to a smooth runny paste with cold water, and stir into the mushroom mixture, using just enough to produce the desired thickness. Consistency preferred by most persons is that of thin white sauce. Serve piping hot on crisp toast or in patty shells. Chopped parsley sprinkled over each serving makes an attractive garnish. 5 servings.

1045   BAKED ONION SLICES

5 large onions, sliced	1½ cups hot water
2 chicken bouillon cubes	2 tablespoons butter

Arrange peeled and sliced onions in greased baking dish. Dissolve bouillon cubes in hot water and pour over onion slices. Dot with butter and bake, uncovered in a moderate oven (375° F.), 45 to 60 minutes or until tender. If they become dry, add more hot water. 5 servings.

1046   BROILED ONIONS

Peel 2 large Spanish onions and slice a little less than ½-inch thick. Brush both sides of slices with melted butter and place on broiler, about 4 inches below heat. When onions begin to be tender, in about 8 to 10 minutes, brush tops with butter and move nearer to heat, so they brown nicely. It is not necessary to turn onions over. When done or just barely tender, sprinkle with salt and chopped parsley. 5 servings.

Note: Sliced onions are equally nice pan-fried in butter. Cooking should be done slowly. Lift carefully from pan with pancake turner or large spatula to preserve shape.

1047   BUTTERED ONIONS

Peel off outer skin from 2-lbs. walnut-size onions and pierce several times with a skewer. If they are quite large, cooking time may be shortened by cutting in quarters. Drop into two quarts of boiling salted water and cook moderately fast, uncovered, from 20 to 30 minutes, or until onions are barely tender when pierced with a fork. Drain and add 2 or 3 tablespoons melted butter. 5 servings.

1048   CREAMED ONIONS

To make creamed onions, add to Buttered Onions (1047) 1 cup thin cream; or substitute 2 cups thin or medium White Sauce (919) for the butter, the last 5 minutes of cooking.

1049   ESCALLOPED ONIONS

2 lbs. medium-sized onions   ⅓ cup buttered bread crumbs,
2 cups thin white sauce   or ½ cup grated cheese

Peel onions. Slice about ¼-inch thick, cover with boiling salted water,
1 teaspoon salt to 1 quart water and cook rapidly, uncovered, until
onions are tender, from 5 to 7 minutes. Drain, add White Sauce (919),
and turn into buttered shallow casserole. Sprinkle with buttered bread
crumbs (1118) or grated cheese and bake in a hot oven (425° F.) until
golden brown. Serve immediately. 5 servings.

1050   FRENCH-FRIED ONIONS

1 cup all-purpose flour   6 tablespoons water
¼ teaspoon salt   2 to 3 large onions, about 1¼
½ cup evaporated milk   lbs., peeled and sliced about
2 tablespoons salad oil   ¼-inch thick
1 egg white, unbeaten

Sift flour, measure and resift with salt into mixing bowl. Add milk,
oil and egg white, and beat until smooth. Add water to make a medium
thin batter. Separate onion slices carefully into rings and dip into the
batter so each ring is completely covered. Drop batter-covered rings a
few at a time into deep fat heated to about 375° F. and fry until golden
brown. Lift out and drain on absorbent paper or paper towelling; sprinkle
with salt. Serve hot as a garnish and accompaniment for meat. These
fried rings if kept in a warm oven should stay crisp for 15 to 20 minutes
after frying. 5 servings.

1050a   PAN-FRIED ONIONS

1½ lbs. onions   ½ teaspoon salt
3 tablespoons butter or bacon
  fat

Either white or yellow onions may be used, but white ones have a
milder flavor. Peel the onions and wash, then remove thin slices from
root and stem ends, and slice onions thin. Heat the fat to sizzling hot
in a skillet, add onions, sprinkle with salt, cover, reduce heat and cook
until delicately browned on under side, 4 to 5 minutes. Now turn onions
over carefully using a spatula or pancake turner and brown other side and
cook until barely tender through. Serve at once. 5 servings.

1051   GLAZED ONIONS

1¼ lbs. small white onions
¼ cup butter

3 tablespoons sugar
¼ teaspoon salt

Choose onions the size of hickory nuts. Cover with boiling water, drain and peel very carefully, then pierce 2 or 3 times with skewer. Now cover with boiling salted water and simmer, uncovered, until barely tender, about 15 minutes. Combine butter, sugar and salt in saucepan, and heat slowly, stirring constantly until melted. Drain onions, place in syrup and cook a few minutes, turning frequently to coat entire surface with syrup. 5 servings.

1052   ONIONS au GRATIN

1½ lbs. small white onions
2 tablespoons butter
3 tablespoons flour
1½ cups milk

¾ teaspoon salt
⅓ cup buttered bread crumbs
   (1118)
½ cup grated sharp cheese

Peel onions, pierce them with a skewer and cook uncovered in 3 pints of rapidly boiling salted water, 1 teaspoon salt to 1 quart water, until almost tender. Drain and place in a buttered baking dish. Cover with white sauce made of butter, flour, milk and salt (919). Sprinkle with buttered bread crumbs and top with the grated cheese. Bake in a moderately slow oven (325° F.) until nicely toasted, 20 to 25 minutes. For escalloped onions, omit the cheese. 5 servings.

1053   STUFFED ONIONS No. 1

5 large Spanish onions 2 lbs.
2 cups cooked rice (174)
½ cup chili sauce

2 tablespoons melted butter
¼ lb. cheese, grated, 1 cup
Salt to taste

Peel onions, remove thick slice from stem end and scoop out ¼ cup pulp from center of each onion. Pierce onions through several times with a skewer to help keep their shape. Drop onions into 4 quarts boiling salted water, 1 teaspoon salt to each quart of water, and cook until just tender, 25 to 30 minutes. Drain and remove core from centers of onions, forming cups. (Centers may be cooked until done and served creamed.) Combine hot rice with chili sauce, butter and all but ¼ cup of grated cheese; season to suit taste. Fill onion cups with this mixture and set on a buttered baking sheet. Sprinkle remainder of grated cheese over tops. Place in a moderately hot oven (425° F.) or under the broiler, watching carefully, until cheese is golden brown and stuffing hot through. 5 servings.

1054 STUFFED ONIONS No. 2

5 medium onions, 1½ lbs.	Dash pepper
½ cup chopped cooked ham	½ cup evaporated milk
¼ cup chopped green pepper	⅔ cup water
½ cup soft bread crumbs	½ cup buttered bread crumbs
1 tablespoon melted butter	(1118)
½ teaspoon salt	

Peel onions and cut a slice from the top of each. Parboil onions as in 1053 until almost tender; then drain and scoop out centers. Chop centers and the raw slices cut from tops and combine with ham, green pepper, soft bread crumbs, and melted butter. Add seasonings and stuff into onion cups. Place in a buttered baking dish. Mix milk and water and pour around onions. Cover top of onions with buttered crumbs. Bake in a moderate oven (375° F.) until tender, about 30 minutes. 5 servings.

1055 BOILED GREEN ONIONS IN CHEESE SAUCE

4 bunches green onions	1 cup water
3 tablespoons butter	¾ teaspoon salt
¼ cup flour	1 cup grated cheese
1 cup evaporated milk	

Trim off roots and ends of green stems of onions. Wash onions and boil until tender in barely enough salted water to cover, 1 teaspoon salt to 1 quart water. Meanwhile, melt butter, blend in flour, add milk and water, and stir over direct heat until sauce boils and thickens. Add salt and cheese, stirring until cheese is thoroughly blended with sauce. Drain onions and pour sauce over them. Onions may be cut in 1-inch lengths, but there is less shrinkage if they are left whole. 5 servings.

For creamed green onions, omit cheese.

1056 OKRA AND TOMATOES

2½ cups sliced okra	3 medium tomatoes or 2
3 tablespoons butter or bacon fat	cups cooked tomatoes
	Salt and pepper to suit taste
2 medium onions, sliced	1 teaspoon sugar

Choose young tender okra pods. Pods should be easily pierced with thumbnail. Rinse thoroughly in cold water, but do not rub pods. Remove stems and cut in ½-inch thick slices. Put butter or bacon fat into skillet, add the sliced onion, then tomatoes, sprinkle with salt and pepper, cover and simmer about 3 minutes. Then slide okra slices over top of tomatoes to preserve green color. Sprinkle with salt, pepper and sugar.

Cover and continue to simmer until okra is tender, about 5 minutes. Then stir vegetables together. Season to taste. Serve hot. 5 servings.

1057   **BUTTERED PARSNIPS**

Choose firm parsnips, allowing one good-sized parsnip per serving. Scrub and scrape to remove any blemishes or discolorations. Split lengthwise in halves. Add boiling water to cover, and 1 teaspoon salt for each quart of water. Heat to boiling, cover pan, then reduce heat and boil gently until the parsnips are tender, from 20 to 30 minutes, depending on tenderness and size. Drain thoroughly. Then pour melted butter over them and cook in the butter until browned on all sides, watching carefully and turning frequently. Parsnips scorch easily because of their high sugar content. Serve hot.

1058   **FRENCH-FRIED PARSNIPS**

| 3 medium-sized parsnips | ⅓ cup milk |
| 1 egg | Bread crumbs or salted flour |

Scrape parsnips and cut in quarters lengthwise, then cut once crosswise. Cover with boiling water and cook until just tender. Avoid cooking so long that they get soft and mushy. Drain. Beat egg; add the milk. Dip the strips in this mixture and then in either bread crumbs or flour. Fry in deep fat which has been heated to 375° F., until golden brown. Drain on absorbent paper and serve hot. 5 servings.

1059   **PARSNIP STEW**

| 2 lbs. pork shanks | 2½ cups diced potatoes |
| 4 cups diced parsnips, about 4 parsnips | 1 tablespoon salt |

Wipe the pork shanks with a damp cloth. Simmer from 2 to 3 hours in a quart of water, or until almost tender enough for meat to fall from bone. About 40 minutes before serving time, add diced parsnips and more water if necessary to cover. Twenty minutes later add potatoes and salt. Continue cooking about 20 minutes. Remove bones and skin from shanks. For color, add a little caramel (1121), a few drops of brown vegetable coloring, or some kitchen bouquet. 5 servings.

1060   **BUTTERED OR CREAMED PEAS**

Shell 2½ lbs. peas. There should be 2½ cups shelled. Wash in cold water, drain and cook immediately. Add boiling water to come ½-inch over peas, then add salt in proportion of 1 teaspoon to 1-qt. water. Boil gently uncovered until peas are tender, from 20 to 30 minutes depending on age and size of peas. Add more boiling water if needed. When peas are done, liquid should barely cover them so that draining will not be necessary. Add 2 tablespoons butter, or drain peas and add a medium White Sauce (919). Reheat and serve immediately. 5 servings.

Note: Equal quantities of drained, fresh boiled peas and carrots or celery may be combined and buttered.

1061   PEA AND POTATO CASSEROLE

2 lbs. potatoes	5 tablespoons flour
¼ cup butter	¼ teaspoon salt
1 cup hot milk	¼ lb. sharp cheese, diced
¾ teaspoon salt	1 egg yolk beaten with
No. 2 can peas	1 tablespoon milk
3 tablespoons butter	

Wash and pare potatoes, then cook in boiling salted water in a covered pan until tender. Drain, saving liquid. Add the ¼ cup butter, half the hot milk and the ¾ teaspoon salt and beat until potatoes are a stiff, fluffy mass. Drain peas, and make a white sauce with the 3 tablespoons butter, flour, ¼ teaspoon salt, the rest of milk and liquid from peas and potatoes (919). Stir in cheese until blended. Add peas to sauce and heat. Spread ⅔ of the hot mashed potatoes over bottom and sides of a casserole, and pour the creamed peas into the center. Pipe remaining potatoes over top of peas in a lattice, or drop in puffs from a tablespoon, not covering the peas entirely. Brush top of potatoes with egg yolk mixture. Brown in a moderately hot oven (400° F.) and serve immediately. 5 generous servings.

1062   PEA LOAF

No. 2 can peas	Pepper
1 cup fine dry bread crumbs	1 cup evaporated milk
1 egg, slightly beaten	3 outer leaves lettuce,
1 teaspoon grated onion	chopped fine
½ teaspoon salt	

Drain peas, saving liquid. Mash peas thoroughly and add remaining ingredients and pea liquid, mixing just enough to blend well. Pour into well-buttered bread loaf pan (6-cup size) and bake in a moderately slow oven (325° F.) 50 to 60 minutes, or until a sharp knife inserted in center comes out clean. Unmold onto platter and serve with Celery Cream Sauce (904) or Carrot Sauce (903). 5 servings.

1063   STUFFED GREEN PEPPERS No. 1

Choose 5 green peppers of uniform size and shape and which will stand upright. Wash thoroughly. Cut a slice from the stem end and scoop out seeds and dividing membranes. Parboil about 2 minutes in boiling water. Remove and drain thoroughly. Stuff with the following mixture:

1 medium onion, chopped	No. 2 can cream style corn
2 fresh tomatoes, peeled, chopped	1¼ teaspoons salt
	¼ cup buttered bread crumbs
2 tablespoons butter	(1118)

Sauté onion and tomatoes in butter until onion is slightly soft. Add corn and salt and heat to bubbling. Stuff mixture into parboiled green pepper cases, top with buttered crumbs, and place peppers in a buttered shallow baking pan. Bake in a moderately hot oven (400° F.) until crumbs are toasted and stuffing is hot, from 25 to 30 minutes. 5 servings.

Note: ½ lb. hamburger, browned and seasoned, will add flavor and food value to the above mixture.

1064   STUFFED GREEN PEPPERS No. 2

Prepare 5 green peppers as in recipe 1063. Wash thoroughly and boil 1 cup rice (174). Drain and rinse with hot water; again drain well. Chop 10 slices bacon and fry until crisp; then add bacon and 2 tablespoons bacon fat to the cooked rice and toss to blend rice and bacon fat. Stuff into parboiled pepper cases, placed in a buttered baking pan or casserole. Bake uncovered in a moderately hot oven (400° F.) until peppers are tender and rice is crispy and brown. 5 servings.

1065   STUFFED GREEN PEPPERS No. 3

5 green peppers	1½ cups medium white sauce
2 cups chopped, cooked macaroni (171)	(919)
	Buttered bread crumbs
½ cup grated sharp cheese	(1118)
½ to 1 cup cooked lima beans	

Prepare green peppers as for Stuffed Green Peppers No. 1. Combine macaroni, cheese and lima beans with the hot white sauce. Stuff into parboiled green pepper cups, top with buttered crumbs and place in a buttered casserole. Bake in a moderately hot oven (400° F.) until peppers are tender and crumbs are toasted. 5 servings.

569

1066   STUFFED GREEN PEPPERS No. 4

4 medium size or 2 very large green peppers	½ lb. ground beef
2½ slices bread from 1-lb. loaf	1 bouillon cube
2 tablespoons chopped onion	⅓ cup hot water
2 tablespoons chopped celery	½ cup cooked tomatoes or tomato juice
2 tablespoons butter	⅓ cup buttered fine crumbs

Select and prepare peppers as described above. Cut bread into ½-inch cubes and toast. Sauté onion and celery in butter 2 minutes. Add beef and sauté with constant stirring until it becomes a grey color. Dissolve bouillon cube in hot water and add it and the tomatoes to meat mixture. Heat thoroughly. Fold in bread cubes. Fill peppers with hot mixture. Top with buttered crumbs. Bake in a greased shallow baking dish in a moderate oven (350° F.) 15 to 20 minutes, then 5 to 10 minutes in a moderately hot oven (400° F.) to brown tops. Serve immediately. 4 servings.

1067   BAKED POTATOES

For perfect baked potatoes, which should be mealy and dry, a baking type of potato (Russet) is essential. Scrub the potato thoroughly and place in a moderately hot oven (400° F.) until soft. An average-size potato, 10 ounces will take from 40 to 55 minutes to bake soft through. Choose potatoes of uniform size and shape so they will get done at the same time. Test for doneness by squeezing potato in hand, through a pot holder or several thicknesses of a dry towel; or by piercing with a sharp-tined fork. To serve, split the potato across the top with two gashes at right angles, and press the sides so the baked contents are pushed up. Top with a pat of butter and a dash of paprika and serve with plenty of additional butter and salt. Allow one average-size potato for each serving.

1068   BOILED POTATOES

For boiling, select waxy potatoes which hold their shape well. Some good varieties are Rural, Early Rose and Ohio. Wash, scrape or pare 2 lbs. potatoes and cover with either cold or boiling salted water, 1 teaspoon salt to 1 quart water. Cover and cook at moderate rate until tender when pierced with a fork, from 20 to 30 minutes, the time depending on the size. If the right amount of water is added in beginning, there will be little water to drain off. Watch the last few minutes of cooking to evaporate excess moisture, shaking kettle gently to prevent scorching. This will give potatoes a mealy appearance on the outside. Transfer potatoes to a well heated covered dish to keep them hot. Pour over them 2 or 3 tablespoons of the fat and the brown residue left in skillet after frying ham or 2 or 3 tablespoons of melted butter.

Large potatoes may be cut in halves or quarters to hasten cooking. Small new potatoes are often boiled with their skins on; skins will slip off easily when done.

Note: Any water that is drained from boiled potatoes contains valuable nutrients. Save it for making soup or gravy, or to boil other vegetables.

1068a   RICED POTATOES

Put hot, boiled, pared potatoes into a ricer that has been heated by dipping it into boiling water. Rice the potatoes directly into a hot serving dish. A good way to heat the dish is to pour boiling water into it and let stand a few minutes; pour out, then dry quickly. Add a few shakes of paprika to the top of riced potatoes, then drop on a pat or two of butter. Cover and serve immediately, with or without gravy.

1069   PARSLEY BUTTERED POTATOES

Choose small boiling potatoes of uniform size. Scrape and cook as for Boiled Potatoes. Drain thoroughly and replace over heat for a minute to evaporate excess moisture; then turn into hot serving dish and pour melted butter over them, turning so each potato is coated all over. Sprinkle with finely chopped parsley and serve immediately. Ham or bacon fat may be used instead of butter.

1070   CREAMED POTATOES No. 1

5 or 6 medium size potatoes	Salt and pepper to taste
1 cup cold water	Chopped parsley, if desired
1 cup cream, milk *or* evaporated milk	

Wash potatoes, pare thinly, and cut in ½-inch dice. Add water, cover kettle and boil gently until half done, about 5 minutes; then add cream or milk and seasonings, again cover and continue cooking slowly until potatoes are done and sauce slightly thickened. Just before serving, sprinkle with a little chopped parsley if desired. 5 servings.

1071   CREAMED POTATOES No. 2

5 or 6 medium size potatoes	1½ cups thick White Sauce (919)

Wash potatoes, pare thinly and cut in ½-inch dice. Barely cover with salted water, 1 teaspoon salt to 1 quart water, cover and cook moderately fast until done, about 10 minutes. Drain thoroughly and add cooking water to hot white sauce to produce desired thickness. Combine with potatoes. May be kept hot over boiling water if necessary. 5 servings.

Variation: White sauce may be increased to 3 cups and 2½ cups cooked peas may be added.

1072   CREAMED POTATOES WITH CHEESE

1 quart potatoes cut in ½-inch dice, 5 to 6 medium
¼ lb. cheese, grated

2 cups medium White Sauce (919)

Cook potatoes in a covered pan in just enough boiling salted water to cover until tender, about 10 minutes. Meanwhile stir cheese into hot white sauce. Add drained potatoes. Serve hot with sprinkling of chopped parsley or dash paprika. 5 servings.

1073   AMERICAN-FRIED POTATOES

Thinly pare 5 or 6 firm boiling potatoes and slice thin. Melt 2 to 3 tablespoons shortening in a heavy skillet. When fat is hot, lay in the sliced potatoes, sprinkle with salt, cover skillet and cook slowly. When under side is beautifully browned, in about 10 minutes, turn potatoes carefully with pancake turner; cover, and continue cooking 10 to 15 minutes longer, until potatoes are tender in center and crisp on bottom. 5 servings.

1073a   GRATED POTATO PATTIES

3 cups grated raw potatoes, about 2½ lbs.
1½ teaspoons salt

2 teaspoons grated onion
¼ cup bacon or ham fat
¼ cup hot water

Thoroughly mix grated potato, salt and onion. Shape quickly into 5 patties and place in hot fat in a 10-inch heavy skillet. Brown well on both sides; then add water, cover, reduce the heat and cook 10 minutes longer, turning at end of 5 minutes. Serve hot. 5 servings.

1074   ESCALLOPED POTATOES

5 or 6 medium-size potatoes
3 tablespoons flour
1 teaspoon salt

1½ cups milk, scalded, *or* 1 cup evaporated milk and ½ cup water
2 tablespoons butter

Wash potatoes, pare and slice thin. Combine flour and salt. Arrange ⅓ of the potatoes in bottom of a greased baking dish; sprinkle with

⅓ of the flour-salt mixture; repeat. Pour on scalded milk and dot with butter. Cover and bake in a moderate oven (375° F.) for 45 minutes, then uncover and bake 15 to 30 minutes longer, or until potatoes are tender. 5 servings.

1075   QUICK ESCALLOPED POTATOES

2 tablespoons butter	1¾ cups milk
2 tablespoons flour	5 cups sliced potatoes
¾ teaspoon salt	

Melt butter in saucepan, stir in flour and salt, then add milk slowly, stirring constantly until sauce boils and thickens. Now add potatoes and heat with occasional stirring until the sauce boils again. Pour potatoes and sauce into a greased casserole, cover and bake in a moderate oven (350° F.) for 30 minutes or until potatoes are tender. Serve hot. 5 servings.

1076   FRENCH-FRIED POTATOES, WHITE OR SWEET

Baking potatoes are best for French-fried white potatoes; sweet potatoes, not yams, are best for French-fried sweets. Wash and pare thinly, then cut into slices about ⅜-inch thick, lengthwise of the potato. Cut these slices into strips ⅜-inch wide, and dry thoroughly in a clean towel or with paper toweling. Place a handful of strips in a frying basket and lower carefully into deep fat heated to 375° F. and far enough so the fat just covers them. Cook until they are light golden-brown. Lift out of the fat, drain thoroughly in the basket, then turn out onto paper toweling or absorbent paper; sprinkle with salt. Do not cook too many potatoes at one time; there should be only a single layer in the basket. Allow 1 average-sized potato for each serving.

French-fried potatoes may be kept hot without losing their crisp freshness if they are spread out on flat baking pans after thorough draining on paper toweling and placed in a slow oven. Do not attempt to keep them more than half an hour.

1077   MASHED POTATOES

6 medium-size potatoes	about ½ cup hot milk
2 tablespoons butter	Salt to taste

Wash and pare potatoes thinly, and cook as directed for Boiled Potatoes (1068), until soft when pierced with a fork. Drain thoroughly, saving the water. Mash potatoes thoroughly or put them through a ricer which has been heated by running hot water through it. Add butter and hot milk and beat vigorously over low heat, using a fork or wooden spoon, until very light, fluffy and white. Beat in salt to suit taste. Pile into a hot serving dish, leaving surface fluffy, then top with a pat of butter and a dash of paprika. Serve immediately. 5 servings.

Water drained from potatoes should not be discarded, as it contains valuable minerals. Use it for making gravy or vegetable soup.

1078   POTATO DUMPLINGS

2 cups rice boiled potatoes,
3 medium size

2 eggs, beaten

1 teaspoon salt

1 teaspoon grated onion

1 tablespoon chopped parsley

½ cup toasted ¼-inch bread cubes

½ cup all-purpose flour, sifted with ½ teaspoon baking powder

Combine ingredients in order given, mixing thoroughly. Drop by tablespoonfuls on top of boiling Beef Stew (502), Sauerbraten (505) or sauerkraut about half an hour before serving; cover tightly and allow to steam 25 minutes. Serve dumplings on or around the stew. 5 servings.

1079   STUFFED BAKED POTATOES

5 large baking potatoes,
3 lbs.

½ to ⅔ cup butter

1 teaspoon salt or to taste

½ cup hot milk

½ cup grated American cheese

Choose baking potatoes of uniform size and shape. Scrub thoroughly and bake in a moderately hot oven (400° F.) until they are soft all through when pierced with a fork, from 50 to 60 minutes. Cut baked potatoes in half lengthwise, scoop out and combine with butter, salt and hot milk. Mash, then whip with fork or wooden spoon until light and fluffy. Pile lightly into the potato shells, sprinkle with grated cheese, and return to the oven, or to broiler until the top is toasted. If they are to be served with creamed or à la king meat, make a depression in the center when stuffing the potato into the shells and omit the cheese; after toasting, pour the meat mixture into and over the hot potato. 5 servings.

Note: Cheese may be omitted from this recipe if desired.

1080   POTATOES O'BRIEN

5 medium baking potatoes,
2 lbs.

1 tablespoon butter

1 medium onion, chopped

1 canned pimiento, chopped

½ teaspoon salt

Pepper to taste

1 teaspoon chopped parsley

Wash and pare potatoes thinly and cut into ¾-inch dice. Fry in deep fat heated to 360° F. until golden brown; drain. Melt butter in a skillet and sauté the onion until soft and yellow. Add potatoes and pimiento and toss about until well mixed and until hot through. Add seasonings, turn into a hot serving dish and sprinkle with chopped parsley. 5 servings.

If preferred, the potatoes may be sliced and pan-fried rather than fried in deep fat, adding the onion and pimiento the last few minutes of cooking.

1081   POTATOES au GRATIN

6 medium-size boiling potatoes   ¼ lb. cheese, grated
2 cups thin white sauce (919)

Wash potatoes, pare thinly and slice quite thin. Combine potatoes and white sauce in saucepan and heat gently until sauce bubbles. Arrange layers of the creamed potatoes in a buttered casserole with grated cheese between layers and on top. Cover casserole and bake in moderate oven (375° F.) until potatoes are tender, about 25 minutes. Then remove cover and brown top, either in oven with temperature increased to 475° F. or under broiler. 5 servings.

For variation in color and flavor, add diced green pepper or pimiento, or both, to the creamed potatoes just before turning into the casserole.

1082   HASHED BROWN POTATOES

Shred 5 large cold boiled potatoes on coarse shredder. Heat 4 tablespoons butter or bacon fat in a heavy 9-inch skillet until hot. Add potatoes, patting out lightly in a uniform layer. Cover skillet and cook gently until lightly brown on under side, then carefully turn potatoes over, using pancake turner or large spatula, and cook until brown on other side. Lift out onto serving plate and serve at once. 5 servings.

1083   ROAST POTATOES

Pare 6 to 8 medium-size boiling potatoes, 2 to 2½ lbs., and place in roasting pan around the roast meat, 1 to 1½ hours (depending on size of potatoes) before the roast is to be done. When potatoes are browned on under side, turn over to brown other side and continue baking until tender when pierced with a fork. To shorten cooking time, potatoes may be parboiled, cooked until almost tender, then baked with the roast for 30 minutes, or long enough to brown well.

Note: New potatoes may be used, but they take longer to cook and never become dry and mealy like old potatoes. Potatoes boiled until barely tender make handsome "roast" potatoes when fried in deep fat (360° F.) until golden brown.

1084   BOILED SWEET POTATOES

Sweet potatoes are of two types: (1) The long slender old-fashioned kind which is red or yellow in color, and has a firm, dry texture. (2) The yam, which is fatter and less tapering, much deeper in color and considerably more moist. If a mealy potato is preferred, the sweet potato should be chosen. If a moist, waxy one is desired, the yam should be selected. Either may be boiled, baked or candied.

Choose potatoes of uniform size, allowing 2 lbs. for 5 servings. Small slender sweet potatoes may be boiled whole; larger ones should be cut in halves or quarters to hasten cooking. Paring is so difficult when raw that the skin is usually left on until they are cooked, then the skin comes off easily. Scrub the potatoes very thoroughly, halve or quarter if necessary and drop into rapidly boiling water. Boil 15 to 25 minutes or until tender when pierced with a fork; drain and peel. Serve with plenty of butter and salt.

1085   BAKED SWEET POTATOES

Choose sweet potatoes of uniform size and similar shape so the baking time will be the same for all of them. Allow 5 medium-size potatoes for 5 servings. Scrub thoroughly and place in a shallow baking pan. Bake in a hot oven (450° F.) until tender when pierced with a fork, about 30 minutes for medium-size potatoes. Serve whole or remove from the shell and mash, seasoning with butter and salt.

1086   MASHED SWEET POTATOES

Cook sweet potatoes by boiling (1084) or baking (1085). Remove from skins and mash. Add butter, allowing about 3 tablespoons for 5 medium potatoes, and salt and sugar or strained honey to suit taste; then whip until fluffy with a fork or wooden spoon. 5 servings.

A little grated orange rind and a dash of sherry whipped into the seasoned potatoes add interesting flavor.

1087   CANDIED SWEET POTATOES

5 medium-size sweet potatoes or yams	1 cup brown sugar, packed, or granulated sugar
½ cup water	¼ teaspoon salt
	2 tablespoons butter

Scrub potatoes, then pare thinly. Heat the water, sugar and salt to boiling and put potatoes, left whole or cut in halves, into the hot syrup, turning to coat all over. Cover tightly, reduce heat and cook slowly, turning potatoes from time to time until just tender, or from 1 to 1½ hours. Add butter, turning potatoes to mix well and continue cooking 5 minutes longer. Serve hot with the syrup over them. Sweet potatoes may also be glazed by heating peeled potatoes and syrup in a covered pan in a moderate oven (375° F.). Turn occasionally and add butter just before serving. 5 servings.

Variation: Cooked sweet potatoes, peeled, left whole or cut in halves, may be drizzled with melted butter, sprinkled with sugar and baked in a moderately hot oven (400° F.), uncovered, until hot through, brown and sugar-crusted.

1088   ESCALLOPED SWEET POTATOES AND APPLES

5 medium-size sweet potatoes or yams	¾ teaspoon salt
	½ cup brown sugar, packed
2 tart apples	3 tablespoons butter

Scrub potatoes, pare and slice. Pare, core and slice apples. Arrange in alternate layers in a buttered casserole, sprinkling each layer of potatoes with salt and each layer of apples with sugar. Dot with butter, cover casserole and bake in a moderate oven (375° F.) until both potatoes and apples are very tender and flavors are well blended, about 45 minutes. 5 servings.

1089   BUTTERED RUTABAGA

2 to 2½ lbs. rutabaga	3 tablespoons butter
4 cups boiling water	1 tablespoon flour
1 teaspoon salt	Salt to suit taste
2 teaspoons sugar	Chopped parsley

Slice rutabaga into ½-inch thick slices, then peel slices and cut into 1-inch wide dice or wedges. Put into a 3-qt. saucepan with water and salt and boil covered until just tender, 25 to 35 minutes. Drain off ¾ cup of the cooking water. Melt butter, blend in flour, add cooking water and stir over direct heat until sauce boils. Add sugar. Add salt to suit taste. Now pour sauce over hot rutabaga and reheat. Then turn into vegetable dish and sprinkle finely chopped parsley over top. 5 servings.

1090   MASHED RUTABAGA

1¼ lbs. rutabaga, sliced   1 teaspoon sugar
   ¼-inch thick and pared   2 tablespoons butter
 3 medium potatoes, 1 lb.,   1 egg, beaten
   pared and cut in half   Salt and pepper to suit taste
1½ teaspoons salt

Place rutabaga and potatoes in separate saucepans and add 3 cups
boiling water and half the salt to each. Cook covered until tender, 20
to 25 minutes. Drain both vegetables, saving liquid. Rutabaga pot liquor
makes a delicious vegetable cocktail; potato water should be used for
gravy, soup or cooking other vegetables. Mash rutabaga and potato
separately; then combine. Add sugar, butter and beaten egg, and beat
vigorously until mixture is smooth and fluffy. Add seasoning to suit taste.
Addition of potato to the rutabaga makes it much milder in flavor and
gives the mixture a fluffy consistency. 5 servings.

1091   CREAMED SALSIFY

 3 cups sliced salsify, 1 large   2 tablespoons flour
   bunch   1 cup milk
1½ cups boiling water   1 chicken bouillon cube
 ¼ cup fine cut celery   ¾ teaspoon salt
 3 tablespoons butter   Dash pepper

Remove tops from salsify and discard. Wash salsify roots and scrape
off all blemishes. Slice about ⅛-inch thick, and immediately cover with
boiling water. Add the celery, cover and simmer until salsify is tender
or for about 15 minutes. Meanwhile make a white sauce of the butter,
flour and milk (919). Drain liquid from salsify and measure; there should
be ½ cup. If there is more, evaporate to ½ cup; if there is less make up
with water. Add salsify and liquid to the sauce. Reheat and stir in bouillon cube and seasonings. Makes 5 servings.

1092   SAUERKRAUT WITH APPLES

 3 or 4 tart cooking apples   3 tablespoons butter
   No. 2½ can sauerkraut *or*   3 to 4 tablespoons sugar
 1 quart bulk sauerkraut   ½ teaspoon caraway seed

Peel apples, core and cut in eighths. Alternate layers of kraut and apples
in a 3-qt. saucepan. Add enough water to cover and rest of the ingredients, heat to boiling; then reduce heat, cover and simmer until apples
are very tender, or from 20 to 25 minutes. Most of the liquid should be

evaporated. Watch carefully while cooking rapidly until all liquid has evaporated. Turn into a hot serving dish and serve immediately. 5 servings.

Note: If apples have tender red skins, leave skins on for beautiful color.

1093   SPANISH RICE

1 small onion, chopped	2 teaspoons sugar
¼ cup chopped green pepper	3 cups hot boiled rice (174)
3 tablespoons butter	Salt and pepper to taste
2 cups canned tomatoes	

Sauté onion and green pepper for 5 minutes in butter. Add tomatoes, sugar, rice and salt and pepper; bring to boiling point and simmer gently 5 minutes more. Serve hot. Grated Parmesan cheese sprinkled over top is a pretty tasty garnish. 5 servings.

1094   BUTTERED SPINACH

Wash 2 lbs. spinach very thoroughly through several cold waters; if necessary wash each leaf separately to remove all sand and grit. Discard bad leaves and any tough stems. Put spinach into 3-qt. saucepan, add 1⅓ cups boiling water and 1 teaspoon salt and cook 5 to 10 minutes or until just tender, turning occasionally. Drain thoroughly and pour melted butter over spinach. Serve immediately. 5 servings.

1095   CREAMED SPINACH

Clean and cook spinach as directed above (1094). Drain thoroughly. Add 1 cup thick White Sauce (919) and 1 teaspoon grated onion for each 2 lbs. spinach. Mix lightly and reheat if necessary. Serve at once.

1096   SAVORY CREAMED SPINACH

1½ lbs. spinach or No. 2 can	¾ teaspoon salt
3 tablespoons butter	Pepper
1 small onion, chopped fine	1½ cups milk
¼ cup flour	

Wash and cook spinach according to directions (1094), or use canned spinach. Drain, chop fine. There should be 1¼ to 1½ cups. Melt butter in saucepan, add chopped onion and cook until soft; blend in flour, salt and pepper. Add milk and cook over direct heat, stirring constantly until sauce boils and thickens. Fold in chopped spinach and reheat if necessary. Serve hot. 5 servings.

1097   CREAMED SPINACH DE LUXE

1½ lbs. spinach *or* No. 2 can	3 tablespoons flour
1 teaspoon sugar	1½ teaspoons salt
3 tablespoons butter	1 cup milk
½ clove garlic, chopped fine, *or* 1 small onion	1 cup thin cream

Cook spinach as for Buttered Spinach (1094), adding the sugar to the cooking water; or heat canned spinach in its own liquor with the sugar. Drain thoroughly. Meanwhile melt the butter in a saucepan, add the chopped garlic and cook until soft; blend in the flour and salt and add milk and cream. Stir constantly over direct heat until sauce boils and thickens; then add the drained spinach which has been chopped, mix well and reheat until the sauce bubbles up. Serve immediately. 5 or 6 servings.

1098   SPINACH WITH BACON AND EGG

1½ lbs. spinach or No. 2 can	Salt to taste
5 slices bacon	3 hard-cooked eggs (395)

If using fresh spinach, wash thoroughly and cook as for Buttered Spinach (1094). If using canned spinach, heat to boiling in its own liquid. Meanwhile pan-broil bacon until done. Drain hot cooked spinach and combine it thoroughly with crumbled bacon and as much of the bacon fat as desired for seasoning. Season to taste and serve with sliced hot hard-cooked eggs. 5 servings.

1099   SPINACH WITH CHEESE SAUCE AND BACON

2 tablespoons butter	1 cup grated cheese
3 tablespoons flour	No. 2 can spinach, well
1 cup evaporated milk	drained; *or* 1½ lbs. fresh
1 cup water	spinach, cooked
Salt to taste	5 slices bacon

Make a white sauce of the butter, flour, milk, water and salt (919). Add grated cheese and stir until thoroughly melted. Put drained spinach in a buttered baking dish and pour cheese sauce over it. Top with bacon slices which have been half cooked. Bake 15 to 20 minutes in a moderate oven (350° F.). 5 servings.

1100   SPINACH MOLD WITH CHEESE SAUCE

1½ lbs. fresh spinach   3 eggs, separated
 2 tablespoons butter   ¼ cup butter
 2 tablespoons flour   ¼ cup flour
½ cup milk   2 cups milk
 1 teaspoon onion juice   1 teaspoon salt
½ teaspoon salt   ¼ lb. cheese, diced or grated
   Pepper

Wash spinach thoroughly, drain and place in a 3-qt. saucepan; add 1 cup boiling water and cook until just tender, 5 to 10 minutes. Drain and chop; there should be about 1½ cups. Make a thick White Sauce (919) of the next 6 ingredients and cool slightly. Beat egg yolks slightly, add the white sauce slowly and stir until well blended. Add spinach and fold in the egg whites which have been beaten until stiff. Turn into a well-buttered 4-cup ring mold which has been lined in the bottom with waxed paper; set in a shallow pan of hot water and bake in a moderately hot oven (375° F.) about 30 minutes, or until a knife inserted in the center comes out clean. Meanwhile, make a white sauce with the remaining butter, flour and milk (919), adding salt and cheese at end and stirring until melted. Unmold spinach ring on hot serving plate and serve with the cheese sauce. 5 servings.

Note: Center of the ring may be filled with buttered onions (1047) if desired.

1101   BAKED ACORN SQUASH

Scrub squash thoroughly; cut in half and scrape out the seeds and the fibers, using a spoon. Butter cut surfaces, place cut side down on a baking sheet and bake in a moderately hot oven (400° F.) for 30 to 45 minutes, or until inside is very soft. Turn cut side up, place butter in the cavity of each half and on the rim, sprinkle with a little salt and brown sugar and replace in the oven until the sugar is melted and the rim of the squash is toasted to an appetizing brown. Serve in the shells with additional butter. One good-sized squash serves 2.

1102   BUTTERED SUMMER SQUASH

Any variety of summer squash (Butternut, Patty Pan, yellow Crook-neck, Zucchini, etc.) may be cooked by this method. Allow 2 lbs. for 5 servings. Choose young, tender squash; it should be easy to pierce the skin with the thumb nail. Wash thoroughly and cut into slices ½-inch thick. Do not pare off skin and do not remove seeds. If squash is mature and therefore tougher, it may be necessary to peel thinly and remove the large seeds. Measure 3 or 4 tablespoons butter into a 3-qt. saucepan. Heat until melted, then add squash. Add salt, allowing about ¼ teaspoon to each pound of squash. Cover pan and cook gently until tender, about 6 minutes for young squash. Remove cover, add a dash of pepper if desired and serve immediately.

1103   PAN-FRIED SUMMER SQUASH

Choose young, tender squash. Wash thoroughly and remove any blemishes. Slice crosswise ½-inch thick without removing skin or seeds. Dip slices in beaten egg diluted with ¼ cup milk and seasoned with salt and pepper; then dip in fine dry bread or cracker crumbs or flour. Fry in butter or bacon fat until golden brown on both sides. Squash should be done through by this time; if not, reduce heat, cover skillet and cook 2 or 3 minutes longer. Two pounds squash serves 5.

1104   SUMMER SQUASH MEDLEY

2 tablespoons butter	1 teaspoon salt
1 cup chopped celery	½ cup water
1⅓ cups chopped onions	Pepper to taste
2 medium summer squash	Paprika

Melt butter in a 3-qt. saucepan, add celery and onions, cover tightly and simmer 10 to 12 minutes, stirring occasionally. Peel squash if skin cannot be easily pierced; split and scoop out seeds and fiber. Dice. There should be about 5 cups. Combine with celery and onions; add salt and water. Cover and simmer 10 minutes or until tender. Add pepper and serve piping hot with paprika on top. 5 servings.

1105   STUFFED SUMMER SQUASH

5 tender Patty Pan squash	¼ cup butter
½ cup chopped green pepper	1 teaspoon salt
½ cup chopped celery	Pepper to taste
2 cups corn cut from cob or	¼ cup hot top milk
No. 2 can whole kernel corn	

Wash squash carefully, do not pare. Place in a 4-qt. saucepan, cover with boiling water and cook rapidly about 15 minutes or until tender when pierced with fork, or place in covered casserole and bake in a moderate oven (350° F.) until tender, about 30 minutes. Meanwhile, sauté green pepper, celery and corn in the butter until celery is soft. Drain squash, split crosswise, scoop out centers; combine centers with sautéed vegetables and seasonings. Heap mixture into squash shells, set in baking pan and pour a little hot milk over filling in each. Cover and bake in a moderate oven (350° F.) about 10 minutes. Serve hot. 5 servings.

1106   BAKED WINTER SQUASH

In general, the most satisfactory way of cooking the hard-skinned winter squashes—Hubbard, cushaw, etc., is to bake them. Split the squash in half, using a saw-tooth knife to saw apart or use a cleaver if necessary, then remove seeds. Hubbard squash may be cut in serving size pieces, if desired. Place halves or pieces, cut side down on buttered baking sheet, bake in a moderately hot oven (400° F.) until tender when pricked with a fork. This takes from ½ to 1½ hours, or longer for large Hubbard squash. Remove from oven. Small squash may be served "on the half shell" with butter and salt. Larger squash should have the tender pulp scooped out and mashed with butter and salt, whipping up until smooth and fluffy. Three pounds squash serves 5.

For a more elaborate dish, the mashed buttered squash may be sweetened with honey or maple syrup, have some chopped nuts added, then placed in a buttered casserole and the top covered with marshmallows. Place in a hot oven (425° F.) until the marshmallows are just toasted.

1107   BRAISED ZUCCHINI SQUASH

¼ cup butter	¾ teaspoon salt
1 medium onion	Few grains pepper
8 small Zucchini squash	½ cup water

Melt butter in a skillet and sauté thinly sliced onion until soft. Wash tender young squash, remove a small slice from stem and blossom end, and cut squash in half lengthwise. Put squash cut side down into butter, pushing the onions to one side. Heat slowly until slightly browned on under side, then turn over, add salt, pepper and water. Cover tightly and continue cooking for about 12 minutes, or until vegetables are tender and liquid is evaporated to about 1 tablespoon. Carefully remove squash and onions to hot platter and garnish with broiled tomato slices or parsley. 5 servings.

1108   BUTTERED SWISS CHARD

Allow 1½ to 2 lbs. chard for 5 servings. Wash the leaves thoroughly, discarding any discolored tough leaves; then strip the green leafy part from the thick fleshy midrib, and cook like Spinach (1094). The midribs require longer cooking than the green leaves and should be cooked separately in a small amount of salted water like Asparagus (981), either whole or cut in 1-inch lengths. Drain and add melted butter. Combine leafy part and midribs and serve hot.

1109 ESCALLOPED TOMATOES

No. 2 can tomatoes or 4 large fresh
2 cups soft bread crumbs, toasted

1 medium onion, chopped
¾ teaspoon salt
1 tablespoon sugar
2 tablespoons butter

Combine tomatoes with the toasted bread crumbs and stir in onion, salt and sugar. Turn into buttered casserole. Bake in a moderate oven (375° F.) from 15 to 20 minutes or until hot through. 5 servings.

1110 PAN-BROILED TOMATOES

5 large tomatoes, 2½ lbs.
½ cup butter or half bacon fat
1 teaspoon thyme

¼ teaspoon salt
1½ tablespoons grated onion

Wash tomatoes and cut out the cores and the blossom ends. Melt butter in a skillet, add the thyme, salt and onion and simmer gently until onion is soft, about 5 minutes. Slice tomatoes 1 inch thick, or cut them in half crosswise. Lay them in the seasoned butter and cook at simmering point, spooning the fat up over them from time to time. When they begin to soften on under side after cooking 1 or 2 minutes, turn carefully, using a pancake turner or large spatula and continue cooking about the same length of time on the other side, spooning fat over the top. They should not be cooked until mushy. Transfer to a hot platter and pour the savory butter over them. More salt may be wanted by some. Garnish with parsley and serve immediately. 5 servings.

Variation: To the ½ cup butter melted in the skillet, add instead of thyme and onion, ⅓ cup grated raw carrot, 1 teaspoon celery salt and a dash of pepper. Simmer 2 or 3 minutes or until carrot is soft; then add the sliced tomatoes and cook as described above.

1111 STEWED TOMATOES

1 small onion, chopped or grated
1 tablespoon butter

No. 2½ can tomatoes
¾ teaspoon salt
1 teaspoon sugar

584

Put onion and butter into saucepan and simmer until onions are soft and yellow. Add tomatoes, salt, sugar, heat to boiling and simmer 5 minutes. Serve immediately with a little sugar, if desired. 5 servings.

1112   STUFFED BAKED TOMATOES

5 large tomatoes, 2½ lbs.	Salt to taste
5 slices white bread, cut in ½-inch dice and toasted	Dash pepper
¼ lb. sharp cheese, grated	¼ cup butter, melted

Cut a thin slice from the stem end of each tomato. Scoop out center with a spoon, leaving walls at least ⅓-inch thick. Chop tomato centers and combine with remaining ingredients, tossing lightly to mix well. Stuff mixture into tomatoes, heaping up generously. Place tomatoes in a buttered shallow baking pan. Any left-over stuffing may be placed around the tomatoes. Bake in a moderately slow oven (325° F.) for 20 minutes. Serve immediately. 5 servings.

1113   MACARONI, TOMATO AND GREEN PEPPER CASSEROLE

7- or 8-oz. package macaroni	1 teaspoon salt
3 tablespoons chopped onion	3 green peppers
2 tablespoons butter	2 oz. sharp cheese, grated
No. 2 can tomatoes	

Drop macaroni into 3 quarts rapidly boiling water with 2 teaspoons salt, and boil, uncovered, about 20 minutes or until tender. Sauté onion in butter until soft and yellow. Add tomatoes and simmer gently about 5 minutes. Add drained macaroni and salt, mix well and continue simmering about 10 minutes longer. Wash, quarter, and remove seeds and membranes from peppers; boil for 6 minutes in 1 quart water with 1 teaspoon salt. Then drain and arrange in buttered casserole. Fill casserole with macaroni and tomato mixture; sprinkle cheese on top. Bake in a moderately hot oven (400° F.) 15 minutes or until cheese is golden brown. 5 or 6 servings.

1114   BUTTERED TURNIPS, WHITE OR YELLOW

Wash 2 to 2½ lbs. turnips thoroughly, then cut in ½-inch slices. Pare each slice, then cut into dice, if desired. Turn into saucepan, cover with boiling water, add salt (1 teaspoon to 1 quart water), and boil vigorously, uncovered 15 minutes; then reduce heat, cover and simmer until tender, 10 to 15 minutes longer, by which time very little liquid should remain. Serve turnips in remaining liquid or thicken it with thin flour-water paste (1125). Or drain off, chill and use as vegetable cocktail. Add 3 tablespoons butter, a dash of black pepper and 1 teaspoon sugar to each pint of turnips with additional salt to suit taste. Instead of butter, the drained turnips may be combined with 1½ cups medium White Sauce (919), if preferred. 5 servings.

Variation: Small white turnips may be cooked whole or may be scooped out to form cups for peas.

1115   VEGETABLE PLATES

Any desired combination of three or more vegetables, cooked separately according to the directions for each and combined with plenty of butter, makes a good vegetable plate dinner. One of the vegetables should be potatoes and the others should be chosen for contrast in color, flavor and texture. Suggested combinations are:

1. Cabbage wedges, sliced carrots, green beans, potatoes.
2. Spinach, small whole beets, small buttered onions, potatoes.
3. Braised celery, peas, carrots cut in quarters lengthwise, potatoes.
4. Cauliflower, broiled tomatoes, Zucchini squash or asparagus, parsley potatoes.

Broiled bacon (544) or a poached egg (391) is an attractive garnish for any vegetable plate if desired. Cheese sauce (920) or white sauce (919) served over one of the vegetables adds interest and appetite appeal.

1116   RICE AND VEGETABLE SOUP CASSEROLE

1 cup uncooked rice	¾ cup water
10½-oz. can condensed vegetable soup	½ cup grated cheese
	Buttered bread crumbs

Wash rice thoroughly, drop gradually into 2 quarts rapidly boiling salted water, 1 tablespoon salt, and boil gently 15 to 20 minutes or until grains are just soft when pressed between thumb and fingers. Stir occasionally with fork. Drain and rinse with hot water. Combine rice with the soup, water and grated cheese; mix well and turn into buttered casserole. Sprinkle buttered crumbs over top and bake in a moderate oven (375° F.) for 30 minutes. 5 servings.

1117   PREPARING CANNED VEGETABLES

The liquid in which most canned vegetables are packed consists of water, a small amount of seasoning and the vegetable juice that cooks out during processing of the can. This liquid contains some of the food value of the vegetable, especially the minerals, as well as some flavor. It should not be discarded.

To prepare canned vegetables so they will have the maximum flavor and food value, drain the liquid into a saucepan and boil it briskly over direct heat until it is concentrated to about ⅓ its original volume. This takes a few minutes if boiling is rapid. Then add the drained vegetables to the liquid and reduce heat, simmering until they are hot through. Add butter and continue heating until it is melted. Canned vegetables require no cooking, only heating to make them palatable.

DEEP FAT FRYING

* * * * * * * *

WHO doesn't like crisp, fresh-fried doughnuts, crullers and French Fries, especially when homemade? A deep fat frying thermometer is a "must" but so are perfectly balanced recipes for Deep-fat Fried Foods to be appealing and easily digestible.

* * * * * * * *

Foods fried in deep fat are almost always popular because of their crisp, flavorful crust, and such crusts are impossible to produce by any other method of cooking.

Fried foods will not be fat-soaked, which is a frequent objection, if they are cooked at a temperature which will quickly form a crust before the fat has a chance to penetrate. The frying will not be "smelly" if the fat is watched and never permitted to get too hot. For this reason, a frying thermometer is essential to success. The fat will not break down and have to be thrown out after 2 or 3 fryings if it is never allowed to become overheated, but half a dozen and sometimes as many as a dozen fryings—with coolings and reheatings between—may be done with the same 2 or 3-lb. lot of fat.

It is only when fat is heated to or beyond the smoking point that the substance which gives it acrid flavor and odor is developed. This substance is acrolein, which is also responsible for much of the reputation of fried foods being indigestible. Since the smoking point of most shortenings is considerably higher than the correct frying temperature, this point needs never be reached under the eye of a careful cook.

The only reliable check on the temperature of deep fat is a frying thermometer clipped inside the kettle throughout the frying. The bread test often mentioned in recipes is not a satisfactory substitute for a thermometer. It is difficult to cut bread cubes to precision—an inch in size, and the variation in the moistness of bread is sure to affect the time required to brown. Then homemakers are sure to vary in their judgement when a cube of bread has acquired a certain degree of brownness. Furthermore it is impossible to keep a check on temperature variation during frying by this method.

Many homemakers avoid cooking fried foods because they feel they must be eaten immediately when done. A well fried food, however, after being thoroughly drained on absorbent paper or paper toweling, can usually be placed on a shallow pan and kept warm for as long as half an hour in a slow oven. Doughnuts and crullers may be re-heated in a paper sack, in a moderately hot oven, just like hot breads, and will be nearly as good as when fresh.

See recipes for Deep Fat Frying—Doughnuts, Croquettes, French Fried Foods in Index.

LEFTOVERS

PUT the leftovers to tasty, eye-appealing use, and give the food budget a lift. Here's a short chapter that tells you how it can be done.

◆ ◆ ◆ ◆ ◆ ◆ ◆ ◆

Food leftovers may be regarded as clear gain or as clear loss, according to whether your family is willing to accept them gracefully in a new dress, or insists that leftovers are only good for chicken feed.

Meats are the most generally accepted leftovers, and some home managers go so far as to choose a larger pot roast, or a larger ham or turkey than the family requires, in order to have some left for sandwiches, hash or croquettes; or for various casserole dishes the next day. Here are two examples of how a big meat cut can be economically and appetizingly used:

1. Whole pork shoulder makes an economical, imposing, and delicious roast. Serve it hot the first day, cutting big juicy slices from the shank-end. The next day serve barbecued pork slices; the following day have hot or cold pork sandwiches for lunch; and finally, serve hash or jellied meat loaf or croquettes, accompanied with a creamed vegetable.

2. A whole ham is practical for even a small family. Have the butcher saw it in two and cut 3 or 4 half-inch steaks from the center to be broiled for dinner for 2 nights. For another day, roast the butt end—a fine main dish for Sunday dinner. Several days later prepare a boiled dinner with the shank end; or cut off thin slices to pan-broil for breakfast or for sandwiches, then use the bone for making soup.

Vegetable leftovers are less easily used as only small amounts are usually left. However, two or even more kinds may be combined, to be served as a vegetable or in salad or soup. When leftover vegetables must be reheated, leave some of their own pot liquor on them and heat them in this, or if there is none, add a little water and butter.

If good care is given to the foods while they are stored, they will remain in good condition till the next day; but it should be remembered that the vitamin content will lessen on standing. Cool the food and place it in closed containers, air-tight if possible, to prevent the absorption of any foreign odors and flavors and to prevent drying out. Then be sure that the food goes straight into the refrigerator and stays there until it is used.

In preparing leftovers, avoid chopping or cutting them up too small. Let the pieces be large enough to be readily identifiable. Do your disguising in some other way than by reducing the food itself to a point where it is unrecognizable.

In the recipe section of this book will be found recipes for many good leftover dishes. So Home Manager, it's up to you to check these recipes and fit them to your leftover foods while they still retain their form, color and vitamin content.

MISCELLANEOUS RECIPES

1118   BUTTERING BREAD CRUMBS

Melt 1½ to 2 tablespoons of butter in a skillet or shallow saucepan. Add ½ cup sifted dry bread crumbs, then stir over moderate heat until crumbs are well coated and slightly toasted. Use to sprinkle over au gratin or casserole dishes to give a temptingly toasted, delicate crust when baked.

1119   USES OF STALE BREAD

Never let stale bread become moldy. Even when it is quite hard and old it may still be used for toast. If making toast is not practical, place the bread in a slow oven (250-300° F.) and dry out until very hard and crisp. Then place it in a large paper sack and roll it with a heavy rolling pin until it forms fine crumbs. Or put the bread through a food mill that has its screw loosened. These crumbs may be sieved if desired, and will be as good as bought crumbs. Store in jar with a perforated top.

Slightly stale bread, which is neither hard nor moldy, though it may have lost its appeal for eating as bread, can be used with complete satisfaction in bread puddings, escalloped tomatoes, stuffings for meat or poultry, and many other cooked dishes.

1120   RE-HEATING QUICK BREADS

Leftover muffins, biscuits and shortcakes may be freshened successfully if they are sprinkled very lightly with water and placed in a paper sack, then snugly closed at the end, and heated in a hot oven (400° F.) until piping hot.

Another way of heating them is to split them and toast under the broiler or in a hot oven. This produces a crisper texture and a different flavor from the fresh bread, whereas the other method makes them taste much like freshly baked breads.

1121   CARAMELIZING SUGAR

Put 2 cups granulated sugar in a heavy skillet and heat, stirring constantly until sugar melts to a light amber-colored liquid. Watch carefully —a dark amber liquid has a scorched flavor. Carefully add 1½ cups boiling water, and simmer until caramel dissolves, stirring frequently. Cool and store in a covered jar to use as coloring for stews and gravies, and as delicious sweetening for custards, ice cream or candy.

1122   CARROT STICKS

Choose rather small, tender carrots. Keep in refrigerator until ready to serve. Wash well and scrape clean, then rinse in cold water. Now cut in quarters lengthwise, or in small strips. Never soak strips in water. Serve immediately.

1123   RENDERING CHICKEN FAT

Put chicken or other poultry fat into a shallow baking pan and place in a slow oven (250-300° F.) until fat fries out. Drain off the accumulated fat from time to time to avoid overheating and strain. Store in closely covered container in refrigerator. Chicken fat is a delicious substitute for butter, in cakes or cookies, or for frying potatoes, or wherever small amounts of fat are used for cooking. The cracklings left add delicious flavor to biscuits and cornbread.

1124   MELTING CHOCOLATE

Break chocolate into 1-ounce or ½-ounce pieces and place on a square of waxed paper; put into top of double boiler over hot, not boiling water. To hasten melting, cover the pan. When fully melted, carefully lift out the waxed paper and scrape the chocolate off with a spatula. Another method which prevents melted chocolate from sticking to the pan is to rub the bottom of the pan with butter; then put the chocolate in and melt over hot water as described above. Scrape out with a rubber scraper. Chocolate need not be grated or shaved to melt it successfully. Never melt chocolate over direct heat, as it scorches very readily.

1125   FLOUR-WATER PASTE FOR THICKENING GRAVY, ETC.

Sprinkle 2 tablespoons flour over ¼ cup cold water in a small jar; cover and shake it vigorously until blended. This amount thickens 1 cup milk to a good average thickness when stirred in, brought to boiling point, and simmered 2 or 3 minutes.

1126   SOURING FRESH OR EVAPORATED MILK

When a recipe calls for sour milk or buttermilk and there is none in the house, fresh milk or evaporated milk in the proper dilution may be soured by adding vinegar. Use 1 tablespoon vinegar to each cup of fresh milk or diluted evaporated milk. Stir well and use just like sour milk.

1127   SUBSTITUTING EVAPORATED FOR FRESH MILK

If you wish to use evaporated milk in a recipe for baked goods which calls for fresh milk, dilute the evaporated milk with water in the proportion of 2 parts water to 1 part evaporated milk. For example, in a recipe calling for 1 cup fresh milk, use ⅓ cup evaporated milk diluted with ⅔ cup water.

For other cooked foods, such as custards and sauces, dilute the evaporated milk with an *equal* quantity of water. This produces a milk which is the equivalent in food value of the same amount of fresh milk. For example, in a recipe for cocoa calling for 1 quart fresh milk, use 2 cups evaporated milk diluted with 2 cups water.

For whipping and in general when evaporated milk is being substituted for cream, it should be used full strength.

1128   WHIPPING EVAPORATED MILK

Have the evaporated milk thoroughly chilled. This may be done by any of 4 methods: (1) Pack the unopened can in ice and salt, as for freezing ice cream. (2) Place the unopened can in the freezing compartment of a mechanical refrigerator. (3) Pour the milk out into a bowl surrounded by ice and salt. (4) Pour the milk out into a freezing tray. Chill until ice cold, but do not freeze.

Have bowl and beater chilled. Pour milk into a cold bowl and whip immediately and rapidly. Addition of 1-2 teaspoons of lemon juice to each cup of milk either before or after it becomes stiff with continued beating will make it hold its stiffness better. Sugar may be beaten in just as with whipped cream.

Evaporated milk will not turn to butter no matter how long beating is continued. If it fails to whip successfully, it needs to be colder. You can re-chill and re-whip it without fear of its turning to butter.

Evaporated milk increases in volume about three times when whipped.

1129   PLUMPING RAISINS

Wash raisins and turn into colander. Cover, place over boiling water and let steam 5 minutes. Cool. This makes them taste better in cake, cookies, etc.

Butter is more than just a nutritious food with a delicious flavor; it can be highly decorative as well, as the illustration shows. All these attractive little butter pats, balls, curls and blossoms can be made by any enterprising housewife armed with a sharp knife, a pair of wooden paddles, a butter curler, and a mold or two. They are easy the first time, easier the second, and fun no matter how often you make them.

Butter balls: Have butter firm but not so cold that it crumbles. Dip wooden paddles into boiling water, then into ice water; let them stand in ice water until ready to use, and return to the ice water whenever you put them down for a minute. Cut butter into 1-inch square pats about ⅓-inch thick, and quickly press into a rough ball with the fingers. If weather is warm, butter may be held under ice water while pressing into shape. Place a ball on the grooved side of one paddle, and holding this steady, place the other paddle lightly over the butter. Now roll it round and round, exerting scarcely any pressure until the butter takes the shape of a ball with burry or waffled markings. A little practice will reveal how little pressure is required to shape the ball. Let balls stand in ice water a few minutes, then place in refrigerator on waxed paper until ready to use.

Butter roses: Using about ½ teaspoon butter, make small balls with the paddles. Then turn the paddles over, place a ball on the smooth side of one, and with the smooth side of the other, spank the ball flat, making it a little less than ⅛-inch thick. With fingers, roll up this flat sheet to form a narrow tube, and use for center of rose. Make a flattened disc for each petal, and arrange around the tightly rolled center, curling tightly or spreading out according to whether a bud or a full-blown rose is desired. After the addition of each petal drop the rose into ice water. The petals may be handled more easily without breaking if the butter has first been squeezed and worked in ice water until waxy and pliable. Put finished roses on waxed paper and place in the refrigerator until ready to serve. (Much larger butter roses may be made in the same way, using more butter for each petal.)

Curled butter pats: Have butter well chilled; cut in pats about ⅓-inch thick. Dip a sharp knife into hot water, and starting at the corner of the pat, shave a thin layer upward toward the center. The knife should make a 60 degree angle with the butter surface. Do two corners or all four, and decorate with tiny sprigs of parsley if desired.

Butter curls: Have the butter moderately hard. Work on a ¼-pound stick of butter, drawing the chilled butter curler along the surface to remove about ⅛-inch strip of the butter that curls up as you draw the curler across the stick of butter. A little practice will enable you to get just the right thickness to curl well.

Butter molds: Prepare butter molds (plunger type) like the wooden paddles, by dipping first into boiling and then into ice-cold water. Have butter firm but not hard. Cut into pats ½-inch thick, and cut out with the chilled mold, holding the plunger up; then lower plunger and press down to mark the design into surface of the pat. Remove excess butter around edge of mold, then push the molded butter out onto waxed paper. Store in refrigerator until ready to serve.

1131   BROWNING FLOUR

Spread white flour about ¼-inch thick in the bottom of a heavy skillet, and place over moderate heat, stirring frequently until flour takes on an even tan color. Cool, then store in a glass jar or other moisture-proof can or container. Browned flour has only about ½ the thickening power of white flour, so a sauce or gravy recipe calling for ¼ cup white flour will require about ½ cup browned flour. The browner the flour, the less its thickening power will be.

1132   STEAMING

Steaming means cooking by application of steam rather than by dry heat or heat from boiling water. It is adapted to cooking certain vegetables, especially yellow and white ones, and to fruit puddings and fruit cakes. In modified form, it is applied to many other foods; for example, baked custards are always placed in a pan of water in the oven.

Special steamers resemble large double boilers in which the upper pan has perforations in the bottoms permitting the steam to circulate through. These are a great convenience, but if the budget or the storage space will not permit the purchase of a steamer, it is possible to improvise one with equipment which may be already on hand. A good-sized saucepan, an enamelware colander which fits inside it, and a lid which will cover the pan tightly with the colander in place, will make a perfectly satisfactory steamer. The water in the saucepan should never be permitted to touch the bottom of the colander when steaming is being done.

A covered roasting pan may be converted into an oven steamer by placing a trivet or wire rack in the bottom, which will lift the foods above the surface of the water. This is useful for puddings and small fruit cakes. Steaming may also be done in an ordinary double boiler if the water in the lower pan is not permitted to touch the upper pan. Excellent steamed pudding may be made by pouring the batter directly into the top of the double boiler, covering it, and cooking over shallow boiling water until done.

1133   PARBOILING

Parboiling simply means cooking partially in boiling water. It may refer to cooking to various degrees of doneness that can range from blanching to boiling until not quite tender. For example, green pepper cases which are to be stuffed and baked are usually immersed in boiling water for 2 or 3 minutes; this is virtually blanching, since it intensifies the green color and destroys the enzymes which ordinarily destroy the color during cooking. It also takes out some of the strong flavor. The parboiled peppers are nowhere near to being fully cooked, but the parboiling process contributes some to the better appearance, flavor and texture of the finished product.

Potatoes are often boiled until almost tender, then drained, and their cooking finished in the roasting pan with a roast of meat. Onions to be baked may be parboiled until it is easy to scoop out the centers for stuffing. Dried beans which are to be baked are sometimes parboiled to reduce the baking time.

1134   LARDING MEAT

Larding means introducing into lean meat long narrow strips of fat salt pork or bacon. The strips may be inserted in slashes made with a sharp knife, or a special larding needle may be used to thread the fat into the meat. The inserted fat melts and bastes the lean meat, thus conserving the meat juices and helping to make the meat more tender.

1135   USE OF CANNED FRUIT JUICES

When canned fruits are drained for use in salads, the juice is sometimes difficult for the homemaker to dispose of. Here are some suggestions:

1. Use instead of water in making fruit gelatin.
2. Combine with water or ginger ale and a little lemon or lime juice as a beverage.
3. Combine with milk or buttermilk (13) to make a nutritious and flavorful after-school beverage for children.
4. Thicken with corn starch and use as a sauce for corn starch pudding (350) or leftover cake.
5. Use instead of water to moisten prepared mincemeat.
6. If several kinds of fruit juices are on hand at one time, mix them together as an appetizer-cocktail.

1136   CHOPPING PARSLEY

Chopped parsley adds so much to many foods in appetizing color, fresh flavor, and food value (parsley is one of the richest sources of vitamin A known), that it is worthwhile to know a quick and easy way of preparing it. The usual method of chopping it in a wooden bowl or with a knife on a bread board is not as efficient as it might be, and makes a good deal of dishwashing.

The easiest way is to put the leaves of the washed parsley into a small narrow glass like a jelly glass. Then with a pair of kitchen shears, snip the parsley leaves until it is finely divided into clean cut bits. This method prevents the bits from flying about, and there is nothing to wash except the glass and the tips of the shears.

Parsley should be chopped just before using to be at its best in color and food value. The leaves may be stripped from the coarse stems and put in a glass, and the glass covered and placed in the refrigerator an hour or two ahead of time, ready to be quickly snipped up when needed.

1137   GRATING OR SHREDDING AND GRINDING FOOD

Food graters come in various sizes, and it is important to choose the right size for the food to be grated, in order to make it as attractive as possible. Owning a set of graters and shredders makes it possible to choose a very fine size for grating whole nutmegs; a slightly coarser one for grating orange or lemon rind; a still coarser one for raw carrots; and a large shredder for cabbage to be used in slaw.

Using too fine a grater for carrots and other raw foods, such as raw potatoes and apples, reduces them to a mush and deprives them entirely of the interesting form they should retain. The same effect may be produced by moving the material being grated back and forth over the shredder; if it is moved in one direction only, the food remains in attractive loose shreds.

Grated or shredded food should be handled as little as possible, especially if it is to be sprinkled over a dish as a garnish, like grated chocolate or cheese. It should be grated just before it is used, for finely divided foods dry out, oxidize, become discolored and lose flavor, attractiveness and food value much more rapidly than foods in large pieces. If it is necessary to let a grated food, such as grated lemon rind, stand for a few minutes before using, it should be folded up in waxed paper to prevent loss of aroma and flavor.

Foods are conveniently grated or shredded onto waxed paper; then when the grated food has been measured, any excess may be wrapped up in the paper and discarded.

Graters and shredders should be made of stainless materials, and should be thoroughly cleaned after each use. Every bit of food that may be clinging to the rough side should be carefully removed by rinsing with running water and brushing if necessary. When onion has been grated, it is especially important to remove every trace of odor, so none will be imparted to the next food to be grated.

Everything that is true of grating food is also true of grinding. The size of knife used should be carefully chosen, the ground food should be treated in the same way, and the grinder should be cleaned scrupulously and thoroughly dried to prevent rusting.

TABLE 22. COOKING TEMPERATURES FOR CANDY*

Thread stage	230–234° F.
Soft ball stage	234–238° F.
Medium ball stage	238–245° F.
Firm ball stage	245–250° F.
Hard ball stage	250–265° F.
Soft crack stage	265–272° F.
Medium crack stage	272–290° F.
Hard crack stage	290–310° F.
Caramel stage	320–345° F.

*Whether you use a candy thermometer or not, the cold water test is an invaluable aid in determining when the candy is done, since it reflects atmospheric conditions as temperature does not. The test is made as follows:

Into a cupful (or more) of cold but not iced water, drip several drops of the boiling hot candy. Test immediately by forming the drops into a ball with the fingers.

SOFT BALL STAGE: At this stage the drops form a ball that can just be picked up, but will collapse when removed from the water.

MEDIUM BALL STAGE: At this stage the ball in the water will be fairly firm but will lose its shape when lifted out.

FIRM BALL STAGE: At this stage the ball in the water has a putty-like feel and holds its shape out of water.

HARD BALL STAGE: At this stage the ball when removed from water will be hard enough to make a sound when tapped against a plate.

SOFT CRACK STAGE: At this point candy is too hard to shape into a ball in water, but it forms a firm ribbon that bends when lifted out.

MEDIUM CRACK STAGE: At this point the ribbon holds its shape out of water without being brittle.

HARD CRACK STAGE: At this point the ribbon remains brittle when removed from the water.

CARAMEL STAGE: This stage begins at the point where the color becomes a light amber, and continues through to a dark amber color. If caramel becomes too dark, it will have a disagreeable flavor.

CAUTION: Always remove the pan of candy from heat while the COLD WATER TEST is being made; otherwise there is danger of overcooking while testing is being done.

At the *soft ball stage*, the drops form a ball that can just be picked up but will collapse when removed from the water. At the *medium ball stage*, the ball in water will be fairly firm but will lose its shape when lifted out; at the *firm ball stage* the ball in water has a putty-like feel and holds its shape out of water. At the *hard ball stage*, the ball when removed from water will be hard enough to make a sound when tapped against a plate.

At the *soft crack stage* the candy is too hard to shape into a ball in water, but the firm ribbon it forms will bend when lifted out. At the *medium crack stage* it will hold its shape out of water without being brittle. At the *hard crack stage* it will remain brittle when removed from the water. The *caramel stage* begins at the point where the color becomes a light amber, and continues through a dark amber color; if allowed to progress too far the caramel will develop a disagreeable burned flavor.

Caution: The pan of candy should always be removed from the heat while the cold water test is being made; otherwise there is danger of overcooking while testing is being done.

GLOSSARY OF TERMS USED IN COOKING

• • • • • • • •

IF you were going to have a mousse for dinner, would you marinate, freeze, or julienne it? Would you frizzle, fricassee or fry a sausage? Is pot liquor intoxicating? What's the difference between cutting, and cutting-and-folding? Can you poach other foods than eggs? This chapter defines dozens of the terms constantly heard in modern cooking. Study them and you won't need to look puzzled when your neighbor uses them so glibly.

• • • • • • • •

À la . . . . in the manner or fashion of.

À la mode . . . . such as (1) Beef à la Mode, prepared by marinating and braising in the marinade; (2) Pie à la Mode— wedges of pie served with a scoop of ice cream.

Aspic . . . . originally a savory meat jelly, often containing diced meat and other foods; now used for gelatin dishes other than desserts, such as tomato aspic.

Au gratin . . . . literally, with a crust; usually of cheese or fine bread crumbs, or both.

Bake . . . . to cook by dry heat in an oven.

Barbecue . . . . to roast slowly on a spit or over coals in a specially prepared trench, usually basting with a highly sea- soned sauce; used loosely of any meat served in such a sauce.

Baste . . . . to spoon liquid over a food while cooking to prevent drying out. The liquid is usually meat drippings, melted butter or shortening, or a mixture of these with water; or the juice of the food itself may be used.

Beat . . . . to manipulate a food mixture, usually a batter, with a brisk regular circular and lifting motion which in- corporates air; also, to use a mechanical egg beater.

Blanch . . . . to dip food in boiling water for a minute or so, then dip immediately in cold water and drain. This pro- cedure loosens skins on nuts such as almonds, after which skins can be easily slipped off; in fruit such as tomatoes and peaches. It also destroys enzymes, and sets the color in vegetables to be frozen.

Blend . . . . to mix two or more ingredients thoroughly.

Braise . . . . to cook by browning in a small amount of fat, adding a small amount of water or other liquid from time to time, then simmering gently, covered, until tender.

Broth . . . . a thin soup; also the liquid in which meat, fish and vegetables have cooked; contains bits of solid material and sometimes fat. See Stock.

Brown . . . . to cause a food to become brown, by sautéing, frying, toasting, broiling or baking.

Canapé . . . . a type of appetizer made by topping small pieces of plain or toasted bread with well-seasoned spreads and fancy garnishes.

Caramelize . . . . to melt sugar and cook until golden brown.

Casserole . . . . (1) an earthenware, glass or metal dish for baking; (2) a combination of foods, usually with cream sauce, baked in such a dish.

Chop . . . . to cut into irregular small pieces.

Chowder . . . . a kind of stew, originally applied only to fish or clam stews, now also applied to many mixed vegetable stews, usually without meat other than chopped bacon or salt pork.

Confectioners' sugar . . a pulverized sugar combined with a little cornstarch, used for cake icings, etc.

Cream . . . . to soften a fat with a spoon or beater; also to combine the softened fat with sugar.

Creole . . . . a well-seasoned tomato sauce containing green pepper and chopped onion.

Cut into . . . . to incorporate fat into a flour mixture by dividing it finely with knives or pastry blender.

Cut and fold . . . . to blend a mixture by using two motions; (1) cutting through the mixture with the edge of a spoon or other implement; (2) sliding the implement along the bottom of the bowl and bringing it up at the side so as to lift the lower portion of the mixture and fold it over the upper portion; these motions are repeated until blending is complete. The object is to mix without loss of air, as when blending stiffly beaten egg whites into a cake batter.

Dice . . . . to cut into small pieces of uniform size and shape, approximately cubical.

602

Dissolve . . . . .to pass into solution in water or other liquid; also to cause to pass into solution.

Drain . . . . .to free from liquid.

Dredge . . . . .to coat with flour or fine bread crumbs by sprinkling or by rolling the food in them.

Escallop . . . . .to bake food, usually a mixture with white sauce and topping of crumbs or crumbs and cheese, in a baking dish or casserole; originally, to bake in a scallop shell. Same as Scallop.

Fillet . . . . .a boneless piece of fish or lean meat.

Filet mignon. . . . . .a slice of beef tenderloin, sometimes wrapped in bacon; cooked by broiling.

Frappé . . . . .a liquid mixture frozen to a mush.

French . . . .(1) to trim meat away from the end of a bone, as a lamb chop;
(2) to flatten boneless meat with a cleaver, as a slice of beef tenderloin;
(3) to cut into thin slivers, as green beans.

French fry . . . . .to fry in deep fat.

Frizzle . . . . .to sauté until the edges become curly, sometimes crisp, as chipped beef or thinly sliced ham.

Fricassee . . . . .to cook meat, usually cut in pieces, by braising; the meat is most commonly fowl, rabbit or veal.

Frost . . . . .to cover a cake with icing or frosting.

Glaze . . . . .as noun—a shiny coating applied to certain foods, such as baked ham, fruit cake, rolls, etc.; may be a mixture of sugar and fat, sugar and water, egg white, cornstarch, etc.;
as verb—to apply such glaze, either with or without heat.

Grate . . . . .to obtain small particles of a food by rubbing it back and forth on a grater.

Gravy . . . . .a sauce similar to cream sauce, made with meat drippings, flour and milk, water, cream, sour cream or broth, etc.

Ice .... as noun—a liquid mixture frozen until firm but smooth;

as verb—(1) to chill by addition of chopped or crushed ice, as a beverage;

(2) to cover a cake with icing or frosting; same as Frost.

Irradiate .... to enrich with added "sunshine" vitamin D, by exposure to ultraviolet light.

Julienne .... to cut into long slender pieces, as vegetables and sometimes cooked meats.

Lard .... to introduce fat into a lean meat by threading slivers of fat salt pork or bacon through it.

Liquor .... the liquid in which a food is packed, as oysters or canned foods. See also Pot liquor.

Lukewarm .... of a temperature about blood heat, or 100-110° F.

Marinade .... a mixture, usually of vinegar or lemon juice and water, or a well-seasoned oil and vinegar dressing, in which certain foods are seasoned.

Marinate .... to let stand in a marinade.

Melt .... to become liquefied, usually through the application of heat.

Meringue .... a stiffly beaten mixture of egg white and sugar; may be cooked or uncooked.

Mince .... to chop or cut into very, very small pieces.

Mousse .... a type of still frozen desert consisting chiefly of flavored and sweetened whipped cream.

Parboil .... to cook partially in boiling water; cooking is usually completed by some other method.

Pan-broil .... to cook in a skillet with just enough fat to prevent sticking.

Pan-fry .... to cook in a skillet with shallow fat.

Pasteurize .... to apply heat below the boiling point to a food for the purpose of destroying certain organisms, especially those which cause fermentation. Applied commercially to milk; in the home principally to fruit juices which are being preserved.

Pipe .... to force through a pastry tube, as cake icing.

Poach .... to cook food in a hot liquid in such a manner that it retains its original shape.

Pot liquor . . . . the liquid in which vegetables have been boiled.

Pot roast . . . . a large piece of meat, usually a less tender cut, cooked by braising rather than by baking or roasting.

Powdered sugar . . . . . white sugar partially reduced to powder.

Punch . . . . any beverage composed chiefly of mixed fruit juices.

Purée . . . . as noun—the smooth sauce so obtained; originally, a thickened soup;
as verb—to rub through a sieve or colander, obtaining a thick smooth sauce.

Ramekin . . . . a small individual casserole dish.

Rice . . . . to press through a potato ricer.

Roast . . . . to cook by dry heat. See Bake.

Roux . . . . the paste of melted fat and flour which is the basis of all cream sauces and gravies.

Scald . . . . (1) to bring just to the simmering point, as milk; (2) to pour boiling water over, as in cleaning a pan.

Scallop . . . . see Escallop.

Score . . . . to cut part way through, as through the fatty covering of a ham and around the fatty edge of steak.

Sauté . . . . to pan-fry foods cut small in shallow fat, turning frequently.

Sear . . . . to brown the surface of meat quickly by exposing it to a high temperature during the first few minutes of cooking. This has recently been discarded as a practice of meat cookery because it increases weight loss and loss of juices.

Season . . . . to add salt, pepper, spices, herbs, etc. for purpose of improving the flavor.

Shred . . . . use shredder and rub foods in one direction only to produce strings or threads of food such as carrot or cocoanut. Shredders come perforated in 4 sizes: (1) Fine, for lemon rind. (2) Medium, for carrots, cocoanut, etc. (3) Coarse, for raw beets to be quick-cooked or for cooked potatoes to hash-brown. (4) Coarser for cabbage. The cutting holes in a shredder are cut out and bent outward, and food can be cut only by rubbing in one direction. The cutting holes in a grater are punched through, and food is rubbed in both directions, and the particles are much finer.

Simmer . . . . to cook in water just below boiling point, very gently.

Sherbet . . . . see Ice—as noun. Sometimes made with milk rather than water.

Skewer . . . . as noun—a long metal or wooden pin for fastening meat;
as verb—to fasten meat with such a pin.

Soufflé . . . . a baked dish made basically of milk and eggs, to which separately beaten egg whites give an airy lightness; means literally, "puffed up."

Spatula . . . . a sort of flexible knife with rounded end and without sharp edges. Available in many sizes.

Steam . . . . to cook by steam rather than in boiling water; usually without pressure.

Steep. . . . . to allow a substance to stand in liquid below the boiling point, for extraction of flavor, color or other qualities, as tea.

Stir . . . . to mix food materials with a circular motion to blend them and produce a uniform consistency.

Stock . . . . liquid in which meat, fish and sometimes vegetables have been cooked.

Toast . . . . to brown by means of direct heat or oven heat.

Torte . . . . strictly, a hard meringue baked in the form of a cake; any cake baked in a torte pan, especially one with a meringue topping baked on.

Toss . . . . to mix by lifting lightly and repeatedly, usually with a fork, or a fork and spoon.

Truss . . . . to fasten into position with skewers and twine, as a fowl.

Whip . . . . to beat vigorously with a rotary beater or wire whip so as to incorporate air.

XXXX sugar . . . . see Confectioners' sugar.

INDEX